THE A. W. MELLON LECTURES IN THE FINE ARTS
delivered at the National Gallery of Art, Washington, D.C.

1952 Creative Intuition in Art and Poetry *by Jacques Maritain*
1953 The Nude: A Study in Ideal Form *by Kenneth Clark*
1954 The Art of Sculpture *by Herbert Read*
1955 Painting and Reality *by Etienne Gilson*
1956 Art and Illusion: A Study in the Psychology of Pictorial Representation *by E. H. Gombrich*
1957 The Eternal Present: I. The Beginnings of Art. II. The Beginnings of Architecture *by S. Giedion*
1958 Nicholas Poussin *by Anthony Blunt*
1959 Of Divers Arts *by Naum Gabo*
1960 Horace Walpole *by Wilmarth Sheldon Lewis*
1961 Christian Iconography: A Study of Its Origins *by André Grabar*
1962 Blake and Tradition *by Kathleen Raine*
1963 The Portrait in the Renaissance *by John Pope-Hennessy*
1964 On Quality in Art *by Jakob Rosenberg*
1965 The Origins of Romanticism *by Isaiah Berlin*
1966 Visionary and Dreamer: Two Poetic Painters, Samuel Palmer and Edward Burne-Jones *by David Cecil*
1967 Mnemosyne: The Parallel between Literature and the Visual Arts *by Mario Praz*
1968 Imaginative Literature and Painting *by Stephen Spender*
1969 Art as a Mode of Knowledge *by J. Bronowski*
1970 A History of Building Types *by Nikolaus Pevsner*
1971 Giorgio Vasari: The Man and the Book *by T.S.R. Boase*
1972 Leonardo da Vinci *by Ludwig H. Heydenreich*
1973 The Use and Abuse of Art *by Jacques Barzun*
1974 Nineteenth-century Sculpture Reconsidered *by H. W. Janson*
1975 Music in Europe in the Year 1776 *by H. C. Robbins Landon*
1976 Aspects of Classical Art *by Peter von Blanckenhagen*
1977 The Sack of Rome, May 1527 *by André Chastel*
1978 The Rare Art Traditions *by Joseph Alsop*
1979 Cézanne in America *by John Rewald*
1980 Principles of Design in Ancient and Medieval Architecture *by Peter Kidson*
1981 Palladio in Britain *by John Harris*

BOLLINGEN SERIES XXXV·6·II

S. GIEDION

THE BEGINNINGS OF ARCHITECTURE

The A. W. Mellon Lectures in the Fine Arts · 1957
The National Gallery of Art, Washington, D. C.

BOLLINGEN SERIES XXXV · 6 · II
PRINCETON UNIVERSITY PRESS

PUBLISHED BY PRINCETON UNIVERSITY PRESS, PRINCETON, NEW JERSEY
IN THE UNITED KINGDOM: PRINCETON UNIVERSITY PRESS, GUILDFORD, SURREY

THIS IS PART TWO OF *The Eternal Present*, THE SIXTH VOLUME
OF THE A. W. MELLON LECTURES IN THE FINE ARTS,
WHICH ARE DELIVERED ANNUALLY
AT THE NATIONAL GALLERY OF ART, WASHINGTON.
THE VOLUMES OF LECTURES CONSTITUTE NUMBER XXXV
IN BOLLINGEN SERIES SPONSORED BY BOLLINGEN FOUNDATION

FIRST PRINCETON / BOLLINGEN PAPERBACK PRINTING, 1981

For this edition, the color plates (pp. 247-262) have been printed in monochrome.

The Eternal Present I: The Beginnings of Art AND *II: The Beginnings of Architecture* WERE PREPARED WITH THE ASSISTANCE OF JAQUELINE TYRWHITT

Library of Congress Catalogue Card No. 80-8733
ISBN 0-691-09789-9
ISBN 0-691-01835-9 PBK.
LAYOUT BY THE AUTHOR AND HERBERT BAYER MAPS BY LIAM DUNNE

PRINTED IN THE UNITED STATES OF AMERICA
BY PRINCETON UNIVERSITY PRESS, PRINCETON, NEW JERSEY

wild (at our first) beasts uttered human words
— our second coming made stones sing like birds — . . .

E. E. Cummings (1963)

FOREWORD

The Beginnings of Art, the first volume of THE ETERNAL PRESENT, dealt with prehistory. The present volume, *The Beginnings of Architecture*, deals with the first high civilizations, Egypt and Sumer. The two volumes are independent of each other, yet related by a common interest—the problem of constancy and change.

It is a problem that does not end with prehistory nor with the first high civilizations. It permeates the entire history of mankind. At no time, however, did the problem of constancy and change, rooted ineradicably in the human soul, flare up with such intensity as it did during the first high civilizations, following upon the fundamental changes caused by the establishment of a strictly differentiated social order.

The Eggshells of Prehistory. Since time immemorial, man had lived in isolated, independent groups. Even in the context of the new stern, hierarchical society, certain of man's primeval beliefs lived on with a remarkable constancy.

Among the most notable was the role of the animal, venerated throughout prehistory as a being mightier and more beautiful than man. The constancy with which this veneration persisted side by side with the worship of anthropomorphic deities—the transmutation of animals into deities and deities into animals, and the granting of immortality to animals through mummification—bears witness that at no time during the entire Egyptian period was the prehistoric bond with the animal severed.

Creating an Anthropomorphic Cosmos. The establishment of the state coincided with the establishment of a pantheon of anthropomorphic gods in which each deity possessed a clearly differentiated physiognomy, had a particular task to perform, and was part of a patriarchal family with a dictatorial ruler at its head.

Closely connected with the conception of individual, anthropomorphic gods was the recognition of the human body—more especially the female body—as beautiful. Delicacy in its sculptural treatment was achieved in the Fourth Dynasty, and thereafter the portrayal of the female body has remained a supreme goal of the sculptor's art.

Constancy and Change in the Mode of Expression. The differences between paleolithic art and art of the high civilizations leap to the eye. The astonishing thing is the constancy with which certain constituent elements of paleolithic art live on. The most telling qualities of prehistoric art endure: the stress upon outline and the sinking of reliefs into the stone. Although the uneven rock walls of the caverns have been replaced by plane surfaces, the sunken relief persists as a light-catcher, the illumination of one rim of the sunken outline being emphasized by a dark line of shadow along the other even in the glaring sunlight of the New Kingdom pylons.

The Origins of Monumental Architecture: Mesopotamia. The creation of the first man-made temple is synonymous with the emergence of monumentality. The prehistoric Al 'Ubaid acropolis of Tepe Gawra XIII, with its open plan of three temples, and the large temples of Uruk (ca. 3000 B.C.) were not surpassed or even equaled throughout Mesopotamian history.

Ziggurats: Stairways of the Gods. The ziggurat, the temple tower, originated early but did not reach its culmination (as in the ziggurat of Ur) till around 2000 B.C., half a millennium later than the pyramids. Ziggurats, in contrast to the pyramids, were accessible and stood within the precincts of the city. Their sequences of terraces afforded opportunity for Sumer's most inspired architectonic invention: the monumental stairway.

Beginnings of Stone Architecture and the Ka: Egypt. It was the grave that gave birth to the first stone architecture. The sacred precinct of Zoser's mortuary temple at Saqqara, with its step pyramid and galaxy of inner courts, was built of the "eternal" material for one sole purpose: to provide an eternal existence for the Ka of the dead king.

Pyramids: Rites and Space. The form of the pyramid consists of four equal isosceles triangles converging on a single point. Plane surfaces, the constituent element of Egyptian architecture, reign supreme—a triumph of abstract form.

Through its symbolic impact the pyramid merges and even competes with eternity. Human endeavor has never again achieved such sublime simplicity in materializing man's irrepressible urge to link his fate with eternity. Immaculate precision makes logic merge with enigma and mystery.

The Great Temples and the Eternal Wandering. Ground plans of the great temples of the New Kingdom correspond to Egyptian belief, which accepted no standstill in life or death. Their layout expressed the idea of an eternal wandering. Except for the dark cella in which the image of the god was preserved, every part was conceived as a place of passage. Even the great hypostyle halls, with their forests of columns, formed passageways for the king and his procession taking the sacred statue of a god on his wandering to another sanctuary. No interior space was provided for the community as, for example, in a Christian church.

Foreword

Hatshepsut and the Cosmic Inner Court. The terraced mortuary temple of Queen Hatshepsut was built in the rock amphitheater of Deir el Bahari and represents the radiant climax of Egypt: a rare unity of architecture and sculpture which remained unsurpassed. Like all Egyptian architecture, this temple is oriented vertically, its finely articulated man-made structure being embedded with great daring within the immense verticality of the rock amphitheater.

Supremacy of the Vertical. One of the great changes from prehistory, with its equal rights of all directions, was the advent of the vertical as an organizing principle to which everything had to be related. This occurred at the beginning of the high civilizations, with the rise of architecture. The pyramid, the ziggurat, and monoliths in the form of steles and obelisks expressed the vertical as the connecting link with the cosmos.

The horizontal is the line of repose: the vertical is the line of movement. Yet horizontal and vertical belong together, connected by the angle of ninety degrees, which, together with them, acquired an extraordinarily powerful position. Axis and symmetry are consequences of this new principle of organization.

The penetration into Egyptian art of the vertical as an organizing principle is overwhelming. In reliefs all figures are projected onto a vertical plane, and in sculpture a vertical axis passes through the body, forming the line of intersection of two vertical planes crossing each other at right angles. This method of representation was retained throughout three millenniums.

The meaning of the squared grid, invented by the Egyptians, was not to facilitate the reproduction of the external appearance of things, but to project their absolute proportions onto the vertical plane.

The First Architectural Space Conception. Space conception is an automatic, psychic recording of the visible environment. It develops instinctively, usually remaining in the unconscious.

The first space conception in architecture encompasses the high civilizations of Egypt and Sumer and also Greece. The common denominator, despite deep-rooted differences in almost every sphere of life, was a common attitude toward the placing of volumes in limitless space. The pyramids of Giza and the Acropolis of Athens give perhaps the clearest expression of the attitude toward architectural space throughout this long period. Differences between them are more obvious than their underlying common approach to space.

In neither the Greek nor the Egyptian civilizations was there any development of interior space that could compare with the immense force their builders knew how to express when confronting their structures with the open sky.

ACKNOWLEDGMENTS

This volume, like the first, is the outcome of the A. W. Mellon Lectures in the Fine Arts, given at the National Gallery of Art, Washington, 1957. The studies on which it is based have extended over some fifteen years.

I wish to acknowledge assistance given to me from many different quarters.

John Marshall of the Rockefeller Foundation kindly helped to open a number of doors to me in Egypt and Iraq.

I was able to spend some weeks in the resthouse of the late Zakaria Goneim, Chief Inspector of Antiquities, Saqqara, at the time he discovered the untouched entrance to the unfinished pyramid.

I had the privilege of being introduced to all parts of the Zoser complex at Saqqara by Jean-Philippe Lauer, whose indefatigable efforts have resurrected the first architecture in stone.

Also at Saqqara I was able to meet and talk with W. B. Emery.

Herbert Ricke, Director of the Swiss Egyptological Institute in Cairo, kindly gave me permission to reproduce some of his important reconstructions of pyramid-age structures.

In Iraq, the officials of the Baghdad Museum, under the late Director-General of Antiquities, Naji-al-Asil, were very helpful. Fuad Safar, excavator of Eridu and Hassuna, then engaged on studies of the painted temple at Al 'Uqair and the ziggurat of Aqar Quf, gave me much precious advice.

At Nasiriya, in southern Iraq, the Governor was most hospitable and provided us with jeeps and an escort for our excursions through the desert.

At Uruk (the modern Warka) we were warmly received by Heinrich Lenzen and A. Falkenstein and acquainted with the pertinent problems of this extensive site.

In England, the Keepers of the Departments of Egyptian and Western Asiatic Antiquities of the British Museum in London and the Keeper of the Department of Antiquities at the Ashmolean Museum in Oxford were of great assistance in assembling the necessary material.

In Munich I had the benefit of advice from Professor H. W. Müller and also from Dr. J. von Beckerath, an outstanding scholar on questions of Egyptian chronology, to whom I am particularly indebted for his kindness in writing an essay providing a detailed insight into the thorny problems of precise dating in the first high civilizations. Publication of this volume was too far advanced for this essay to be inserted in full, but excerpts are included in Part I.

In Paris I received much assistance from Marie-Louise Tisserant, of the Department of Egyptian Antiquities of the Louvre, until her recent death in a motor accident.

Very special thanks are due to my friend William Stevenson Smith, Curator of the Department of Egyptian Art of the Museum of Fine Arts, Boston, for his patient counsel while I worked in the Museum library and his unfailing assistance with endless matters of fact and detail in the preparation of this volume.

At Harvard University, as for the first volume, I wish to express my indebtedness to the constant help of the library staffs of the Graduate School of Design, the Widener Library, and the Fogg Museum. Most of the drawings adapted from other plans or based on the author's sketches were made by Tao Ho, a student of architecture at the Graduate School of Design.

My friend G. E. Kidder Smith kindly gave permission for the reproduction of some of his brilliant photographic work. Most of the photographs, however, were taken by the author. Typography and layout are by Herbert Bayer, based on a preliminary dummy prepared by the author.

As she did for the first volume, Professor Jaqueline Tyrwhitt (Graduate School of Design, Harvard University) has undertaken or supervised all aspects of translation and shouldered the heavy burden of putting this book on its feet.

A summary of this entire two-volume work constituted the first Gropius Lecture at Harvard University, April 15, 1961, under the title "Constancy, Change and Architecture."

S. GIEDION

Doldertal, Zurich
August 1963

The "eye" in the margins of the text refers to an illustration on the page indicated. An original color illustration is indicated by "col." A page number alone refers to a textual passage. "I" indicates a reference in Volume I of the present work.

TABLE OF CONTENTS

The maps follow p. 526

PART I THE DIFFERING DESTINIES OF EGYPT AND SUMER

The Differing Destinies of Egypt and Sumer

Constancy and change in the archaic civilizations

The problem of constancy and change during the first high civilizations lies at the root of our inquiries. We approach Egypt and Sumer in terms of a continuity from prehistory rather than looking back from the standpoint of Greece. Greek art is not taken as the universal standard against which perfection and less than perfection can be assessed. Thus the question immediately posed is: What were the elements of prehistory that still lived on in the bloodstream of the high civilizations?

In the earliest high civilizations, as in prehistory, the separation of belief from reality, the sacred from the profane, was not yet accentuated. The isolation of
52 ff reality, symbolized by the dethronement of the animal, had begun, but was not yet complete, at any rate in Egypt.

The study of continuity helps to elucidate the problems of change, which contain the seeds of future development. It enters into the new experiences of organizing wide territories and of building up community life in newly formed cities. The position and the development of architecture are linked to these new dimensions.

In a period so full of symbolic expressions reaching far back into prehistory, architecture cannot be dealt with in isolation. Like sculpture and painting, architecture was not created to please the eye in the first instance. The statues in
107 ff which human beauty is for the first time discovered and expressed—especially the beauty of the female figure—were placed in eternal darkness or in inaccessible locations.

The form of the pyramids is a typical expression of relationship between the sacred and the profane. The strictest geometrical precision is united with a longing for eternity. In this sense Plato, attuned to Egyptian thought, considered the laws of geometry to be eternally constant and unchanging. The form of the pyramid and the superb imagination which gave shape to Egypt's nascent architecture is but the tip of the iceberg, which emerges above the water while the main mass lies hidden below the surface. Thus the beginning of architecture can
320 ff only be treated with reference to the religious background from which it arose.

Egyptian architecture has the closest links with the principles of sculpture and relief. The laws of composition that govern a pyramid and a sculpture are identi-
148 ff cal. In approaching Egyptian architecture we must be aware of Egyptian modes of expression in sculpture and relief—above all, relief, which is bound as closely to Egyptian architecture as prehistoric animal reliefs to the rock walls from which they are hollowed out. Egyptian reliefs are of a special kind: sunken re-

liefs. They never project beyond the wall surface, in contrast to the high reliefs 157 of Mesopotamia and, later, Greece. It is interesting to note constancy and 161 change in the interpretation of the different needs of prehistory and the archaic civilizations by the use of similar artistic means. Prehistoric reliefs never project beyond the natural surface of the rock, and though in Egypt the irregular rock 1:371 ff walls become flat, smoothly polished planes, the reliefs remain embedded in their surface. The discovery of the expressive qualities that lie within the flat plane is one of the fundamental inventions of Egyptian art. As soon as Egypt had found herself, everything became subject to the laws of the plane surface.

Primeval art was concerned with the delineation of outline, whether engraved in clay, bone, or rock. Mastery of the outline was fundamental to primeval art. The Egyptian reliefs were also cut into the stone. Methods altered with changing situations but the principle remained the same. An Egyptian artist was often termed "Drawer of contours," which was, as Hermann Junker demonstrated with great philological insight, a privileged social position. In burial rituals the painter stands, bearing his offerings, next to the highest official of the dead master (1959, p. 52).

The sunken relief is among the most typical products of Egyptian art. It is true that most writers lay more emphasis on the three-dimensional statues, which anticipate the Greek development. The reliefs were brightly painted, and thus as close to painting as to architecture: in them the Egyptians' exceptional narrative gift is unfolded.

Sunken outlines had acted as light-catchers for flickering torches in the primeval caverns. They acted similarly in the half-darkness of the funerary chambers of the pyramid age and even, later, in blazing sunlight on the great pylons of the New Kingdom. The synthesis of wall, sculpture, and structure, which must be continually resolved anew throughout the history of architecture, here achieved perfection for the first time.

Likenesses and differences between Egypt and Sumer

Aside from the general problems of constancy and change a special problem arises in connection with the first two high civilizations. This is the basic difference between Mesopotamia and Egypt, expressed in different attitudes toward life, and in the different destinies of the two countries as well. Two sculptures can be instanced to demonstrate these differences: one comes from the

1. EGYPTIAN LION'S HEAD *of rose granite from the mortuary temple of King Ne-user-ra. A sculptural marvel of innate dignity and peaceful strength*

2. MESOPOTAMIAN LION *of terra cotta. One of a pair of furiously snarling predators which guarded the city gates of Tell Harmal*

pyramid age, around 2400 B.C., the other from the peak period of ziggurat building, around 2000 B.C.

Behind the hall of columns of the pyramid temple of King Ne-user-ra (Fifth Dynasty), Ludwig Borchardt found the more than life-size head of a striding lion. There were but a few isolated details upon which to base its stance and its position within a deep niche before the innermost part of the temple (1907, pp. 69–70).

4 This lion's head of rose granite is a sculptural marvel of innate dignity and reposeful strength. The head emerges from the mane as from a wreath. The mouth is shut, indicated only by a curving line. The ears are barely pricked, the eyes half sunken. The planes are handled masterfully, and by disregarding minutiae the work has been raised to an awe-inspiring level, as in the earlier sculpture,
37 from the time of King Narmer, of the god Thoth in the form of a baboon. Its discoverer termed it incomplete, perhaps because the final polish is lacking, but it is certainly a complete work of art.

By analogy to Mesopotamian representations this lion has been considered a temple guardian. It is far more likely to be a personification of the king. This lion is no symbol of defense: "It is a symbol of the ruler" (Schweitzer, 1948,
73 p. 25). The majestic Sphinx of Giza bears the head of King Chephren, whose peaceful lion's body has similarly been interpreted as guardian of the necropolis. Its actual meaning was nearer to later Egyptian interpretation when—its original significance having been forgotten—the Sphinx was considered to represent the god Horus.

An indication that the lion of Ne-user-ra is no guardian is given in the only well-preserved relief from this temple, found close to the striding lion. This depicts an intimate scene in which the jackal-headed god Anubis presents the enthroned king with the *ankh,* the sign of life (Borchardt, 1907, p. 16).

5 The two earthenware lions of Tell Harmal, which crouch on either side of the gate to this small Sumerian city close to Baghdad, display a terrifying brutality. At first sight they seem to consist solely of menacing open jaws with bared fangs. Flaring nostrils and protruding eyes are emphasized by strongly sculptured eyebrows, their hackles are raised, and their ears pricked. A pair of eternally furious predators. All else is but a foil: their squat bodies, extended claws, and the en-
57 circling manes that hang in coarse tufts like the woolen robes of Sumerian priests. This remained the standard type of representation till the days of Babylon, when Nebuchadnezzar had a frieze relief of sixty lions in many-colored enamel erected on either side of his processional way. Like the monsters of Tell

Harmal fifteen hundred years earlier, they snarl with open mouths, flaring nostrils, and raised hackles: eternally ready to attack the stranger.

The different natures of these Egyptian and Mesopotamian lions express the different destinies of the two countries. Some regions seem condemned to follow a certain course from start to finish. Mesopotamia, whose north and south were subject to constant invasions from the Asiatic highlands, was assigned a tragic destiny from the start.

Attitude toward death

The origin of every religion lies in man's longing to make contact with supernatural forces so that he may gain knowledge of the future. To this is added another, more encompassing and inextinguishable human desire, the longing for a prolongation of life, for a continuation of existence after death. Man's attitude toward death and the hereafter changes. This presents a key to the nature of a religion and, consequently, to a people's attitude toward its destiny. This is particularly marked in the case of Egypt and Sumer, whose cultures developed simultaneously.

The Egyptians' optimistic approach to the hereafter shows their special gift for overlooking, or at least lightening, the dark side of human destiny. Life on earth was just a beginning. Death was but a way station, a bridge to an eternal and wonderful existence. The famous Pyramid Text that opens "O King N thou art not gone dead, Thou art gone alive" (§134; tr. Piankoff, 1957, p. 7) enshrines a basic concept of the Egyptians.

Eternal continuity in the hereafter required co-operation on the part of the living. The departed needed a permanent—an eternal—dwelling place on earth. Even into the Late Period, sun-dried bricks were considered adequate for the houses and palaces of the living, but the dead required an indestructible material: stone. The rise of stone architecture can, in the first instance, be attributed to the Egyptian conception of the nature of death. **264 ff**

Life in the hereafter was an almost directly material reproduction of life on earth, but more magnificent—almost divine. The belief in the continuation of earthly life with all its ramifications was so strong that in King Zoser's mortuary complex at Saqqara everything was foreseen that could contribute to his royal **277 ff** existence: from government buildings to his private quarters under the pyramid and under his southern tomb. The complex also expresses what lay nearest to his heart: the eternal perpetuation of his ruling power. The largest courts are given over to ensuring this through the renewal of the king's royal majesty by

means of the Heb-Sed, or jubilee, festival. The Heb-Sed court was bordered by
284 chapels of the forty-two provinces which paid tribute to Zoser. Two stones were
placed on the axis of the great court between which the king probably ran the
ritual Heb-Sed race to give evidence of his manly vigor. In his underground
267 mansion Zoser had himself thus portrayed.

This extravagant program was not carried on by the pyramid builders of the
following Fourth Dynasty. The growing influence of the priesthood demanded
320 ff an increasing concentration upon the ritual by which the dead king was transformed into a deity. The desire for an enduring dwelling called stone architecture to life, but stone temples only rose to monumental dimensions in the New
Kingdom, when Egypt set about becoming a world power.

Among the measures necessary to ensure continuity of life was the preservation of the earthly body. This gave rise to the science of mummification. That
48 this privilege of eternal life was also extended to animals is a hint that, even to
the last, they were not banished from equality with mankind, and that all creatures were included in a single community.

As an additional safeguard, at least during the peak period of the Old Kingdom, mortuary statues of the dead—or rather Ka statues—were placed in the
326 mastaba tombs of the nobles and in the valley temple of King Chephren.

The dead consumed the same nourishment as the living, and so they needed
regular offerings placed before the false doors to their tombs. The dead lord was
438 pictured sitting on a stool and relishing the sight of a great stack of abundant
offerings. We have these rites to thank for many of the most beautiful reliefs
and, in the New Kingdom, for magnificently colored murals in the necropolis of
Thebes, in which all the produce of the lands of the dead lord is brought to care
for his needs. The painters did their best work in the service of the cult of the
dead.

The grain in the fields of the hereafter grew twelve feet high, and to ensure
the perpetuation of these harvests, laborers were needed to work in the fields of
Osiris. Egypt soon relinquished the slaughter of laboring slaves, whose graves
271 have been discovered around the First Dynasty mastabas in north Saqqara. In
the Old Kingdom, live sacrifices were replaced by statuettes of servants placed
inside the tomb, and from the time of the Middle Kingdom even these were
superseded by small figurines (ushabtiu) in stone, terra cotta, or wood, which
were magically given life to undertake hard labor in the Osirian fields (Speleers,
1923, p. 24). Similarly, figurines of female servants served as concubines to the
dead lord.

Death possessed every privilege. This conviction must have existed from very early times. W. B. Emery found a boat for the use of the dead next to a royal mastaba from the First Dynasty in north Saqqara, and another in Heliopolis. 272 Other, more modest graves by the side of the Nile also had small boats buried beside them.

Like the stars and the sun-god Ra, the dead were caught up in a cosmic wandering. They did not remain perpetually within their tombs, nor perpetually in the hereafter. Some idea of existence after death is given in a funerary text from the Eighteenth Dynasty: "Thou goest in, thou comest out, while thy heart is glad in the favor of the Lord of Gods. . . . It so happens that thou livest again. *Thy soul will not be kept away from thy body*. . . . Thou receivest what is upon earth. Thou hast water, thou breathest the air, thou drinkest to thy heart's content" (Piankoff, 1957, p. 3; my italics).

The ordinary dead were accorded the grace to live like gods. A late hymn to Amon-Ra runs: "Ancient One who early arises as a youth, who takes hold of the limits of eternity, who circles on high, passing through the Netherworld in order to give light to the land with what he has created" (p. 13).

Death betokened no end, it was a translation into the cosmic cycle of the eternal renewal of life. The process of thought on which this is based can be dialectically termed a unity that goes beyond the present: "All that lives and all that grows is the result of an inexplicable and completely mysterious co-operation of heterogeneous factors. . . . Conflicting forces, one might say mutually exclusive forces, combine in the creation of a new state" (p. 29).

It was in Sumer that expression was given for the first time to the tragedy of human existence and the fateful destiny that all must endure: "Man, suffering, striving, doing, as he is and was and ever shall be" (Burckhardt, 1868; tr. 1943, p. 82), man without appurtenances, naked as the celestial goddess Inanna, who, stripped bare in her descent into hell, stood naked before the queen of the nether world. Mankind appears in all its desperation, terrified of death and clutching at present existence, at earthly possessions, at whatever is to hand.

Even the hero Gilgamesh, one-quarter man and three-quarters god, was bound to follow the course of human destiny. His sufferings were but the fate of everyman after death. The spotlight is not on the adventures of Gilgamesh and his friend Enkidu, as it is on Hercules, whose exploits were so much emphasized by the Greeks (e.g., on the metopes of the temple of Zeus at Olympia). The recurrent theme in the Mesopotamian tablets is the severing of relations between two humans caused by the early death of one. After the death of Enkidu, Gilgamesh rushed across the country in a terrified agony of despair, distraught with fear of his own death. He could get no rest until the gods permitted him to meet the shade of Enkidu in the nether world. The two recognized each other, but the news Gilgamesh brought back from the nether world was the destruction of all hope. Enkidu told him: "My body . . . has dwindled, is full of dust, into dust it has sunk" (Pallis, 1956, p. 687).

Gilgamesh desperately desired to avoid the same fate, and the rest of the epic recounts his combat with death by means of a frantic search for the plant of eternal life. When at length he finds it on the floor of the ocean, a serpent, emerging from the waves, eats it while Gilgamesh is bathing. The concept of a preordained fate ruling both the fortunate and the unfortunate, a theme developed two thousand years later in the *Iliad*, is here grimly prefigured in the Gilgamesh epic.

These differing attitudes toward death were mirrored in the two peoples' differing conceptions of the nether world. To the Egyptians it was a place of renewed strength and rebirth. Every evening the sun in its cosmic journey passed through
131 the body of the goddess Nut so that it might next morning be born from between her thighs. Age-old chthonic versions of the creative powers of the earth here have been blended together by the Heliopolitan priesthood.

The nightly journey through the underworld of the sun-god Ra in his boat was beset with dangers which were only there to be happily overcome.

The Sumerian vision of the nether world was of a place totally inimical to life, a place of misery and despair: "Like the Hebrew *Sheol*, the *Kur* [the Sumerian nether world] is the dark, dread abode of the dead. It is a land of no return, whence only exceptionally the shade of a once prominent figure might be called up for questioning" (Kramer, 1959, p. 197).

Kur was a place of restless longing for what has been, for life: "After his death," says S. N. Kramer, describing a poem published in 1919 by Stephen Langdon, "the great king Ur-Nammu comes to Kur. . . . After 'seven days,' after 'ten days,' had passed, the 'wail of Sumer' reaches him. The walls of Ur which he had left unfinished, his newly built palace which he had left unpurified, his wife whom he could no longer press to his bosom" (1956, pp. 182–83).

In "Inanna's Descent to the Nether World," Kramer (pp. 186–93) retranslated and reassembled, from broken and scattered tablets, a story upon which many scholars had worked since 1914.

When Inanna, goddess of love and queen of heaven, went into the nether world, she was stripped naked, bereft of her divinity, and killed by the death-dealing eyes of her sister, Ereshkigal, queen of the nether world. Her corpse was suspended from a stake. Only through ruse and magic could she return from the nether world, and then only under the surveillance of demons, on the condition that she deliver a substitute. She could find none until, coming to the city of her lover, Dumuzi (Tammuz),

She fastened the eye upon him, the eye of death,
Spoke the word against him, the word of wrath,
Uttered the cry against him, the cry of guilt:
"As for him, carry him off."
The pure Inanna gave the shepherd Dumuzi into their hands.

It was Kramer who discovered the end of the story. Up till then, Dumuzi and Inanna had been considered the greatest pair of lovers in Sumerian mythology. He was a vegetation-god like Osiris, and when Inanna was prematurely bereft of him it had been believed that she descended once more into the nether world to bring him back to earth. The cold-blooded inhumanity of the new version gives us an insight into the extreme pessimism of the Mesopotamian world. What is expressed in this Sumerian poem was repeated again and again until the tumultuous history of the Land of the Two Rivers ended.

Influences upon the beginnings of architecture

Unlike Egypt, in Mesopotamia there could be no impetus to create an architecture based on such vague and intangible convictions and such an abysmally pessimistic approach to life after death.

The dead had to rest beneath the earth. There was nothing for them in heaven. Everyone must descend to the nether world, to the "land of no return." It would thus be senseless to erect permanent dwelling places for the dead. So Mesopotamian graves were simply covered with earth, and thus it remained. The serried rows of so-called kings' graves in the Royal Cemetery of Ur, which date from the First Dynasty of Ur (ca. 2500 B.C.), are but underground charnel houses. The most sensational of them, found by C. L. Woolley, belonged to Queen Shubad, who was buried there with eighty sacrificed members of her household. The golden vases and inlaid harps show a cultural standard which bears comparison with the elaborate furnishings, inscribed with hieroglyphs, found in the tomb of Queen Hetep-heres, the mother of Cheops. But architecturally, Mesopotamian tombs were without significance. Yet this was the period when the great pyramids of Cheops, Chephren, and Mycerinus were storming the heavens.

Mesopotamian graves always remained the same. The crypts of the Assyrian kings of the eighth century B.C. found at Khorsabad also had no superstructure.

361 ff The Egyptians' cult of the dead gave birth to their finest architectural achievements. The state temple of the New Kingdom at Karnak is the most impressive,
415 ff but the mortuary temple of Queen Hatshepsut at Deir el Bahari is the masterpiece.

The hopeless nothingness into which the events of Sumerian mythology flow mirrors the fate of Mesopotamia. Few records of power combats between city-states, such as those between Lagash and Umma in the early historic period, have been found, and these have had to be pieced together from the few scattered
60 inscriptions. The earliest account, on the Vulture Stele, describes the victorious campaign by Eannatum of Lagash against the city of Umma (ca. 2460 B.C.). This struggle continued on and off for a century, until finally both were conquered by the mighty Sargon of Akkad. Half a millennium later the same scene was replayed in the Isin-Larsa period (ca. 1960–1700 B.C.) till this power struggle was brought to a decisive end by the great Hammurabi of Babylon. The same story is continually repeated, varying only in dimensions. Finally the world empires of Babylon and Assyria alternately extinguished one another until Cyrus the Persian put an end to the independent existence of Mesopotamia forever.

A long sequence of pitiless conquerors carried out widespread destruction on both sides. On the occasion of one revolt, Assurnasirpal III of Assyria (883–859 B.C.) ordered "all the chief rebels flayed and the scaffold [which he had erected for this purpose] draped with their skins . . . others . . . impaled on stakes above the tower" (Schmökel, 1957, pp. 252–53).

When Assurbanipal, the otherwise cultivated leader of Assyria, conquered Babylon in 648 B.C., the devastation was carried to such extremes that even the bones of previous kings were exhumed. He boasted: "The sepulchres of these earlier and later kings . . . I destroyed, I devastated, I exposed to the sun. . . . I laid restlessness upon their shades" (Champdor, 1957; tr. 1958, p. 88). This conqueror's power reached to the margins of the then known world, with the exception of Egypt. Less than half a century later, however, in 612 B.C., Assyria was decimated, and Nineveh razed to the ground. "Nineveh was buried under a heap of ashes; her arrogant warrior-people had been driven off to the bottom of Nergal's nether world, where each newcomer receives as his only sustenance the sixty sicknesses that are to afflict him throughout eternity, where he becomes but one more spectre among the drifting shadows, dreaming forever of a return to earth to devour the living" (pp. 91–92).

Babylon's magnificence was renewed for the last time by Nebuchadnezzar: its resplendent ziggurat, Etemenanki—the Tower of Babel—its great Ishtar Gate, and stately processional avenue. Barely twenty years after Nebuchadnezzar's death Babylon was conquered by Cyrus, in 538 B.C. The Babylonian kingdom became a Persian province. Seldom in history has destiny rolled with such recurrent ruthlessness, and simultaneously with such cinematic compression.

Periods of Egypt and Sumer: dates and disparities

In comparing the disparate structures of the two archaic civilizations, the dates for their beginnings are particularly important, for both in turn took the lead. Unhappily there is no agreement—no *communis opinio*—in determining the start of the historical era. For earlier periods we have only relative datings as to their time and duration, derived from the position and thickness of the strata in which their artifacts were found.

Even after the invention of script—around 3000 B.C.—there are but the barest evidences of tangible history. Early Sumerian clay tablets are inscribed with reckonings of goods in the temple communities and, in the first two dynasties of Egypt, the few hieroglyphs found on funerary steles or as seal impressions on vases only give the name of the dead lord or the name of the reigning monarch.

Later in Egypt the "king lists" become available. These are tablets on which the names of the successive kings are engraved within their cartouches. They date from the period of the New Kingdom. Sety I placed the Tablet of Abydos in his temple to honor his seventy-six antecedents. The Tablet of Karnak was placed in the festival hall (Akh Menou) of Tuthmosis III, and the Tablet of Saqqara was found in the tomb of the royal scribe of Ramesses II. Only one of the papyrus lists, which were also placed in the temples, has been found: the greatly damaged Turin *Canon of Kings*, from the time of Ramesses II.

These lists contain several versions of the number of years each Pharaoh reigned. In addition, there are several fragments of a history of Egypt written by the Egyptian priest Manetho around 250 B.C., which now seem more reliable than had long been thought. Alan Gardiner throws light on these and other sources in his *Egypt of the Pharaohs* (1961, pp. 46–68).

Apart from these, we have the aid of certain astronomical indications from Egyptian texts. Foremost among these are the so-called Sothis dates. The rise of the star Sothis (now called Sirius) occurred simultaneously with the annual onset of the Nile floods and marked the beginning of the new year. Few statements relating to this event can be astronomically determined (Parker, 1950), and only two such dates are really certain, one in the Middle Kingdom and one in the New Kingdom. Parker places the important inauguration date of the Egyptian calendar shortly before 2900 B.C. At that time the year opened with the appearance of the star Sothis, in contrast to the earlier calendar, which, as with almost all primitive peoples, was based on the phases of the moon.

The Egyptologists pride themselves on the discovery of these astronomical dates, which place them on a surer footing than the Sumerian scholars. R. A. Parker's highly illuminating work turns on mathematical arguments, difficult for the nonmathematician to follow. He is less interested in the exact dating of individual kings or dynasties than in the important date of the opening of Egyptian history.

The "short" and "long" chronologies

It is now possible to make a thorough revision of the earlier, too ancient datings of the prehistoric and protohistoric periods of Egypt and Mesopotamia, and, beyond this, for the historic period. Today preference is given to the so-called short chronology. But the date of the opening of the historic period, which plays an important role in both high civilizations, is still under discussion.

The British Museum, the Metropolitan Museum of Art in New York, and the Museum of Fine Arts in Boston place the beginning of the historic period at 3200 B.C., while J. Vandier of the Louvre holds to the date of 3300 B.C.

The importance of establishing dates for the beginnings of the historic period in Egypt and Sumer is illustrated by the work of a great scholar who, in 1925, calculated that the date for Egypt should be pushed back to 4186 B.C., so that its achievements would have a thousand-year priority over similar ones in Mesopotamia (Meyer, 1925, p. 46). In 1941, Alexander Scharff sought clarification of this famous and much disputed question of which could claim seniority (p. 6). These inquiries were quite understandable, since it was only in the thirties and forties that excavations in Mesopotamia probed down to virgin soil and that Mesopotamia's priority in the fourth millennium could be firmly established (as in Tepe Gawra and Hassuna in the north, Eridu and Uruk in the south).

To arrive at direct comparisons between Egypt and Sumer we need a chronology jointly established by Egyptologists and Sumerian scholars. Though comparative tables appear in almost every book, they rarely agree. It is only possible to compare the major trends.

As early as 1926, Scharff had attacked the long chronology of E. Meyer. In Scharff's view, the Early Dynastic period opened in 2850 B.C. In his last book, in which he dealt with Egypt and A. Moortgat with the Near East (Scharff and Moortgat, 1950), the chronologies of Egypt and Mesopotamia were almost synchronized.

W. F. Albright is also in agreement with the short chronology for both Egypt and Mesopotamia (1946, p. 364). Later he stated more explicitly: "We are now safe in approximating the chronology of Scharff and Stock, from which the independent chronology, defended by the writer since 1925, seldom diverges by over fifty years" (1954, p. 30).

Since then, on the basis of Parker's studies and his precisely evaluated relationships between the datings of individual periods and, above all, the beginning of the Egyptian state, J. von Beckerath has pushed back the beginning of the First Dynasty slightly. After a careful sifting of dates, working backward, von Beckerath came to the conclusion that the First Dynasty began in 2950 B.C. plus or minus fifty years (von Beckerath, 1961, pp. 31–32). However, from the viewpoint of our book the divergence of this date from the one currently employed, 2850 B.C., is not material, since in any case no precise links are possible with the Sumerian development. In summarizing, von Beckerath comes to the conclusion that "research has now attained such a general measure of certainty that only the Early Period (First and Second Dynasties) and details of the so-called Intermediate periods between the chief periods (the Old, Middle, and New Kingdoms, and the Late Period) remain unclear" (1961, p. 28). I am keeping to his dates.

How carefully the Egyptologists have probed into the matter of datings can be seen in the following comparative table sent to me by von Beckerath in connection with the duration of the Old Kingdom:

Dynasties	Scharff 1950	Parker 1950	Helck 1962	Hayes 1962	v. Beckerath 1962
VI–VIII	ca. 190 years	187 years	187 years	ca. 185 years	187 years
V	" 130 "	160 "	141 "	" 150 "	152 "
IV	" 120 "	113 "	113 "	" 120 "	118 "
III	" 50 "	50 "	55 "	" 55 "	52 "
Total	" 490 "	510 "	496 "	" 510 "	509 "

The Differing Destinies of Egypt and Sumer

Comparative chronology can provide certain insights. There is, for example, the question: When was human beauty first recognized? Throughout prehistory the human face and the human posture were considered inferior to those of the
104 animal. Then German archaeologists working in Uruk found a lovely female countenance, in transparent alabaster, which reflects the whole Sumerian melancholy. It was found in a Jemdet Nasr stratum of about 2800–2700 B.C. In
109 Egypt female beauty was first recognized some centuries later, though it then encompassed the entire female figure.

The periods of Mesopotamia

Histories of Egypt and the Near East describe the various periods of each country. We shall here touch only on those which occur in this book.

PREHISTORIC BEGINNINGS: The prehistoric periods in Mesopotamia are named after the locality where the artifacts of each period were first discovered. In historic time the names of cities often take the place of localities.

Hassuna period: This north Mesopotamian village culture goes back to around 5000 B.C., with richly informative settlements and decorated pottery that ranges
101 from simple triangles scratched upon convex vessels to a masklike female face
100 upon a vase neck. It is related to the painted pottery of Samarra, which itself
454 has connections with the highly developed animal drawings on the pottery of Iran (Giyan, Sialk, Susa).

Al 'Ubaid period: Named after a mound of ruins not far from Ur; its pottery is spread over almost the whole of Mesopotamia. In this period temple building at-
196 tained its greatest elegance. The finest attainments were the acropolis of Tepe
202 Gawra in the north, around 3500 B.C., and Temple VII at Eridu in the south, both built about the same time.

Al 'Ubaid pottery acquired highly sensitive shapes, such as the flattened liba-
243 tion vessels with very slender spouts—the so-called tortoise vases. Sculpture, on the other hand, did not progress beyond idol figurines such as the bird-headed
I:177 female figures from Ur, or the countless figurines found in Tepe Gawra and many other places.

Uruk period: Around 3000–2800 B.C. Named after the chief cultural center of Sumer, the city of Uruk, the biblical Erech and contemporary Warka. This was the city of the fertility-goddess Inanna. In the precinct of her sanctuary stood a
203 temple (Uruk level IV) never surpassed in Sumer in size or elaborate articulation.

The use of script in this period marks the opening of the historic era.

Jemdet Nasr period: Around 2800–2600 B.C. Although the period is named after a mound of ruins thirty kilometers northeast of Babylon, the chief finds come from Uruk: numerous reliefs, a tall alabaster ritual vase dedicated to the 121
goddess Inanna, and the lovely female face referred to earlier. Probably there 104
were greater works of sculpture than we know of in the preceding Uruk period, for the perfection of the Jemdet Nasr period can scarcely represent a beginning phase. Cylinder seals also attained perfection.

Protoliterate period: This appellation derives from the Chicago School and is used "to designate those cultural phases in early Mesopotamian history in the course of which writing first appeared and developed until it reached the stage in which the phonetic principle . . . began to be employed. . . . We include in this term the later part of what has been called 'Uruk period' and the whole of the 'Jamdat Nasr period' " (Delougaz and Lloyd, 1942, p. 8, footnote).

EARLY DYNASTIC PERIOD: This appellation is widely used; the period is frequently subdivided into First, Second, and Third Early Dynastic. It embraces the period from 2600–2350 B.C., from the time when Sumer was split up into a number of rival city states until its conquest by Sargon of Akkad.

Mesilim period: Around 2600 B.C. Named after King Mesilim of Kish, a city not far from Babylon, it begins the Early Dynastic period. In the Mesilim period the dominance of the priestly office makes inroads on the notion of royalty despite the continued existence of the priest-king. This is the period in which, for the first time, a spacious king's palace was discovered, with courts, halls, and columns (Palace A at Kish). Apparently also to the Mesilim period belongs "the first great wall of world history, which should archaeologically be shifted to the Mesilim period, the 9.5-kilometer-long double wall of Uruk, with its more than eight hundred semicircular towers, but only two gates" (Schmökel, 1957, p. 19).

First Dynasty of Ur (Ur I period): Around 2500 B.C. Renowned for the discovery of the Royal Cemetery of Ur, with its "death pit." Copper sculpture was developed to full three-dimensionality in the temple of King A-anni-pad-da at Al 'Ubaid (6 km. from Ur). At the same time the city of Lagash was growing, seventy-five kilometers north of Ur. The grandson of this city's founder, Eannatum (ca. 2460 B.C.), inscribed upon his Vulture Stele the first account of wars 60
and battles.

Akkadian period: Around 2350–2150 B.C. Named after the newly founded capital of Sargon of Akkad. The first conqueror on a large scale, he also created the first standing army—5400 men. Like the later dictators of Babylon and As-
65 syria, he was deified. This is the period when the cylinder seals blazon the dethronement of the animal.

After two centuries of unified rule the state was split up by the invasion of the Guti (ca. 2200–2075 B.C.). After their displacement came the final renaissance of Sumer.

Ur III period: Around 2065–1960 B.C. Under King Urnammu the largest ziggurats (temple towers) were built in Sumer. Standards of house building reached a level unsurpassed even today in the Near East: the patio houses of
186 around 2000 B.C.

The main theme of the fragmentary reliefs on the Urnammu stele is the erec-
123 tion of the great ziggurat of Ur, but they show also that king and god now stand on an equal footing.

This brings to a close the Sumerian culture, which for more than two millenniums had formed the basis of Mesopotamian learning and architecture.

114 A generation earlier, under the rule of the pious priest-king Gudea, the city of Lagash was producing the finest portrait statues of Mesopotamia. Their humanity outshines not only the later representations of Assyrian rulers in obvious poses of might; even in Egypt there are no portrait statues which combine such gentleness with such an awareness of human destiny.

Babylon: Around 1830–1530 B.C. During the few centuries of the old Babylonian empire's existence, the earlier Sumerian knowledge was assimilated and expanded. In comparison with other periods of Mesopotamian history this was a quiet, almost gentle time: a creative pause for breath.

Babylon first came to full power with the rise of Hammurabi (1728–1686 B.C.). The dates of Hammurabi's reign were independently ascertained by German and American scholars, and establish a fulcrum for the short chronology.

He cast off the divinity of the Akkadian kings and spoke of himself as "Shepherd of the people." After the conquest of Mesopotamia, the organization of human communications was his innermost desire. The famous Hammurabi Stele in the Louvre, with its three hundred laws, gives proud evidence of this.

There is little to report of artistic works from this period. In poetry, the epic *Enūma Eliš* does not, like the epic of Gilgamesh, deal with affairs of human destiny. It is a creation myth in which the gods wage a grisly battle for existence against the primordial earth mother Tiamat (Pritchard, 1950, pp. 60–72). There was, however, a deepening and expansion of scientific knowledge. It is inessential that the Pythagorean theorem has not been found set down in its accepted form. It expresses, and grew out from, the Mesopotamians' interest in determining relationships between astral constellations and human affairs. As we shall see, the content of the Pythagorean theorem was undoubtedly known at the time of Hammurabi, as a small tablet with cuneiform writing in the Babylonian 473 collection of Yale University shows. The people of Mesopotamia were the finest logicians and mathematicians of their time. But one must beware of setting their scientific aims on a parallel with those of today. What we call science was for them but a by-product of the foretelling of human destiny. In the forefront, just as in prehistory, stood their longing to make contact with supernatural forces. Spells, magic, predictions, were not only part of their religion—they were systematically and officially organized. In contrast to later times, they were all closely bound up with official religious beliefs. G. Contenau, an eminently dependable scholar, considers magic a most important element in the life of the state (1947). The belief that man possesses a certain sensitivity that can enable him to foresee future occurrences, or, as we would now say, that he can develop mediumistic powers, lay at the basis of the Cabala, for example, as Contenau points out. Man, made in the image of God, also bore within himself certain supernatural powers.

On the circuitous routes to the knowledge of contemporary atomic physics, which often contradict ordinary logic and rationalism, we have begun to be less certain than the Positivists that we understand what is taking place: an attempt at systematization of the nonmaterialistic powers at work in man.

Omens, the prediction of future occurrences from certain definite signs, constituted the motivating force of Babylonian scientific observations. As Otto Neugebauer, the best scholar of the scientific knowledge of antiquity, says, astronomical determinations were undertaken "to provide empirical material for omina; important events in the life of the state were correlated with important celestial phenomena, exactly as specific appearances on the livers of sacrificial sheep were carefully recorded in the omen literature (1951, p. 95).

Kassite period: Around 1560–1150 B.C. The rule of the Kassite mountain people fell like a blight on the Sumerian, Babylonian, and Akkadian cultures. Little is left from the many centuries of their dominion. The best insight into this dark

126, 127 period is given by the *kudurru* (steles), with their assembly of symbols of deities. These boundary stones, which were preserved in the temples, reveal a preponderant interest in agriculture and, bound up with it, a great respect for titles to land. There appears to have been little interest in the founding or development of cities. The Kassites' legacy to architecture is just as barren: a small temple to Anu in Uruk, whose façade with its figures of deities deviates
235 from Mesopotamian tradition, and the ziggurat Aqar Quf (ca. 1400 B.C.), whose steepness would have appeared barbaric to Mesopotamian eyes.

This long cultural bloodletting had its consequence upon the final development of Mesopotamia. It is true that knowledge was further refined. King Assurbanipal assembled objects from the Sumerian and Akkadian cultures in his library at Nineveh, and an antiquarian interest in buildings of the past arose, much as in the contemporary Saite period in Egypt. But nothing new was inaugurated. A development of four millenniums came to an end in an atmosphere of frustrated expectations, just like Gilgamesh.

The periods of Egypt

The periods of Egypt, early and late, have a crystalline simplicity compared to the lacerated fate of Mesopotamia. Unlike Mesopotamia, Egypt's early period gives no hint of its later development—it bears no comparison with Mesopotamia's early period and is almost provincial. It will be touched upon only fragmentarily here.

PREHISTORIC BEGINNINGS: In Upper and Lower Egypt there were village communities. These were extremely primitive right up to the threshold of the historic period. The oldest agriculture developed in Lower Egypt. Cylindrical granaries were found in the neolithic villages of the Faiyum, west of the Nile and about fifty miles south of Cairo, and reed huts in neolithic Merimdeh, on the west bank of the Nile delta. Early Ma'adi and El 'Omari, near Cairo, had round and oval huts, and in Ma'adi we meet a custom that goes back to Mousterian times: burial of the dead beneath the dwelling.

In the south, information is obtained mostly from the many cemeteries, and these give their names to the different periods. Their absolute dating is still conjectural.

Tasian period: Fifth millennium. Named after Deir Tasa, about twenty miles south of Assiut. Few relics, one of them a black, tulip-shaped beaker with simple triangles inlaid with white.

Badarian period: Fourth millennium. Named after El Badari, just south of Deir Tasa. Primitive pottery and figurines, such as the compact clay figure of a woman with a heavy head, large incised eyes, and hatched vulva. Other sculp- 1:177
turally interesting seated female figurines also appear at this time, with fully 75
developed breasts and powerful thighs.

Amratian period: Second half of the fourth millennium. Named after El 'Amrah, south of Abydos; sometimes also called the Nagadah I period, after Nagadah, about fifteen miles north of Thebes. Primitive figurines in terra cotta and ivory; pottery vessels engraved with animals, men, and latticelike hatchings. Occasional glimmerings of later cosmic concepts appear, as on an oval dish on 129
which the Mountains of the East and of the West, the morning and the evening sun and its daily and nightly orbits, are drawn in white.

Gerzean period: Reaching into the historic period. Named after El Gerza, south of Cairo. By far the most important preliminary period in northern Egypt. Imagination is visibly less constrained, as shown in the different types of ships with superstructures and human figures drawn upon pottery vases, as well as a 360
wall painting in Hierakonpolis from this period. Cosmetic palettes were also further developed.

Egypt was now eagerly seeking new means of expression and adopting motifs from the more advanced Sumerians (Kantor, 1944, pp. 110–36; 1952, pp. 239–50).

The Old Kingdom: The period of groping and searching also encompassed the first two dynasties, the Early Dynastic period (ca. 2950–2650 B.C. Scharff gives 2850 B.C.). The breakthrough occurred in the Third Dynasty, whose duration was as short as it was glorious. Such a sudden eruption of the imagination as appears in the mortuary complex of King Zoser at Saqqara has seldom been ob- 274
served in architectural history. The Third Dynasty is included in the so-called pyramid age by reason of Zoser's step pyramid. We do not wish to depart from customary usage, although the program of the Zoser complex is quite different from the priest-ordained ritual of the dead of the Fourth Dynasty pyramid complexes (2591–2473 B.C.). This transposition of complicated ritual into architectural form at Giza leads to a high point in Egyptian history in the 316
twenty-sixth century.

A period of decline set in slowly in the Fifth Dynasty (2473–2321 B.C.) and accelerated in the Sixth Dynasty (2321–2160 B.C.). The highly centralized power structure split apart, and with it the state. There followed the First

Intermediate period (ca. 2134–2040 B.C.), a time of misery and decay leading to sheer anarchy and the rise of powerful feudal overlords (nomarchs) in the provinces. Anyone wishing to study the state of development at this period must seek his information from the tombs of the nomarchs.

THE MIDDLE KINGDOM: 2040–1785 B.C. Egypt recovered herself in the Middle Kingdom, the shortest of the three great periods of Egypt. We are now very far from the ingenuous assurance of the Old Kingdom, when, especially at its summit, everything was directed toward one eternal ascent. All existence had been disrupted by anarchy and destitution, and toward the end of the Middle Kingdom new calamities were already threatening. If one looks into the faces of the leaders of these later days one finds them deeply engraved with lines of worry about the future.

In the meantime, however, there was a period of peculiar intensity, whose obscure sources have recently been elucidated as far as possible (Winlock, 1947). We have only fragmentary indications of the political events and the works of art. Both in the north and in the south only isolated relics of the temples of the Twelfth Dynasty have survived from which their dimensions may be inferred. Our only knowledge of the temple of Sesostris I (1971–1929 B.C.) in Heliopolis comes from his obelisk, the first of its kind. His Heb-Sed pavilion near the temple of Karnak, its columns engraved with the most delicate reliefs,
364 was found broken up and buried beneath an Eighteenth Dynasty pylon, and was carefully pieced together again.

The reunification of the Two Lands proceeded from Upper Egypt, the impetus coming from Thebes. The internal warrings between the nomarchs, the rulers of Thebes, and the kings of Herakleopolis were brought to an end by Mentuhotep II. It was he who again brought unity to the kingdom, in 2040 B.C., and he held it securely together throughout the fifty years of his reign. Only a few years after his death the short-lived Eleventh Dynasty also expired.

Mentuhotep's tomb is the most important of those of the Middle Kingdom if
413 one judges from the standpoint of originality. It lies in a valley at Deir el Bahari, beside the much later mortuary temple of Queen Hatshepsut. In conception it lies between the tombs of the nomarchs and Hatshepsut's mortuary temple.

In the Twelfth Dynasty (1991–1785 B.C.) King Amenemhat I left his residency in the north to build himself a new capital south of Memphis, near the entrance to the Faiyum. The notion of royalty had lost some of its divinity. The Amenemhats and Sesostrises carried out intensive land settlement projects.

They built canals and transformed the area around the Faiyum into a fertile region.

The *genius loci* imposes itself. For the last time in the north, royal graves take the form of pyramids. But means for creating a solid construction were lacking, as was the conviction that the god-king was the indispensable intermediary for eternal life. The brick pyramids of Lisht and Dahshur, erected within sight of the pyramids of Sneferu, did not even survive their own time. Thus it came about that the granite pyramidion, the peak of Amenemhat III's pyramid 448 (1842–1798 B.C.), was recovered intact with its evidences of the highly refined reliefs of the late years of the Twelfth Dynasty.

After the First Intermediate period art had to recover its form-giving powers. The statues of the unifier of the kingdom, Mentuhotep II, are still retrogressive. The coming subtlety appears in the sunken reliefs, as in the scene of Queen Kawit's toilet, with its deeply engraved outlines. From the beginning of the 155 Twelfth Dynasty, however, a certain hardness can be observed, as in the relief of the god Ptah embracing King Sesostris I (1971–1929 B.C.), from one of the 92 columns of the reassembled pavilion at Karnak.

It was only toward the close of the Middle Kingdom that art rose to its highest intensity: in the sculptures of King Sesostris III (1878–1842 B.C.) and Amenemhat III. These are the most singular of that period. The eternal youth characteristic of the Old Kingdom is no more. These statues were not placed in inaccessible tombs. They stood in the temple, like those of Gudea in Lagash (ca. 2000 B.C.). But they do not bear the benign yet impersonal features of the Asiatic. These statues fall between the unapproachable severity of Zoser in his 291 serdab and the somewhat effeminate expressionism of the Akhenaten portraits. Their combination of bitter experience and lofty majesty has no counterpart in other periods of Egyptian art.

This represents one side of Egyptian life in the early second millennium. It was otherwise in the realm of private life. Here, in the reliefs, paintings, and jewelry, a rare delicacy emerged. Painting and jewelry attained astonishing subtleties of color. This appears, for example, in the painting of the inner walls of a wooden chest from Deir el Bersheh, in central Egypt (Museum of Fine Arts, Boston), where birds, fruit, and offerings are painted directly onto the brown cedarwood in warm, bright colors, leaving the wood between them untouched. The art with which the color is applied gives a striking translucence to the objects, such as is achieved today by the use of similar techniques in the paintings of Joan Miró.

The same sheen appears on the colored stones which stud the jewelry found in the graves of the princesses at Lisht. Semitransparent precious stones set between thin gold threads in the perforated royal breastplates (pectorals) give a shimmer to the plumage of a falcon almost like the painting on the wooden sarcophagus from Deir el Bersheh. The carving of the slender wooden figures of
462 bearers of offerings found in the same grave shows the same delicacy as the reliefs of the period. Cyril Aldred's small book *Middle Kingdom Art in Ancient Egypt* (1950) contains a concentrated evaluation of the art of this time, and W. Stevenson Smith is an excellent guide through the involvements of its history (1958, pp. 88–120).

The New Kingdom: The Second Intermediate period set in as furtively as the First. Its limits are even more vague, since the Hyksos invasion can only be firmly determined a century after the breakdown of central authority. The Hyksos, who built their capital, Avaris (now identified with Tanis), on the eastern Nile delta, were not a homogeneous racial group. They have left little behind them other than countless tax collector's scarabs, which are found everywhere in the provinces.

One cannot consider these "shepherd folk," as they were called in antiquity, as simple barbarians like the Kassites, who at that time were conquering Mesopotamia. The Hyksos' advanced technology enabled them to conquer Egypt. In his chapter on "Hyksos Importations into Egypt," Winlock says that the Egyptian "was not practical. . . . The Egyptian had not made a single important development over his ancestors in any practical thing which would go to make life less arduous. He was always content to live as his forebears had, until some outsider forced him to adopt a new way of life" (1947, p. 150).

The Hyksos brought with them the horse and the chariot, such as were used many centuries earlier in Sumer. Their most significant importation was the short bow made up of several thin layers of wood, or wood and horn, glued together: as far as we know, the earliest version of plywood. From the Hyksos the Egyptians learned to improve the technical efficiency of their arrows, daggers, helmets, shields, and other implements of war, so that an up-to-date arsenal was in readiness for the New Kingdom's world conquests (pp. 158–63).

The New Kingdom is sometimes considered to have lasted from about 1550 to 715 B.C., when the strange Nubian kingdom, from far in the south, near the Fourth Cataract of the Nile, extended its rule over Egypt. But von Beckerath considers it more correct to terminate it at the end of the Twentieth Dynasty (1080 B.C.). The great period of the New Kingdom covered the Eighteenth and

Nineteenth Dynasties (ca. 1550–1198 B.C.). This period, including the years of transition, lasted about half a millennium, comparable in length and brilliance to the Old Kingdom. These two periods above all embody the creative side of the Egyptian nature.

The Eighteenth Dynasty: From the time of Ahmose (1552–1527 B.C.), who expelled the Hyksos, the Tuthmosids of the Eighteenth Dynasty presented a series of sharply delineated rulers. Tuthmosis I advanced on the Nubians and thrust them back almost to the Fourth Cataract. He also started the grandiose development of the temple of Amon at Karnak. His daughter, Hatshepsut (1490–?1469 B.C.) introduced the concept of large-scale, long-term planning. Tuthmosis III, who destroyed much that Hatshepsut had built, erected his festival hall (Akh Menou) at the east end of the Karnak complex: perhaps the ultimate in structural skill attained by Egypt. 369

The mortuary temple of Queen Hatshepsut in Deir el Bahari shows a mastery in handling space, adaptation to a vast landscape, and great architectural independence. Egyptian architecture never again achieved such majestic and at the same time so deft a command of spatial relationships. 262 col

Tuthmosis III presented a dramatic contrast to Hatshepsut. He conquered the greater part of western Asia, and under him the bounds of Egypt were extended farther even than under the Ramessides. He achieved world power for Egypt for a longer time than was granted to either Babylon or Assyria.

The dimensions and colossal statues of the mortuary temples of King Amenhotep III (1400–1362 B.C.) foreshadowed the gigantic scale of the Ramessides.

In the temple of Luxor, also dedicated to Amon, the reliefs in the innermost area—like those in Hatshepsut's mortuary temple—satisfied the desire to produce evidence of the divine origin of the monarch. As always in Egypt, reliefs present the art of the period at its most subtle. In the tombs of high Theban officials such as Ramose, they attain an insurpassable delicacy.

After the short interlude of Akhenaten (Amenhotep IV) and his Amarna period (1362–1345 B.C.) the new dynasty opened.

The Nineteenth Dynasty: The Ramessides came from Avaris (now identified with Tanis), which they rebuilt as their capital. They were the last dynasty of world renown. Ramesses II (1290–1224 B.C.) towers over their other kings. As so often, there is difficulty in establishing exact dates. It is known that Ramesses II reigned for sixty-six years, and in recent studies Parker has shown that two different datings are possible for him: 1304–1238 B.C., and 1290–1224 B.C. For historical reasons, von Beckerath accepts the later date: 1290–1224 B.C. (1961, p. 30).

Throughout his long reign he was equally famous as a general and as a fanatical builder. One still finds traces of his buildings everywhere in Egypt. His most
386 colossal work was the completion of the great hypostyle hall at Karnak. Monumental dimensions were the master stroke. But there was no tendency, as in the Old Kingdom, to achieve monumentality by reduction to the barest essentials. Now individual building elements acquired colossal dimensions, as, for example, the columns of the great hypostyle at Karnak. Not only were there colossal statues of Ramesses II from Memphis to Thebes and farther up the Nile to the rock temple of Abu Simbel, but even the reliefs surrounding the great hypostyle at Karnak acquired a gigantic scale. Only when their scale is reduced, as in the figure of the queen, who scarcely reaches the knee of the colossus of Ramesses,
381 does the former Egyptian grace again shine through.

After the death of Ramesses II (1224 B.C.) the curve of Egypt's fate took a rapid downward turn. In the following Twentieth Dynasty (1198–1080 B.C.) nine more kings bore the name of the great Ramesses, but only one of them, Ramesses III (1195–1164 B.C.) had much character. He was the author of the temple and palace at Medinet Habu, in which the tradition of the New Kingdom
87 lives on in the human proportions of the paintings and the fine web of reliefs that covers the walls.

THE MILLENNIUM-LONG FINALE: The Egyptian culture did not come to an abrupt end. It proved itself stronger than its conquerors. After the fall of the New Kingdom the divided country was ruled by the priest-kings of the sacred city of Amon at Thebes, and by the kingdom of Tanis in the north (Montet, 1952). Libyan and Nubian Pharaohs followed: the Twenty-second and Twenty-third Dynasties at Bubastis. Then came the Nubians (Kushites) of the Twenty-fifth Dynasty. They were educated as Ethiopian kings, but Egyptian influence was dominant and all took over the culture of the Egyptian ruling class.

Saite period: 664–525 B.C. The most interesting phenomenon of the Late Period was the Twenty-sixth Dynasty, from the delta city of Sais. These rulers, probably of Libyan origin, temporarily gave new life to the finest Egyptian traditions. It is possible to see the great Saite interest in the art of the Old Kingdom and in the portraits of the Middle Kingdom as just a neutral antiquarianism, like the care with which they rebuilt monuments of the Old Kingdom, even creating new entrances to Zoser's tomb beneath the step pyramid. But it was more than this. It should not be confused with the rebirth of antiquity in the Renaissance, or with the nineteenth century's sniffing about for styles in all past periods. The Saite period was engaged in a despairing but most interesting attempt to permeate the present with the past in order to create a new continuity. That the actual situation of Egypt at the time doomed this effort to failure is another matter. The strength was lacking to inaugurate a fourth great period in Egypt.

That this was not simply an epigonic imitation is shown by the bronze animal statuettes made to be placed as votive offerings in the temples, as for example falcons, ibis (the bird of Thoth), or the numerous cat statues dedicated to the goddess Bastet, which enclosed mummies of cats. These form part of the revi- 40
talizing of the animal cult in the Saite period and were standardized products. However, the Egyptian sculptural tradition lived on in them: not so much to express the external appearance of the animal as its characteristic essence. No cat ever had quite the proportions or sat quite so upright as the cats of Bastet, but it is exactly those traits which give them their fascination.

An insight into the art and psychology of the Saite period and the final phase of the Egyptian development is of the greatest interest to us today. This research is just beginning (Bothmer, Müller, and De Meulenaere, 1960).

There was over a century of Persian rule. There was the conquest by Alexander the Great. Then three centuries under the Ptolemies. Finally Egypt became a Roman province.

The most noteworthy feature is the persistence of the religio-cultural structure, which was maintained for almost a millennium after the end of the New Kingdom. Translated into our period this means from the time of Charlemagne to the nineteenth century: in other words, the entire span of European civilization from the midst of the Dark Ages to the Industrial Revolution.

The Egyptian culture absorbed all conquerors as soon as they came under its spell. Even under foreign rulers such as the Hyksos (Fifteenth and Sixteenth Dynasties) and the Persian rulers (Twenty-seventh Dynasty), the sequence of the Egyptian dynasties was continued—from the First to the Thirtieth Dynasty.

It was the Egyptians' mythopoetic imagination that sustained the great vitality of their civilization. The notion of kingship changed from that of the divine king of the pyramid age to that of the king as an instrument of the favor of the gods in the Late Period. But the tradition of kingship persisted throughout, and with it the king's direct relations with the gods. Alexander the Great, the Ptolemaic kings, and the Roman emperors up to Domitian all assume the ritual gestures and garments of the Pharaohs and stand before the gods in the manner of the great rulers of Egypt's prime.

PART II THE EGGSHELLS OF PREHISTORY

The problem of constancy and change undergoes considerable extension during the first high civilizations, which arose in Egypt and Sumer in the course of the fourth millennium B.C.

It no longer only concerns constancy and change within certain phases of culture, as in prehistory, however long they endured. With the advent of the high civilizations the question arises: What prehistoric traditions still live on in Egypt and Sumer? What is changed and what is radically new?

I:passim

In this volume we shall show how certain prehistoric phenomena persist until the end of Egypt's existence, and in what context changes appear which will be inherited by the Mediterranean civilizations.

A strong cord that was never wholly severed connected the earliest high civilizations with prehistory. Kurt Sethe, who published the Pyramid Texts, opens his *Urgeschichte und älteste Religion der Ägypter* with these words: "It has rightfully been said of the people of Egypt that, unlike other nations, their eggshells always remained with them" (1930, p. 1). Sethe's point was that the Egyptians always clung to their original conceptions and experienced no difficulty in juxtaposing the old with the new and the new with the old.

Perhaps one should go even further: the Egyptians never completely lost the eggshells even of their prehistory. The cord which connected them with their prehistoric development was never entirely severed. Indeed, this continued linkage was at the basis of their nature; it accounts for what is to us largely incomprehensible—the inseparability of the probable and the improbable, logic and illogic, science and mysticism. Similarly the inner bonds between the animate and inanimate worlds, between men, animals, plants, matter, and the cosmos, were never sundered. Mentally this is not difficult to grasp, but emotionally it is a world we cannot enter.

For the Egyptians, the animate had direct relations with the inanimate: the living with the dead.

Their reverence for the animal reflects their reverence for everything imbued with life. This most important primeval tradition stressed a direct communion with the animal world. In other words, the acceptance of the relation between society and natural species, the reverence for the animal, was maintained, as A. R. Radcliffe-Brown (1952) has found it maintained among primitive peoples today. However, in the first high civilizations, this primeval tradition underwent a special kind of development with the creation of a new world of gods.

Their attitude toward the animal is their strongest link with the prehistoric conception of the oneness of all life. The consequences arising from this are everywhere apparent.

We of today, with our firmly anchored acceptance of the supremacy of man and his dominion over plants and animals, our religion based on the Book of Genesis and our logic based on the Greeks, find Egyptian ideas as illogical as they are untenable: such as the identification of the god of creation (Atum) with a lizard or the identification of the sun-god (Ra) with a dung beetle. That this identification of the highest gods with the most insignificant creatures was possible at all betokens an imagination rooted in a world closed to us, a world in which an unbroken cord linked creature with creature, expressed not only as a pictured representation but as a sacred reality. Only if we understand the religious conviction that no discrimination was conceivable within the realm of animate matter can we comprehend that an insignificant insect and the cosmic godhead could be one and the same.

The animal and the symbol held dominion before the advent of the organized world of gods. Veneration of the animal finally vanished with the ascendancy of the Greek and later the Christian *Weltanschauung*.

In the earliest historic periods, animals were not differentiated as high and low, noble and base. Then, animals which in later times were almost ignored received godlike veneration or were theologically identified with gods as their earthly manifestations.

Originally the four male gods of the Ogdoad created at the cult center of Hermopolis were frogs and the four female goddesses were serpents.

Centipedes had their sanctuary.

Scorpions were the companions of Isis, who appears herself "in the form of a scorpion-goddess" (Kees, 1941, p. 59). Selkhit, the enigmatic goddess of death, who from the Mountain of the West takes the setting sun into her arms, is presented as a headless female bust with arms similar to those of a scorpion, and 1:217
at the beginning of the New Kingdom she is shown entirely as a scorpion (Jéquier, 1946, pp. 240–41).

The black dung beetle (scarab), which ran everywhere over the sands of the desert then as it does now, pushing a ball of dung before it, was Khepri, the
self-creator, identified with the morning sun. The ball of dung was the ball of 134
the sun raised aloft between his forelegs, for the scarab was "the earthly manifestation of the formless [highest] god Atum" and was, possibly from the very beginning, connected with the "primeval mount" at Heliopolis, "the first firm spot of the world beginning which separated itself from the chaos of the primeval ocean Nun" (Kees, 1941, p. 215).

We are immediately confronted by the question: What forms did the cult of the animal go through during the first high civilizations? It was in the veneration of individual animals that the prehistoric tradition lived on most forcefully. Later the animal cult underwent a change: the animal acquired divinity. A specially selected animal became the incarnation of an anthropomorphic god, and thus the god himself. The Egyptian development, with its more intensive cult of the dead, presents better evidence of this transition than that of Sumer.

Sumer, on the other hand, offers us a better insight into the continuance of prehistoric imagination in the position occupied by hybrids. Hybrids, composite
1:485 ff creatures, arose in primeval times from man's longing to find a form that would make contact with those invisible powers with which his fate was intertwined. In Sumer, the inexhaustible varieties of prehistoric hybrid forms were reduced to a few types. Animal hybrids incorporated by accumulation the powers of the different animals which composed them, such as the bird Imdugud, which had
56 the body of an eagle and the head of a lioness, and animal-human hybrids like
63 the bull-man.

The continuance of prehistory is also manifested by the stress laid on fertility symbols. In this context, we shall concern ourselves with the female figure as a
74 ff fertility symbol and with the transformation of primeval idols ("Venus figurines") into the Great Mother and goddess, as well as the transformation of an animal into a cosmic and anthropomorphic godhead (cow > Hathor). A male
82 ff fertility symbol, the Egyptian ithyphallic god Min, also reaches back into prehistory.

89 ff Finally, we shall touch on the prehistoric connections of one of the most complicated theological notions: the Ka.

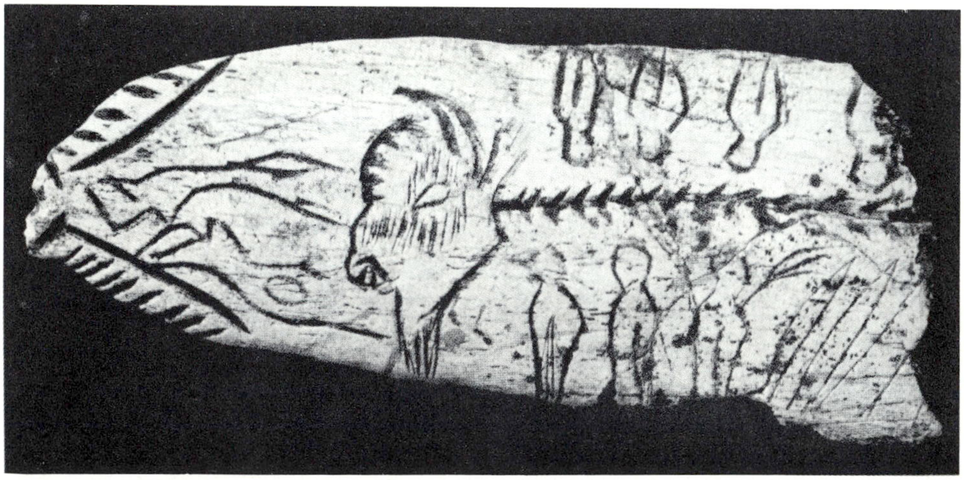

3. MAGDALENIAN BONE ENGRAVING: *Burial of bison accompanied by human mourners. Chancelade (Dordogne)*

THE ANIMAL AND THE ARCHAIC HIGH CIVILIZATIONS

We have designated the role the animal filled in the ritual life of prehistory as sacred, but sacred in the sense used by primitive peoples. They do not separate the sacred from daily life. They do not transfer it to the celestial sphere. For them, sacred and profane are bound together: both spheres are sacred. As mentioned earlier, Mircea Eliade calls this conception the "ambivalence du sacré" 1:278 (1949; tr. 1958, p. 26). The animal was simultaneously an object of veneration, and food. Though killed, it still possessed a fearsome power. Its spirit lived on. Every precaution had to be taken not to arouse its anger and revenge. It was essential to do everything possible to assure its re-entry into existence. This relation with the animal continues throughout the entire primeval period and, though rapidly vanishing, persists among primitive peoples today.

A ritual attitude toward the animal was so deeply embedded in the human spirit that it survived throughout the first high civilizations, especially in Egypt. The veneration of the animal and the belief in its soul persisted, though the nature of such belief changed with changing conditions.

In this context a distinction must be made between the individual animal as object of veneration and the animal as a divinity. The individually venerated animal is any animal of its kind. Its existence does not end with its death. The dead animal and the dead man both compel awe and veneration, the animal possibly more than the man. Magdalenian bone engravings exist which show solemnly festive animal burials, but none has yet been found depicting a human burial. left

The divine animal belongs to the first high civilizations. In Egypt it is a carefully selected example of its species, bearing signs, known only to the learned few, which indicate that it is a personal incarnation of the god—or that, even more, so long as it lives, it is the god himself. The concept of the divine animal is a re-reflecting process. What the theologians present as a divinity is projected back into the being of a specially selected animal.

Transition from sacred animal to deity

At the opening of the historic period there are certain indications of the transition from the animal considered as sacred to the animal considered as god. Animals entered the ambit of the newly emerging world of gods either as the living incarnation of a deity (the bull Apis, the ram Khnum) or as the image of the god in animal form (Thoth as a baboon or as an ibis). 37

During the period of transition from the prehistoric to the historic periods

in Egypt, one is aware, when comparing representations of human figures with
1:455 those of animals, of the strong wind of prehistory with its millenniums of tradition. Incontestably the animal retains its primacy. The human figures, when they exist, are difficult to recognize, just as in earlier periods of prehistory.

Certainly a few exceptions occur in the Early Period, such as a half life-size limestone head (Ashmolean Museum) from Hierakonpolis, whose meaning is far from clear. Some unpretentious 4- to 8-centimeter faïence figurines,
36 almost malachite green, are more informative. They were found in the necropolis at Abydos where Flinders Petrie had earlier unearthed small animal and human statuettes of the same material (1903, pls. 5–6). At first glance one is obliged to ask oneself whether these small humanlike figures can in fact represent human beings, so close are their posture and appearance to those of an animal. On closer inspection a human, though masklike, divided forehead and nose become clearly recognizable. The largest male figurine has the long-drawn-out head that we recognize from the Magdalenian period. It is stretched so far forward that it forms one continuous line with the back, like that of a hyena. The arms rest upon the ground like posts, and are reminiscent of hippopotamus sculptures from the same period (Museum of Fine Arts, Boston). The fingers are depicted by lines engraved upon the pedestal: an ancient prehistoric tradition. All these figurines come from the time of the unification of the two kingdoms of Egypt, or perhaps somewhat earlier.

The supremacy of the animal also appears in the selection of topics. Animals play a far greater role in the Predynastic period than humans. The pictures on the plaster wall at Hierakonpolis, dating from late-Gerzean times—the last phase of prehistory—are predominantly of animals, though some actively
360 handled human figures already appear. Animals also predominate in the rock engravings of the Wady Hammamat, the desert valley which is the closest link between the Red Sea and the Nile. These are now believed to be of the same period.

Several of the ceremonial cosmetic palettes of the First Dynasty have no figures of humans. One such (Ashmolean Museum) was found in the temple of Hierakonpolis. It shows a tumult of wild animals of the greatest vitality. As in prehistory they are disposed freely in space. Since no care was taken to organize them in relation to the neighboring horizontals and verticals, it is still customary to speak of their chaotic lack of grouping and to the absence of spatial coherence. This approach will in time become just as inadmissible as the criticism of prehistoric works according to the rules of visual perspective. Actually this free disposition is one of the last expressions of the prehistoric space conception.

Other small and insignificant reproductions of animals give a more intimate expression of popular beliefs. These objects, measuring only a few centimeters, were laid in graves or used as amulets to afford protection or confer strength. The most varied species are represented: mice, hares, cattle, antelope, crocodiles, lions, etc. In the environs of the oldest temple at Abydos innumerable such miniature animals were found, including sacrificial cattle, hooded falcons, baboons, and frogs.

Animals were honored for special attributes they were assumed to possess. The frog—like the snake—being a chthonic creature seemingly emerging from the earth, was a symbol of nascent and ever-renewed life. Its great fertility bound it to the goddess of birth, and possibly also to the fertility-god Min. When placed in a grave it gave assurance of life in the hereafter.

The eight godheads—the four divine couples—of Hermopolis represented primordial powers, in contrast to the Heliopolitan sun-based religion. These were the powers that existed before world order was established: the primeval ocean, the twilight, endless space, nothingness (Bonnet, 1952, p. 5). As symbols of their origin, these chthonic deities bore the heads of frogs and snakes. As stated earlier, frogs and snakes belonged to the extensive category of creatures honored for their protective powers. They were in no way gods.

The transition from sacred animal to deity was contemporaneous with the establishment of an anthropomorphic world of gods at the beginning of the organization of empire states. In addition to Hermopolis with its eight gods incorporating the chthonic powers, there came Heliopolis, an ancient center now risen to eminence with the sun-god, Atum-Ra, as its supreme deity. The newly founded capital of Memphis made a third center, whose chief god was Ptah, "Lord of the mighty word." He achieved creation by the power of the word, in contrast to spitting or masturbating like the god Atum at Heliopolis. Ptah, like the simultaneously instituted Pharaoh, operated by commands issuing from the heart, the seat of ideas, and the tongue, the seat of speech. Ptah, the intellectual, was a priestly invention *par excellence*. He was depicted as a mummified human **45**
figure, but his earthly incarnation was the bull Apis.

The god Thoth was somewhat different. One of the most pluralistic of all the gods—inventor of the art of writing and himself an author, protector of scribes, founder of astronomy and all intellectual pursuits—Thoth was a typical Late product. Even he, however, bears traces of the transition from sacred animal into animal as deity. Possibly because his origins as a sacred baboon became lost

4. FAÏENCE FIGURINES *showing men in animal-like postures. Early First Dynasty*

in the mists of prehistory, Thoth was finally elevated to the leadership of the eight deities of Hermopolis. He is also sometimes shown in the form of an ibis (probably originating from the Nile delta). His appearance as a baboon establishes the moment when the animal rose to the majesty of a deity. How this transition took place and what had been the earlier attributes of the baboon we do not know. But numerous malachite-green faïence figurines of baboons found in Abydos, Hierakonpolis, and other places can be dated from the prehistoric and protohistoric periods.

right

The 52-centimeter alabaster figure of the god Thoth in the form of a baboon (Staatliche Museen, Berlin) marks the culmination of the transition. God is present in animal form. The pediment of the statue is inscribed with the barely legible name of King Narmer, who had it made as a votive temple offering. The baboon's posture is similar to that of the little faïence human figurines. Traces of color show that it, too, was painted blue-green. The form is still blocklike, abstract. The arms, planted on the ground between the massive thighs, spring

5. THE GOD THOTH *in the form of a baboon, often called the Baboon of Narmer. Egypt's earliest sculptural masterpiece. First Dynasty*

6. MUMMIFIED GAZELLE *surrounded by vases. Heliopolis, Predynastic period*

7. MUMMIFIED GAZELLE. *Esna* (*Upper Egypt*), *Saite period*

from the shoulders in one unwavering curve. With the new dimensions a new monumentality has arisen. The knees project with imposing strength yet are firmly integrated with the block. One senses latent vigor and highly tensed nerves, just as one does in the much later lion's head from the pyramid temple of Ne-user-ra, which shows the same masterly use of sculptural planes. 4

We quote Hedwig Fechheimer's felicitous description of this figure when she first published it: "In this unified form, built up of mighty projecting and colliding planes, the eye of the observer is everywhere conscious of the primordial cubic stone" (1927, p. 88). Scharff considered this alabaster baboon to be the first "classic Egyptian sculpture" (1939, p. 450) and thought it strange that animal sculpture should be so much in advance of representations of the human figure in stone: "The reason for the great superiority of animal sculpture in the Early Period must sometime be studied more exactly" (ibid., footnote).

These reasons must be sought in the prehistoric development during which means of representing the animal, but never the human, were brought to the highest perfection. Several centuries were to pass in Egypt before the human figure would become an object of artistic concern. It was only in the Fourth 107 ff
Dynasty that the sculptural beauty of the human form was first discovered.

Thus it is understandable that in the great revolutionary period of the unification of the two kingdoms, Egypt's first monumental and datable sculpture should be the deity appearing in the form of an animal.

8. MUMMIFIED DOG *surrounded by animal bones, emerging from debris above the unfinished pyramid. Saqqara, Saite period*

Veneration of the individual animal

The earliest tokens of animal veneration are some bear skulls and thighbones
I:286 ff found in stone chests in the Drachenloch, a small cavern in the eastern Swiss Alps, 2445 meters high. They stem from the early Mousterian period, about 50,000 B.C. Their reverent manner of preservation was to make possible the animals' re-entry into life.

The animal burials from the Magdalenian era raise the question whether they demonstrated veneration of the animal in addition to providing for his re-entry into life.

The same question arises in the early animal cults of Egypt. Few real facts are known about the Predynastic period. But in 1950, when preparing the foundations for a new building in Heliopolis, today a suburb of Cairo, F. Debono came upon a Predynastic necropolis with seventy-three graves. These he designated as "probably parallel" to Nagadah II and the Merimdeh period. "The necropolis in question is situated at the extreme north of the racecourse of modern Heliopolis. The dead were covered with mats, the skins of animals" (1950, unpublished Mss.).

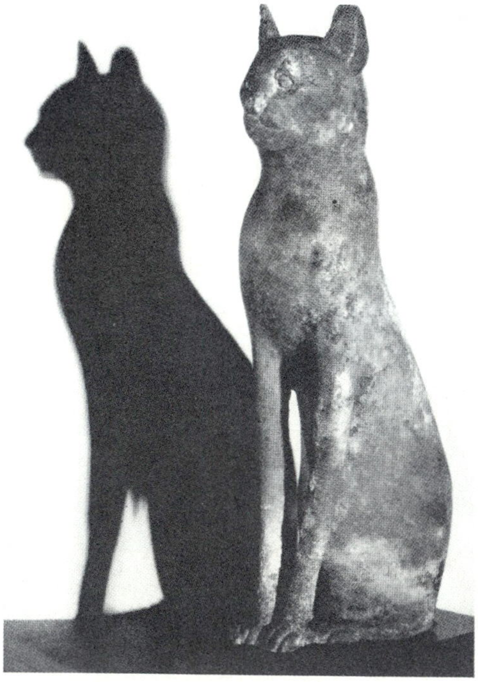

9. BRONZE CAT *containing mummy of a cat. Twenty-second Dynasty or later*

Six gazelle graves were found: "They were buried with the same care, and often greater care, than the humans. Remains of mats were existing upon the bodies of certain gazelles." They were richly accompanied by grave-utensils. "In one tomb, the gazelle was almost entirely surrounded by vases. This is the 38
first time animals have been found buried in a human cemetery" (ibid.).

In Saqqara, a necropolis used from the time of the First Dynasty, and in nearby Abusir, the favorite necropolis of the Fifth Dynasty, were revealed "enormous pits, winding underground passages, and deep wells enclosing thousands of cattle, sheep, dogs, birds, etc." (Gaillard and Daressy, 1905, preface).

The veneration of the individual animal ended only with the end of Egypt itself. It extended even into the Roman Empire. Also, the reserving of a section of the human cemetery was continued, as at Heliopolis: "One knows in fact that in practically every necropolis one finds beside the [human] tombs a section reserved for the burial of animals" (ibid.).

The climax of the animal cult occurred in the Saite period. Embalming, which by preserving the earthly body would guarantee a further existence, became the usual procedure for animals. A mummified gazelle from Esna, Upper Egypt, 38
shows the careful workmanship. It is wrapped first in cloth bands impregnated with resinous matter and then in papyrus stems. The horns and ears are also carefully enwrapped.

Mummified animals are so numerous that the excavators simply leave them among the rubbish. One almost stumbles over them. During the excavation of the Third Dynasty unfinished pyramid at Saqqara, I saw a mummified dog of the 39
Saite period emerge surprisingly from the debris.

To this late period of animal veneration belong the numerous bronze cat statuettes, which, aside from details of ornament, are much alike. They were standardized products, almost mass produced. The sensitive modeling of the left
body, with its slender limbs compressed into the mass and its attentive head, makes each of the many examples appear like a rare original. Sculpturally these animal statuettes are among the finest products of the Late Period. Most come from the animal necropolis of the city of Bubastis, the Nile delta capital of the Twenty-second Dynasty. Its local deity was Bastet, who was sometimes represented with a cat's head, similar to the lioness-headed Sekhmet of Memphis. 71

The striking proliferation of the animal cult in the Late Period was due chiefly to the loosening of the priest-controlled religious system as the state's independent existence declined. As "the creative strength of theology diminished, and consequently the gap between popular beliefs and theology became insurpassable, the animal cults, with other elements of popular beliefs, became the sole focus of religious life. From their incorporation in the popular beliefs we can understand their tenacious hold throughout all historic changes, so that they live through the most widespread systems and most powerful gods . . . they remain alive in the minds of the people and only disappear when they do" (Otto, 1938, p. 58).

This attitude toward the animal was not only an Egyptian popular belief which could not be dislodged, it was also the oldest tradition of mankind that lived on. The Egyptian theology, which was so clever in adaptation, had for outward and inward reasons to allow animals and anthropomorphic gods to mingle and blend with one another. Only the later religious proclamation of the supremacy of man caused the final overthrow of the animal.

The animal as deity

The adoration of the animal in primeval times passed through the millstones of theology and was assimilated into the anthropomorphic process. As a result, certain selected animals became divine and incarnations of the highest deities. Each animal during its lifetime was the god himself and enjoyed the same veneration. The god took on its form. A sacred awe protected it from slaughter. During the long period of the cult of the bull Apis, scholars have found only two mentions of his slaughter. Herodotus recounts (III, 29, 64; tr. Powell, pp. 211, 229) that the Persian king, Cambyses, who killed the sacred animal, was terribly punished by the affronted deity—he fell into madness and suffered a painful death; a similar fate befell another evildoer who had eaten of the sacred flesh (Hopfner, 1913, pp. 85–86). However, Gardiner considers that the first is "more than improbable by the evidence from the Serapeum," where a bull sarcophagus is said "by its inscriptions to have been dedicated by the king himself" (1961, p. 364).

It is the destiny of all high civilizations to be ever in danger of overspecialization. Only the fields vary in which this occurs. In Egypt, religion became the realm of overspecialization. Society was partitioned into professional organizations charged with the selection and care of the divine animals. In the case of the most famous of these, the bull Apis, twenty-nine different signs of his divinity had to be noted by specially trained connoisseurs. Other specialists were assigned to act as his grooms, others to deck him in festal attire, and there were special members of the priesthood whose task was to embalm him after death. Specialists for apes, cats, jackals, vultures, and many other animals were formed into separate professional organizations (ibid., p. 21). Thus the divinity of the animal resulted in a ritual bureaucracy covering every stage of its existence.

Apart from the few selected animals which were proclaimed to be direct incarnations of deities, others enjoyed the position of sacred and inviolate temple animals (Wiedemann, 1912, pp. 22 ff.). These were not incarnations of gods and therefore not divine, but they could be neither slaughtered nor offered in sacrifice. "Such an act was considered worthy of death" (Hopfner, 1913, p. 22). Nor could they be allowed to putrefy: they were embalmed and buried in mass graves.

The incarnations of gods in Egypt ranged from the lion and the crocodile to the shrewmouse, but the main cults were confined to domestic animals, understandably among an agricultural people. The bull was no longer the wild bull, the ram no longer the wild ram who, with his enormous curving horns, had appeared on the early ceramics of Iran and cylinder seals of Sumer to give 454 458

10. SARCOPHAGUS OF APIS *in the Serapeum at Saqqara. Nineteenth Dynasty. After Mariette*

11. RELIEF OF APIS, *the divine bull, standing on a pedestal before a worshiping scribe. From a Nineteenth Dynasty sarcophagus. Serapeum, Saqqara. From Mariette*

strength to the deceased. But for the main cults the same animals—bull and ram—were still chosen because of their powers of procreation and their fecundity. In the forefront of the priestly animal cult stood the bull: Apis, the white left bull of Memphis, the black Mnevis bull of Heliopolis, and other bulls of lesser renown.

Apis: a re-reflecting process

The animal as a divinity represents a re-reflecting process linking the newly created anthropomorphic gods with the primeval animal cults and permitting an animal to assume the being of a deity whom it will embody throughout its lifetime. The cult of the bull Apis, holding sway over a longer period than the Christian Era, shows how strongly the animal continued as the primal source of religion. Veneration of the bull, which arose in prehistoric times—witness the 1:408 ff colossal bulls painted in the cave of Lascaux—existed in Predynastic Egypt. Various nomes, or provinces, held the bull as sacred and displayed his symbol on their standards. Even in the First Dynasty, an ostracon shows a drawing of the bull Apis, with his characteristic markings (Otto, 1938, p. 11). The Apis bull was driven onto the sown lands to make them yield, in a ceremony called the "Running of the Apis." This ritual is depicted upon a porphyry bowl of Horus Aha in an early First Dynasty inscription (Simpson, 1957, pp. 139–42).

In Egypt the bull was venerated for its powers of procreation. This is different from the function of the Sumerian bull-man, who was primarily the protector of 63 the herds.

The monumental development of the Apis cult took place at the time of the

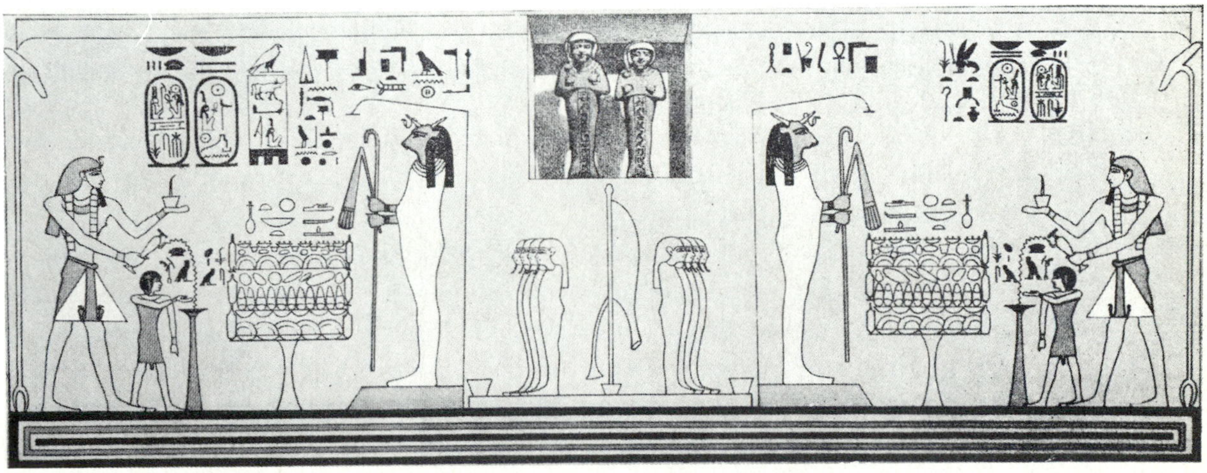

12. RELIEF OF APIS *in the mummified form of the god Ptah with a bull's head; before him Ramesses II and his son. Serapeum, Saqqara. From Mariette*

New Kingdom and continued until the late Ptolemaic period, and it required numerous buildings. The cult's burial place, the Serapeum, at Saqqara, lay in the midst of the oldest necropolis of the Egyptian kings. It stands witness to the most elaborate development of the animal cult.

Before Auguste Mariette discovered the entrance to the catacombs of the Apis graves in 1851 his eye had fallen upon a small sphinx that lay three-quarters buried in the sand (today in the Louvre). He followed the description of Strabo and unerringly deduced that this sphinx formed the beginning of an alley which led down to the Serapeum. The way to the entrance doors was also marked by pylons. Mariette then found himself in a long passage; right and left
43 stood sarcophagi of bulls within high barrel vaults hewn directly into the rock (1855). Tombs were found dating from the Eighteenth Dynasty, from the time of Amenhotep III, founder of the temple of Luxor, and his successors. In the Nineteenth Dynasty, under Ramesses II (1290–1224 B.C.), these burials achieved an astonishing splendor.

Almost all the sarcophagi were plundered and empty when Mariette found them. Only one tomb was untouched. Here lay an Apis mummy bearing a pectoral of Ramesses II (now in the Louvre). The atmosphere of holiness which clung to this mortuary city was so strong that the son of Ramesses II, Kha-em-Wast, high priest of Ptah in Memphis, was himself buried in the same vault.

The sarcophagi of the mummified Apis bulls are made of syenite, basalt, or limestone. They are unusually large: 3 to 4 meters high, 4 to 5 meters long, and more than 60 tons in weight. On the upper row of one of the reliefs the
44 striding Apis bull stands upon a pedestal with the disk of the sun and the uraeus between his horns. Before him is a lotus flower. A royal scribe, in a position of adoration, stands by an offering table. Above the Apis hovers the Udja eye of Horus, with the body of a vulture. In a lower row the adoring scribe appears once more with a companion.

Upon another sarcophagus, Apis has the mummified form of the god Ptah
45 with a bull's head. Before him the Pharaoh Ramesses II and his son Kha-em-Wast are making offerings.

What was the life of the Apis bull? Some information has recently come to light. Within the walls of the temple of Ptah in Memphis the architectural historian Alexander Badawy discovered the ground plan of the luxurious palace in which the Apis bull lived out his life and in which he was embalmed. In 1954, John Dimick, of the University Museum of Philadelphia, uncovered the bull's living quarters and the mighty alabaster table which served for his embalming

(1958, p. 183). A cartouche of Ramesses II was found in the sanctuary, and it was possible to ascertain that a complete renovation had been undertaken in the fifth century B.C., a further indication of the undiminished veneration of Apis in the Late Period.

The white bull Apis, who remained a deity throughout his life, presents the best example of the re-reflecting process. The deification of each specimen of this animal occurred as a result of the belief that certain distinctive markings proved him to be an incarnation of the god Ptah himself.

Apis was the outcome of priestly speculation and popular beliefs (Otto, 1938, pp. 23–24). Through the interconnection of Ptah and Apis the popularity of the animal was brought into the service of a theologically higher animal-divinity (p. 25). "This was not simply a cunning artistic stroke of the priesthood, but an outcome of the Egyptian mode of thinking" (p. 32).

The magic arising from the recognition of Apis as god upon earth appeared in the continual extension of his powers. Besides being the incarnation of Ptah, Apis gradually absorbed other of the highest gods. He incarnated the primal creator, Atum, and became Apis-Atum, and finally he absorbed the god of vegetation and death, Osiris: "The most fruitful union of Apis was with Osiris . . . between these two fertility-gods there was a natural bond of relationship" (p. 27). As a consequence of this union, Apis also took on the character of a god of death.

When the Greeks took over the Apis faith a new god arose—Serapis. "This name is the Grecian form of the Egyptian Osiris-Apis. . . . This god, revered alike by Greeks and Egyptians, was used by Ptolemy I . . . to create a Serapis cult which bound both peoples together in the new capital of Alexandria" (p. 29).

During the last phases of Egyptian history, this cult came more and more into the center of religion. Thus it was understandable that the Ptolemies continued the Apis burials in the Serapeum.

The ram cult

The ram cult was also widespread and prominent. Its most southerly sanctuary was the island of Elephantine, encircled by the rapids of the First Cataract. There the ram-headed god Khnum was "Lord of the dark waters"—i.e., the cataract—and thus guardian of the source of the Nile (Badawy, 1937, p. 22). That rams were honored as his incarnation is clear from the closely packed rows, 49 in the necropolis, of granite sarcophagi containing mummified rams. The

13. MUMMIFIED RAM *incarnating the god Khnum, faced with a painted plaque painted with cult scenes. Elephantine (Upper Egypt)*

above mummies bore gilded horns and upon their breasts lay painted plaques indicating the relation of the deified ram to the female ruler of the locality.

In the New Kingdom Khnum was certainly also a creator-god. In the Birth Room of the enclosed sanctuary of the temple of Luxor is a relief which depicts right a ram-headed, male-bodied god, modeling upon a potter's wheel the newborn Amenhotep III and his Ka.

Khnum was also associated with the highest god of the New Kingdom and became absorbed by him. The visitor to the religious center of Thebes is constantly reminded of the important role of the ram as the personification of the state-god Amon-Ra. The long avenue leading to the great temple of Amon-Ra 51 at Karnak is flanked by dense rows of ram-sphinxes: their heads bear the flat spiral horns of the domestic sheep and their bodies are those of lions. The sacred barge which carried the deified statue of Amon-Ra bore golden rams' heads upon its prow and stern. Upon the bark of the sun, the god Ra at midnight 362 took on the form of a ram seated within the solar disk.

14. KHNUM AS CREATOR-GOD *fashioning upon a potter's wheel Amenhotep III and his Ka. From an Eighteenth Dynasty relief in the Birth Room, temple of Luxor. Drawing by Schwaller de Lubicz*

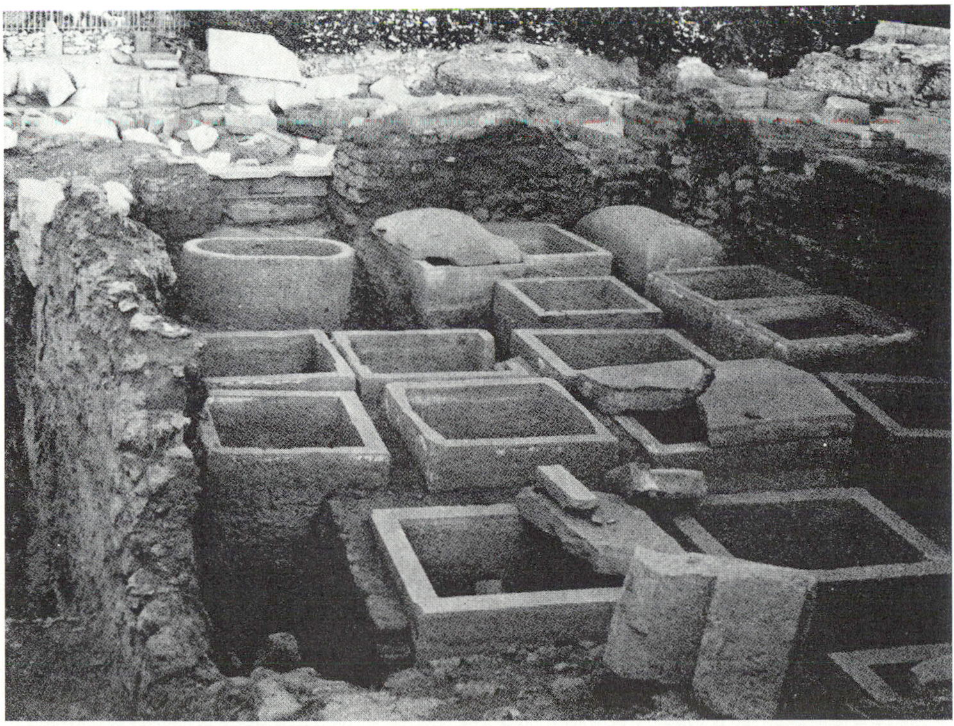

15. RAM SARCOPHAGI. *Necropolis, Elephantine (Upper Egypt)*

Even the foreign conquerors of Egypt came under the disquieting spell of the powers that emanated from the animal cults—the Persians as well as the Greeks. Not only the Ptolemaic kings treated the divine animals with great honor and granted tax exemption to the districts protected by them (Hopfner, 1913, p. 95), but Alexander the Great represented himself as the son of Amon-Ra and struck coins on which he was represented with the horns of a ram (p. 91).

The ram was an early symbol of fecundity because of its extraordinary generative powers: "That the sacred ram within the temple is an embodiment of the god of generative power is apparent from the animal at Menes [one of the great cult centers] where the women shed their garments before him and even had sexual intercourse with him," as Theodor Hopfner recounts on the authority of various classical writers (p. 95).

Animals and marks of distinction

The continuity of the primeval veneration of the animal can frequently be sensed in the first high civilizations. Animal attributes were a sign of dignity and power among the highest of the social hierarchy. The Pharaoh had a bull's tail fastened to his girdle on occasions of high festival: "The *sed-heb* or Tail festival, when the king was invested with the tail, was one of the most important of the royal ceremonies. A sacred dance, performed by the Pharaoh . . . is often represented as taking place in a temple before Min, the god of human generation" (Murray, 1952, p. 26).

The Egyptian priests wore a panther skin when performing their sacred functions. On Mesopotamian cylinder seals, the priests of Enki, god of the deep waters, were covered with the form of a fish, the head serving as a kind of tiara. These were all relics of prehistory, which sought to ennoble a different kind of dignity through adoption of an animal *Gestalt*.

In Mesopotamia the horned crown was maintained with especial constancy
as the sign of a god. In prehistory, a horn was a symbol of strength and fertility,
1:473 as it first appears in the raised left hand of the Venus of Laussel. The horned
69 crown continued to be a symbol of the anthropomorphic gods of Mesopotamia
throughout the entire changeful history of that land. Horns were also placed
218 at the corners of the high temple of the ziggurat as signs that this was the
abode of the deity.

Why it was Mesopotamia and not Egypt that held the horn in such high esteem may be found in a very early tradition. A striking characteristic of the ceramics of the fourth millennium from Mesopotamia (Samarra) and Iran

16. SPHINX REPRESENTING AMON-RA, *with ram's head and lion's body, protecting the king between his paws. From the western alley of sphinxes, Karnak*

(Susa, Sialk, Tepe Musyan) is the dominance of the animal. All emphasis was placed upon the horns, the body sometimes being almost entirely suppressed. Horns, such as those of the ibex, which frequently recur, were not simply fertility symbols. They also were thought to possess the secret power of renewing life. "The position of a deity in the Babylonian pantheon was shown by the number of horns worn. The great gods and goddesses had seven horns" (ibid., p. 25).

454

457

The bison held a prominent position in the mythology of both archaic civilizations, and it is easy to understand that the bison horn would be brought into the anthropomorphic world of gods as a symbol of especial dignity.

The fading of the animal cult

In Egypt one of the longest chapters of the history of mankind was finally brought to a close: the veneration of the animal. It gradually diminished during the late days of Egypt, after a last hectic flicker during the Saite period (664–525 B.C.), regarding which the attitude of Greek sources differs from that of later Roman ones.

Herodotus, who visited Egypt in the fifth century B.C., thus in the aftermath of the Saite period, grants considerable space to an objective view of animal veneration there. And even Plutarch, in the first century A.D., sees the animal cults as the "outcome of the most deep-going philosophical speculation" (Hopfner, 1913, p. 4). In a comprehensive work on the animal cults of ancient Egypt, Hopfner gives a list of the more important passages on the subject in classical writings, from Herodotus to Aelian, around A.D. 200 (pp. 10–11, 187–90). From Hopfner's list one can note how the Roman attitude began to alter around the beginning of the Christian Era. The jurist Cicero and the naturalist Pliny the Elder treat animal cults either with harshness or with scorn.

The decisive attack came from the Judaeo-Christian dogmatists. In the words of the Jewish philosopher Philo of Alexandria (died ca. A.D. 50): "Can anything be more ridiculous than this cult? Naturally strangers, coming to Egypt for the first time, must laugh themselves sick" (ibid., p. 4).

Condemnation followed from clerical writers as well as from the fathers of the church, such as John Chrysostom (fourth century A.D.), who saw the animal cults as mere stupidity. All this opposition was essential from the standpoint of Christian dogma, since the animal cults, as part of the inseparable oneness of the world, stood in opposition to the transcendent spiritual conception of God.

Christian dogma is dedicated to a universal process: the extraction of man from an all-encompassing oneness. Contempt for the animal was based on the ever stronger conviction of the pre-eminence of man. The first signs of this appeared with the anthropomorphization of the universe.

The indeterminate, all-pervasive primeval longing for contact with invisible powers found an echo in the new conditions of the archaic high civilizations. It appeared most directly in ceaselessly changing hybrid forms with human bodies and animal heads.

The reason why, in primeval times, hybrid creatures had a human body and an animal head can be easily understood. Man thus took on the animal's superiority—its strength and its impenetrable mystery. These human-animal creatures reach far back into the early Aurignacian period, to the bird-headed 1:487 female idol traced in the clay of the cavern of Pech-Merle.

The greater strength of the animal should afford a better contact with the invisible powers. An endeavor to make sharp distinctions between man and animal in these impenetrable religious desires can lead nowhere. Intangibility was the essence of the prehistoric hybrid.

Through a combination of the special characteristics of various animals, even greater power could be attained. This was believed from the earliest beginnings, when man, using different colored clays, attempted to depict upon smooth rock walls the outlines of strange monsters. One need but recall the great serpent, 1:308 three meters long, with the head of a beast of prey and gigantic fangs, drawn in the cavern of La Baume-Latrone in southern France.

Also from Aurignacian times is a demonic thing, a large animal-like head 1:181 ff from La Ferrassie (Dordogne), composed of so many separate features that it can be attributed to no existing animal species.

Even more fantastic are the minglings of parts of various animal bodies and heads into one composite creature, such as are found in the almost inaccessible sanctuary of the cavern of Pech-Merle. Here is a medley of a rhinoceros, a 1:322 lioness, and three gazelles, whose bodies cannot be distinguished from one another.

These representations of composite bodies must have continued through thousands of years. A seal of the third millennium, from the Uruk–Jemdet Nasr period, shows three wild goats which share the same body; one has its head below lowered and another is looking backward.

17. COMPOSITE FIGURE: *Three wild goats sharing the same body. Impression from a steatite stamp seal. Early third millennium*

Hybrids in Sumer

In the period of the creation of the anthropomorphic pantheon, man-animal hybrids appeared in Sumer. They played a greater role there in the earliest phase than in Egypt. This was due both to the earlier onset of Sumerian civilization and to the longer continuance there than in contemporaneous Egypt of a pictorial imagery of the prehistoric world.

When with difficulty one penetrates the remote world of the Sumerian seals, one finds in the earliest specimens animals, always animals, covering the surfaces with symbolic meaning. Very few human figures appear, usually indeter-
65 minate in meaning and placed in relation to the animals. In the Third Early Dynastic period combat scenes multiply, between animal and animal and man and animal. At this time seated gods also appear upon cylinder seals, recognizable by their double-horned headgear. But these gods bear grotesque animal or bird heads, and figures of another type, whose gigantic eye sockets occupy
65 almost the whole of their heads, are no less fantastic. They are hybrids, as indeterminate as any in prehistory. They are intermediaries like the bird-
I:177 headed female figurines from Ur.

In the hybrid figures of prehistory one draws near to the core of religious longing. In the high civilizations they bridge the way to the anthropomorphic gods. They were transitional phenomena.

In contrast to prehistory, the archaic high civilizations limited themselves to only two types of hybrids: the composite animal and the animal-man.

In Sumer there were certain animal hybrids, like the lions with twining serpent-necks (cylinder seal, Baghdad Museum, 10759; Frankfort, 1954, pl. 8B), which also entered Predynastic Egypt under Mesopotamian influence. These are often treated like heraldic ornaments. Other hybrids play no special
56 role, except for the lioness-headed eagle Imdugud, who appears frequently during the formative period of the gods.

Among the animal-men there were fish-men and scorpion-men who guarded the door to the underworld in the Gilgamesh epic. Upon a lyre from the First
right Dynasty of Ur, a scorpion-man is depicted with a human body and scorpion garments. He is less frightful than many other figures from the royal tombs of Ur.

Imdugud, the lioness-headed eagle

Imdugud, the lioness-headed eagle, must have possessed a special attraction for the Sumerians. It is a typical hybrid arising from the desire to accumulate power.

18. SCORPION-MAN *with human body: Detail from a lyre. First Dynasty of Ur*

Imdugud "symbolizes a speedy and powerful attack by incorporating in one personage both the king of the birds, the eagle, and the king of the beasts, the 56 lion" (Dhorme, 1949, p. 103).

But this is only one of its meanings. Imdugud is predominantly a mythical bird, a creature mingling the cosmic and the earthly or chthonic "who decrees the fates and utters the word": so does Kramer translate the Sumerian narration on a stele (1956, p. 235), in which the hero of the saga, Lugalbanda, at the end of the world, has lost his way back to his city of Uruk and tries to find it again through a trick. "He is determined to first win the friendship of the *Imdugud*-bird who decrees the fates and utters the word which none may transgress" (ibid.). He wins Imdugud by feeding the young birds in her nest during her absence. Thereupon the bird shows him the way home from this "far-distant land of Zabu" which is "a journey from which none return" (ibid.). Imdugud is the bird who knows all and who determines destiny.

Imdugud is always presented on seals and reliefs as a female bird, with the mane-free head of a lioness, but never in a maternal function. A pair of bulls bow in adoration before the hovering bird upon a seal from the Third Early 65 Dynastic period (British Museum 116724; Wiseman, 1959, p. 22).

In contrast to the symbolic representations of Imdugud upon reliefs and seals, epic narratives bring out a maternal aspect. In the Gilgamesh epic she nested, with her young, in the crown of the tree of the goddess Inanna (p. 223).

Normally Imdugud hovers with widespread wings above heraldically organ-

19. LIONESS-HEADED BIRD IMDUGUD *with two deer: High relief in copper (42 in.). From the Early Dynastic temple at Al ʻUbaid*

ized Sumerian animals—lions or stags, wild animals like herself. Sometimes she
65 appears to be attacking them with her talons and beak.

In the beginning this lioness-headed eagle was usually depicted in profile,
63 with folded wings, as E. D. Van Buren (1935, p. 239) shows in a series of illustrations. Imdugud appeared in the early Jemdet Nasr period: "One of the earliest representations . . . appears on a cylinder seal which is at least as early as Uruk III, the early Jemdet Nasr period" (p. 238). A large-scale
above representation of Imdugud with two deer occurs upon a copper relief from the
163 Early Dynastic temple of Al ʻUbaid, to which we will return because of the sculptural projection of the relief. Henri Frankfort sees no aggressive action in this scene: "The gesture does not represent aggression but affinity: the same deity is symbolized by bird and deer" (1954, p. 30).

This becomes more understandable in representations in which Imdugud
right holds two lions in her talons, as in a relief upon a pierced slab of Dudu, high priest of King Entemena. The hole in the slab served to hold a ritual mace. The main motif shows Imdugud, next to the donor, with the two lions who, one might almost say, gaze amicably up at her.

20. IMDUGUD *grasping two lions with her talons: Relief on pierced square slab meant to hold ritual mace. Lagash, Early Dynastic period*

On Entemena's silver vase from Lagash, in the Louvre, Imdugud hovers above a frieze of lions, stags, and ibexes.

No other representation conveys the power of this mythopoeic atmosphere with greater immediacy than the mace of King Mesilim of Kish, around 2600 B.C. The lioness-headed eagle, her eyes and tongue encrusted with jewels, extends the heavy burden of her outspread wings over the upper surface of this 59
ritual mace. This is the mighty storm bird, carrier of thunder and rain, bearer of

21. IMDUGUD *on face of votive macehead of King Mesilim of Kish near Babylon. The encircling frieze of lions carries the first recorded source of the history of this land; ca. 2600* B.C.

22. IMDUGUD *on upper surface of the mace (see fig. 21): The lioness-headed goddess with outspread wings*

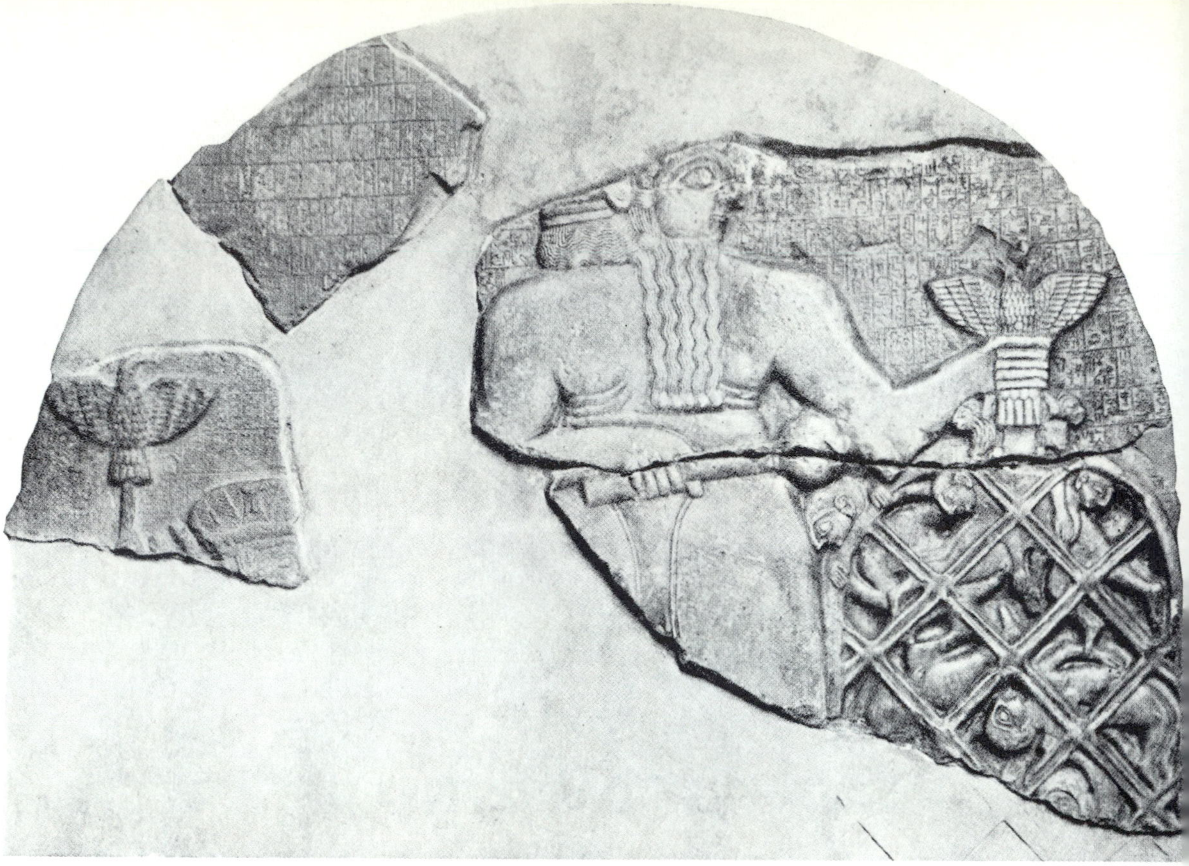

23. VULTURE STELE *describing victory of King Eannatum of Lagash: A tiny Imdugud appears in the giant fist of the god Ningirsu. Ascendancy of anthropomorphic gods now fully established; ca. second half of third millennium*

fertility. Conjunction with the mace brings her warlike aspect to the fore.

58 Around the macehead is a frieze of male lions whose manes bear an inscription. Plastically, both Imdugud and the lion frieze are strikingly simplified. This mace, carrying the name of King Mesilim of Kish, presents the first recorded source of the history of this land. Kish is described as the oldest of the sovereign cities. It lay only a few miles east of Babylon and some fifty miles from the site of Baghdad, and belonged to the Mesilim period (named after the king), which followed the Uruk III–Jemdet Nasr period, when Sumerian sculpture was in its first bloom. This is a sign that the highly developed culture of the south was again penetrating into the north.

Imdugud represented the mighty bird of destiny who ruled alone and independently. She was bound to no city, to no god, and appeared in many places (Van Buren, 1935, pp. 237–51), until she suffered the fate of many other animals and animal hybrids and, in Lagash (Telloh), became the emblem of the anthropomorphic city-god Ningirsu, son of the storm-god Enlil and himself a storm-god and a war-god.

Upon the famous vulture stele in the Louvre, Imdugud, in the hand of the left gigantic god Ningirsu, fastens the net in which enemies of King Eannatum have been captured. This vulture stele, from the second half of the third millennium, is a highly meaningful historical document. It shows the subservience of the ancient bird of fate and the rise to dominant power of the god.

The 1.8-meter-high fragment of limestone is adorned on both sides with representations and inscriptions that recount the life of Eannatum down to details of his campaign against the city of Umma. Upon the face, occupying two-thirds of the height of the stele, stands Ningirsu, wearing a stiffly pressed skirt and with a great beard reaching to his naked chest. He is gigantic in proportion to the human figures. In one hand he carries a mace with which he has just struck a prisoner on the head. In the other the storm bird Imdugud, holding two lilliputian lions in her talons, serves as a clasp to close the net. The great bird almost disappears within the enormous hand of the god. The final ascendancy of the new anthropomorphic gods could not be more strikingly represented.

The bull-man

No lion-headed bird can be found in primeval times. It is otherwise with the animal-man hybrids, of which the most important is the bull-man. During the period before anthropomorphic gods rose to importance, a bull with a human head is found on seals and reliefs, reclining, or standing upon his four legs. The bull-man of Sumer, who appears in the third millennium, is related to the far more savage and fantastic hybrids of primeval times. A leaping bull-man from 62 the Magdalenian period (cavern of Les Trois Frères, Ariège) shows very distinctly the continuous alternations between man and animal. A powerful imagination is at work as the hybrid continually changes its animal and human form from part to part and limb to limb. Its short horns, huge eyes, and nervous nostrils all recur in the Sumerian bull-man; the herds and domestic animals fall under his protection and do him reverence, as is shown upon many cylinder seals.

The principal relations between hybrids and animals were rather different. In the same cavern of Les Trois Frères another bull-man is playing a musical 1:499 ff instrument and driving before him a series of amazing animal hybrids: reindeer with bison heads, etc.

A comparison of this primeval musician with a representation upon a cosmetic palette from the last Predynastic period of Egypt is informative. This palette from Hierakonpolis, as M. A. Murray points out, shows a conceptual linkage between the hybrids of primeval times and those of Egypt. On the palette, now in the Louvre, "is a representation of a man who is disguised as a jackal. He wears a jackal's head and skin over his head and back with the tail dangling behind, his hands and feet are uncovered and are clearly human. He plays on a flute, and like his palaeolithic prototypes he is dancing. Like the Ariège masker he is in the midst of animals. . . . He performs on a musical instrument" (1934, p. 251; fig. in Quibell and Green, 1902, pl. XXVIII).

The conceptual link is especially noticeable in the human feet—it is a human being with an animal's head.

High above the swarming animals in the cavern of Les Trois Frères is the
1:500 most famous of all hybrid representations, the "sorcerer" with reindeer horns, human beard, and enormous eyes. In his shamanlike form he draws the hunted quarry magically toward him.

The Sumerian bull-man, especially in the period of animal domestication, appears more often as a protective spirit against the onslaughts of savage animals, a combative defender.

The most plastically interesting representation of the bull-man, with the body
right of a bull and the face of a man, is in relief upon a roughly square limestone plaque from Al 'Ubaid, of the time of the First Dynasty of Ur. This shows a wild bull, as though escaped from the primeval period, clambering up a moun-

24. PREHISTORIC BULL-MAN: *One of the prehistoric hybrid creatures. Cavern of Les Trois Frères (Ariège), Magdalenian period. From Bégouën and Breuil*

tain. The Imdugud bird, with folded wings, sits perched upon its back and, symbolizing the combating forces of preservation and destruction, "rends the beast's hindquarters with its sharp teeth" (Van Buren, 1935, p. 237).

A cylinder seal of the Third Early Dynastic period leads us into the atmosphere of a religion in which the bull-man played a leading role. Upon the upper register: "On each side of a mountain surmounted by a three-branched plant lies a man-headed bull raising one foreleg to rest its hoof on the mountain" 65

25. BEARDED BULL-MAN *climbing a mountain: Imdugud with folded wings is perched upon his back. The prehistoric bull-man has reversed his traits and become almost domesticated. Relief on limestone plaque from Al 'Ubaid. First Dynasty of Ur, ca. 2500* B.C.

(p. 245). The plant signifies "perhaps the 'sacred tree' or the 'tree of life' " (Wiseman, 1959, p. 21). The bird Imdugud again sits on the back of each of these bulls, tearing at their flesh. At either side, two figures stand ready, dagger in hand, to stab the lioness-headed eagles. The scene does not represent a battle but has an undefined symbolic meaning. The bull-man is the guardian of the sacred tree, the protector of life. Of the two "heroes," whose heads mainly consist of a single enormous eye, little can be said except that they represent "mythological figures" (ibid.). In the lower register the religious atmosphere is heightened. Two bulls bow their heads in reverence before an eagle with outstretched wings.

Sumerian man's tragic attitude toward life is expressed in endless combat between man and man, animal and animal, man and animal—an ever-recurring theme of early seals and reliefs.

In primeval times there were representations of beasts of prey who had fought unto death, such as a creature with a great stream of blood flowing from his mouth, in the cavern of Pech-Merle. Of the battle leading to this end we
1:321 have no knowledge. Probably there was none. What was depicted upon the rock in this secret position was an active symbol, the representation of a wish that demanded fulfillment.

Throughout the whole history of Mesopotamia, scenes of combat are constantly depicted, in complete contrast to Egypt where such scenes lasted barely beyond the period of early Sumerian influence. In the final third of the Early Dynastic period, battle scenes between animal and animal and man and animal increase in number. Earlier peaceful sequences of strongly abstract animals, of running ibexes, or goats interspersed with fish and frogs, or of
458 animals juxtaposed upside down as in primeval times, vanished before the flood of combat scenes.

This is the period in which the bull-man lost his animal-like stance. He now stands upright. And not only that: although he retains two animal legs, the upper part of his body has become humanly slender. He still bears the horns and ears of a bovine, such as were always retained by the Egyptian cow-goddess Hathor. His human face has become ever more strongly emphasized, framed within a pointed or a large, squared-off ceremonial beard. The bull-man is one of the most frequently represented figures during the third millennium, the period of transition from hybrids to anthropomorphic gods.

Upon a seal from Tell Agrab of the Second Early Dynastic period, two such

26. RECUMBENT BULL-MEN *flanking a mountain, with Imdugud on their backs. Three branches sprout from the mountaintop (tree of life?). Impression from cylinder seal of Third Early Dynastic period*

27. BULL-MEN WITH HUMAN ARMS *attacking a lion assaulting a cow. Impression from cylinder seal. Tell Agrab, Second Early Dynastic period*

28. BULL-MAN AND HUMAN FIGURE *repressing rampant lions and bulls by magic force: Central figure probably vegetation-god Tammuz. Impression from cylinder seal of Third Early Dynastic period*

65 bull-men, with bull's hindquarters and human upper body, are about to fall upon a lion that has attacked a cow.

The bull-man often accompanies a human figure whose meaning is not exactly determined. Frequently he can be identified with the Sumerian god of vegetation, Tammuz, who also signified a combination of procreative and protective powers. Upon a seal from the Third Early Dynastic period (British Museum), the bull-man appears with a bearded "hero," naked except for a
65 three-stranded girdle and a mystifying headdress. This purely human hero appears to hold off two rearing bulls, more through magic than strength as, ever more strongly, the bull-man holds off two rampant lions. He subdues them simply by thrusting his arms against their breasts. It is a magic scene of destructive forces held in check. Frankfort points out in connection with a similar scene that "the struggle between lion and bull stands for a conflict between divine forces, and one may surmise that the lion represents the destructive aspect of the Great Mother, an aspect which was recognized but believed to be held in check as a rule" (1954, p. 12).

In the Protoliterate era, in which the bull-man has not yet been traced, the
161 figure of the bearded "hero" appears in full plasticity, in the friendly embrace of animals, upon vases from the Jemdet Nasr period (e.g., ibid.). Since the "hero" has often been identified with Tammuz, the divine herdsman, his head-
65 dress upon the seal might represent plant symbols of the god of vegetation.

The bull-man in the Late Assyrian period

The bull-man recurs among the colossi of the Assyrian empire, but in a radically altered form. He stands before the gigantic palaces of the kings as a guardian and a force to ward off evil. In front of the king's residence and in the throne
right room of Khorsabad built by Sargon II (722–705 B.C.), striding and yet statically frozen despite his giant wings, he stands again as a bull on four legs. But on this bull's body are a smooth courtier's head and features, which we isolate in our picture to draw attention to the perfumed atmosphere of the carefully trimmed beard and coiffure. Two ornamental horns, the insignia of a deity, curve smoothly around a fezlike headdress.

This figure has arisen from two different prototypes, the bull-man and the lion, which in the early periods had served as guardians of the temple. In the
211 temple of Al 'Uqair lions are painted to right and left of the altar, and in

29. HUMAN-HEADED BULL: *Head of colossal granite winged bull from Khorsabad. Late Assyrian period*

5 the small temple city of Tell Harmal (ca. 2000 B.C.), near Baghdad, they crouched before the entrance with wide-open, snarling jaws.

Among the best of the surviving human-headed bulls from the Late Assyrian period are two in rose granite which guard a door in the inner town wall of Nineveh. They came to light in 1941 as the result of an earthquake and now stand upon the site, protected by a wooden roof.

The bull-man, first the outcome of a profound fatalistic faith, has become a decorative vestige. However, these colossi still hint at his earlier significance in Mesopotamia. But instead of being guardian of the herds and wrestling with the savage powers of nature, he has become a gigantic amulet to frighten away the evil spirits which beset the ruler within and without his palace gates.

Subjugation of the animal

Reliefs and cylinder seals inform us of the slow process of subjugation of the animal throughout the third millennium. At first animals appear alone in their majesty. Then, in the Early Dynastic period, man enters, in the form of the
65 bull-man or the hero, suppressing rampant lions and bulls.

In the following period the attitude toward the animal becomes distinctly different, simultaneously with the rise of the first world conqueror, Sargon of Akkad. This is the time when the king became himself divine: no longer the priest-king but the god-king. On the stele of Naramsin, one of Sargon's successors, the king has assumed the divine insignia: a horned crown.

The subjugation of the animal is further revealed in another seal on which the bare right leg of the goddess Ishtar emerges from beneath her long woolen
right robe as she treads firmly upon the back of a crouching lion. In one hand the goddess wields a toothed sword and in the other "a leash (double in the upper part) attached to the mouth of the lion. I take it that the weapon fits in clearly with the character of the goddess, while the other also connotes her power which can quell even such a creature as a lion, which was, of course, her special animal" (Letter to the author from H. J. Kantor, March 11, 1962).

Hybrids in Egypt

Hybrids assumed great importance in Egypt because of the persistence of animal cults. They were inextricably interwoven with the great Egyptian deities whose form immediately betrays their continuous kinship with the animal world. Many of them were habitually represented as hybrids, others as animals.

30. THE GODDESS ISHTAR AND THE LION: *The goddess subdues the lion by placing her bare foot upon its back and holding a leash attached to the lion's mouth*

The animal forms reach back to primeval times, the hybrid forms occur mostly during the transition from divine animal to anthropomorphic god. In many cases the actual sequence of transformation from animal to hybrid can be followed from existing representations.

Out of the darkness looms Suchos, an influential crocodile-headed god whose "noble crocodile's form came forth from the Nun [the primeval ocean]" (Bonnet, 1952, p. 757). Anubis, jackal-headed god of the dead, was the embalmer who could give new life to the mummified body. His parentage is uncertain: "Texts of the high period never name his father or his mother and refer to no place of origin" (Garnot, 1948, p. 48). He too stands alone, like Suchos, the fertility-god Min, and Hathor, who never lost her cows' ears and whose origin is lost in the mists of prehistory.

Horus, the protector of the king, was a falcon before he adopted hybrid form. Seth, with his grotesque head, descended from an animal of indeterminate race. Many interpretations have been attempted, but without success. Horus the sun-god and Seth the desert-god were incorporated into the family of Ra by Heliopolitan theologians. But earlier they had been entirely separate.

Among the mother-goddesses thought to have existed before any life came into being was the fertility-goddess Mut, who is sometimes even represented as an ithyphallic androgynous creature (Lanzone, 1883, III, p. 335; pl. CXXXVI), but is normally shown as a seated lioness-headed woman. Mut is often intermingled with Sekhmet, goddess of warfare, who also bears the head of a lioness. Both of them eventually became connected with the highest gods: Mut as the consort of Amon-Ra, Sekhmet as the consort of Ptah, supreme god of Memphis.
right One of the hundreds of Mut or Sekhmet statues is shown here. It still stands in the fertility temple of Mut at Karnak.

Of all these composite beings, the Sphinx at Giza is perhaps the most intriguing, since in it god, god-king, animal, and sun cult all merge together.

The Sphinx

The Sphinx, a lion with a human head, was hewn out from the living rock: an enormous boulder remaining within the stone quarry excavated for building the pyramid. It is a sculptured mountain. Even so, it is not really a freestanding sculpture, since it is surrounded on three sides by the rock walls of the quarry.
72 It is curious to note that this most colossal sculpture of Egypt is actually hollowed out of the rock like a sunken relief. Its horizontal back lies level with the
73 surrounding desert; only the head projects above the horizon, giving the whole its well-known aspect. Since the body lies within its large U-shaped bowl of rock walls, it has repeatedly been covered with sand. Even in the last century it has had to be cleared three times.

The Sphinx faces to the east. For us this is a simple point of orientation, but for the pyramid age it meant the rebirth of the sun and the reappearance of the gods. The west was the direction of death—the realm of the dead—but the east meant the continuance of life.

What was the significance of the Sphinx?

Originally it represented King Chephren, wearing his royal headdress and ceremonial beard. This was ascertained by Mariette, who excavated the body of the Sphinx and found Chephren's temple lying protected between its two great paws.

Even in Predynastic times, a kind of sphinxlike creature had existed, with "the body of a lion, and the head of a hawk or eagle . . . provided with wings" (Hassan, 1953, p. 145).

In Heliopolitan theology the king became a sun-god after death: "The Giant Sphinx would therefore represent Chephren as the Sun-god acting as the

31. LIONESS-HEADED SEKHMET: *One of the many statues of this Egyptian goddess from the temple of Mut at Karnak. Eighteenth Dynasty*

32. BODY OF THE SPHINX *from the north, rising from horizontal strata of natural rock. Giza, Fourth Dynasty*

guardian of the Giza necropolis" (Edwards, 1961, p. 108). The Sphinx records the moment of closest identity between god and Pharaoh: between the invisible and the visible.

After the pyramid age the original significance of the Giza Sphinx seems to have been forgotten. It became incorporated in the solar cult, identified as the god Horus of the horizon. The sphinx upon a granite stele of King Tuthmosis IV utters these words: "I am thy father, Hor-em-akhet-Kheperi-Ra-Atum" (Hassan, 1953, p. 222). This means the sun in all its phases. Actually one

33. HEAD OF THE SPHINX *from the south, showing the rock structure of the face and parts of the body*

cannot speak of a real forgetfulness of the original significance of the sphinx, since its form was always pluralistic in meaning.

The Sphinx of Giza remains unique in size and impressiveness. The numerous colossal statues of the Ramesside kings of the New Kingdom, placed before the pylons of their temples or—as at Abu Simbel—hewn directly out of the rock face, never attain the mystic power that still emanates from the Sphinx despite its mutilated features. 380

CONSTANCY AND CHANGE IN FERTILITY SYMBOLS

Constancy and change have seldom been so interwoven as in the sequence from fertility symbol to venerated animal and then to goddess. The different stages are so intermingled that one can scarcely be distinguished from another.

From fertility idol to goddess

In prehistory all human beings played insignificant roles in comparison with the major animals, but the female—the generator of the species—was more important than the male. The woman is the visible bearer and molder of life Desires for fertility and procreation are concentrated in the female form. This
I:437 was expressed in the naked and pregnant Venus figurines from the early Aurignacian period, and stressed by their exaggerated buttocks, breasts, and sexual triangle. They were not goddesses but potent magic symbols, able to bring new life to birth or to renew the life of the dead, beside whom they were buried in later times.

With the beginning of agriculture, in the fifth and fourth millenniums, a different type of Venus figurine appeared. This type, found in many early Meso-

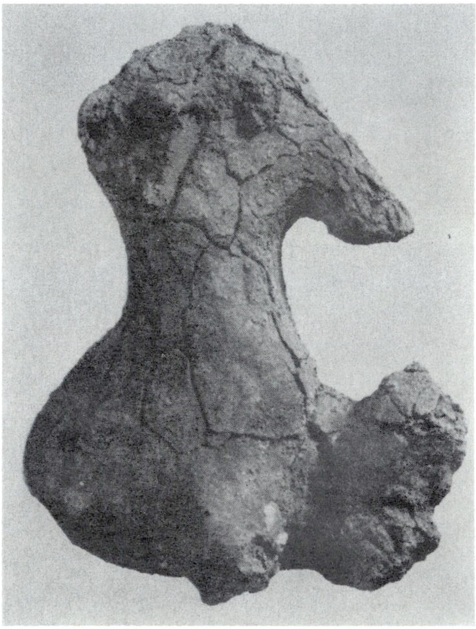

34. SEATED CLAY FIGURINE: *Armless fertility idol with protuberant buttocks. From level V, Hassuna (northern Mesopotamia). Early fourth millennium*

potamian settlements, such as Jarmo, Hassuna, Arpachiyah, and Tepe Gawra, is a seated figure with horizontally outstretched legs, molded of clay and unfired. Somewhat later these figurines were joined by a slender standing type (Ur), much like that of the Magdalenian period of prehistory, but this type was heavily outnumbered by the seated figurines.

The rough sculptural treatment of a figure from level V in Hassuna, northern Mesopotamia, gives a moving insight into a helplessly floundering search for plastic expression. **left**

A figurine from Deir el Ballas in Upper Egypt comes from an early period for **below**

35. SEATED CLAY FIGURINE *with powerful thighs and well-developed breasts. From Grave 394, Deir el Ballas (Upper Egypt). Protohistoric period, Nagadah I*

Egypt, the protohistoric (Nagadah I, sequence dating 34). It is, however, later than the Hassuna figurine. Its face, though indistinct, is not veiled. It has no arms. Its breasts are fully formed, its powerful thighs stretched forward and covered with the cuplike hollows which, throughout all prehistory, were em-
1:132 ff ployed to strengthen the power of a fertility symbol. Its attitude has been likened, not without foundation, to the posture of giving birth. Such figures are still earth-bound and as much tied to chthonic concepts as the Aurignacian Venus figurines. Whether they set forth a personal request or whether we already find here the representation of a more generalized form—the earth mother or the Great Mother—is uncertain.

The leap from fertility charms to the Great Mother, and thence to a goddess or goddesses, came about with the creation of an anthropomorphic pantheon; afterward, a male god assumed undisputed supremacy in a male-oriented society. The change from the fertility idol to the more generalized concept of the earth mother and then to the anthropomorphic goddess was, as Erich Neumann has stated (1955, pp. 185–86), obscured by the rising dominance of the male and the male gods. The patriarchal principle ushered in the bloodthirsty warring period preceding the foundation of the first states. The creation of a world of gods and the foundation of states were contemporaneous.

When the god Atum spat or masturbated to create Tefnut and Shu, or the god Amon-Kamutef created his mother, the natural process seems to have been reversed.

All this led to a division and a masking of the primeval fertility beliefs which were bound up with the female process. Hermann Kees was struck by the scarcity of myths relating to a goddess who "did not admit the need of help from a neighboring god but was able to create life from her own forces" (1941, p. 162). Yet the long prehistoric tradition of the supremacy of the female role remained alive and could not be entirely dismissed even up to the end of Egyptian history.

When questions of the origin of the universe began to disturb the human mind, the goddess who had evolved from the ancient fertility idols acquired a self-generative character. She was considered the daughter and mother who created her begetter, and was often thought of and indeed sometimes represented as an androgynous being, a female counterpart to Amon-(or Min-) Kamutef.

Legends tell of the "male-female primeval force" of the goddess Neith, "the terrible arrow-goddess from Sais" (ibid.). Sethe also stresses that Neith, "without detracting from other theological precepts, acted as the oldest of all the gods: 'the great one, the mother of the gods,' who was already born when nothing else existed and who, therefore, was considered androgynous, like Ptah from Memphis" (Sethe, 1930, p. 68).

Even in Isis, who was closely woven by the priesthood into the family of the Heliopolitan gods and transformed into a loving wife and gentle mother, we meet traces which point to the original autonomy of this sorcery-filled goddess and to the mystery of her conception, achieved by her own power, thus hinting at her inherent bisexuality (Kees, 1956, p. 139). The legend of the murder of Osiris and her finding the scattered parts of his body reads like a Greek myth. It is not surprising that Plutarch, the comparative biographer of the first century A.D., selected it in his story *De Iside et Osiride* and that the cult of Isis penetrated the Hellenistic world and slowly expanded over the entire Roman Empire.

Hathor

The direct sequence—primeval charms, earth mother, goddess—is not the only route. There are other ways: from animal to cosmic deity. But whether the starting point is charm or animal, the meaning remains the same: the desire for fertility.

The cosmic projection arose from the "fetishistic local gods" (Sethe, 1930, p. 6) which appear on the Predynastic standards of the different districts. In historical times, certain of these were transformed into celestial cows whose bodies were the universe and whose legs formed four pillars upon which the heavens rested.

The earliest accounts are contained in the Pyramid Texts. But these derive from the Fifth Dynasty, when the priesthood had already attained its dominance.

Among the various celestial cows that persisted was Hathor, the nurturing all-mother, who, even when she took on a human body, never wholly lost the signs of her animal form. Originally she was probably a wild cow, although this can only be proved for another of the cow-goddesses (Bonnet, 1952, pp. 403–4). In Predynastic times she appears, together with a calf, as the emblem of one of the nomes. Hathor had several companions, among them Nut, who was also depicted as a celestial cow.

The link between female animal and earth mother can also be observed in yet another celestial cow, Methyr, whose name means "Great flood." She arose from the primeval ocean and bore the sun and "set this child of hers between her horns" (Sethe, 1929, p. 93). The link that binds these heavenly kine together is the primeval maternal fertility symbol that, while still retaining its animal form, was transposed to the cosmic sphere.

None of the other mother-goddesses of Egypt had so enduring an influence as Hathor, whose chief distinguishing characteristic was the plurality of her aspects: fertility idol, self-begetting goddess, cow from the marshes of the Nile delta, anthropomorphic goddess in close attendance upon the king. Hathor was simultaneously guardian of the Nile delta, of the marriage bed, and of the necropolis of Thebes: donor of life and protector of the dead. She bequeathed to mankind the joys of life and the powers of love: "From ancient times Hathor was honored as the goddess of joy with dance, song, and music" (Hermann, 1959, p. 23). Her instrument was the sistrum.

In the form of Hathor the beauty of the female body found, for the first time, full plastic expression. In her final phase she became the goddess of love. The ritual hymns to her, which go back to the Middle Kingdom, are, as Alfred Hermann makes clear (p. 25), forerunners of individual love poems:

I say of her that I take pleasure in her aspect
My arms make (the gesture)
Come to me, come to me.

The interwoven threads of Hathor's significance are scarcely possible to disentangle. **below** Even her neckband, or *menit*, carries on the traditions of a fertility symbol. It has a kind of counterweight whose stylized form goes back to a fertility idol in the shape of a female torso. In Eleventh Dynasty graves at Deir el Medineh (Barguet, 1953, p. 103) the counterweight was replaced by the scarab, Khepri, symbol of the rising sun: growth and transformation. The inscription states that the deceased touching the sacred object is given abiding life and constantly renewed youth (p. 109).

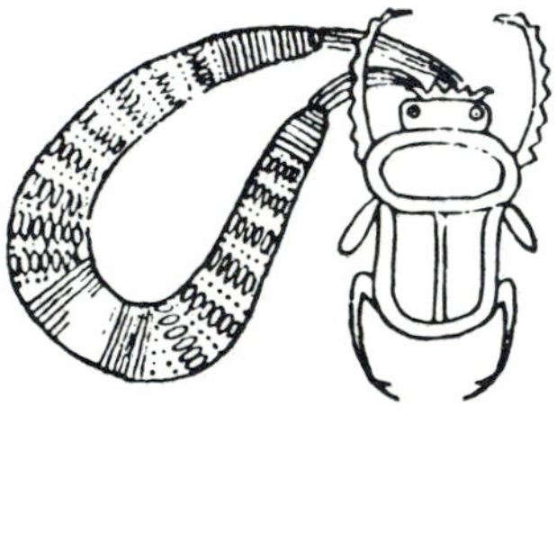

36. NECKLACE OF HATHOR *fastened by a scarab, symbol of recurring life, which acts as a counterweight. From a tomb at Deir el Medineh. From Barguet*

Prehistoric links

Hathor shows more traces of her prehistoric origins than any other goddess. Her head was depicted four times on the upper corners of the Predynastic Narmer below palette: a hybrid head with human features intermingled with cows' ears and horns. This representation remained constant into Roman times.

An Amratian tablet reaches even further back than the Narmer. According to below its finder, Flinders Petrie, it represents the head of a cow with five-pointed stars at the tips of its ears and horns, and another resting on its point above the forehead. In *The Beginnings of Art* we compared this representation with the late- I, 114 neolithic abstract human figures from eastern Spain: headless, with hands and feet ending in starlike forms.

How should this mysterious palette be interpreted? Abstract head of a cow or abstract female torso? Legless torsos were common both in Mesopotamia and Egypt. Women with curving upraised arms are a standard type of Amratian figurine. There were no goddesses in Egyptian prehistory, but it may well be that in this and other such representations interweaving cow, mother idol, and

37. PREDYNASTIC SLATE PALETTE *representing the abstract head of a cow, its horns, ears, and forehead tipped with stars. Probably simultaneously a representation of the torso of a precursor of the goddess Hathor. Amratian period. From Petrie, et al.*

38. HATHOR HEAD FROM NARMER PALETTE: *One of the four Hathor heads from this palette, which extends to form an abbreviated torso as in the Amratian palette*

goddess the transformation process had its origin. A. J. Arkell compares the Amratian tablet to other early representations incorporating stars and suggests a cosmic relationship: "Probably the resemblance of the new moon to a cow's horns was the reason why a cow-goddess was first associated with the sky. She would then soon be thought of as giving birth to the moon and the stars at nightfall. In this way seems to have arisen the concept of Hat-hōr, 'the house of Horus' the sun-hawk" (1955, p. 126).

Hathor and kingship

From the beginning, Hathor was closely associated with the king, as the Narmer tablet shows. In the pyramid age, in the first blaze of the anthropomorphic
469 deities, Hathor appears in a series of triads as companion to King Mycerinus of the Fourth Dynasty, the backs of their hands touching. In these triads where she stands with the king and a goddess of one of the provinces, Hathor still bears her curving cow-horns, though her wholly female form conveys the impression
109 of a close human relationship with the king. A fragment of one of these triads,
107 which will be described later, brings out clearly how here the full beauty of the female body was for the first time given plastic expression.

The close connection between Hathor and the kingship gained additional ritualistic strength at the beginning of the New Kingdom, when she was made guardian of the necropolis of Thebes. With this she became more of a protectress than a companion. In her original form as a wild cow she strides out from a
right barrel vault in the rock face of Deir el Bahari, sheltering the Pharaoh Amenhotep II beneath her body. Elsewhere he was depicted kneeling beside her udder to drink her sacred milk: "He wished thereby to prove that she was his divine mother, and the complacent manner in which she yields him her milk sufficiently shows that she admitted the legitimacy of his claim" (Maspero, 1912; tr. 1913, p. 112).

Even more dignified is the scene in the Hathor shrine of Hatshepsut's mortu-
423 ary temple at Deir el Bahari, where the sacred cow stands proudly in profile upon her boat emerging from the Nile marshes, the disk of the sun between her horns. Beneath her head stood Queen Hatshepsut, whose figure was later erased. Only Hathor's neckband—the *menit*—remains undamaged, encircling the necks of both Hathor and the queen as if in an embrace. This delicate gesture of encirclement was later used when a woman wished to show a man her affection (Hermann, 1959, p. 21).

Hathor's cult continued unabated throughout Ptolemaic times, and even later. Her image traveled annually up the Nile from her cult center at the temple of

39. HATHOR EMERGING FROM BARREL VAULT: *Relief from the Hathor chapel of Amenhotep II*

Denderah, near Thebes, to celebrate her marriage with her son Horus at his Ptolemaic temple at Edfu.

In *The Beginnings of Art* we followed the transformations of a deity from a mountain stag to the many-breasted Artemis Ephesia. Here the transformation always remained within the orbit of fertility rites. The transformations of Hathor cover a much wider range, even though she never relinquished attributes of her earlier phases, but incorporated them always within her expanded significance: from fertility charm to love poem. Like many other gods, Hathor was a collective symbol.

1:217 ff

In popular belief she remained the tangible symbol of female fertility. More than any of the other divine cows, she retained her nurturing mother aspect, and she appears in many different forms as the helper of women. In a litany from the Late Period, eighteen forms of this great goddess were recounted (Bonnet, 1952, p. 280).

Inanna

In Sumer there were also various kinds of fertility-goddesses. But there the situation was much simpler and less entangled in myth. Most prominent is Inanna. Before Inanna assumed human form she appeared as a primeval symbol, a long, cometlike pole of bound reeds, usually depicted (as upon an alabaster
120 vase from Uruk) paired near a priestess and (upon cylinder seals and reliefs) jutting out from the roofs of the cattle stalls, showing her to be protector of the domestic herds. But even in the earliest tablets from the time of the Gilgamesh epic, Inanna, protector of arable fields and domesticated animals, had changed into a love-hungry Venus and soon afterward into a bloodthirsty goddess of war.

122 ff Inanna, in contrast to the Egyptian fertility-goddesses, belonged to the highest rank of the Sumerian hierarchy. She, her father the god of the moon, and her twin brother the god of the sun formed the supreme triad. Inanna was identified with the most brilliant star of the evening sky, Venus. Later this
123, 127 planet, with eight or twelve rays enclosed within a circle, will become her symbol, and "little by little the goddess of war and love will absorb the other female personages of the pantheons of Sumer, Akkad, and Assyria" (Dhorme, 1949, p. 74).

As with the Egyptian goddess Hathor, popular belief clung to her primeval function as a fertility-goddess. Further, the populace saw her as "the mother of sorrows who listens to prayer, who intercedes with the angry gods and succeeds in appeasing them. . . . A profound feeling of tenderness animates the hymns and prayers addressed to her" (ibid.). Both Hathor and Inanna exemplify the dynamic transformations of the earliest gods.

Min as idol and as god

Human representations in Egypt in the early days did not always represent anthropomorphic gods. One of the few Egyptian gods who certainly stems from the reservoir of prehistory is Min. This god can be followed throughout the whole course of Egyptian history, beginning with his unusual Predynastic
85 statues from Coptos, up to the Ptolemaic period. It was in the New Kingdom, which liked to revive early customs, that Min achieved his greatest renown: he

was absorbed by the sun-god Amon-Ra, who came to be portrayed as ithyphallic, in the likeness of Min.

Even at the extreme end of Egypt's most brilliant period the beautiful reliefs in the second court of the temple of Ramesses III (1195–1164 B.C.), at Medinet 87
Habu, show the high regard paid to Min and to his festival of the renewal and promotion of fertility.

Min as idol

The Min statues from Coptos are not representations of a god. They are fertility idols. When Petrie found them at Coptos, unrelated to any definite stratum, their large size, unusual for prehistory, presented a riddle. They are unique, and could even arouse suspicion were it not for the reliefs upon their sides. These, as we have shown earlier, are so close to prehistoric representa- 1:206 ff
tions that they can be directly compared with the themes and the methods of depiction of the Magdalenian period. They show that stags' antlers, known to 85
be one of the oldest symbols of fertility, were at the same time the oldest symbol associated with the god Min. Antlers can also be recognized in his hieroglyph, which has been variously interpreted as a fetish symbol resembling a "wooden bolt," or as a thunderbolt. The traditional interpretation of the antler is as a symbol of fertility and renewal of life. That this was so, even in the fourth millennium, can be seen in the ibexes on mortuary pottery vessels from Samarra 454
and Susa, with their enormously accentuated horns in comparison with their puny bodies.

The feather, which appears above the Min symbol on the Min reliefs, represented in primeval times (as French prehistorians have recently discovered) 1:200
an abstract form of the phallus.

Many views have been put forward regarding the place of origin of this god of fertility and his migration into Egypt. He has been thought to come from Somaliland (Punt), from Asia, and from Libya. This is of less importance than his general derivation. He is rooted in the traditions of primeval times. His body is formed like a pillar, his right arm pressed close beside his body and his left 85
hand holding his ithyphallic member. The body is covered with many large cupules (cuplike hollows), which were associated throughout primeval times with the desire to induce fertility. Close to where his legs are broken off are two 1:132 ff
diamond shapes with a crossline. This form has been identified by C. Hentze, from Magdalenian bone engravings, Mesopotamian cylinder seals, and also 1:198
from China, as a vulva symbol.

In addition, there are the reliefs on the flap at the side of the figure which

I:205 repeat a Magdalenian motif: an animal's head with outstretched tongue reaches toward vulva symbols (conch shells). These reliefs tell something more. Their motif does not, like most Predynastic Egyptian symbols, belong to the imaginative world of the farmer. It reaches back to the period of the hunter, to primeval times.

These Min idols are overlaid with various symbols of fertility and procreation. The repeated juxtaposition of male and female symbols points to an androgynous being. The name Min later became Min-Kamutef, the "Bull of his mother," which means he is her begetter. "The meaning of this begetting is self-creation. . . . It signifies god as the first beginning in that god created himself and there was no one before him" (Bonnet, 1952, p. 364).

The priests of Heliopolis, in one of their accounts of the creator-god Atum, state that he formed Shu, god of the air, and his sister and wife Tefnut, goddess of the moisture, by masturbation (Pyramid Texts, §1248; tr. Mercer, 1952,

40. HEAD OF MIN, *fertility-god, belonging (according to Flinders Petrie) to the torso in the Cairo Museum. Coptos, Predynastic period*

41. STATUE OF MIN: *Large cupules on body, vulva symbols near base. Coptos*

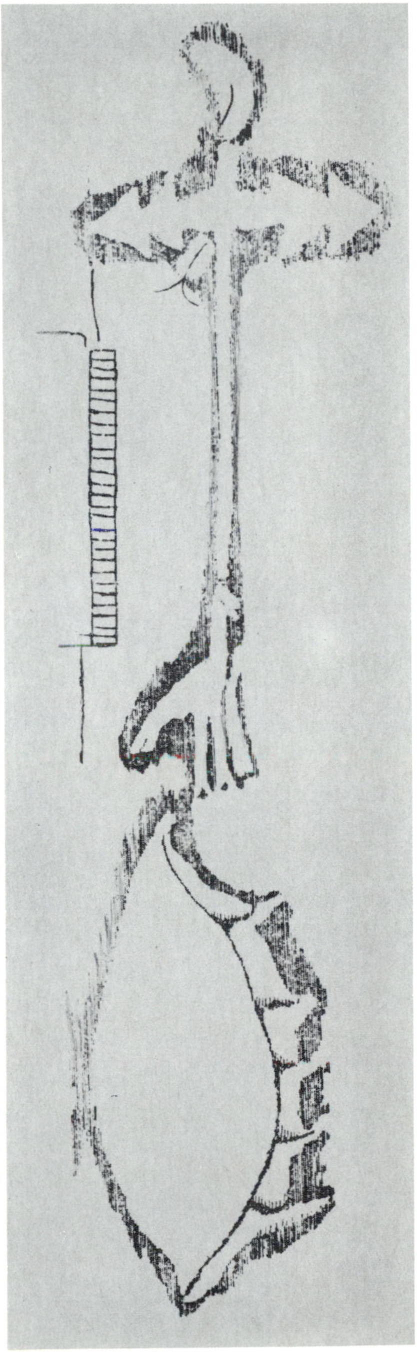

42. SYMBOL OF MIN: *A horizontal two-headed dart crossed vertically with an abstract feather, in relief upon the right thigh below the extended right arm. From Flinders Petrie*

43. RELIEF OF MIN *in characteristic attitude: Ithyphallic, one upraised arm and one leg. To his right, three large lettuces, symbols of fertility. From a Seventeenth Dynasty temple limestone block re-used in the temple of Tuthmosis III at Coptos*

III, p. 621). If one compares this myth with the posture of the archaic statue of Min, one perceives how Egyptian theologians were always concerned to incorporate age-old traditions into their system.

Among the Min statues at Coptos, Petrie only found one head—now in the 84
Ashmolean Museum, Oxford. It probably belongs to the Min statue in the Cairo Museum. This head, with its indications of a beard, is not so damaged as it may appear. As in all prehistoric figures, the face probably never had any distinct features.

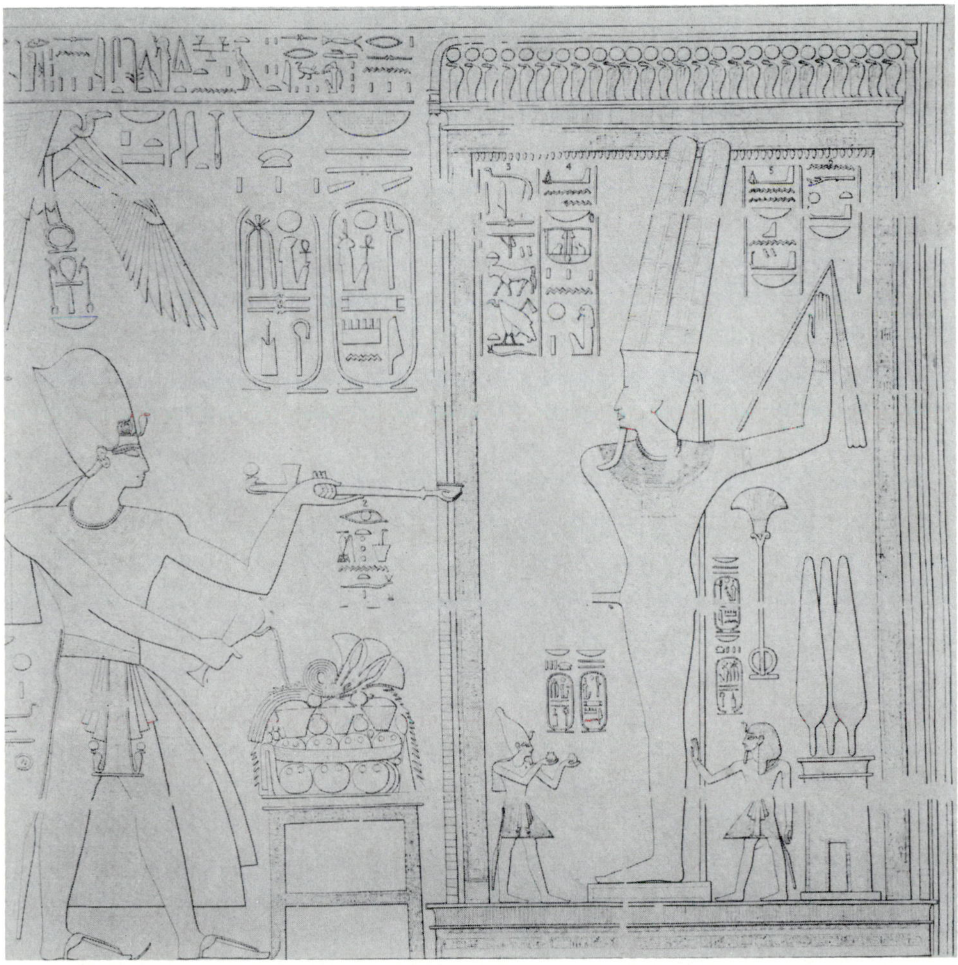

44. MIN AND RAMESSES III. *Medinet Habu, Twentieth Dynasty. From Nelson*

Min as god

1:217 ff In the case of Artemis Ephesia the transition was complicated, passing through many different stages. With Min it was simple. The primeval fertility idol was incorporated into the Egyptian pantheon, where he assumed the mummified likeness of other deities, in particular Ptah and Osiris. Both of these have certain connections with Min, Ptah as the god of creation and Osiris as god of vegetation. With Osiris this form is easily understandable as a result of the fate he endured. Min, like all primeval idols, was without destiny. He stood alone.

His deified form was depicted according to persistent hieratic rules and remained unchanged up to the Ptolemaic period. Min, the earlier idol of procreation and of pervading procreative force, stood upon a pedestal, imprisoned in the wrappings of a mummy. This has sometimes been interpreted to mean that Min even as a corpse still possessed the power to create life (Bleeker, 1956, p. 49). But the enclosure of this idol from Coptos within the form of a mummy appears today more like a typical theological inversion.

In Min's deified form, only one foot and one arm are visible. The idol from Coptos had one arm pressed close against the side of his body. Now it has been 86, 157 jerked above his head. "The upraised arm in Egypt is a typical gesture of wargods" (p. 46).

Through the seeming absence of the other arm the figure appears mutilated. But it has been stressed: "It is certain that Min clasps the phallus with it" (p. 48).

Upon his head Min bears the divine emblem—two tall, upright feathers that strengthen still further his incorporation into the hierarchy of the gods.

Like the reliefs on the side of the Coptos statues, a palette from the Gerzean period, the final Predynastic stage, shows the symbol of Min in a simplified form: a horizontal, two-headed dart crossed vertically by an abstract feather (Massoulard, 1949, pl. LXV, 1). In the graves of Helwan this symbol of Min appears, carved out of ivory.

Min remained a stranger in the community of the gods of light, such as Horus and Isis, with whom he was sporadically associated. He remained alone until approached by the highest god, Amon, who first appears as the local god of Thebes in the Middle Kingdom. Amon assimilated Ra, the sun-god, and became Amon-Ra. Finally he assimilated Min, the ancient fertility-god from nearby Coptos; and even in the Twelfth Dynasty Amon had assumed an ithyphallic form so that he exactly resembles the god Min "and is treated exactly like him. . . . Behind him stand the same attributes: the curious conical pillar and the tree or lettuce plant. . . . The same ceremonies were performed before both gods: the offering of lettuces and the ladder. The same titles to address them: 'High with feathers' referring to the headdress, 'He with the uplifted arm' referring to the posture of the arm, 'Whose beauty is admired' referring to his erect phallus, and, above all, the most significant 'Bull of his mother' which expresses the self-genesis of the god" (Sethe, 1929, pp. 19–20). This was the moment when Amon approached so near to the ancient fertility-god that he completely took over his appearance, "so that he formed with him . . . but one and the same god" (Gauthier, 1931, p. xi).

THE KA AND PRIMEVAL CONCEPTS

There is a bridge to the religious concepts of primeval times where one would least expect it. This is the notion of the Ka, which was further elaborated by the Heliopolitan theologians and incorporated into their religious system. They complicated the theory of the Ka so much that it became "one of the most elusive problems" (Faulkner, 1955, p. 141).

The Ka played a dominant role among ideas relating to the spirit. Whenever the Egyptians came to formulate their thinking, they strove to find ways to approach the continuity of the life beyond from as many sides as possible: the mummified body, daily offerings and attention, and the reliefs and paintings in the tombs. The agricultural products and handicrafts depicted there were realities in the prehistoric sense: that is, they were active operating symbols and not 1:92
just remembrances of things past. The survivors had continually to renew exactly specified meals to ensure the well-being of the dead. Equally real were the *ushabtiu*—small, painted, mummylike figures which were buried with the deceased to serve him in the hereafter, to perform any heavy labors, or, if they were female, to supply sensual pleasures.

As a further assurance of the afterlife, the soul was split into seven species. Each had a special function. Among them two had the leading roles: the Ba and the Ka. The Ba comes nearest to our Christian individual soul. In the New Kingdom, the Ba soul was represented as a sinister bird with a human face and

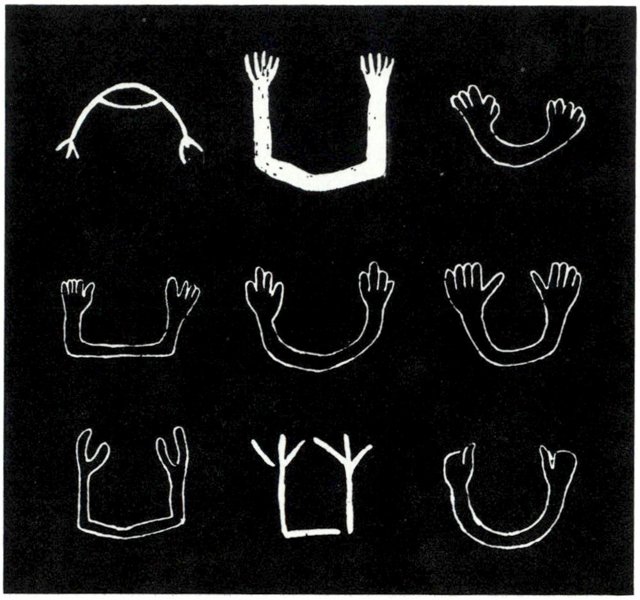

45. KA HIEROGLYPHS: *Drawings of the earliest forms used. From H. U. Petrie*

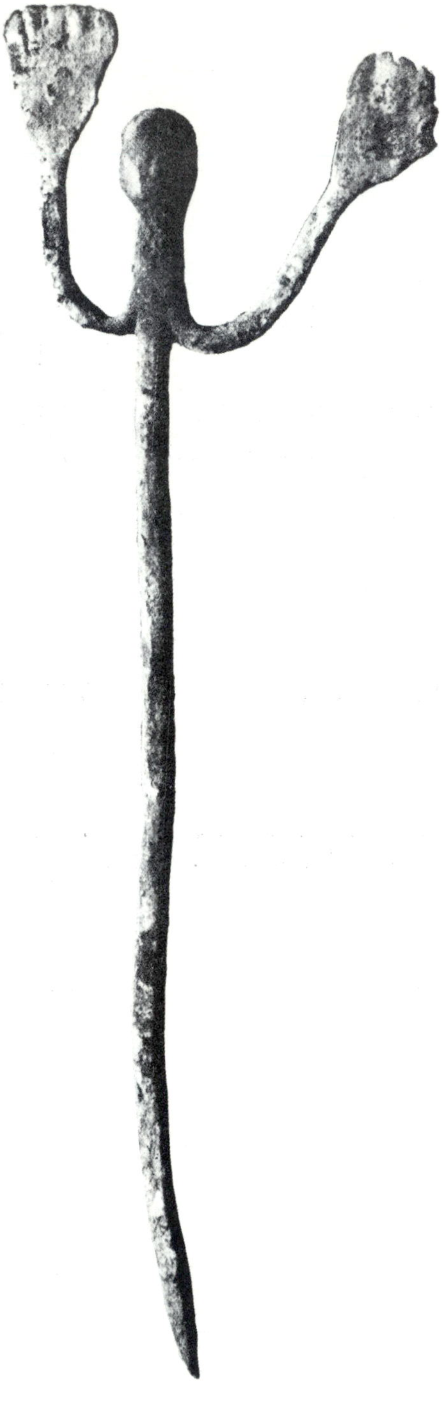

46. MAN WITH UPRAISED ARMS: *This force-dispensing gesture is universal, from Scandinavia (cf. vol. I, fig. 63) to Africa. Hand-forged iron figure found standing in the ground before a tomb. Bandiagara (Mali), several hundred years old*

often with human hands. At the moment of death, this soul left the body in the form of a bird. It is depicted sitting on a tree and pecking at the fruits of the earth. The notion of the Ba soul played a secondary role in Egypt.

It is typical of Egypt that in the foreground should be not the personal, individual Ba soul but the Ka, which had a much wider cosmic significance. The concept of the Ka has interested Egyptologists in recent years, since it is seen as a key to the nature of Egyptian religion. In apparent agreement, the Ka is interpreted as a kind of "vital force." "The closest approximation to the Egyptian notion of the Ka is 'vital force.' . . . The Ka, according to this view, should be impersonal and should be present in varying strength in different persons" (Frankfort, 1948, p. 62). It is a cosmic, divine force—a force which emanates from the god and which was serviceably built into the new social hierarchy. The king, at the summit of the hierarchy, received the Ka from the sun-god. He was the possessor of the Ka, which he then dispensed to the people. Through the Ka, the king was the human manifestation of the god (Greven, 1952, p. 33). "The Ka is not only a divine force which relates the king with his ancestors and with the deity, but it also relates the people with their ruler, and through him with the godhead" (Jacobsohn, 1939, p. 60).

The Ka was a vital and invisible force. How should it be transferred from the god to the king? The force-bestowing manual gesture appears strongly on a Swedish rock engraving of a demon or a god with upraised arms. The relation 1:117
of this primeval gesture of the outpouring of vital force by the overdimensioned hands, and the closeness of its meaning to the primitive Ka hieroglyphs of the First and Second Dynasties, has been suggested in *The Beginnings of Art.* The 1:115 ff
gesture is universally found from Scandinavia to the heart of Africa, where a wrought-iron figure of relatively recent date still shows the same upraised and left
overdimensioned hands.

The Egyptian hieroglyph for the Ka consists of two upstretched arms with outspread fingers. It has been suggested that this hieroglyph is similar to another which signifies "to encompass, to embrace" (Kees, 1956, p. 44), and which indeed appears the same, only in a reversed position. The strength-giving power of this gesture of the upraised arms goes back to prehistory, and is still preserved in the crude hieroglyphs of the First Dynasty. It shows how the divine left
power was transferred. The friendly gesture of the embrace has never been presented with so many shades of meaning, so forcefully, and so frequently, to bring out the close relations of man to man and man to god.

The one who is transferring the Ka lays his arms from behind upon the one

47. HEAD OF CHEPHREN *embraced by the wings of the falcon-god Horus: A gesture simultaneously transferring the Ka and protecting the king. Fourth Dynasty*

48. SESOSTRIS I AND PTAH: *The god embraces the king at his jubilee (Heb-Sed) festival to invest him with renewed powers of life. Relief from fragment of a pillar from Sesostris' jubilee temple. Middle Kingdom*

who is to receive it, as, for example, the falcon-god Horus lays his wings upon left the shoulders of King Chephren, possessor of the Ka. "The transference of the Ka was called by the Egyptians 'to protect' " (Spiegel, 1953, p. 113, par. 165).

The embrace of a god does not always signify transference of the Ka; it can also mean giving or renewing strength and power. On a fragment of a pillar of the jubilee temple of King Sesostris I, Middle Kingdom, discovered buried in the foundations of a pylon, the god Ptah embraces the king at the time of the left Heb-Sed festival, and invests him with the renewed power of life and strength which was the inner meaning of this jubilee festival.

The conception of the coming of the Ka from the god must have made a great impression on the Egyptians. Recall the relief in the Birth Room of the temple 49 of Luxor depicting the ram-headed god Khnum with a potter's wheel on which he models two figures: the unborn king, Amenhotep III, builder of Luxor, and his invisible double, his Ka. Ursula Schweitzer—a Basel Egyptologist who died too young—took the scene, of which this is only a fragment, to have wider implications, in that the queen first brings the Ka into the world and after that her son (1956, p. 63).

The richest insight into the mysterious changes and wanderings of the Ka concept has been given by Schweitzer. On the basis of Maspero's famous theory of the Ka as "a second exemplar of the body, of less dense matter than the matter of the body" (Maspero, 1878, quoted by Schweitzer, 1956, p. 13), she traced the development of the Ka concept beginning with the First Dynasty.

From the Middle Kingdom, in the Twelfth Dynasty, there is a rare wooden statue of King Hor, found near the south brick pyramid of Dahshur. The king stands in his naos (chapel), bearing the Ka hieroglyph on his head. It is a Ka 94 statue, since the king is naked.

Mortuary statues were closely related to the Ka: "The Egyptians did not consider mortuary statues just as likenesses of the dead. They were existentially connected to the dead through the Ka" (Greven, 1952, p. 32). It was not the mummy but the mortuary statue which possessed the Ka. The continuance of life after death was largely assured by the bearer of the Ka—the mortuary statue. For this reason there were often many of these, and they were carefully protected in the serdab, or statue chamber, which was usually "connected with the outer world by a slit through which incense could be dispensed" (p. 33).

As a preparation for the reception of the Ka there was the so-called ceremony of the "Opening of the mouth," such as occurred in the valley temple of Chephren. Even today it is thought-provoking to see, through the narrow slits of

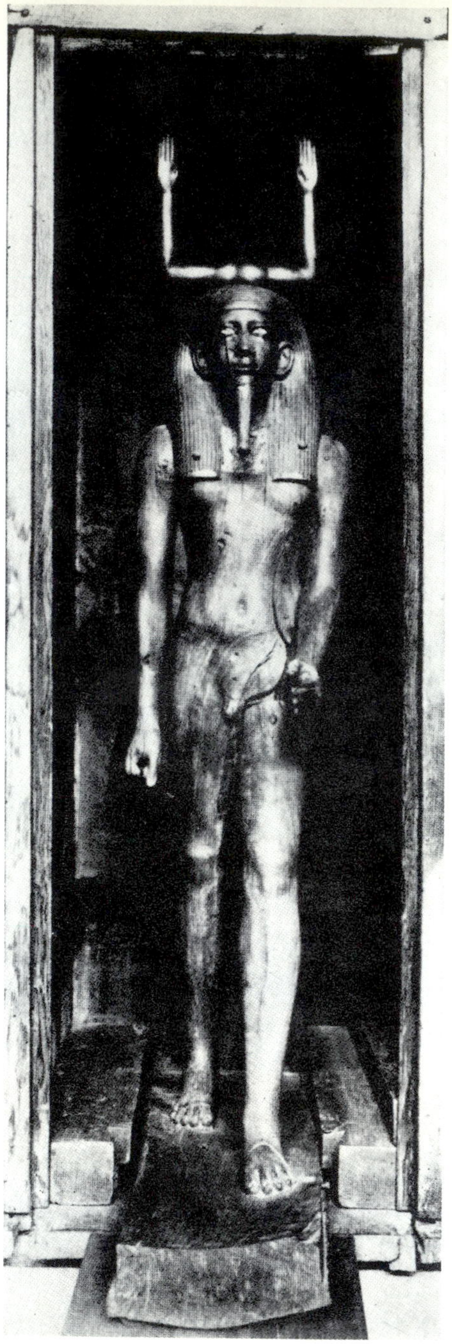

49. HOR WITH KA HIEROGLYPH: *The king stands in his naos bearing a Ka hieroglyph on his head. Wooden statue. Middle Kingdom*

290 the stone wall, how the eternally vigilant mortuary statue of King Zoser sits waiting for his Ka to return to him.

In this belief another significant primeval conception lies hidden: symbol and reality are synonymous.

PART III CREATING AN ANTHROPOMORPHIC COSMOS

To gain insight into the formation of the anthropomorphic world of gods one must make careful use of the word "deity." This term is often used loosely and unclearly.

In prehistory there were no gods. When human figures were represented, they were fertility symbols. This may be the chief reason that female figures
1:434 ff were usually shown pregnant and with exaggerated breasts, buttocks, and sexual triangle. In Sumer, Egypt, and elsewhere, toward the end of the prehistoric era, a more slender female type slowly began to emerge, but it retained the traditional emphasis on the sexual triangle. The relatively few male figures
1:204 ff in prehistory were mostly shown as ithyphallic, also expressing the desire for fertility and procreation.

The prehistoric female fertility image has been called by a variety of names: idol, earth mother, Great Mother, and also *grande déesse* or mother-goddess. This vagueness can easily lead to confusion. Through the tens of thousands of years from the Aurignacian-Perigordian era to the dawn of systematic agriculture in the Middle East, female figurines appear, always modeled with stress on those parts most important for reproduction. These are magic images of wish fulfillment—fetishes, some would say—and their purpose is to procure fertility. They have no deeper meaning, any more than have the engravings on bone or cave wall of ithyphallic men, sometimes alone, sometimes following a female. They are earth-bound. This fundamentally sets them apart from the god concept evolved at the beginning of the historic era, or possibly shortly before.

Everything indicates that the religious notions of prehistory never freed themselves from the earth, but were concentrated upon facilitating entry and re-entry into an earthly existence in which no distinction was observed between man and animal.

The gods of the pantheons were quite otherwise. Each possessed a clearly outlined physiognomy, had particular tasks or attributes, bore a name, entered into relations with other gods, and was part of a patriarchal family with a dictatorial ruler at its head. Prehistory's crude hankering after fertility and procreation had given place to an organized ruling household. The ever-increasing host of gods and their assemblies, especially in Mesopotamia, have been likened to a parliament.

The decisive change that came about with this creation of undying gods with human forms was their transference into the cosmos. This transposition is of fundamental significance for the further development of religious thought. It was the starting point for all later religious systems, with their increasing emphasis upon the transcendental factor.

In a certain sense, the religion of the first high civilizations represents a transitional stage. The deity is still to some extent earth-bound: he can take up his abode temporarily in dwellings created especially for him.

The Sumerians built their god of the deep waters a palace of lapis lazuli at Eridu. In this temple at the summit of the ziggurat occurred the sacred coupling. This ritual has had a long survival: even to this day, the Sultan of Surakarta in Indonesia must ascend a tall tower for his ritual marriage with the Queen of the Sea.

In Egypt, the pyramidion at the peak of the obelisk was the abode of the god 448 or, like Amon at Karnak, he lived in his cult figure in the dark cell of his temple. Yet he could come and go, and was able to undertake journeys. His real home was the cosmos.

This cosmic transfiguration induced a powerful upsurge in imaginative thought, and gave rise to questions which have not yet ceased to disquiet mankind. There is the eternally unsolved cosmogonic question: how and by whom was the world created? There are also cosmologic problems: what are the relationships between the earth, the heavens, and the heavenly bodies, and what order do they obey?

TEMPLES WITHOUT IMAGES

One continually comes up against the inner difficulties that must have beset the human spirit in the anthropomorphic representation of the newly created gods. They are evidenced by the absence of images of the deity in the earlier temples. In the temple strata of around 3000 B.C., no anthropomorphic statues of gods were found. This cannot be ascribed to chance, especially in Mesopotamia, where the early stages of development are more easily followed and compared than are those of Egypt.

There it is as true for the north as for the south, where the sixteen levels of Eridu, from the fifth millennium until the building of the ziggurat around 2000 B.C., yielded no trace of any representations. The altars were bare. Only in one of the upper levels was a temple found with its floor covered with fishbones that hinted at the possible existence even then of Enki, god of the deep waters, to whom the famous ziggurat was later erected. The same phenomenon can be observed in the north. It is true that the twenty levels of Tepe Gawra disclosed numerous female figurines of clay (fertility symbols), as well as sacred vessels, but no trace of the statue of a god.

There are many other instances, but the most outstanding is the religious center of Uruk (the Biblical Erech). In the highly developed temple complex from its peak architectural period (Uruk IV), the excavators indicate the different temples simply by letter—*A*, *B*, *C*, *D*—for there is nothing to indicate consecration to any particular god.

Altars without gods, veneration of a featureless supreme being, existed even in Greek civilization. K. Schefold (1959, p. 128) notes that in Olympia there was no statue of Zeus except in the classical temple, and that the famous late-Hellenistic Zeus altar at Pergamum (ca. 180–160 B.C.) bore no cult statue of the god. The podium of the altar remained bare.

A reluctance to represent the supreme being in human form is easily understandable. Apart from a natural diffidence about presenting the godhead as analogous to man, which also occurs in later religions, there was at that time a further obstacle: the veneration of the animal that had occupied the forefront of man's sentiments since his earliest beginnings.

The archaic civilizations displayed a certain diffidence in the representation and exposure of their deities. Generally they were personified in connection with the god-king, sometimes as reliefs, more rarely as sculptures in the round. The legitimacy of the Pharaoh as god-king appeared most distinctly, and com-
469 paratively late, in the triad groups of King Mycerinus of the Fourth Dynasty, where the god-king alternated with the great protective goddess Hathor as the central figure. These sculptural groups had no continuation. In the New Kingdom their place was taken by large colored reliefs, such as those of Sety I at Abydos. The divine origin of the ruler was also stressed in the New Kingdom by the intercourse of the queen with Amon-Ra, who approached her in the shape of the king (reliefs in Hatshepsut's mortuary temple at Deir el Bahari and
137 Amenhotep III's Birth Room in the temple of Luxor).

Statues of deities in human form were not exposed even in the New Kingdom. Although colossal statues of the ruler were placed in a most conspicuous position before the pylons, the gods themselves were represented there only by symbols
375 —by the age-old sacred posts, now grown to monumental masts, and the obelisk
380 as seat of the highest god. A colossal statue such as that of Athena Promachos on the Acropolis, whose golden spear-tip flashed rays seen by ships at sea, would have been unthinkable in the archaic civilizations.

FROM MASKS TO THE HUMAN COUNTENANCE

The religious structure of the first high civilizations was founded upon the discovery of the human form and the human face. Without this, its entire edifice could not have been built up. Only after man had begun to consider himself beautiful could his own image be used as a model for the object of his worship. Only then could eyes receive their glow, the mouth its attraction, the figure its grace.

For this to occur, the primeval conception of man as inferior to the animal had first to be overcome. Previously, male and female bodies had served only as fertility symbols. With a few rare exceptions the face was hidden, or merely 1:487 ff
indicated. It was shown clearly only among hybrid creatures with a human body and an animal head, such as the shaman in the cavern of Les Trois Frères (Ariège).

What are today called masks were, for primitive and primeval man, a means of transformation into another being, another nature, and a means of contact with supernatural powers. In this roundabout way, fragments of the human face were allowed to appear. Masks led to the unveiling of the human countenance.

The masked face from Hassuna

Hassuna, in northern Mesopotamia, is one of the earliest known settlements; it throws much light on village culture during the transition from the neolithic period into the age of copper. But there were extraordinarily few representations of human beings. Seton Lloyd and Fuad Safar, who with the greatest care excavated the seven-meter strata in 1943–44, noted that "apart from a female 100
face modeled and painted on a Samarran vase" all representations were "crude and rather incomprehensible unbaked clay figurines of the primitive 'mother- 74
goddess' type" (1945, pp. 262–63). The vase fragment came from one of the deepest strata (level V), and thus from the copper age. Further, it was brought into the village from cultivated Samarra.

Beneath meeting eyebrows, the slightly protruding eyes, round as marbles, have elongated slits such as are usual in masks. Upon each cheek are three vertical strokes or tattoo marks. The sides of the face are lost amid parallel zigzag vertical lines; the lower part is crossed by three parallel horizontal lines. The remaining space is filled by black triangles, their points directed downward. Triangles, like those scratched on the earliest urns from Hassuna, appear to be

50. MASKED FACE *modeled and painted on neck of vase. From level V, Hassuna (northern Mesopotamia). Early fourth millennium*

51. GOLD PENDANT AS FERTILITY SYMBOL: *Vulvalike form, with sketchily indicated breasts and navel but oversized sexual triangle. From El Ajjul (Gaza), Late Period*

52. FEMALE FIGURE ON JAR HANDLE: *Face and body reduced to the utmost, but enormous sexual triangle hatched below handle. Buffware pot from Cemetery A, Kish (Mesopotamia). Fourth millennium*

an age-old symbol for the promise of future life: a triangle with "the apex pointed downward signified the female" (Stone, 1927, p. 5).

In nearly every grave of Cemetery A in Kish, a handled jar was found: "No
101 less than three specimens were found in burial 40" (Mackay, 1929, p. 142). The handle takes the form of a mother-goddess. Face and body are reduced to the utmost, only eyes, nose, mouth, and the small breasts being shown. "Sometimes . . . the eyes and breasts also have the pupils and nipples indicated" (p. 145). Immediately below the handle is an enormous triangle with herringbone hatching. Its size, in comparison with the rest of the figure, stresses its significance upon these mortuary vessels. Upon the shoulder of the jar, above the projecting beading common in vessels of this type, two concentric rows of hatched triangles reinforce this significance. The oldest pottery from Hassuna also has a row of triangles, but they are vertically disposed upon its body.

This fertility symbol lived on through long ages. Gold pendants from a late
100 period found in El Ajjul, Gaza, "indicate by breasts, navel and vulva sketchily added to the Hathor head a gradual development from the symbol to the anthropomorphic idol of a mother-goddess" (Barb, 1953, p. 200).

The female face from Uruk

Almost a millennium lies between the masked face from Hassuna and the female
104 head of translucent alabaster from Uruk. This sculpture was found, almost uninjured, by H. Lenzen's expedition in 1939, its face turned upward amid the rubbish from an early Jemdet Nasr building. It therefore stems from the beginning of the third millennium. There is nothing else like it from this period. The gypsum heads found in Jericho, from much earlier, cannot be counted as works of artistic expression.

The appearance of this almost life-size face at so early a period is like the bloom of a miraculous flower. Such perfection is not attainable without antecedents, but these are hidden from us. Suddenly it presents what had till then not existed—the gentle charm of a human countenance: a perfect oval, a harmonious accord of brow, cheeks, and chin—delicate but tense—and expressively sensitive closed lips.

Lenzen gives this description: "The eyebrows repeat in the beautifully arched lines the almond-shaped, incised eyes and grow together above the indented root of the nose, conforming to the Sumerian ideal of beauty" (1939, p. 85).

What does this portrait signify?

There is nothing to indicate that it is the likeness of a goddess. As Lenzen perceived, the head is "far removed from supernatural godlike features" (p. 86). Not a goddess, but probably—as in prehistory—a medium between man and the unseen powers is here represented, in the form of a priestess who personifies, in her entire bearing, the highly bred product of a city culture.

The head is not the remnant of a statue, for the back of it is flattened. Almost simultaneously, another marble head was discovered, in Tell Brak in northern Mesopotamia, which belongs to the same period and of which the back part is also lacking (*Illustrated London News*, May 20, 1939, p. 883). The neck of the Tell Brak head is elongated and becomes thinner at the base, a sign that it too is an isolated head and not part of a statue. Its masklike character is especially clear in its abstract ears, incised eyes, slanted and oversized, and puffed-up lips.

A comparison of the two heads but confirms the uniqueness of the lady of Uruk: over her face lies quietness.

The mouth

The shimmer of melancholy and tragedy that hovers over the face from Uruk loses nothing by comparison with a fragment of a female head from the Eight- 105
eenth Dynasty, but between them lie about fifteen hundred years. The tremendous distance covered in the artistic conquest of the human countenance by the time of the New Kingdom is fully expressed in this fragment of a head of Nofretete or Queen Tiy (Hayes, 1959, II, pp. 259–60). Its immediacy and its attempt to come as close as possible to naturalness—closer than in any other period in Egypt—are typical of the short Amarna period. Though the fragment is carved from one of the hardest of stones, yellow jasper, it is vibrant with life. Once tightly pressed lips have become warm and rounded. Their sensual moistness is even more pronounced in this fragment than in the famous Nofretete head now in Berlin.

The eyes

Accentuation of the eyes plays a prominent part in giving life to representations of the human countenance. This did not exist in primeval sculpture. Later, full of the delight of new discovery, sculptors gave eyes unusual vivacity through inlaid color, as in the Uruk head, or the oversized hypnotic eyes of the statues of Tell Asmar.

53. FEMALE HEAD *almost life-size: First appearance of the gentleness of the human face, though still somewhat masklike. The features are somewhat flattened, and the sides of the cheeks are almost at a right angle to the frontal plane. White marble. Uruk, early third millennium*

In the famous limestone statue in the Louvre of a scribe from the Fifth Dynasty, everything is concentrated upon the eyes. The scribe sits naked, with folded legs, his body held stiffly upright. His eyes, of alabaster, black stone, silver, and crystal, stare penetratingly into the distance, as though alert to receive a message from eternity that must be transferred immediately to the papyrus roll spread out upon his lap. It has been suggested that the figure may represent the governor of a nome: a nomarch. 106

54. MOUTH OF NOFRETETE OR QUEEN TIY: *In the fifteen hundred years between the Uruk head and this fragment with its rounded cheeks and sensual lips, human beauty was both discovered and conquered. Yellow jasper. Amarna period, Eighteenth Dynasty, fourteenth century* B.C.

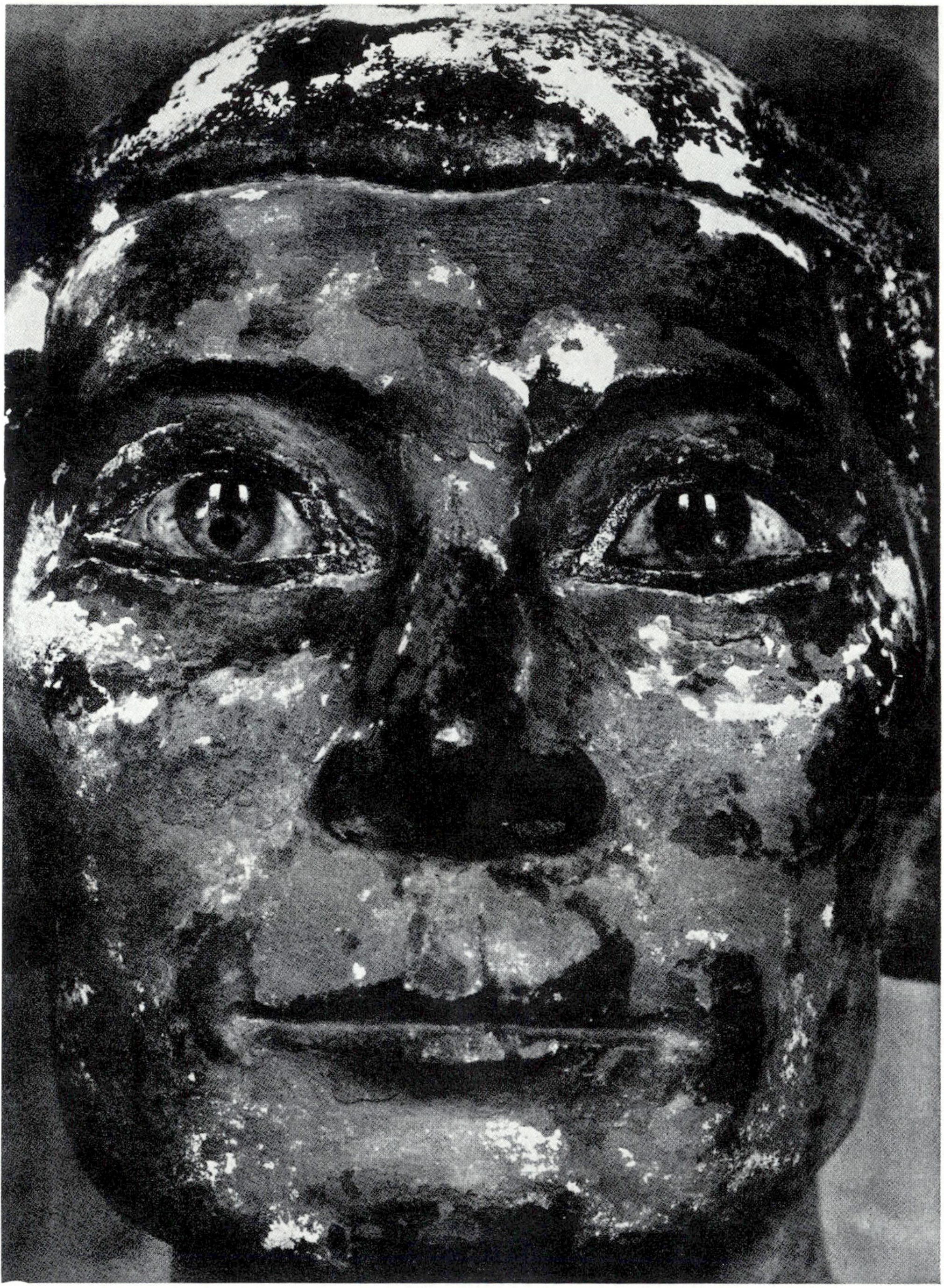

55. FACE OF THE LOUVRE SCRIBE: *This famous polychrome statue is naked, a papyrus roll on its lap. Emphasis is concentrated upon the strongly modeled head and, above all, on the brilliant crystal eyes staring into the distance. Fifth Dynasty, third millennium*

As Egypt became conscious of its artistic powers, which had slumbered below the surface for so long, the Sumerian prelude began to pale.

The decisive event was the discovery of the human body. First steps were sculptures such as the Ka statue of King Zoser, of the Third Dynasty, the reliefs 291 of him in his underground chambers at Saqqara, and those of Hesy-ra of the 267, 169 same dynasty. From the standpoint of the plastic treatment of the body, a great distance divides the Zoser statue from that of Chephren, of the Fourth Dynasty, in which the bodily structure is forcefully displayed.

Under Mycerinus, a generation after Chephren, realization of the plastic qualities of the female body awoke, and with this a desire to give sculptural ex- 469 pression to the great intensity of its perfect interflow of forms. From this time on, the female body remained among the highest goals of sculpture. We have no measure of what this daring manifestation meant to the people of the Fourth Dynasty.

Female beauty manifested

The sculptural groups of King Mycerinus, standing with the goddess Hathor on his right and a god or goddess of one of the nomes on his left, offer the best insight into the discovery of female beauty. G. A. Reisner unearthed several of these triads from the rubble of Mycerinus' valley temple at Giza in 1908–10. The four groups which could be reconstructed—others remain as fragments—are in the museums of Cairo and Boston. The large group in Cairo will be con- 468 ff sidered later from another point of view. Here we are concerned with a highly original aspect of these sculptures—their plastic treatment of the female body.

Gaston Maspero was Director General of the Service des Antiquités at the time they came to light. With French subtlety, he at once recognized their artistic finesse, observing that the sculptors "who executed the schists were much more skilled" than those who worked in alabaster (tr. 1913, p. 48). Maspero stressed the mastery of the artist who could handle such an "ungrateful material" as schist "with the same suppleness as if he had been kneading the most ductile clay" (ibid.).

He recognized that "the women are especially remarkable with their full round shoulders . . . the belly strong and well designed, the thighs full and graceful, the legs vigorous, one of the most elegant types created by Memphian

56. FRAGMENT OF MYCERINUS TRIAD: *Slate stele (80 cm.) with the goddess Hathor, King Mycerinus, and a badly damaged male god (not shown). From Mycerinus' valley temple, Giza, Fourth Dynasty*

57. GODDESS HATHOR: *Detail of fig. 56. One of the earliest representations of female beauty. The human body has become a dignified vehicle for a deity*

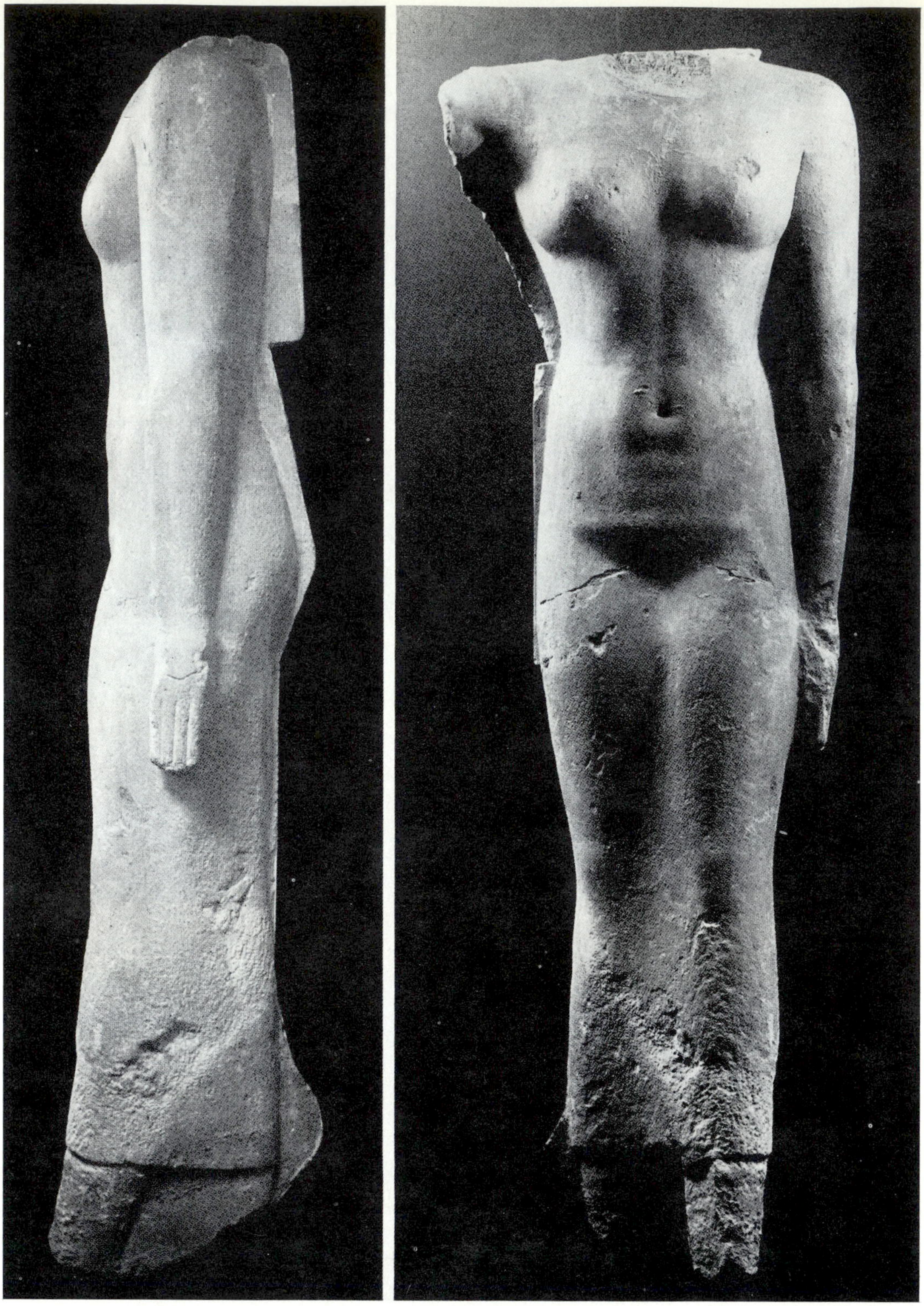

58. TORSO OF A WOMAN: *Two views of life-size figure forming part of a family triad. From Fifth Dynasty tomb of Ra-wer, Giza*

Egypt" (ibid.). But these figures were not merely elegant and graceful, they were the first appearance of female beauty in art.

Fragment of a Mycerinus triad

In the complete groups, attention is quickly absorbed by the heads—the faces,
the heavy wigs, and Hathor's headdress with the sun disk between her two 469
cows' horns. In the fragments, these involvements with contemporaneousness
are banished. Nothing distracts attention from their timeless aspect—the plastic 109
mastery of the female figure.

The last century did not lay much value upon fragments. Like a broken teapot, each statue had to be made complete. Today there is a different attitude. The intensity contained in a torso has been revealed to us by a long line of sculptors, from Maillol and Rodin to Lehmbruck, Brancusi, and Arp. The Hathor fragment described below fully achieves what Maillol always sought in studies of the human body: the harmony that exists in the interplay of the body's architectonic and surface tensions. That this should first have been represented in the period which built the pyramids is not surprising.

A fragment of one of the Mycerinus triads, among the most beautiful Egyptian sculptures in existence, was recently brought from the study collection of the Museum of Fine Arts in Boston to the exhibition hall, through the initiative of W. S. Smith. It is of greenish-black slate, eighty centimeters high, and has been described by E. L. B. Terrace (1961, p. 41).

Only part of the king's body remains—a strongly modeled, forward-striding 108
central figure. His left-hand companion is also greatly damaged. But by grace of chance the body of the goddess Hathor is preserved intact. Head and feet are lacking. This brings out even more strongly the quality of the torso, the masterly combination of bold, curving outlines and careful treatment of detail.

The broken cylinder of the neck is framed by the ends of Hathor's wig. Her 109
shoulders take on a gentle curve. The line of the left one runs into her loosely hanging arm, whose hand once held the right hand of the king. Her arms are clearly separated from the body. The outline of the torso flows unbroken from below the shoulder joint to below the knee. The hips are barely indicated.

The body details are molded with similar subtlety. Plastic modulation is concentrated upon the torso, the forms purified through a slight process of abstraction. The full breasts protrude as hemispheres, free of naturalistic details. A deep groove runs vertically upward from the navel, ending between the breasts.

The group was once polychrome. But in its present state the light that glides over this Hathor figure shows even better the delicacy of the sculptural treatment. Although the goddess is clothed in a long garment her body appears nude, since it shines through the close-fitting fabric as through glass. Even the skin becomes a transparent membrane. A gentle hollow marks the end of the torso, and the muscular parts of the belly are made visible by slight horizontal undulations. Every inch pulsates with vitality. A body made for procreation has become a beautiful and sacred vessel for the incarnation of a goddess.

Torso of a woman

110 Close kin to the Hathor figure in the fragmentary Mycerinus triad is a life-size figure made of Tura limestone, in the Worcester (Mass.) Museum (Cott, 1935–36, p. 17). It has been tentatively established that the piece comes from a family group taken clandestinely from a tomb at Giza (Cooney, 1945, pp. 54–56). Other figures from this group are in the Brooklyn Museum and in Kansas City.

Outlines and body modeling are very similar to the Hathor fragment, though not quite its equal in subtlety. This may be partly because the workmanship of Fourth and Fifth Dynasty sculptures was less perfect in alabaster and limestone than in harder stones like schist and basalt (Maspero, tr. 1913, p. 48).

The stance is the same. Although the position of the left leg hints at a forward movement, it is overshadowed by the quietude that radiates from the clearly symmetrical structure of the figure, with its unalterable interplay of simple organic forms.

Nothing in these aristocratic bodies reminds one of the animal-like prehistoric fertility figurines or idols. A new ideal female form arises here for the first time, never later to be abandoned: the representation of woman at the peak of her youthful beauty.

This radical transformation had far deeper roots than a mere change in erotic taste. In primeval times all interest was concentrated upon the reproduction of the species, alike of animals and men. In highly civilized Egypt another demand attained supremacy—the desire to live on endlessly, in perpetual youth. In other words, the female nude was without erotic significance both in prehistory and in the first high civilizations. The change began in Greece. Before that time the female body was a container either of fertility or of the imperishable youthfulness of the hereafter.

One small inheritance remains from prehistoric tradition: the care with which the belly region is indicated, with its typical accentuation of the sexual triangle, common to all fertility idols from Aurignacian times onward. In Egyptian statues, the shape is usually marked by a slight horizontal ridge.

The pyramid age was, during the Fourth and part of the Fifth Dynasty, an age of sculpture. At the time of Mycerinus, Egyptian sculpture showed a momentary interest in the highest form of plastic expression—sculpture in the round. It would seem but a moment to the Greek development of the fifth and fourth centuries B.C. But this was not the direction taken by Egyptian sculpture. It remained bound to the stone. 148 ff

The human body in Sumerian sculpture

In seeking to know how the nude body was handled in Sumer, one searches in vain for a representation of the Sumerian goddess of love, Inanna, that could in some way serve as a parallel to the Hathor figure.

Sumerian priests stood naked before the deity. They had to be handsome and well built. One could imagine that this religious background would engender an 115, 120
interest in mastering the representation of the human body. But it did not occur. The tendency was, rather, to conceal the body within long, bell-shaped, kilted 123
gowns. The upper part was still naked in Early Dynastic reliefs and statuettes, 57
but it also was soon covered by the heavy woolen robe. Only arms and legs remained free, as in a series of stone figurines from the temple of Tell Asmar (Baghdad Museum; Oriental Institute, Chicago). Most of the figures are bearded, with large, wide-open eyes, their hands crossed in an attitude of prayer.

This tradition was maintained throughout three millenniums. Its end products were the gigantic, but somehow sterile, reliefs from the last Assyrian period, when the body was completely enveloped down to the feet. It may well be that these ritual garments explain why—in contrast to Egypt—there was no plastic investigation of the human body in Sumer.

Yet Sumer had a short period during which even the handicap of the cumbersome knitted robes was surmounted, and expression given to human dignity and inner piety. The large diorite statues of the priest-king Gudea of Lagash 114
(Telloh), most of them in the Louvre, convey an unusually strong expression of deep earnestness and pious meditation (Parrot, 1948). Here everything is concentrated upon the features. The body itself is scarcely apparent. It is buried beneath the heavy gown, as beneath a coat of armor. Only the hands speak.

Gudea reigned shortly before and at the beginning of the Third Dynasty of

59. SEATED STATUE OF GUDEA, *priest-king of Lagash, with the ground plan of a temple on his lap. The form of his body disappears beneath his heavy garment, except for the finely modeled hands clasped in prayer; ca.* 2100 B.C.

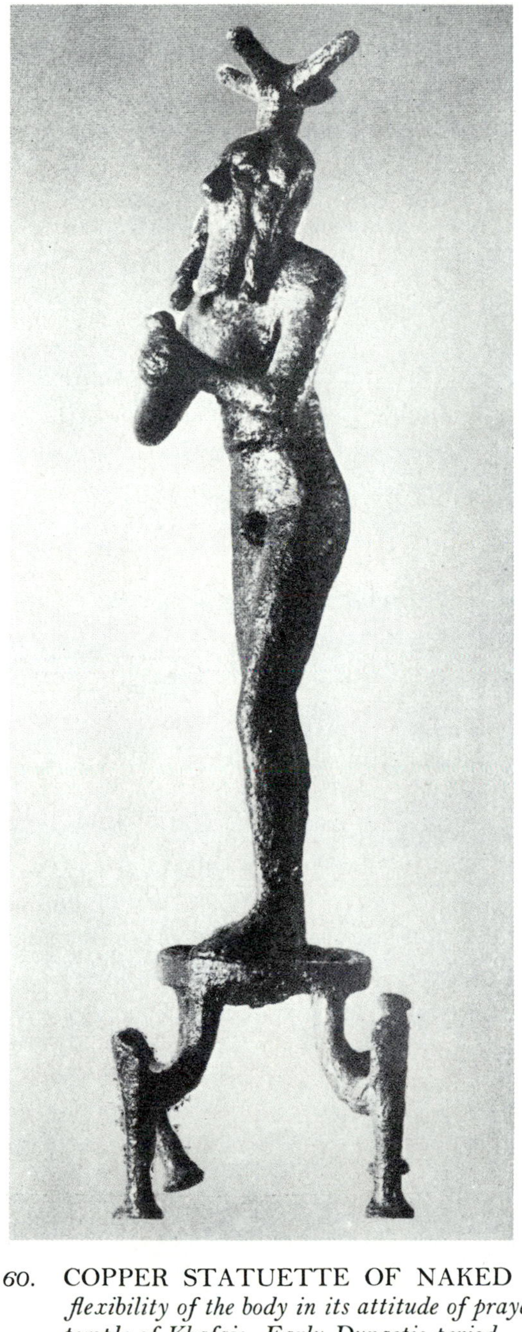

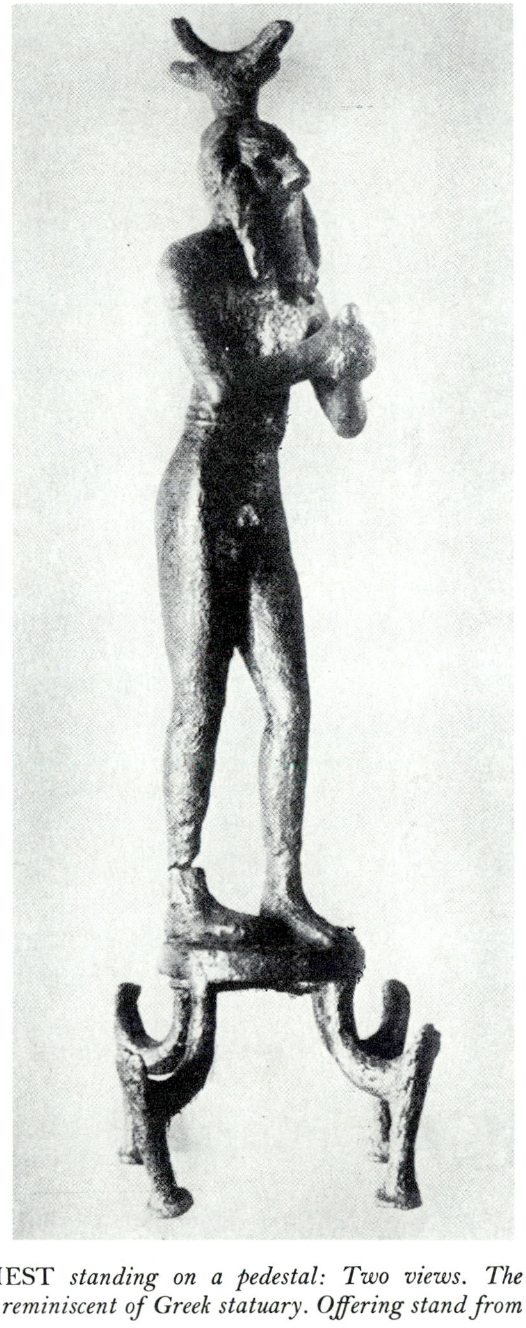

60. COPPER STATUETTE OF NAKED PRIEST *standing on a pedestal: Two views. The flexibility of the body in its attitude of prayer is reminiscent of Greek statuary. Offering stand from temple of Khafaje. Early Dynastic period*

Ur, thus about half a millennium after the Mycerinus sculptures. His statues stood, as lasting intercessions of the priest-king, in a public temple erected to the city-god Ningirsu and other deities. This is very different from Egyptian mortuary complexes, which were inaccessible to the people.

The Gudea statues are pure sculptures in the round and were certainly free-standing. The largest one, in the Louvre, portrays Gudea in his most distinguished capacity, as temple builder. Upon his knees lie the ground plan of a temple, a yardstick, and a measuring peg, just as, in a somewhat different form, they are perpetuated upon the stele of his younger contemporary Urnammu of Ur.

159 ff The sculptured limestone vases of the Protoliterate period in the third millennium pushed high relief to extreme limits. The two deer upon a large
56 copper panel from Al 'Ubaid are also three-quarters in the round, parts of them springing forward beyond the frame. Such instances would seem to imply that a strongly sculptural development lay ahead. Nothing of the sort occurred. The promise of an early sculptural impetus in Sumer evaporated.

The starting points of this never-developed tendency must be sought among minor objects. In the temple of Khafaje, in central Mesopotamia, Frankfort and P. Delougaz discovered several copper statuettes of the Early Dynastic period,
115 representing priests naked except for a girdle (Frankfort, 1939b, pls. 98–103). They were raised up upon an airy, four-branched pedestal that served as an offering stand in the temple. Their hands are clasped in an attitude of prayer.

These figures have no vertical axis, no median plane. The body has become flexible. Arms curve freely, opening out into space, and wide-apart legs create a spatial tension. The torso is bent slightly forward in a momentary turning movement. This audacious conquest of the third dimension could never have occurred in Egypt, whose artistic canons stood in direct opposition. Three-dimensional movement in sculpture was only developed further in Greece. The Mesopotamian episode was cut short.

APPEARANCE OF ANTHROPOMORPHIC DEITIES

There is still much difference of opinion about just when the anthropomorphic deities first appeared. The question deeply affects the history of man, but there are few definite clues to lead us to an answer.

Both literary and pictorial sources are extremely scarce. In literature the Gilgamesh epic, probably written down in the latter part of the third millennium, about 2600 B.C., gives the best insight. Gilgamesh, a typical example of the newly created hero figure, appears to have reigned only a few centuries earlier as king of Uruk, thus approximately in Uruk III or Uruk IV, the Jemdet Nasr period and the time of the first great architecture.

In the epic, the world of gods is already well established. We meet the entire range—the anthropomorphic goddess Inanna, the demon Humbaba, Gilgamesh, the mortal hero seeking immortality who stands between god and man, and his hybrid companion Enkidu. All are woven into the action, which is already imbued with the tragedy that saturates Mesopotamian history and art.

In Egypt, more prone to visual than to literary expression, pictorial representation offers the best source of information, since the Pyramid Texts, though they certainly reach further back, were only chiseled into the walls of a pyramid mortuary chamber in the Fifth Dynasty.

In prehistory, as we have seen, there was always a reluctance to represent the human figure. Both high civilizations, Egypt and Sumer, seem at first to have felt similar restraint at representing the human forms of their newly created anthropomorphic gods.

Opinion differs as to whether at first only symbols were used, such as the sacred reed-bundle of the goddess Inanna in Sumer, or the shield with crossed 120 arrows of the goddess Neith in prehistoric Egypt. Did the symbols exist earlier, independently? Were they only taken over by or assigned to the later anthropomorphic deities? Did these abstract symbols go through a transformation similar to that of the celestial cow Hathor, who assumed human form, or of the heavenly constellations in both Sumer and Egypt, which became anthropomorphic gods? Such questions can scarcely be answered unequivocally.

The prehistoric reluctance to depict the human countenance and the tendency to replace it with animal-like faces or animal heads also lingered in Sumer and Egypt at the beginning of history, when the anthropomorphic pantheon was created.

The effort to thrust monotheism back to the early Mousterian period—some fifty millenniums ago—has now been abandoned. Relations with unknown forces took on no circumscribed forms during the whole of prehistory. There are no established representations of gods in human form before the historic period. What evidence exists is scarce and doubtful. In the Ashmolean Museum, for example, there is a basalt figurine, fifteen and one-half inches high, of a man with a hanging beard and a penis sheath. It has been described by W. S. Smith (1958, pp. 13–14), who thinks it may be a god. We also know of a small drawing from the First Dynasty, often called the god Ptah.

In major First Dynasty representations, animal-gods are shown still in their animal form as mighty protective lords. The god of the kings, Horus, had not yet acquired his later hybrid form—a falcon head upon a human body. On the **below** beautiful limestone relief from the tomb of King Zet in the Louvre, Horus is still completely a falcon. He perches upon a rectangle containing the hieroglyph for the king's name—a serpent—and a representation of the entrance to the palace; thus he protects both the person and the abode of the king.

The creation of the pantheon of divinities runs parallel with the creation of the state. The opinion of the Dutch philosopher of religion, G. van der Leeuw, that God "is a latecomer in the history of religion" (1933; tr. 1938, p. 104), becomes more and more credible.

Sumer

No pictorial representations of deities were found in early Sumerian temples, nor in the temple of Al 'Ubaid dedicated to the mother-goddess Ninhursag and

61. STELE OF KING ZET: *The god Horus, who has not yet acquired human features, appears as an enormous falcon protecting both the king—represented by his signature, a serpent—and the entrance to the palace. From Abydos, First Dynasty*

ascribed to the First Dynasty of Ur, nor in the great temples of Uruk III. The naked figures with priestly girdles that appear on stone reliefs and vases of 161 Uruk III and elsewhere, either engaged in battle or protecting the sacred animals, are not gods. Neither are the bull-men who often appear in pairs on seals 65 and reliefs. But this does not mean that no gods of the Sumerian pantheon existed at that time.

The alabaster vase of Uruk

An alabaster vase, part of a large collection of finds (1933–34) from two rooms 121 of a building in the latest Uruk III level, shows perhaps better than any other find the uncertainty surrounding the human appearance of the deity. This vessel, approximately three feet high, displays in four bands of successively larger size a presentation of offerings. The lowest band shows the world of edible plants; immediately above it are the domesticated animals; along the third band is a procession of naked priests bearing libation vessels and offerings in cone-shaped baskets. Finally, in the broad top band, the procession with its gifts nears 120 the sanctuary, indicated by the sacred reed-bundle symbol.

"The great alabaster vase," writes its finder, E. Heinrich, "lay fallen over and crushed beneath the weight of the masonry above it, so that it had broken into fifteen pieces. . . . Even before its burial on this site . . . the vase had been broken and repaired with the help of copper bands" (1936, p. 15).

Is the robed female figure before the sanctuary the fertility-goddess Inanna herself, or a priestess? A conclusive answer is not possible, since a decisive fragment is lacking: the headgear of the central female figure. Did she wear the horned crown, which in later representations is the distinctive sign of a deity? Frankfort believes the two reed-bundles establish the figure as a divinity, "for such a bundle is the pictographic prototype of the character with which her name was written in historical times" (1954, p. 10).

A hint that it is the priestess rather than Inanna herself who is represented on this alabaster vase comes from two other sources of the same period. A seal in the Baghdad Museum shows an offering scene with two similar conical baskets of fruit standing on the floor. Before them are two man-high reed-bundles without priestess or goddess (1939b, pl. V c). In the temple of Inanna at Uruk was a trough, also contemporary with the alabaster vase. It 120 depicts the sacred flock of sheep returning to a reed hut which shelters their lambs. The presence of the goddess is announced by two tall Inanna symbols which rise above the reed hut. Another reed-bundle, probably paired, protects

62. URUK ALABASTER VASE: *Detail. The most conspicuous objects are the more than human-sized reed-bundles, symbols of the goddess Inanna. To the left a naked man offers fruit in a conical jar. The setting implies that the figure receiving the offering is a priestess. Early third millennium. Drawing by Heinrich*

63. RELIEF ON STONE TROUGH: *The largest objects are the reed-bundles of Inanna which project high above the sacred barn. Same period as Uruk vase*

64. URUK ALABASTER VASE: *About three feet high. The three lower bands of reliefs represent plants, animals, and human bearers of gifts. The upper band shows the offering scene before the sanctuary of Inanna. Early third millennium*

the rear of the flock. The placing of these symbols in this scene comes very close to that on the alabaster vase.

Heinrich does not decide whether one should accept "the person who receives the offerings as the goddess herself or only as her representative, as a priestess" (1936, p. 16).

Knowing the hesitancy to represent clearly-featured deities in this period, there seems no reason to regard this undoubtedly dominant figure as a deity.

From the middle of the third millennium, representations of anthropomorphic deities exist on reliefs and on cylinder seals. The so-called vulture stele reveals the situation at this period more clearly than any other representation, with its
60 daring attempt to portray the god himself in effigy. Ningirsu, the protective god of Lagash, is shown grown to mountain height, invincible and pitiless.

This oversize representation of the deity indicates the newness of the attempt to give a human shape to an immortal. Later on, the god is shown no larger
right than the mortals, sitting on his throne like an earthly king and distinguished only by his tiara of horns.

The astral gods of Sumer

With the creation of anthropomorphic gods the primeval conception is expanded; primeval man's immediate nearness to and direct contact with the animal fade into the background. Larger dimensions take their place: the world and the underworld, water and floods, air and storms, heaven and the heavenly bodies—all are bound into the anthropomorphic process. In detail, the methods by which this transformation took place were different. The principle remained the same.

Prehistory had never given definite form to the invisible power, but with the first high civilizations came the rationalization of the intangible in the form of humanlike gods. Man projected himself into the infinite. Embedded in religious images are the germinal forms of that *hubris* which man would later invoke in his desire to become master of all nature.

The moon-god Sin, or Nannar (Sumerian), was the sickle moon. He was the oldest of the three supreme astral gods and father of the other two—the sun-god Shamash or Anu (Sumerian), and his twin sister Ishtar or Inanna (Sumerian). The sun-god was the intercessor with the moon, from whom the day would be born.

Upon a ten-foot stele of King Urnammu of Ur, assembled from small stone
right fragments, the moon-god Nannar appears in the uppermost row, seated on a throne with Urnammu standing before him and receiving his command to build

65. URNAMMU STELE: *Detail. The moon-god Nannar, oldest of the three astral gods and lord of the city of Ur, sits on a throne. Before him stands Urnammu being commanded to build the ziggurat of Ur. The size of the astral bodies indicates their importance. End of third millennium*

the ziggurat of Ur, of which the moon-god was considered the proprietor. The strength of the cosmic component in the outlook of the time is brought out by the size of the heavenly bodies in this relief. A sickle moon surmounted by a star is its most outstanding feature, at the summit of the stele and larger than the enthroned god.

127 The symbol of the sun-god Anu was a sun wheel with four undulating spokes (sun rays).

Inanna, the third member of the triad, was the goddess of Uruk, the religious center of Sumer. In this aspect she was daughter to the moon-god Nannar. She was also depicted as daughter to Anu. When she was one and when the other depended upon the city. In Ur, she was the daughter of Nannar, but in her own city of Uruk, where beside her shrine stood the huge temple precinct and ziggurat of the "Lord of the pantheon," Anu, she was daughter to this supreme godhead. She appears in this aspect in the epic of Gilgamesh when she laments before Anu the hero's captivity. All this shows Inanna's importance in Mesopotamia. In Sumer's so expressly male and patriarchal pantheon she attained an extraordinary prominence, which she held until the fall of Babylon. In her anthropomorphic form she became a wildly passionate woman—something unknown among the goddesses of Egypt.

82 In the beginning, Inanna had been a fertility-goddess. Her early symbol, a bound bundle of reeds, was typical of a newly established community based upon the care of fields and kine. This symbol probably antedated her anthropomorphic form and her transplantation to the heavens.

During the course of the third millennium the cosmic identification was completed. Inanna was then incarnated in the shining planet Venus, the brightest object in the early evening sky. But her metamorphosis was to go further. In the epic of Gilgamesh, around 2600 B.C., she was an aggressive, lusting woman; by the time of Gudea of Lagash, around 2000 B.C., she had become a bloodthirsty war-goddess, and this she remained.

127 The three most striking heavenly bodies—moon, sun, and Venus—form an astral triad that recurs under different names in the later Mesopotamian period. The Tower of Babel was dedicated to the sun-god Marduk, and the famous portal of Babylon, through which the New Year festival procession had to pass, bore the name of Ishtar (Inanna).

Apart from this triad—moon, sun, Venus—there was a second, consisting of An (or Anu), chief regent of the Sumerian pantheon; Enlil, the storm-god and executor of fate; and Enki, god of handicrafts and of the life-giving waters of wisdom. Some Sumerian scholars add to this triad the great mother-goddess Ninhursag (Kramer, 1956, p. 84).

The domain of the gods Anu, Enlil, and Enki was no longer confined to individual stars. It ranged over whole sections of the firmament. "Between the three rulers of the visible world, the astronomers divided the celestial zone delimited by the Tropics of Cancer and Capricorn. This part of the firmament was separated into three routes: a central band, on either side of the equator, formed the route of Anu; the band to the north the route of Enlil; the band to the south the route of Ea [Enki] (Dhorme, 1949, p. 36).

In addition to the great triads, there were almost uncountable numbers of lesser astral gods, each linked to a certain constellation. Even the god of hell, Nergal, was identified with the planet Mars.

Kudurru: symbols and astral deities

According to when one dates the first downfall of Babylon, Mesopotamia was ruled for about four hundred years by wild tribesmen from the Zagros Mountains. This whole period, particularly its opening, is little known. Among its few architectural remains is the steep ziggurat of Aqar Quf, which still stands near 235 Baghdad at Dur Kurigalzu, the Kassite capital founded in the fifteenth century B.C.

The most important artistic evidences of the Kassite period are their numerous steles, called *kudurru,* which are now in museums everywhere—the Louvre, the

66. WINGED CENTAUR FROM A KUDURRU. *From Boll*

67. KUDURRU: *Astral symbols representing Kassite deities emerge near a ziggurat. The dragon represents Nabu, god of wisdom; the double lightning flash, Adad; the scorpion, the goddess Ishara. A scepter terminates in a chimeralike head; ca.* 1500 B.C.

British Museum, Baghdad, etc. These *kudurru* are in the shape of the boulders that lie scattered over the highlands of Kurdistan whence the Kassites had come. They are often considered boundary stones which guaranteed property rights (King, 1912). Contenau, however, states that "they are the authentic deeds, documents, which were never placed in the fields . . . but in the temples in the custody of the gods" (1931, II, p. 896). They are also sometimes deeds of donation of property. Their inscriptions recount the duties and rights of the property owner: blessings on those who follow the rules, curses on those who break them. To increase their efficacy, symbols of the gods were added and,

68. KUDURRU FROM UR: *Surmounted by planet Venus, moon, and sun. This boundary stone is dominated by the demoniac expression of the astral symbols of Kassite deities; ca. 1500* B.C.

more rarely, the familiar scene of a personage offering to an enthroned god. The quantity of symbols rather than representations is new, and is explained as due to the limited space available. This can scarcely be the reason. Neither earlier nor later in Mesopotamia were there such fantastic and enchanting assemblies of symbols of the astral deities. They possess the chimeralike fantasy of the Asiatic hinterland that later appeared in the animal style of Luristan.

It has long been recognized that a centaur is portrayed on one of the *kudurru*
125 in the British Museum. This ithyphallic winged figure has two heads and two tails, and is loosing an arrow from a bow (Boll, 1903, p. 189). A similar centaur appears in the Hathor temple at Denderah, where, in Roman times, the twelve constellations of the zodiac were depicted (p. 191). The centaur there represents Sagittarius. The centaur from the shadowed history of the Kassites was accompanied by a scorpion, the adjacent sign of the zodiac. This strange resemblance between representations a millennium apart would seem somehow related, though we cannot prove it, to the rise of astrology in Mesopotamia (p. 182). Egyptian representations of the constellations, around the same period as the
143 ff *kudurru*, in the tombs of Senmut or Sety I, had nothing to do with the signs of the zodiac.

A strange, demoniac atmosphere emanates from these stones and their sym-
127 bols. On one the cuneiform inscription is compressed into the lower part of the stone and is dominated by a group of symbols. These represent a mixture of old Sumerian deities with others brought in by the Kassites. At the top are the Sumerian triad: the Venus star Inanna, the crescent moon Nannar, the sun Anu. Below them is a row of temples surmounted by symbols of the Kassite gods.

On a *kudurru* from Ur in the Baghdad Museum a group of astral symbols
126 emerges near a ziggurat: a dragon for Nabu, god of wisdom; a double flash of lightning for Adad, god of lightning and the beneficent rain; and in the upper part, the scorpion-goddess Ishara and a kind of scepter terminating in an animal with an elongated snout.

The Kassite *kudurru* with their excitable demoniac symbols were a reflection back from the anthropomorphic gods to the symbol. They are the expression of a savage mentality, far removed from that of the cultivated Mesopotamians.

Humanization of the course of the sun in Egypt

The principle by which the Egyptian universe became anthropomorphic was the same as in Sumer, but it was carried through quite differently. It was penetrated by the optic awareness of the Egyptians as well as their mythopoeic disposition.

It is true that the Mesopotamian gods had families and history. But in comparison to the lives of the Egyptian deities, their lives were static. In Egypt one image followed on the heels of another. Although, indeed, the mythopoeic dramatization of images was only fully developed in the New Kingdom, with its great gift for narration, its roots ran far back. It was the course of the sun, the cycle of the twenty-four hours, that always rekindled the imagination.

Even before the birth of the gods an incorporation with the cosmos had been announced. A Predynastic ceramic dish in the Cairo Museum portrays in abstract form the course of the sun from east to west. At the two ends of this oval-shaped bowl, two circles with rays indicate the position of the sun in the west and the east. In the center stand the Mountain of the East and the Mountain of the West in the form of two isosceles triangles. A number of zigzag lines which are interrupted by the two suns indicate the enclosing primeval ocean. The passage across the heavens and the distinction between the morning and the evening sun are already seen individually. In this Amratian dish a scene is set which will be enlivened by mythopoeic and anthropomorphic sun worship. below

Among the many theological systems of Egypt, none was more popular and none underwent more artistic elaboration than that of Heliopolis. The city had been an influential religious center even before the founding of the kingdom, and it retained its magical powers of attraction until the Grecian period. No part of its theological system excited so much pictorial representation as the

69. OVAL AMRATIAN DISH: *Abstract portrayal of the orbit of the sun during day and night. Two isosceles triangles indicate the Mountains of the East and of the West, white zigzag lines the oceans of the sky and of the nether world. Amratian period*

cosmologic concept. Rooted in sun worship, it was based on the daily cycle of the twenty-four hours, the continual change from day to night and from the rising to the sinking of the sun.

135 The sun itself was transported in two ships, a ship of the day and a ship of the night. While the ship of the day crossed over the ocean of the sky, the ship of the night traversed the nether world, the primeval ocean. The night sky, when the moon takes over from the sun, played a far less prominent role, just as the moon in Egypt had far less importance than in night-oriented Mesopotamia. In Egypt the moon was represented by the god Thoth, who was far more renowned as the inventor of writing and as the god of wisdom than in his secondary function as god of the moon.

We know of no more dramatic representation of the path of the heavenly bodies across the arc of the sky and the nightly struggle of the passage through the underworld. It gave rise to ever-new variants, ever-new pictures of how the sun disappears in the west and is reborn, and of what happens from hour to hour on both sun ships. The manifold meanings and polymorphic transformations of form of the sun-god Ra and his companions here come to fruition.

The theological invention of the nine gods of Heliopolis (the Ennead), with their simultaneous incorporation of animals, was a master stroke of priestly imagination as great in its way as the architectonic imagination of the pyramid age. At the head of the Ennead was the sun-god Ra, whose children were Shu, god of the air, and his wife Tefnut. Geb, the earth-god, and Nut, the sky-goddess, were born of this union; their children in turn were Osiris and Seth, and the goddesses Isis and Nephthys.

In one form or another, the various family connections of the Ennead were woven into the cosmologic scene. The violent severance of earth and sky belongs to the myths of humankind. In Egypt it became highly anthropomorph-
right ized. The severance of heaven from earth recurs continually. It is caused by Shu, who stands with both arms stretched above him to hold his daughter Nut, goddess of the heavens, apart from her husband and twin brother Geb, god of the earth, so that the coupling twins shall be forever separated.

This momentary acrobatic situation was, with Egyptian charm, transposed into an eternal continuity. The goddess Nut remains a graceful, slender woman despite her long, outstretched body which suggests the Egyptian notion of the heavens as a huge platter. The four pillars which support the sky must also be shown; they are the stretched-out hands and feet of the goddess, which touched the earth with the tips of their elongated fingers and toes. In another version,

70. NUT, GODDESS OF THE SKY, *swallowing the winged western sun, whose rebirth in the morning is indicated by another winged ball at her feet. Detail of relief below. Nineteenth Dynasty*

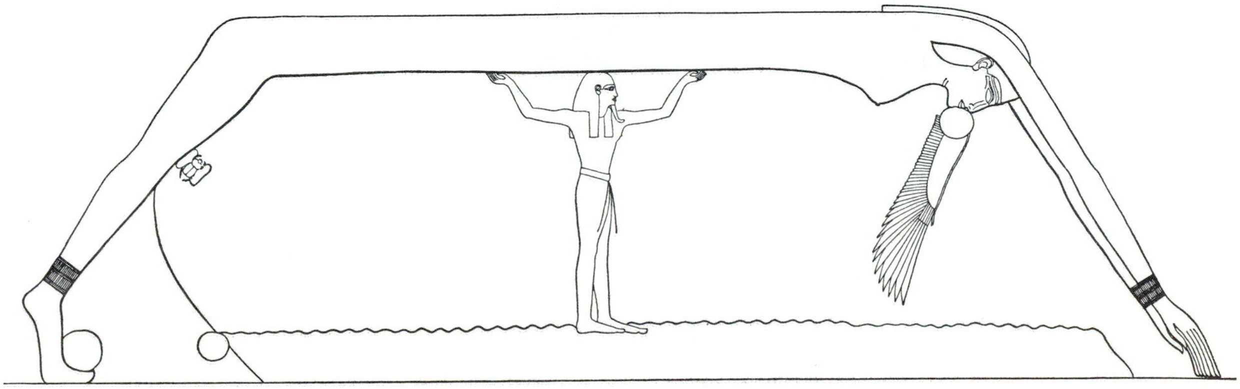

71. NUT, GODDESS OF THE SKY: *The god of the air, Shu, separates his daughter Nut from his son and her husband, Geb, god of the earth, here indicated only by an undulating line. Relief from the cenotaph of Sety I at Abydos. Nineteenth Dynasty. Drawing after photograph taken by Calverley*

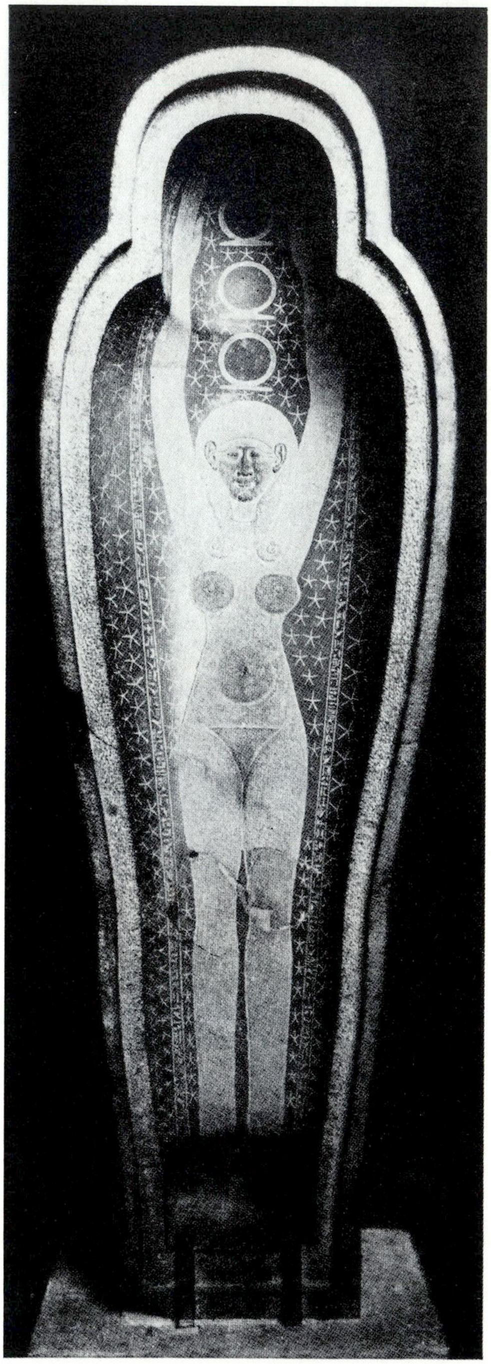

72. NUT, GODDESS OF THE SKY: *Nut bends over the dead as she does over the earth. Five-pointed stars border her body, and above her head is the threefold symbol of eternal return. Painting on underside of sarcophagus lid. Late Period*

the sky is represented as the body of the cosmic cow, Methyr or Hathor, whose four legs constitute the four posts of heaven.

One of the most beautiful representation of Nut covers the ceiling of the enormous cenotaph sarcophagus of Sety I in his mortuary temple at Abydos. The distortions of the proportions of Nut's body, which by no means conform to 131 the Egyptian canon, do not destroy the charm of this figure. She is simultaneously as delicately balanced and as tremendous as the course of the world. Her body sparkles with stars. "Against the mouth of Nut the sun disk is figured, apparently with folded wings" (Frankfort, 1933a, p. 73). This represents the sun-god Ra, and the inscription states: "The Majesty of this god enters into her mouth in the Netherworld. The Netherworld is opened when he sails in it. The stars enter after him . . . and they hasten to their places. . . . In the left half of the picture the sun is seen three times: once in the soil by itself, once on the foot of Nut, apparently still inside the earth, and finally as a beetle flying along Nut's thigh" (pp. 73–74). Nut swallows the sun each evening and gives birth to it each morning. Eternally between her mouth and her vulva it undergoes a daily renewal of life: "The Majesty of this god comes forth from her hinder part" (p. 74).

In the Late Period, Nut's function was popularized. Her regenerative power then became available to normal mortals. She became a goddess of death. Along the inside of the lids of sarcophagi from the Saite period stretches the arched left and slender figure of the goddess, protecting and bestowing life on each dead body over which she bends.

The connection between Nut and the passage of the sun, though the best known, is only one interpretation of her role. She could also suddenly become Hathor, who strides out from the Mountain of the West, in her form of a cow, to receive the stars.

In a Theban grave of the Eighteenth Dynasty a headless goddess with projecting breasts receives the sun in her outstretched arms. Is she Nut? Or is she, as others maintain, the less clearly defined scorpion-goddess Selkhit emerging from the Mountain of the West? (Jéquier, 1946, pp. 240–41) In this headless figure, with her black-tipped breasts, we see a continuance of primeval repre- I:217 sentations.

The path of the sun never ceased to excite the mythopoeic side of the Egyptian nature. Sethe has gathered together many of these images (1928). At their root lies the belief that the sun is the source of all life. The way in which ever-new versions of the journey of the sun and of the birth of the sun came for-

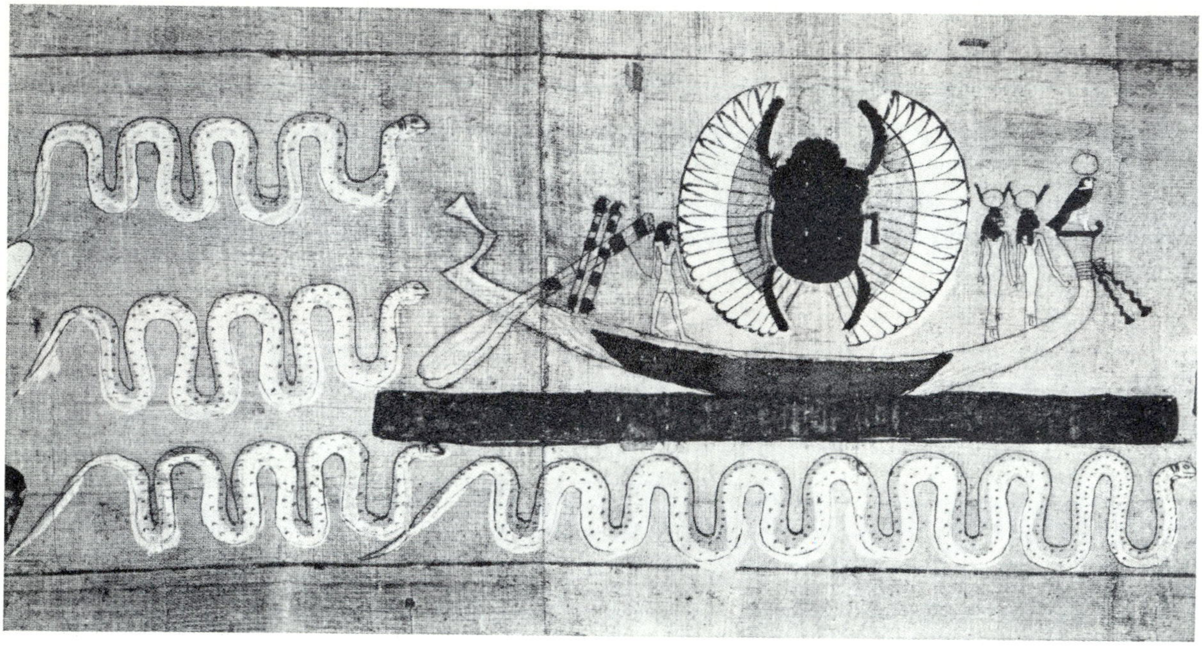

73. THE WINGED KHEPRI *in the solar barge: The sacred ship on the water. At the prow a hawk surmounted by a disk and two Hathor figures. At the stern a Horus-god stands near the rudder. Papyrus of Nesi-Khonsu B. Twenty-first Dynasty. From Piankoff*

ward is a sign of how the Egyptians were fascinated by the eternal recurrence of change and permanence, the eternal wandering and return. We find here a phenomenon parallel to the processional journeyings of the statues of the gods from one temple to another. The notion is also reflected in the architectural organization of the great temples, as well as in the earlier pyramid complex, with its valley temple, causeway, mortuary temple, and the pyramid itself, from which the heavenly ladder conducted the dead king up to the sun. An eternal wandering.

On the lid of the gray granite sarcophagus of the priest Taho in the Twenty-sixth Dynasty (Saite period), the transference of the sun from his nocturnal ship to his day ship is most delicately represented. Two goddesses stand, one in either prow, their arms extended horizontally, and the great weightless ball of the sun gently rolls from one outstretched hand to the other. The length of their arms is intentionally exaggerated.

right

It was not necessary for the sun to be born each day from Nut. The bark of

74. TRANSFERENCE OF THE SUN *from the ship of the night (right) to the ship of the day (left): The ball of the sun, like a weightless balloon, just touches the long, outstretched arms of the goddesses standing in the prows. A deeply engraved Horus dominates each boat. Sarcophagus of the priest Taho. Twenty-sixth Dynasty*

the sun could instead be raised from the nether world by Nun, god of the primordial ocean (Jéquier, 1946, fig. 21).

The birth of the sun could also be consummated by symbols. In the Leiden Papyrus the sun is raised up to the sky by two human arms which grow out from the *ankh*, the sign of life, which itself emerges from the *djed*, the symbol of eternal duration. Isis and Nephthys, the one belonging to the day, the other to the night, kneel upon the earth in adoration, while on either side dog-headed apes greet the rising sun.

The sun takes on different forms at different hours. In the morning it appears as Khepri, the scarab, at midday as the falcon with the sun disk encircled by the uraeus serpent, at night as the ram. **left**

The disk of the sun can also appear in human form, usually with a ram's head, in the center of the sun boat, which was manned on either side by gods. These were the "untiring" circumpolar stars.

The orbit of the sun seldom penetrated so deeply into man's consciousness as in the valley of the Nile, with its directly north-south orientation. Across the vast expanses of the desert the sun blazed with absolute dominion. It furnished a point for an untiring imagination that transposed reality to a mythical religious sphere. The daily journey of the sun became an ever-renewed battle between light and darkness, between the forces of good and of evil, which were continuously undergoing anthropomorphic transformations.

On the structure of Egyptian and Greek mythologies

The direct contrast between Greek and Egyptian mythology throws further light on the Egyptian attitude toward the anthropomorphic deities.

Greek mythology was concerned with human relations, human tragedy, and human fate. Individual human experiences were built into the forms the Greeks created: in sculpture the human figure took on a three-dimensionality totally unknown before. Although gods of the Greek pantheon were concerned with cosmic symbolism—Apollo, Demeter, Dionysus—this aspect remained in the background.

A relief in the Birth Room of the temple of Luxor depicts the divine origin of **right** Amenhotep III. It shows the god Amon meeting with the mother of Amenhotep; they are seated together upon the hieroglyph for "heaven." Their feet rest weightlessly upon the hands of two goddesses, Selkhit the scorpion-goddess, and Neith, goddess of arrows. "Selkhit is closely linked with Neith, both goddesses together are handmaidens who assist at the birth and in the care of the divine infant" (Roscher, IV, p. 652). Neith is here no goddess of war. She is "the great mother of god, Amaunet, who appears in prehistory . . . [and] created the seed of gods and men" (Bonnet, 1952, p. 515). Conception and birth are simultaneously symbolized. All expresses a joyous festival.

Very different is the case of Alcmene and Zeus-Amphitryon, a single erotic adventure wherein the god took the form of Amphitryon to gain his ends, and Alcmene felt herself guilty as soon as she realized what had occurred. In the case of Amenhotep III, it is a ritual fertility proceeding that is represented; it was repeated with each king, since it was presumed that every Egyptian king was directly conceived by god.

The intimacies of Zeus are the outgrowth of individual eroticism. From the Greek period on, eroticism took the place of fertility symbolism. Hence the exaggeration of individual erotic experiences. Again and again this results in human tragedy or—as in the *Iliad*—in altering the fate of whole peoples.

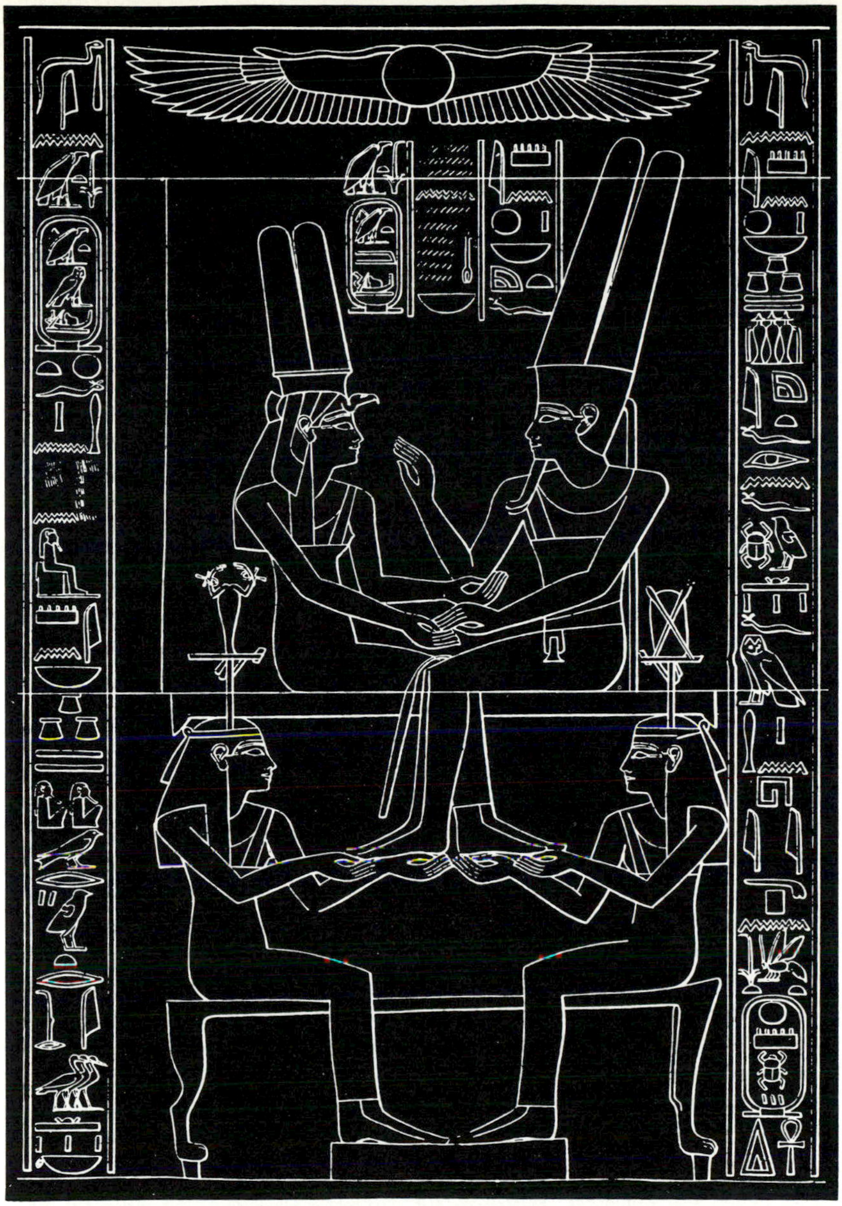

75. AMON AND THE QUEEN: *To symbolize the act of theogamy, their hands meet and their feet are crossed. Below them sit the goddesses Selkhit and Neith, who will nurse and protect the infant Amenhotep III. From an Eighteenth Dynasty relief in the Birth Room, temple of Luxor. Drawing by Schwaller de Lubicz*

In the Egyptian sphere, the oneness of the world in the form of cosmic symbolism was paramount. Tragedy and the fates of individuals were of little account. The period of individualism had not yet dawned. When the matter came up it was in connection with the possibility of projecting memory into the afterworld. This occurred in the New Kingdom with the independent-minded Queen Hatshepsut and with the religious revolutionary King Akhenaten, who unseated the pantheon of gods and installed in their stead Aten, disk of the sun, as the single supreme godhead.

One of the few tragic episodes in the history of the Egyptian gods was the dismemberment of Osiris by his brother Seth. After the battle between Horus and Seth, the matter was resolved satisfactorily for all parties through a reorganization of the cosmic laws.

It is no accident that it is from late classical sources (Plutarch) that we are informed of the sacrificial role played by Osiris' wife Isis, and of the developed sequence of feasting, death, dismemberment, and the reassembling of the body of Osiris, even down to the smallest detail.

Egyptian mythology does not enter matters of individual fate. It deals with cosmic powers whose unending flood overwhelms and humbles man. Instead of the fates of individuals with their differentiations of personalities, it is concerned with subtle differences in cosmic occurrences such as are scarcely observed in other cultures.

INTERDEPENDENCE BETWEEN MAN AND ASTRAL BODIES

The notion of a connection between astral bodies and human destinies is part of a universal concept that the cosmos contains nothing fundamentally dead or inimical.

Early, precise observations of the stars and their movements reflect a longing to establish the interdependence between stars and earth, stars and man. The connection between the sun and the seasons of the year was manifest; the connection between the moon and the earth, the moon and growth, was more mysterious. Wholly intangible was the relation with more distant constellations, such as the circumpolar stars, which ever point to the North Pole and never sink below the horizon: the Egyptians named them the "untiring."

The demand for a relationship was differently felt in Egypt than in Mesopotamia. Both countries used observations of the stars to establish seasons of the year, to orient their buildings, and for various other practical purposes. But then their paths diverged.

In Mesopotamia, scientific knowledge and the foretelling of destiny were inextricably amalgamated. In an often retold dream of that great figure of the early period, Gudea of Lagash, the goddess Nisibis appeared to him not only as the goddess of intelligence, wisdom, mathematics, and writing; she also "bore the tablet of the good star"—in other words, she was simultaneously goddess of astrology (Dhorme, 1949, p. 283). "For the Sumerians and Akkadians, the sky was, in effect, a great map on which their destiny was inscribed. Men called the constellations 'the writing of heaven' or 'the writing of the firmament' " (p. 282).

The great complexity which once encompassed the relations of stars and earthly happenings in Mesopotamia has not been explored. How far the resulting tradition was based on experience, on mythical thought, or on pure superstition is a complex question today left hovering in mid-air, though it demands elucidation just as do the Mesopotamian symbols, also neglected in research. It is no longer sufficient to sweep them under the rug with Cartesian logic.

The Egyptians pursued a purpose different from that of Mesopotamia. When they depicted the stars in a sepulchral chamber, they did it simply to inform the 143 dead of the paths of the astral bodies and so to guide him in his eternal wanderings.

The relationship between man and stars in the first high civilizations was thus fundamentally different from ours, which involves far greater knowledge of new astronomical worlds, their distances, and their temperatures. The concept of infinity has never before been so forcibly hammered into men's minds. The entire structure of present-day knowledge requires that it reject all mystical connection between cosmic and earthly happenings.

Today, nevertheless, many observations from earlier times live on without context. Among them is a belief that there is a relationship between the phases of the moon and the best time to sow seeds or breed animals. It is probably impossible to know how far back these and similar, certainly greatly distorted, notions reach. They stem from a time when there was still an undisturbed belief in the interdependence of man's fate and the cosmos.

The Egyptian mythopoeic imagination was kindled by the day, the Mesopotamian by the night. Until the end of the pyramid age the fundamental experience in Egypt was the radiant light of day and the sun; in the Land of the Two Rivers it was the starlit night sky and the moon. This difference ruled the thought of the two civilizations.

The Egyptians based their calendar on the sun year of 360 days, Mesopotamia on the moon year of 345 days. In Mesopotamia, "the month began with the evening when the new crescent was for the first time again visible just after sunset. The Sumero-Babylonian day also began in the evening" (Mercer, 1957, p. 110). In Egypt, the beginning of the year was connected with the first appearance of the star Sothis (our Sirius), in the early morning sky.

The experience of the night side of life, and the feeling of being utterly at the mercy of destiny, permeated Mesopotamian existence. Later, the Greeks took over the idea of destiny, without being led into the deep pessimism already revealed in the depressing adventures of Gilgamesh, around 2600 B.C. This interest in destiny was closely linked with a desire to fathom in advance the will of the gods. The stars were identical with the deities. They influenced all happenings and were thus guides to man's fate. Everything depended upon whether the initiate was able to read the decisions of the gods from the movements of the stars. It has not been clearly proven just when this sort of belief in the stars arose. But it must be closely linked with the anthropomorphization of the universe, and thus it must have found its form shortly before or at the beginning of historical times: "Collections of astrological omens were made in Sumero-Babylonian times . . . as early as the time of Sargon" (ibid., p. 82).

In Egypt the situation was quite different. The Egyptian disposition was like the quiet, mathematically calculable flow of the Nile, in complete contrast to the eternally unpredictable behavior of the Euphrates and Tigris and the sudden catastrophic cloudbursts of Mesopotamia. These regional, structural differences were expressed in the differences of certain deities. Gods like Enlil, at once creator, storm-god, and executor of destiny, or Adad, the god of lightning, had no parallels in Egypt.

Egypt, as far as we know today, took no refuge in astrology. There have been recent attempts to prove that the meaning of the stars only rose to prominence in Hellenistic times (Nilsson, 1943). This would be true for Egypt, where the meaning of the stars first became influential under the Ptolemies, via Asia Minor. In Mesopotamia, as we have seen, it was quite otherwise.

The Egyptians' knowledge of the stars and their movements was based on highly developed observation. Using the most primitive means, they were able to fix the position of the polestar, and from this to lay out with astounding precision the north-south axis of the Cheops pyramid. Sights taken upon the stars were also used to determine the position of the cornerstones of temples, upon which great importance was laid. Special offerings were buried at these points, as at Deir el Bahari.

The annual rise of the fixed star Sothis occurred almost exactly at the start of the rise of the Nile floods. Annually it again became visible for the first time in the early morning, shortly before sunrise. The Nile year and the Sothic year corresponded with one another. Sothis and its astronomical variations played a most influential role in Egyptian history (Scharff and Moortgat, 1950, pp. 32–37). All these are scientific observations that have nothing in common with astrological decrees.

The astronomical ceiling of Senmut's tomb

The Egyptians seemed impelled to endow abstract conceptions with sentient form and poetic charm. We have few insights into the cosmic dream world of the starlit night sky that first appeared on sarcophagus lids of the Middle Kingdom. Of them, none is more intensive than the astronomical ceiling of Senmut's tomb 143
in Deir el Bahari. We shall linger upon it, since it presents the attitude of the Egyptians to the stars more clearly than the scanty written descriptions. It contains an inimitable juxtaposition of precise astronomical facts with dreamlike poetic images, of the same delicacy as the reliefs in Hatshepsut's temple above it. There is no hint of astrological problems. What is drawn is the cosmos itself as the eternal calendar, with the personification of certain cosmic happenings.

The great architect Senmut had the daring to make a mole-like burrow for 415 ff
himself almost beneath the temple court of his masterpiece. Then came his downfall, and probably also that of his queen. The entrance to his tomb was covered with debris. Through thirty-four centuries it lay forgotten, until rediscovered by H. E. Winlock of the Metropolitan Museum, New York, in 1925–27.

More than a hundred steps lead steeply down to the level, exceedingly simple funerary chamber with its drawing of Senmut's portrait just by the entrance. The incompleteness of the tomb is evident from the roughhewn steps of the low entrance tunnel. Only the flat, segmented ceiling of the chamber, with its engraved configurations of stars, has had its surface smoothed. Immediately below, one peers into the black, never-used grave-pit. The project was of the utmost simplicity, and the intense concentration of cosmic representation in so compact a space, together with the tragic situation that caused this tomb to remain unfinished, renders it one of the most moving impressions of Egyptian destiny.

The drawings were finished only in black and white, but their fine line and freshness of execution surpass the colored versions of the starlit heavens on the ceilings of the tomb of Sety I in the Valley of the Kings, and in the mortuary 144
chapel of his son Ramesses II (Ramesseum, Thebes, ca. 1250 B.C.). These seem already to have a hint of classical rigidity.

It is the night sky to which we are introduced, the realm of the stars into which we enter. But the deities of the day move in their boats in this nocturnal society. To them are added the constellations and, with mathematical precision, the delineation of the eternal calendar.

The astronomical ceiling of Senmut's funerary chamber measures approximately ten by twelve feet, and is divided into two parts. A border of several right rows of five-pointed stars surrounds each one. In the middle of the central separating band is the cartouche of Queen Hatshepsut—a hint that the drawing dates from the period when the great architect still stood in the glory of her queenly favors as privy councilor of the sovereign's right.

Immediately springing to the eye are twelve circles in one area, identified as the twelve months: "The circles subdivided into 24 sectors are a new feature of an astronomical ceiling; the connection with the subdivision of the day into 24 hours is obvious" (Pogo, 1930, p. 312).

The other, southern part of the ceiling also has temporal indications, this time in columns. The twenty-two short columns (reading from right to left) contain the principal stars belonging to the thirty-six ten-day "weeks" or Decans of the stellar year (Bull, 1923, p. 283). Each week was ruled by the decan star that rose at its start, and each month had three "weeks."

Below this band of short columns, groups of stars hover in free rhythm. It is not difficult to imagine how glittering this star canopy would have been if it had ever been painted.

A special position was granted to a constellation of four stars. The central 144 star is framed by three curious lines. These indicate "an egg represented in the Egyptian manner, slantwise with a triple outline. . . . It reminds one of the world egg, the origin of the earth" (Röder, 1928, p. 2). This constellation, Sah, had long been associated with Orion. Following one of the later texts, S. Schott identifies the central star with its three companions as Orion (Mercer, 1957, pp. 73–74).

This calendarlike abstract representation now moves into the anthropomorphic sphere. Beside the constellation of Orion, the god Sah himself is represented as a youth, strolling onto his boat, with backturned head, a scepter in his left hand, an outstretched sign of life in his right. He is accompanied by stars. Two have alighted on the bow and stern of the boat.

In the neighboring boat stands a slender goddess with raised right arm, a scepter and sign of life in her left hand. Above her crown hovers the rising sun. She is Isis, the loveliest figure on the whole ceiling. With charm, and at the same time with authority, she carries out her dominating role. She was called

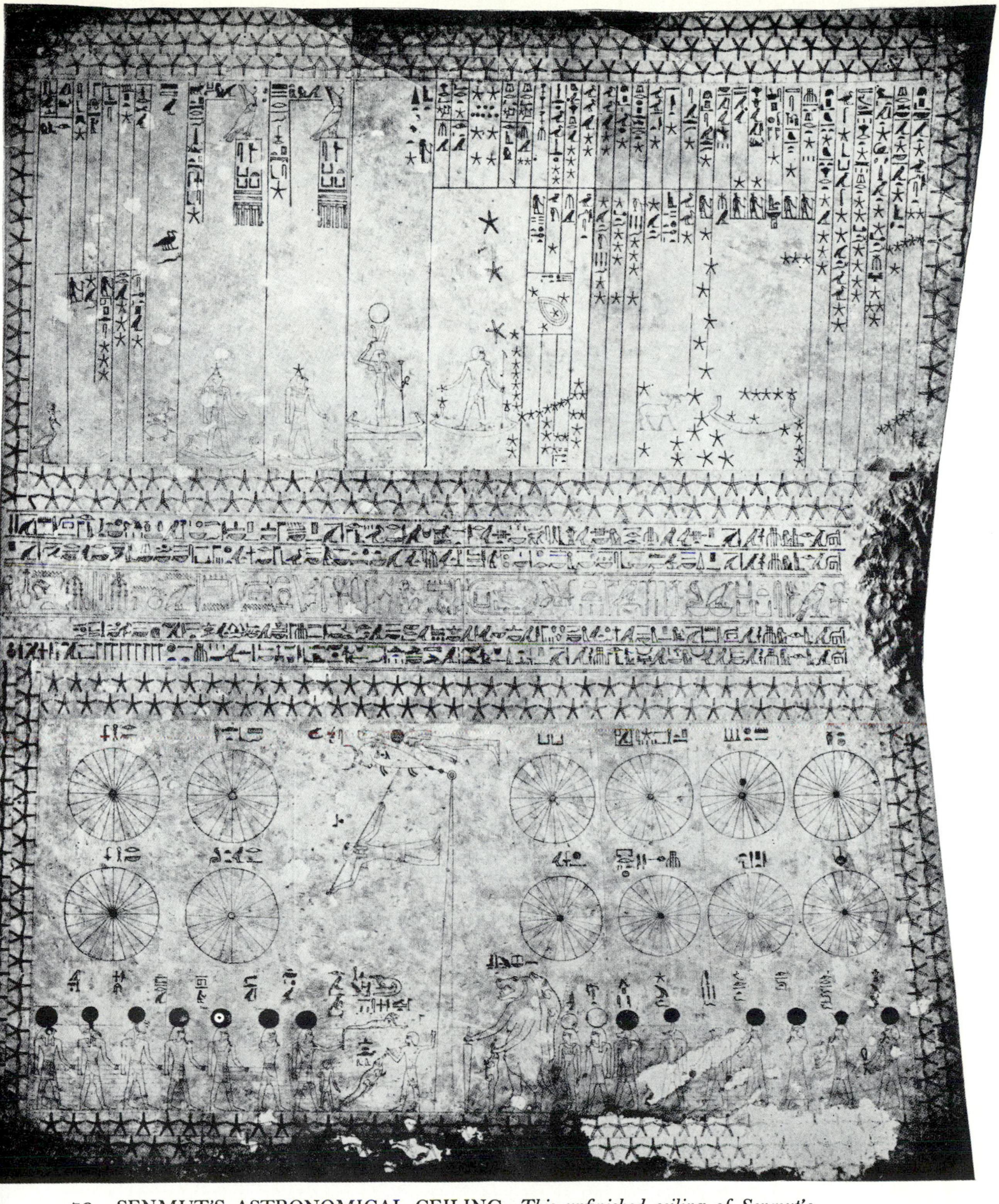

76. SENMUT'S ASTRONOMICAL CEILING: *This unfinished ceiling of Senmut's funerary chamber (10 x 12 ft.) was the first of its kind. The upper part shows the thirty-six weeks of the Egyptian year, the lower part twelve circles representing the twelve months. Both include scenes of deities drawn with the utmost delicacy. Unpainted drawings from Deir el Bahari*

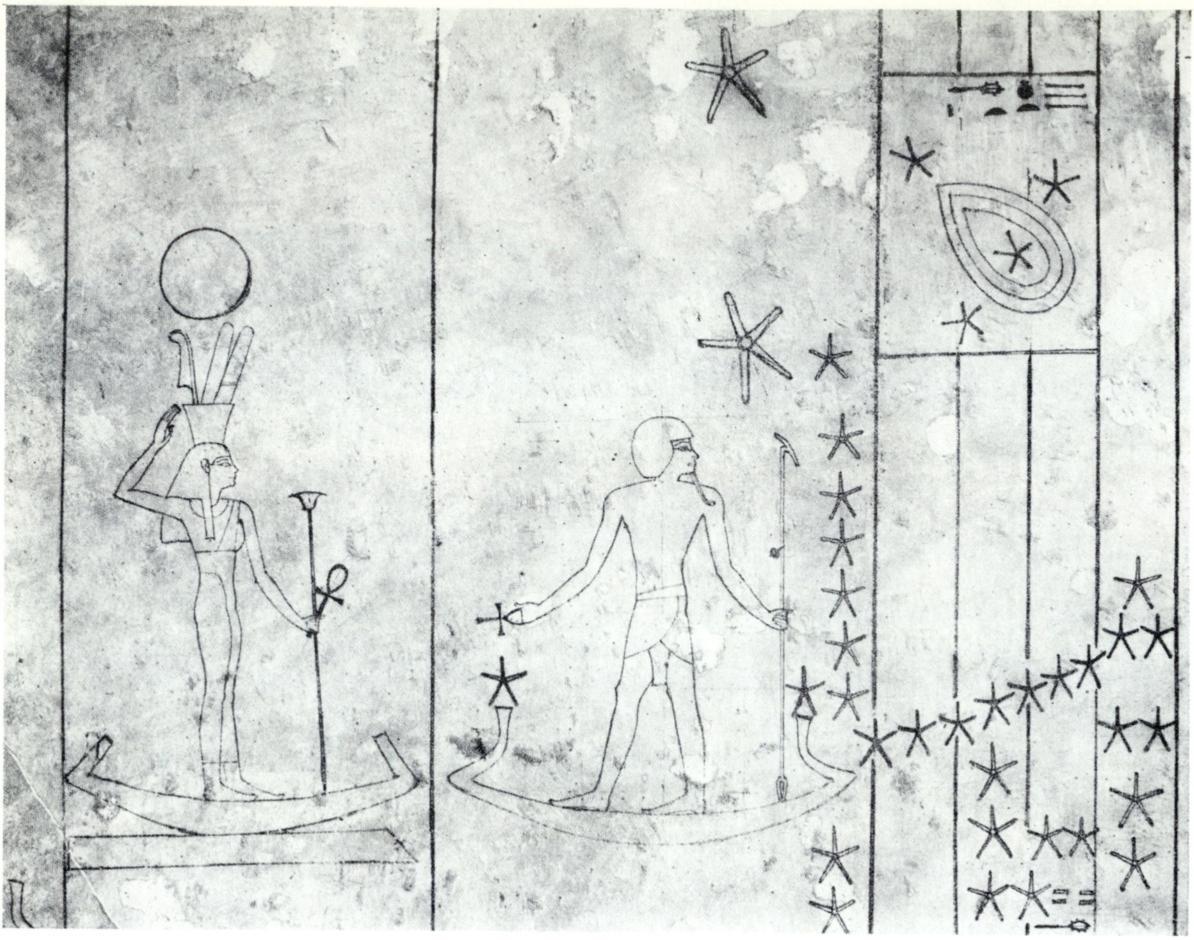

77. SENMUT CEILING, SOUTHERN PART: *To the right, a constellation of four stars, the central one framed by three eggshell-like outlines, probably the constellation of Orion (Sah). Below, a drawing of Sah standing in his boat, a star at stem and stern. Nearby, another boat with the slender goddess Isis, the rising sun above her head*

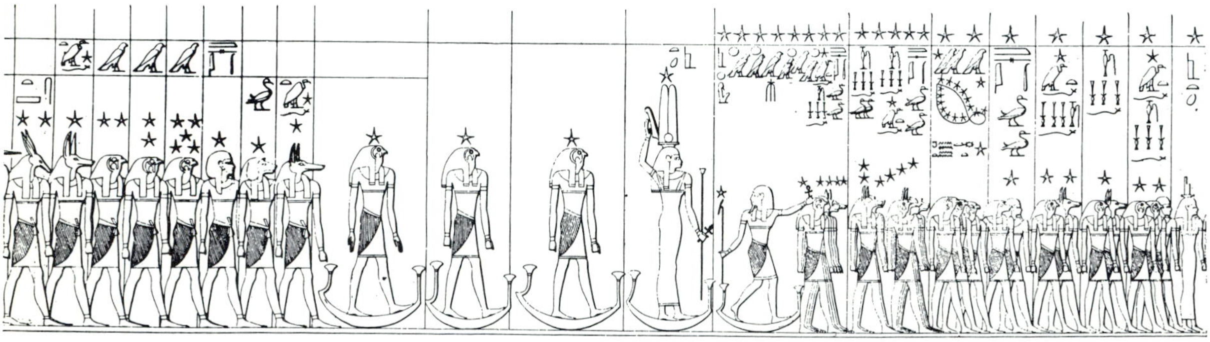

78. CONSTELLATION IN TOMB OF SETY I: *Constellations approximately the same as those in Senmut's tomb appear in the tomb of this Ramesside king. The row of animal-headed deities can here be more easily recognized. From Lepsius*

79. SENMUT CEILING, NORTHERN PART: *Symbolic group of a falcon-headed god, probably Horus (the morning star), directing a staff against a strangely formed bull with a tail of three stars. This sinking night constellation probably represents Meskhit, our Great Bear*

queen of the decan stars. She guides them, since she was identified with Sothis.

Apart from these purely abstract or anthropomorphic forms, other stars appear as rows of hybrid gods, with human figures and animal heads, as well as whole constellations in purely animal form. Thus there is a symbolic group, in the northern sector, of considerable artistic fascination. A falcon-headed god, 145 probably Horus, who was identified with the morning star, directs a long staff (spear?) against a strangely formed bull: long body drawn out to a point, fragmentary legs, straight tail to which the three round stars are attached. It is the Egyptian constellation of Meskhit.

Some recognize Meskhit as "the well-known Egyptian representation of the constellation Ursa Major" (Pogo, 1930, p. 309). Others doubt the identification of the Egyptian constellation of the bull Meskhit with our Great Bear (Röder, 1928, p. 4). But this is not important in our context.

To us this scene appears as a mythopoeic parallel to the Orion-Isis scene. That symbolizes the dawn of the new year, this the daily rising of the morning star in the form of the god Horus, who sets his spear against the sinking constellation of night, Meskhit.

Associated with the assaulted bull, standing far back, is the goddess of death, Selkhit, bearing on her head the disk of the evening sun and above it her symbol, the scorpion. Selkhit is often merged with Nut, goddess of the sky. Like her, Selkhit received the sun disk at evening; when this happens, she is shown head-
1:217 less, with outstretched arms.

One cannot overlook two long lines that stretch from the last round star of the bull's tail across the entire northern part of the ceiling. What do they mean? Sighting upon the stars to establish the precise delineation of a ground plan? They have been brought into connection with the ceremony of the stretching of the cords, and Pogo (1930, p. 310) refers to a passage from Brugsch: "I have grasped the peg . . . I observe the forward-striding movement of the constellations. My eye is fixed on the Great Bear. I . . . determine the corners of your temple" (Brugsch, 1883, p. 85).

Pogo has investigated the astronomical import of this ceiling and has reconstructed the position of the stars at that period; he believes that this kind of representation is based on a tradition that reaches far back.

The eternal calendar and the interplay of constellations are there as guides for the departed, not as predictions of destiny. They indicate to the dead how the months and years, through which he may eternally continue his life, follow one another. In Egypt the dead need pose no questions to destiny.

PART IV CONSTANCY AND CHANGE IN THE MODE OF EXPRESSION

SCULPTURAL TENDENCIES IN EGYPT

The great differences between paleolithic art and the art of the archaic high civilizations leap to the eye. The astonishing thing is that certain constituent elements of primeval art continue to live on. This cannot be revealed by a simple comparison of forms. The continuity only comes to light when one probes into methods of representation. Then it appears that the methods we considered the 1:293 ff most telling qualities of prehistoric art—the stress upon outline and the hollowing-out of reliefs—were continued throughout the entire Egyptian epoch, though the process changed to meet a new requirement: the polished stone surface instead of the rough rock face.

The Egyptian was bound to stone as primeval man was to rock. This relation with stone was easy and natural in Egypt, though not in Sumer. The limestone blocks for the pyramids needed only to be transported across the Nile from 72 Tura. The Sphinx at Giza was born from a single spur of rock left over from the construction of the pyramids. The granite quarries of Aswan in the south were inexhaustible.

The Egyptians' preference for stone was due to their desire for eternal duration. For their earthly life, humble bricks—even unburned bricks—sufficed, up to the Late Period.

The painted pottery of Predynastic Egypt bears no comparison with the superb painted pottery from Iran and Mesopotamia. But, in contrast, the stone vases of the Predynastic period and of the First Dynasty remain unsurpassed to this day for the beauty and variety of their form. Every difficulty was overcome to carve them out of the hardest of stones: syenite, diorite, basalt. Later dynasties re-used them to lay beside their dead. Thirty thousand were found in Zoser's mortuary complex at Saqqara, ranging from squat, thick-walled vessels to those of the utmost slenderness, with walls so thin as to be transparent. Jean-Philippe Lauer, who brought the Zoser complex to light, stowed them away in drawers, as in the storage rooms of a warehouse.

Plane surfaces as a constituent element in art

The fundamental invention of Egyptian art was the discovery of the possibilities of expression inherent in plane surfaces. This is valid for the whole of art: architecture, painting, and sculpture. Everything was submitted to the laws of the plane surface. Through the use of this abstract element with the utmost restraint, the highest form of expression was achieved. The pyramids of the Fourth Dynasty, and the obelisks and pylons of the New Kingdom, present the discovery of the surface and its possibilities of expression as an eternal contribution to the development of architecture.

Sculpture in the round also came under the rule of the plane surface. Its three-dimensionality was reduced to the utmost. The limbs of statues were projected by a few parallel or superimposed upright planes. The surface and projection onto the surface is also a feature of Egyptian painting. The body and its limbs are not depicted as they appear at one moment in time, but rather as they are. What a decisive influence this emphasis on the surface had upon Egyptian reliefs will immediately become apparent.

Outlines

To represent an object by drawing its outline is almost a natural gesture. Whenever primitive man tried to give vent to his urge for representation he turned to the outline. The origin of this procedure lies in Aurignacian art, when man traced the first outline of an animal in the cavern clay. What is astonishing is the 1:293 ff great intensity with which a simple outline could capture the actual nature of the animal.

This becomes apparent if one thinks of the use of the same procedures in African rock drawings. Engravings exist on the rock walls and loose blocks of North Africa and the Sahara (Graziosi, 1942). These follow the same prehistoric principles of representation but remain bound to their primitive forms, lacking the further development and powers of suggestive expression of Aurignacian art.

The representation of an object by its outline has persisted through all periods, including the present. The relative age of rock engravings can only be judged by the nature of the patina and the depth of the lines. Rock engravings were forerunners of the sunken reliefs which Egyptian art developed to such perfection. Not far from the valley of the Nile, numerous petroglyphs have been found (Massoulard, 1949, pp. 91–106), the oldest apparently dating back to the late stone age or the copper age. A number were found later at watering places in the Nubian desert (Frobenius, 1933, pls. 32–40). Their discoverer himself describes them as "small and petty when compared to the monumental works of the West" (p. 54).

The case is not very different with numerous other rock engravings. Near

80. FIRST DYNASTY RELIEF *of a bird: As in prehistory, the outline is formed by hollowing out the surface of the stone. Fragment of limestone stele from Abydos*

81. FIRST DYNASTY STELE: *The rough surface, smoothed only in the hollows, strengthens the outlines. Limestone stele belonging to a royal attendant. From Abydos*

ancient Coptos, where the Nile is only about one hundred miles from the Red Sea, a caravan route approaches from across the Arabian Desert. Here, in 1932–37, numerous rock paintings were discovered in the Wady Hammamat by H. A. Winkler (1938, I). But these too give little insight into the beginnings of the Egyptian development.

The Egyptian development becomes interesting immediately before and during the First and Second Dynasties. Here one must refer to existing source material. Perhaps the most immediate insight into this first phase of awakening Egyptian art is given by Petrie's collection of fragments from the royal tombs of the First Dynasty (1901). These tombs were found in Abydos, in raised positions around the crown of a hill. Whether the kings were actually buried here, or in other graves discovered by Emery in north Saqqara, has not been finally decided.

Hollowed-out reliefs of the early dynasties

The inscriptions and drawings found by Petrie upon unpretentious fragments of stone vases, of pottery, alabaster, ivory, slate, and ebony almost all have the hesitating engraved outlines of primeval times and North Africa. And yet everything is altered. This is not only due to the hieroglyphs but to something that will later become all-powerful: the orientation to vertical and horizontal and the consequent right angle. Even when the lines are somewhat slanting, the germ is there and the direction is foreordained. We also gain here a rare insight 374
into the reed architecture of a sanctuary of this period.

Reliefs on fragments of steles also show the unsureness of an experimental period, as for instance the relief of a bird on the fragment of a First Dynasty left
stele in the Ashmolean Museum, found near the cenotaph of King Wedymu in the Thinite Royal Cemetery at Abydos; also another limestone stele, belonging to a royal attendant, found in the neighborhood of the cenotaph of King Zer left
(1901, p. 33). These fully preserve primeval methods. The outline originates from the hollowing-out of the stone, just as in the reliefs upon the sides of the Min statues from Coptos.

A comparison between these reliefs and a small Venus figurine embedded in 1:444
the rock, which was recently discovered in Les Eyzies (Dordogne), and was carved some fifteen to twenty millenniums earlier, shows how employment of the same methods leads to similar results. This certainly does not imply a direct connection. It relates to a natural occurrence. Just as the child, in a few years, experiences the long early development of humanity, so new developments briefly restore earlier stages of human experience. This is what happened in the art of the first dynasties.

Among the few remaining monuments from Abydos are two approximately five-foot steles of King Peribsen, found near his tomb at Abydos. "They are cut 152
in very compact syenite, and much polished" (ibid.). They have rounded corners. Petrie, who does not say much about procedure, emphasizes that they had to be photographed from the side: "The best result was from the side, by reflections"

82. SECOND DYNASTY STELE: *The whole surface is smoothed and the relief skillfully hollowed out. This is an early stage of the fully developed sunken relief. Syenite stele of King Peribsen with rounded corners. From Abydos*

(ibid.). It is the experience of every photographer of primeval reliefs that they can only be captured with the use of side lighting—*lumière frisée.* 1:528

A further link with prehistory is found in the three great statues of Min from Coptos, whose iconographic relations with prehistory have already been described. Petrie, their discoverer, stresses that the reliefs found upon their flanks were made "by hammering the outline as a slight hollow around the figures" (1896, p. 7). 85

The sunken relief as a light-catcher

The common characteristic of primeval and Egyptian reliefs is that both were sunk into the stone. It has already been stressed that primeval reliefs never projected beyond the profile of the surrounding rock. Again and again a part of the rock surface remains untouched, so that the animals appear to live within the rock itself. A sheet of cellophane would stretch smoothly across the entire relief, unbroken by any projection of the modeling. This holds true even for the most strongly plastic prehistoric reliefs, such as the great frieze of horses at Cap Blanc (Dordogne), where the bodies of the horses are often hewn half a meter deep into the rock wall. 1:382

In accordance with the totally different situation in Egypt, the sunken relief changes without relinquishing its basic principle. Rock walls are replaced by plane surfaces, but these polished walls are treated in the same manner as the rough structure of the rock. They never lose their inner unity.

The smooth surfaces that came with the beginning of stone architecture must have had a great fascination for their inventors. The gigantic walls of the pyramids repulse any plastic treatment. One could almost say that they inhibit any disturbance of their smooth, polished surfaces by inscriptions or reliefs.

The relief comes as a fundamental innovation in the architectural conquest of the surface through the way its outline is now produced. It is still derived from a hollowing-out process, but this no longer takes the curving shape of a shell. Instead, the surface is immediately penetrated at an angle of ninety degrees. This right angle forms a knifelike edge of great plastic significance. The side caught by the light is illuminated as though by a strip of neon lighting, while the other side is emphasized by a dark line of shadow. The effect of these sharp edges is so intense that outlines are fully visible even under the most glaring sunlight. Even on the black asphalt beloved by the Late Period, the outlines of a figure are brought to life on the sunlit side and stressed by a deep black line on the shadow side. 158

83. OLD KINGDOM SUNKEN RELIEF: *Sharply incised outlines on this false door catch the light even in the half-dark funeral chamber of Theta. Giza, Fourth Dynasty*

The sunken relief operates as a light-catcher. It first appeared in the half-dark tomb chambers of the Old Kingdom. As G. Jéquier points out, "the sunken relief, which gives figures an extremely fine silhouette, is formed on one side by a line of shadow, on the other by a track of luminosity" (1924, p. 83).

By the Middle Kingdom, the sunken relief with its sharp edges was already fully developed. It was used on a comparatively small scale, as in an Eleventh Dynasty relief, on the limestone sarcophagus of Kawit, showing the dressing of a lady's hair. The outlines of head, shoulders, and arms are more deeply cut than those of the body surface, body details, and jewelry. The continuous changes of light and shadow, to which the sunken relief is so responsive, become especially striking in details.

☞ right

84. MIDDLE KINGDOM SUNKEN RELIEF: *Now the surface is incised at a ninety-degree angle. The knife-sharp edge intensifies the outline by its clean-cut separation of light and shadow. Detail of limestone sarcophagus of Kawit, showing the hairdressing of a lady. Eleventh Dynasty*

The full development of the Egyptian sunken relief came about in the great building undertakings of the New Kingdom, a millennium after its first appearance.

As a gatherer of light and shadow, the sunken relief was destined to cover the mighty temple walls with representations that live within the wall surfaces without destroying them. The surfaces of pylons, obelisks, even the shafts of colossal columns in the half-dark hypostyles, were covered with hollowed-out reliefs, sometimes of considerable depth, as in the hieroglyph "Son of Ra." A scene from Pylon VII at Karnak, in which Tuthmosis III is shown slaying prisoners, shows how sharply the outlines still appear in bright sunlight.

156
378

Huge sunken reliefs were also spread across the walls of the half-dark hypostyle halls, reminding one of their early use in the Old Kingdom mastabas. Details of a scene of Ramesses II offering to the god Min, from the south wall of the great hypostyle at Karnak, were then only visible to a limited extent.

157

85. NEW KINGDOM SUNKEN RELIEF: *Emblem of the "Son of Ra" with cupule (5 cm.) containing an embedded sphere. Karnak*

The sunken relief was never abandoned in Egyptian architecture, not even in the Late Period and Roman times. During the Saite period, which saw revivals of many of the different epochs of Egyptian art, the sunken relief attained the utmost finesse. On Saite sarcophagi, hewn from a solid block of stone, scenes depicting the relations of the dead with the orbit of the sun are etched in lines as fine as those of seventeenth-century copper engravings. Such subtle treatment of a hard stone surface has never since been attempted.

On a black stone from the Thirtieth Dynasty (fourth century B.C.), the
158 kneeling King Nectanebo I is engraved in sunken relief. The Ptolemaic kings continued to ornament the walls of their temples at Edfu and Philae in the same manner; so did the Roman emperors in the temple of Denderah near Thebes, where they are portrayed in the likeness of Egyptian Pharaohs.

86. NEW KINGDOM SUNKEN RELIEF: *On the half-dark south wall of the great hypostyle hall at Karnak the sunken relief is still used as a catcher of light. Relief of Ramesses II offering to the god Min. Nineteenth Dynasty*

87. LATE PERIOD SUNKEN RELIEF: *Even on a black stone in poor light, the outlines of this sunken relief are clearly marked by light and shadow. Relief of King Nectanebo I. Thirtieth Dynasty*

In the subsequent history of architecture the sunken relief is comparatively seldom employed. But it may be recalled that—in a simpler form—it has been used in our own period by Le Corbusier in his Unités d'Habitation at Marseilles and Nantes. On their outer walls he has hollowed out reliefs which live within their concrete surfaces.

The abiding quality in all Egyptian reliefs was the supremacy of the plane surface. To achieve this the relief need not always be sunk in, especially when upon an intimate scale. What was essential was that it be always delicate and always remain within the atmosphere from which it had grown, emerging only as though shimmering through it. This held from the beginning: in the Third
267 Dynasty reliefs of Zoser striding through his "otherworldly" dwelling deep

below his pyramid, as in the wood relief of Hesy-ra in the Cairo Museum. The 169
early Fourth Dynasty bearers of offerings (personified estates) to Sneferu in the valley temple of his step pyramid at Dahshur follow the same law, as does
the Fifth Dynasty mastaba of Ti at Saqqara, where the surface reliefs are doubly 453
stressed by a second delicate outline. Through this extremely low relief a springtime delicacy developed, as in the reliefs in the pavilion of Sesostris I at Karnak.

In western European art one would expect such a budding, springlike period to grow toward the sculptural and baroque. Nothing of the sort occurred in Egypt. The New Kingdom flat reliefs became, if anything, even more delicate and graceful.

The reliefs of Hatshepsut's mortuary temple at Deir el Bahari present the narrative charm in which the New Kingdom excelled, whether they depict her
expedition to the land of Punt or the majestically striding cow Hathor. 423

Of the different kinds of relief—sunken, low, and high—only the delicate low relief and the sunken relief respect the plane surface. This is especially true of the sunken relief which, as in prehistory, always lies dormant within the stone. When, after a long development, sunken reliefs covered the gigantic surfaces of Egyptian temple walls, their interconnection with the stone achieved a complete unity with architecture.

SCULPTURAL TENDENCIES IN SUMER

The attitude of Sumerian civilization toward reliefs was quite different. From the beginning, Sumerian reliefs protruded from the surface plane. The surface was reduced to a back cloth, before which the sculptural scene unrolled. This started with the invention of cylinder seals, whose endless sequences unroll upon a neutral background. Their plastic energy is astonishing, even in the Early Dynastic seal impressions, where the play of light and shadow enables the figures of men and animals to spring out from the flat surface (Frankfort, 1954, pl. 39C). It can easily be argued that, given the small scale of the cylinder seals, nothing else was possible. But the way in which the felicitous invention of the cylinder seal was plastically developed was deeply rooted in the Sumerian *Kunstwollen* (artistic volition).

The Sumerian development was based upon plasticity and contrast. The earliest decisive advance appeared in the Jemdet Nasr period, which is put by some around 3000, by others around 2600 B.C. Its center was Uruk, and it is more

88. SUMERIAN HIGH RELIEF: *A lion attacking a bull, its whole head projecting from the ritual vessel of yellow limestone. Uruk III period, early third millennium. From Heinrich*

89. SUMERIAN HIGH RELIEF: *A tremendous desire for three-dimensionality is expressed in the limited volume of this limestone vase from Uruk, on which two bearded heroes (?) protect two bulls from attack by a mythical bird (Imdugud?). Uruk III period*

90. SUMERIAN INLAID FRIEZE: *A sequence of cattle inlaid in mother-of-pearl contrasts strongly with a background of black bitumen. Part of frieze from temple of the mother-goddess Ninhursag at Al 'Ubaid. Early Dynastic period*

exactly known as the Uruk III period. Its material was stone. It produced a rare
104, 121 female countenance, a tall alabaster vase, and various ritual stone vessels. Upon
160 one of these, made of yellow limestone and twenty centimeters high, is a lion who seems less concerned with his vicious attack upon a bull between his claws than with pushing his overlarge head directly out into the void. A smaller lion which stands peering forward near the spout of this libation vessel seems totally unconnected.

Upon the fragmentary upper part of a limestone vase of the Sumerian Late
161 Protoliterate period (Uruk III), the tumult of battle among various creatures is brought out within the smallest volume: two bearded men fight with two bulls, upon whose backs sit mythical birds. The birds and the "heroes" are oversize in comparison to the bulls. The way one bearded man grapples with both bulls suggests the action of a protective guardian rather than of an attacker. Is it Imdugud, the great bird of prey, who is attacking the bulls?

The vehemence of sculptural high relief is here pushed to an extreme. Between the neck of the vessel and the outward-springing bodies of the men is a perforation, a form of cutting free from the related background, especially clear in the right-hand figure.

With this first appearance of fully sculptural treatment of the human body, every effort was made to break free from the surface. Under a quite different set of assumptions, the tendency was carried further in fifth-century Greek and in Hellenistic art.

In one of the temple friezes from Al 'Ubaid, strongly contrasting elements left
have been combined. Cattle, ranged one behind the other in procession, are made of mother-of-pearl inlaid against a background of black asphalt. A copper rim heightens the sculptural effect.

What here appears in germinal form is fully developed in a large copper panel that probably stood over the door of the same temple. It shows Imdugud, the 56
lioness-headed eagle, with two stags. The relief is explosive, the figures three-quarters in the round. The eagle's lioness head, the antlers of both stags, and even their tails, spring well beyond the heavy frame. Such exuberant plastic figures would have been unthinkable in Egypt.

Sculpture in the round

The freestanding sculpture of Mesopotamia had beginnings similar to those of the reliefs. Here too the desire was for three-dimensionality in representations of animals and men. Objects are modeled on every side, like the offering stand from the First Dynasty of Ur (British Museum), with an upright ram standing amidst widely spaced leaves and flowers (Frankfort, 1954, pl. 28), or the copper statuettes of priests of the Second Early Dynastic period from the altar of the 115
temple at Khafaje.

A high relief in copper of lowing cattle, attached to the front of the Al 'Ubaid 164
temple, shows a striking tendency toward three-dimensional sculpture: the head of one of them being thrust forward almost completely in the round.

A row of rather large copper bulls is believed to have stood before the façade of the same temple. A single figure gives an idea of their impressiveness. Few 165
other sculptures from this early period show as clearly the extent to which the desire for three-dimensionality had come to be expressed.

An unusual impression of high-strung vitality emanates from this heavily oxidized copper figure. But the oxidation is a chance augmentation. What is certain is the sense of instantaneous movement: head turned sharply to the right, tail slightly curved, feet poised momentarily upon the ground, with the hind legs wide apart and the front legs closer together.

Every detail is carefully considered, from the shape of the hooves to three folds of skin above the eyes. The belly falls like a bag: one senses its fleshiness. Such a vivid grasp of naturalism would be impossible in the Egyptian method of representation. With a three-dimensionality hitherto unknown, this animal takes possession of the space around it.

When H. R. Hall and C. L. Woolley discovered the bull in 1919 it was completely flattened out. They state: "The body was first carved in wood, a mere trunk without head, legs, or tail; these were made separately. . . . Then this core was given a thin coating of bitumen and over it were hammered plates of thin sheet copper" (1927, p. 84).

This great three-dimensional impulse of the first half of the third millennium was never carried further in Mesopotamia or the Near East. Time waited for Greece to drive sculpture in the round to an unforeshadowed development.

The strongly plastic handling of Sumerian reliefs can be seen in a square, pierced tablet from Lagash, which Frankfort takes to be a "support for a mace" (1954, p. 33). It depicts Dudu, high priest under Entemena. Above is the
57 lioness-headed eagle Imdugud with two lions, to the left a calf, half kneeling, and to the right Dudu, wearing a kilt, the upper part of his body bare.

Broad bands separate each subject from the others, effectively destroying the background surface.

This propensity for strongly plastic modeling, which arose in the first part of the third millennium or shortly after, later faded. But its principle—sculptural figures before a neutral background—was never to be dropped. It can be followed throughout Near Eastern art, from the stele showing the victory of
60 Eannatum of Lagash over his enemies—the so-called vulture stele—and the
123 stele of Urnammu depicting the erection of the ziggurat of Ur around 2000 B.C. up to the huge reliefs of the Late Assyrian kings of the eighth century B.C. from the palace of Sargon II at Khorsabad. Here the figures of the king and his cour-

91. SUMERIAN HIGH RELIEF: *The head of a cow pushes forcefully out from a copper panel once attached to the wall of the Al 'Ubaid temple. True sculpture in the round is achieved and the relation of the relief to the wall has become nonexistent. Early Dynastic period, middle of third millennium*

92. COPPER STATUE OF STANDING BULL: *Highly developed three-dimensionality. All details of the body are shown in full immediacy and vivacity.* H. *62 cm. From the temple at Al 'Ubaid, Early Dynastic period, ca.* 2500 B.C.

tiers are oversize and the whole scale of the relief has become pretentious (120 in. high). Nothing exists apart from it: the background surface has become totally absorbed (ibid., pl. 96). More modest in scale, but just as insipid emotionally, are the long sequences of figures ranged one after the other on the walls of the stairway of the palace of Darius and Xerxes at Persepolis, finished in the fifth century B.C., just before the decay of the great Persian Empire. 461

THE USE OF COLOR

The glowing freshness exhibited by the colors both of primeval times and of Egypt comes from the use of the same imperishable materials: earth colors, giving yellow, brown, and reddish hues. Then as now, ocher was used: ocher, whose reddish pigment seemed to symbolize blood and was thus strewn over the dead both in Aurignacian times and in Predynastic Egypt.

Black was obtained from a kind of carbon, as in primeval times, when it was used with the manganese oxide of the caverns.

With the discovery of copper and its oxidation, new hues came into the color scale. The intense blue and, above all, the sharp malachite green at first exercised an enormous fascination. Mixed with a binding material, the latter was used as a cosmetic for ritual adornment on occasions of high festival, and this use persisted. The noble cosmetic palettes of the First Dynasty have in the center a circular cupule in which to rub down the malachite. Palettes were given to the dead so that they could adorn themselves properly on ritual occasions, or, like the famous Narmer palette, they were consecrated by the king to a temple: in this case to a sanctuary in Hierakonpolis, Upper Egypt.

The blue, which looks so luminous in pictures and the intensity of which has never again been attained, "consisted of a crystalline compound of silica, copper and calcium" (Lucas, 1948, p. 392).

These imperishable, radiant colors and the avoidance of shadows expressed fully the optimistic nature of the Egyptians.

Although, particularly in the New Kingdom, palaces and private houses were painted, as in Tell el Amarna, the funerary monument always was and always remained, from the pyramid age on, the true field for painting. This was so from the beginning of the Third Dynasty (remains of painting in the Hesy-ra chapel at Saqqara), through the beginning of the Fourth Dynasty (painting in Atet's mastaba at Medum and the rock graves of Beni Hasan), up to Hatshepsut's magically delicate paintings at Deir el Bahari and those in the deep rock-tombs of the Ramessides in the Valley of the Kings near Thebes.

PREHISTORIC AND EGYPTIAN METHODS OF REPRESENTATION

The custom in prehistoric art of representing the body of an animal in side view, the legs and hooves from the front, the head in profile, and the eye again from the front, Abbé Breuil called *perspective tordue.* This method of representation does not imply twisted or distorted perspective. It has nothing to do with perspective. It means the simultaneous representation of an object frontally and in profile, in order to set forth its true character in the clearest form.

Not only the Egyptian and Sumerian, but all archaic art, including the early Greek, retained this simultaneity of representation, e.g., showing the head in profile and the eye frontally. This resulted from the supremacy of the new con- **Part XI**
cept of order. From then on, everything had to be projected onto the vertical or horizontal plane, with the vertical playing the more important role.

The comparison of a rare prehistoric relief with a famous Egyptian relief may give a closer insight into the continuity and change of means of representing the human figure.

A prehistoric relief: the man of Laussel

The prehistoric relief of a standing man (height 47 cm.) was found in the sanctuary of Laussel (Dordogne), slightly above the Aurignacian level. It belongs 1:474
to the comparatively short period, reaching from the Solutrean to the Magdalenian age, during which prehistoric sculpture flourished. After this, sculptural development was discontinued for thousands of years, until it reappeared with the utmost vehemence in Sumer and Egypt.

The upper part of the body of this standing man from Laussel is turned to the right, with the left shoulder forward—a posture today called the boxer's stance 168
(in contrast to the wrestler's position). The outstretched left hand is still partly extant, the raised right hand only just indicated. It is unimportant in this context whether we have before us an archer or, as was later assumed, a spear-thrower. The heavily damaged head is indicated in profile, the upper part of the body in a three-quarter turn. The right side of the chest is slightly modeled and the line of the thorax is suggested, as is the navel. Two deep horizontal lines across the hips, indicating a girdle, are conspicuous.

The lower part of the body with the right leg slightly advanced is shown, like the head, in profile. This narrow-hipped male figure is remarkably slender. Its

93. PREHISTORIC RELIEF *of a standing man, from Laussel (Dordogne).* H. 47 *cm.*

94. THIRD DYNASTY RELIEF *of Hesy-ra: Wooden panel (height of figure 54 cm.). From his tomb at Saqqara*

outlines are incised with a firmness and sensitivity normally found only in the representation of animals.

This relief from the early Solutrean period and an Egyptian relief both show the so-called boxer's stance: body turned to right and left shoulder advanced. In both, head and legs are in profile. The Egyptian relief also retained the girdle and the nakedness which, in solemn rituals, was often carried over from primeval
115 times, as in the copper statue of a priest from Khafaje.

An Egyptian relief: Hesy-ra, Third Dynasty

Ten millenniums or more lie between the Third Dynasty relief of Hesy-ra
169 (height of figure 54 cm.) from his Saqqara tomb (ca. 2630 B.C.), and the relief of the prehistoric man. The intensity of this wood relief of one of the great officials of the court of Zoser shows the first efflorescence of Egyptian art. It is the most beautiful of the five standing and sitting representations of Hesy-ra that Mariette found in the niches of the inner corridor of Hesy-ra's tomb.

The head is modeled in sharpest profile. The outline of the upper part of the body is simplified almost to the form of a trapezoid. The accentuated shoulders are turned frontally, while the slender, boyish hips and legs, in walking position, are seen from the side.

It is the representation of a man whose every feature betrays that he was accustomed in life to command. All details in this wood panel are engraved almost microscopically. Each strand of hair in the wig is clearly marked. In his left hand, Hesy-ra holds a staff, together with writing equipment—the stylus with its case, bag of colors, and board with attached inkwell—turned into the frontal plane. His right hand grasps a horizontally held scepter.

The entire posture is concentrated on a moment of action, with mouth, nose, eyebrows, and jaw tense and prominent. The fact that the eye is placed in the frontal position is hardly noticeable. In spite of the relentless expression, all brutality is absent. The carefully elaborated details emanate a harmony and charm which is part of the mystery of these early times, found also in the reliefs
267 of Zoser's "underground residence" in his tombs at Saqqara.

The details of the Hesy-ra relief appear so spontaneous that one tends to forget that everything was calculated and arranged to the last detail. With the head in profile, the shoulders and the upper part of the body *en face*, and the extremities viewed from the side, the vertical plane becomes a constituent element in the structure of the relief. Everything appears to be turned about the vertical plane. Front view and side view form two planes at right angles to each other. Everything is related to this.

The contrast between this convention and the freedom of direction of the primeval relief from Laussel lies in the reduction here to two planes standing at right angles to each other.

How are the different parts of the body projected onto these two vertical planes? It may be that the side and the front views were considered as of equal importance, although the side view was most frequently employed and always used for the great numbers of figures ranged in sequence that appeared throughout Egyptian art. The freedom the Egyptian artist allowed himself lay in the choice of which detail of the body was to be represented frontally and which in profile. This is already conspicuous in the placing of the eye *en face* while the head is viewed in profile.

Although every detail is carefully indicated, the representation evades immediate grasp. How are the chest and the lower part of the body portrayed? Frontally or in profile? Where does the borderline lie?

This question was raised in 1887 when Adolf Erman noticed—or, as Heinrich Schäfer expressed it, "discovered"—that the navel in the Hesy-ra relief is drawn to the side. Also the nipple and the swelling of the breast are shown in profile. Erman explains this as follows: "The body comes out in the most confused fashion. The shoulders are given in front view, whilst the wrist is in profile, and the chest and lower part of the body share both positions. With the chest, for instance, the further side is *en face,* the nearer in profile, the lower part of the body must be considered to be three-quarter view, as we see by the position of the umbilicus" (tr. 1894, p. 398).

Everything seemed to tally in this explanation, which grew out of the nineteenth-century approach to pictures. But in 1919 Schäfer pointed out that this "naturalistic" interpretation was "impossible and confusing" (p. 170), for it could never have occurred to an artist of the Old Kingdom that the various elements with which he built up his picture needed a logical mediator.

A three-quarter view would mean the transfer of our modern viewpoint to the Egyptian way of seeing things, but this viewpoint is incompatible with the Egyptian mentality. "There is not a single definite example in the entire period of the Old Kingdom which shows an individual body or part of a body—in this case the human belly—in three-quarter view" (p. 172).

Schäfer rightly objects to the notion of a three-quarter position. His next step, however, is incomprehensible to us, for he assumes that in the relief of

Hesy-ra a profile view of the chest follows the frontal placing of the shoulders. He finds support for this in the outline of the breast with the nipple and the sideways-pushed navel. The contour to the left is explained as the line of the back (p. 173).

This puts the entire method of portrayal in question, and thus affects the whole of Egyptian art. On what principle is the separation of two planes effected, one of which must stand at right angles to the other?

In this case, where does the division come between the shoulders seen *en face* and the chest seen in profile? Everything else is clear in the Hesy-ra profile relief, but here the portrayal suddenly becomes blurred. A sudden jump from one plane to the other at this point is inconceivable, since in Egyptian art the clear swiveling of the plane is always found at the joints.

However, when the head is shown from the side, its most important part, the eye, is shown frontally. Thus, when the trunk is represented frontally, the breast is shown in profile. This simultaneous representation of side view and front view, which in part went back to prehistoric times, became a general rule.

The place where the frontal view of the upper part of the body joins the lateral view of the lower parts and the legs is located on the decisive borderline, just above the hip joint. The breast itself is pushed to the side at an angle of ninety degrees.

This separation of the human body into its natural parts and joints—head; shoulders, chest (upper part of the body); pelvis and legs (lower part of the body)—occurs in this portrayal in the sequence which, once established, is continuously repeated in Egyptian art: lateral–frontal–lateral views. **479 ff**

During nearly three millenniums, up to their last works in Roman times, Egyptian sculptors never changed this method of representation. Reliefs of male or female bodies were always portrayed with a single breast, usually the left one, as in the sculptor's model at the Metropolitan Museum of Art in New York, **right** where a Ptolemaic queen of the second century B.C. is represented in the form of a goddess. On its own soil the long Egyptian tradition proved stronger than the new impact of Greek development.

95. PTOLEMAIC RELIEF: *Upper part of body is depicted frontally with one breast in profile. This method of simultaneously representing front and side views had been used for nearly three millenniums. Sculptor's model of a Ptolemaic queen. Second century* B.C.

PART V THE ORIGINS OF MONUMENTAL ARCHITECTURE: MESOPOTAMIA

Mesopotamia is the birthplace of architecture.

In early Mesopotamian temple buildings, a curious phenomenon can be observed that stands in contrast to the later development of both the archaic high civilizations. This is the care taken in shaping the interior space of the shrine. It is as if we stood at the origin of the space development which set in some millenniums later with the Pantheon in Rome, and which still continues today: the molding of interior space.

Part XII

How did this early trend toward forming a temple by hollowing out its interior space and giving ample access to the ordinary people arise? Why was it interrupted and cut short?

Direct contact with the deity drew to an end with the rise of the first empires. An all-powerful mediator then came between man and god: the priest-king. Free access to the deity gradually diminished. The image of the god was placed in a dark cell to which none but the mediator had access. This phase appears in its most monumental form in Egypt. The shaping of the interior space had become meaningless from a ritualistic point of view and thus an architecture developing from the formation of interior space dwindled away.

I:371

Earlier we indicated how in prehistory an age of sculpture could begin, vanish for thousands of years, emerge again under quite different social and cultural conditions, and thereafter remain permanently in the foreground. Something similar to this occurred at the dawn of architecture.

In the early temple precincts, e.g., Eridu, Tepe Gawra, Al 'Uqair, Tell Asmar, Uruk, the interior of the temple was well articulated. How could this anticipation of later development come about at the beginning of architecture?

The basis for it is to be found in the relations between man and the invisible forces. In prehistoric times the most secret rites were performed in hidden places, in inaccessible depths of the earth. There, too, the most sacred symbols were depicted.

During the great period of upheaval, when the first stable human settlements were coming into being, a gradual change took place in man's relations with the invisible powers. How was contact to be made with them in the age of agriculture? And what form was to be given to the place where man held intercourse with them?

The earliest temples provide information about the time of their building and the architectural form that was developed. The dwelling place, the abode for the god, was erected on the model of the human shelter.

In prehistory there were many signs that man could build a shelter for himself: a lean-to of wattle and daub against a rock wall, or a hut formed in one of many different ways. But when more permanent settlements came about in neolithic times, fragile, tentlike shelters were gradually replaced by solid dwellings. Such a solid dwelling would house both the living and the dead, as well as, in a corner, female figurines or charms promising fertility. The house was all in one: the house of the living, of the ancestors, and of the helpful, protective household spirits.

When, in the fifth millennium man built the first small sanctuary in Mesopotamia, it signalized a separation of the world of the spirits from his private abode. Though this first shrine, built in Eridu, was still shaped like a house, it 191 served the whole community as a center for intercourse with the surrounding invisible forces, and its offering table and altar provided opportunities to serve them.

So, in the earliest stage of the development of architecture, the temple took the form of a human habitation in which invisible forces, and later the deity, were presumed to dwell.

From the ground plan of Sumerian temples it is quite clear that in this early period the faithful had direct access to the altar and to the entire interior. The earliest temple contained an offering table or altar. It was only much later, after the anthropomorphic gods were installed, that an image of the god was placed at the farthest end.

The architectural model for the earliest temples was the newly developed blocklike dwelling house, rectangular or almost rectangular in ground plan. This regular rectangular house, which has remained even to this day the standard form for a dwelling, had evolved only after centuries of experimentation with innumerable variants.

THE FORMATION OF THE HOUSE

This is not the place to go into details of the complicated and by no means yet clear development of the human shelter, even though investigations into its origins are becoming increasingly refined. The subject is no longer left solely to the archaeologist. He has been joined by a team of specialists in the fields of climate, paleolithic botany and zoology, the domestication of animals, and the uses of carbon 14 (Braidwood and Howe, 1960). The development of the human dwelling, from prehistoric structures to the patio house in Mesopotamia around 2000 B.C., is given here in the briefest outline. The rectangular house, with rectangular ground plan and upright, rectangular walls, was the end product of an immeasurably long development.

Prehistoric structures

The primeval plan for a hut was a circle, that form which is the basis of so many prehistoric symbols. Like birds who build themselves round or oval nests, man just scraped out for himself round or oval hollows in the ground.

The Magdalenian reindeer hunters of Ahrensburg, near Hamburg (ca. 12,000 B.C.), have left numbers of stones arranged in circles. These were used to hold down the walls of their tents. Their discoverer, A. Rust, assumed that each site was used only once by the hunters. Sometimes a second band of stones was added to protect the hollowed-out dwelling floor from flooding by rain water (1958, pp. 47–54).

It seems that the earliest verifiable dwelling places were trough-shaped or saucer-shaped depressions in the ground. The most numerous examples are in Russia: in Gagarino (Tambov), "where S. N. Zamiatnin discovered the lower part of a habitation in the shape of a shallow pit, the walls being strengthened with a row of stones" (Golomshtok, 1938, p. 325), in Kostienki (Voronezh), and many other sites from the Aurignacian and Solutrean eras. A number of female cult figurines were found in these dwellings, which are believed to have been roofed.

These dwellings gave rise to the view that "the technical germ of the house is . . . the straight or curved wind shelter, in other words the roof. This gives rise to the two basic ground plans of all architecture, the curvilinear and the rectangular structure" (Menghin, 1939, p. 427). It is known that wind shelters were used in the Aurignacian-Perigordian era, as D. Peyrony indicated on good evidence: "They established a shanty beneath the rock overhang of La Ferrassie by leaning timber up against the cliff and securing the base with stones and rubble" (1934, p. 90).

It is far more probable, however, that the starting point for the house was provided by the form of its dwelling area rather than the shape of its roof.

The circle around a fire, the circle around the hearth, had pride of place, and circular or oval single-roomed huts appear as a primitive form of dwelling over the entire world, sometimes grouped to make a many-roomed house.

The forms of human habitations in Aurignacian times may always remain unknown. The Magdalenian age, which reaches some ten to twenty millenniums back, left representations of various shelters, which give hints of some kinds of construction then existing.

Prehistoric man did not record the objects of his immediate environment, and it is scarcely possible that his rock engravings represent ordinary human dwelling places or "animal traps"—a name often given to his tectiform or rooflike symbols. It is more likely that these engravings depict soul houses or ancestor houses for the spirits of men or animals. Such sacred shelters are still numerous in existing primitive cultures, and a Predynastic Egyptian model house of burnt clay with a tray for offerings to the dead belongs in this category.

La Mouthe

The concept that prehistoric rock engravings of shelters represent soul houses comes out perhaps most graphically in a hut of posts and branches shown on the rock wall of the cavern of La Mouthe (Dordogne). This occupies a position of 180 special importance and is, certainly not accidentally, superimposed over a great number of small animals visible in Abbé Breuil's drawing. The repeated rhomboid-shaped parts of the roof seem to be leaning against a rock wall supported by posts.

We have noted earlier how the art of the Pacific Northwest Indians shows an 1:182 amazing similarity to the earliest prehistoric sculptures. It also appears likely that the "secret shrine" of a Nootka Indian whaler can provide some insight 180 into these early representations of shelters, since it is known that the small puppets it contains embody the souls of earlier whalers.

Font-de-Gaume

Numerous tectiform engravings of roofed structures, often clustered together as

96. REPRESENTATION OF PREHISTORIC HUT *in the cavern of La Mouthe (Dordogne): The hut is superimposed over a number of carefully incised and painted animals. Its rectangular roof is seen on the right from above, supported upon posts that are drawn not straight but curved. Magdalenian period. Drawing by Breuil*

97. MODEL OF SECRET MAGIC SHRINE *of a Nootka Indian whaler on Vancouver Island*

98. TECTIFORM *representing skeleton construction of a prehistoric hut, incised high on the rock wall of the cavern of Font-de-Gaume (Dordogne). Magdalenian period*

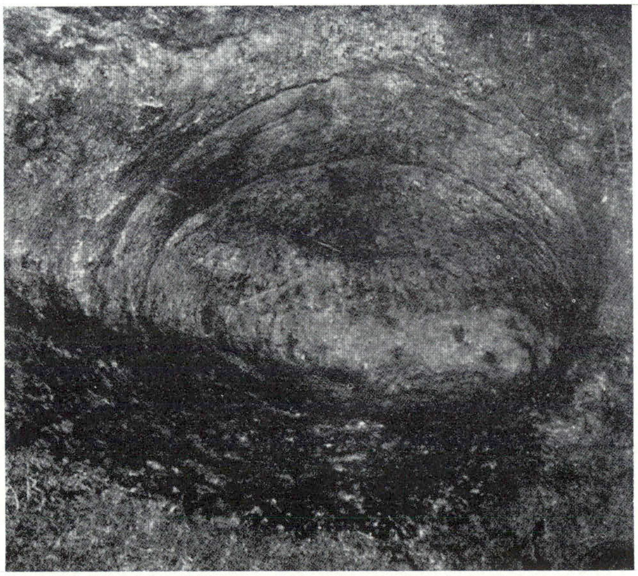

99. VAULTLIKE ENGRAVING *on a natural hollow in the cavern of Font-de-Gaume (Dordogne): The real significance of this apparent barrel vault is unknown*

181 in the cavern of Font-de-Gaume, show an astonishingly advanced knowledge of frame construction.

Barrel vaults also seem to have been known, as indicated by repeated parallel
181 lines engraved on a natural rock niche, also in the cavern of Font-de-Gaume.

Neolithic Egypt

Man-made circular and oval pits or hollows have also been noted in neolithic Egypt. Along the shore line of the former Faiyum lake, G. Caton-Thompson found numerous large circular fire pits or hearths, as well as straw-lined granary pits, many three to five feet in diameter and around a foot deep (Caton-Thompson and Gardner, 1934, pp. 24, 41–42). In northern Mesopotamia "great spherical grain bins built of clay, coated outside with bitumen and sometimes lined with gypsum plaster" (Lloyd and Safar, 1945, p. 262), were also found in the lowest levels of Hassuna.

In Merimdeh, southwest of the Nile delta, Junker excavated two irregular rows of oval huts which were at times almost kidney-shaped (1940, p. 10). These also were slightly sunk into the ground like the saucer-shaped dwelling places of Kostienki, Russia. Round "cellars," built, curiously enough, just before the breakthrough of the rectangular house, have been found dug into the ground up to one meter in depth, as at the early settlements at Ma'adi (Menghin and Amer, 1932, p. 19) and El 'Omari, both about six miles from Cairo.

In referring to the development of tombs in Upper Egypt, Scharff states that "these were at first circular or oval pits which became rectangular as a consequence of being lined with tiles made from Nile mud" (1939, p. 439).

Khirokitia

The standard form of the house was only established after long groping: round houses, oval houses, houses with sloping walls pitched to meet together, and the rectangular house. There were also numerous combinations of round houses
185 and rectangular houses, as in the fourth-millennium settlement of Arpachiyah, excavated by M. E. L. Mallowan. All had been tested out before the strictly rectangular house emerged and, with it, the temple bounded by rectilinear walls.

On the island of Cyprus, forty miles from the coast of Asia Minor, a settlement of several hundred circular domed huts (tholoi) has been discovered at Khirokitia. Forty-eight were excavated and precisely recorded by P. Dikaios. He found the "total deposit of about 4 m. packed with tholoi, small and large. . . . Some of the Khirokitia tholoi have a noteworthy feature in common with those of Arpachiyah, namely, the rectangular antechamber" (1953, p. 333). But this chamber is very much shorter. Khirokitia is early in comparison to other settlements in the Aegean area. In absolute chronology its dwellings are now dated to the middle of the fourth millennium, with 3700 B.C. as the upper limit. Arpachiyah dates from the beginning of the fourth millennium, but the stone vessels of Khirokitia cannot be compared with the elaborately designed ceramics of Arpachiyah. Khirokitia was a frontier settlement. Just where upon the Asia Minor mainland its direct antecedents lie has not as yet been ascertained.

The most interesting feature of the Khirokitia dwellings is their internal organization. They had an upper floor covering half the area of the ground floor. This division is still usual in the rectangular house plans of the Greek islands, and Le Corbusier reintroduced the age-old principle in his Pavillon de l'Esprit Nouveau, Paris, 1925. When he visited the Greek islands in 1933, together with several friends, he took out his tape measure, and I remember his delight when he found that the floor-to-ceiling heights of the houses (226 cm.) corresponded exactly to the dimension he liked to use and later incorporated in his Modulor system.

Orchomenus

Even in a comparatively late period of development—Orchomenus in Helladic Greece (ca. 2000 B.C.)—Heinrich Bulle found a row of stone circles (up to 6 m. in diameter), sometimes widened to an oval shape, directly upon the rock base (Wace and Thompson, 1912, p. 195). It was only above these that the first approximately rectangular plans were found. ☞ 184

Earliest Jericho

The excavations of Jericho by Kathleen Kenyon still remain enigmatic in the whole story of the development of the house and the human settlement (1957). Their amazing fortifications and partly excavated rectangular houses can be dated back to pre-pottery ages, and—according to carbon 14—to between the middle of the sixth and the middle of the seventh millennium.

Çatal Hüyük

Still more astonishing are the discoveries of a new civilization in Anatolia' made by James Mellaart at Çatal Hüyük, about 250 kilometers south of Ankara. Çatal Hüyük (double hill) covered a city of several thousand inhabitants, encompassing thirty-two acres. So far, during the seasons of 1961, 1962,

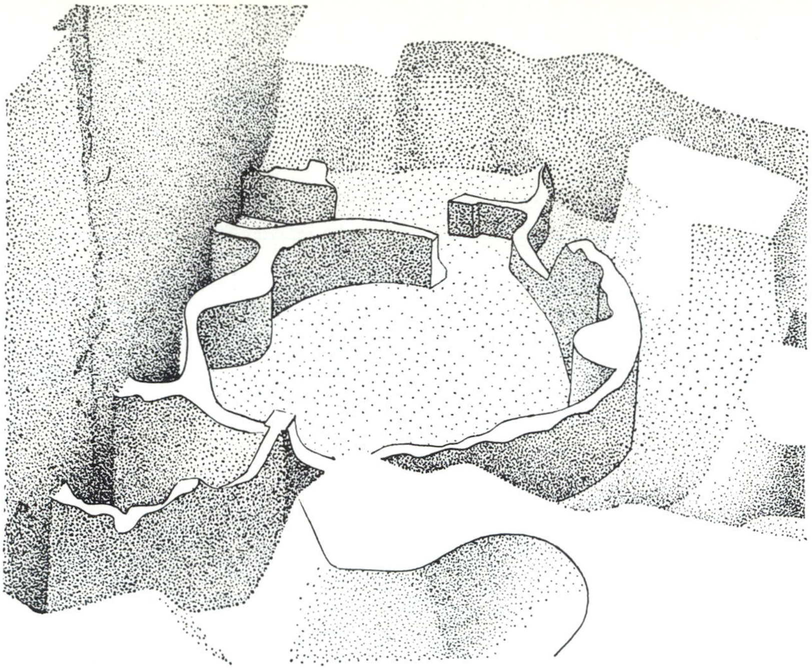

100. BUILDING AT TEPE GAWRA: *Circular structure, about five meters in diameter, with one entrance. Very early use of buttresses. Sanctuary or secular dwelling? Stratum XIX, fifth millennium. Drawing after Tobler*

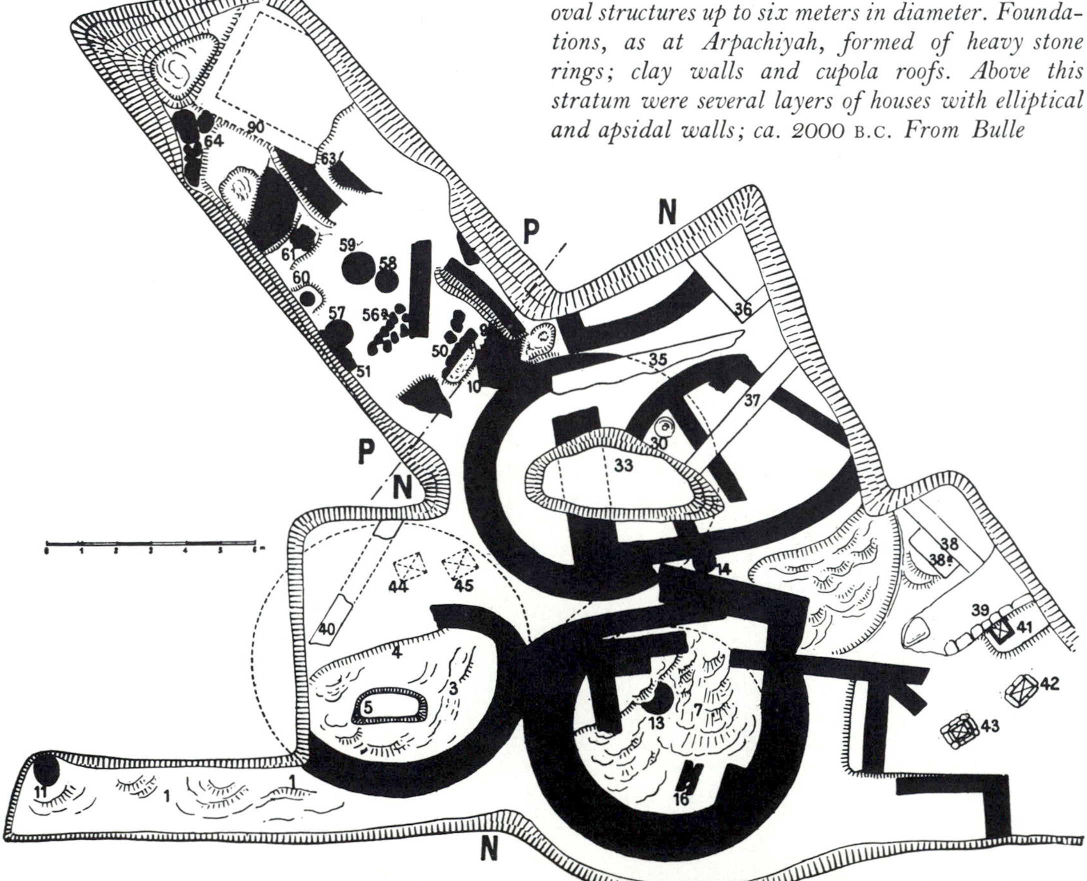

101. SETTLEMENT AT ORCHOMENUS: *Early Helladic settlement in Boeotia, Greece. Circular and oval structures up to six meters in diameter. Foundations, as at Arpachiyah, formed of heavy stone rings; clay walls and cupola roofs. Above this stratum were several layers of houses with elliptical and apsidal walls; ca. 2000* B.C. *From Bulle*

102. HOUSE AT ARPACHIYAH: *Circular stone foundation of a beehive house with long chamber. In this settlement on a fertile plain the stone circles had diameters of up to ten meters. Exceptionally finely designed ceramic bowls were found in these primitive structures. Fourth millennium*

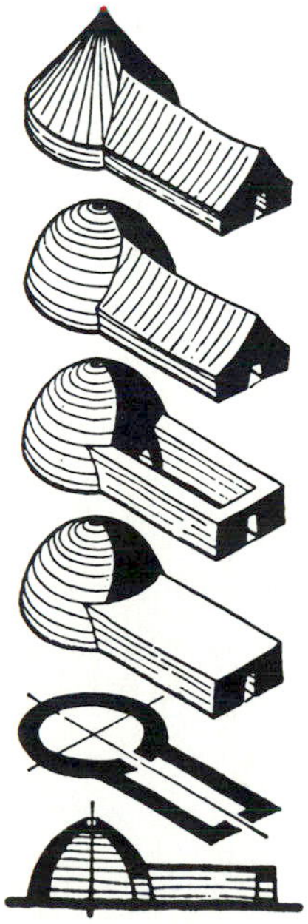

103. BEEHIVE HOUSES: *Reconstruction of the different types of beehive house with long chamber found at Arpachiyah. Drawing by Mallowan and Rose*

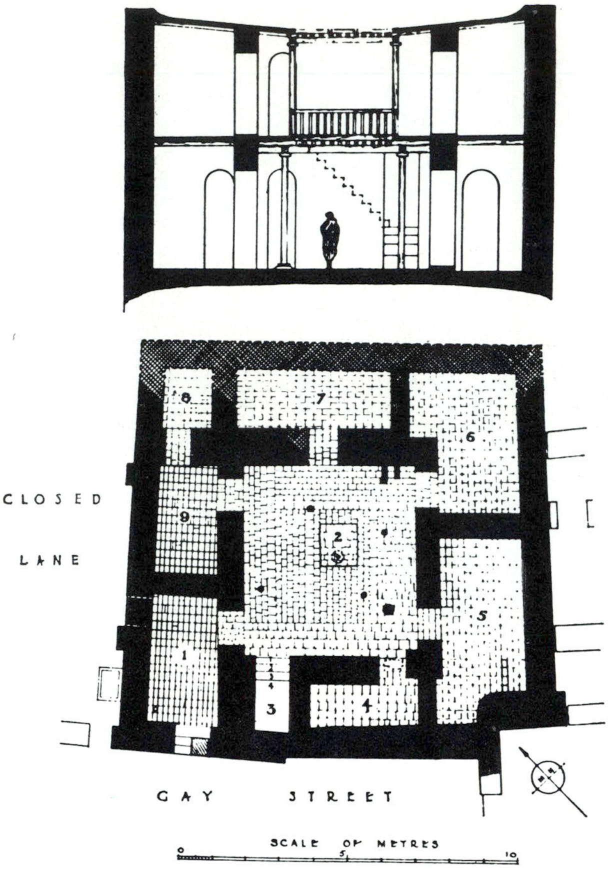

104. PATIO HOUSE AT UR: *The single-family house consisting of a central courtyard surrounded by well-organized rooms was never superseded in the Orient; ca. 2000* B.C. *From Woolley*

and 1963 Mellaart has unearthed ten strata which he dates back to the sixth and seventh millenniums. In level VI he cleared a complex of forty well-equipped chambers, including four shrines, all with rectangular or nearly rectangular walls. However, "not a single house was entered directly from a courtyard or the street: on the contrary the only way in and out was via the roof" (1963, p. 54). From level II to level VIII the shrines contained large bulls' (or cows') heads similar to the bucrania of several millenniums later found by Emery around a mastaba in north Saqqara (1961, p. 71). Nothing at all like this city has been found in the birthplace of architecture—Mesopotamia. Here in Anatolia a civilization existed whose origins and aftermath are unknown: which apparently came and went without further development. A new chapter of the unexplored sixth and seventh millenniums opens.

105. STREET AT UR, *with rounded corner; ca. 2000* B.C.

Hassuna

In northern Mesopotamia all transitions of settlement can be followed, from the hunting nomads to the shepherds, and on to the food gatherers and farmers. The transition can here be established from circular tents with a ring of stone weights, and circular houses, to houses whose steeply pitched walls come together to form the roof, and, finally, to the strictly rectangular house.

Hassuna, a settlement on the upper reaches of the Tigris not far from Mosul, was excavated in 1943–44 by Lloyd and Safar. Until R. J. Braidwood discovered Jarmo on a spur of the Kurdish uplands, Hassuna was considered the most ancient Mesopotamian settlement known in the north. Its different levels bring out the stages of transition leading up to a stable settlement. The lowest level

(Ia) was a camping site of not wholly settled people with hearths: "An oval hearth . . . lay upon a foundation of sherds and pebbles set in a kind of primitive cement" (Lloyd and Safar, 1945, p. 271). Of the next settlement (Ic) only fragmentary curvilinear adobe walls survived. Above this the houses already began to approach rectilinear forms. The founding of Mesopotamian settlements is put at "about 4750 B.C. ± 325 years" (Braidwood, 1957, p. 130).

Earliest Tepe Gawra

In the lower levels of Tepe Gawra, also in the north of Mesopotamia (strata
184 XVII–XX), circular structures were found which were about five meters in diameter and could only be studied fragmentarily (Tobler, 1950, pls. XLII, XLV). Their excavator, A. J. Tobler, was not certain whether these round buildings, or tholoi, were sanctuaries or dwelling houses (p. 43).

Through years of the most careful concentration, E. A. Speiser, and later Tobler and his colleagues from the University Museum in Philadelphia, investigated twenty successive levels of the cult center of Tepe Gawra. Their work threw light on the development of the earliest temples and dwelling houses, and the striking parallelism of this development, level by level. A further five or six levels had to remain undetermined. Only two test probes could be made, twenty-seven meters deep. These showed no "building remains" (ibid., p. 48). On this site, with its continuous record of building activities far back into neolithic times, it would have been especially interesting to know the forms of the earliest structures.

The patio house around 2000 B.C.

The earliest development of houses, both in the south and north of Mesopotamia, ran parallel with the development of the temple. Both consisted of a long rectangular room—a *Langraum*—with small chambers on either side.
190 In the beginning the ground plans were so similar (as at Tepe Gawra) that it is difficult to distinguish one from the other. The temple retained its long rectangular form up to the last centuries of Assyrian and Babylonian culture. In contrast, the human dwelling tended toward a square ground plan with rooms surrounding an open inner court. This form was achieved by about 2000 B.C., at the time of the Third Dynasty of Ur.

During his excavations of Ur in 1926–27, Woolley discovered a whole new
223 urban quarter of highly developed town houses. His first vivid description of

them follows: "The real interest of the work lay in the discovery of a well-
preserved town quarter of the time of Abraham; on the main level we unearthed
streets and houses which throw a new and unexpected light on the social and 187
domestic conditions of the period. . . . [In contrast to] a single-storied building
in mud brick, consisting of three or four rooms opening up on an open yard . . .
burnt brick was freely used, the quality of the construction, bricklaying etc., was
remarkably good, the buildings were often of two stories, and both in ground
plan and in elevation the house of a well-to-do citizen. . . . The essential
feature of the ground plan is the central courtyard, a rectangle surrounded by 186
chambers which open on to it. . . . Nearly always the court was paved with
burnt brick . . . and generally there was in the middle of it a drain-top leading
down to a deep vertical drain" (1927, pp. 387–88, 390). On the ground floor
were kitchen, liwan, lavatory, and entrance lobby. "The upper floor serves the
family for residence" (p. 394). Room heights were 2.50 meters.

Thus, after approximately three millenniums of continuous development, the human shelter reached a level of comfort for the Near East which has never been surpassed. Europe at this time was still experimenting with round and oval huts, as at Orchomenus.

THE FORMATION OF EARLIEST TEMPLES

At the opening of history in Mesopotamia, around 3000 B.C., the form of the temple was already fully developed. It represents the first monumental type of architecture. What followed, throughout the changing destiny of this country, was but a further development of tendencies which were already apparent in the third millennium, during the Early Dynastic period. This can be traced through a long succession of ruling powers, through the Babylonian and Assyrian dynasties, up to the end of the historic existence of Mesopotamia in the sixth century B.C.

The relation of the people with the deity is revealed by the position of the sanctuary within the temple precinct, the position of the cella within the sanctuary, and finally by the position of the image of the god. All point to an ever-increasing distance between the deity and the people. Later arrangements of the sanctuary aimed at increasing this severance.

In the beginning, the entire sanctuary stood open to the believers. There were different entrances, as in a Christian church. Walter Andrae comments very

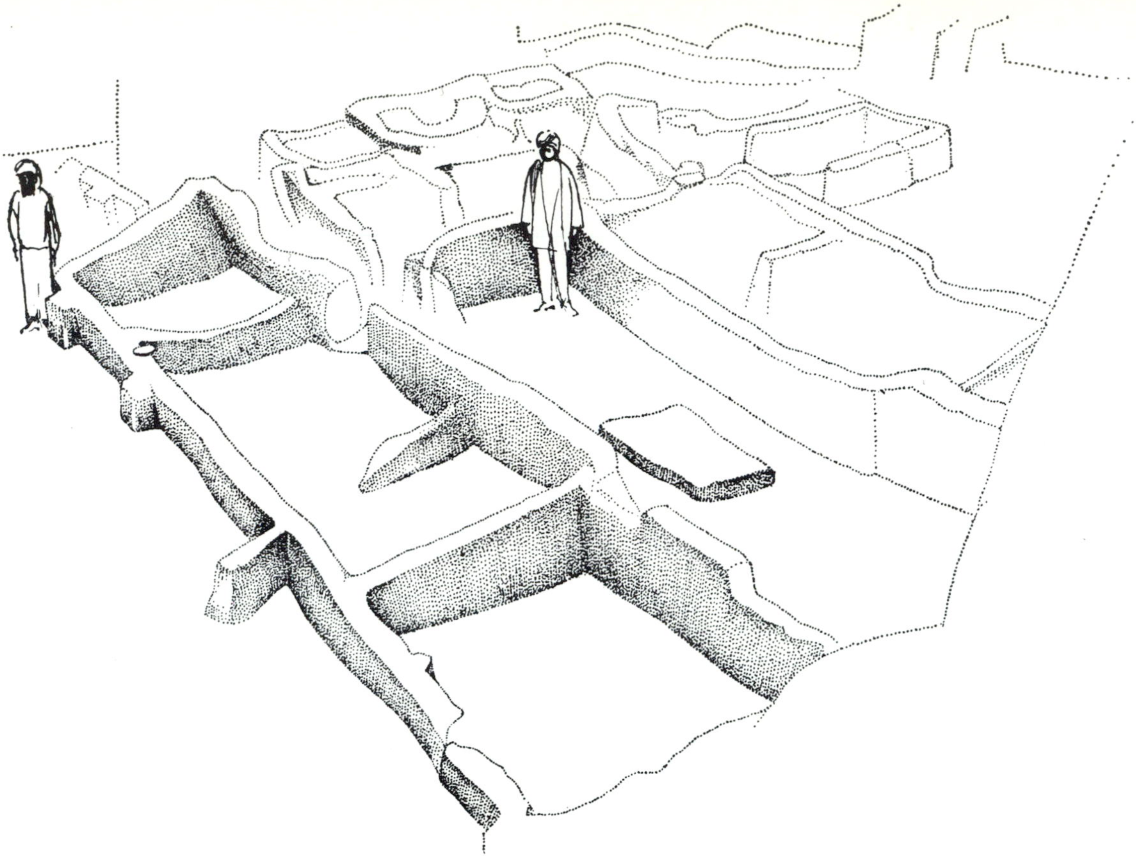

106. TEMPLE AT TEPE GAWRA (*northern Mesopotamia*): *A long central chamber and low offering altar distinguish this from a secular dwelling house of identical ground plan. The Langraum was retained throughout the entire Mesopotamian development. Stratum XVIII, fifth millennium. Drawing after Tobler*

perceptively on this free access to the sanctuary: "Life in these temples must be imagined as flowing freely through them. A coming and going is possible on every side, in strong contrast to the enclosure [*Ausschliesslichkeit*] of the later Akkadian-Babylonian temple precincts which, with few exceptions, were built like a fortress with one single entry point" (1939, p. 658).

Slowly the distance widened. First a few steps were introduced, then this
202 became a raised platform as at Al 'Uqair and in the so-called white temple at
209 Uruk. The temple of Al 'Uqair was raised upon a smaller second platform, standing upon a platform walled about like a fortress.

This development took place during the Protoliterate or formation period of Sumer. But, once within the temple, the faithful were still immediately related to the altar and offering table.

107. SHRINE AT ERIDU (*southern Mesopotamia*): *Earliest known shrine at Eridu, resting on virgin soil. Miniature in size, less than four meters square, but already incorporating a central offering table and an altar in a recessed niche. Stratum XVI, pre-Al 'Ubaid period, fifth millennium. From Van Buren*

Interior space up to the third millennium

The most unexpected feature of protohistoric temple architecture was, as already noted, its accent on the perfection of interior space. This approach was in strong contrast to the diminution of the importance of interior space which set in with the beginning of the historic periods.

In place of the hollowing-out of inner space there then arose massive volumes. The formation of a plastic architecture, an architecture of volumes placed in space, became and remained the highest ambition of architects throughout the next three millenniums.

The devaluation of interior space proceeded step by step, parallel with the mounting rigidity of the hierarchical social structure. A magnificent disposition of volumes in space—the ziggurats and pyramids—rose to full splendor relatively late. The ziggurats, those many-tiered temple towers, first achieved monumental proportions around 2000 B.C.

The temple as an enclosed space to which the people had free access, where man could stand face to face with his god, was halted in its development at the start of history. All the Mesopotamian excavations of recent decades have provided further verification of this.

191 In the south, in Eridu (Abu Shahrein), Lloyd and Safar in 1946–49 excavated
the most ancient "house of god" yet known, dating back to pre-Al 'Ubaid times
231 (fifth millennium). Above it they found a long succession of increasingly
differentiated temples, whose ruins were finally incorporated in the huge raised
platform upon which the ziggurat of Urnammu was erected shortly before
2000 B.C.

In the north, in Tepe Gawra, Speiser and Tobler uncovered twenty levels giving an insight into the beginnings of an elaborate temple community starting before the Al 'Ubaid period and only ending around 1500 B.C.

The scanty remnants of foundations which must be linked together to form ground plans seem as isolated in time and space as stars in the firmament. Yet despite all lacunae, it is possible to trace the outlines of the conception of inner space that evolved over fifteen to twenty centuries prior to the third millennium.

The earliest sanctuary at Eridu was built on virgin sand and only measured
191 12 x 15 feet (Frankfort, 1954, p. 2). Its earth walls were not yet placed precisely
at right angles to one another, but certain essential elements of later temples
were already present in embryo—from the remains of the wall buttresses which
projected into the interior space, to the organization of the shrine itself: ". . . a
doorway facing an altar in a niche-recess, a central offering table showing traces
of burnt sacrifices. In this building Al 'Ubaid ware had entirely disappeared,
replaced by a new and unfamiliar type only slightly resembling those of Tell
Halaf and Samarra" (Van Buren, 1949, pp. 123–24).

The earliest temples at Tepe Gawra in the north (in the lowest levels yet
excavated) also belong to the pre-Al 'Ubaid period. Here too one can perceive
the outline of the standard form. The temple in one of the deepest levels—
190 stratum XVIII—had "a long central chamber, on either side of which were
smaller auxiliary rooms. The religious character of the edifice is established by
a rectangular podium located slightly to the rear of the central chamber, or
sanctum" (Tobler, 1950, p. 44). The construction of the building is still very
crude: walls of rammed earth which do not meet at exact right angles, and re-

inforcing buttresses, as at Eridu, which project both to the inside and the outside. These buttresses indicate, in an embryonic form, something that will later be carried to a high degree of refinement, and special attention will be paid to the three temples on stratum XIII in which this development reached its full perfection.

The acropolis of Tepe Gawra

To understand the evolution of protohistoric architecture it is not enough simply to compare the ground plans of important buildings. In one case in particular we are able to observe the relation of a temple to its immediate environment: the three temples at Tepe Gawra, stratum XIII. It was recognized immediately that this discovery was of fundamental significance for the earliest cultural history of the Orient (Moortgat, 1945, p. 42). Here in Tepe Gawra XIII one can recognize more vividly than almost anywhere else the leap forward of this early architecture to a monumental form, and gain an understanding of the handling of interior space.

The situation is approximately as follows: Tepe Gawra, fifteen miles northeast of Mosul, consists today of two mounds divided by a depression. These 194 mounds doubtless still contain many interesting secrets, particularly in the lowest levels where, unfortunately, excavation was very limited. Speiser made some test diggings here in 1927. Actual excavations were undertaken between 1931 and 1938 by him and others under the sponsorship of the University of Pennsylvania, and the results were published in two handsome and meticulous volumes (Speiser, 1935; Tobler, 1950).

The excavations extended through twenty levels: the first nine covering the entire site, the rest taking in less and less of the area. Tepe Gawra, as we have seen, was a place of continuous settlement throughout long ages. It was abandoned around 1500 B.C.—and forever. Here no conqueror raised a ziggurat over the ruins.

It was the open plan of the three temples of stratum XIII and the unexpected architectural sensitivity of one of them that prompted me to visit the site and see it with my own eyes. Naturally I could not expect to see the remains of any buildings, for each stratum had to be completely cleared to allow the one below it to be examined. The site now again lies covered with turf and grazed by sheep, as it had for more than three thousand years before it was excavated.

Its situation in the landscape, however, remains unaltered. To the south the

108. VIEW OF TEPE GAWRA, *a very early small religious center near the Kurdish highlands: Two mounds separated by a depression where the acropolis once stood. Over twenty levels of habitation indicate a continuous settlement flourishing through nearly three millenniums, ending 1500* B.C.

right

relics of past ages are again buried in the sand, for storms have swiftly obliterated what the spade so painstakingly revealed. Yet Tepe Gawra still retains something of the original aspect of the site. The fields of grain begin to mist over with green and, about a mile and a quarter away, groves of thousand-year-old olive trees spread out above the Kurdish village of Fadhilyeh. Beyond it, in the distance, stretch the sharp horizontal contours of a range of hills—the Jebel Maklub—herald of the Kurdish highlands. Tepe Gawra, whose ancient name remains a riddle, lay aside from the great military route between Assur and Babylon—no strategic stronghold to excite an invading conqueror. It was a modest religious center, almost villagelike in character, set within a gentle landscape and without an extensive hinterland, neither a proud regional center like Uruk nor a simple village like Hassuna. I inquired of the inspector who accompanied us whether remains of earlier settlements existed around the mound. The reply was not encouraging.

The structure of the Tepe Gawra mound itself shows a close and intimate grouping of temples and private houses, the latter often astonishingly spacious. If it was in fact a temple settlement, as has been assumed, it can throw some light upon the first beginnings of this system. The site was not so completely organized as, for example, the later site of Khafaje, where the temple storerooms and workshops were built between the double walls of the great temple courtyard (Frankfort, 1933b, p. 68). At Tepe Gawra the relationship between temple and dwelling houses is more like that in small medieval towns than in the forbidding Assyrian temple-fortresses. 220

Allowing for the relativity of prehistoric dating, the early fourth millennium may be taken as the period of the rise of Tepe Gawra XIII. This is determined by its position amid the other levels excavated and by the colored pottery found there. There were three temples: the earliest, whitewashed eastern shrine built of disproportionately large sun-dried blocks, each over half a meter in length; the central, or purple temple; and the northern temple, the only one to be considered here. 196

These three temples, which do not stand exactly at right angles to one another, are grouped in a U-formation and frame an open space rather than an enclosed courtyard. This did not come about accidentally or without fore-

109. THE MOUND OF TEPE GAWRA, *with distant view of the Kurdish highlands*

110. THE NORTHERN TEMPLE: *Excavation of stratum XIII at Tepe Gawra. Only a few courses of sun-dried brick remained. The temple was probably lighted by triangular windows. The highly differentiated modeling of its interior space has no counterpart from this period*

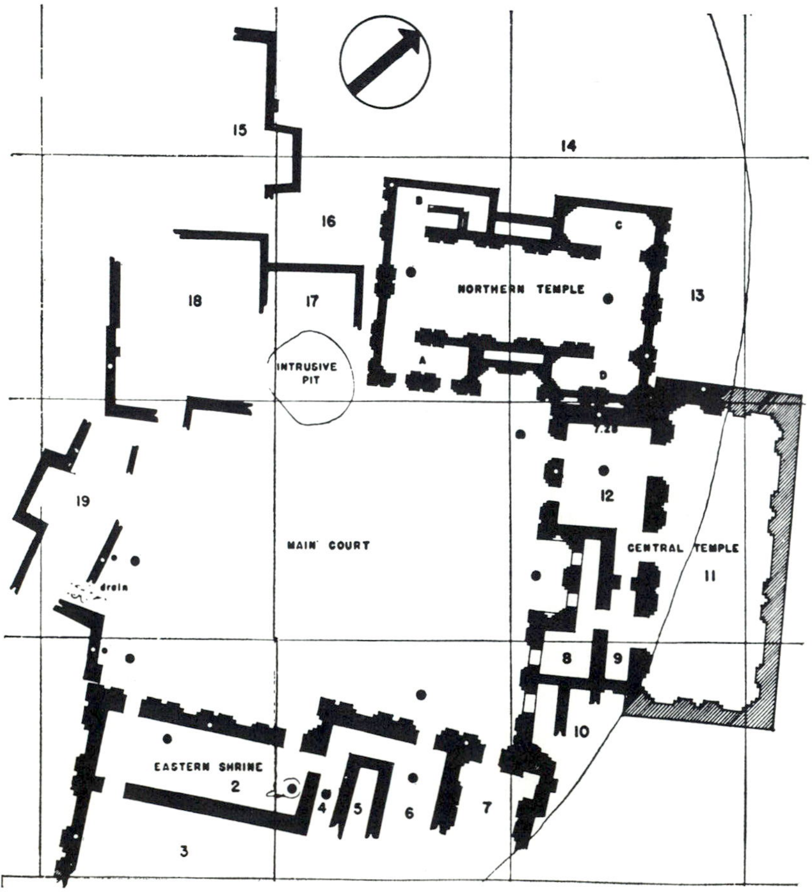

111. ACROPOLIS OF TEPE GAWRA: *Ground plan of stratum XIII. Three small shrines form a roughly U-shaped open court. Though modest in size compared with the later monumental temples of Uruk, they afford an insight into the advanced standard of architecture in the Al 'Ubaid period. Early fourth millennium. From Tobler*

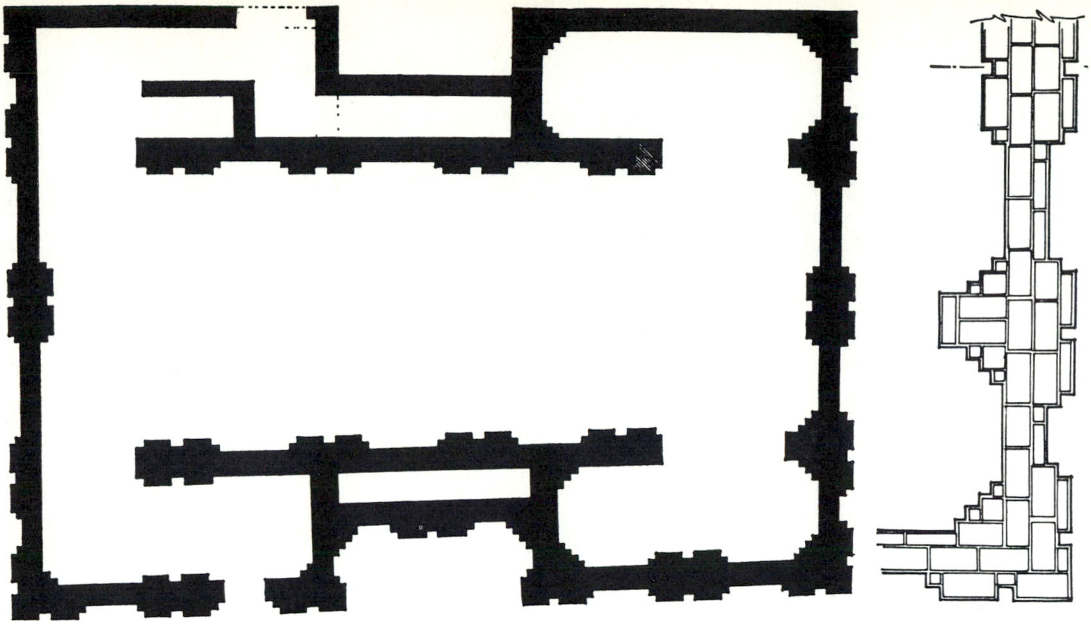

112. NORTHERN TEMPLE: *Ground plan and section through wall. The articulated buttresses with small pilasterlike strips occur both inside and outside. In contrast to later temples, the walls are extraordinarily thin. From Tobler*

thought, for the excavators found that the space between the temples had been carefully leveled and smoothed, first with fine gravel and then with fine clay. Thus a U-shaped form was developed around a well-formed, level, and integrating open space. The spatial organization was emphasized by a large, deeply recessed niche on the axis both of the central temple and of the whole court. "The remaining side of the court was closed off by a number of thinner, undecorated, and disconnected walls which formed no recognizable buildings" (Tobler, 1950, p. 30), but which in no way disturbed the spatial relationship of the three connected temples.

Of the three, it is the northern temple in which the inception of monumental architecture is most unmistakably displayed. The delicacy and sensitivity of its surface modeling were unsurpassed by any later Mesopotamian building. As in a bud, this modest temple (8.5 x 12.25 m.) enfolded all that was later to be expanded to gigantic dimensions in the great centers of power and administration, Ur and Uruk. When I visited Warka (the modern Uruk), one of the archaeologists working there referred to the northern temple in Tepe Gawra XIII as "pocket-sized." This it is, in comparison with the 120,000-square-meter temple precinct (the Eanna) at Uruk. But the northern temple of Tepe Gawra XIII was as significant for the development of early monumental architecture as Brunelleschi's Pazzi chapel for the development of the early Renaissance. There, just as in the modest dimensions of the Florentine chapel, one can detect the characteristic features of later ambitious structures. above

197 What first strikes the eye is the dominating, elongated central hall, whose spatial connections and separations were most subtly achieved. By and large, the ground plan differs very little from that of other temples, such as the white 202 temple at Uruk or the late Temple VII at Eridu. Just as in them, the walls bounding the central area are organized as a succession of recessed niches. The astounding features of the northern temple are the delicate articulation of the 197 encircling walls, which are as thin as concrete panels, and their express utilization to organize the interior space. This consisted of a single space which, through the deliberate arrangement of its walls, was divided into a dominating central hall with, at either end, a symmetrically disposed rectangular space at right angles to the main axis. The strength of the central hall was increased by the addition of two freestanding partitions; these created large side niches, one of which formed a small vestibule that served as an antechamber or preparation for entry into the main sanctuary. These niches also indicated their later development as "side chapels." The organization of the walls created an interlocking space impossible to take in at one glance—which would naturally give rise to doubts as to whether it could conceivably have been built in Protoliterate times, were it not for its position in the sequence of strata and for other undoubted finds that place it firmly in the Al 'Ubaid period.

The most sacred part of the northern temple was its spacious open cella at the northern end. Its encircling walls were even more strongly modeled than others in the building. The jutting freestanding panels merged the central hall with the cella and at the same time created two large side niches—pockets of space. The articulation of the walls in the rest of the building seems merely a preparation for that of the cella. The pair of projecting buttresses on the central axis still have only two pilasters, but the buttresses to right and left of them are bordered by four pilaster shafts. This is a tremendous development from the clumsy buttresses of other temples in the strata immediately beneath.

The architect of the northern temple must have possessed a feeling for the total unity of a building, a feeling for the interrelation between the interior and exterior faces of the walls. The cella buttresses with many pilasters penetrated the wall and repeated their form on its outer surface. Their fourfold pilasters were also echoed in all corners of the chapel-like niches. All in all, the modeling and organization of the walls of this temple exhibit the refinement and delicacy that exist only in monuments of great architecture.

No trace of an altar platform or offering table was found in the northern temple, in contrast to the lower strata. We do not know why this was, but in any case, very few objects were found in this stratum. Among those few was an incense burner that, as we shall see in the next section, may give some idea of 200 the exterior appearance of the temple. "The overhanging ledge surmounting the object may reproduce the eaves of the building, and while there is no other evidence to suggest the presence of windows in any of the stratum XIII buildings, the triangular openings of the incense burner make such an assumption entirely reasonable" (ibid., p. 144).

This Al 'Ubaid temple makes it impossible to explain the form of the earliest brick architecture in purely materialistic terms, as an imitation of walls of wooden planks. Both inside and outside surfaces of all the temple walls, apart from the outer face of the rear wall, were rhythmically molded with stepped pilasters. This was new, and a great stride forward from erecting simple supporting buttresses. The power of a creative imagination was here able to transform a humble material, an unlikely material—sun-dried brick—into a structure replete with spiritual force.

ARCHITECTURE, POTTERY, AND ABSTRACTION

The design of the walls of Tepe Gawra XIII, with the interrelated modeling of their inner and outer surfaces and their astonishing thinness, stands in strong contrast to temple walls at the peak of the Sumerian period, when, as in the temple of Inanna at Nippur (ca. 2000 B.C.), they were ten to thirteen feet thick (Haines, 1956, p. 266). The explanation must be sought outside the realm of architecture.

At this early period, the same material—clay—was used to make thin-walled pottery vessels, hard and resonant as a bell. A race of people lived here who were able to turn the thinnest and most delicately modeled vessels on the potter's wheel, whose hands were accustomed swiftly and simultaneously to mold both inside and outside faces of these exquisite examples of the potter's craft. Shortly thereafter, pottery declined from its eminent position and architecture failed to fulfill its early promise of a refinement of proportions in the service of a far-reaching hollowing-out of interior space. Other trends, based on other premises, came to the fore in Sumer, as in Egypt.

Does this imply that the earliest monumental architecture was derived from

113. BEAKER FROM TEPE GAWRA: *The surface is organized with vertical lines, like the temple buttresses. The single triangle suggests a symbolic meaning. From stratum XIII. From Tobler*

114. INCENSE BURNER FROM TEPE GAWRA: *Probably the triangular perforations not only show the shape of the temple windows but—as everywhere in the protohistoric period—operate as a fertility symbol*

pottery? That is certainly not the intention. But the forms of both pottery and architecture grew from the same ruling principle of the time: abstraction. The origins of monumental architecture are rooted in abstraction. This can explain the organization and division of its interior space. Both the articulation of the temple walls and the surface decoration of the pottery vessels testify to this, as can be observed from any random fragment. In stratum XIII at Tepe Gawra, a beaker was found whose decoration the excavator described as "admirably balanced, and well adapted to the contours of the beaker to which it was applied." He then added: "The design suggests a comparison with the triangular windows and long, vertical grooves to be found on the incense burner from this stratum. . . . It is not improbable that we have in the central decoration of this beaker a stylized representation of an entrance to one of the temples" (Tobler, 1950, p. 143).

left

left

Pottery was not a model for architecture, nor was architecture a model for pottery. The basis and background for both embraced a common conception: abstraction and symbolism.

We are here at the close of that use of abstraction as a universal means of expression which had attained absolute dominance in the neolithic period. In the northern temple of Tepe Gawra XIII another aspect of this long tradition came to fruition. How can one explain the crystal-clear structuring of the interior of this temple, its abstractly modeled surfaces, and the organization of its divisions, except as the outcome of an imagination trained through long ages to create forms for which no direct image exists in nature?

GROWING DISTANCE BETWEEN DEITY AND PEOPLE

We can gain insight into the time sequence of the formation of inner space and the modeling of the entire building by a comparison of four temples: the temples of Tepe Gawra XIII in the north, and Eridu VII, the white temple, and Temple D at Uruk in the south.

The earliest of these is Tepe Gawra XIII, from around 3500 B.C. or probably even earlier. The latest is the white temple of Uruk, from the Jemdet Nasr period, between 2800 and 2600 B.C. Temple VII of Eridu and Temple D at Uruk fall between these dates.

The interior of Tepe Gawra XIII, though differentiated in form, is a single

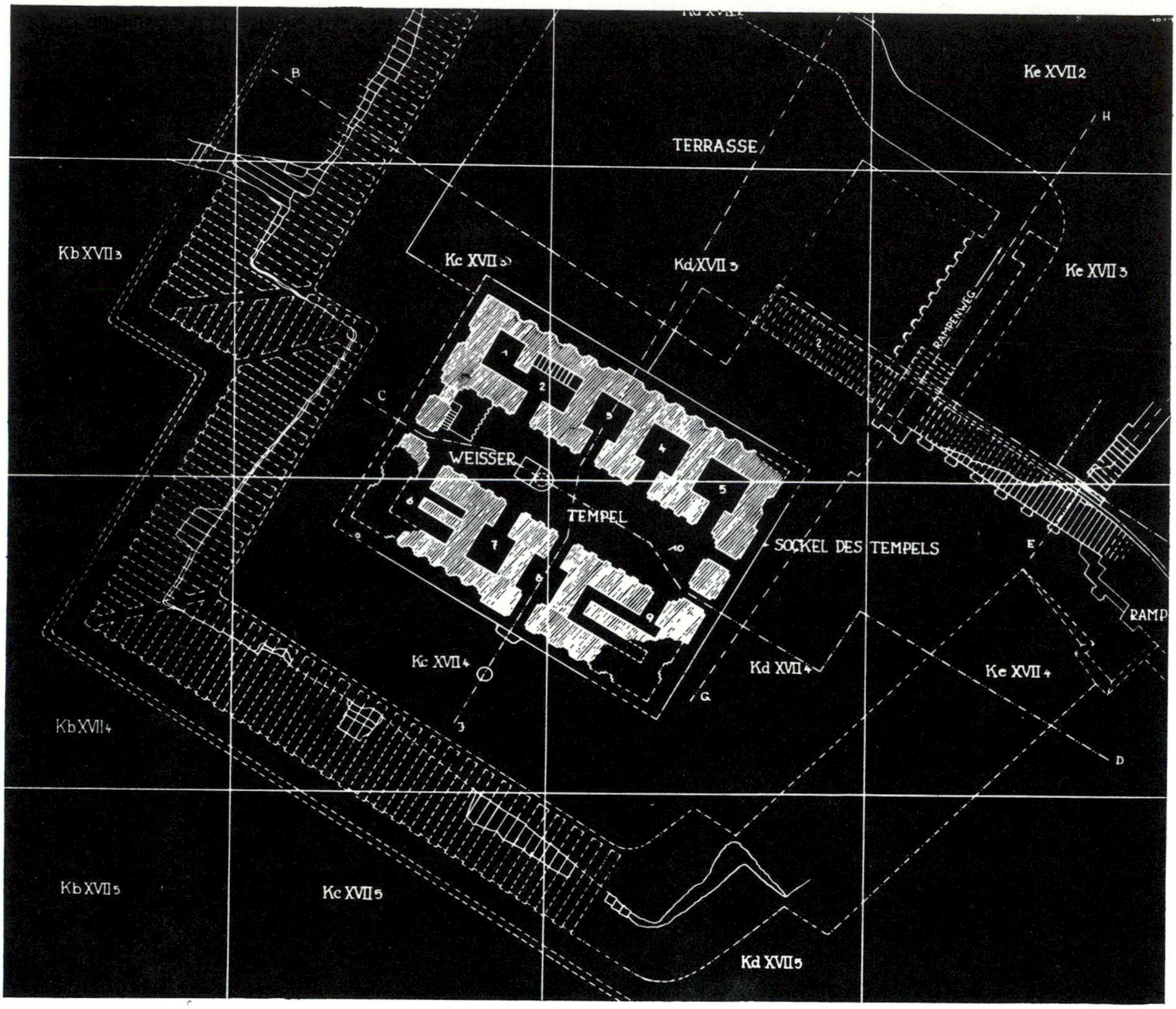

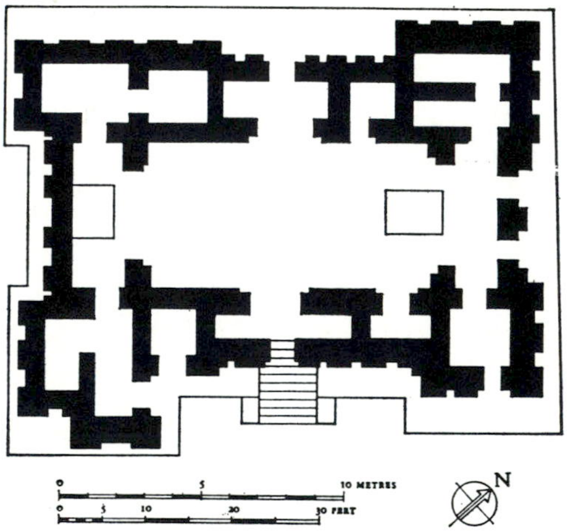

115. PLAN OF WHITE TEMPLE, URUK: *Sited on a high terrace approached by steps, with entrance on three sides. Later than 3000 B.C. From Lenzen*

116. PLAN OF TEMPLE VII, ERIDU: *Strongly accentuated corners and alternate buttresses and recesses along the walls. The long chamber can be entered from three sides. From Frankfort*

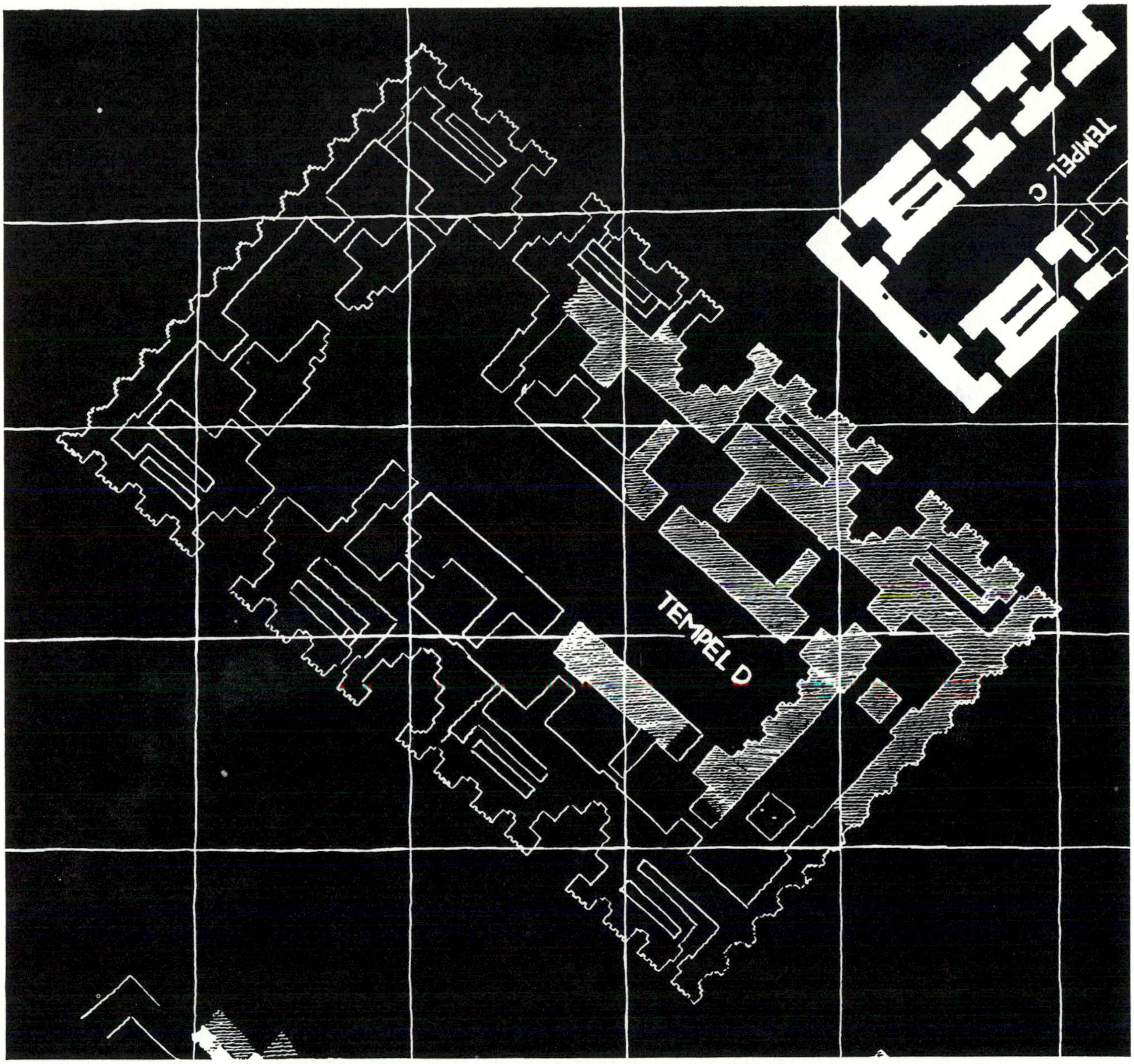

117. PLAN OF TEMPLE D, URUK: *The largest of all the Sumerian temples (50 x 80 m.), it shows full mastery of modeling exterior and interior space. The refinement of the deep recesses in its outer walls indicates the high standard of the period. Uruk IV, ca.* 3000 B.C. *Drawing by Lenzen*

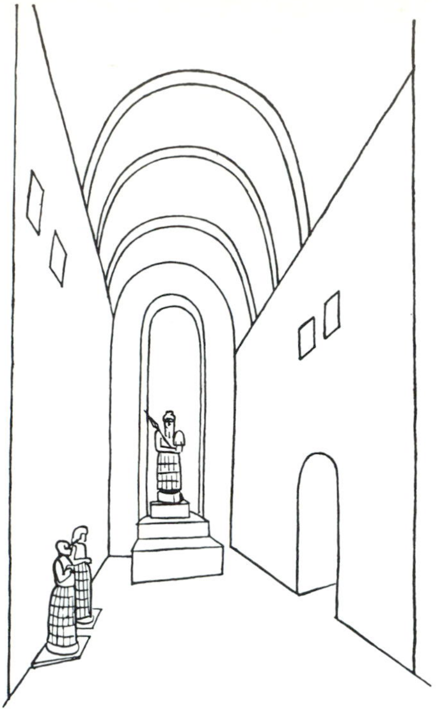

118. SINGLE-CHAMBER SHRINE AT TELL ASMAR: *It is not certain that a statue to the god Abu stood on the altar as shown. Drawing after Lloyd, from Delougaz and Lloyd*

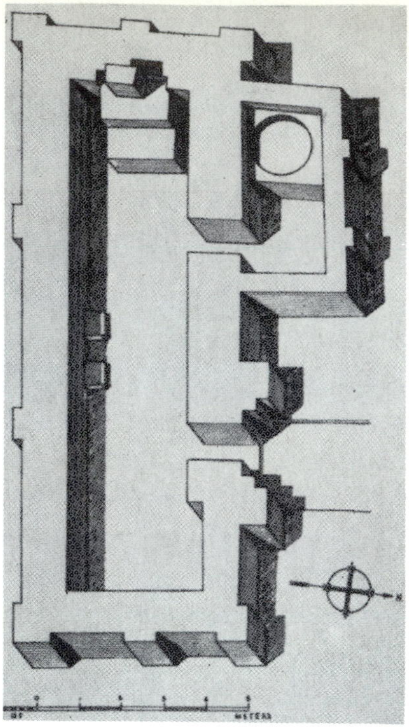

119. EARLY DYNASTIC SHRINE AT TELL ASMAR: *In this period the temple had a single entrance near the end of the long chamber. From Frankfort*

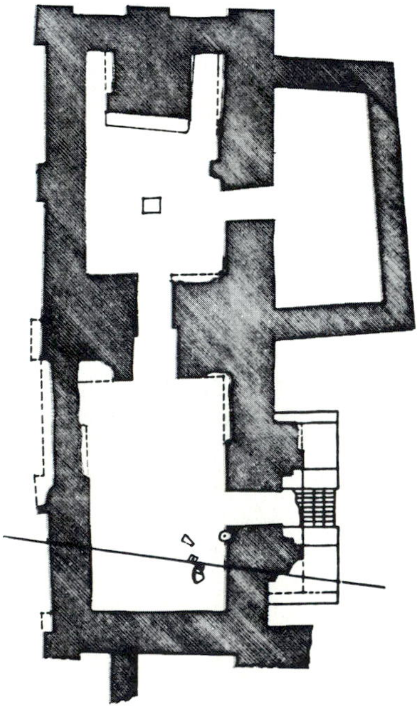

120. AKKADIAN SHRINE AT TELL ASMAR: *Near the beginning of this period, the shrine was divided in two by the thickest wall. From Delougaz and Lloyd*

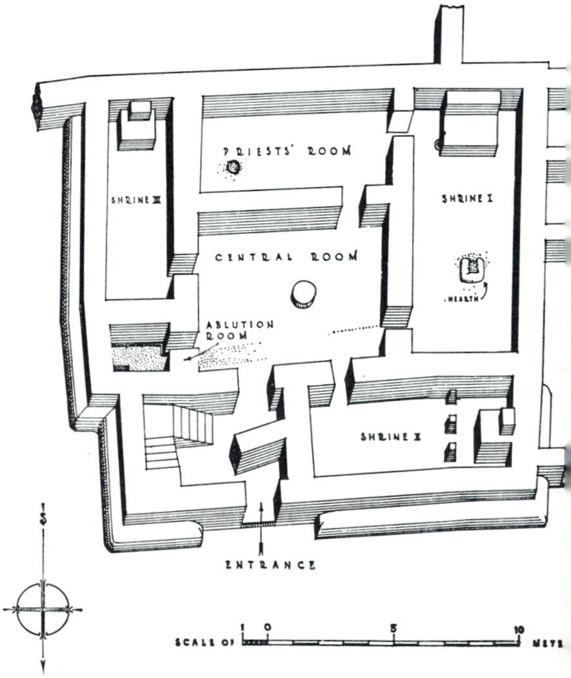

121. THE THREE SHRINES OF TELL ASMAR, *Second Early Dynastic period. The whole complex has only one entrance from outside. From Frankfort*

room. As in a building of today, the interior space is divided by two screens 197
which help to form open niches at either end.

The outline of the plan of the larger Eridu Temple VII is very close to Tepe
Gawra XIII, though the strongly accentuated corners have become bolder, the 202
walls thicker, and buttresses alternating with shallow recesses surround the whole structure. Despite the general similarity of external plan, the tendency to move away from a free-floating space embracing the whole interior is already clearly marked. Instead, emphasis is laid on a long, stretched-out cella with smaller auxiliary rooms alongside.

The white temple of Uruk is by far the best known of all Protoliterate sanctuaries. Uruk was the foremost religious center of Sumer. It was still a proud, rich city in the time of the Seleucid kings in the fourth century B.C. Its gods, who were considered the owners of the city, were Anu and Inanna. A long line of mythological kings ruled at Uruk, including Gilgamesh. The fine reliefs on
its famous alabaster vase give the earliest representation of an exuberant agri- 121
culture in the Jemdet Nasr period.

The white temple stands high upon a platform raised over the ruins of its
predecessors—a token of the great accomplishments of this same space con- 202
ception at the end of the Protoliterate period, early in the third millennium.

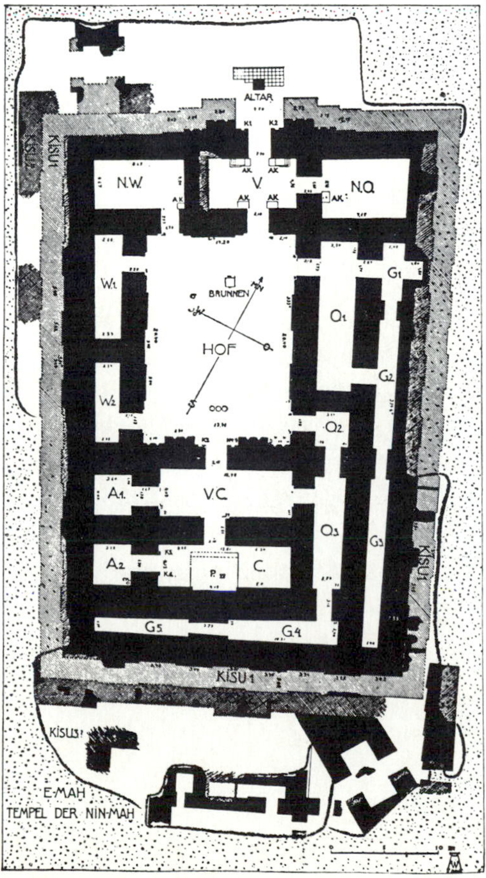

122. PLAN OF E-MAH TEMPLE, BABYLON: *This temple of the goddess Ninmah shows how the tradition of the Langraum persisted to the end. Separation of the faithful from the deity has now become emphasized by a sequence of barriers. Sixth century* B.C. *From Koldewey*

This temple acquired its name because its mud-brick walls were covered with whitewash. It was dedicated to the high god Anu, lord of the heavens: "Its ground plan is approximately rectangular (17.50 x 22.30 m.). The most important part of the temple is the central chamber, 18.70 meters long and 4.85 meters wide, bordered on the northeast side by five rooms and on the southwest by two rooms and two stairways" (Lenzen, 1942, p. 8). Lenzen draws attention to the fact that the temple at Tell Brak in Syria, on the Khabur River, a tributary of the Euphrates, excavated by Mallowan in 1937–39, which is roughly of the same period as the white temple, has almost exactly the same proportion of length to breadth (p. 29). Thus, both in the north and in the south, the same ground plan and the same space conception were developed.

Many large temples were built in Uruk, since, as the city of Inanna and seat of Gilgamesh, it was a singularly important religious center. The largest temple
203 was found in the archaic stratum, Uruk IV. Known as Temple D, it measured 50 x 80 meters and was built around 3000 B.C. The interior was T-shaped and the deeply recessed outer walls showed the highly refined technique attained at this period. It is not until churches of the Gothic and baroque periods that we again find exterior walls treated in so plastic a manner.

The separation of the cella

The inner court. In the pre-Sargonid period, before the middle of the third millennium, a growing severance between the deity and the faithful became apparent. Instead of many entrances there was only one, placed toward the far end of the cella. Then an antecella was inserted before the cella. An inner court further helped to accentuate the distance.

The distance between deity and people came to be expressed architecturally toward the beginning of the period of Sargon of Akkad, around the twenty-fourth century B.C.

A major gap exists in our knowledge of this period, for we do not know where the newly founded capital city of Akkad was actually situated. It was the residence of Sargon, the first great conqueror, king of "the four corners of the earth," whose rule extended to the Mediterranean coast and even beyond.

A faint reflection can be gathered from Eshnunna, a small Sargonid city at Tell Asmar, excavated between 1931 and 1933 by Frankfort, Delougaz, and Lloyd. Eshnunna lay on the Diyala River, not far north of where it flows into the Tigris below Baghdad. Here a series of temples was built, one over the other, starting in the Protoliterate period and ending at the beginning of the Akkadian period. Four versions of the earliest shrine from the Protoliterate period were found, all with irregular ground plans.

Above them was a series of three square temples built during the Second Early Dynastic period. Here three small shrines were assembled around a common inner court, each with a single entrance opening onto it. The only connec- 204
tion was through one doorway to the court. This may be partly because the temple lay in the midst of the town and was surrounded by private houses, like a baroque monastery. It was in the second of these square temples that the excavators made their greatest find, "a hoard of statues buried beneath the floor" (Delougaz and Lloyd, 1942, p. 189).

This sequence of temples had "four principal building levels" (p. 192), the last two entering into the Akkadian period. Having neither niches nor transepts, in contrast to earlier temples such as Tepe Gawra or Eridu VII, the nave ap- 196, 202
peared extremely long. It was entered on the long side, toward the far end from the sanctuary. The ratio of length to breadth was as great as four to one. Only one very small adjoining room existed, which the excavators "presumed to be a kitchen in which sacred food was prepared" (Frankfort, 1934, p. 44). Because of the thickness of the walls, and for other reasons, the excavators consider they were roofed by a semicircular vault of mud bricks spanning three meters. "It is known that the Sumerians had already mastered the principle of the brick arch, and . . . there is no reason to suppose that the construction of a vault over a span of 3 meters, by means of a movable wooden centering, would be beyond their architectural ingenuity" (Delougaz and Lloyd, 1942, p. 196).

The tentative reconstruction of the nave gives some idea of the appearance 204
of the interior, even though its height may be somewhat exaggerated. In contrast to the early temples of north and south, the modeling of the interior had become extremely simple: no buttresses, no niches, only one strongly concentrated space.

It would seem that we are here only a step away from the Romanesque churches of southern France with their barrel vaults. Instead, the envelopment of both the faithful and the rituals within a single space was drawing to its close.

This occurred even in the third and fourth building levels of this single-shrine temple. "The shrine was then divided into two separate compartments by a wall with a doorway in it" (ibid., p. 192). This new dividing wall is thicker than any other in the building, and the doorway is small. The ritual altar and offering table have now become severed from the people, and the space for ritual and thé space for the people is of the same size. The single entrance to the temple has been monumentalized.

It is logical that this severance occurred just at the outset of the Akkadian period. Again and again Akkadian cylinder seals portray the anthropomorphic gods in dialogue with Sargon, and he himself was sometimes depicted with a horned crown, the insignia of a god.

The dividing wall in the latest single-shrine temples of Tell Asmar points to the beginning of a process which was to become ever stronger: the severance of the deity from the people.

There are many instances in which the further growth of the Mesopotamian temple can be followed. The isolation of the god grew constantly greater. The image stood in a dim light, or in total darkness. The plan of the sanctuary was adapted for this purpose and the tradition remained unchanged up to the end. The temple normally continued to be a rather humble rectangular structure even when it was placed upon a most conspicuous site, like the temple to the
205 goddess Ninmah (the Great Mother), built by Sardanapalus and, later, Nebuchadnezzar, toward the start of the sixth century B.C. This Babylonian temple stood between the Ishtar Gate and the palace, beside the broad processional way of the great New Year festival. One had to pass through several doorways and vestibules to reach its inner court. The cella containing an image of the goddess lay on the axis of the court, upon a higher level, and an antechamber was placed before it. "It appears probable that the secular folk were not allowed to penetrate beyond the antechamber. Access to the cella was evidently intentionally rendered difficult by the postament, which projected almost as far as the door" (Koldewey, 1913; tr. 1914, p. 59). The antecella was connected with the cella by a single small opening facing the image of the goddess, which probably stood in complete darkness.

POLYCHROME ARCHITECTURE AROUND 3000 B.C.

Apart from architectural articulation of the walls, both internally and externally, a refined enrichment of architectural surfaces had also come into being before 3000 B.C. Polychrome cone mosaics covering the massive semi-engaged columns of the temple complex of Uruk IV have been preserved, and the rich-
165 ness of the high reliefs and the freestanding copper bulls in the Ninhursag temple

123. MODEL OF PAINTED TEMPLE, AL 'UQAIR: *The buttresses of the curved lower terrace are similar to those used later in building the ziggurats. Before 3000* B.C.

at Al 'Ubaid, about half a millennium later, indicate the advanced development of Sumer at this period.

The fullest insight into the use of color on interior walls is afforded by the so-called painted temple of Al 'Uqair, about forty miles south of Baghdad. In this man-made sanctuary the prehistoric urge to give form to what is essentially immaterial can again be recognized. We cannot expect the great richness of the prehistoric symbolism of the cavern walls, whose images were the outcome of thousands of years of experience. We stand here at a new beginning. above

By the use of highly refined techniques, Lloyd and Safar were able to rescue the exceedingly fragile and fragmentary frescoes of the painted temple and thus open up for us a reliable view of the manner in which the temple interior was painted—around 3500 B.C. according to them (1943, pp. 132–58), though it may have been nearer to 3000 B.C.

The ground plan of this temple was normal: a long hall with small chambers

124. ALTAR FRESCO IN PAINTED TEMPLE: *Here we can glimpse the surface treatment of a protohistoric façade. The recesses between fluted buttresses are covered with triangular and diamond-shaped patterns. The horizontal cornice has two ornamental bands, the upper one probably protruding*

along both sides; the façade articulated into a series of niches and fluted but-
202 tresses. Its dimensions were almost identical with those of the white temple of Uruk. Like this, too, it was raised up on a high terrace. "The wall faces inside the building were also carefully mud plastered. Every surviving square foot bore traces of color washes or painted ornament. The almost insuperable difficulty of preserving or even recording more than a small percentage of these frescoes" is then recounted by Lloyd (ibid., pp. 139–40). When first exposed, they were as bright as the day they were applied more than five thousand years before, but they faded within a few hours. Nevertheless it proved possible to establish the system followed in painting the interior walls. First came "a band of plain color, usually some shade of red, forming a dado about 1 meter high all round the room. Above this there would be a band of geometrical ornament about 30 cm. high" (p. 140). Finally, on the upper part of the walls, a running frieze of animals and human figures upon a solid white ground.

The altar was treated with special care. It was of considerable size: the solid brickwork was 2.60 meters wide with a projection of 3.60 meters. "On the right side a flight of six shallow steps" (ibid.) led up to its surface. Naturally, at that period, no statues of the god yet stood upon it. Upon the face of the altar and both sides, right and left, were found "the best-preserved paintings in the building" (ibid.). Here by chance we are given a singular insight into the total treatment of the façade of a protohistoric temple: "The design on the front is of

125. LION FRESCO IN PAINTED TEMPLE: *The large spots which make this lion appear to be a leopard may be a survival from prehistoric times. Another lion found by Layard at Eridu also had circles marked on his body*

an architectural character, and one sees in it the representation of the façade of a
210 building, the altar itself, in fact, being treated as a miniature temple. On the but-
tresses even the three flutes are represented by vertical lines, while the recesses between are filled with a geometric pattern comparable to the mosaic ornament found in a similar position in several temples at Warka [Uruk]. . . . The vertical stripes representing buttresses were painted alternately white and yellow" (pp. 140–41). The recesses between the buttresses were filled alternately with diamond-shaped and triangular patterns, both of ancient symbolic meaning. These are also the dominant motifs of the Al 'Ubaid pottery and of the mosaics on the columns of the temples of Uruk and Al 'Ubaid.

The horizontal cornice of a temple façade was also skillfully brought out on this altar painting by two long horizontal bands, one filled with a rhomboidal pattern, the other with rectangular checkers. These bands were separated from one another by an unbroken line of darker paint.

Right and left of the altar, like protecting guardians, two "excellently pre-
211 served animal figures" (p. 141) were painted (now in the Baghdad Museum):
one "couchant," the other sitting.

Lions or leopards? Lloyd puts it thus: "Both are what one would normally in heraldic painting call 'lions'; but, since they are covered with black spots on a white ground, perhaps the word 'leopard' would be more appropriate" (ibid.). All later guardians were lions. It is very possible that we have here a late survival from prehistoric times and that the "leopard" with its heavy outline stems from a far-distant ancestry. Are its unnaturally large black spots not reminiscent of the dots and disks of Aurignacian times or the large black dots on the two
I:149 horses of Pech-Merle, which were in no way intended to represent a piebald
horse?

Iconographically it is interesting to note that the jaws of these guardian
"leopards" were already threateningly agape, as was later the case with all the
4 f Mesopotamian lions, in contrast to the lions of Egypt, which were depicted in
brooding tranquillity.

The mud-brick temples of Mesopotamia were often solidly decorated with rich colors, enabling the base material from which they were formed to be forgotten. On the exterior façade, a somewhat excessive degree of subdivision in the ornamentation demonstrates that this was but a beginning—a first experiment. The interior handling of color was far more free: to some extent it reminds one of some of the small painted Romanesque churches still to be found in Alpine areas.

ON THE SIGNIFICANCE OF THE EARLIEST MONUMENTAL ARCHITECTURE

The first appearance of the man-made temple is synonymous with the appearance of monumentality in architecture. The age-old yearning to establish contact with invisible forces was, for the first time, given an architectural form. The sequence of temples in the numerous strata at Eridu, Tepe Gawra, Uruk, and elsewhere showed no signs of the anthropomorphic images of gods which appeared later with the rise of kingly rulers.

In the graves and tombs of Tepe Gawra, of which more than four hundred were discovered, numerous objects were found: beads, buttons, stamp seals, figurines of animals, pendants, and amulets. In the lowest levels and in the soundings at the base of the mound, small crude fertility figurines were found—a perpetuation of earlier Venus statuettes. They "may be considered as representations of the Mother Goddess. . . . Nearly all specimens conform to a standardized type in which the woman . . . is always shown holding her breasts, which are rather prominently modeled. Heads are merely pinched" (Tobler, 1950, p. 163). This makes apparent why, in the Early Dynastic period, the power of Inanna-Ishtar, goddess of fertility, love, and war, was so great.

Also, the white temple of Uruk and the painted temple of Al 'Uqair yielded no signs amid their relics which could point to an anthropomorphic pantheon. It was only after the Akkadian period that these appeared in full abundance.

It is not certain whether the long, stretched-out cella of the early temples ever contained the image of a god at its far end. In the temple of Tell Asmar, Frankfort 204 and his associates found ten figures "which seem to have formed the complete sculptural furniture . . . buried together under the floor beside the altar" (Frankfort, 1954, p. 24). These statues (most of which are now in the Oriental Institute in Chicago and the largest one, a man and a woman, in the Baghdad Museum) raise the question of the appearance of deities in their anthropomorphic form. Whether the tallest figure, which was about thirty inches high, can really be identified as Abu, god of fertility and vegetation, is not absolutely sure. Even though he is larger than the others he holds his hands in the same position of prayer as they do.

The religious equipment found in these early temples consisted merely of an altar and an offering table. It is consequently uncertain whether the religious center of Eridu was, from its beginning, dedicated to the service of a definite deity or, to put it more strongly, whether in the fifth millennium Enki, the

Sumerian god of water and wisdom, whose cult had its center at Eridu, existed at all. Indeed, it seems highly improbable. The first definite signs of his existence appeared only in one of the upper levels (Temple VII), where "the whole of its floor was a layer of *fishbones*, nearly six inches deep" (Lloyd, 1947, p. 581), which were taken to be offerings to Enki, god of the waters, though there was no image of the god.

The organization of the interior space of the temples before 3000 B.C. testified to a desire to attain direct contact with invisible powers with no intermediary aid of anthropomorphic deities. This represented just as great an achievement of
I:293 ff the creative imagination as the first drawings of Aurignacian man. That was the earliest beginning of art, this the earliest beginning of architecture.

The tragedy of archaeological excavations is that the scanty remnants spared by the reluctant earth must again be obliterated—this time forever—in order to uncover the strata below them. Only memories remain, so far as they can be recorded in plans and photographs. But these memories should be kept alive.

In these simple structures of sun-dried clay the flame of inspiration burned brightly. There is no question of arousing feelings of inferiority or a desire for imitation, but an understanding of this early development should form part of the groundwork of education in art history and architecture: not so much to record the facts as to strengthen belief in the power of human imagination. The first beginning of architectural history lies here in these early temples, and here alone. With the single exception of the ziggurats, Mesopotamian architecture, from this point on until it reached its close in the sixth century, was obscured by the radiant phenomenon of the Egyptian development.

PART VI ZIGGURATS: STAIRWAYS OF THE GODS

After the preliminary period, which encompassed the first beginnings of monumental architecture and ended with the opening of recorded history, there came a break. The conception of architecture as the molding of interior space was not disrupted suddenly, but a change became noticeable as soon as power over men and the means of production came to be concentrated in the hands of a single man.

The urge to build began to move in the direction of erecting massive volumes: volumes placed freely in space. Parallel with this concentration came an increasing suppression of interior space. In the architecture of palaces or temples, wherever they arose in the ensuing period—in the Middle East, Egypt, or Crete—it can be observed that rooms have become long and narrow, just like
204 the Sumerian cella toward the Akkadian period. When large halls were needed, they were filled with a forest of gigantic columns, as in the Egyptian temple of
509 Karnak or, nearly a millennium later, in the hundred-pillared throne room of Darius at Persepolis.

The grandest expressions of this urge to place enormous volume in space are the ziggurat and the pyramid. Their massive construction attained dimensions previously unknown. They are both the manifestation of a dominant ruling power and the expression and symbol of contact established—as far as was humanly possible—with the superhuman forces.

DIFFERENCES BETWEEN ZIGGURAT AND PYRAMID

Even though the ziggurats took on their monumental form more than half a millennium later than the pyramids, we will discuss them here in relation to general developments in Mesopotamia.

Differences between the two were apparent from the beginning. Only when these are fully appreciated can one come to an understanding of their dissimilar forms. Both pyramid and ziggurat retained—from the beginning to the end of their development—the distinguishing features of their different origins. Their subsequent development can always be traced back to their different starting points.

Differences between Ziggurat and Pyramid

The ziggurat arose within the city of the living as a temple or altar upon a staged tower within the temenos (temple precinct). It was accessible to its summit.

The pyramid arose in the desert within a necropolis—a city of the dead. It was totally inaccessible.

The ziggurat was normally dedicated to the god to whom the city "belonged" —in Ur the moon-god Nannar, in Eridu the water-god Enki, in Nippur the storm-god Enlil. This introduced a notion of eternity.

The pyramid was both the tomb and the eternal abode of the king as son of the sun-god Ra. Even with its highest spiritual significance as the king's daily link between this world and the next, each pyramid was allotted to a particular king, who was immediately succeeded by another.

With their polished limestone or granite surfaces, the pyramids stood amid the desert sands, untouchable. In whatever sacred awe the ziggurat was held—however unapproachable it was to the common people—its monumental flights of steps made it accessible, and at the same time ate into the solid mass of its volume. The ziggurat, with its temple or offering place on the topmost platform and, later, a lower temple in the temenos, was the abode of the god. Here, at an annual festival, he was joined for one night by a priestess in sacred marriage (*hierosgamos*), after which the priestess was probably sacrificed.

The ziggurat was part of the organism of the city. Though it stood within a walled inner court with a forecourt, it still belonged to the city and was involved in its life. In its classic period, as at Ur, the most important civic buildings—the palace of the king, the treasury, and the dwelling of the high priestess—all stood in close proximity to the ziggurat.

The ziggurat may be considered older or younger than the pyramid according to the point of view adopted. It was older if one accepts as its starting point the terraces, raised on one or two steps, that formed the base of many temples around 209
3000 B.C.: the germ of its classic form. It was much younger than the pyramid if one considers its independent existence to have begun with its many-stepped form, which appeared around 2000 B.C., during the Third Dynasty of Ur.

Earlier staged towers may have existed. They appear on cylinder seals before this time, but their dimensions in this small scale cannot be calculated, and no actual ones have yet been discovered.

Pierre Amiet has traced the urge toward the vertical (*culte en hauteur*)—deeply rooted in the notion of the ziggurat—back to its origins as a stepped altar (1951, 1953, 1959). The best-known representation is upon the uppermost

120 band of the great alabaster vase from Uruk (Jemdet Nasr period), where a stepped altar is shown accompanied by the emblems of the goddess Inanna. It "could be mounted for the presentation of offerings or for prayer" (1951, p. 85). This illustrates the basic function of the ziggurat: to provide an offering place to the deity. High altars figure frequently upon Early Dynastic cylinder seals. They could be mounted by ladders and perhaps also by steps. They served as landing stages to the "god in his boat" who hovers above them. Upon them he could consummate his sacred marriage with the priestess, by which "he brings to the world the renewal of life in all its forms" (p. 88).

The most rewarding representation of a very early staged tower is upon a seal from the Protoliterate period; it came from Susa, of whose earliest architecture practically nothing remains. This seal shows "the most ancient definite
below image of a temple on a high terrace" (1953, p. 28). A tall structure rises above a high substructure articulated with recessed panels. Before it three prisoners are massacred by the king as an offering to the deity (ibid.). Six large horns project from the towerlike structure, like those that appeared two millenniums later on a relief of Assurbanipal, also from Susa. On the early-third-millennium seal they seem to be an enlarged version of the abstract bulls' heads painted on the mortuary vessels found in fourth-millennium graves as bestowers of strength; these are sometimes shown singly, and sometimes in a chain as on the
454 vessel from Tepe Musyan.

The pyramid was the result of a sudden urge of such passionate intensity that it can almost be said to have arisen overnight. From the mastaba, whose sloping walls were only a few meters high, there was a sudden leap to the

126. FORERUNNER OF THE ZIGGURAT: *Towerlike building on buttressed terrace. From a third-millennium cylinder seal found at Susa, now in the Louvre. Drawing by Amiet*

stepped pyramid of King Zoser (2643–2624 B.C.) at Saqqara, the experimental structure and gradual enlargement of which can be closely traced. 297 ff

Within a few decades after this, the pyramid acquired its standard form, attaining a massivity and magnificence during the Fourth Dynasty, under Sneferu and Cheops, that were never to be achieved again.

The great age of the pyramids covered only a few centuries. With the ziggurat it was quite otherwise. Throughout the existence of the Land of the Two Rivers, the ziggurat remained the central monument of its religious cult. It was held in high esteem in every period: Sumerian, Akkadian, Kassite, Babylonian, Assyrian. Even Alexander the Great, when he entered Babylon, wished to restore the famous ziggurat Etemenanki, the Biblical Tower of Babel, but he died before he could do so.

A final resurgence of ziggurat building took place under his successors, the Seleucid kings. During the height of their power, in the third century B.C., one of them constructed a ziggurat for Anu, god of the heavens, in the age-old religious center of Uruk. The building of this structure followed the traditions of almost two millenniums, and it is to this event that we owe our clearest insight into the ceremonies and significance of the ziggurat (Falkenstein, 1941, pp. 244 ff
27–29).

Both ziggurat and pyramid derive their existence from man's awakened urge toward the vertical as a symbol of contact with the deity, contact with the sky. The ziggurat required more than a millennium to reach its zenith, the limit of its possibilities; the pyramid required only a century.

THE CLASSIC FORM OF THE ZIGGURAT

The form of the ziggurat—a tower composed of a series of stepped terraces with a temple on its summit—held good throughout Mesopotamian history. Its eminence, however, began to diminish after the collapse of the Neo-Babylonian empire in 538 B.C. But ziggurats remained standing for centuries, and the successive foreign rulers of the country prided themselves on their regard for them: the Seleucidae on their erection of new ones and the Parthians on their restoration of old ones.

The customary idea of the ziggurat is based on the Biblical description of the Tower of Babel (Gen. 11:1–9) and on Herodotus' account of his visit to Babylon (Ravn, 1939; tr. 1942). Upon a fifth-century Greek, the strange shape of the Etemenanki ziggurat must have made as deep an impression as its height and the brilliant colors of its seven terraces.

The actual form of the ziggurat was rather different in its early stages in the protohistoric period from its classic development around 2000 B.C., though its series of superimposed, receding steps remained constant.

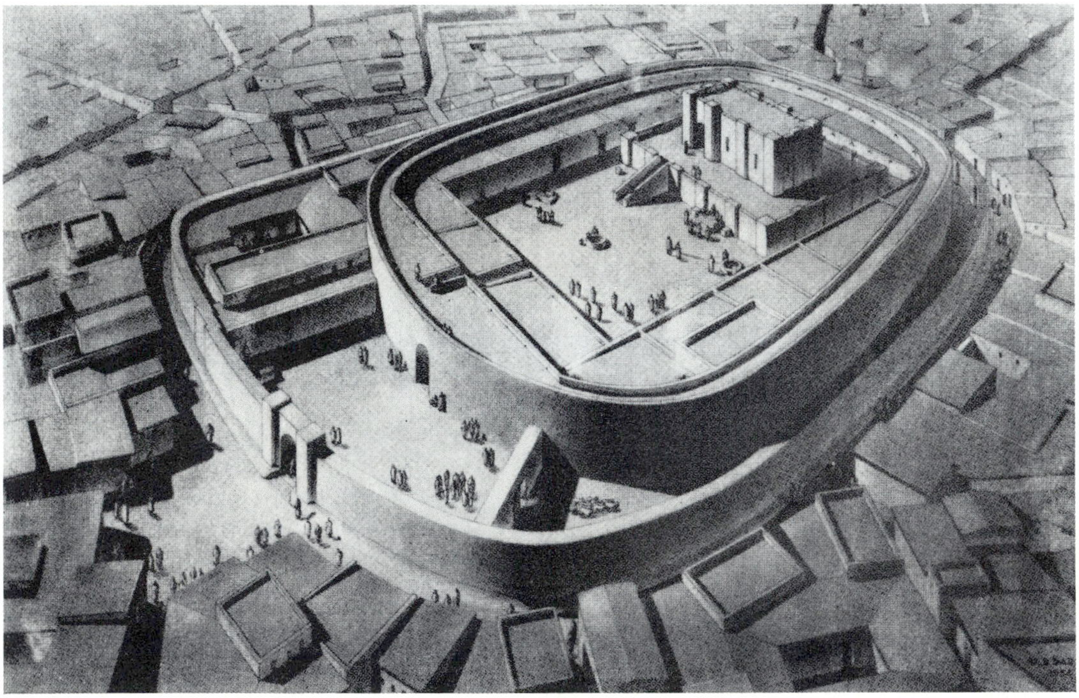

127. THE OVAL TEMPLE, KHAFAJE: *Raising the sanctuary on two terraces creates a certain separation from the surrounding dwelling houses, but it is still closely associated with workshops of the temple community. From Delougaz*

The raised terrace of the Ur I temple of Ninhursag at Al 'Ubaid was six meters high, that of the white temple at Uruk, twelve to thirteen meters from 202 the ground. In the temples of Al 'Uqair and Khafaje there were indications of the 209, left beginnings of a third level. Raising the level of the sanctuaries at these sites tended to separate them from more secular structures, but even in the final version of the temple at Khafaje a certain intimacy between the sanctuary and its surroundings is still discernible.

The oval shape of the terraces of the temple of Khafaje is reminiscent of the earliest architectural development. Delougaz discovered that the temple at Al 'Ubaid stood on a similar oval terrace (1940), so it is possible that these two temples are approximately contemporaneous. The whole of the Khafaje temple structure was surrounded by dwellings, an arrangement not unlike the setting of many large cathedral closes within the residential organisms of medieval cities. The buildings surrounding the oval terraces also served as warehouses for the temple stores.

When the ziggurat achieved its classic form, all this vanished. Supplies needed for the temple community were then housed elsewhere. The chambers along the inner side of the enclosing walls of the courts were, for the most part, offering places—as at Ur and Uruk.

The ziggurat of Ur

The ziggurat of Ur arose in the midst of the highest culture then existing. It was not completely isolated. Even today the ziggurats of Eridu and of Al 'Ubaid are within view from its summit. It stood in an urban and an agricultural landscape, well irrigated by numerous canals: a scene past imagining today, when nothing can be seen on the journey from Eridu to Ur save swarms of locusts clattering against the windows of the car. At that time the Euphrates flowed past the two harbors of the city of Ur. Not far away, it joined the Tigris, and shortly after flowed into the sea near Eridu, which was linked to Ur by a canal. Thus Ur, standing upon the highest strategic point of this level land, was destined to become the capital city of the earliest civilized state.

Its ziggurat was one of the first to attract the attention of archaeologists. As early as 1854, excavations were undertaken by J. E. Taylor, British Consul at Basra, but the great discoveries were made between 1922 and 1934 by Woolley. Beneath the ziggurat he found parts of buildings dating back to a thousand years earlier.

The period of the Third Dynasty of Ur, which saw the classic form of the ziggurat, was the final and most glorious upsurge of Sumer, after a long period of servitude. None of its rulers was more renowned than Urnammu, founder of the dynasty and builder of the ziggurats of Ur, Eridu, Al 'Ubaid, and Nippur. The ziggurat of Ur is by far the best preserved of these today. It must have continued to inspire a holy awe, for even the last king of Babylon, Nabonidus, continued to add to Urnammu's work, burying cylinders recounting his additions in each of the four corners of the uppermost terrace. Even the name of Cyrus the Great is linked with the ziggurat of Ur. Like every religious edifice in Mesopotamia from start to finish, the ziggurat was erected diagonally to the points of the compass, though, as in the case of the temples, the rectangular ground plan (here 200 x 150 ft.) made this orientation somewhat approximate.

right

227

Urnammu had permitted himself what was a great luxury at that early date: he decked the floor of the first terrace with a layer of burned bricks, 2.5 meters thick. Their superb workmanship has held up to the present day, and it is to them that we owe the survival of the original form of this ziggurat.

128. STELE OF URNAMMU: *Detail. King Urnammu* (*2065–2046* B.C.), *the great ziggurat builder of the Third Dynasty of Ur, stands to the right with builders' tools on his shoulder. Before him Nannar, the moon-god, wearing his four-horned crown. Behind him a servant. To the left, fragments of a scene representing the erection of the ziggurat of Ur*

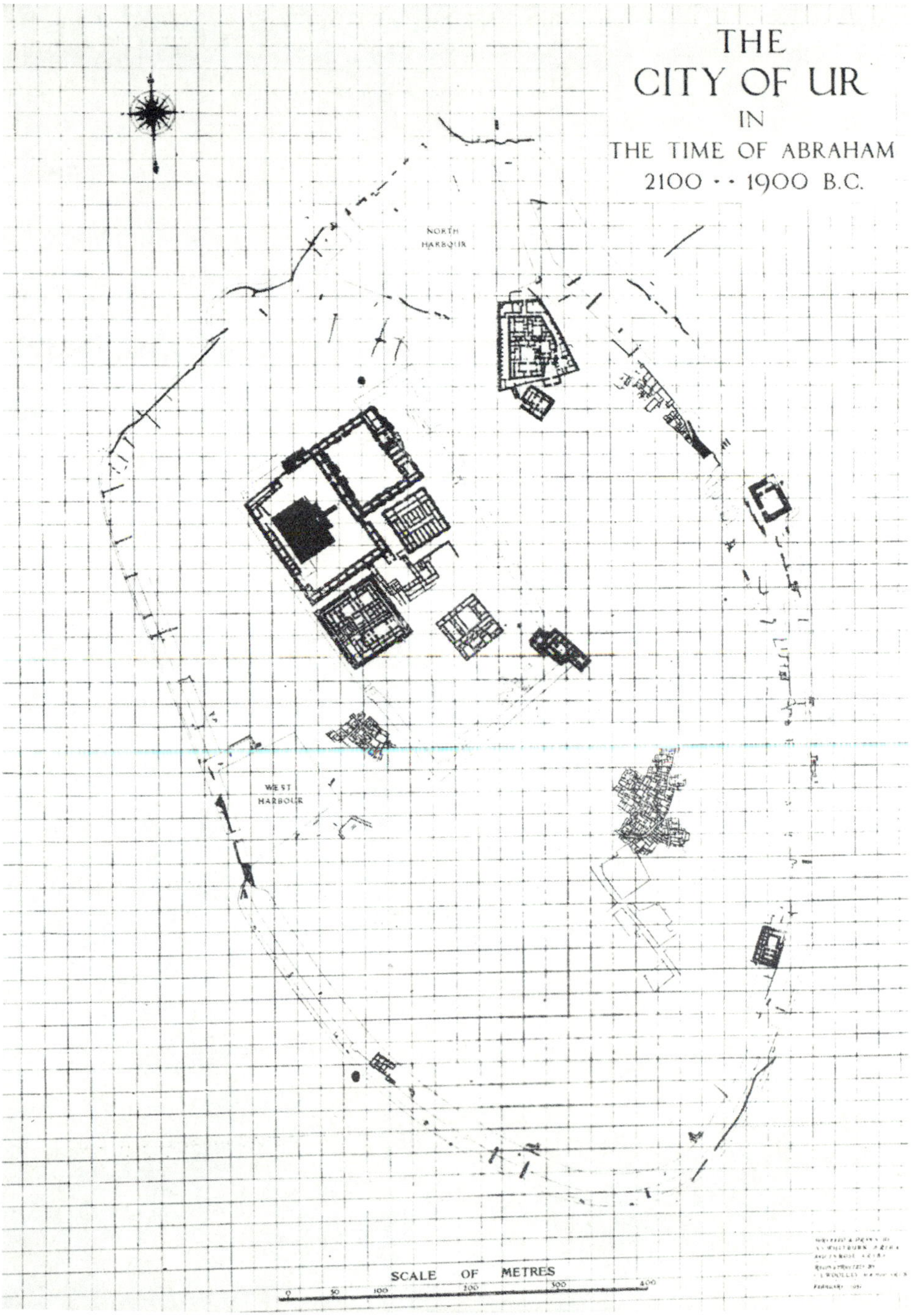

129. MAP OF THIRD DYNASTY UR: *Ziggurat and sacred precinct to the left. The densely built so-called quarter of Abraham to the right. Harbors on the Euphrates to the north and west; ca. 2000* B.C. *From Woolley*

Ziggurats: Stairways of the Gods

According to Sumerian concepts, the city of Ur and its ziggurat belonged to
222 the moon-god Nannar. In the second row of the great stele of Urnammu, the
king is shown as a royal building craftsman, carrying a pickax on his shoulder.
123 Above him sits the moon-god upon his throne, with a long flowing beard and a
four-horned crown—an ax pressed against his side and, in his hand, "an emblem conventionally known as 'the ring and staff' and often interpreted as a symbol of justice. This is probably correct, but on this stele the symbolic objects are recognizable for what they are, namely, a measuring rod and line" (Frankfort, 1954, p. 51).

It is difficult to establish whether the stepped tower of Ur had any direct forerunners or whether, like Zoser's stepped pyramid, it was a sudden creation. In any case it is the first demonstrable structure with three levels. It is also the earliest ziggurat with such wonderfully preserved terraces, niches, and sloping walls. These rose to a height of 15 meters above the court in which the ziggurat stood. A second and a third terrace followed until a total height of 21.33
226 meters was attained.

130. VIEW FROM THE ZIGGURAT OF UR: *Baked bricks on the top of the ziggurat occupy the foreground. Beyond them stretch the buried temples and city of Ur. The dark line on the horizon indicates the limits of the city*

The monumental stairway

The first level, bound up with religious concepts, afforded an opportunity for
the most inspired architectonic invention of Mesopotamia: the monumental
stairway. Flat against the northeast wall, two symmetrically opposed stairways 226
made a dignified descent into the temple court. The main stairway, on the central axis of the ziggurat, jutted far out from the structure and united with the 227
two side stairways on the level of the first terrace, where it was bridged over
with a tower. From this point the central stairway narrowed and led to the
uppermost terrace. This created a tremendous perspective for the priestly
processions. A huge pier buried in the body of the ziggurat supported this flight 228
of stairs.

A small stairway had been used earlier to lead up to the terrace of the temple
at Uruk, and a broader one to the terrace of Temple VII at Eridu. Temple 202
towers with several terraces are shown on early cylinder seals, but no actual ones
have yet been discovered.

At Ur, for the first time, the bridging of a difference in levels—a purely technical expedient—became a constituent element of monumental architecture. The broad central stairway started far off from the body of the ziggurat and its continuation reached the uppermost terrace. The notion of a ladder between heaven and earth was marvelously portrayed. Characteristically, it was not the satisfaction of purely material needs but the desire for a symbolic realization of the link between god and man that gave rise to this new and expressive architectonic form.

A building 21.33 meters high is a very limited goal. But men are obliged to use limited means to project limitlessness, and the desire for eternity—for limitlessness—was manifested here by a limited edifice. Building was a sacred enterprise. It was the medium of union between man and god.

131. LEFT-HAND STAIRWAY *of the ziggurat of Ur*

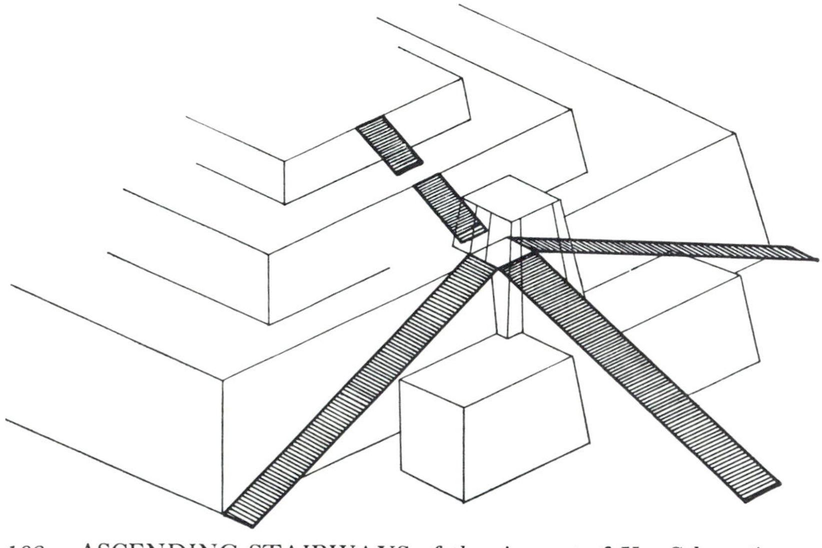

132. ASCENDING STAIRWAYS *of the ziggurat of Ur: Schematic drawing after Lenzen*

133. THE CENTRAL STAIRWAY, *which protrudes boldly from the ziggurat of Ur*

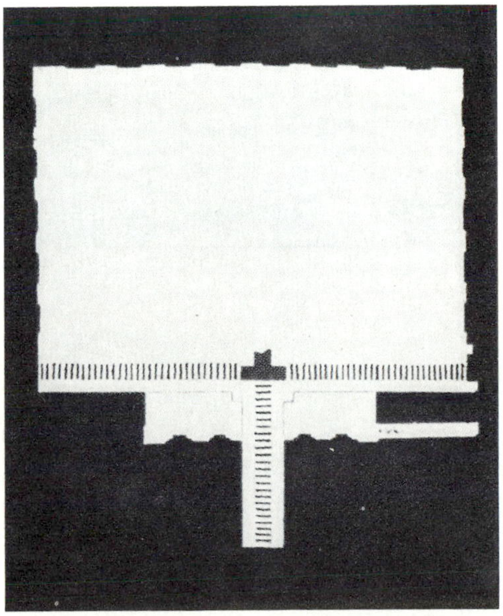

134. SCHEMATIC GROUND PLAN *of the ziggurat of Ur, indicating its compact mass and three-branched stairway*

135. FOOT OF LEFT-HAND STAIRWAY, *showing the baked-brick structure of the ziggurat of Ur*

The ziggurat of Eridu

Eridu, one of the oldest religious centers, was the city of Enki, the friendly god of the deep waters and of wisdom. It lay within sight of both Ur and Al 'Ubaid, amid fertile gardens on the shores of a sea that has since withdrawn some below hundred miles.

The ziggurat of Enki was for centuries one of the religious landmarks of Sumer. It was erected shortly before 2000 B.C. by that same great builder, Urnammu, and his son Shulgi, above the remains of sixteen levels of earlier 230, 231 temples which were excavated in 1946–49 by Lloyd and Safar. They found objects from the graves of a large cemetery which gave insight into the apparently idyllic lives of the population of Al 'Ubaid times: a small clay model of a sailing 230 ship, the earliest known, was found in the grave of a child. Today the ziggurat of Eridu lies again beneath the sands. Remnants of the two lowest stages and 233 some marble steps from the stairway are all that now remains. From the rear it looks like a slope covered with newly fallen snow.

The significance of this ziggurat and the awe in which it was enveloped may be gathered from a hymn recorded many centuries after its erection, in the time of Hammurabi, first king of Babylon. Some passages from a recent German translation indicate the intimate relations of the god Enki with his ziggurat.

136. THE ZIGGURAT OF ERIDU *at the time of its excavation, its buttressed walls visible on the extreme right*

137. ERIDU TEMPLES AND ZIGGURAT: *Photomontage of the various levels excavated, from the ziggurat at the top to the earliest sanctuary on virgin soil*

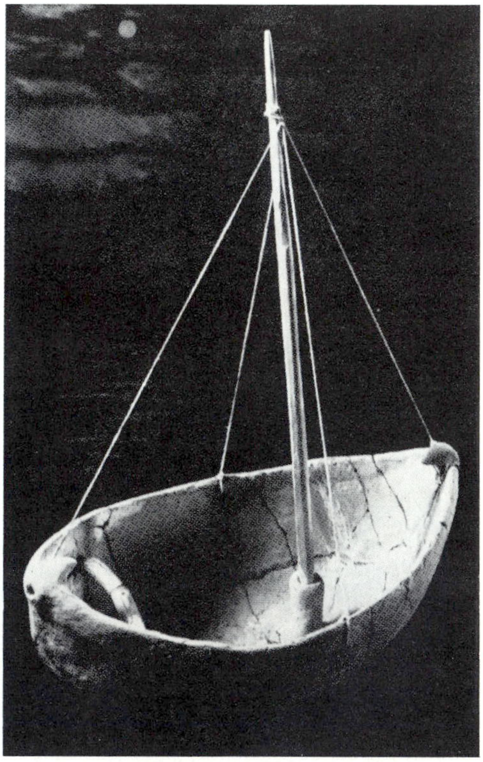

138. PREHISTORIC SAILING SHIP: *The earliest known model. From a child's grave in the Eridu cemetery, Al 'Ubaid period*

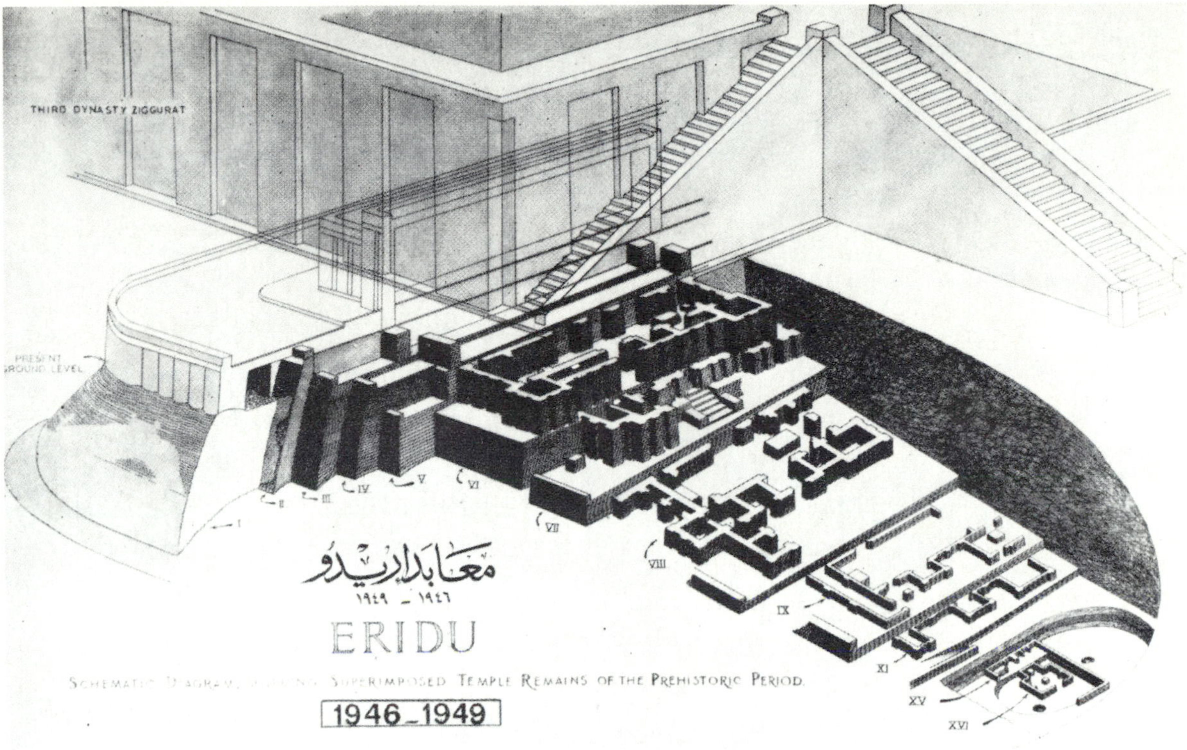

139. ERIDU TEMPLES AND ZIGGURAT: *Drawing of the superimposed levels. The most interesting is Temple VII (see fig. 116)*

In the Eridu Hymn (Falkenstein and Soden, pp. 133–37 *passim*) the god himself designs his temple with his "holy stylus of reed":

Then the Lord of Apsu [the deep waters], the King Enki,
Enki, the lord who determines destiny,
Built his house all of silver and lapis lazuli . . .
He built his house in Eridu on the shore (of the sea).

The structure itself then comes to life and begins to speak. Perhaps this is not merely a poetic fiction, for the Sumerians had gods of the pickax and the brick mold. These were survivals from primeval animism and from totemism.

His brickwork speaks aloud and takes consultation (with its lord),
The summit bellows like a bull.

Then Enki's messenger goes up to the ziggurat and says:

In thee a mighty high place has been founded

Holy heaven is at thy threshold . . .
House built on the rim (of the land), created for
the perfected divine power.

Finally the hymn ends with a banquet to Enlil, the god of heaven and father of Enki, who has invited all the other gods. Enlil says:

Great gods who have come here . . .
My son has built himself a house, the King Enki,
He has made Eridu rise up like a mountain from the earth . . .
He has built his house of silver adorned with lapis lazuli.

The Eridu Hymn, though recorded relatively late, yet has the atmosphere of that early period when the material, the human, and the divine were closely bound together—a period which had far more in common with prehistory than with the outlook of today.

In preparing a dwelling for a divine guest, the first thing to consider was its correct location. The most important problem was not the building itself but the selection of its site. When a completely new temple was to be erected, it was first necessary, throughout the history of Mesopotamia, to discover the wishes of the deities regarding the site. This is expressed symbolically in the Eridu Hymn when the god Enki himself draws the plan with his "holy stylus of reed."

It is for this reason that in places like Eridu, a sequence of temples is found lying one above the other. Each new builder felt reassured of the god's acceptance of this site. Later rulers took the utmost pains to track down the records of earlier foundations, which were engraved on cylinders, prisms, and small cones of baked clay. The last king of Babylon, Nabonidus (555–538 B.C.), dug "eighteen cubits below the floor of the temple of Sippar" (Dhorme, 1949, p. 184) to find the foundation records of the temple builder Naramsin who had reigned seventeen centuries earlier.

140. THE ZIGGURAT OF ERIDU, *present condition: View from the back, taken in 1954*

LATE FORMS OF THE ZIGGURAT

The classic form of the ziggurat developed little further during the periods of Babylonian, Kassite, Assyrian, and finally Neo-Babylonian rule. Indeed, its standard type remained almost unchanged for more than fifteen centuries.

André Parrot has counted thirty-three ziggurats in twenty-three cities (1953; tr. 1955, p. 26), but only two from the lengthy later periods are dealt with here: Aqar Quf, from the time of the Kassites, and the Neo-Babylonian Tower of Babel, Etemenanki.

Outside Mesopotamia, ziggurats continued to be built in increasingly elaborate settings. One of the finest is the ziggurat of Choga Zambil near Susa, built in the thirteenth century B.C., and excavated by R. Ghirshman (*Illustrated London News*, July 13, 1957, p. 76). The sides of its square base measure 350 feet and the outer enclosure was pierced by three gateways, the Royal Gate being guarded by four thirty-foot towers. This led into a vast forecourt containing an avenue of fourteen tables of sacrifice and a large jar for ablutions.

The ziggurat of Aqar Quf

right The temple tower of Aqar Quf (ca. 1400 B.C.), twenty miles northwest of
Baghdad, is one of the few remains of about four hundred years of Kassite
19, 125 domination over Babylon and Sumer. As we mentioned earlier, the Kassites
were warrior tribes from the Zagros Mountains, who swept across the great
plains of Mesopotamia with their horses and war chariots. Little is known of
them. Their strangest relics were sculptured boundary stones—*kudurru*—which
were placed in the temples or out in the fields to keep the land inviolate.

126 A *kudurru* stele from about the fifteenth century B.C., now in the Baghdad Museum, not only displays the usual array of simple divine symbols—sun, moon, and stars—but the space bounded by its rounded top was filled in with pictures of ziggurats and fabulous animals that convey a somewhat gruesome impression despite their artistic charm.

The ziggurat of Aqar Quf was the outstanding monument of Dur Kurigalzu, the newly founded government center named after its builder, Kurigalzu I. The elongated area covered by this city was shaped almost like a boat. Excavations by the Iraq Directorate General of Antiquities in 1942–43 uncovered the approaches to the ziggurat, its stairways and neighboring buildings, including the temple and palace (Baqir, 1944, pp. 5–10).

141. THE ZIGGURAT OF AQAR QUF: *Very steep slope, ca. 1 in 10;* H. *ca. 57 meters. The only great monument remaining from about four centuries of Kassite rule; ca.* 1400 B.C.

This tower is still remarkably well preserved. Seventeenth-century travelers believed it to be the Tower of Babel. Even today, on close approach its height (57 m.), suddenly rising from the desert sands, is impressive. The ground plan is approximately square—69 x 67.6 meters. It is far higher and steeper than the ziggurats of Urnammu, the slope being more than one in ten (9 cm. in 1 m.). Its foundations rest directly upon virgin limestone.

235 The photograph shows the ziggurat from the south. The main approach was by a central stairway with two side stairways. The three niches, which come out so strongly in the photograph, have no connection with the original structure.

We do not know the exact form of the ziggurat of Aqar Quf, despite its imposing height. The astonishing solidity of its structure bears the hallmarks of long experience. "After every eight or nine courses of bricks there is a layer of reed matting, bedded in about 8 cm. of sand and gravel. The reeds are almost unaffected by time and still have a strong tough texture. They have also been used to make great plaited ropes about 10 cm. in diameter, which at short intervals run right through the structure from side to side and act as reinforcement" (ibid., p. 6).

The intervening layers of reeds and holes for the reed ropes are visible in the photograph. In principle this structure does not depart from Sumerian building methods. In Sumer also, the main mass of the tower had been built up from layers of sun-dried bricks and reed matting, with reed ropes used both to drain off water and as a means of reinforcement. The craftsmanship is quite remarkable, and the steepness of the slope most unusual. It reminds one more of the
127 boulderlike Kassite boundary stones than of the quietly consistent rise of the Sumerian ziggurats.

Etemenanki: the "Tower of Babel"

The stepped form of the ziggurat persisted. But the number of stepped terraces, their height, and the lavishness of their adornment increased steadily. They were used for ever more elaborate ceremonies.

The Neo-Babylonian ziggurat Etemenanki may have been the Tower of Babel. Its height is estimated at seventy-five meters by some, by others at even ninety meters. Though this cannot be accurately established, it does give an idea of how height continued to increase during the last phase of Mesopotamian temple development. Etemenanki probably had seven terraces. Upon its highest platform one or more temples were raised. Its adornment was magnificent. The stepped terraces were faced with strongly colored, glazed bricks, each terrace in a different color. Nothing is left of this splendor today but a pond of stagnant water. After Robert Koldewey left in 1917, the inhabitants of the small town of Hilla, nearby, robbed the uncovered surfaces of all remaining bricks. below

The ziggurat continued to be the center of religious life throughout these later periods. Etemenanki stood within an almost square temenos, whose sides measured about four hundred meters. Outside this court stood the temple, Esagila. Both were dedicated to the city's god, Marduk.

The ziggurat was approached by a truly majestic *via sacra*, built for the New Year festival that took place at the autumn equinox. It was probably the longest and most ostentatious processional way that has ever been erected. It spilled over two sides of the walls of the ziggurat's courtyard; passed across the first stone bridge ever laid over the Euphrates River; went through the Ishtar Gate,

142. SITE OF ETEMENANKI (*Tower of Babel*): *Only a pool showing the level of the subsoil water indicates the position of the great ziggurat of Babylon. After Koldewey stopped excavating in 1917, inhabitants of the neighboring town stole every brick from the uncovered walls*

flanked by its massive towers, and ran between the shining glazed bricks of its approach walls, adorned with more than five thousand animals in relief. At this stage the processional way was 12.5 meters above the level of the plain and was paved with white and red marble slabs.

Exaggerated pomp is often a by-product of despotic power, insecurity, and formalism. These ruins give an almost unbearable impression of this. Koldewey's large model of the city stands in the small museum at Babylon, and the eye seeks in vain here, as in the plundered reality outside, for anything that can give rest and satisfaction to sight or mind. What is the value of such a majestic processional way when it stands totally unrelated to anything else, falling away on either side into banality? Even with no knowledge of its imminent end, one could not but sense that uneasy sterility which so often sets in as soon as outward pomp takes the place of inner intensity. Babylon is an early instance of this: perhaps the first.

From 1899 to 1917 Koldewey could only clear the sacred precinct as far as possible and investigate its monuments, for the work of an excavator has seldom been so hampered by mountains of debris. Shafts sunk deep below the ground (Wetzel and Weissbach, 1938, pl. 5)—a tribute to the period that developed underground railways—laboriously groped for the plan of the temple Esagila. But darkness still reigns over most of the city itself, which spreads over several square miles below countless mounds of sand. Wandering among these seemingly endless hillocks covering a buried city of a million or more inhabitants, it is impossible to evade the disturbing reflection that this was the first time that an ever-recurring fate caused an overlarge city to sink into utter oblivion.

BUILDING AS A ROYAL ACTIVITY

We can only grasp the inner content of early architecture if we direct our attention to the significance attributed to building as an activity. In ancient times, building was considered a sacred task calling for the highest levels of human imagination. The holy aura that surrounded it is symbolized by the hymn in 231 f
which Enki, god of the deep waters, himself designed his ziggurat at Eridu. Building linked man with god. Both Gudea of Lagash and Urnammu have testified to this in written and pictorial records.

The clay cylinder seals of the priest-king Gudea reflect great unrest among the Sumerian people. Recent research suggests that the reigns of Gudea and Urnammu partly overlapped. Gudea, deeply disturbed, was seeking the correct location and plan for a temple to the city's god, Ningirsu, son of the storm-god Enlil. This was revealed through dreams in which the god conveyed his wishes to Gudea, who then "bowed his head" and fulfilled the requirements.

A desire for the direct intervention of the god had induced the wish to build. Cylinder seals disclose the immediate cause: "A great drought. The flood waters do not rise." Then follows the promise: "When the foundations of my temple have been laid, the flood will come . . . fertility . . . oil . . . wool . . . from the cracked earth water shall spring" (Scharff and Moortgat, 1950, p. 278).

The numerous diorite and alabaster statues of Gudea are among the loveliest products of Neo-Sumerian sculpture. The largest of them, now in the Louvre, 114
shows the priest-king as a temple builder; he is seated, with the temple plan, a stylus, and a ruler upon his knees.

Urnammu, the great builder of ziggurats, was also a social and moral reformer. He framed what Kramer, who deciphered it, has called "the oldest law code as yet known to man" (1956, p. 49). We say "as yet," for the three hundred famous laws of Hammurabi of Babylon, on the Louvre stele, have twice in recent years been superseded by more ancient codes. Urnammu's fragmentarily known laws give, however, a side light on the growing humanity of Neo-Sumer. They are "of very special importance for the history of man's social and spiritual growth. For they show that, even before 2000 B.C., the law of 'eye for eye' and 'tooth for tooth' . . . had already given way to the far more humane approach in which a money fine was substituted as a punishment" (p. 50). This human background affords a glimpse of the spirit of the period that produced the classic form of the ziggurat.

Ziggurats: Stairways of the Gods

The stele of Urnammu was found in the forecourt of the ziggurat of Ur, its fragments scattered over the pavement of the courtyard. Although many pieces are still missing, what remains sets forth the greatest concern of this last period of Sumer: the actual building of the ziggurat of Ur. At the summit of the stele
123 are the all-powerful gods in the form of the major constellations, with the anthropomorphic moon-god seated upon his throne. In what remains of the
222 second row one can make out two figures, the king, with builders' tools on his shoulder, and a companion.

The belief that the royal builder, the man who stood in closest relationship to the gods, should work with his own hands upon the building, persisted to the end of Mesopotamian history. E. Dhorme cites the texts of Nabopolassar, one of the Neo-Babylonian monarchs: "For my lord Marduk, for him, I bowed down my neck, I kilted up the garment which clothes my royalty, I carried bricks and clay upon my head" (1949, p. 187).

THE SIGNIFICANCE OF THE ZIGGURAT

Opinion varies as to the meaning of the ziggurat. The theory that ziggurats were erected over the graves of kings or gods has been abandoned (Etemenanki was at one time regarded as the grave of Marduk). This idea was derived from Greek and Roman sources.

Andrae, the brilliant excavator of Assur, described the ziggurats as "earth mounds, which the earliest inhabitants of this marshy plain, threaded with arms of the river, erected as dwelling places both for god and man to protect them from the dangers of inundation" (Lenzen, 1942, p. 3). This rational explanation is easily understandable; the actual facts were only realized later, after excavations at Uruk, Tepe Gawra, Eridu, and elsewhere. In the protohistoric Al 'Ubaid period and in the following Early Dynastic period, temples were built
upon "high terraces," as Lenzen called them, above the accumulated ruins of 231
earlier temples, as in Eridu.

As a result of his experience as an excavator at Uruk, Lenzen does not consider the ziggurats to be towers. Instead he speaks of them as "high terraces" or "stepped terraces" (pp. 51–55). He had tunneled into the Anu ziggurat of Uruk from all four sides and had discovered signs in the archaic levels that earlier buildings had already been covered over before Urnammu raised his fourteen-meter-high ziggurat above them (pl. 10).

Ziggurat and sacrifice

The significance of the ziggurat is closely bound up with ritual sacrifices. In the Jemdet Nasr period, long before ziggurats were built, high altars were places of
sacrifice. An early-third-millennium cylinder seal from Susa is the first known 218
representation of a thronelike sanctuary upon a raised terrace where a sacrifice is undeniably depicted. A bearded priest-king, ruler of Susa, shoots three men with arrows from his curved bow (Amiet, 1953, p. 28); they are prisoners who would be offered to the deity along with captured booty. Offerings also played an important part in Egyptian religion, but there their greatest role was to provide nourishment for the dead or for the gods.

Royal statues—including those of Gudea—were not self-glorifications, like 114
statues of Roman emperors: they were personal intercessors who stood in the temple, within sight of the god, to plead for the king's longer life. The sacrifices
so profusely offered in Mesopotamia were concerned with the welfare of the 245

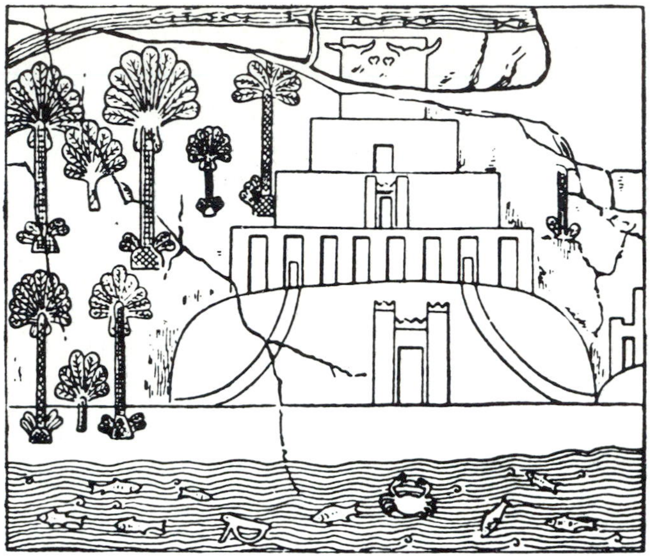

143. REPRESENTATION OF A ZIGGURAT: *Assyrian relief found at Nineveh. Seventh century* B.C. *From Parrot*

living, not the dead. This was true even in the early periods. The most beautiful vessels made in Al 'Ubaid times were libation vases—the so-called tortoise vases. Each was formed from two shallow dishes placed one over the other, with a long and elegant spout ending in a flattened disk that ensured a ceremonious outpouring of the liquid.

right

Drink offerings appear again and again on seals and reliefs. On a limestone plaque from Ur naked priests pour libations before the moon-god Nannar and onto an altar. The great temple complexes offer many indications of the unusual significance of sacrifices and offerings in Sumer. They include burnt offerings—for the prolongation of earthly life, not for the benefit of those already in the nether world.

right

In Uruk no sign of a temple was found in the archaic strata around the Anu ziggurat: "Instead, another remarkable phenomenon appeared. In this early Jemdet Nasr period, places of sacrifice appeared in three locations which were connected to one another by long tracts" (Lenzen, 1942, p. 12). These places of sacrifice were examined and recorded in stratum after stratum (pls. 4–9). They were ranged one after the other, in the form of long troughs. Later these were grouped within a series of rectangular cells in which the burnt offerings were

144. LIBATION VASE FROM ERIDU: *These "tortoise" vases are among the finest ceramics of the period. Small white dots are painted upon them, and, above the spout, a white triangle—a fertility symbol going back to the oldest prehistoric traditions. Al 'Ubaid period, fourth millennium*

145. LIMESTONE PLAQUE FROM UR *with central perforation: Used as a stand for a votive object. Upper register: a naked priest pours a libation before the seated moon-god Nannar. Lower register: a naked priest pours a libation onto an altar before a temple or ziggurat*

made. They were so numerous that the whole place looks almost like a slaughter yard. At Ur, chambers full of wood ash were found in the court of the ziggurat. At first these were taken to be "temple kitchens." Since then opinion has inclined to the belief that they were the sites of burnt offerings. This sacrificial impulse is also expressed in the form of the ziggurat. It soars up against the sky line, a gigantic sacrificial altar. It is by no means certain that temples stood upon each of the terraces. Lenzen, for example, found no traces of them in so sacred a site as the Anu ziggurat in Uruk.

The ziggurat is depicted as a high altar in a frequently reproduced Assyrian
242 relief from the seventh century B.C., part of which is in the British Museum and part in the Louvre. It represents a near-classic form of ziggurat with four steps. The topmost step has a pair of horns at each of its four corners. "This latter detail is of the greatest importance, for not only does it confer an undeniably religious character upon the monument, but in fact likens it to a giant altar. It is known that altars were actually provided at the four corners with horns, one of the uses of which was to assure complete sanctuary to any who laid hold on them" (Parrot, 1953; tr. 1955, pp. 33–34). And Dhorme remarks: "In this last detail . . . the ziggurat comes near to the horned altars whose function we know not only in Israel but also in Mycenae and Crete. Thus the ziggurat could be considered as a high place where sacrifices might, from time to time, be performed" (1949, p. 179).

No accounts exist of the rituals from the Sumerian period to the end of Mesopotamian history. It is only from a Seleucid text (Uruk) that we can gain some insight into the conduct of a sacrifice upon a ziggurat. The text, which deals with the Anu ziggurat in Uruk and is translated by Falkenstein, states: "In the first night watch, on the roof of the high temple of the ziggurat . . . when (the star of) the great Anu of heaven comes out," a feast was laid out upon a golden table for Anu and Antum (his wife) as well as for the seven planets, and most exact instructions were given for this entertainment of the god of the ziggurat: the flesh of cattle, sheep, and birds, beer of the first quality, and "outpressed wine poured from a golden ewer," as well as every kind of fruit, also honey and aromatic spices, "spread on the seven golden incense burners." How far this account is also true for the earlier period is unfortunately not known (1941, p. 29).

Mesopotamian rituals endured for long periods, and it is unlikely that new rites would be invented in the last throes of a declining culture. Parrot has thus assumed, with full justification, that the Seleucid rituals "are almost certainly connected with beliefs of immensely greater antiquity" (1953; tr. 1955, p. 62).

Slowly attention has been drawn to the symbolic meaning of the ziggurat. Falkenstein, who deciphered the earliest clay tablets from Uruk, believes no too narrow or too simple explanation should be accepted, since "we still have far too little information on the cult significance of the ziggurats" (1941, p. 28).

The names borne by different ziggurats—"House of the Mountain, Mountain of the Storm, Bond between Heaven and Earth" (Frankfort, 1954, p.6)—imply that they created a link between heaven and earth.

During the Assyrian and Babylonian empires, their relation with cosmic symbolism came to the fore. The seven terraces of Etemenanki, each of a different color, were supposed to relate to the spheres of the seven planets. But these possible astrological indications have, in fact, little connection with the original significance of the ziggurat.

Frankfort relates the idea of the ziggurat with the idea of the sacred "mountain" which, wherever it arose, betokened the center of the world. "The signifi-

146. VOTIVE BRONZE: *Modeled offering scene before a ziggurat. From Elam*

cance of the ziggurat was symbolical, and the symbolism could be expressed in more than one way. The same idea, which was unequivocally expressed in a high artificial mountain, could also be rendered by a mere platform a few feet high," and the earliest temple platforms "already represented the sacred 'mountain' " (ibid., p. 7).

To take a stand upon one single meaning of the ziggurat is to be quite out of tune with the mentality of the period. A number of ideas are woven into the phenomenon: the rock as the first thing to emerge from primeval chaos; the mountain, which, wherever it arose, represented the center of the universe; the earthly throne of the god; and—what seems to come closest to the Sumerian outlook on life—the ziggurat as a monumental site for the offering of sacrifices.

Just as most of the symbols of prehistory circled around the idea of fertility, most of the concepts of the Sumerian culture and its successors circled around the idea of sacrifice.

I. THE FIRST CAPITAL IN STONE: *Papyrus column from northern building of the Zoser complex. Saqqara* (*cf. p. 287*)

II. THE ONLY ENTRANCE *to the Zoser complex* (*cf. p. 278*)

III. ENTRANCE TO THE ZOSER COMPLEX *seen from the processional passageway (cf. p. 282)*

IV. COLONNADED PROCESSIONAL HALL: *View toward the great court. Zoser complex* (*cf. p. 282*)

v. GREAT COURT *with Temple T in the foreground. Zoser complex* (*cf. p. 283*)

VI. HEB-SED COURT *with its chapels. Zoser complex* (*cf. p.* 284)

VII. THE BENT PYRAMID OF SNEFERU. *Dahshur* (*cf. pp.* 306 *ff.*)

VIII. CASING OF THE BENT PYRAMID (*cf. p.* 312)

IX. THE FIRST TRUE PYRAMID: *Sneferu's third pyramid; his bent pyramid in the background. Dahshur (cf. pp. 309, 311 f.)*

x. CHEPHREN'S VALLEY TEMPLE: *Interior view from the entrance. Giza* (*cf. pp. 325 f.*)

XI. PYRAMID AT EVENING: *Chephren's pyramid, Giza* (*cf.* *p. 505*)

XII. PYRAMID AT MIDDAY: *Cheops' pyramid, Giza (cf. p. 315)*

XIII. THE GREAT HYPOSTYLE HALL *seen from the west. Karnak* (*cf. p. 385*)

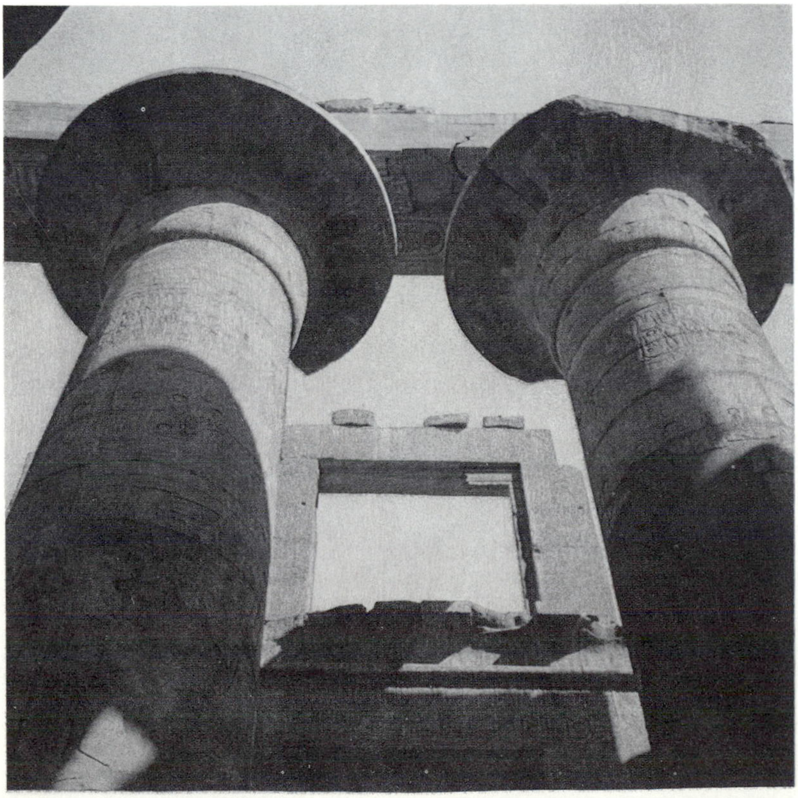

XIV. ROOF SLAB *with four small holes for letting in daylight. The great hypostyle hall, Karnak (cf. p. 391)*

XV. WINDOW OF CLERESTORY *without its stone grille. The great hypostyle hall, Karnak (cf. p. 391)*

XVI. STRUCTURAL MEMBERS OF THE FESTIVAL HALL *of Tuthmosis III. Karnak* (*cf. p. 372*)

XVII. VAULTING OF THE HATHOR CHAPEL *in Hatshepsut's mortuary temple. Deir el Bahari* (*cf. p.* 427)

XVIII. HATSHEPSUT'S MORTUARY TEMPLE *with its terraces* (*cf. p. 425*)

PART VII BEGINNINGS OF STONE ARCHITECTURE AND THE KA: EGYPT

THE EGYPTIAN RELATION TO STONE

One of the greatest achievements of Egyptian civilization was to sever stone from the rock and to make of it a building material unsurpassed to this day. The choice of this unyielding material, which demanded great labor and high skill to give it the desired form, was directly based upon Egyptian religious convictions.

A longing for an eternal material was always present in the inner feelings of the Egyptians, and the use of stone went far back into their prehistory, i.e., the Predynastic period. Stone vessels—jars, bowls, vases of the hardest rock, such as basalt, porphyrite, and diorite—have been found in prehistoric graves and had already reached their highest perfection in the First Dynasty. In a queen's tomb at Saqqara, Emery found in 1955 three transparent dishes of rock crystal, six to eight inches across, one of them less than two millimeters thick (1956, fig. 7).

Stone, the least perishable material, was at first reserved for the dead. Its use was long denied the living. Its enduring qualities made it the ideal substance from which to build resting places for the dead, and it was the grave that gave birth to the first stone architecture. Its early development was a long process, continuing throughout the early dynasties. Then, like a bolt from the blue, a radiant stone architecture suddenly appears full-fledged, at the beginning of the Third Dynasty, in Zoser's mortuary complex at Saqqara.

Preludes in clay: the mastabas of north Saqqara

Saqqara lies a short hour's drive south of Cairo. At no other place in Egypt, throughout the millenniums, have so many dead found their resting place as here in the immediate vicinity of the ancient capital, Memphis. That city long ago vanished beneath cultivated fields. Of its appearance, its temples and palaces, even its extent, only the vaguest notions exist. The unburned bricks of which it was built have crumbled into dust.

All that remains is the necropolis on the desert rim: Saqqara. Everywhere, one is aware of the millenniums. Potsherds from every dynasty lie on the crests of wavelike dunes, many as yet unexcavated. One comes across human bones, whitened and reduced to a brittle shell, that crumble like incandescent lamp filaments when picked up. Dominating the view of the rugged desert plateau to the south is the silhouette of the step pyramid of King Zoser. It marked the dawn of the pyramid age. At the far end of the necropolis, in north Saqqara, there is a long row of great mastabas of First Dynasty kings or high officials.

Reisner opens his monumental *Development of the Egyptian Tomb Down to the Accession of Cheops* by pointing out that from its very beginning the Egyptian tomb had a twofold function: it was both a burial place and an offering place (1936, p. 1).

Up to the Late Predynastic period, Egyptian tombs were simply shallow circular or oval holes or pits, in which the dead were buried in a contracted position, just as they had been during the long prehistoric ages. "Side by side with these open-pit graves, in the same cemetery . . . occurs the earliest improved type of Egyptian grave, the open pit lined with c.b. [clay brick] and roofed with wood and c.b." (p. 5). Then, like the houses, these graves gradually became rectangular. They also became deeper, larger, and subdivided, until quite an elaborate substructure had come into being.

To this substructure under the earth was added a superstructure above the earth. Its form differed in Upper and Lower Egypt. Herbert Ricke explains this difference as an outcome of two different ways of life. In the fertile delta area of the north (Lower Egypt), the early farmers lived in small settlements (Faiyum, Merimdeh). Their dead were buried beneath the floors of the dwellings, or their tombs were modeled after the houses of the living. In the south (Upper Egypt), lived wandering herdsmen who buried their dead in the gravel, building above them a small cairn or tumulus.

W. S. Smith comments on this contrast "drawn between the nomads of the south, with their tentlike dwellings and grave mounds, and the settled inhabitants of the north, who built in brick and copied their houses for their tombs. This does not seem to allow sufficiently for the possibilities of development in the villages and towns of the agricultural communities, which must long have outnumbered any nomad elements up and down the Nile Valley" (1958, p. 24). But throughout Egyptian history, earliest habits are ineradicable, and there seems little doubt that in essence Ricke's hypothesis is closely related to the Egyptian habit of mind.

The superstructure in the north gradually acquired a low, flat-topped form with sloping, paneled walls: the mastaba (Arabic for "bench").

The introduction of stone as a building material can be followed in the tombs of the First and Second Dynasty necropolises of Abydos, Helwan, Saqqara.

Among more than a thousand graves in the cemetery of Helwan were some in which the wooden posts and walls of sun-dried brick had been partially re-

147. WALL IN ZOSER'S SUBTERRANEAN CHAMBER: *The blue faïence tiles are designed to imitate reed matting. The hieroglyphic djeds in the shallow arch symbolize eternal duration. Saqqara. From Firth and Quibell*

placed by stone slabs. Helwan had no royal graves. It was a cemetery for lesser people.

In a mastaba on the escarpment of north Saqqara, heavy stone portcullis blocks were found at the foot of the descending passage, protecting the dead from intruders. There were two portcullises, one behind the other.

270

The great mastabas of the kings of the First Dynasty were uncovered on the opposite side of the Nile, at Saqqara, by Emery, starting in 1935. (There had been earlier excavations, but circumstances did not permit them to be completed.) The mastabas lie at the northern limit of this huge necropolis, which

148. RELIEF IN ZOSER'S SUBTERRANEAN CHAMBER: *King Zoser running his ceremonial race. Saqqara. From Lange and Hirmer*

stretched south even beyond the pyramid and mortuary complex of King Zoser. Emery's careful and meticulous classifications have given us new insight into the different periods of the First Dynasty. Many gaps have been filled and many questions answered. Many others still remain to be solved.

The proud row of royal graves provided an unexpected view of the early development of the mastaba. Emery's three volumes, richly illustrated with excellent axonometric drawings, present a wealth of information that we shall only summarize here.

The type of the mastaba always remained the same, but the tomb became progressively larger and more elaborate. The superstructure was built of sun-
272 dried bricks, with panels and buttresses in the form known as a palace façade. In Tomb 3503 this was faced "with mud plaster covered with a white gypsum

149. RELIEF OF HEB-SED FESTIVAL *of King Sesostris III on lintel: A high point of the festival was the new coronation of the king on the thrones of Upper Egypt (right) and Lower Egypt (left). Middle Kingdom*

stucco" (1954, II, p. 129). These white buttressed niches were an embryonic form of the huge limestone enclosure wall with which King Zoser surrounded 248 col, 274 his mortuary precinct.

The outer walls that encircled the mastabas were plain—devoid of articula- 272 tion. Outside them lay subsidiary burials of servants sacrificed to serve the king 271 in his afterlife. The grave of Queen Meryet-nit (Tomb 3503) was surrounded by twenty-two subsidiary burials. "This barbaric custom did not survive in the burial customs of the Second Dynasty" (1958, III, p. 98). Barbaric as it was, it was never carried out on the scale of the death-pit of Queen Shubad at Ur some centuries later. Beyond these burials, in several instances, remnants were found 272 of a solar bark.

The substructure was increasingly subdivided, finally including nearly fifty chambers and magazines—a custom still preserved in the subterranean quarters of Zoser's tombs. A photograph of a mastaba from the reign of Wedymu (Tomb 273 3506) shows the central rock-cut pit of the substructure and a stone doorway at the foot of a flight of stairs descending from ground level to the pit. The buttressed inner walls of the superstructure are also apparent.

Though their inner structure changed, these mastabas never altered their general form. But one of the inexplicable leaps of the human imagination occurred at the beginning of the Third Dynasty, when the great genius of Imhotep inspired him to raise a large vertical structure and to use stone as the building material.

Imhotep the builder

A half-mythical yet historic figure hovers over the birth of stone architecture: Imhotep. Two millenniums after his death, he was raised to the stature of a god of healing. While he was alive, Zoser entrusted to him the highest office of the land. He was grand vizier, also " 'chief judge,' 'overseer of the King's records,' 'bearer of the royal seal,' 'chief of all works of the King,' 'supervisor of that which Heaven brings, the Earth creates and the Nile brings,' 'supervisor of everything in this entire land' " (Hurry, 1928, pp. 6–7). Imhotep's universality, scarcely conceivable for later periods, could only occur in the early stages of a high civilization, when everything had first to be invented, then organized.

Though his existence had not been doubted, the first direct proof of it from his own period came to light in 1925–26, when the Zoser complex was slowly freed from sand and rubble. Near the step pyramid, Firth discovered remnants

150. STONE PORTCULLISES *at entrance to mastaba tomb: Two heavy granite portcullises at the foot of the stairway leading from ground level guard the entrance to the substructure of Tomb 3500 in north Saqqara. First Dynasty*

of a statue of King Zoser on the base of which beautifully executed hieroglyphs give a direct account of Imhotep's existence. "This begins with a series of titles, followed by the name of their holder, one Imhotep . . . The Chancellor of the King of Lower Egypt, Chief under the King (of Upper Egypt?), Administrator of the Great Mansion, Hereditary Noble, Heliopolitan High Priest, Imhotep" (Gunn, 1926, p. 192).

This points up Imhotep's rare combination of powers as organizer, statesman, and creative spirit. In addition, as the inscription states, he was high priest of Heliopolis. We do not know whether the title of high priest existed before the Third Dynasty, but the first recorded mention "so far known seems to be that on the famous fragment of the statue of Djoser from the Step Pyramid" (Baumgärtel, 1955, p. 8).

Priestcraft, magical healing, and medicine were closely interrelated in ancient

151. MODELED WALLS OF A MASTABA: *The superstructure of the tomb is bounded by carefully molded and recessed brick paneling like that developed in Mesopotamia. Tomb 3503, north Saqqara, First Dynasty*

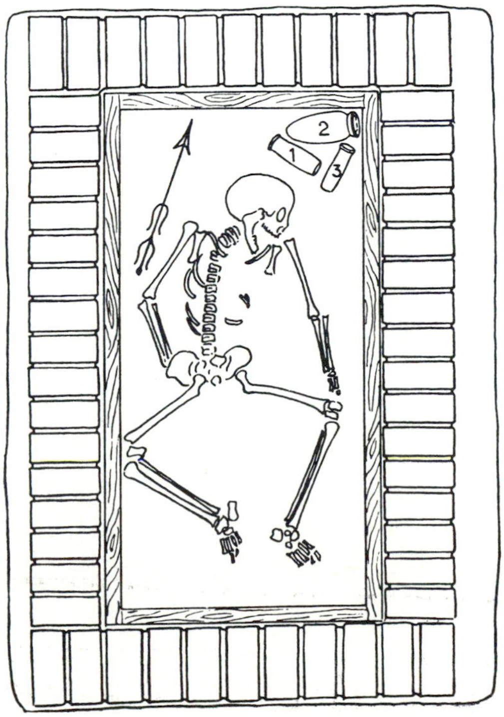

152. SUBSIDIARY BURIAL *with sacrificed retainer: Tomb 3506, north Saqqara. First Dynasty. From Emery*

153. MASTABA AND SUBSIDIARY GRAVES: *View of the modeled walls of Tomb 3506 (65 x 25 m.), showing subsidiary graves in the foreground*

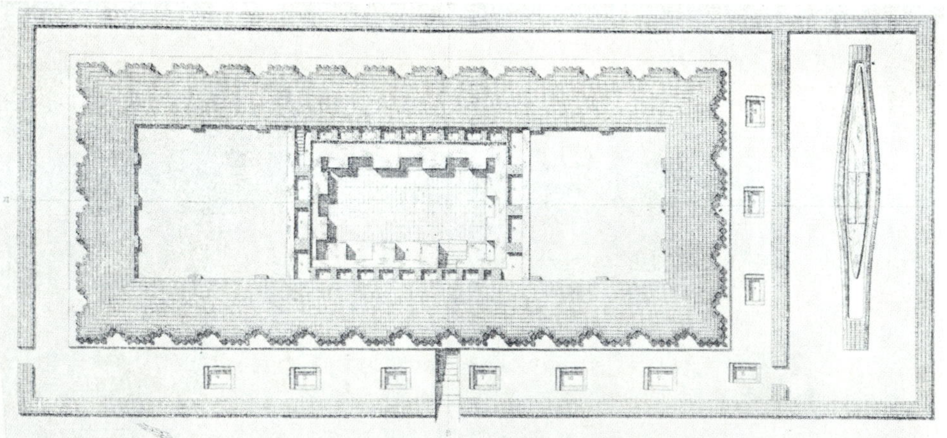

154. GROUND PLAN OF MASTABA: *Ground plan of Tomb 3506 with ten subsidiary tombs and a boat grave all within the same walled enclosure. The descending central stairs lead to a stone doorway. From Emery*

155. SUBSTRUCTURE OF MASTABA: *The stone doorposts and lintel of Tomb 3506 from within the substructure*

156. SECTIONS OF VAULTED SUBSIDIARY GRAVE: *Drawings of one of the subsidiary graves of Tomb 3500. From Emery*

Egypt; all three contained the same basic elements. This is a relic of prehistoric culture.

The Greeks made demigods of warrior heroes, the Egyptians of men of wisdom. Imhotep's reputation as a magical healer was far greater and more enduring than his reputation as organizer, statesman, or architect. In the Old Kingdom, not long after his death, he was revered as a demigod of magical healing and medicine. Statuettes of him in many museums show him without the insignia of a god: "The demigod stage appears to have lasted from the reign of Mycerinus until the beginning of the Persian period" (Hurry, 1928, p. 56)—more than two millenniums. Finally, in the late Saite period, when there was a renaissance of Old Kingdom cults and arts, Imhotep was raised to the rank of god of medicine, or, more accurately, of the magical arts of healing. As such, he was one of a triad that included Ptah, the Memphite god of creation, and Ptah's lioness-headed wife Sekhmet, a fertility-goddess.

Imhotep's title as god of medicine must be employed with care, for, as Maspero cautioned long ago, "it is in virtue of his powers as a magician that Imhotep was deified" (Hurry, 1928, pp. 69–70, quoting Maspero)—in virtue, that is, of his art of magic as therapy.

Our only tangible record of Imhotep is his architecture. A tradition as long-lived as that of his powers of magical healing credits him as architect of Zoser's mortuary complex. First confirmation of it was the inscription found by Firth. Second is an inscription found in the Wady Hammamat, a valley on the caravan route from Coptos to the Red Sea, which lists twenty-five generations of architects, going back to Imhotep, the son of Kanofer, " 'chief of works of the South- and of the Northland' " (ibid., p. 193).

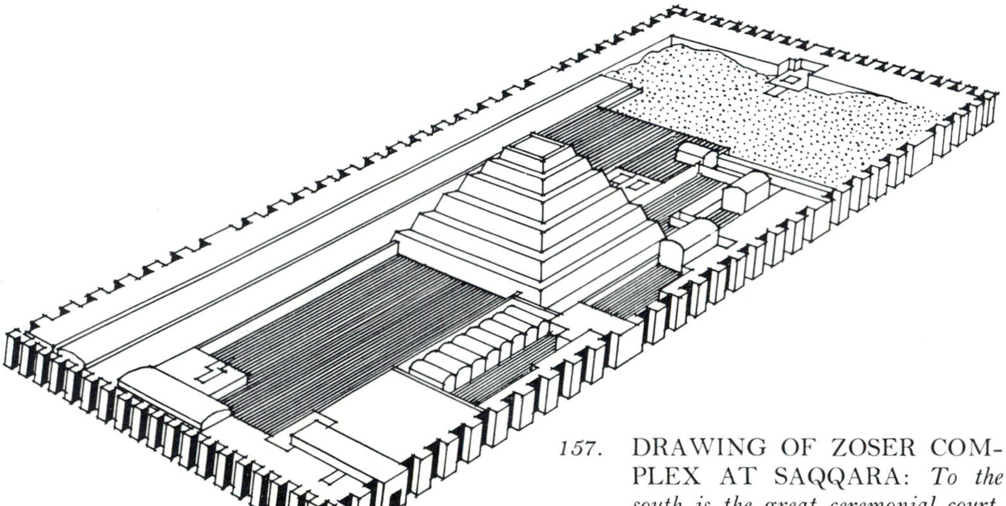

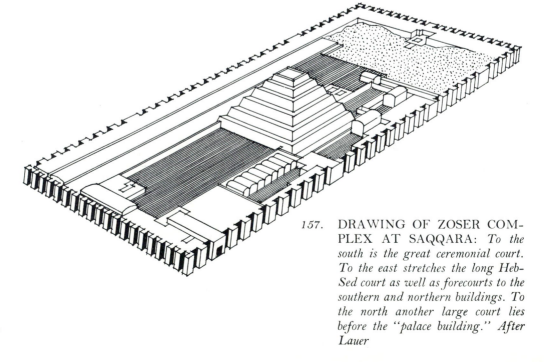

157. DRAWING OF ZOSER COMPLEX AT SAQQARA: *To the south is the great ceremonial court. To the east stretches the long Heb-Sed court as well as forecourts to the southern and northern buildings. To the north another large court lies before the "palace building." After Lauer*

IN THE SHADOW OF THE KA

The beginning of stone architecture is inseparably bound up with the concept of the Ka, and it was for the Ka of the founder of the Third Dynasty, King Zoser, that stone architecture first came into being.

The Ka, as we have seen, is a kind of vital force emanating from the god to his son the king. The king was the only earthly possessor of this cosmic and divine force, but he could dispense it to his subjects. The desire for an eternal continuation of earthly existence found its expression in stone architecture, for only stone could provide an indestructible container for the Ka. The Ka hieroglyph, two vertically upstretched arms, is closely related to the prehistoric 90
gesture of bestowing force, and one of the spells in the Pyramid Texts reads: "Atum, so put thine arms . . . about this pyramid, as the arm(s) of a *ka*, that the *ka* of N. [the king] may be in it, enduring for ever and ever" (Utterance 600; tr. Mercer, 1952, I, p. 253).

King Zoser's mortuary complex at Saqqara gravitates about the step pyramid —the first of all the pyramids—which we will discuss in Part VII. Surrounding the pyramid is a vast walled enclosure within which are shrines, altars, courts, gateways, storehouses, tombs, etc. It was the king's Ka who resided in the subterranean palace chambers, who issued his orders in the government building, ran his ceremonial race in the large court at the time of his jubilee festival, wandered through the entire precinct, closing behind him the ever-open carved stone doors leading to chapels and other buildings, and departed on journeys through the many dummy doors in the high enclosure wall.

Zoser had two tombs within the complex. His mummy was deposited in the one below his step pyramid. The other, attached to the south enclosure wall, was only discovered in 1928 by Firth and Lauer. At the end of small passages hewn deep down into the rock, a totally unexpected marvel came to light: the low walls were covered with small blue tiles, each of them convex and scarcely larger than a brooch. Their glaze is still brilliant as a butterfly's wing. Mrs. Firth's watercolors of the chambers of Zoser's southern tomb give a vivid im- 266
pression of the sudden surprise of this scene amid eternal darkness. The tiles represent reed matting set in wooden frames here represented by stone posts carved to resemble wood. Surmounting them are shallow arches filled with a row of *djeds*—the hieroglyphs for eternal duration. Between the tile sections are some of the loveliest reliefs of the Old Kingdom. They show Zoser running his 267
ceremonial race, and include his titles in beautifully carved hieroglyphs.

We are here in the intimate domicile of the Ka: bedchamber, reception room, and nearby—still in miniature, but large enough to be accessible—storage chambers for all his personal needs.

Entrance to the two groups of almost identically equipped tomb chambers is exceedingly complicated. Those below the pyramid had been discovered in 1842 by Karl R. Lepsius, and parts of them sent to the Berlin Museum. Whether the duplication of these tombs was due to the separation of the burial of the king we are not certain. As ruler of Lower Egypt, his body was buried below the pyramid to the north, but the canopic vases containing his entrails were placed in the southern tomb as a symbol of his domination over Upper Egypt.

The Heb-Sed festival for the Ka

Why did the Ka need so large a complex? Because the creative vital force from time to time needed regeneration. The strength of the king, like that of nature itself, needed periodic renewal. This was effected at the Heb-Sed festival, at the jubilee of the king's reign. We do not know the exact intervals at which the jubilee recurred. Normally it was thirty years, or the span of a generation. "It has been supposed, with some reason, that the royal power was originally granted only for thirty years, after which the king would be deposed and perhaps also killed" (Drioton and Vandier, 1938, p. 147). This was to spare the land from declining because of his sinking vitality (Spiegel, 1953, p. 138, par. 209).

Just as the Ka cannot be likened to our concept of the soul, so the Heb-Sed festival cannot be compared with a contemporary royal jubilee. "It was not a mere commemoration of the king's accession. It was a true renewal of kingly potency" (Frankfort, 1948, p. 79). It was not confined to the person of the king, but was also "a renewal of all those beneficial relations between heaven and earth which the throne controls" (ibid.).

This required time. The festival lasted for five days filled with highly complex ceremonies. The king, seated first upon the throne of Upper Egypt and then upon the throne of Lower Egypt, received declarations of loyalty and gifts from the provinces. The thrones, surmounted by a double baldachin, stood back to back upon a platform approached at either end by several steps. The form of the vaulted awning had existed in the early part of the First Dynasty, and had undergone few changes since (Badawy, 1954, p. 66).

268, 374

During the second part of the ceremonies the king became active. It was necessary for him to display his physical powers. In a special pavilion he dis-

carded his royal garments and his crooklike scepter, then set out to run a ceremonial race between the two fixed stones which still remain in the large court. This sprint was regarded as a dance over the "field" that symbolized the two lands of Egypt. It grew out of ancient fertility myths, and a cylinder seal of the First Dynasty shows an early king running his ritual course just like Zoser in the relief in his blue-tiled underground chamber. But on the cylinder 267
seal the king is accompanied by the bull Apis, whose traverse of the fields ensured their fertility (Vandier, 1952, I, pp. 862–63).

The relationship between the bull Apis and the king's ceremonial race was preserved. P. Lacau says the first record that the bull was indeed Apis appears on a relief which represents Queen Hatshepsut as a Pharaoh, together with a bull. This was on one of the blocks from her chapel later buried in the foundations of the pylon of Amenhotep III at Karnak (1926, fig. p. 131).

ARCHITECTURE FOR THE KA OF KING ZOSER

The sacred precinct of Zoser's step pyramid is in every respect a venture into the unknown under the impetus of an unshaken and powerful faith in the existence of the Ka. While the complex attains a scale hitherto unheard of, every aspect reveals its experimental nature. A new chapter opens, for this is the first time man has attempted to create architecture from stone. From the heavy portcullis blocks of the mastabas, this weighty material—stone—now 270
comes out of the darkness into the exuberant light of the sun.

A new kind of imagination was demanded of the architect when he approached this "eternal" material instead of working with mud bricks and reed or wood posts. Many details of the masonry betray his hesitancy in handling his new material. The blocks are small and the drums of the engaged colums seldom 280
exceed ten inches in height. At the same time Imhotep had the courage to erect a structure 204 feet high, with a craftsmanship that has withstood all ravages of 252 col
time.

Only through Lauer's rebuilding have we gained a vivid impression of Zoser's mortuary complex. Firth drew attention from 1924 to 1931 to the various parts of the complex: enclosure wall, entrance hall, Heb-Sed court, etc. Lauer arrived in Saqqara in 1927 with J. E. Quibell, and after the early death of Quibell he concentrated with inflexible determination upon rebuilding the great complex

158. ONLY ENTRANCE TO ZOSER COMPLEX: *A narrow ever-open doorway (1 x 6 m.) through a fortresslike entrance tower*

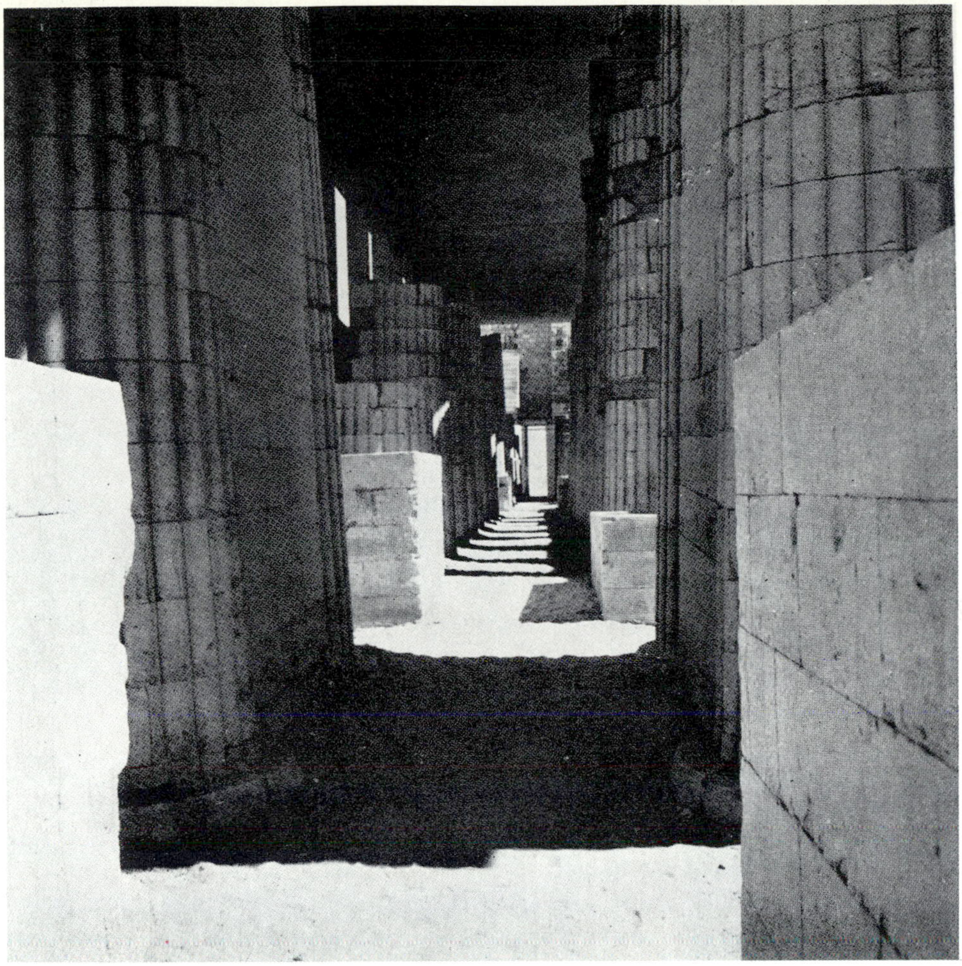

159. COLONNADED PROCESSIONAL HALL: *Ribbed engaged columns terminating tonguelike protrusions form niches along both side walls. Roofed with flat slabs. Lighting from oblique-angled slits near the ceilings of the niches*

160. SECTION OF PROCESSIONAL HALL. *Drawing after Lauer*

(Firth, Quibell, Lauer, 1935). There are other great excavators, but Lauer is unique. Like Borchardt and Ricke, he is an architect by profession, but he has dedicated his life to reconstructing the Zoser complex. When I revisited Saqqara
286 at the end of 1960, Lauer, in his sun helmet, surrounded by his workmen, stood before one of the chapels in the Heb-Sed court. He was about to raise its back wall to the original full height of the shrine. He has stuck to the task of restoring to Zoser's monument some of its early brilliance. Without his careful piecing together of its original fragments we could never have experienced the magnificence of man's earliest architecture in stone.

274 Zoser's complex embraces a rectangle of some thirty-five acres, within a
248 col paneled wall of beautiful limestone ten meters high. This may or may not have symbolized the "white wall" of sun-dried brick that surrounded Memphis, the newly founded capital of Menes, first king of Upper and Lower Egypt. The
271 paneling—a sequence of rectangular projections and recesses—recalls mastaba

161. RIBBED COLUMNS, PROCESSIONAL HALL: *Detail. The drums of the columns seldom exceed ten inches in height*

162. END OF PROCESSIONAL HALL: *The end facing onto the ceremonial court is formed by a sort of hypostyle hall. The passageway widens to include four pairs of engaged columns. A stone Ka door stands permanently open in the left foreground. Note: The protective concrete-slab roof on supports is modern*

and palace frontages of the First and Second Dynasties. This surface treatment subsequently lost its architectural importance. It did not disappear, but was relegated for the most part to the outside of sarcophagi, especially in the Old Kingdom.

Interior spaces: the processional hall

The Egyptians never showed great interest in the elaboration of enclosed interior space. Many of the buildings of the Zoser complex were dummies, con-
288 sisting of a stone façade directly backed with rubble—like a stage set. Some of
them have fragments of interior space, but only as a kind of gesture. It is other-
250 col, 281 wise with the long processional hall that sets the pace for the entire complex.
279 Its shrouded lighting, slanting through horizontal window slits, and the conception of a sacred inner space as a hall of passage persisted. Even the gigantic
259 col hypostyle of the temple of Karnak followed this earliest conception.

Many false doors were indicated upon the enclosure wall, to allow King
Zoser's Ka freedom of movement. But there was only a single entrance for the
278 living. Through it passed Zoser's procession on the occasion of his festival.
This door, no more than a meter wide, stood eternally open and formed part of a
249 col, 286 fortresslike tower of considerable height. On entering through a passage into a
tiny trapezoid court, one is confronted by two wide doorways, each with an
ever-open stone door carefully carved in place. A second short passage is fol-
281 lowed by another ever-open stone door. All could apparently be closed by the
Ka between the dates of his festivals.

We now enter the first large stone hall—fifty-four meters long. It is a processional way, like the later hypostyle halls of the New Kingdom, as in the
392 Luxor temple. Zoser's hall of passage was flanked by twenty engaged columns of
red-painted limestone upon either side, which formed the ends of short trans-
279 verse tonguelike walls projecting from the long outer walls, and thus created a
series of open chapels. It is interesting that the center aisle had already become
higher than those on either side, so that only a dim light could penetrate the
326 small slits high up in the outer walls. This system lasted: we see it in Chephren's
370 valley temple of the Fourth Dynasty and in Tuthmosis III's festival hall in the
Eighteenth.

Like the entry, the exit from the ceremonial passageway was spatially en-
281 larged, not by a court but by a covered hypostyle-like enclosure. Four pairs of
ribbed and engaged columns were connected by cross walls. There is an obvious
tendency toward the creation of larger interior spaces, but the time of the freestanding supporting column has not yet arrived.

Exterior spaces: the galaxy of courts

What always interested the Egyptians was placing volumes in space, making immediate the contact between a man-made structure and the cosmos.

Large inner courts, surrounded by colonnaded porticoes, were also conceived in relation to the sky. Stars and sun were painted upon the ceilings of their ambulatories. The development of the inner court began with the funerary 328 temples of the Fourth Dynasty and continued thereafter. Their peristyles were an indispensable introduction to the sanctuary, which was never relinquished. Finally, in the terraces of Hatshepsut's mortuary temple, they were, so to speak, 262 col built into the cosmos.

In Zoser's complex a galaxy of courts radiates from the step pyramid. But 274 these are not inner courts in the later sense. None possesses even the germ of a colonnade. They are in truth piazzas in the city of the Ka: the great court for the ceremonial race surrounded by buildings, the smaller Heb-Sed court bordered with two rows of chapels, the piazzas before the "government building" and the "king's palace." None of these forms part of an actual building. Their symbolic meaning is different from that of the inner courts of the Fourth Dynasty temples. Even so, they are prototypes of what is to come. They gave courage to create large-scale open areas within a building complex.

The great court of the ceremonial race

On the longitudinal axis of the great court of the complex stand two B-shaped blocks between which Zoser's Ka would continue to run his ceremonial race at the jubilee festivals. There is also a square altar with a ramp (sun altar?) and the temple named "T" by Lauer, which was thought by Ricke to be the pavilion 251 col in which the Ka of the king could be divested of his royal raiment before running his ritual course. It was separated from the court by a low wall that probably contained an entrance.

Along the west side of this court stretches the long façade of dummy storehouses. Its eastern wall backs onto the Heb-Sed court. The step pyramid occupies the north side, leaving an opening to an offering court. The main feature toward the south is the vaulted southern tomb of the king, attached directly to the enclosure wall of the precinct. Its real significance is still unknown.

The Heb-Sed court

In this court the king's Ka was reinvested with royal power to rule over Upper

below, 252 col and Lower Egypt. The east and west sides were lined with chapels for each of the provinces (nomes). Beside each chapel entrance hung a limestone door
286 pivoted permanently open upon its carved socket. Upon entering the chapel,
right one has to circumvent a screen wall (*couloir à chicane*) to obtain access to a small offering niche; no view of the cupboardlike niche is possible from the entrance.
right Fences charmingly sculptured in limestone separate one chapel from the next, and were certainly derived from the customary wooden fences. Behind the chapels rose tall dummy buildings consisting of a series of façades of high
286 vaulted shrines, one of which Lauer was reconstructing to its full height in 1960.

At the south end of the court, a great stone platform approached by two flights of steps supported the two coronation thrones with their canopy.

In the northwest corner of the court, standing in a shrine, four statues were
287 once attached to a wall (Zoser with his wife and daughters).

Courts of the northern and southern buildings

Following the most careful research, Lauer has reconstructed the limestone
288 façades of these two buildings with their arched cornices, tall engaged columns, and pendent leaf capitals that were never repeated.

Ricke was concerned here, as in the whole complex, to discover the significance of these two dummy structures. He arrived at the conclusion that they were replicas, reduced in size, of the government buildings of Upper and Lower Egypt, which may have stood in Memphis. He believed he could recognize
289 representations of a timber skeleton construction with nonbearing walls of mats, reminiscent of the tent palaces of Upper Egypt.

The southern building is approached from the east face of the step pyramid across a respectable plaza.

The fluted ribs of the tall shafts on both façades bear an apparent resemblance

163. RECONSTRUCTION OF HEB-SED CHAPELS: *The east side of the Heb-Sed court with its row of tall dummy shrines fronted by low chapels (cf. col. pl. VI). From Lauer*

164. INTERIOR OF A HEB-SED CHAPEL: *The dividing wall enforces a zigzag access (couloir à chicane) to the offering niche. Graceful fences in stone symbolize separation from the the next chapel*

165. GROUND PLAN OF HEB-SED CHAPEL *showing entrance, couloir à chicane, and offering niche. Drawing after Lauer*

166. PIVOT OF KA DOOR: *Every detail of this opened Ka door is executed in stone, including the pivot and socket, as everywhere in the Zoser complex*

167. JEAN-PHILIPPE LAUER RECONSTRUCTING A HEB-SED CHAPEL. *December 1960*

to the profile of a Doric column, but this is entirely illusory. Their corrugated surfaces never became popular in Egyptian architecture. Like the paneled recessed walls, they induced a strong play of light and shadow that did not correspond to the Egyptian ideal of a plane surface. The Egyptians preferred perfectly circular columns, or the papyrus-stem columns whose prototypes stand 250 col
along the processional passageway of Zoser's complex. About eleven hundred years later, Senmut used proto-Doric columns in the open colonnades of 431
Hatshepsut's mortuary temple.

On the east wall of the northern building are three engaged papyrus columns beneath an arching cornice. All essential attributes of this emblematic plant of Lower Egypt are indicated: the bell-shaped cup of the flower, and the triangular 247 col
stem which almost springs out from the wall. This first capital in stone is imbued with all the freshness and vitality of early spring. It is perhaps the most exciting of the many architectural details that first came into being in Imhotep's mortuary complex for King Zoser. The papyrus column, it is well known, never disappeared from Egyptian architecture; it always represented the power of organic growth shooting up toward the sky.

In a final court on the north face of the step pyramid is the serdab, a com- 290
pletely enclosed, cupboardlike chamber containing the statue of Zoser. Adjacent are the remains of a large building considered by Lauer to have been a mortuary temple, but by Ricke the palace of the king's Ka. The latter opinion seems the more convincing, not only because mortuary temples were customarily situated on the east face of the pyramid, but also because the elaborate rituals connected with them were developed during the Fourth Dynasty.

168. FEET OF FOUR LIFE-SIZED FIGURES *in Heb-Sed court: Probably Zoser, his wife, and two daughters. This would have been the earliest group of its kind*

169. FAÇADE OF NORTHERN BUILDING, *partly reconstructed, showing the rubble backing of this dummy structure*

170. FAÇADE OF NORTHERN BUILDING: *Reconstructed to its full height. Drawing from Lauer*

171. ENGAGED COLUMNS WITH PAPYRUS CAPITALS *on east wall of dummy northern building. These are the origin of all later variants of papyrus columns used throughout Egyptian architecture, even into Roman times (Philae)*

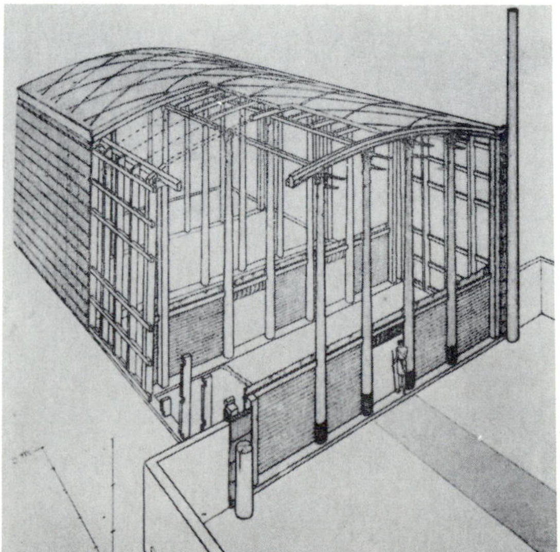

172. STRUCTURE OF A GOVERNMENT BUILDING *of Upper Egypt: A timber skeleton developed from a tented palace. Ricke has suggested that the northern and southern buildings represent government palaces of Upper and Lower Egypt. Drawing from Ricke*

THE ZOSER STATUE IN THE SERDAB

Many works of sculpture have disappeared, or have left only insignificant
287 remnants, such as the feet of the four human figures which once stood upon a raised platform in the northwest corner of the Heb-Sed court, probably representing Zoser, his wife, and their two daughters. If complete, they would be the first life-size statuary group of human figures, long antedating the well-known
469 groups with King Mycerinus at the end of the Fourth Dynasty.

The statue of Zoser that Firth found in 1924–25 at the northeast corner of the
right pyramid was almost undamaged (1925, p. 149). There sat the king in the darkness of his paneled closet—his serdab. Only two round holes cut at eye level in the wall facing him linked him with the outside world. Through them he could receive the odors of incense and his crystal eyes could gaze out into the void.

The original limestone statue of the king, now in the Cairo Museum, has been replaced with a good cement copy from which one receives an uncanny impression of the ever-vigilant ruler sitting in darkness. His face is undamaged except for the eyes and nose. Even this disfigurement fails to detract from the majesty that emanates from his high-held head, with its deep-set eyes and its modeled cheekbones. His left hand, the fingers close together, lies flat upon his knee. This position was to be retained by all later statues of Pharaohs. Zoser's right arm, bent at a right angle, lies across his breast.

173. STATUE OF ZOSER IN HIS SERDAB. *Drawing after Firth*

174. SEATED STATUE OF ZOSER *found in his serdab*

He wears the garments ordained for the Heb-Sed festival, the ritual headdress falling to the shoulders, and the ceremonial beard.

In this statue, if anywhere, one senses the great dignity, and perhaps also the tragedy, inherent in the god-king. It is also the first movingly human representation in Egyptian art.

The few small statues that have come down to us from the Second Dynasty bear no comparison with this one. Particularly if one looks for the expressive power of the human countenance, which is so decisive for all future development, one must cast the net wider. We do not know exactly how many centuries lie be-
104 tween the grieving, enigmatic face of the priestess of Uruk from the Jemdet Nasr period and the statue of King Zoser. The Sumerian alabaster head is far closer to human tragedy than Zoser's immutable countenance. But his statue is in the line of the conquest of the human image as the highest form of art.

As the whole Zoser complex was destined for the Ka, so was this statue of the dead king. It, not the mummy, was the seat of the Ka when he returned from his wanderings. For this reason there were often later several such statues, each carefully protected within a serdab, since "the Ka, as the source of divine being, is the guarantor of eternity" (Greven, 1952, p. 33). Therefore one protects it and hides it, as in the serdab, "for with the destruction of this representation his eternal existence also ends. The Ka has no free existence of its own, it needs an external form in which the divine can make its appearance" (ibid.).

Since the king was the only human possessor of the Ka, the first Ka statue could only "stem from a royal tomb. According to the present state of knowledge, it is Zoser's statue that fits this designation" (ibid.). Thus it is understandable that the greatest sculptural intensity was concentrated upon this enclosed statue, which was one with the pyramid and stood in the closest relation to the tomb deep below the earth.

Tectonic elements

Zoser's complex contains the beginnings of many features that later became constituent elements in the development of space and form in Egyptian architecture. At the same time, the eye can readily test in the irregularities and corrections of the stonework in the Zoser complex how unaccustomed to handling this material the early builders were. Thus it is even more astonishing to behold the richness of imagination expended upon every detail.

Among the tectonic elements which first appear here are the cornice, the torus molding, stone corner posts and columns (Badawy, 1954, pp. 79–83). Of these forms, the stone column may be selected as witness of the continuity of Egyptian tradition. The compound shafts of bundled reeds in Zoser's processional hall 250 col grew to monumental dimensions in the Fifth Dynasty, and similar papyrus-bundle columns were erected as late as the first century A.D. in the Isis temple on the island of Philae. The open papyrus flowers upon the columns of Zoser's "gov- 247 col ernment buildings" later swelled to monstrous proportions along the main pas- 259 col sageway of the great hypostyle hall at Karnak. The polygonal columns—often called proto-Doric—of Temple T and the "government buildings" reappear 251 col comparatively rarely later, as in the Middle Kingdom (Mentuhotep's mortuary 288, 410 temple), and in the New Kingdom (Hatshepsut's mortuary temple). 431

Life on earth and life beyond

Stone architecture grew from an immutable conviction that life in the hereafter was a direct continuation of earthly existence, with its recurrent festivals and its daily round of activities. But this continuance depended on many precautionary measures, from simple offerings "causing his name to live," to mansions in which the dead might live forever. The form of the final home changed many times during the history of Egypt, but the conviction remained that life in the beyond, like life on earth, never stood still. Its movements were bound up with the eternally recurrent cycles of the stars and the sun. The vital force—the Ka—wandered continually to and fro from earth to heaven.

Never was the life on earth so directly projected into the life beyond as in the sacred precinct of Zoser's step pyramid. Its courts and buildings served one exclusive purpose—to provide an eternally renewed existence. Everything radiates a joyous optimism.

The Zoser complex stands between the comparatively humble mastabas of the kings of the first dynasties and the dramatically organized pyramid complexes of the Fourth Dynasty, ruled by the complicated ritual and overpowering might of the priesthood. In Saqqara a gentle smile seems to hover over the entire complex. This optimism reappeared but once, in the mortuary temple of Queen Hatshepsut at Deir el Bahari, about eleven centuries later. But the idea of creating a whole architectural setting for the use of the Ka was never to recur.

PART VIII PYRAMIDS: RITES AND SPACE

Pyramids are the triumph of pure abstract form.

With his own hands, man makes his work stand erect and confront the limitlessness of cosmic space. Through its symbolic impact the pyramid, man-made, merges and even competes with eternity. Only a few perforated Gothic spires—those shrieks in stone from man to sky—express a similar intense demand for penetration of the eternal by man's temporal existence, but the artistic means are radically different.

In one respect above all, the pyramids are unique. Human endeavor has never achieved such sublime simplicity in materializing man's irrepressible urge to 257 col link his fate with eternity. It is this absolute simplicity and immaculate precision that merges mathematical logic with enigma and mystery.

THE PLANE AS A CONSTITUENT ELEMENT OF ARCHITECTURE

The standard form of the pyramid, the so-called true pyramid, consists of four equal isosceles triangles converging on a single point. The geometrical body formed by these four triangular planes reveals great wisdom of construction. Each of its sides is precisely oriented to the four cardinal points. The standard form was never changed.

No later period has had either the impulse or the courage to sacrifice everything else in order to express its urge toward eternity by the purest abstraction. The pyramids had no reliefs, no inscriptions, no detailing of any kind. Only smooth, dazzling planes, inaccessible to human approach. The power of the plane becomes sublime.

253 col These immense triangular surfaces were faced with highly polished limestone, 226 or even rose granite. Unlike the Mesopotamian ziggurats, they had no flights of steps. They repulsed the touch of mortals. Each was the abode of a dead king, who wandered from his eternally sealed chamber in the heart of the pyramid to travel over the sky by day and through the dangers of the underworld ocean by night.

Plane surfaces always form a background for the tectonic elements displayed upon them, and the gradations of the step pyramid represent a move toward the relentless planes of the Cheops pyramid. From the latter to the obelisks and pylons, the plane surface never ceased to be a constituent element of Egyptian architecture.

THE EXPERIMENTAL PHASE OF THE PYRAMID

In comparison with prehistoric and early historic Mesopotamian development, one could almost say that Egypt remained half asleep. Although in the First and Second Dynasties there are some indications of the imaginative strength that was to come, they are few and spread out over centuries. The decisive change occurred in the Third Dynasty.

The pyramids went through an experimental phase marked in every respect by gropings for form and structure. But measured against the slow, steady flow of normal Egyptian development, the transition to a standard form was attained with astounding speed, in little more than half a century. Development in our period proceeds at a hectic pace, yet it took the same time for iron construction to proceed from its beginning to the creation of the Eiffel Tower.

The transitional period started with the step pyramid of Zoser at the beginning of the Third Dynasty and ended with the three pyramids of Sneferu at the beginning of the Fourth Dynasty. The certainty of form and construction acquired during this experimental phase led in one generation to the unsurpassed perfection of the Cheops pyramid.

252 col
257 col

The step pyramid of Zoser, Third Dynasty

It is an enormous leap from the flat-topped mastaba tombs of the First and Second Dynasties to the step pyramid of Zoser. The sixth stage of this pyramid attained a height of 204 feet. It was, in a way, man's first skyscraper, his first tall building. Its contemporaries must have held it in great awe. This awe persisted. Even the Saite kings carried out large-scale renovations of its interior, and graffiti made by pilgrims in the time of Ramesses II testify to a marveling reverence and a yearning for a renewal of early piety.

272

What gave the impetus for this unusual structure? It was the outcome of a belief in the godlike nature of the king, who after death would become one with the deity. The need to represent and to facilitate his doing so may have brought about the urge that led to the pyramids, whose form is rooted in cosmic representation.

No other pyramid shows as impressively as Zoser's the emergence of the architectonic spirit. It could not have been created without the architectural genius of Imhotep, and even so, the concept of the step pyramid emerged only during the course of its construction.

175. ZOSER'S STEP PYRAMID: *This southern corner of the west face shows the differing sizes of blocks and courses which mark the transition from a mastaba to a step pyramid*

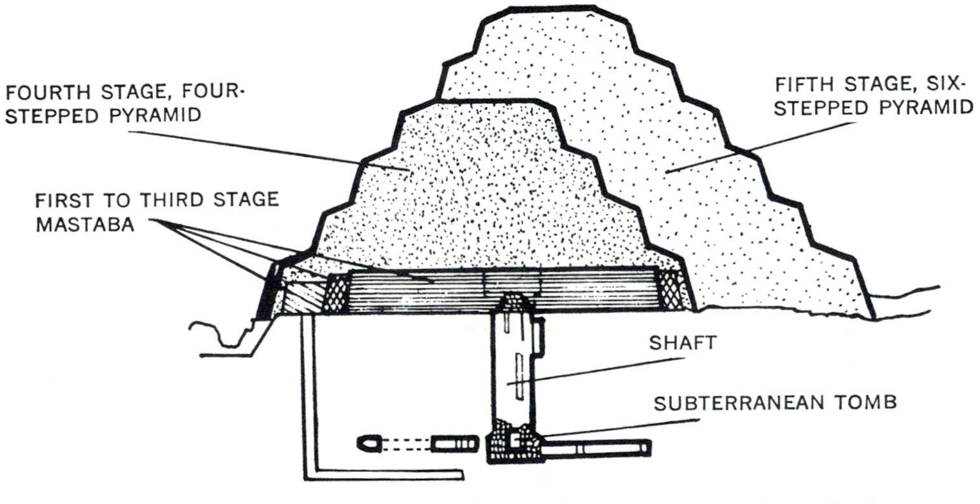

176. STEP PYRAMID: *East-west cross section. The high degree of experimentation is apparent, moving from the first mastaba, with its deep, symmetrically placed shaft, to a four-step and then a six-step pyramid, the shaft becoming increasingly eccentric. The final leap from a four-step pyramid demanded the greatest audacity. Drawing after Lauer*

Lauer distinguishes six stages—in his words, "six projects" (1936, pp. 12–26). The first three encompass the point of departure, the mastaba together with its enlargements. The last three deal with the actual pyramid, first with four steps, finally with six.

The mastaba, first to third stage

A mastaba was planned; but square, larger (about 200 ft. sq.) and higher (26 ft.) than usual. One side was then extended and the whole refaced with Tura limestone. A second extension of the east side reinstated the square ground plan which formed the basis for the step pyramid. left

The step pyramid, fourth to sixth stage

The fourth stage announces a change of plan. The whole is transformed into a four-stepped, square-based pyramid, constructed asymmetrically over the mastaba. In the fifth stage the decisive verticality is achieved. The center of the pyramid is shifted to the northwest and two more steps are added. The sixth stage consists in a slight enlargement of the height and volume and "is just a simple modification of the casing" (Lauer, 1936, p. 21). The entire structure was, as usual, faced with Tura limestone.

Today its flanks lie exposed. In their hesitant but most ingenious masonry one senses the experimental nature of the grandiose project. In this first stone architecture great caution governed the dimensions of the blocks, for the builders were still used to the size of clay brick, but no later method proved so successful in resisting time. left

The subterranean tombs

The same experimentation appears in the underground burial chambers with their many ramifications.

At the bottom of a square shaft ninety-two feet deep, constructed during the erection of the pyramid, lay Zoser's burial chamber. Lauer found nothing but a black, mummified foot. From this burial chamber, passages lead out on all four sides. Their numerous branches contained the graves of members of the royal family, including that of an eight-year-old child.

Here, as in his southern tomb beside the enclosure wall of the complex, Zoser established an astonishing underground residence for his future life. In the scaled-down replicas of rooms from his palace at Memphis, the whole friendliness of his complex is revealed. Suddenly, some twenty-eight meters below

ground, we are amid the joy of life. The tile wall coverings simulate reed mat-
266 ting, just as they did in the southern tomb, and the lunettes above them contain
267 delicate reliefs, of the king running his ritual course at the Heb-Sed festival.
Their quality can be compared with the wooden reliefs found in the tomb of
169 Hesy-ra, one of Zoser's court officials.

The dead king retained an intimate closeness to daily life, even in the depths of the earth.

This naïve projection of an earthly existence into the beyond, this demand for an eternal present which pervades the entire Zoser complex, was never to be repeated. The overpowering rituals of the sun cult supervened. This cult was already present in the Zoser complex, but there it formed only part of the whole: it was bound up with the realm of the Ka and with the renewal of power at the Heb-Sed festival. In the Fourth Dynasty, the intimate relationship of death to life was replaced by an elaborate ritual to which the dead king was submitted by the priesthood. It was this ritual that determined the program of the later pyramid complexes.

An unfinished step pyramid of the Third Dynasty

Not far from the southwest corner of Zoser's complex, Zakaria Goneim, Chief Inspector of Antiquities at Saqqara, found an unfinished pyramid of King Sekhemkhet, one of Zoser's successors. Between 1951 and 1955 Goneim excavated parts

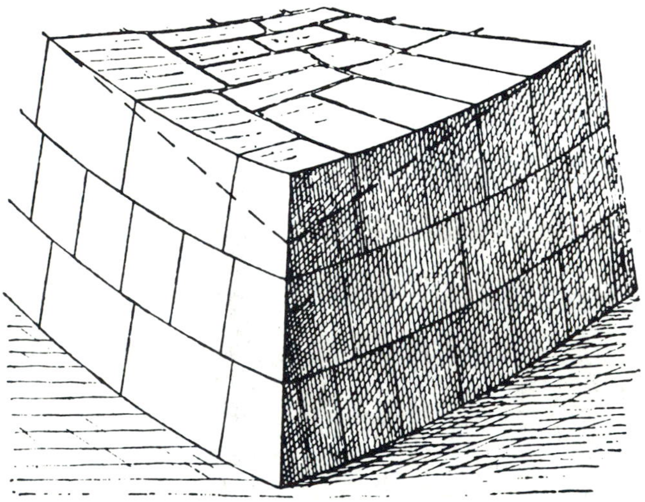

177. CORNER OF A STEP PYRAMID: *Schematic drawing showing how a line bisecting the corners is avoided by tilting the courses as indicated by the dotted line. From Lauer*

178. CORNER OF UNFINISHED PYRAMID: *Here the slight uptilting of the courses is readily apparent. Pyramid of Sekhemkhet, Saqqara. Third Dynasty*

179. CORNER OF UNFINISHED PYRAMID *from above*

310 of this never-completed complex. The enclosure wall was paneled like that of Zoser, and the pyramid also followed his system.

300, 301 During the period of excavation one could learn much about how builders solved the problem of constructing pyramid corners.

The most impressive part of this unfinished pyramid was the monumental en- right trance to its substructure, between two high retaining walls cut deep into the rock bed. In February 1954, I was living as Goneim's guest at Saqqara. One evening he stormed in full of excitement: "The entrance is untouched!" And it was. But when, months later, they penetrated the innermost chamber and opened the sealed alabaster sarcophagus, they found it empty. This disappointment, together with other misfortunes both during and after his excavation of this buried pyramid, may have contributed to Goneim's early death. In autumn 1958 he was found drowned in the Nile.

The three pyramids of Sneferu

Sneferu, founder of the Fourth Dynasty, was a great experimenter in pyramid building. He built three pyramids for himself, and each is different. Probably his first was the one at Medum, which had been started by Huni, the last king of the Third Dynasty. This pyramid stands in complete isolation some forty-five miles 254 col south of Giza and thirty south of Dahshur, where he built the other two close together.

Medum

The pyramid of Medum is a forerunner of the standard form, though it passes 305 through two step-pyramid stages (the first with seven steps, the second with eight) before arriving at the smooth unbroken surfaces of the true pyramid. Its badly damaged third and fourth steps still loom above the waste of debris and desert sand, and some fragments of its smooth final surface remain. It had once presented the aspect, unusual for Egypt, of a great tower with stepped layers rising at an angle of seventy-five degrees. Like Zoser's step pyramid, that at Medum was built in several stages, though its original center was never shifted.

In the first, seven-stepped stage, there was a nucleus and "six thick coatings of masonry, diminishing in height from the centre outwards. . . . Each of the coatings, which inclined inwards at an angle of about 75°, consisted of a core of local stone cased from top to bottom with Tura limestone" (Edwards, 1961, pp. 65–66). The smooth limestone cladding indicates that at first this was considered the final solution.

180. UNTOUCHED ENTRANCE TO UNFINISHED PYRAMID, *blocked by a roughly built wall*

181. OPENED ENTRANCE TO UNFINISHED PYRAMID

182. ENTRANCE TO UNFINISHED PYRAMID, *showing the high, carefully built, and slightly stepped retaining walls*

183. STELES BEFORE MORTUARY TEMPLE, MEDUM: *These two round-headed steles stand before a small mortuary temple attached to the east face of the pyramid. The offering table is buried under the rubble filling in the little court before the temple*

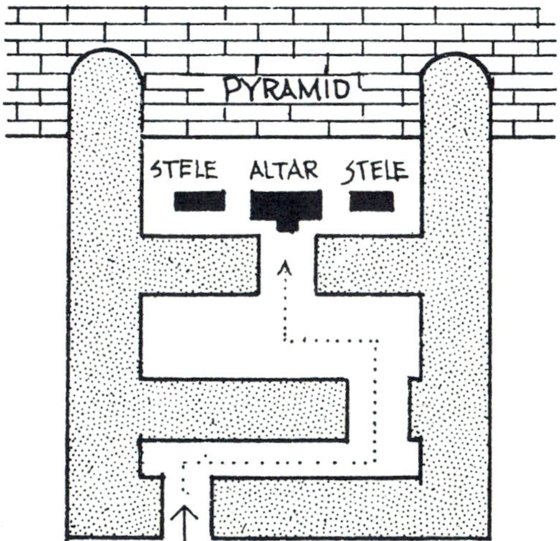

184. GROUND PLAN OF MORTUARY TEMPLE, MEDUM: *The asymmetric entrance from the temple forecourt is protected by a couloir à chicane. Drawing after Flinders Petrie*

185. EAST FACE OF PYRAMID OF MEDUM: *Only a few of the towering steps of the pyramid remain. The two steles from fig. 183 can just be seen rising above the roof of the nine-foot-high mortuary temple. The simplicity of Medum's small temple court with its offering table and two steles was maintained in the great pyramids at Giza, though fronted by the new monumental courts of the offering temple*

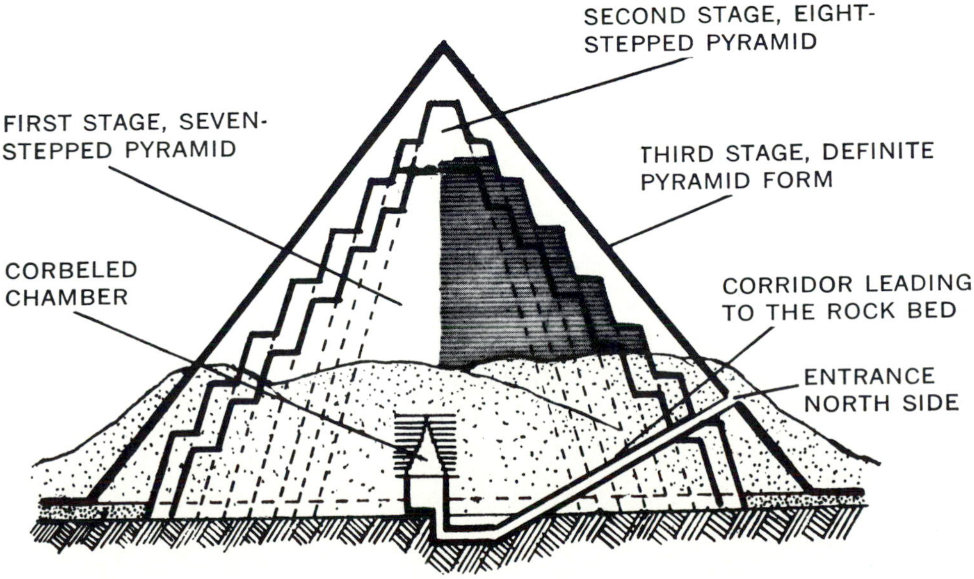

186. PYRAMID OF MEDUM: *North-south Cross Section. Drawing after Flinders Petrie*

In the second, eight-stepped stage, the height seems to have been considered
305 insufficient. "The top step was raised by about 45 feet and each successive step
was built up to a level somewhat higher than the one above it in the previous design" (p. 66). The construction was the same. Rough blocks were placed on the smooth surface of the steps, and the whole was again encased in limestone.

In the third stage, the polished steps were again hidden by rough-hewn blocks and, as a final procedure, an uninterrupted plane surface was created on all four sides by enclosing the whole within a polished stone casing. This led to the definitive pyramid form. It cannot be ascertained whether the stages followed immediately upon one another or whether there were interruptions. Probably the latter. It is even possible that there was an exchange of experience between the builders of the pyramids of Medum and Dahshur. "Varille noticed that one finds the same carrier's marks upon blocks of the Medum pyramid and upon the blocks of the rhomboidal pyramid [the bent pyramid], and he concludes that the same team worked on the two monuments" (Vandier, 1954, II, p. 15).

It is tempting to explain the new form of the pyramid with its smooth triangular surfaces as the outcome of technical innovations, but this is not sufficient.
345 The standard form grew from new ritualistic needs, as A. Moret and others have
long recognized. All three Sneferu pyramids differ basically from Zoser's, and
the difference corresponds to a change in program. Gone forever are the architectural representations of daily earthly life. The smiling aspect of the Zoser
complex has given place to the stern ritual necessary to transform the dead king
into a living god. The essential architectonic organization (which we will dis-
320 cuss later in this section) is here represented on the smallest scale—valley temple, causeway, mortuary temple—before reaching the final sepulchral chamber
within the pyramid. We know scarcely anything of the valley temple. The causeway can just be recognized. Only the small mortuary temple remains, attached
304, 305 to the center of the east face of the pyramid. It is little larger than one of the
Heb-Sed chapels of Zoser's complex.

Dahshur: the bent pyramid

253 col The first of the two pyramids that Sneferu built at Dahshur has a steep slope in
its lower part—54 degrees. The angle of the upper part diminishes to 43 degrees. The total height was about 336 feet. One explanation of the "bend" was that the pyramid had been "finished in haste," and it was confirmed in 1839 "that the stones in the upper part were laid with less care than those below" (Edwards, 1961, p. 71). But "Varille believes it would be preferable to call it the 'double pyramid' or 'the pyramid with two slopes.' He does not believe the dou-

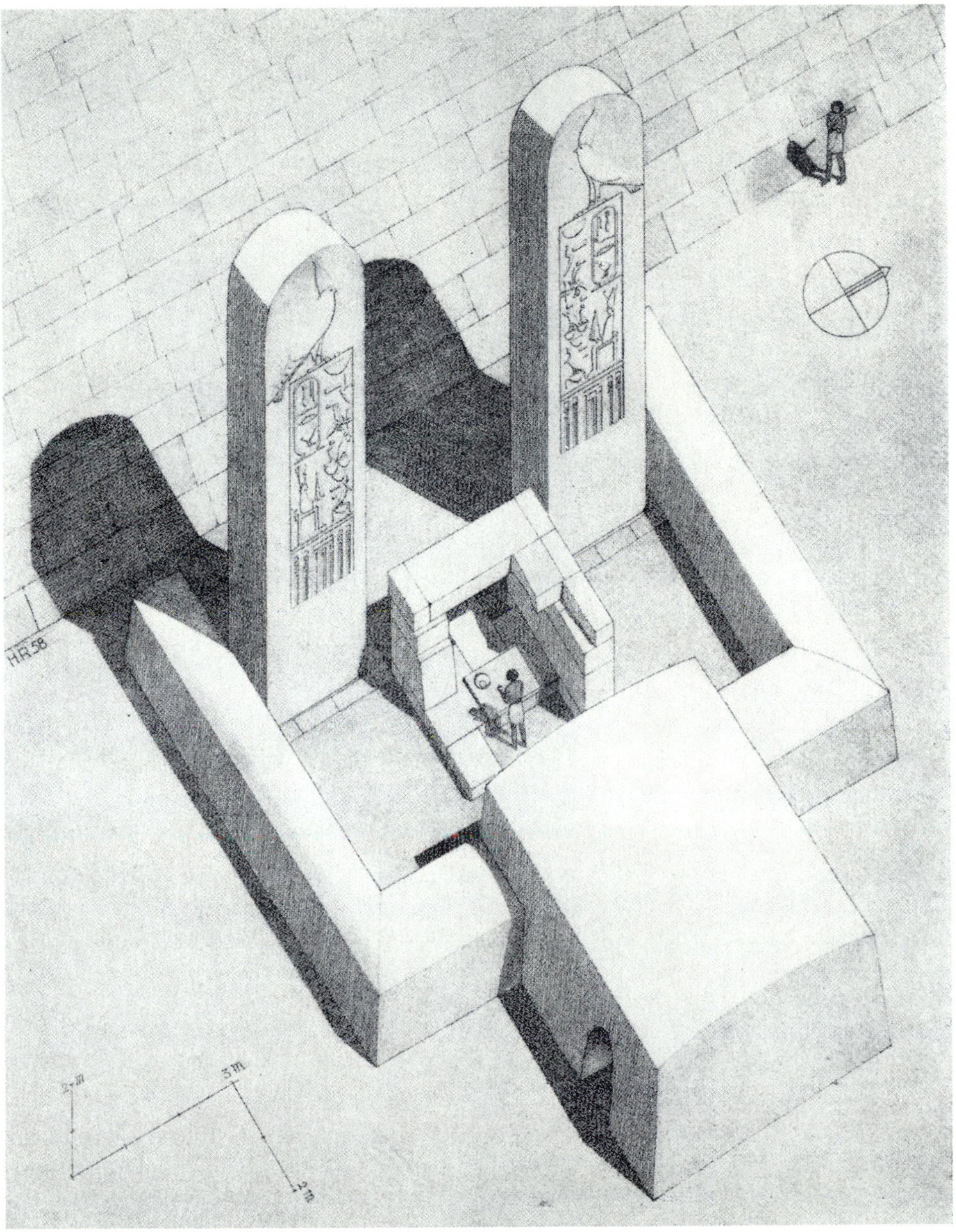

187. OFFERING TEMPLE OF BENT PYRAMID, *Dahshur: Ricke's careful reconstruction gives a good insight into the simple form of the offering temple at the beginning of the Fourth Dynasty. The elements are the same as at Medum: entrance covered, altar in the open and between two steles placed directly before the pyramid. From Fakhry*

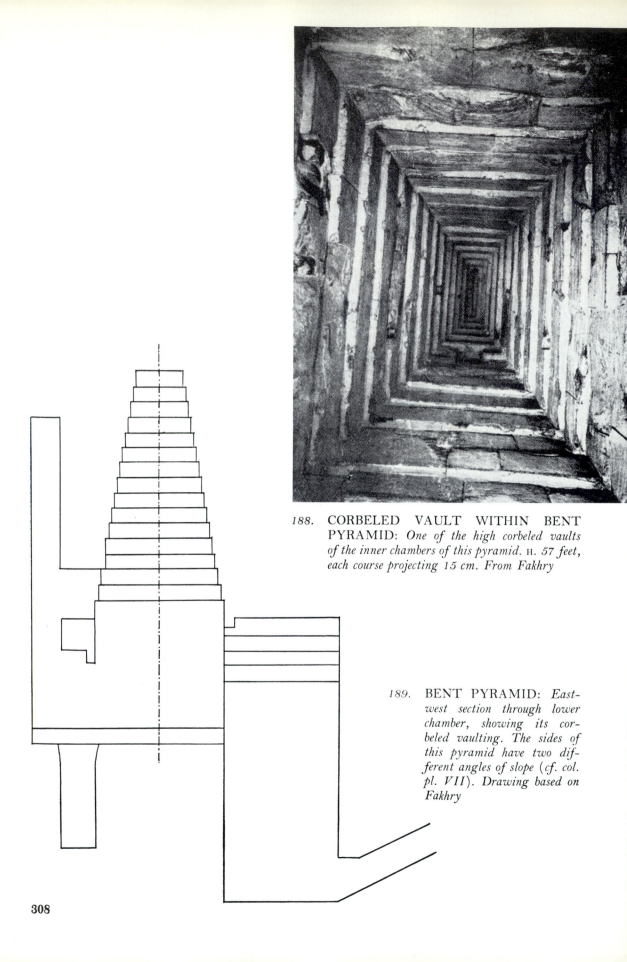

188. CORBELED VAULT WITHIN BENT PYRAMID: *One of the high corbeled vaults of the inner chambers of this pyramid.* H. *57 feet, each course projecting 15 cm. From Fakhry*

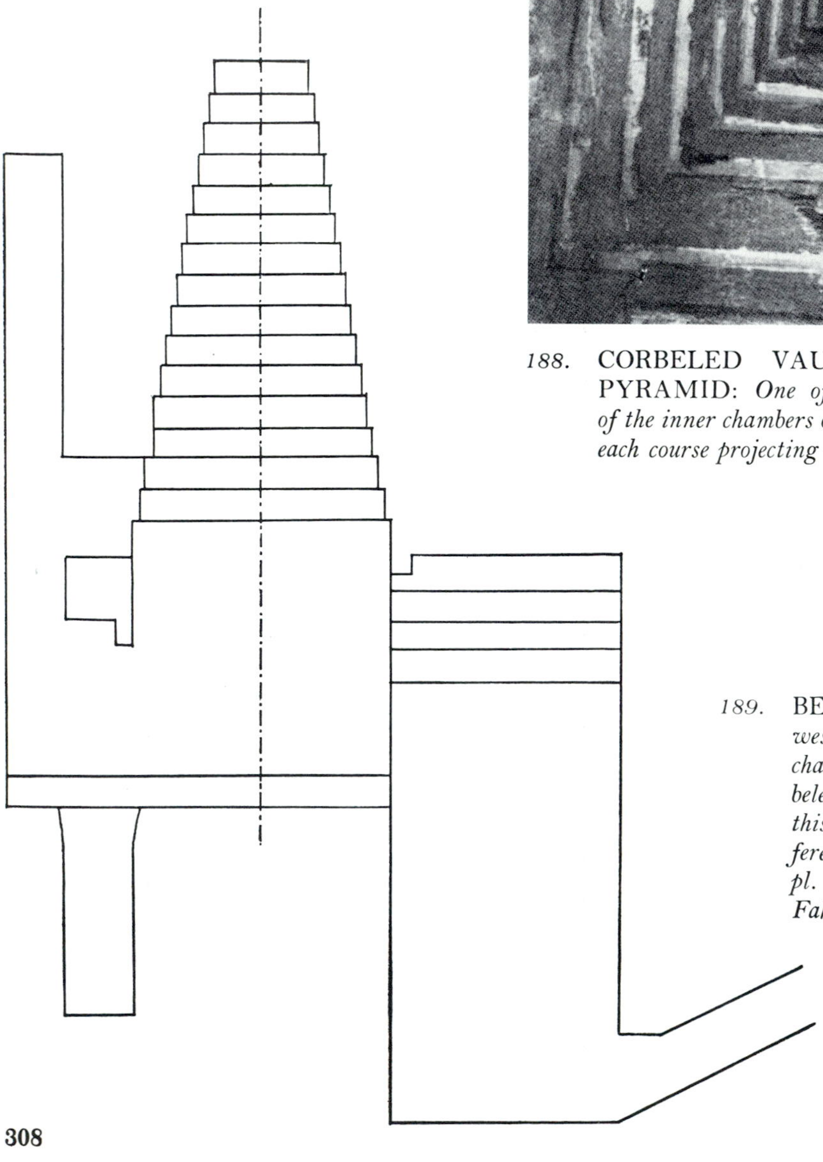

189. BENT PYRAMID: *East-west section through lower chamber, showing its corbeled vaulting. The sides of this pyramid have two different angles of slope (cf. col. pl. VII). Drawing based on Fakhry*

190. SNEFERU'S NORTHERN PYRAMID: *The first true pyramid, near his earlier bent pyramid (cf. col. pl. IX). No facing stones are left upon its sides and the corners are rounded. Structure of red sandstone from a local quarry. Blocks of considerable dimensions. The base covers as much ground as that of Cheops' pyramid*

ble slope is the result of the architect's irresolution. For him it corresponds to the characteristic of duality which is expressed by the pyramid itself (it contains two burial chambers), and is only the materialization, in architectural terms, of a symbolic idea" (Vandier, 1954, II, p. 16). This theory is reinforced by the low walls of the valley temple, which show a similar bend.

The bent pyramid has not only two different slopes; it also has two independent chambers. One is entered, as usual, from the center of the north side of the pyramid. The other is entered from the west side—which was never repeated. The downward-sloping corridor from the north entrance ends in a rectangular chamber fifty-seven feet high. This height is achieved by an astonishingly audacious corbeled construction: "Every course projects 15 cms on all the four sides" (Fakhry, 1959, p. 47). Thus we can see that even in a period of searching for the standard form of the pyramid, builders had skill and courage to tackle im- left

318 pressive vaulting problems. The magnificent Grand Gallery of the Cheops pyramid, leading up to the burial chamber, also employed corbeling along its two parallel walls.

The valley temple of the bent pyramid has only recently been excavated by Ahmed Fakhry, with reconstruction by Ricke (ibid., pp. 106–17). Here to some extent we can study the emerging pyramid complex: valley temple, causeway, offering temple, pyramid.

The dimensions of the ceremonial areas are larger than those at Medum.
307 Though the offering temple, which leans against the pyramid, is only slightly larger, the valley temple already has a highly developed ground plan: a roofed

191. ENCLOSURE WALL OF UNFINISHED PYRAMID: *Its blocks, though small (50 cm.), are already double the size of those used in the Zoser complex. Saqqara, end of Third Dynasty*

192. GIGANTIC BLOCKS *of so-called temple of the Sphinx, near Chephren's valley temple: Within a single century the Egyptians learned how to handle stone blocks, from small bricks to megalithic stones weighing thirty tons. Fourth Dynasty*

anteroom, a spacious inner court with two rows of five pillars standing before six niches containing statues of the king and carved in one piece with the walls of the niches.

Dahshur: the first "true pyramid"

Upon the desert plateau, about half a mile north of the bent pyramid, Sneferu built the first pyramid to achieve the standard form. It is now often called the red pyramid after the color of its blocks, which came from a local quarry. Originally,

like the others, it was covered with a smooth facing of Tura limestone. Today
309 its corners appear rounded. The area around it has not been completely excavated.

Its slope (43° 30′) is almost the same as that of the upper part of the bent
pyramid. Its proportions appear squat. The slope of the Cheops pyramid is only
257 col eight degrees steeper, but how much greater upward thrust results from that
small increase in the angle of inclination!

Only in Dahshur, undisturbed by tourists or the debris left by excavations, can
we appreciate the emanating power of the pyramids. Here in the desert the earth
appears as though seen from astronomical heights: intangible, immaterial. Here
254 col there is nothing else. The two pyramids resting upon an endless plain confront
only the cosmos. The heavens arch over them like the figure of the goddess
Nut. Everything earthly has fallen away and man grasps what it means to stand
before eternity.

On the experimental phase

Only rarely in the history of architecture is it possible to take so close a look at the creation of a monumental form as it is in these mighty constructions. The process can be discerned in every aspect: extension of experience in technical knowledge, in ritualistic organization, in the symbolic content of the newly arisen form.

Growing experience in the handling of stone

We find ourselves in the midst of technical advances without parallel in Egyptian history. The new problems of using stone as a building material were solved
with astonishing quickness—within a single century. Dimensions of the stone
blocks grew ever larger, from the small, twenty-five-centimeter ashlars of
331 Zoser's complex to the large limestone blocks of the Giza pyramids, and up to
the megalithic boulders of eighteen to thirty tons that compose the so-called
311 temple of the Sphinx near Chephren's valley temple.

253 col Large areas of the casing of the bent pyramid at Dahshur still remain; they
show that builders even then knew how to construct these immense sloping
planes solidly and firmly. The polished surfaces are composed of a mosaic of
wedge-shaped blocks, each about two meters long, driven into the body of the
pyramid. One place where the surface is damaged looks like a glacier crevasse,
and we can see from it the marvelous instinct for craftsmanship that made possible such daring experiments.

Even more impressive than the craftsmanship of the period is the engineering
knowledge that made possible the stable construction of the steeply sloping
sides of the pyramids. The courses are built independently, at a steep angle,
so as to counteract disruptive forces such as expanding joints. As Auguste
Choisy observed in *L'Art de bâtir chez les Égyptiens* (1904), the independent
sloping layers of the pyramid support one another. Probably Imhotep invented 298
these inclined courses when he changed the earlier mastaba into Zoser's step
pyramid. Mastabas were built with the traditional horizontal courses, but in
the step pyramid the courses followed the angle of the slope (Lauer, 1936, I,
pp. 17–18). Where two courses meet at a right angle, a line bisecting the angle
must be avoided. This was managed by tilting the courses slightly as they
approached the corners. The two abutting courses could thus be joined upon a
curved bed without splitting the joint, as Lauer shows in his drawing. The 300
system can be observed best in the unfinished pyramid (Goneim, 1956, pp.
52–54). Our photograph shows the slight uptilt of the corner blocks as well as 301
the inward curve of the entire course.

CONSTRUCTION FOR ETERNITY

Pyramids are fundamentally different from mountain masses. Their sloping sides are constructed in independent layers, like the annular rings of a tree translated into an abstract engineering technique.

It is in Zoser's step pyramid that we can first trace the growing experience
298 in structuring with stone. The static principle by which solidity could be guaranteed this tall structure came about through the newly invented superimposition of sloping walls, which demanded highly precise craftsmanship.

The pyramids were constructed with an astonishing insight into the laws of statics and of the movement of forces. Volumes piled up like heaps of rubble cannot resist earthquakes or the ravages of time, and the pyramids of later dynasties, which did not follow the wise principles of the early times, have crumbled and lost their form.

This play of forces within the pyramid has been analyzed by a Swiss engineer,
317 H. Rössler (1952). He explains that the great resistance of the pyramids is only partly due to their enormous dead weight. Much comes from fortifying forces whose strength increases with height. One of Rössler's diagrams indicates how the horizontal thrusts at every level are directed toward the central core to reinforce the structure. Because of the slope of the walls, thirty-five per cent of the vertical thrusts are transmitted to the inner core, reaching from base to summit, the remainder being carried down by gravity into the rock bed. Thus the stability of a pyramid increases with its height. Rössler compares the pyramid's series of almost independent sloping layers with the expansion joints of concrete construction.

We do not here enter into a discussion of the way the pyramids were erected (Lauer, 1948, pp. 161–85), but it may be noted that the principal theory, since the time of Borchardt (1928), has been that there were ramps running perpendicular to the face of the pyramid. I. E. S. Edwards suggests that construction ramps may have run parallel to the sides rather than perpendicular to them (1961, p. 221), and, in 1953–54, Goneim records: "On three sides of the structure I found traces of what are almost certainly construction embankments. . . . Had the pyramid been completed, the ramp and embankments would gradually have been removed as the casing-stones were put on" (1956, p. 71).

Recently both Rössler and the Egyptologist Dows Dunham have suggested that the pyramid itself provided its own working platform. Dunham also points out that the work was much more complicated than a modern engineer might assume, since "there is no evidence as early as the Fourth Dynasty for any knowledge of the wheel, the pulley or the derrick. . . . We also know that the Egyptians of the Pyramid Age did not have draught animals and that the power used must needs be that of men hauling on ropes" (1956, p. 161). He discards the notion of perpendicular ramps as impractical and considers construction ramps encircling the body of the pyramid and growing simultaneously with it "a plausible suggestion" (p. 165). This suggestion is incorporated in a model (Museum of Science, Boston) of the Mycerinus pyramid under construction.

The great pyramid of Cheops, Fourth Dynasty

Unsurpassed in height, size, and excellence of construction, the Cheops pyramid 257 col
has almost become a symbol for the whole of Egyptian architecture. Since it is the best known of all the pyramids, we will say little about it here.

It is exactly square, each side 756 feet; height 481.4 feet; slope $51^\circ 52'$. No hesitation whatsoever existed with regard to its exterior form. All was conceived at a single stroke. With this pyramid the experimental phase is over. The precision of its orientation to the four cardinal points is stupendous—it differs no more than $3'6''$ from the exact north-south orientation (Lauer, 1948, p. 186).

The interior planning was changed three times. But the entrance corridor 316
on the north side, starting about fifty-five feet above ground level and sloping downward at an angle of $26^\circ\ 31'\ 23''$, remained unaltered. It has been suggested that this angle, prolonged toward the sky, met the polestar at the time the pyramid was constructed.

First phase: the entrance corridor continued straight on, boring deep down into the rock bed—a system already outmoded—terminating in a never-used chamber lying deep under the vertical axis of the pyramid.

Second phase: a change in direction. A most ingeniously concealed passage led upward from the entrance corridor, turned onto a horizontal level, and ended in a chamber with a low, corbeled roof, similar to that in the Medum pyramid.

Third phase: the final change. The ascending corridor of the second phase now continued on, unbroken, straight into the heart of the pyramid. Up to this point of juncture the corridor is less than a man's height. One has to bend low to pass along it. Then, suddenly, the cramped passageway opens up into the 318
Grand Gallery, 153 feet long and 28 feet high. Its walls, composed of enormous blocks of highly polished limestone, rise vertically in seven sections, each slightly corbeled forward. Sneferu's experimental rectangular chamber fifty- 308

193. BIRD'S-EYE VIEW OF CHEOPS' PYRAMID: *Color lithograph by Karl Richard Lepsius, ca. 1850. From Lepsius*

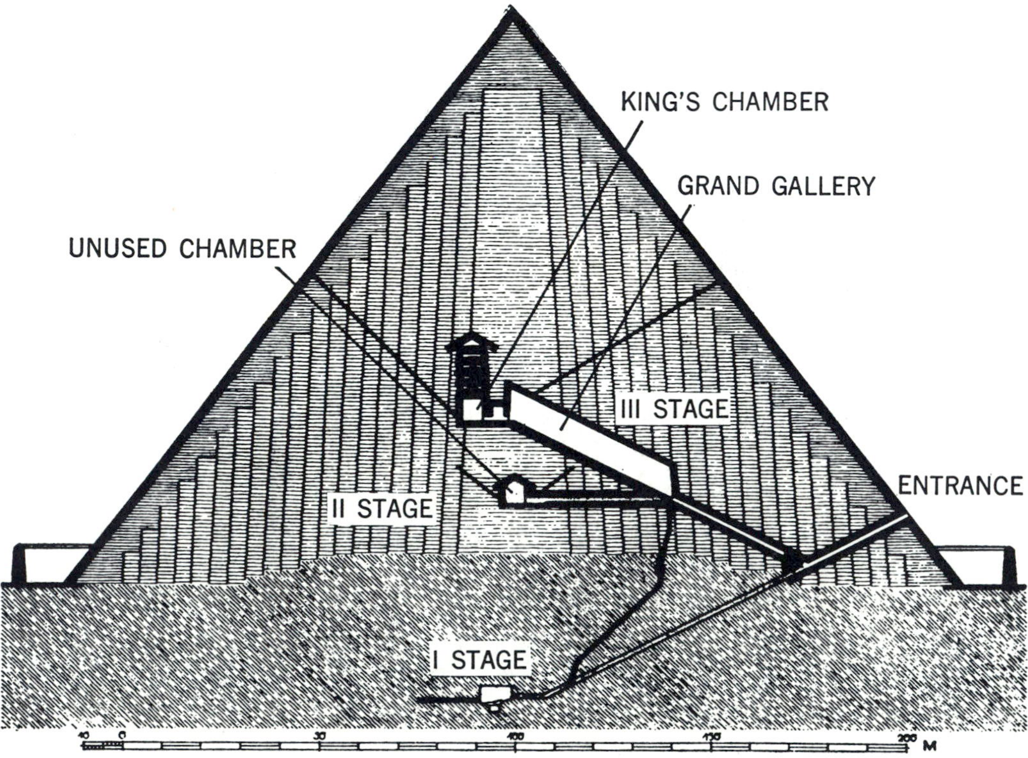

194. CHEOPS' PYRAMID: *North-south cross section showing the changes made in its interior plans. Drawing after Borchardt*

seven feet high in the bent pyramid at Dahshur is here continued on a monumental scale.

The jointing in this gallery is so fine that an Arab historian remarked that neither a needle nor even a hair can be inserted into the joints of the stones. To construct the enormous body of the pyramid the Egyptians used the precision of a watchmaker. The large blocks that form the gallery walls could not have been brought in along the low corridor leading from the pyramid entrance. Borchardt proved that the Grand Gallery was constructed during the process of erecting the pyramid (1932, pp. 5–12).

The Grand Gallery was used once only: when the mummy of the king, lying in his wooden coffin, was carried along it to his funeral chamber. The marvelous great boat found in 1954, untouched, on the south side of this pyramid, was also probably used but once: to bear the body of the dead king from his royal residence to the valley temple.

If ever proof were needed that this architecture—sealed forever, inaccessible to all human beings once the funeral rites were ended—was created as an offering to invisible powers, whether Ka or god-king, it is here.

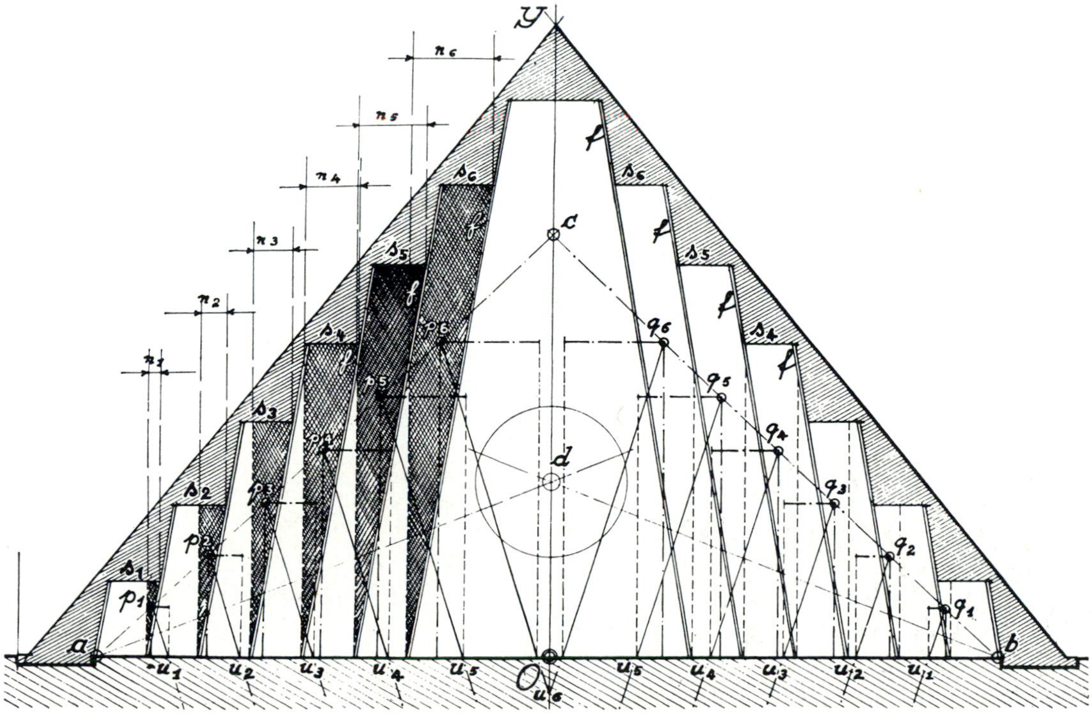

195. THE INTERIOR DYNAMICS OF A PYRAMID: *H. Rössler, a Swiss engineer, calculated that the horizontal thrusts are directed toward the central core at every level, and thus reinforce the stability of the structure. Thirty-five per cent of the vertical thrusts are transmitted to the inner core, reaching from summit to base. Only the remainder of these thrusts have to be carried down into the rock bed. Stability increases with the height of the pyramid. From Rössler*

At the end of the Grand Gallery is a high step. Beyond it a low passage leads below into a kind of antechamber, once protected by three granite portcullises, and thence into the granite-lined funeral chamber of the king, forty meters (some 130 ft.) above ground level. His extremely simple sarcophagus, without any inscriptions, had been set in place, near the northwest corner of the chamber, during construction of the pyramid. Its cover has never been found, and the sarcophagus was empty.

The walls of this funeral chamber are oriented to the cardinal points. Its dimensions (34′ 4″ x 17′ 2″) as well as those of the sarcophagus have been scrupulously analyzed for symbolic implications. The extreme precision of its measurements and the exact north-south alignment has always given the Cheops pyramid a special position, and some of its implications will be discussed below (pp. 472ff).

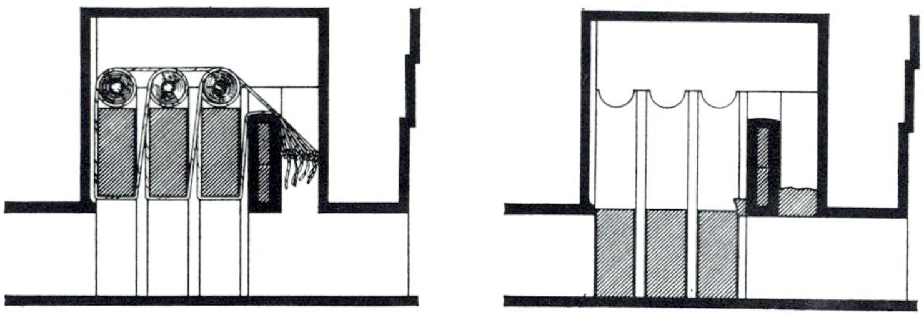

196. THREE PORTCULLISES, CHEOPS' PYRAMID: *At end of Grand Gallery. These protected the entrance to the King's Chamber, which contained his sarcophagus. From Borchardt*

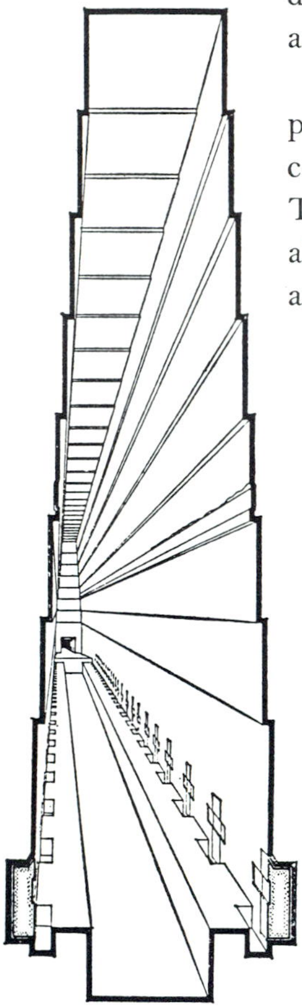

197. THE GRAND GALLERY, CHEOPS' PYRAMID, *leading to the King's Chamber:* L. *153 feet,* H. *28 feet. Corbeled vault with seven projecting courses. From Edwards*

THE LATER PYRAMIDS

The abstract form of the pyramid never vanished from Egyptian memory nor from the vocabulary of architecture. But the enthusiasm which engendered the construction of pyramids did not endure. The perfection they attained in the Fourth Dynasty remains unique—like the Parthenon.

It is not our task to follow their later fate in detail, for it has been recorded fully by others (Lauer, 1948, pp. 86 ff.; Vandier, 1954, II, pp. 101–209; Edwards, 1961, pp. 133–204). A few words will suffice.

Even the Fifth Dynasty pyramids were impermanent. That built in Saqqara by the first king, Weserkaf, from rough blocks, is now but a heap of rubble. Those of his immediate followers, Sahura, Neferirkara, Ne-user-ra, are in little better condition. They were built as a modest triad in Abusir, a few miles from Saqqara. Their heights ranged between fifty and seventy meters.

In the Middle Kingdom, the Twelfth Dynasty kings removed their capital from Thebes and established it again in the north. Their brick pyramids (in Dahshur, Lisht, Lahun) were erected upon a cross network of retaining walls.
These did not hold their form, and little is left of them. The beautiful pyramidion 448
of Amenemhat III, of indestructible basalt, is the only complete capstone of a pyramid extant. Like the pectorals and other jewelry found in the tombs, it shows the highly refined craftsmanship of the period.

Much more significant than these offshoots is the mortuary temple, in the
Theban necropolis, of Mentuhotep, founder of the Middle Kingdom. Here the 410
pyramidal form was used to crown a new building type; it no longer indicated the tomb center, beneath which lay the actual grave.

During the decay of the monarchy and the rising influence of the feudal lords,
royal burial customs changed. Rulers adopted the type of rock-tomb, cut directly 403 ff
into the cliff face, that had been used by the governors of Elephantine during the 406
Sixth Dynasty. Mentuhotep gave this type its monumental form. The pyramid lost its exclusive quality when it ceased to be solely a prerogative of the king.

It often happens that in remote places on the fringes of civilization age-old habits are kept alive or are redeveloped from the beginning. This occurred with the pyramid. In Nubia, between the Fourth and Fifth Cataracts, Ethiopian rulers erected about one hundred and eighty pyramids between 750 B.C. and A.D. 350. These repeated the development from simple gravel mound to pyramid.

Ethiopian kings ruled Egypt for a century. Beneath the first of these southernmost pyramids lay Piankhy, founder of the Twenty-fifth Dynasty. Dunham has carefully traced the development of these diminutive pyramids (1950), but they have nothing in common with the sublime heights of their Egyptian forebears. They sit huddled together like the huts of an African village.

THE PYRAMID COMPLEX

Rites and architectural form

The appearance of stone architecture is linked to another innovation: setting an architectural stage for a highly elaborated ritual. The transposition of symbol and rite into architectural form is never absent from the history of architecture. But in no later period has it so complicated a symbolic content as here in this initial phase.

Every detail of pyramid planning, of the shapes and proportions of the spaces, their number and placement, had symbolic and ritualistic significance. This is
374 an enormous stride in development from the reed temples of the First Dynasty,
204 and even from the Mesopotamian temples, which always retained their original simple organization.

The theme of the whole complex was the stages that had to be gone through to transform the dead king from a still earthly, transient being into an eternal deity. The sequence was approximately as follows: the dead body was cleansed and then prepared for eternity (mummified). These proceedings gave rise to a valley temple on the borders of vegetation, isolated from yet connected to the fertile land. But the king was more than a cadaver. His ties with Upper and Lower Egypt and the assurance of his continued existence were given expression in the form and structure of the valley temple, by means of whole rows of tomb statues, etc.

The location of the desert plateau, about one hundred feet higher than the Nile valley, led to the creation of a causeway up which the mummy of the king was borne to its last station, the pyramid temple, situated on the east side of the pyramid. This was the scene of the priestly rituals and recitals by which the king was transformed into a god before being laid forever in his sarcophagus within the heart of the pyramid.

Initial phases

That these ritualistic observances attained an uncanny elaboration shows the enormous power wielded by the priesthood. Every step in the transformation of the dead king into a god is echoed by its architectural setting.

Like the standard form of the pyramid, this did not occur all at once. Sneferu's

three pyramids, the one at Medum and the two at Dahshur, show stages both in the development of the true pyramid and of its three associated elements: valley temple, causeway, and pyramid temple. But, at Medum as well as at Dahshur, these were of modest proportions compared to the pyramids near them or to Zoser's imposing complex. The causeways that connected the fertile river border with the small offering temples were left uncovered, exposed to the drifting sands. At both Medum and Dahshur the offering places beside the Sneferu pyramids were extremely primitive. The one at Medum was simply 304
a room-sized court with a small altar for offerings to the dead king. On the right and on the left was a stele. Immediately in front of the offering place stood a modest hutlike structure, merely a kind of protective barrier to exclude the unauthorized from this sacred place. The small dark building consisted of a blocked entrance passage that can only be traversed by making a double turn (*couloir à chicane*). These we know from entrances to the many offering chapels 285
in Zoser's Heb-Sed court.

Of the valley temple at Medum almost nothing is known. Thus it was with the greatest interest that Egyptologists awaited the excavation of that of the bent pyramid at Dahshur, which Fakhry undertook in 1951–55. They hoped this would provide information about the earlier stages of the complicated layout of Chephren's valley temple at Giza. "The building that was raised at the lower end of the causeway was, through its position far from the edge of the cultivation and through its planning, so very different from that of the valley temples known to us since Chephren, that one hesitates to call it a valley temple," says Ricke (Fakhry, 1959, p. 106). Fakhry assumes that on the rim of the cultivated land there may be another valley temple.

The Dahshur valley temple, with its inner court and its two rows of closely spaced columns with statue niches behind them, reminds one of the mortuary temples as they developed during the next three generations. It has little in common with the later valley temples. The different spaces needed for performance of valley temple rituals are missing. The elaborate rites developed so strongly under Chephren and Cheops still seem to appear all of a sudden.

Their skeleton, however, existed already: valley temple, causeway, offering temple. "Nevertheless, if the general scheme according to which the southern pyramid of Sneferu was arranged is to be regarded as a preceding step in the organisation of the layout in all later royal pyramids, then our building must also be regarded as the starting point for the development of the later valley temple, and even as the first of valley temples" (ibid., p. 110).

Final phase

The sudden ritualistic expansion that appeared under Sneferu reached its climax in the huge complex erected by his son Cheops. Some social change must have taken place. Generally speaking, the enormous increase in rites and rituals must have resulted from extraordinary gains in power by the clergy. In the huge, newly created halls and pillared courts, hymns to Osiris and Nut and the spells recorded in the Pyramid Texts could resound with the utmost impressiveness. All is new. The divinity of the king, and its cult, reach climax.

Step by step, the scanty remnants of the experimental period show how hesitantly the complicated ritual evolved until it found its ultimate form in the pyramid complexes at Giza.

Heliopolis had been the ancient religious and cultural center, whose beginning is lost in the mists of time. Here a highly organized and ingenious priesthood had grown up which—as always in Egypt—combined interlocking elements of the north and the south.

"The imaginative power of the priests of the Old Kingdom had become so great that they were able to unite two completely different myth cycles—the Osiris myth [from the north] and the old royal myth of the battle between Horus and Seth [from the south] . . . and also to work out the system of the nine gods of Heliopolis [Ennead] and transmit all this to posterity in a poetic form. . . . Although unfortunately no exact dating can be given for this spiritual event, it must certainly . . . have occurred in the first half of the Old Kingdom . . . i.e., in the first half of the third millennium" (Scharff, 1947, p. 35). The belief that the Pyramid Texts stem from a very early period is now obsolete. In Scharff's view they were drawn up in the Third or Fourth Dynasty (p. 16). They, like the rituals, were new in the pyramid age, even if their content reached back to a much earlier period.

The pyramid complexes of Giza grow out of this whole religious movement. The mighty, indispensable intermediary in both ritual and royal power was the priesthood. Only the priests could fulfill what they had themselves promulgated. The new architecture in stone was a necessary adjunct to this highly elaborated ritual. With great ingenuity, Ricke and Schott attempt to discern in the organization of the ground plan a direct projection of certain spells from the Pyramid Texts, and even the expansion and contraction of certain cults, such as that of Osiris (1950).

It was not only the amalgamation of the religious traditions of the south and the north, but also the influence of the desert landscape that gave rise to the architectonic organization of one of the most complicated series of rituals ever invented by man: the sequence of the river passage, the valley temple, the causeway, the pyramid temple, and the pyramid itself.

The relation between these rites and the architecture they produced can perhaps be best seen in the valley temple of Chephren and the pyramid temple of Mycerinus.

The valley temple of Chephren

The valley temple of Chephren is the only Fourth Dynasty sanctuary that still preserves its former grandeur. This is probably because it lay hidden beneath the desert sand until detected in 1853 by the sharp eyes of Mariette, who came upon it from behind when clearing sand from around the Sphinx. The front of the temple, which had doorways six meters high, remained under the sand until the beginning of this century. The only adornments on the sloping walls of polished rose granite from Aswan were beautiful hieroglyphs in relief, recording the name and titles of the king.

The entrance to the interior did not lead directly to its goal. The simple baffle-wall entry (*couloir à chicane*) to the little offering temple at Medum, which 304
still preserves the deep-rooted prehistoric notion of protecting the sanctuary from the view of the uninitiated, here achieves high monumentality.

The two entrances for Upper and Lower Egypt are symmetrically organized, and appear in plan almost like two interconnecting pipelines. Their vestibules 325
stretch up 9.40 meters into the building fabric. Walls, floors, and ceilings are of polished granite. Both vestibules end in a blank wall. All other spaces are lower. A narrow passage leads at right angles into a long rectangular antechamber whose height is only about four meters.

From here one enters the cross hall of the T-shaped hypostyle by means of a short central passage.

What was the function of the different spaces?

There is no complete agreement as to whether the body of the king was cleansed and embalmed elsewhere (Grdseloff, 1941, pp. 10–12), or whether these procedures took place on the roof of the valley temple (Drioton, 1941, p. 1013). In any case the main purpose of the valley temple would be to accomplish the rites of purification of the embalmed body and the ceremonies of the "Opening of the mouth" of the Ka statues of the king, as elucidated by Grdseloff.

198. POST AND BEAM CONSTRUCTION, CHEPHREN'S VALLEY TEMPLE: *Detail. The monolithic granite pillars of the center aisle support massive granite architraves*

199. CENTER AISLE OF CHEPHREN'S VALLEY TEMPLE, *looking toward the antechamber (cf. col. pl. X)*

200. GROUND PLAN OF CHEPHREN'S VALLEY TEMPLE, *147 feet square.* H. *43 feet. Walls extremely thick. Drawing after Hölscher*

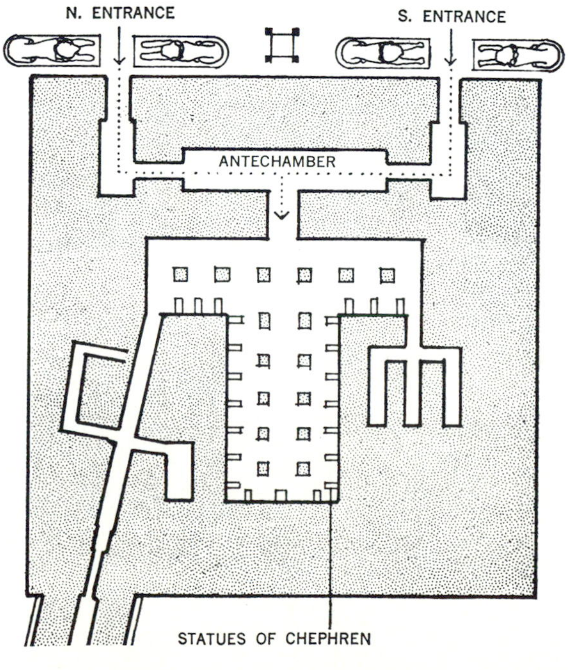

The T-shaped hypostyle hall

255 col, 325 The great T-shaped hypostyle hall with its sixteen monolithic granite columns has also been variously interpreted. Most see it as a single space and the below scene for the "Opening of the mouth" of the twenty-three statues of the king which lined its walls. Only after the priests had performed this complicated ceremony could the statues receive their Ka.

Ricke, however, does not see this hall as one unified space. He considers the cross hall to be the ritual embalming site and the long nave the scene for the "Opening of the mouth." "Their monumental form is an expression of the ideal distinction between the handicraft of mummification in a workshop and the ritual embalming in a cult center" (1950, p. 96).

For the execution of these rites, which culminated in the ceremony of the "Opening of the mouth," it is most likely that the coffin containing the mummy was brought into the empty space in the center aisle of the mouth-opening area. "The ritualistic connection of the embalming place and the place for the 'Opening of the mouth' . . . is made impressively visible in the building form of the

201. LEFT AISLE OF CHEPHREN'S VALLEY TEMPLE: *Reconstruction. Only a partly obstructed, dim light could enter narrow horizontal slits cut through slabs in the roof and wall, as earlier in Zoser's ceremonial passageway. Twenty-three diorite statues of Chephren stood around the walls of the T-shaped chamber. From Hölscher*

valley temple of Chephren through its highly ingenious juncture of a two-aisled cross hall with a three-aisled nave" (p. 98).

No hesitation whatsoever is apparent in the use of these large blocks of stone, the square-cut monolithic columns and heavy beams. Horizontal and vertical 324
meet directly with no intermediary. A stern architecture, fully in accord with the mournful rituals for which it was designed and which shaped every detail of its structure.

The causeway

Sometimes, as here, the archaeologist has to have the talents of a detective to track down the narrow, completely asymmetrical entrance to the roofed causeway, which ran in one straight line for more than a quarter of a mile.

The mortuary temple of Mycerinus

The mortuary temples attached to the pyramids of Cheops, Chephren, and Mycerinus express the culmination of the newly developed funeral rites for the dead monarch. Two functions were combined and yet separated in the same building: a place of veneration and an altar for offerings.

The first was intended for daily services venerating the dead king, and large endowments were set aside so that these could continue eternally. The main feature of this area was a large inner court where hymns and prayers were chanted or recited.

The first appearance of the inner court in its full magnitude was in the
mortuary temple attached to Cheops' great pyramid, but only remnants of its 328
surrounding black basalt pillars remain. Researches by Lauer and Ricke give us some conception of the grandiose pathos of its architecture (Lauer, 1948, p. 95). The walls bore reliefs of which some fragments have been found. The square black pillars of the peristyle gave a monumental frame to the daily services in the large, skyward-oriented inner court—a feature destined to play an outstanding role thereafter in Egyptian ritual architecture.

The second function of the mortuary temple—the offertory—was carefully secluded from the court of veneration. It was the most intimate part of the temple. The offering table itself and one or two large steles were directly attached to the pyramid, to be as near as possible to the resting place of the
king. They retained the same modest size as at the pyramids of Medum and 304, 307
Dahshur.

202. PLATFORM OF CHEOPS' MORTUARY TEMPLE: *Nothing remains of this earliest known monumental building except the remnants of a few square columns, as in the foreground*

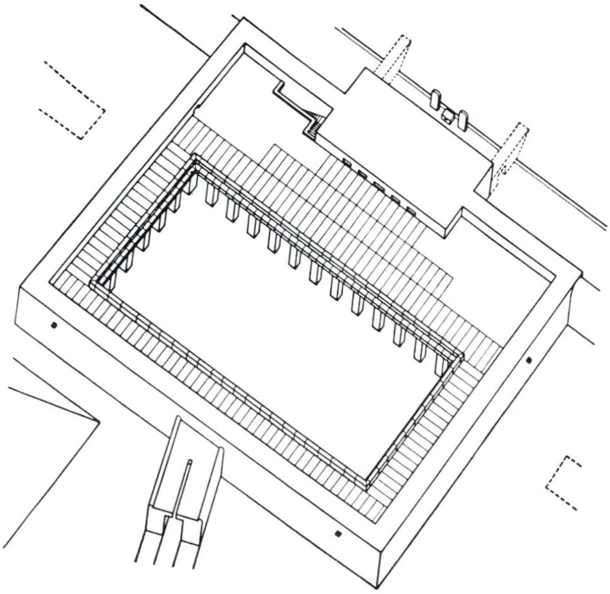

203. RECONSTRUCTION, CHEOPS' MORTUARY TEMPLE, *adjacent to his pyramid. Drawing by Ricke*

204. AERIAL VIEW OF MYCERINUS' PYRAMID *showing east face with adjoining mortuary temple. From Reisner*

The dual purpose of the mortuary temple as a court of veneration and an offertory can best be seen in Mycerinus' building, even though this was never fully completed owing to the disturbed situation at the beginning of his reign and to its relatively brief duration. above

The original plan was to construct the temple of local limestone, but in the end, limestone blocks were only used for the foundations and the core of some of the walls. The rest was brick covered with whitewash. Ricke crystallized Mycerinus' original plan from several different variants (1950, pp. 55–62). Reisner undertook the excavation of the whole complex (1931).

206. DEEP NICHE OF MYCERINUS' MORTUARY TEMPLE: *The huge seated statue was probably placed at its farthest end*

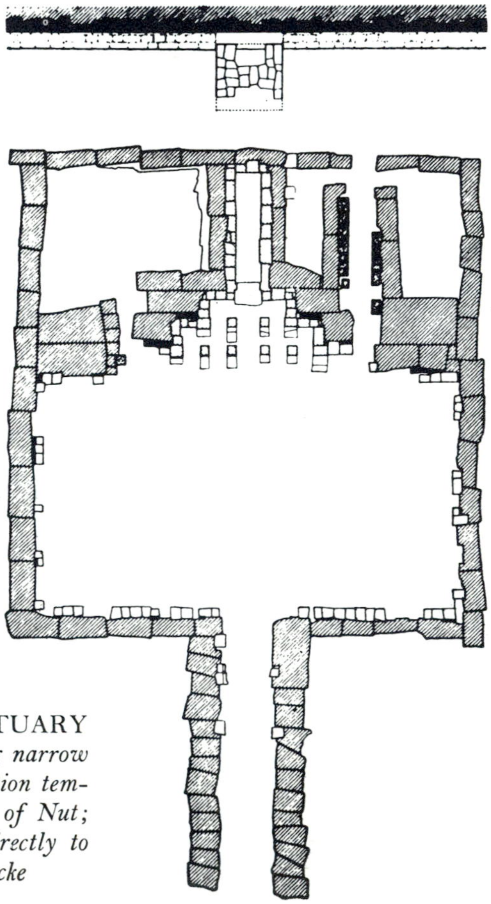

205. COLOSSAL ALABASTER STATUE OF MYCERINUS: *This statue, 7 feet 8 inches high, was found by G. A. Reisner near the mortuary temple, broken in several pieces*

207. GROUND PLAN OF MYCERINUS' MORTUARY TEMPLE *reconstructed by Ricke, showing the long narrow vestibule; large inner court, the center of the veneration temple; deep niche behind the pillars of the Gateway of Nut; and the separated and secluded passage leading directly to the offering table attached to the pyramid. From Ricke*

208. MORTUARY TEMPLE ON EAST FACE OF MYCERINUS' PYRAMID:
In the foreground the ruins of the long, covered vestibule, now in full sunlight

The day side

From the causeway one enters the mortuary temple through a narrow vestibule that leads into the great sun court. The mystical atmosphere of the valley temple with its dim lighting and the long darkness of the causeway has radically changed. All rituals to ensure the future life of the god-king have been com- **left**

209. SECLUDED PASSAGEWAY TO MYCERINUS' OFFERING TABLE: *The walls were faced with blocks of black granite*

pleted. The cosmos in all its splendor may again have right of entry. The architecture expresses that fact in masterly fashion.

A sun court surrounded by pillars, such as Mycerinus planned, had never before been built. Pillars normally stood only before the deep passagelike niche at the far side of the court, forming—according to Ricke—the Gateway of Nut which separated the day-side cults of Ra from the night-side cults of Osiris.

330 A colossal seated alabaster statue of King Mycerinus (7 ft. 8 in. high) was in all probability placed at the farthest end of the deep niche. Reassembled from

several large fragments found by Reisner in the temple area, it now towers above the other Egyptian statuary in the Museum of Fine Arts, Boston. Its unusually athletic torso shows that the king has regained in death the full vigor of his earthly life.

The width of the sun court was narrowed by stages to form the columned passageway—the so-called Gateway of Nut—which terminated in the deep niche. The court was the "public" area where daily services were held for the dead king, and for this reason the whole is sometimes called a veneration temple (*Verehrungstempel*). The duty of caring for and restoring the mortuary temple was laid upon the priesthood, to be met out of the endowments left for the perpetual continuance of the daily services there. In the case of Mycerinus, the original temple was completed only in a somewhat crude manner.

The night side

Near the northwest corner of the sun court a narrow passage leads toward the left pyramid. Right and left it was lined with blocks of black granite. Despite its ruinous condition one receives an instant impression of awe. This passage opens onto the narrow space at the foot of the pyramid within its encircling wall—the most sacred precinct, to which no chamber of the so-called public area had access. In it, directly attached to the pyramid, stood an offering altar with one or two steles, as at Medum and Dahshur. In this final station before the pyramid, 304, 307 utmost simplicity again prevails.

The pyramid complex of the Fourth Dynasty was not developed further as a building type. The sun sanctuaries that appear in the Fifth Dynasty contain no new elements, either in their situation on the rim of the desert or in their structural program. Their ritualistic significance, however, presents an interesting phenomenon.

THE SUN SANCTUARIES OF THE FIFTH DYNASTY

Humanization of the deity

Sun sanctuaries are a peculiarity of the Fifth Dynasty. Each of its first six kings erected his own sanctuary for the Heliopolitan sun-god Ra. Weserkaf, with whom the dynasty opens, built the first one in Saqqara; with the sixth king their use disappeared forever. They represent a short interlude in the Egyptian development during which the fusion of human with divine nature was pushed to such an extreme that these sanctuaries borrowed elements of the royal pyramid complex—that masterly creation for the transformation of a mortal into a deity. In the sun temple, however, it was the deity who assumed human existence. One can go no further.

The cause was to hand. The sun temples of the six kings mark the pinnacle of the Ra cult in Heliopolitan theology. This occurred in the Fifth Dynasty when, as Gardiner records, "the Hēliopolitan priesthood began to wield an unprecedented influence" (1961, p. 84). On the same page he adds: "The dominant position of the sun-god is reflected in a fresh development that now befell the royal titulary. Hitherto the name of the Rē^{c} had appeared only in the cartouches of" kings of the Fourth Dynasty. In the Fifth Dynasty the name of the sun-god appears as part of the praenomen of the king: an all-important change for Egypt.

A legend that the first three kings were the triplet sons of a Heliopolitan priestess and the sun-god Ra is recorded in a Berlin papyrus from the Late Period. It is now thought that the kings of the Fifth Dynasty were the direct offspring of Cheops. Even so, the legend contains an inner truth: the sun sanctuaries were exponents of the Heliopolitan cult, and their disappearance toward the end of the Fifth Dynasty can be attributed to the rapid growth of the Osiris cult. This already heralds the coming Intermediate Period. The radiant confidence which formed part of sun worship disappeared amid the grief and anxiety which beset both the individual and the state during that troubled period.

Upon the walls of the passages and the tomb chamber of the last king of the Fifth Dynasty, Unas, Maspero found in 1881 the first inscribed Pyramid Texts. In them the ever-growing might of Osiris comes out strongly. This development from the highest rise of the solar cult to a flight to the god of the dead, who held the powers of ultimate decision as to future life, encompassed little more than two centuries.

The sun sanctuary of Ne-user-ra

Of the six Fifth Dynasty sun sanctuaries recorded, only one—the complex of Ne-user-ra at Abu Gurob—affords a comprehensive view of their puzzling layout. Borchardt excavated and studied it in 1898–1901 (1905). We can gain from it some comprehension of the inner structure of the Fifth Dynasty fusion of deity with human being. The sanctuary lies on a terrace of leveled sand about twenty minutes' walk from the pyramid and marvelous pyramid temple of its constructor, Ne-user-ra (1907, p. 5). The Nile floods reach to the valley portal which announces the beginning of the sanctuary. This pavilion reminds one in many ways of Chephren's valley temple: sloping walls, separate doorways for Upper and Lower Egypt, and a symmetrical organization of the inner passageways, although of course no hall for the mortuary rites of the king. There is also a roofed causeway that leads from the valley temple to a main area built on an artificially raised and leveled podium. The chief feature of this area was the great sun court in which the priests celebrated daily rites for the king. Access to this sun sanctuary was through an entrance portico. below

All details point to the main purpose: a place of sacrifice, a great court for

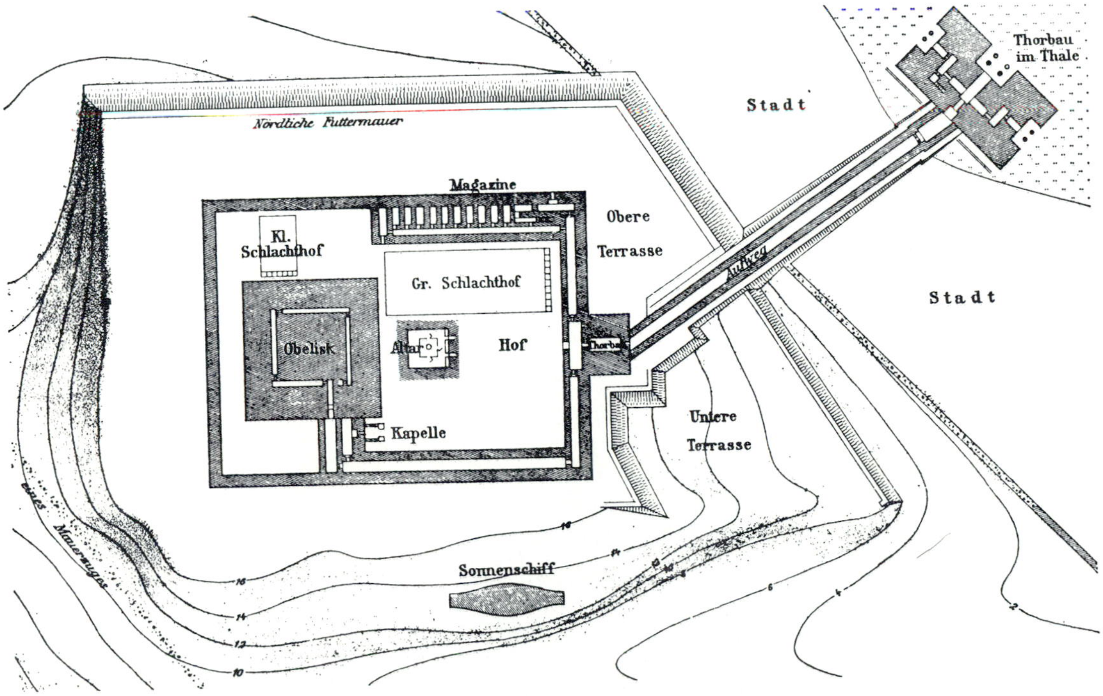

210. SITE PLAN OF NE-USER-RA'S SUN SANCTUARY: *The sanctuary of the sun-god Ra follows the organization of the Fourth Dynasty pyramid complex—valley temple or portal, covered causeway, temple with large court (here 300 x 250 ft.) for sacrifices to the sun-god—before a heavy obelisk instead of a pyramid. Large sun boat outside the enclosure. Fifth Dynasty. From Borchardt*

211. REMAINS OF OBELISK OF NE-USER-RA'S SUN SANCTUARY *at Abu Gurob: The end of the causeway can be seen in the background at the right*

212. SUNKEN RELIEF OF OBELISK: *From chapel of Ti, Saqqara. Painted with green on a granite block in the sun court*

the sacrificial slaughter of animals, with runnels cut into the pavement to drain away their blood, as in the temples of Peru. Ten (today nine) alabaster basins 335, 338 were placed in a row to the right of the entrance; their rims are surrounded with small cuplike hollows like those found later around the fertility altars of Minoan Crete. "Their inner section is like the form of the beautiful vessels of gleaming red pottery known from the Old Kingdom" (1905, p. 48). Perhaps they were basins to receive blood from a cut throat, as Borchardt believed. This was a slaughter area in the grand manner, complete with a mighty alabaster altar 338, 339 immediately before the sun obelisk. In the center of the altar a raised circular platter, reminiscent of the original form of an eating platter, was surrounded by four offering places each in the shape of a *hetep* hieroglyph ⌓, signifying a mat with a circular loaf of bread upon it. These four offering tables were oriented to the cardinal points. The offering table between the two steles at 304 Sneferu's Medum pyramid had a form similar to these, and offering platters in the *hetep* form have been found in many mastabas.

Sun altars of modest size, approached by small steps, also appear in the New Kingdom, such as the altar of the uppermost terrace dedicated to Amon-Ra in 417 Hatshepsut's temple and the one behind Tuthmosis III's festival hall in Karnak, but none had so prominent a position or such sculptural monumentality.

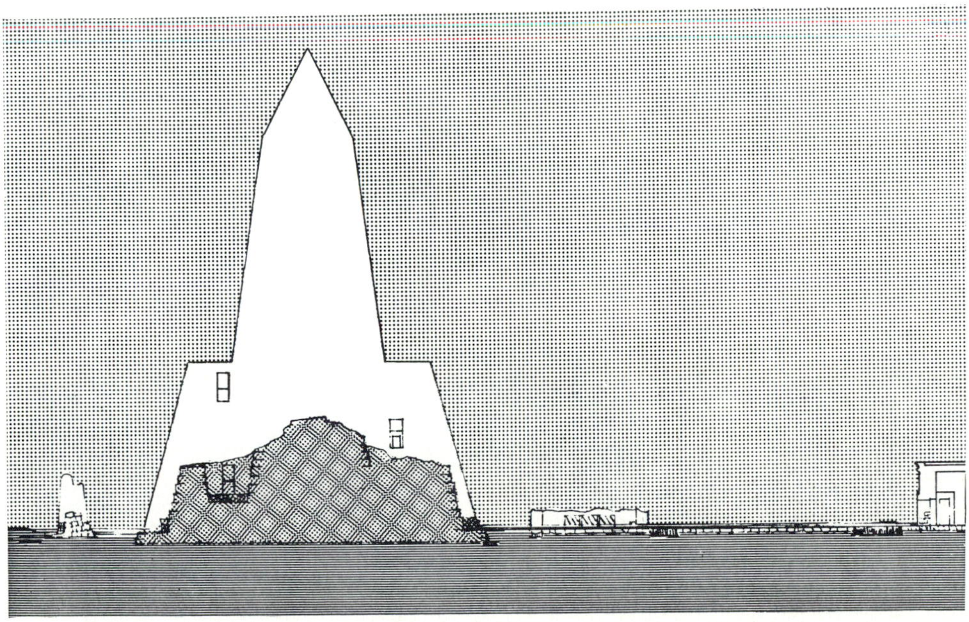

213. RECONSTRUCTION OF OBELISK OF NE-USER-RA. *Drawing after Borchardt*

214. ROUND ALABASTER BASINS WITHIN SUN COURT *on immediate right of entrance from causeway: They were meant to contain the blood of sacrificed animals*

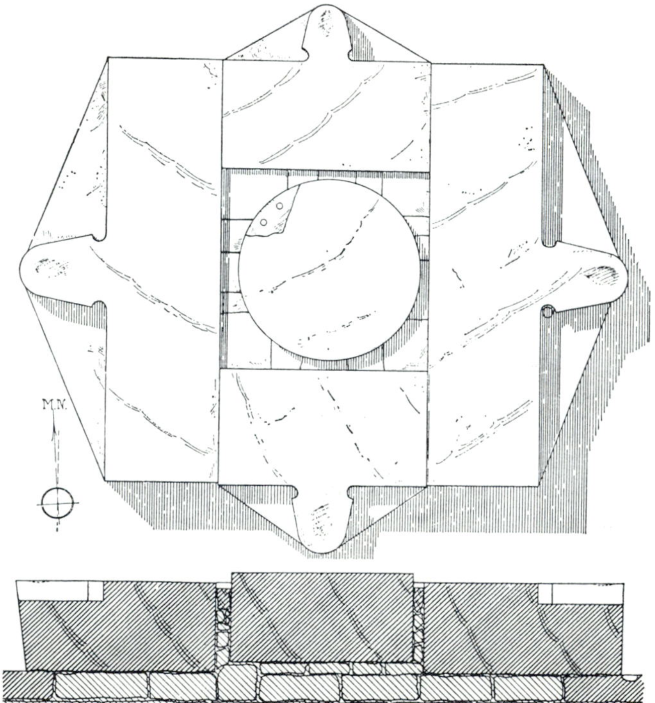

215. PLAN OF SACRIFICIAL ALTAR IN SUN COURT: *A hetep (bread form) on each of its four sides. Raised circular offering table in center. From Borchardt*

216. SACRIFICIAL ALTAR IN SUN COURT, *directly in front of the obelisk*

217. CIRCULAR OFFERING TABLE: *Set within the sacrificial altar. The blood of the sacrificed animals was probably conducted in channels across the court to the alabaster basins*

The sun court of this sanctuary (330 x 250 ft.), which betrays every sign of cosmic orientation up to the magical union through blood, concentrates the significance of the Egyptian inner court without the addition of a surrounding portico. All is directed toward the eternal circle under the protection of the obelisk, symbol of the sun's rays. One emerged into this area from a dark passage that led from the entrance portal into the interior of the truncated pyramid. There was, of course, no corpse to protect. A winding passage led up to the
337 open platform from which the heavy obelisk (built of stone blocks) rose to a height of about thirty meters. Court, altar, obelisk, were all bathed in light.
335 To the south are brick foundations upon which once lay a solar boat similar in dimensions to the marvelously preserved wooden one found on the south side of the Cheops pyramid.

On the meaning of the sun sanctuaries

Are the sun sanctuaries exclusively places of worship, veneration places for the sun-god? All signs indicate it. Their main accent was the towering Ra symbol: the obelisk rising above the truncated pyramid and the place of sacrifice.

The first sun sanctuaries had merely a truncated pyramid, similar to the earlier mastabas and similar in shape to the tomb of Shepseskaf, last king of the Fourth Dynasty. During three seasons from 1955 to 1957, H. Stock and Ricke searched for Weserkaf's sun temple. Little was left of it except for a few revealing details such as a "meager altar of Nile mud bricks" (Stock, 1959, p. 11).

It was Neferirkara, third king and builder of the highest pyramid of the Fifth Dynasty, who first set an obelisk upon the truncated pyramid as a dominating architectural form. Both forms—truncated pyramid and obelisk—can be traced back to symbols of Atum-Ra in the temples of Heliopolis. The truncated pyramid, together with the position of the sun temple on a hill, was conceived
336 as an abstraction of the "high sands" symbol at Heliopolis; the obelisk itself as an abstraction of the benben stone, the first manifestation of Atum-Ra from the primeval chaos (Kaiser, 1956, p. 111).

Yet there are questions whether these sun sanctuaries were destined solely for the god Ra. To judge by Egyptian habit, it is more than probable that they were intended for more than a single purpose.

Each of the six kings built his own sanctuary. What does this mean? Is not the entire project (as has been suggested) a "double"—a second place of veneration? "In other words, should the king maintain, besides his tomb as an earthly ruler, a personal place of worship for himself as one reunited after death with his father Ra?" (Winter, 1957, p. 233)

The significance of the sun sanctuaries of the Fifth Dynasty may be related to the royal mortuary cult (Kaiser, 1956, p. 114). One is reminded of the cenotaphs of the First Dynasty, of the false tomb and the actual tomb that the early kings erected, one in Upper and the other in Lower Egypt, as a double security for their further existence. In the Fifth Dynasty, when the cult of the king as the son of god and the cult of Ra had risen to such pre-eminence that it was possible to readopt the external appearance of the pyramid complex, a fusion of veneration rites for the dead king with those of the sun-god can well be understood.

ON THE MEANING OF THE PYRAMIDS

The meaning of the pyramids has always preoccupied Egyptologists. Not only Egyptologists: astronomers and astrologers, architects and engineers, theologians and mystics, mathematicians and romantic visionaries have continually come up with new interpretations of the nature and inner significance of the great pyramid.

Nothing could be further from my intention than to enter into the interpretative controversies to which the simple, enigmatic form of the pyramid has given rise. Many are recounted by Lauer (1948, pp. 110–60). But I will point out that the theories of the Egyptologists crystallize around two continually recurring and opposing points of view, one materialistic, the other symbolic.

The materialistic concept explains the configuration of the pyramid as the outcome of technical developments, as a culmination of numerous tentative approaches (Speleers, 1935–38, p. 603). This is basically Petrie's view, as he states in his account of the Medum pyramid: "The system by which the construction was carried on bears an evident analogy to the building of the great mastaba tombs in the cemetery of Medum. . . . These wide, flat 'mastabas,' or 'benches,' were added to during the owner's lifetime by coating them with one or two thick masses of brickwork. . . . Such a system exactly agrees with what we see in the pyramid of Medum" (1892, p. 5).

Borchardt, to whom we owe many careful studies of Egyptian architecture, also believes that the form of the pyramid is the result of the efforts of several generations of architects, after many detours and ultimately "perhaps by chance" (1928, p. 40). His approach is based upon construction procedures.

Ernesto Schiaparelli's symbolic approach in 1884

Symbolic ritual begets technical construction, and not contrariwise. The world of the Egyptians was similar to the world of prehistory: filled with symbols in which reality and the hereafter, sacred and profane, were inextricably intertwined. It was a world of the eternal present—the unending continuance of existence. Death was only a bridge leading from one real existence to another; but because of this it had tremendous importance. Probably no other people have made this transition so central to their thinking. Thus no others have ever given it so overpowering an architectural expression.

The relation between the pyramid and its symbolic significance can only be encompassed in a broad sense. The pyramid cannot be considered in isolation, whether as a tomb or as a formal shape. It is bound up with the ascendant solar cult in which the god, the king, and the Ka merge. At the same time, it incorporates age-old concepts too.

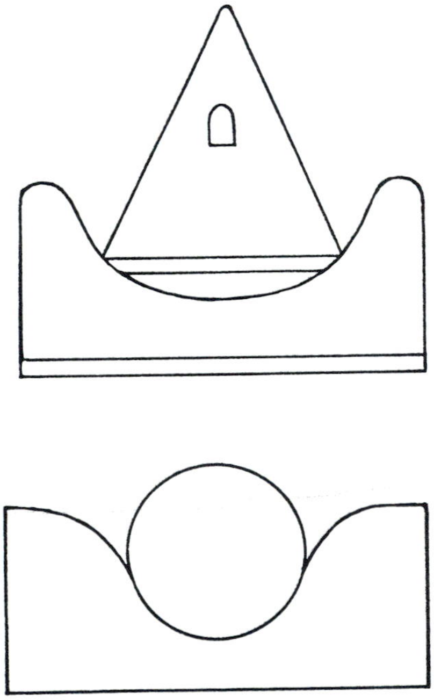

218. SCHIAPARELLI'S RELATION OF SUN AND PYRAMID: *Schiaparelli compares the sun disk between two mountains ("the sun in its horizon") with a pyramid standing in place of the sun*

Scholars have been aware of this from the beginning, but Schiaparelli was one of the first to place on a sound scholarly basis his inquiry into the symbolic meaning of the pyramids. Possessed of the universal outlook of a great scholar, he dared to go into this problem in 1884, at a time when the Pyramid Texts had only just been discovered by Maspero and still lay untranscribed on the walls of King Unas' tomb. Like J. J. Bachofen, Schiaparelli turned to unpretentious tomb inscriptions for clues to the meaning of the pyramids. From small amulets in pyramid form, which were placed beside the dead, he recognized the relation of the pyramid with the sun. Upon one amulet he saw "a pyramid emerging from left between two mountains" (p. 126), which looked like the hieroglyph of the "sun in its horizon."

It is like a defense against later materialistic explanations when Schiaparelli stresses that "the generative conception of the obelisk was not a casual combination of geometrical lines but represented a bundle of solar rays, which emanate from the little pyramid [the pyramidion] which constitutes its upper extremity, and descend vertically to give warmth and fertility to the earth" (pp. 127–28), and recalls the eight sun-adoring cynocephalic (dog-headed) apes at the foot of the Luxor obelisk. (One of these is now in the Louvre.)

The masonry obelisk, as it first appeared in monumental size in the sun sanctuary of Ne-user-ra, had not been known before that time. Its shape, an 337 abstraction of the Heliopolitan baetyl benben, grew out of the shape of the Fourth Dynasty pyramid and was held to thereafter.

From inscriptions, Schiaparelli proved "the simultaneity of the cult of the soul of the dead Pharaoh buried in the pyramid with the cult of the sun represented by the god Ra and other divinities with essentially solar character, above all the goddess Hathor" (p. 132), who was simultaneously known as "Daughter of Ra" and "Mother of Ra": self-procreating, parthenogenetic, the ancient, ever-recurring symbol of life and of the self-renewing sun. Schiaparelli here touches on a current theory that does not regard the pyramid as exclusively expressing the spiritually creative male element. In the Heliopolitan religion, the male principle—Atum-Ra—was the all-highest from which all the other divine forces emanated (Thausing, 1948, p. 124). The female principle "is that which is split off from the highest" (ibid.), but it was also included in the chthonic part of the pyramid as the maternal womb of the earth. This was later expressed on the lids of sarcophagi, where the mother-goddesses Nut, Isis, and Nephthys are shown giving life and protection to the dead.

Schiaparelli's point of departure, in broad outline, was this: the pyramids

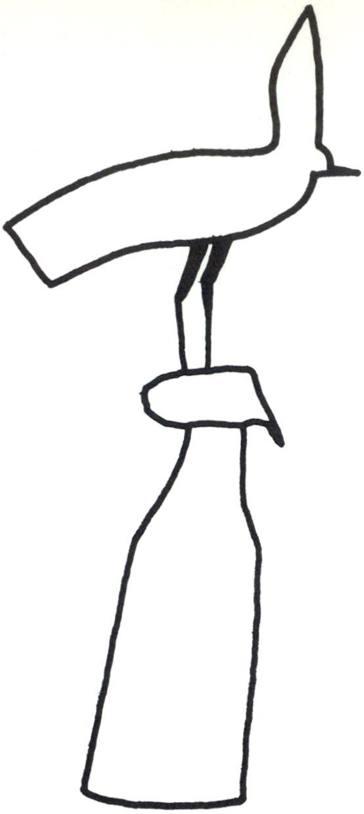

219. BENOU AND BENBEN: *The crested bird from the shoulder of the kneeling man (fig. 220) probably represents the phoenix Benou, and the stone on which he stands the boulder which first emerged from chaos, the benben*

220. KNEELING GRANITE STATUE: *Three royal names are engraved on the right shoulder, also a bird perched on a conical stone. Second Dynasty*

were perceived not as isolated tombs but in a symbolic frame of relationships, which binds them together as similar "cult objects" (*oggetti di culto;* p. 132) with the primeval hill, the monolithic benben in the temple of Heliopolis, and the obelisks before the great temples of the New Kingdom. This conception of the (380) pluralistic meaning of the pyramid has since been widened, but Schiaparelli's approach is still basically valid.

Alexandre Moret: benben, pyramid, and obelisk

Moret, fifty years later, threw more light on the still obscure representation of the sacred benben stone of Heliopolis by showing how it was represented in the first dynasties. He referred to an archaic granite statue from the end of the (left) Second Dynasty. On the right shoulder of this kneeling figure the royal names of three kings are engraved, each in its *serekh*—a rectangle that customarily contained the Horus name of the king—surmounted by the Horus falcon. They are preceded by "a bird with a crest which is not a falcon but probably the phoenix Benou; he holds in his claws the conical end of a stone baetyl whose form is vaguely pyramidal [conical]. I do not doubt that this is the Benou who shines on the ben, as in the Pyramid Text [Utterance 600]" (1935–38, p. 624).

The benben was originally a menhir, like many in the Mediterranean area and in other regions. In Heliopolitan theology it became the primeval hill, which the anthropomorphic god Atum drew out from chaos. Moret saw the relationship between the ben and the monoliths of the neolithic period (pp. 623–24). Referring to the name benben, Moret states that "the doubling of a root signifies repetition, or intensity" (p. 626). We can no longer agree with the opinions he developed from this, though the basic premise still holds good. The current belief is rather that "even the name of the stone is characteristic: benben, since it conceals the root *bn, wbn,* which is bound up with the notion of shining, brilliant, ascending" (Thausing, 1948, p. 122).

The masonry obelisk that appeared in the Fifth Dynasty is indeed "the final (337) development of the baetyl in its regularized form and in its role as the image of the sun" (Moret, 1935–38, p. 625). This is what Pliny the Elder meant when he stated in an oft-quoted passage that obelisks were petrified rays of sunlight.

The "perfect" obelisk as it arose in the Middle Kingdom is "a needle of stone on a square plan, terminating in a pointed pyramidion, with four faces, each of which is an isosceles triangle" (ibid.).

The symbolism of the isosceles triangle

Since the time of Schiaparelli it has been confirmed that the pyramid *Gestalt*, like that of the obelisk, did not arise from a casual combination of geometrical lines nor from a better knowledge of stone techniques, but that "the pyramid in Egypt was a symbol of the radiating sun" (Schiaparelli, 1884, p. 144). We also know that the characteristic triangular shape of its constituent elements was connected with changes in ritual which occurred in the Fourth and perhaps at the very end of the Third Dynasties, with the ascendance of the all-powerful solar cult.

There is general agreement that the form of the step pyramid is associated with the idea of ascending. "A stairway to heaven shall be laid down for him [the king], that he may ascend to heaven thereon," says Utterance 267 of the Pyramid Texts (tr. Mercer, 1952, I, p. 89). This is not very different from the Sumerian view of the ziggurat as an intermediary to heaven, but in Sumer it was thought that the gods had their abode in the temple on its summit. The idea of a ladder was combined with the idea of a mountain rising upward. The ziggurat—the newly arisen mountain—was regarded as the center of the world wherever it stood.

As the step pyramid was replaced by the standard form of the pyramid, the form of an isosceles triangle with two horizontal lines representing the enclosure below walls became the pyramid hieroglyph (*mer*). This, by the way, suggests how late certain hieroglyphs were introduced.

The significance of the pyramid is undoubtedly multiple. One cannot reduce it to the single idea of a tomb, a ladder to the sky, a light cone, or the earthly symbol for the sun-god. It is all these and much more besides. Its all-embracing significance lies in the notion of the eternal wandering which was expressed in 274 Zoser's early pyramid precinct and was given still more cosmic expression in

221. HIEROGLYPHS *of pyramid with enclosure wall* (*Fourth Dynasty*) *and obelisk* (*Fifth Dynasty*)

the Fourth Dynasty pyramid complexes and in the great temples of the New Kingdom.

We finally approach very tentatively the meaning of the pyramid's most important constituent, the isosceles triangle. Where did it come from? How can it be understood? It is an age-old symbol, used in prehistory; when pointing downward it represented the vulva as a fertility symbol. This was shown over and over again in *The Beginnings of Art*. 1:179 ff

In this form it appears frequently during the fourth millennium in Mesopotamia and in Egypt, heavily incised on small female figurines—fertility symbols 1:177 ff called mother-goddesses.

It was transformed during the early Sumerian period into an isolated abstract triangle. The masked face from Hassuna (Mesopotamia)—a fragment of the 100 earliest pottery—shows conspicuously how the residual space is filled up with black triangles, their points directed downward. Triangles painted, hatched, or crosshatched, arranged in rows, are very widespread in the area of the painted-vase culture in Asiatic countries and in Egypt (Baumgärtel, 1955, p. 56).

A fully preserved vase from Cemetery A in Kish (Mesopotamia) has its 101 handle treated as a female figure. The significance of the triangle just below the handle of this tomb vessel becomes even more obvious, since its dimensions are enormous in comparison with the flat, roughly indicated female figure along the handle.

Triangles pointing upward were also often used in the earliest Sumerian 200 period, as in an incense burner from Tepe Gawra.

In Egypt the black tulip beakers of the Tasian period—the oldest ceramics of Egypt—have two rows of almost-isosceles triangles with herringbone hatching: one row pointing upward and one row pointing downward, separated by horizontal bands.

The upward-directed isosceles triangle cannot be pinned down simply as a male fertility symbol. Its pluralistic meaning can incorporate the Mountains of the West and of the East as shown on an Amratian dish, where they are sur- 129 rounded by the primeval ocean and the ocean of the sky. The upward-pointing triangle has also been associated with an uprising flame and the downward-pointing triangle with water always flowing down to the deepest point, again involving aspects of male and female fertility (Schwabe, 1951, p. 154).

The hieroglyph of the pyramidion—the symbol of the sun and abode of the sun-god—is a black triangle.

As to the direction of the triangle, there may have been a change from a chthonic period, when the symbol of female fertility prevailed, to the prevalence of a male hierarchy which found its most complete artistic expression in the pyramids of the Fourth Dynasty.

The symbolism of the square

The pyramid is a volume. Its four triangular planes are but its constituent elements. Their external form arises from the processes of abstraction undergone by the sacred benben stone. The way this was accomplished is typical of the symbolization that underlay everything.

Numbers had not only quantitative properties in the earliest high civilizations, but also qualitative ones, frequently cosmic and divine. The single numbers from one to ten had a special meaning in the different cultures: in the sexagesimal system of the Sumerians, in the decimal system of the Babylonians, and the numbers seven and nine for the Greeks.

Sethe says that one can consider the number four "as, so to say, the sacred number of the Egyptians. . . . The outstanding position of this number is based upon our conception of outer space, the four directions of the heavens (the corners of the world, the supports of heaven . . .), the four winds. . . . The four faces of certain gods and demons (Pyramid Texts, §1207b), or the four horns which certain demonic animals are supposed to possess, one for each direction of the heavens (§470a), are all directly bound up with this conception" (1916, p. 31).

Kees, who enlarged Sethe's theory, thought that one reason for the sacredness of the number four was the natural configuration of Egypt, that it was "incited by the division of the land into 'Upper' (south), 'Lower' (north), 'Right' (west), and 'Left' (east), predestined by the course of the Nile as the central axis. . . . From this complementary reciprocity, the Egyptians derived the four quarters of the world. In accordance with the four directions of the heavens, the sky for them rested upon four pillars" (1941, pp. 167–68). Further examples are the fourfold canopic jars for the intestines, the fact that every purification and consecration must be repeated four times, and many more.

Part XI

The square, as far as we can see, was the most complete plastic expression of the sacred number. Unalterably the square formed the basis from which every true pyramid arose. The interplay between pyramid and cosmos is made clear beyond question by the great precision with which each is oriented to the four cardinal points.

PART IX THE GREAT TEMPLES AND THE ETERNAL WANDERING

Seldom in the history of architecture have the preliminary stages of monumental buildings been so indistinct as in the temples of the New Kingdom.

Such remains of sacred buildings from the Old Kingdom as exist provide no reliable key to the vanished monuments. Temples of the Fourth Dynasty, such
325 as the valley temple of Chephren at Giza, which is the best preserved, are not shrines in the strict sense of the word. They are but a part of the complex cult of the dead and are directly related to the pyramids. The same is true of the sun temples of the Fifth Dynasty, situated at the rim of the desert plateau within
335 the region of the necropolises, for instance the sun sanctuary of Ne-user-ra at Abu Gurob, south of Giza.

Nor can preliminary stages be found for Middle Kingdom buildings. No conclusions can be drawn from the small shrine of the time of Amenemhat III, at Medinet Madi on the edge of the Faiyum, in the north, or from the delightful Heb-Sed pavilion of Sesostris I at Karnak in the south. Maybe the true precursors of the great temples still lie buried in the Nile mud or beneath tilled fields.

I have no intention of recounting the history of the great temples, but only of raising one question: What is the significance of these monumental structures, the greatest in the archaic world in terms of size and of energy consumed?

The colossal temples of the New Kingdom are unprecedented. Their cyclopean dimensions had never existed before and occurred only rarely later. They are manifestations of a world empire that had mastered the art of displaying its power. The temple of Amon at Karnak was officially styled the "Throne of the
before 355 world," and its proportions were in keeping with its name. The precincts were enclosed by a crude brick wall 7500 feet in length and 25 feet thick. Parts of this are still standing, and C. Robichon, the architect and archaeologist, was able to place his studio upon it.

258 col The most spectacular building is the hypostyle hall of the temple of Amon, with its 134 columns. This dates from the time of the earlier Ramessides. If we take a modest temple built during the reign of Sesostris I (1971–1929 B.C.) as the beginning of the building activity associated with the temple of Amon, and the unfinished Pylon I as the end, the whole covers nearly eighteen hundred years.

(It is true that Pylon I is mentioned in an inscription of Sheshonq I, yet it is generally agreed today that it was erected under the Ptolemies [Hölscher, 1943, pp. 139–49]. It was never finished, and it lacks the inscriptions and reliefs which cover the other wall surfaces.)

During the Eighteenth and Nineteenth Dynasties, the names of several great

Pharaohs were associated with Karnak: Hatshepsut, Tuthmosis III, Amenhotep III, Ramesses II. The impressive forecourt of the Ramesside hypostyle was not added till after 950 B.C. by Sheshonq I (925–915 B.C.), founder of the Libyan (Twenty-second) Dynasty, which made its capital at Bubastis in the Nile delta, about forty miles northeast of Cairo. This forecourt, 338 x 276 feet, is the biggest ever built during the first high civilizations.

THE CONCEPTION OF THE TEMPLE

Throughout the long period of the New Kingdom, the basic conception of the temple as tripartite remained unchanged. The actual abode of the god, the innermost sanctuary, was modest in size, and its entrance was sealed. In the temple of Amon, the seal was broken by the Pharaoh in person, on processional occasions. An antechamber housed the sacred bark on which, within a naos, the image of the god was carried during processions. In some temples—Luxor, for instance—the approach to the sanctuary and its adjacent shrines was by open colonnades, but in the type that became the established version the approach was through a roofed hall of columns: the hypostyle. An enclosed court, usually surrounded on three sides by columns, with the high pylon on the farthermost wall, cut the temple off from the outer world.

This architectural scheme, which reappears with many variations in its detail, differs as widely from later Christian cathedrals as the two religious systems they manifest. The ground plan of the great temples corresponds exactly to the profoundest Egyptian beliefs. The Egyptian, who remained faithful to his ancient creed for thousands of years, recognized no standstill in life or in death. His approach to the world was based upon the alternation of constancy and change. Days, seasons, sowing, and reaping, all revolved in perpetual motion with the heavenly bodies and were intimately associated with them.

It was this eternal progression and eternal recurrence, the sublimation of an eternal wandering, that was given form in the organism of the temple. The Egyptian regarded a building, especially a sacred building, with other eyes than ours. Our notion of a work of art as inherently inviolable was foreign to him. All was subordinated to the religious idea. The Egyptian regarded the temple as he did his own body, as something living, growing, decaying, and again coming to life.

The blocks from thirteen different monuments excavated by H. Chevrier from the foundations of the pylon of Amenhotep III (1400–1362 B.C.)—Pylon III, which later formed the back wall of the great hypostyle—cannot possibly be taken for rubble or the result of sacrilegious destruction. They had been carefully placed, and their reliefs were so perfectly preserved that Chevrier was able to reconstruct, from some of them, a gem of Egyptian architecture: the little
364 colonnaded pavilion of Sesostris I, of the Middle Kingdom. The delicacy of its
92 reliefs can stand comparison with those of the early Italian Renaissance.

The exact position of these blocks in the foundations in which they were discovered was not recorded by the excavators at the time and cannot be determined now. That parts of earlier buildings were sown symbolically, like seeds, in later foundations, has been clearly demonstrated by the circle of Egyptologists associated with Alexandre Varille (1909–51), who died prematurely in an accident. In Mesopotamia, precise investigation of the parts of a building lying below ground was a natural archaeological procedure, since there was little else to investigate. It was different in Egypt. There, new studies of foundations, based on their symbolic meaning, led to the discovery by Varille and Robichon of two unique oval shrines; and in the temple to Amon-Ra-Montu at Karnak, they discovered several courses built up of blocks which had been used before, and whose positions, as well as the reliefs upon them, had definite significance (Varille, 1954, p. 23).

This notion of deliberately including stones from an earlier temple in order to give added spiritual force to the new structure is quite foreign to the conception of a Christian church. So is the idea of eternal wandering, which is manifested in the continuous extension of the temple.

The great temple of Amon at Karnak was extended in two directions. Its before 355 entrance was moved steadily forward toward the Nile. New gateways were built, one after the other, in this westerly direction, and their pylons (I–VI) grew like the sections of a telescope; the height of the final Ptolemaic one 382 (Pylon I) reminds us of an early Chicago skyscraper. The second extension stretched southward, with four pylons (VII–X), oriented toward the temple of Mut, consort of Amon.

The interior layout of Egyptian temples further expresses the idea of wandering. With the exception of the small, dark cella, where the god dwelt in his image, and its immediate surroundings, everything was conceived of as a passage. There was no such thing as a fixed, static plan that continued to enclose the same space; with time, the spaces might change in both form and size. There was no major interior space to receive the faithful attending a dogmatic religious service, as in a Christian basilica. It was neither needed nor desired, since the whole was conceived as a place of passage.

To do justice to the structure of the Egyptian temple, we must understand the *cause* of its difference from the church: the predominance of rites over dogma.

Rites, not dogma

One of the bonds between the prehistoric age and the first high civilizations is the prevalence of rites. Rites were far stronger than any clearly defined, rigidly fixed dogma. Dogma in the present sense did not then exist. It would have been

contrary to the spirit of the whole religious structure. How could a dogma be
42 ff established when in Egypt three or four male and female deities existed simultaneously, each being the one supreme creator of the universe? Each was, quite simply, the representative deity of a particular religious center. Heliopolis, the ancient center of worship, had established Ra, the sun-god, as supreme deity in connection with its system of sun adoration. In Memphis, only a few miles away (founded as capital city at the time of the union of Upper and Lower Egypt), Ptah reigned as the chief god. In his function as creator of the universe, the aspect upon which most stress was laid was his power of invention, his creative imagination. Similarly, different centers possessed different numbers of major deities: in Heliopolis there were nine (Ennead); in Hermopolis, in Middle Egypt, there were eight (Ogdoad).

The confusion and contradictions we feel in all this are inherent in the character of the Egyptian gods, with their pluralistic, polymorphic manifestations. The strangest metamorphoses of god and animal were taken for granted, as was the fusion of one deity with another—Isis with Hathor, for example. Just as one Pharaoh often obliterated the name and usurped the statue of a predecessor, so one god took over the character of another, as the imperial
82 ff Amon took over the nature and appearance of the ithyphallic Min. Under such conditions, no clearly circumscribed dogma could come into being.

There was a constant endeavor to achieve some accord among similar deities

222. HATSHEPSUT'S SACRED WAY AT KARNAK: *The sacred way, bordered by sphinxes, on the north-south axis leading from Hatshepsut's Pylon VIII to the sanctuary of the fertility-goddess Mut*

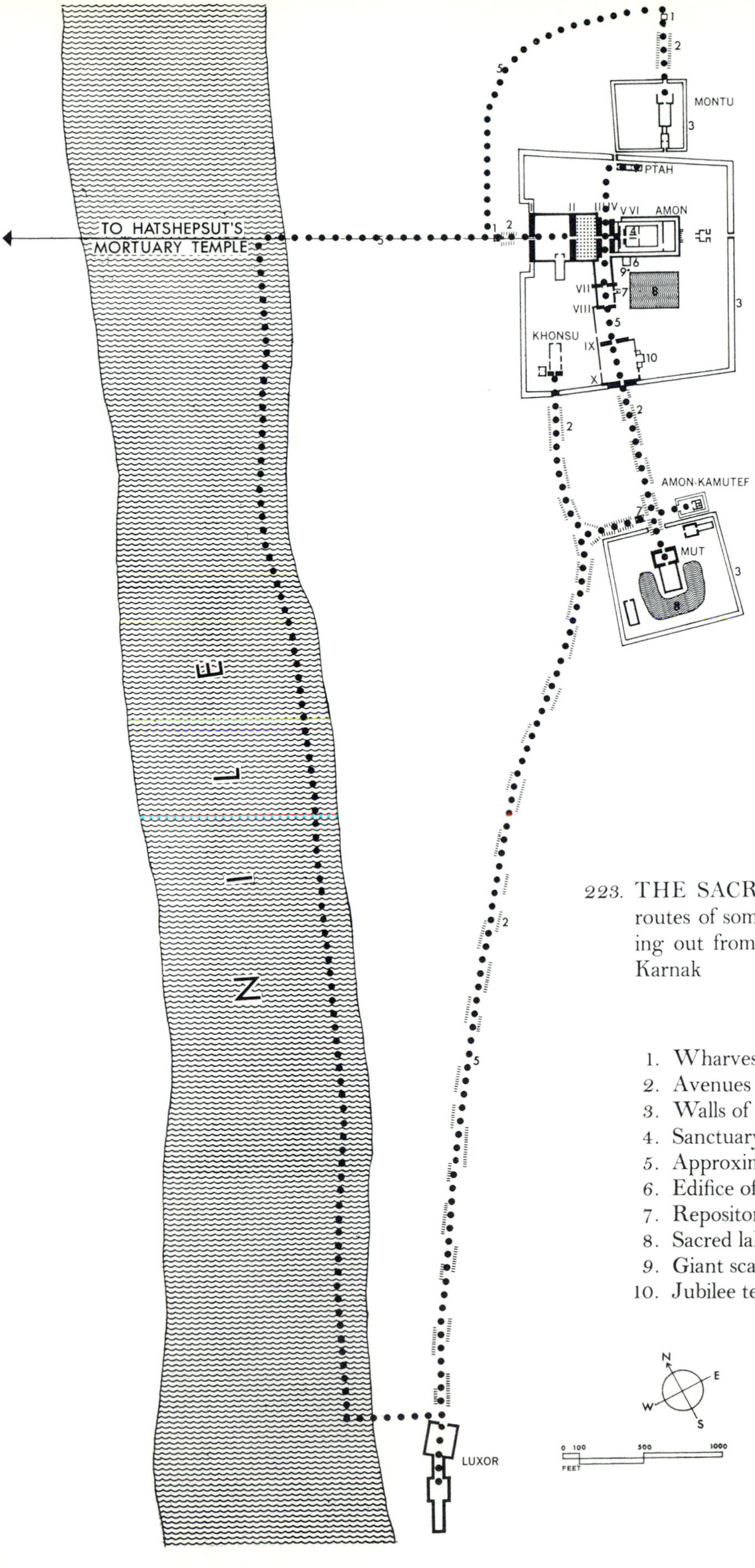

223. THE SACRED WAYS: Approximate routes of some of the Sacred Ways leading out from the Sanctuary of Amon at Karnak

Key

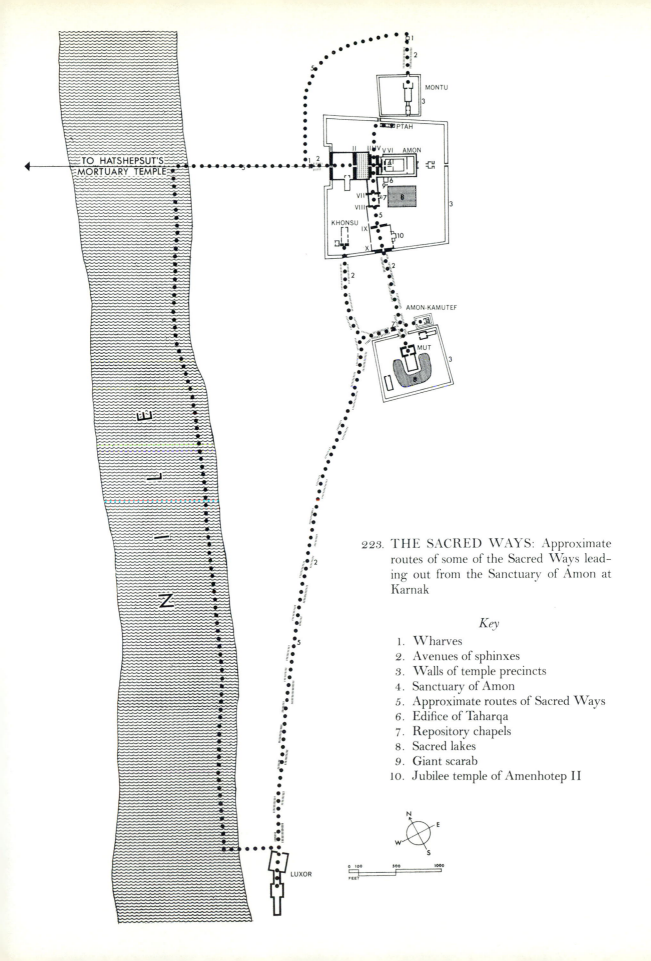

1. Wharves
2. Avenues of sphinxes
3. Walls of temple precincts
4. Sanctuary of Amon
5. Approximate routes of Sacred Ways
6. Edifice of Taharqa
7. Repository chapels
8. Sacred lakes
9. Giant scarab
10. Jubilee temple of Amenhotep II

who differed only slightly in name or attributes. As a result all falcon-gods became united under the name of Horus and most cow-goddesses under the name of Hathor.

The overpowering strength of rites was expressed in the festivals around which religious life circled. The themes of these festivals were not transcendental. They were earth-bound and, like earlier prehistoric rituals, dedicated for the most part to fertility and the propagation of life. The months bore the names of the chief festivals, which sometimes lasted several weeks. The springtime awakening of nature was celebrated at the New Year festival and the eternal renewal of fertility at the harvest festival. Just as in the countless neolithic and bronze age rock engravings of Norway and Sweden everything centered on the seasons, so in Egypt everything was earth-bound and related to earthly existence. Life in the beyond was a copy of life on earth: what had been temporal on earth was transferred to eternity without in any way changing its character.

The main subjects of the large reliefs that unfold along the walls of New Kingdom temples are the processions of these festivals of harvest and fertility. Every incident was deliberate and essential, as was every act performed by the Pharaoh, who accompanied the statue of the god on its annual pilgrimage from 362
one sanctuary to another.

We shall return to these rites depicted in relief on the most conspicuous walls of the temples of Karnak and Luxor. They present what are perhaps the most complicated rituals ever devised by a priesthood. Although they contain the germs of dogma, they are not the outcome of dogma. They replace it.

A dogma is rigidly fixed and must be obeyed in letter and in spirit. It cannot permit the contradictions that are found everywhere in Egyptian beliefs. Dogma in its original Greek meaning signifies something fixed, something legally binding. Dogma involves a law, and two or more differing laws cannot exist side by side.

Ethnologists have often pointed out that the principle of identity, which has been the foundation of logical thought since the Greeks, had no meaning for prehistoric and primitive man. In the domain of religion this is valid also for the first high civilizations. The principle of identity lays down that an object *A* at one moment of time is identical with the same object *A* at another moment of time. The Egyptians were the first to achieve the utmost accuracy in the field of geometrical mathematics by the use of this principle of identity. But logic made no entry into religious rites. In logic, how would it be possible for the believer to recognize his god simultaneously in the form of a beetle, a lion, a goose, and a shrew?

Vagueness and inconsistency in the religious sphere never bothered the Egyptian spirit. Dogmatic controversy never caused religious wars in Egypt. The only serious uproar occurred when Akhenaten (Amenhotep IV) tried to abolish the pluralistic and polytheistic character of Egyptian beliefs and to substitute the absolutism of sun worship (Aten). Despite fundamental differences, it is just this indeterminate quality, this refusal to rationalize relations with the invisible powers, which signifies a continuity with prehistory. Behind it lies the urge to have many ways of making contact with the unforeseeable, unconfined by dogmatic laws. This is perhaps not so strange as it may appear: it is a direct reflection of the never-stable destiny to which everyone is forced to submit.

The sacred ways

The entire interior organization of the temple grew from the most profound beliefs of the Egyptians. These, like nature itself, never came to a standstill. Compared with later ecclesiastical buildings—Christian or Moslem—the Egyptian temple is full of forbidden areas and taboos. The prehistoric tradition of placing sanctuaries in the most hidden places—inaccessible except to initiates—is continued in the dark cella where dwelt the image of the god. The enclosing walls and tall pylons also bear witness to the necessity of shutting off the sacred precincts. A combination of sacred and secular buildings, like a Roman temple in a forum or a medieval Christian church amid dwelling houses, would have been unimaginable.

The idea of eternal wandering left its traces not only upon the interior organization of the temple, but also upon the relation of one sanctuary to another. Each Egyptian temple stood in inner relation to others. An elaborate web of sacred passageways, of sacred approaches, led from one to another.

before 355

Ceremonial processions, with the image of the god hidden in the naos of the sacred bark, wandered at great festivals from one temple to the next, so that the sacred image could be housed for a short time in another sanctuary. Again and again boats—those symbols of movement—are displayed in reliefs on tombs, temples, and obelisks. Boats were inseparably bound up with ceremonial rites.

Boats as symbols of the daily journey of the sun and the wandering journey of the gods and the dead are not limited to a single culture; they can be found almost everywhere. The situation in Egypt differs in that here a high civilization

at the peak of its development employed the symbolism of the boat as the bark
of a deity and gave it a central position in the ritual. The divine barge was preserved in the most holy part of the temple, whose form and construction hark
back to prehistoric times.

Among the partially prehistoric rock engravings in the Nubian desert and in
the Wady Hammamat, and in the representations upon Predynastic ceramics, we
find again and again that boats play a prominent part. According to Helene
Kantor, these boats often have "an upper booth the shape of which is similar to
the hieroglyph for the Upper Egyptian shrine" (1944, p. 124). On a Hierakon- 360
polis wall painting from the late-Gerzean period, or just before the opening of
history, "the largest ship of the wall painting is the most interesting of all, for
on top of the second cabin is placed a lightly built kiosk. . . . Inside is placed a
figure, probably male, faced by another figure standing outside" (p. 115). In
this curving, somewhat S-formed roof and the seated man beneath it, we can
recognize the prototype of the Heb-Sed pavilion for the jubilee of the reign as 268
it appears on a relief from the Middle Kingdom. The Hierakonpolis painting
also shows the form and structure of the divine bark as it was represented even
in the New Kingdom. The ship as a symbol of eternal wandering never lost its 362
deep-rooted significance or its primeval aspect. The deities standing erect in
their boats upon astronomical ceilings, or in the two sun boats of the heavenly 143
oceans finely engraved upon sarcophagi of the Late Period, stand eternally under 135
the spell of a journey that never ends.

Even in the excavations at Helwan, of the First Dynasty (Saad, 1951), boats
were found buried by the side of very humble graves. In 1955 Emery discovered
at Saqqara a funerary boat, also of the First Dynasty, close beside the mastaba 272
of the Pharaoh Wedymu and within its enclosing wall. The most splendid boat of all (41 m. long, 7 m. high) was discovered in 1954, in a perfect state of preservation, at the foot of the south face of the Cheops pyramid. It was built of cedar of Lebanon and had a large cabin; even the ropes that bound its ribs together were still there. The rudder is carved with an arrow: the light, the sunbeam, the arrow of Neith. Opinion is divided as to the purpose of this beautifully constructed boat. Probably it was used to transport the dead king from his residence to the valley temple. It was the fourth found near the great pyramid. Whether these boats were meant to accompany the god Ra on his daily journey or whether—as is now believed—they were vehicles for the journeyings of the dead is of no great importance in this connection.

Just as the dead had their boats, so the little image of the god had his sacred barge, in an antechamber of his cella. We know exactly how the barge rested in the antechamber on a kind of sledge, and how it was borne on the priests' shoulders (Legrain, 1916, p. 6). It never touched the water. When it traveled on the Nile it was transported (for instance from Karnak to Luxor) upon a magnificent Nile barge.

Along the route, there were resting places in the form of repository chapels. These generally had two parallel walls, each as long as the sacred barge, and

224. COLOSSAL GRANITE SCARAB: *Consecrated to Amon-Khepri-Ra. It was carved from the same block as its cylindrical pedestal and stands at the northwest corner of the sacred lake*

were open at either end. They served as stations on the sacred journey from temple to temple, and their careful adornment may indicate that rituals were associated with each halt. Many of them were surrounded by colonnades, and their walls and pillars were often decorated with delicate reliefs, as described by Borchardt (1938). One so ornamented is the charming pavilion of Sesostris I. 364

In all probability, the original route followed by the image of the god was entirely overland. Inscriptions on blocks from the sanctuary of Hatshepsut at Karnak, found in the foundations of the pylon of Amenhotep III, show that the ceremonial progress of Amon, from Karnak to Luxor, during the "Beautiful festival of Opet," still went overland in Hatshepsut's time, resting on the way in six repository chapels (Ricke, 1954, p. 40).

The network of sacred roadways radiating from the temple of Amon at before 355 Karnak led to various sacred places in its immediate vicinity; to the temple of Mut, consort of Amon and mother of the gods; to the temple of Khonsu, the son of Amon; to the sacred lake, indispensable to certain rites, and elsewhere. The north-south axis led mainly to sanctuaries devoted to fertility cults, male and female. The temple of Mut, approached by Hatshepsut's avenue of sphinxes, was 354 built in its present form by Amenhotep III and populated with hundreds of 71 lioness-headed statues of the goddess; it remained in use up to Ptolemaic times. A short distance away stood the sanctuary of Min, the male fertility-god, and close to the temple of Amon himself was the sacred lake, probably devoted to the solar cult and eternal rebirth. It was once bordered with carefully hewn stone blocks, but only fragments of these remain. At the northwest corner of the lake stands a gigantic stone scarab, carved from the same piece of granite as its left cylindrical pedestal. It was dedicated by Amenhotep III to Amon-Khepri-Ra (*khepri* = scarab): the sun of the evening, the morning, and noontime.

In addition to the roadways there was the waterway—the Nile. Ramesses II laid out a monumental approach to it. On the east-west axis of his great hypostyle he built an avenue of ram-headed sphinxes leading directly to the river, 51 just as Amenhotep III before him had built an avenue of sphinxes as a land connection between Karnak and his newly erected temple at Luxor.

When the image of the god, borne from its Karnak sanctuary, reached the east bank of the Nile, its sacred barge was taken on shipboard. The ships used to transport it were made of cedarwood and were of considerable length (130 cubits, about 220 ft.). Their hulls were sheathed in gold and silver "up to the water line. . . . The shrine was adorned with electrum, gold, silver, and jewels" (Wolf, 1931, p. 51).

225. PREHISTORIC NILE BOAT (*Nagadah period*): *With two raised booths, one surmounted by two figures sheltered by a canopy. Drawing upon pottery vessel. From Kantor*

226. PREHISTORIC NILE BOAT (*Gerzean period*): *With two raised booths. On one of them a seated figure, beneath a canopy whose form was retained thereafter for the royal pavilions at the king's jubilee (Heb-Sed) festivals. Wall painting from Hierakonpolis. From Kantor*

On arrival at the west bank, the journey of the sacred image continued overland to the necropolis of Thebes, to the mortuary temples of the rulers of the New Kingdom. The earliest and most splendid approach had been formed by the ramps and terraces of the temple of Hatshepsut at Deir el Bahari. This entire precinct was designed as a reception way for the god Amon, whose barge was slowly borne between the sphinxes of the queen to the sanctuary dedicated to him on the uppermost terrace. This only took place in the few years before Hatshepsut's funerary temple was defaced.

262 col

419

Later—at any rate under the Ptolemies—the wanderings of the gods extended even farther. The image of Hathor was carried more than a hundred miles up the Nile to Edfu for her *hierosgamos* with Horus.

THE GREAT TEMPLE OF AMON AT KARNAK

We will not start with the most spectacular building at Karnak, the great hall of Ramesses II, but with the beginnings of the temple of Amon, the place of his innermost sanctuary, even though this part is beset with questions and uncertainty.

The original limestone temple of Sesostris I (not to be confused with his pavilion, or repository chapel) was the starting point of all later building developments. Its site is today a space vacant except for a few blocks of stone. According to P. Barguet, the temple consisted of a festival (Heb-Sed) hall and three small rooms one after the other, the final one being the sanctuary of Amon, where a pedestal was found, made for a statue of the god and carved with the name of Sesostris I (1953, pp. 145–55). The limestone blocks of this temple have long since found their way to the grinding mills. It is possible that Tuthmosis I, inaugurator of the great building period at Karnak, demolished the temple about the end of the sixteenth century B.C. (Scharff and Moortgat, 1950, p. 124).

The temples of the Tuthmosids

The rule of the Tuthmosids in the New Kingdom marked the rise of Egypt to world power. Tuthmosis I pushed the southern frontiers almost to the Fourth Cataract and the eastern ones to the Euphrates. He became a great builder, an interest inherited by both his daughter Hatshepsut and his grandson Tuthmosis III.

Tuthmosid architecture never strove for the colossal dimensions of the Ramessides who impressed their unmistakable mark on the imperial sanctuaries some three centuries later. Though it attained, at times, huge dimensions (the pylons), it remained delicately structured and never lost touch with the human scale (Hatshepsut's mortuary temple, Tuthmosis III's festival hall). Four of the ten pylons at Karnak were erected by the Tuthmosids. Tuthmosis I built two of these huge portals (now Pylons IV and V), one immediately behind the other. 386
By means of an enclosing wall, he incorporated the ancient temple of the Middle Kingdom into his newly built complex. Whether an open court was thus formed, as appears in Borchardt's reconstruction, is now questioned.

The hypostyle of Tuthmosis I

Between the high walls of his two pylons there was room for a narrow hall set

227. RAMESSES II OFFERING INCENSE BEFORE SACRED BARGE: *He carries a triple incense burner in his left hand, and with his right he throws grains of incense onto it, their trajectory indicated by a curve of dots. South wall of great hypostyle, Karnak*

228. SACRED BARGE IN PROCESSION: *The sacred boat, carried on the shoulders of the priests, contains a small cult statue of Amon which was transported on certain festivals to rest for a short while in another sanctuary. Relief from great hypostyle hall, Karnak. From "Description de l'Égypte"*

229. SACRED BARGE ON PRIESTS' SHOULDERS: *The hawk-headed priests carry the barge in ranks of five, pacing backward and forward and announcing the will of Amon. South wall of great hypostyle, Karnak*

crosswise to the main axis. In his time its wooden ceiling was supported by a single row of wooden columns. This was the hypostyle of Tuthmosis I. The outer pylon, IV, was considerably larger and more massive than the other, and up to the time of Amenhotep III (1400–1362 B.C.) it formed the entrance to the temple of Karnak. Before the two towers of this pylon Tuthmosis set up two granite obelisks. Throughout the age of the Tuthmosids, the main east-west axis, which was later given massive emphasis by Ramesses II's great hypostyle, ended at this pylon. ☞ 365

In the cramped space immediately in front of and behind the innermost

230. REPOSITORY CHAPEL FOR SACRED BARGE: *Resting place for the sacred barge on its processional journeyings, with ramps at both ends and openings all around: earlier used as Heb-Sed pavilion. Sesostris I, Middle Kingdom*

sanctuary, the buildings were so huddled together that by the end of the Tuthmosid era they had become interlocked. This crowding was partly due to Tuthmosis III's efforts to destroy all Hatshepsut's erections.

Hatshepsut's obelisks

In the narrow hypostyle her father had built, Hatshepsut set up two obelisks of
367 Aswan granite, possibly to enhance the entrance to the new sanctuary she had erected behind it. The latter lay between Pylon V and the old temple of the Middle Kingdom and was intended as a shrine for the barge of Amon. To left and right it was flanked by smaller chapels decorated with reliefs. Nothing has remained of this shrine except some blocks with reliefs, which were discovered in the foundations of the pylon of Amenhotep III (now Pylon III). Hatshepsut's nephew and co-ruler, Tuthmosis III, bore the queen such hatred that he destroyed as many of her works as he could. Among them was this red quartzite building, which he partly replaced with one of his own.

Hatshepsut's two granite obelisks, which were just over ninety-seven feet high, had a happier fate. She was particularly proud of them. They were the result of seven months' labor, and their transport from Aswan is recorded on her reliefs at Deir el Bahari. Their pyramidions were of pink granite sheathed with electrum (silver and gold). They were "to rise to heaven, to be seen from far and wide from both banks of the Nile, and to illuminate Egypt like the sun" (Bissing, 1949, p. 161). Tuthmosis III enclosed them within a tower above which soared only the parts sacred to Amon. One of them still stands that way today.

Between Hatshepsut's granite shrine for the barge of Amon and Pylon V, Tuthmosis III built a hall of annals to contain the records of his great feats and campaigns. Some of its beautiful heraldic pillars still remain, bearing, in rarely-used high relief, symbols of the north and south; papyrus and lilies, with small flower buds and long stalks stretching the entire height of the pillars.

This building was squeezed into the huddled complex in front of the innermost sanctuary. If we had nothing else of Tuthmosis III, we would have a very poor picture of the character of the great conqueror. But to the east, just beyond the Middle Kingdom temple, he erected a sacred palace that can stand comparison with Deir el Bahari. In its whole articulation, spatial and structural, it is an apex of Egyptian architecture. Structurally, it was never surpassed. This building, whose real purpose is unknown, is called the festival hall. The architecture of the early Eighteenth Dynasty, which had had its birth at Deir el Bahari, was here further developed.

The tectonic festival hall of Tuthmosis III

At the extreme east of the great temple, even behind the remnants of the Middle Kingdom sanctuary, lies the festival hall, or better, the festival building of Tuthmosis III. Its Egyptian name, Akh Menou ("Brilliant monument"), has been variously interpreted. It served as the place of the royal jubilee festival, and simultaneously as a kind of "temple of fame" glorifying the deeds of the great conqueror. 369

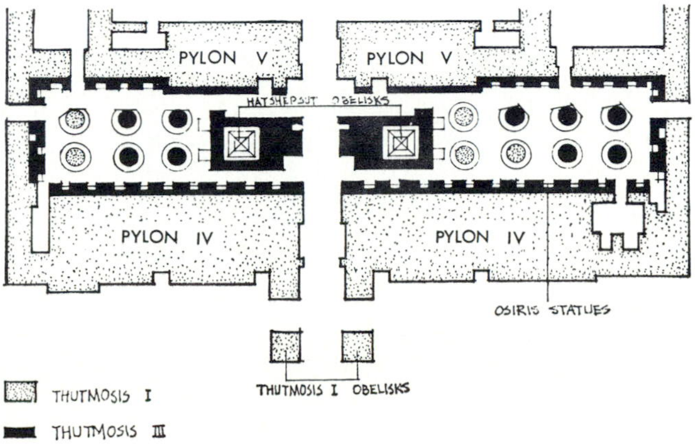

231. GROUND PLAN OF HYPOSTYLE HALL OF TUTHMOSIS I: *This narrow hypostyle hall was originally roofed and had a single row of wooden columns. After Chevrier*

232. LEFT AISLE, HYPOSTYLE HALL OF TUTHMOSIS I: *A row of colossal Osiris statues stands along the northern wall. Hatshepsut replaced the wooden columns with stone ones and planted her two obelisks in the center of the longitudinal axis*

233. CENTER AISLE OF HYPOSTYLE HALL OF TUTHMOSIS I: *One of Hatshepsut's rose granite obelisks still rises over ninety-seven feet high. Around it are remains of the sandstone structure erected by Tuthmosis III to hide it. The height of this obelisk was only surpassed by Tuthmosis III's single one, placed behind his festival hall*

This is a unique building type: a hypostyle hall surrounded on three sides by large and small chambers. It had no successors, and one can well understand that Vandier found it "à vrai dire, assez mystérieux" (1955, II, p. 900).

That the festival hall was included in the processional itinerary of the bark of Amon-Ra is indicated by a repository for the sacred bark close to the south entrance, by the provision of space for turning it around, and by other details, such as the downward-tapering columns of the central aisle, especially the form of their capitals. These are a transformation into stone of the slim wooden columns which, since the First Dynasty, had served to support the canopy of
right the Heb-Sed pavilion. Their circular bases are slashed off along the center aisle, as in the sanctuary of Luxor, to permit the unhindered passage of the sacred bark, carried on the shoulders of the priests.

The Akh Menou was at the same time a thank offering to the principal gods for the success and glory they had bestowed upon Tuthmosis III. This is intimately combined with a display of his person and his deeds. In the Hall of Ancestors Tuthmosis is depicted making offerings to the names of fifty-seven kings whom he regarded as his predecessors: the so-called Karnak Tablet of the Kings, now in the Louvre. One of the columned chambers still contains reliefs of rare plants and animals which Tuthmosis III brought back from his many campaigns in Syria, displaying an interest in the introduction of exotic fauna and flora similar to Hatshepsut's as shown in earlier representations of products of the land of Punt (Somaliland).

This festival hall remained in use over a long period. More than a millennium later, Alexander, in a restoration of one of the chambers, substituted his own image for that of Tuthmosis III sacrificing to the gods.

Tectonic features

In the hypostyle hall new spatial and tectonic features begin to emerge. No other building in Egyptian architecture achieved such an imaginative interaction between tectonic elements and spatial differentiation. The hypostyle hall forms the core of the complex (144 ft. wide, 52 ft. deep). It consists of a triple nave accompanied to right and left by two outer galleries. On three sides about forty chambers were organized, some large, some small, some filled with columns. The entire complex has been meticulously described by Vandier (1955, II, pp. 890–901).

370 The center aisle is slightly wider than the side aisles. It also appears higher, but it is not. In reality all three aisles are the same height. The impression of

234. OUTER AISLE, FESTIVAL HALL OF TUTHMOSIS III: *The Akh Menou. The outer wall of this face has fallen*

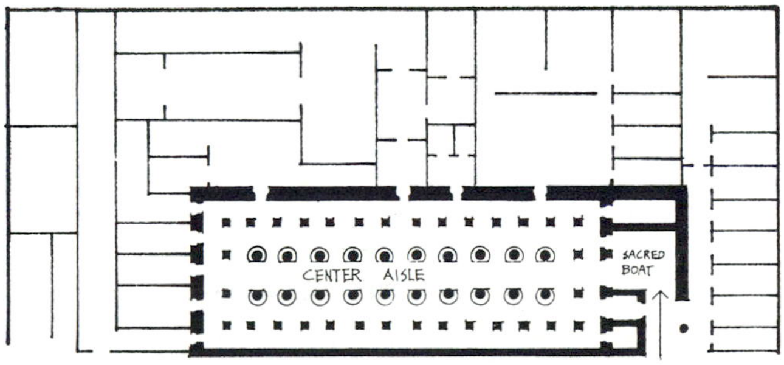

235. GROUND PLAN OF FESTIVAL HALL: *Surrounded by chambers except on the west side. Space is left at the entrance (to the right) for turning the sacred barge in procession. The interesting feature of this hall is the structure of the hypostyle, with its three central aisles and two lower side aisles. After Chevrier*

236. WESTERN AISLE OF FESTIVAL HALL: *The beams which once spanned the side aisle are now cantilevered into space. There were short, square pillars along the side aisle and tall, tapering columns along the central nave*

237. SECTION THROUGH FESTIVAL HALL: *The height of the three central aisles is identical, but the middle one appears much higher. This difference is achieved with much ingenuity by making the square side pillars only the height of the outer aisles and surmounting them by inwardly protruding roofing beams and narrow light slits. Drawing after the author*

238. LIGHTING OF FESTIVAL HALL: *Light slits above the protruding beams of the western aisle*

difference comes about through a subtle interlocking of spatial and tectonic elements. It takes some time to understand the means used to create this ingenious interaction. It cannot be derived from the ground plan and, as far as we know, no elevations or sections of this unique structure exist. We present merely a
370 rough freehand sketch to facilitate orientation.

The central aisle looks higher than the flanking ones, though all are covered by the same flat roof. This is effected by several means. The thirty-two square pillars and the walls that bound the side aisles are considerably lower than the twenty tapering central columns. They are surmounted by a continuous architrave. Above this is the decisive element in producing the impression of differing heights: a series of transverse slabs. These serve as sills below a band of narrow horizontal openings. Following an ancient Egyptian habit, the inner ends of
326 these transverse slabs are cut off at an angle in order to reduce the penetration of direct light, as in Chephren's valley temple about a millennium earlier. The
371 slabs project outward to form the ceiling of the two outer galleries, whose height they determine. The simultaneous protrusion of these slabs on both sides of the vertical supports, into the side aisles as well as into the outer galleries, reveals a spirited architectural ingenuity and a considerable constructive imagination. It is a far cry from the monoliths of Chephren's valley temple, with their grandly simple structure of load and support, to the differentiated construction
260 col of the Akh Menou, where stone beams have become bearing centers, almost as in reinforced concrete construction. The emergence of a subtle structuring of stone architecture can here be glimpsed. But, like the spatial organization of
Part X Hatshepsut's stone terraces at Deir el Bahari, it was never developed further. Neither earlier nor later did Egyptian architecture achieve so complete a mastery of tectonic elements of expression as in this hypostyle hall of Tuthmosis III. And it is of modest proportions. This is an architecture based on the smallest changes of dimension. Spirit, not mass!

Tuthmosis was by nature pitiless. He knew how to hate. On the other hand it is a sign of an inner sense of balance that the greatest warrior king of Egypt here held himself within such distinguished limits.

On the east-west axis of the festival hall, but toward the east, Tuthmosis erected a single obelisk: also a unique occurrence. Its exact placement has recently been rediscovered by Barguet (Vandier, 1955, II, p. 931). It is the tallest known obelisk. The Emperor Constantine brought it to Rome in the fourth century A.D. Today, still solitary, it stands in front of the Lateran palace.

The north-south axis of Karnak

All the buildings so far described were placed immediately in front of and behind the innermost sanctuary of the temple of Karnak, but this east-west axis—the natural orientation for a sanctuary—only acquired its overpowering monumentality in the Nineteenth Dynasty under the Ramessides.

The Tuthmosids had created a monumental axis toward the south. A network of sacred ways already led to various nearby sanctuaries and overland to the before 355 temple of Luxor. This southern axis started almost at right angles to the pylon of Tuthmosis I (now Pylon IV). It was marked by a series of monumental signposts: pylons.

In the time of Hatshepsut the processional way from the north entered inside the precincts of the temple just in front of Pylon IV. A new pylon (now VIII) was built exactly at the point at which the processional way left the temple 376 precincts to the south. Hatshepsut took the main initiative, though whether some start had already been made by Tuthmosis I is not certain. But the generosity with which Pylon VIII is set forward and its plastic relationships recall the spaciousness of the terraces of Deir el Bahari.

PYLONS AS MONUMENTAL BARRIERS

A pylon is composed of high inclined walls and a large entrance to the sacred precincts. Immediately adjacent, to right and left, it is accented by tall flagpoles, obelisks, and colossal statues of the kings. The façades of its gently sloping walls bear sunken reliefs whose delicate but sharply etched outlines stand out even under intense sunlight.

This highly impressive architectural assembly is full of symbolism. The two flanking towers symbolize the mountain ranges that hem in the Nile valley on either side—East and West. They are transmutations of the hieroglyph for
342 Amon-Ra: the sun disk between two mountains, which means "The god is in his horizon."

The cedarwood flagpoles with their pennants were originally "the *ntr*-pole. This was . . . a pole that was wrapped around with a band of coloured cloth, tied with a cord halfway up the stem, with the upper part of the band projecting as a flap at top. Dr. Griffith conjectured that it was a fetish, e.g. a bone care-

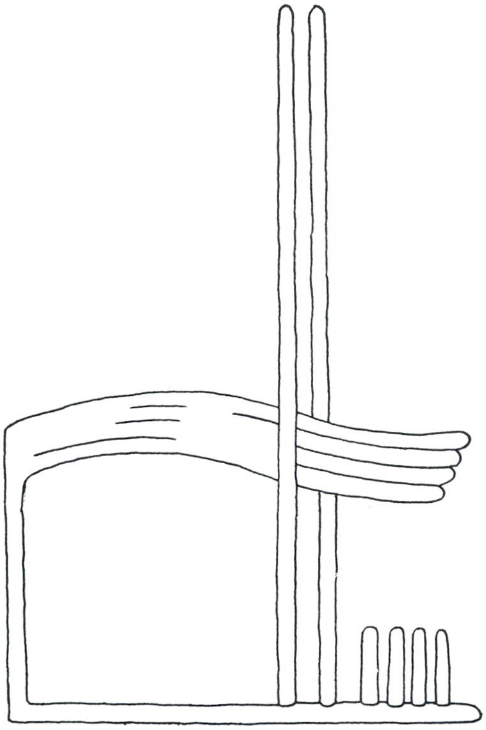

239. FIRST DYNASTY SHRINE WITH TWO HIGH POLES: *From the beginning of the Egyptian empire, two astonishingly high poles were placed before the sanctuary. Drawing after Flinders Petrie*

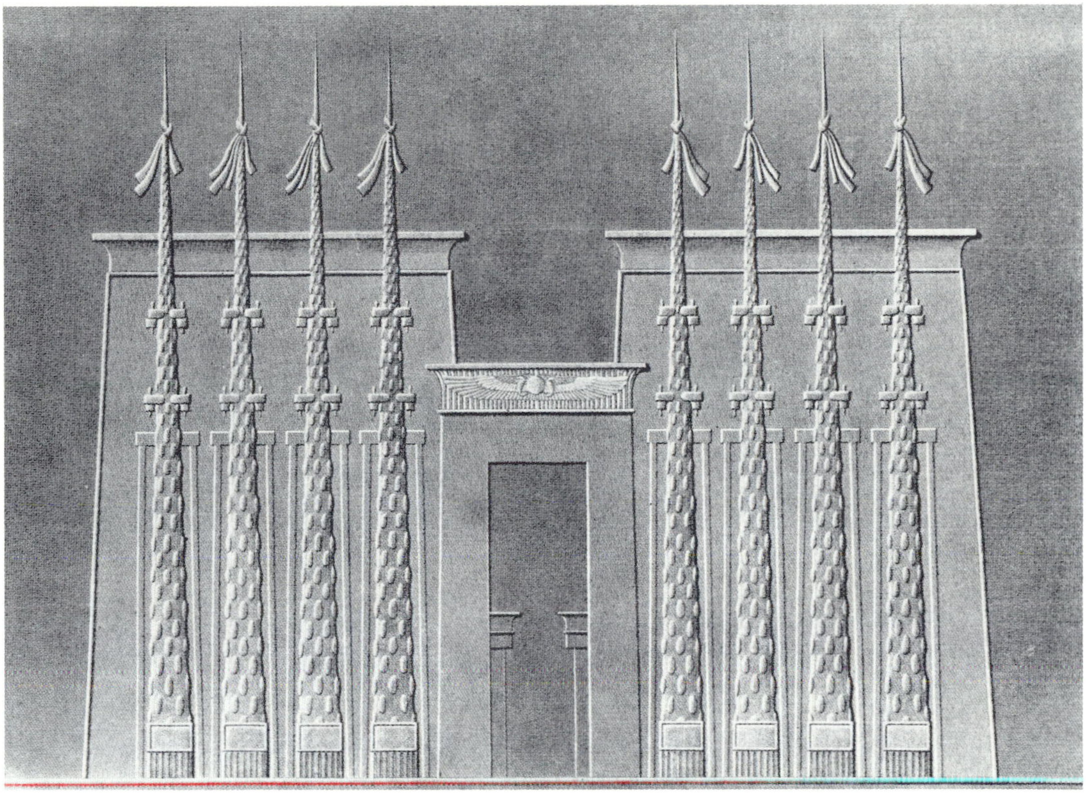

240. PYLON II OF THE RAMESSIDES: *Tall flagpoles with waving pennants rise high above the pylon. Aquatint from a Twentieth Dynasty relief in the temple of Khonsu. From "Description de l'Égypte"*

fully wound round with cloth. . . . As a hieroglyph this wrapped-up pole expresses *ntr*, 'god,' 'divine' . . . gradually it became determinative of divinity" (Newberry, 1924, p. 189).

Thus the pylon symbolizes the entry to the sacred precinct. Its obelisks with their pyramidions signify the abode of the god; its flagpoles the presence of the god; the colossal statues of the kings, the living sons of god. The pylon is a phalanx of divinity. Here the deity displays himself symbolically to the people. All else is secret.

At the beginning of the New Kingdom, under the Tuthmosids, pylons became the most significant features of the great temples. Though the Greek word *pylōn* means an entrance gate, in reality the pylon functioned as a fortresslike

241. HATSHEPSUT'S PYLON VIII OPENING THE SOUTHERN AXIS: *Earliest of the four pylons along the sacred way which led south to various fertility shrines. It is the best preserved of all*

barrier. Here lies its great difference from the Propylaea at Athens. The entrance to the Acropolis, with its receding porticoes, offers the faithful a friendly reception into the sacred enclosure. The pylon commands a halt.

In a thesis now in preparation, a French Egyptologist attempts to prove that the people were not admitted beyond the entrance gate. An examination of the pylons of Tuthmosis I, Amenhotep III, and Ramesses II shows how the great portal shrinks to a small antechamber which, in comparison with the huge mass of the pylons, is not unlike the entrance to a beehive and was certainly well
382 guarded. This may have been different in the case of Pylon I at Karnak, which was erected by the Ptolemies, but it was not built until near the end of the Greek development.

The pylons are the monumental manifestation of a tradition that goes back to

242. PYLON VIII WITH SEATED STATUE OF HATSHEPSUT

243. PYLON VII WITH RELIEF OF TUTHMOSIS III: *Hatshepsut left a generous space between her Pylon VIII and the sanctuaries of the temple of Amon. Tuthmosis III built his Pylon VII within the large inner court. The gigantic relief of the Pharaoh shows him slaying his relatively diminutive enemies. This kind of iconographic representation was preserved from the First Dynasty Narmer palette*

the beginning of Egypt, and perhaps still further—the announcement of an enclosed sanctuary. In the stockades surrounding the court of a reed-hut temple (the sanctuary of Neith) of the First Dynasty, two tall poles bore the triangular emblems of the deity. Another First Dynasty shrine, as drawn by Flinders Petrie, is even more convincing as to the early importance of high poles. On the 374
reliefs of Zoser's "southern tomb" similar poles appear, probably recalling earlier venerated sanctuaries. The New Kingdom pylon with its tall wooden 375, 380
poles and obelisks forbids further entry to the uninitiated.

We have only a fragmentary knowledge of the Middle Kingdom predecessors of the pylon. Of the temple of Sesostris I at Heliopolis, only one obelisk—the earliest known—remains. There are so many gaps in what remains of other temples of this period (Vandier, 1955, II, pp. 595–658) that no definite conclusions can be drawn. The most probable predecessors of its later monumental form are the great gates of the funerary monuments of the Middle Kingdom with their sloping walls.

The tensions felt in the pylon between huge and massive walls, delicate incised reliefs, obelisks, flagstaffs, and colossal statues attached to the wall are full of architectonic excitement. Our present period has again a strong affinity for such dramatic relationships, though it has not yet found the way to master them in a contemporary idiom.

Hatshepsut's Pylon VIII

With her Pylon VIII, Hatshepsut opened up the north-south axis on a grand 376
scale. As in her other buildings, Hatshepsut outwardly followed the established tradition, but inwardly made a number of changes. The form of the pylon is conventional: trapezoidal, with sloping and tapering walls, round fillets at the corners, and a throated cornice molding such as had been customary since Zoser's time. The deeply embedded bases for the tall flagpoles, and the sunken reliefs upon the inner side that show Hatshepsut doing business with the gods, are also traditional. No signs remain of any obelisks.

It is the Tuthmosids who occupy the foreground. Tuthmosis I, Tuthmosis II, Amenhotep I—the forebear of Tuthmosis I—and Hatshepsut herself. This as- 377
sembly of forefathers before a pylon is unusual. Here, in the religious center of the kingdom, Hatshepsut reiterated upon a most monumental scale—as if through a loud-speaker—what was of the utmost concern to her and what her reliefs at Deir el Bahari display in the most varied manner: the legitimacy of her

244. TEMPLE OF LUXOR, PYLON OF RAMESSES II

245. TEMPLE OF LUXOR, RECONSTRUCTION OF PYLON OF RAMESSES II: *Aquatint, 1812, showing the two tall obelisks which then still stood before the pylon. One now stands in the center of the Place de la Concorde (Paris). Two of the statues of Ramesses II were standing figures. From "Description de l'Égypte"*

claim to be Pharaoh. "Even in their present sorry condition the wonderfully harmonious relationships of the statues to the structure remain effective. And the symbolism must have deeply impressed the Egyptian visitor as the sovereigns of the era greeted him at the threshold of the imperial sanctuary" (Bissing, 1949, p. 156).

Tuthmosis III usurped Hatshepsut's colossal statue, which is, by chance, the best preserved of the four. This statue was formerly supposed to have represented an earlier king, but von Bissing ascertained that the figure was Hatshepsut. The whole pylon expresses an indivisible unity. The scale developed here betrays the hand of a master builder. The boxed-up compression of Tuthmosis I's building, a structure unsurpassed until the rise of Hatshepsut, had come to an 377

246. SEATED COLOSSUS OF RAMESSES II: *Detail. Beside the gigantic leg of the monarch stands a miniature figure of his queen. The Egyptians were never afraid of juxtaposing representations in different scales*

247. THE NEVER-COMPLETED PYLON I: *The major part of this pylon, at the main entrance to the great temple of Amon at Karnak, was constructed under the Ptolemies. Portions of the ramps of rough bricks used for its construction still remain in situ*

end. This Pylon VIII gave an impetus to the north-south axis. It was placed so far from the complex that Tuthmosis III was able to set up his own Pylon VII in before 355
the intervening court.

The whole conception of Hatshepsut's Pylon VIII, as well as its bold siting, makes it difficult to believe that it could have stemmed from any other hand than Senmut's. It displays the same broad generosity of treatment as the wide terraces of Deir el Bahari. It also brings to mind the novel placement of the row of colos- 429
sal Osiris figures along the front of the uppermost terrace of Hatshepsut's mortuary temple; in Tuthmosis I's generation they had been ranged against interior 366
walls.

The sacred way led from this pylon to the sanctuary of the lioness-headed Mut. Hatshepsut bordered the long processional way to this southernmost sanctuary of Karnak with an impressive avenue of sphinxes—330 meters behind the 354
enclosure wall erected much later by Horemheb. In Hatshepsut's time the temple of Mut did not exist in its present form, "yet a sanctuary may have stood here even in the Middle Kingdom, if not earlier" (ibid., p. 162). The main builder of the present temple was Amenhotep III. Hundreds of seated granite statues of the goddess Sekhmet-Mut were placed in the temple courts; many of them are now 71
widely distributed in museums.

The southern part of the temple area is still embraced by a sacred lake in an before 355
irregular U-like curve, an unusual shape for an Egyptian body of water. The temple of Mut, like most of the sanctuaries in this part of the Karnak complex, is related to fertility. It may perhaps be not too daring to compare the unusual shape of the sacred lake with that of the womb, as it has recently been shown that the headdress or wig of Hathor (also a fertility-goddess) "repeats exactly the *uterus*-symbol of the Babylonian goddess Ninhursag" (Barb, 1953, p. 199).

A repository chapel with a circumambulatory and a temple built by Hatshepsut are dedicated to Amon-Min-Kamutef (the "Bull of his mother") and reached by a short approach branching off at right angles from the sphinx avenue just before the Mut temple. This resting place for the sacred barge interested Borchardt, who attempted to relate it to Hatshepsut's jubilee (1938, pp. 79–83). In 1954, Ricke made an intensive study of the foundations of both temple and repository chapel. On the fragment of a relief he discovered to whom the temple was dedicated. It was "Amon-Ra-Kamutef, he of the towering feathers, who glories in his beauty, i.e., his powers of procreation" (p. 4, fig. 1). This connection of Amon with Min, the god of fertility, established a kind of preliminary setting for the temple of Amenhotep III at Luxor.

The pylons of the southern axis

Within the precincts of the temple of Karnak the southern axis was emphasized by four pylons (now VII–X) which Mariette named the "pylons of the south." They give somewhat the impression of a series of triumphal arches. Between them lie three courts, with small shrines, for the jubilees of the reigns, inserted in their eastern walls. The processional way led through these four pylons and continued more than three hundred yards along the sphinx avenue to the sanctuary of Mut. Other sacred ways branched off to other sanctuaries. Within the great inner court of Pylon VIII, Tuthmosis III erected a new pylon (now VII). Conventional reliefs of the massacre of defeated enemies covered its walls, and though this is the worst preserved of the pylons, they are still visible.

before 355

378

A scene of the Pharaoh in heroic dimensions, with his mace crashing down on a group of prisoners representing conquered territories and one hand grasping the hair of a group of enemies, is repeated on the front of each pylon. Iconographically this scene goes back to the beginning of the First Dynasty, to the Narmer palette. It formed the background for a purification ritual performed at the moment of entering the sacred precinct.

On the occasion of his thirtieth anniversary, Tuthmosis III built in the eastern wall a repository chapel with a circumambulatory and an exit to the neighboring sacred lake (Borchardt, 1938, pp. 90–93). Behind is the edifice of Taharqa—not really studied or excavated—its walls covered with reliefs related to the cult of Osiris.

Before the last two pylons (now IX and X) acquired their final form under the Ramessides, Amenhotep II built a remarkable jubilee temple fronted by fourteen pillars. Behind it was a hypostyle hall.

All four of these southern pylons, as well as the buildings, suffered many restorations and usurpations by later rulers.

The great hypostyle of Ramesses II

Next to the pyramids, the most spectacular structure in Egyptian history is the great hypostyle at Karnak. It has all the gigantism that marked the age of the 258 col Ramessides, and of all the structures erected by that mighty builder Ramesses II, it is the most important contribution to the history of architecture. No earlier building can compare with the dimensions here given to a covered space, and no later building even attempted such colossal scale. The area is some 6000 square 386 yards: length 338 feet, width 170 feet. It has often been pointed out that it was large enough to accommodate the entire cathedral of Notre Dame in Paris.

These huge dimensions give rise to several questions: What was the purpose of the hall? What actually happened here? What were the structural solutions to the problems thus posed? Finally, how were these expressed in spatial terms?

The hypostyle continues the main east-west axis and gives it its greatest emphasis. Without it, the axis would not have its plastic monumentality.

Its eastern wall is formed by the great pylon of Amenhotep III (Pylon III), in whose foundations the fragments of so many other monuments were buried. Its western wall is Pylon II, erected under Ramesses I. To right and left of the once-small entrance vestibule were two colossal statues of Ramesses II. Fragments of one are still standing. A similar vestibule projected from the pylon of Amenhotep III which had guarded access to the temple. This occasioned some irregularities in the ground plan.

Through Pylon II's later enormous doorway (whose height compares with 388 the Arc de Triomphe in Paris), an overpowering amount of light could penetrate into the interior, in marked contrast to the rest of the building and to the intention of the half-dark colonnaded hall. This gigantic opening was first made under the Ptolemies.

The central passage of the hypostyle, seventy-eight feet high, gives a particularly strong emphasis to the east-west axis. This passage is formed by six columns on either side, whose diameter is the same as that of Trajan's column in Rome (11 ft. 7 in.). This central passage is far wider than those formed by any of the seven colonnades on either side. Its pre-eminence is enhanced by the fact that the interval between it and the lower colonnade on either side is greater than the intervals between any of the latter.

248. THE GREAT HYPOSTYLE HALL FROM THE SOUTH: *From left to right, remains of Pylon II started by Ramesses I; boundary wall; columns of the lower and higher aisles and openings of the window gratings. To the right some remains of Pylon III, built by Amenhotep III, and, finally, the obelisks of Hatshepsut and of Tuthmosis I*

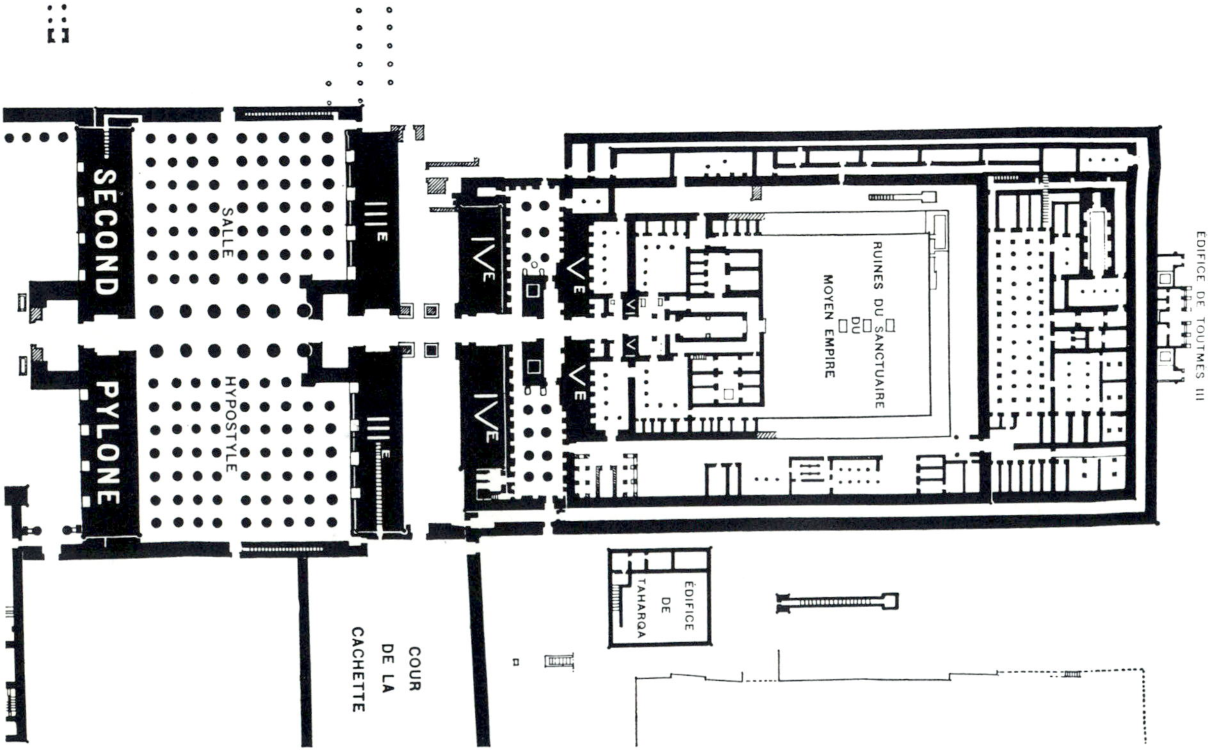

249. GROUND PLAN OF GREAT HYPOSTYLE HALL: *338 x 170 feet, with 134 columns ranged in 16 rows. To the left the large colonnaded court built by the rulers of the Twentieth Dynasty, to the right the buildings of the Tuthmosids. From Chevrier*

This east-west processional way between the high columns was the path the king followed on his procession to the temple of Luxor, bearing a censer in his 362
hand, as we see him in reliefs. Carvings on ceiling slabs along the way constantly repeat the protector of the Pharaoh: the goddess Nekhbet, a vulture with outstretched wings.

The term "hypostyle" appears in Diodorus, first century B.C. (Legrain, 1929, p. 159), to denote a hall with a roof borne on columns. In this dense, column-packed hall of Ramesses II the word acquired quite a special meaning. The 122 lower columns, which are six and a half feet in diameter, seem to shatter space, for the intervals between them are smaller than their diameter. The beautiful eye-level photograph by G. E. Kidder Smith, of the hypostyle at Medinet Habu, 389
brings out the fragmentation of space felt by the present-day spectator. At Karnak the dense rows of lower columns are not arranged symmetrically with the 509
high columns, and this makes the space appear even more filled up. This did not happen by chance; it was intentional.

Despite such crowding of the space, the architectural conception of elevation and ground plan is clearly expressed. Although there is a narrow central aisle in the north-south direction, the principle of the building was to employ every means to stress the dominance of the east-west colonnade as a place of passage; thus even in this gigantic hall there are no altars. It is not a gathering place for a congregation of the devout; it is not a resting place; it is simply a most monumentally conceived place of passage. In its half-darkness ritual functions were performed and oracles delivered. Pronouncements of the deity were received here—for instance, the nomination of the Pharaoh's successor in cases of doubt. The most famous such nomination was that of Tuthmosis III, when the sacred barge bearing the image of Amon halted in its journey before the young prince. Though the incident actually occurred in the small hypostyle of Tuthmosis I, it indicates the purpose of such halls.

The hypostyle at Luxor

The basic conception of the hypostyle as a place of passage and ritual had crystallized even more definitely in the earlier hypostyle of the temple of Amon at 393
Luxor, which was the first example of the final form of the great temples of the New Kingdom.

The peaceful reign of Amenhotep III enabled the major part of the temple to be completed at one time. We have no reliable information about the layout of

250. ENTRANCE TO GREAT HYPOSTYLE HALL: *Through Pylon II, begun by Ramesses I. Before it stands one of the statues of Ramesses II and the low walls of the lodges which guarded the entrance. Within is the central nave. From Jéquier*

earlier Middle Kingdom temples on this site. Later, Ramesses II added a colonnaded court and a pylon at a slight angle to the temple's north-south axis, which did not improve the whole. 392

The architectural rhythm at Luxor flows unusually steadily. The architecture itself is powerful and yet, for Egypt, very delicate, like the outlines of the funerary reliefs of high royal officials on the opposite bank of the Nile. The dewy freshness of forms noticeable in Hatshepsut's work was repeated in this masterpiece of the great-grandson of Tuthmosis III.

251. BASES OF PAPYRUS-BUD COLUMNS AT MEDINET HABU: *These relief-covered columns in a side aisle of the hypostyle are built up from stone drums, like those of Zoser's mortuary complex (see fig. 161). But now the drums have grown to colossal dimensions (diameter up to 4 m.). The intervals between them are so narrow that the columns sometimes seem to form a solid mass*

398 The innermost sanctuary with its side chapels can only be entered through one
narrow door. It is purposefully secluded, like the offering altar of the pyramid
kings. In front of the door is a magnificent colonnaded vestibule, its long side
394 opening onto a large interior court. One can scarcely imagine a more impressive entrance to a sanctuary than this open-sided hall with its four colonnades of eight papyrus-bundle columns each. These columns are so slender that their massing is not at all oppressive. They are more akin to the papyrus-bundle columns of the Fifth Dynasty funerary temple of Sahura than to the colossal columns of the Karnak hypostyle, which was built only fifty years later. It is hard to understand why this open-sided hypostyle did not usher in a new tradition.

395 The spacious interior court, surrounded by a double-columned portico, then
392 closes down dramatically to a narrow hypostyle consisting of a central passage with seven columns, fifty-two feet high, on either side. This hypostyle is conceived as a narrow, tubular passage. Its total width is only sixty feet. The image of Amon was borne between these colonnades on its way from Karnak to Luxor at the "Beautiful festival of Opet."

Chevrier, who did so much for the investigation and preservation of the hypostyle at Karnak, believed, according to Vandier, that the double row of columns of the central aisle of Ramesses II's hypostyle at Karnak actually goes back to Amenhotep III and was built at the same time as the Luxor hypostyle (1955, II, p. 912), and that it also originally had seven columns on either side. Indeed, Chevrier claimed to have found remnants of the last pair of columns beneath the
386 Ramesside Pylon II. This view has not been generally accepted (ibid., p. 924), but the suggestion is extremely interesting, for it lends emphasis to the original conception of the hypostyle as a place of passage, a form still preserved in the Ramesses II hypostyle at Karnak, although at first sight one is confused by the manifold multiplication of the columns on either side.

THE DIMMING OF LIGHT

One of the main differences between the huge Ramesses II hypostyle at Karnak and an early Christian basilica lies in the handling of light.

The Egyptians loved half-darkness, not only in their temples but also in their houses. They liked to place their windows as high up as possible, as in a well-known funerary model of a house of Predynastic times.

We have more precise information about their way of living in the New Kingdom. In one of the houses at Tell el Amarna, "the decoration of the North Hall was concentrated on the upper part of the walls, where at intervals there were small grille windows in the outside walls" (Lloyd, 1933, p. 5).

There are some scanty remains of the palace of Amenhotep III, from the previous generation, at Malkata, Thebes. Smith gives a vivid description of the palace of the builder of the temple at Luxor (1958, pp. 159–72). "The private apartments of the king consisted of a long, columned hall with a throne room, at the back of which opened a bath and an antechamber to the king's bedroom. On each side of the hall there were four suites of rooms for the chief ladies of the harem" (p. 168). In the columned throne room, the windows with their stone grilles and narrow light slits were again placed near the ceiling.

The same manner of lighting, though in huge dimensions, was used in the Ramesside hypostyle at Karnak, which has light-slits similar to those used by 259 col Tuthmosis III in his festival hall, though enormously larger. Eight openings 260 col stretch the whole length of the difference in height between the lower columns and the architrave supporting the ceiling of the center passageway. These clerestory windows would have made it possible to admit a flood of light; instead, they were filled with the typical Egyptian perforated stone grilles. This construction has often been compared with the Christian basilica. Yet in these latter, light was permitted to enter unhindered into the hall. At Karnak, the window grilles acted like heavy curtains.

The desire for half-darkness is even more evident in the light coming from the seventy-eight-foot-high ceiling at Karnak. Small openings (9 x 7 in.) were pierced in the heavy (2 ft. 8 in. thick) ceiling slabs, so that the light entered as though through a keyhole. "Thus the light could only enter in narrow rays 259 col through these little openings" (Legrain, 1929, p. 179). Color plates show one of the windows without its perforated-stone screen and also one of the pierced, once blue-painted ceiling slabs.

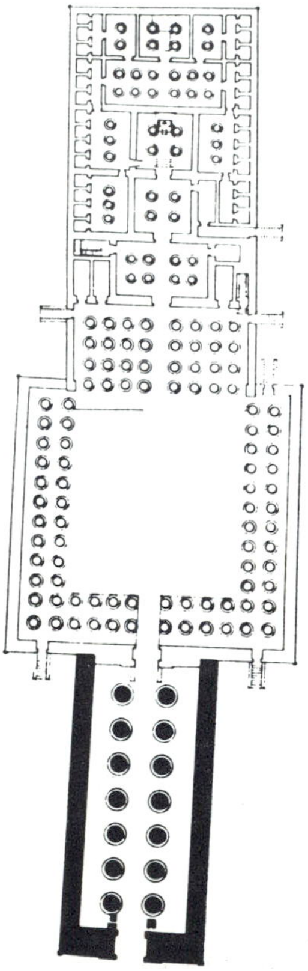

252. HYPOSTYLE HALL, TEMPLE OF LUXOR: *View of the long hypostyle hall of Amenhotep III, originally planned to have three aisles of columns, but hastily finished, after the death of Amenhotep III, by his grandson Tut-ankh-amon with a single aisle bordered by seven papyrus-bundle columns*

253. GROUND PLAN OF TEMPLE OF LUXOR, AMENHOTEP III (*1400–1362* B.C.): L. *621 feet. The whole complex presents a unified plan, from the narrow, elongated hypostyle, across the double-colonnaded inner court, to the sanctuaries shielded by an open-fronted hypostyle with four rows of eight columns each. The main sanctuary of Amon with its many side chambers is at the extreme north end of the temple. From Schwaller de Lubicz*

254. TEMPLE OF LUXOR: *View of the hypostyle hall from the inner court*

255. TEMPLE OF LUXOR, INNER COURT OF AMENHOTEP III: *144 x 168 feet, with excellently preserved papyrus-bundle columns of granite*

256. TEMPLE OF LUXOR: *The hypostyle hall, with the pylon of Ramesses II in the background*

The all-permeating idea of wandering is most clearly expressed by the great reliefs of ritual processions within the hypostyle halls: Luxor, Amenhotep III, fourteenth century B.C.; Karnak, Ramesses II, thirteenth century B.C.; Medinet Habu (west of Thebes), Ramesses III, early twelfth century B.C.

Many sacrifices were offered to the god on his journey. At the same time he performed important acts of state by way of oracles, such as the selection of Tuthmosis III as Pharaoh. "When the god was brought out . . . borne in a
363 barge on the shoulders of the priests, petitions or candidates to different posts were presented to him. The god accepted and rejected. It was probably by moving toward the petitioner or by retreating from him that the god indicated his will" (Piankoff, 1957, pp. 18–19).

The huge reliefs on the walls of these royal temples reveal the great importance attached to ritual ceremonies performed during the wandering of the god. They depict practically every step and every action of the Pharaoh as he, the son and representative of the god, accompanied the sacred barge which contained the god's image hidden within its naos.

It is to these reliefs that we owe most of our insight into the ritual: the route by land and water from one sanctuary to another, the location of the various processional stations, and the sacrifices performed. The sacrificial ceremonies were of the utmost importance. But this was not all: "Ancient writers have told us of kings and priests wearing animal masks during religious ceremonies. The low
362 relief of Ramesses II on the south wall of the hypostyle is the best illustration of these writings" (Legrain, 1916, p. 41). In this relief Ramesses II is depicted pacing backward while facing the sacred barge. In his left hand he holds a triple incense burner and with his right he throws grains of incense onto the ritual instrument. The trajectory of the grains is indicated by a curve of dots.

The hawk-headed priests "who carry the barge play the part of members of the great or little Paout" (ibid.); in ranks of five, pacing backward and forward, they form "a council to whom the decisions of Amon are communicated" (p. 42).

The columns of the hypostyle are densely packed, and the space between them and the wall is so narrow that the camera cannot take the large reliefs in one shot. In the large and unwieldy volumes of *Description de l'Égypte*, first published by order of Napoleon I in the early nineteenth century, the draftsman de-
362 picted the entire scenes. On one of them the priests do not wear animal heads. Their heads are shaven. In spite of some inaccuracies, the nature of the proces-

sion is well expressed: the wooden carrying-poles on the priests' shoulders bear the sacred barge. Upon it may be seen the shrine of the god, the divine feathers, and, at bow and stern rams' heads, the symbol of Amon.

Along the walls of the hypostyle of the Luxor temple, the "Beautiful festival of Opet" is represented. This has been described in detail by W. Wolf (1931). The various stages of Amon's progress from his cella at Karnak to that at Luxor and back are shown in minute detail along a 150-foot band: the king's sacrifice before the barges in the temple of Amon at Karnak; the barges being carried from the Karnak temple to the Nile on the shoulders of the priests; the journey of the barges on the Nile to Luxor, with an accompanying procession on land; the procession of the barges from the landing stage to the temple of Amon at Luxor; the barges set up in the temple of Luxor and the sacrificial offerings; the return journey; finally, the king's act of sacrifice before the barges in the temple of Amon at Karnak (p. 38).

The date of these reliefs is not definitely established. They resemble the Amarna style of Akhenaten (Amenhotep IV) and are ascribed to Tut-ankh-amon (pp. 1–3).

The "Beautiful festival of Opet," which consisted mainly of this processional wandering and the sacrifices connected with it, was fundamentally a fertility rite. This explains the fusion that made Amon sometimes almost indistinguishable from the fertility-god Min, as the latter is depicted in ithyphallic form standing before Alexander the Great in the temple at Luxor. What really happened at this "Beautiful festival of Opet," and the actions connected with what is represented in the reliefs, cannot be fully understood.

Amon, "the invisible one," journeyed in his magnificent barge from Karnak 362
to visit his "southern harem" at the temple of Luxor. In Thebes the ruling deities were a triad of Amon, his consort Mut, and his son Khonsu. Luxor was regarded as the residence of his other consort, Amaunet. But he traveled in company with Mut and Khonsu, who rode in two other barges for which two shrines were prepared at Luxor with direct access to the great vestibule with its quadruple colonnades of slender papyrus-bundle columns.

"Amon had also a number of human concubines headed by the Chief of the Concubines who generally seems to have been the wife of the High Priest, or else his sister or daughter. They probably had their residence in Luxor, the Southern Harem of Amon. It is quite possible that these concubines were no other than the musician-priestesses, the Chantresses of Amon" (Piankoff, 1957, p. 18).

257. TEMPLE OF LUXOR, INNERMOST SANCTUARY OF AMON: *Here the cult statue of Amon rested after its journey from Karnak on the occasion of the "Beautiful festival of Opet." A statue of the god was at one time placed upon the wall behind the altar*

Possibly the Egyptians, with their remarkable understanding of symbolism, did not take these abstruse ideas too literally. In a wider sense, the latter originate in the vagueness and polymorphism which for the Egyptians was bound up with the notion of deity.

Ritual processions in Egypt, Mesopotamia, and Greece

Mesopotamian temples have only been described in their earliest stages, in connection with the first beginnings of architecture. Their late stages, in Babylon, Assyria, and again Babylon, are of less significance.

However, there are similarities in the religious structure of Egypt and Mesopotamia that demand some passing reference.

Mesopotamia developed the earliest codes of law. These were inscribed with precisely defined judicial terms upon steles and clay tablets.

However, there are no sacred writings in Egypt or Mesopotamia—or, incidentally in Greece—out of which religious beliefs clearly developed. None of these peoples possessed a dogma with legal powers. All were concerned with establishing direct contact with the deity. But this contact was confined to the privileged few and consequently—as we have shown—led to the separation of the mass of the faithful from the presence of the deity. Only when the statue of the deity wandered from one temple to another could the people receive a glimpse of the naos in which the sacred statue was enclosed.

In Egypt the sacred ways led from the imperial temple of Karnak, stopping before 355 at various sanctuaries, to the temple of Luxor and across the Nile to the necropolis of Thebes, where Hatshepsut had dedicated her mortuary temple to the god Amon. The Karnak statue of the deity wandered up to the highest terrace of this mortuary temple, into his chapel hewn deep into the rock face.

The Mesopotamian sacred wanderings were just as thoroughly worked out, though differently expressed. The monumental stairways of the ziggurats of around 2000 B.C. were used for the processions of priests which paraded magnificently up and down the three arms of the stairway.

The most grandiose processional way was created near the end of Mesopotamia's existence, in the sixth century B.C. During his reign of more than forty years King Nebuchadnezzar built a processional route in Babylon for the god Marduk, more splendid than any before or since. It formed the background for the greatest annual event, the New Year festival, which celebrated the rebirth of nature: a fertility ritual in which the king played an important role. Just as in the Egyptian "Beautiful festival of Opet," when the statue of Amon wandered to the temple of Luxor in a procession headed by the Pharaoh, the Babylonian statue of the deity wandered in its splendidly decorated chariot and ritual boat from the Tower of Babel (Etemenanki) and the state temple of Marduk (Esagila) along a mile-long avenue to another temple (Akitu). The mighty procession was led in Thebes by the Pharaoh, in Babylon by the king. The purpose of the two festivals was also similar: the fulfillment of fertility rites.

The separation of the faithful masses from the godhead occurred in both countries. In Mesopotamia the same space never accommodated the abode of the deity and the populace. In Egypt the separation was even more radical.

Even Greece did not break with the ancient ritual meaning of the sacred wandering of the god and the exclusion of the public from the temple. There, no divine statues wandered from temple to temple. The wandering was done by the people. In the magnificent three-dimensionality of the Delphian landscape, nature was far more closely incorporated into the procession as it moved from the earliest sanctuaries to the sacred Castalian spring and up the hillside to the temple of Apollo.

In the urban setting of Athens the Great Panathenaean festival was celebrated every four years; it fell in August and was probably united with a harvest festival. The processional route of this greatest festival of the Athenians was filled with ritual significance. It started from the Dipylon gate of the city and wended its way along the Hermes alley and diagonally across the Agora, passing several sanctuaries before arriving at the Acropolis. The procession, bearing new raiment for the statue of Athena, was led by the chief councilor of the city and accompanied by other members of the council, priests, and horsemen. Its importance is brought out by the dominant position its reliefs occupy on the frieze around the Parthenon. In contrast to Egypt, the Parthenon statue of the goddess Athena had grown to gigantic dimensions. During the festival the great temple door was thrown wide open and the goddess made visible to all. But the people, even here, remained outside the sanctuary.

That the people might wander around the temple but never enter within it is common to Mesopotamia, Egypt, and Greece. This condition is one of the reasons why, throughout the three archaic civilizations, the relations of volumes in space remains a hallmark of the first architectural space conception.

PART X HATSHEPSUT AND THE COSMIC INNER COURT

The terraced temple of Queen Hatshepsut (1490–?1469 B.C.) was constructed in the rock amphitheater of Deir el Bahari, on the opposite bank of the Nile from the temple of Karnak. This radiant climax to a sequence of rock-tombs achieves a rare unity of architecture and sculpture, and a new freedom in the articulation of space that was to remain unsurpassed in the Egyptian development.

The mortuary temple of Queen Hatshepsut was not a tomb. Her father, Tuthmosis I, had broken the ancient custom that required every Pharaoh to be buried beneath a pyramid, or at least to conserve the triadic sequence of valley temple, causeway, and mortuary temple, Tuthmosis I chose to place his own funerary monument in a desert valley, filled with boulders, on the other side of the mountain from Deir el Bahari: the Valley of the Kings. The mountain that below forms its background tapers to a pyramid. Here the successive Pharaohs of the New Kingdom continued to be buried until the Twentieth Dynasty, in chambers tunneled ever more deeply into the mountainside. These tombs were sometimes so cunningly concealed that, as when Howard Carter discovered the tomb of Tut-ankh-amon, all the treasures were still undisturbed. Carter and Lord Carnarvon also discovered the tomb of Hatshepsut in which she had also placed a new sarcophagus for her father's coffin. This tomb was found plundered of all else.

258. THE VALLEY OF THE KINGS: *This concealed rock gorge, surmounted by a pyramidlike peak, became the burial place for rulers of the New Kingdom*

The mortuary temple of Queen Hatshepsut marked the end of a development of the rock-tomb that had been in process for almost a thousand years. The basic type was the rock-tombs favored by the nomarchs, provincial governors of Upper Egypt from the Old Kingdom to the Twelfth Dynasty.

At first the nomarchs were simply officials who governed the provinces as servants of the king. With the weakening of centralized power and an occasional waning of the magic aura that surrounded the Pharaoh, they became feudal lords of increasing independence; they left their rock-cut tombs as proud witnesses of their high position.

These nomarchs' tombs began to be built in the Fourth Dynasty. A governor of the fourteenth province, named Khenouke, acquired from King Mycerinus, sometime before 2473 B.C., "authorization to be buried in the district in which he was born" (Vandier, 1954, II, p. 295): in other words, far away from Memphis and the pyramids within whose shadow and under whose protection all mastabas of the nobles had stood until then. This marked the beginning of independence. Toward the end of the Old Kingdom, both emancipation and the destruction of the central power proceeded rapidly.

None of the royal tombs between the Sixth and Eleventh Dynasties shows signs of new architectural forms developed under the influence of the cult of the dead. It was the nomarchs and not the kings who created the new rock-cut type. When Neb-hepet-ra Mentuhotep (2061–2010 B.C.), founder of the Middle Kingdom, built his famous funerary temple in the cliff amphitheater of Deir el 410 Bahari, he was, in principle, following the line of development established by the nomarchs.

The structural form of the rock-tomb can only be comprehended when it is related to the physical structure of Upper Egypt. There are no desert plateaus like those at Giza or Saqqara in Lower Egypt, where the table-shaped mastabas of the nobles could easily be sunk into the ground. Any buildings in the valley bottom of Upper Egypt would risk destruction by the Nile floods, and on both sides the narrow strip was closely bordered by towering cliffs.

The physical structure of this valley was exploited to the full for ritual purposes. The rock-cut tombs of the nobles, hewn halfway up the steep cliff face, 404 show how conscious these provincial governors were of the power they wielded. In a compressed form, the tombs followed the royal sequence: valley temple, causeway, mortuary temple, and tomb. The forms themselves were simplified

259. ROCK-TOMBS OF SIXTH DYNASTY NOMARCHS: *View from the Nile. To the left, tomb of the governor Sabeni; to the right, that of his son Mekhou. Causeways lead up to their tombs from the river bank. Aswan*

and, in the case of the funerary temple and tomb, they became different in kind, for these were hewn directly into the rock face.

Between the Sixth and Twelfth Dynasties, two stages in the spatial organization of these rock-tombs can be recognized: an early one in which the rectangular chambers were cut parallel to the walls of the cliff, and a later one when they penetrated deeply into the rock. In other words, the development moved from transversely cut chambers (*Querraum*) at the end of the Old Kingdom to the perpendicularly cut chambers (*Langraum*) of the Middle Kingdom.

260. SABENI'S TOMB, CAUSEWAY: *Looking across the Nile from the tomb entrance, down the causeway bordered with steps*

Early stage: nomarch tombs of Aswan, Sixth Dynasty

The finest expressions of the early stage, in which the chambers ran parallel to the face of the cliff, are the rock-tombs of two governors of Elephantine (Aswan). These two chambers, which have no separating wall, belonged to a father and his son. The father, Sabeni, lord of the First Nome of Upper Egypt, had the larger chamber to the left; his son, Mekhou, the chamber to the right. 406
Sabeni's chamber contained three rows of six columns which, like his offering

261. SABENI'S TOMB, ENTRANCE: *The side walls formed by the natural sandstone cliff with its many-colored horizontal strata. Two simple steles without inscriptions stand before the entrance*

262. GROUND PLANS OF TOMBS OF SABENI AND MEKHOU: *The two communicating hypostyles of father and son are cut out from the living rock, transversely to the rock face. Based on Brunner*

table and false door, were cut out of the rock face. Mekhou completed the tomb of his father, who had fallen in a campaign against the Nubians. He then made himself a chamber immediately to the right of it, as a funerary chapel. This contained two rows of squared columns, parallel to the two inner rows of his father's chamber.

Two steles without inscriptions flank the entrance to Sabeni's chamber. There left is no decoration. The austere dignity of the design is heightened by the horizontal layers of different-colored sandstone, which greatly impressed Paul Klee; their influence can be detected in his paintings.

These dry facts cannot do justice to what was here accomplished, for in these tombs with their infinitely wide outlook the relation of death with the cosmos can be sensed more powerfully than usual. From their position halfway up the steep cliff wall that rises abruptly from the banks of the Nile, nothing limits the 405 view to the east. Stepping out from their entrances, one is embraced by the cosmic vault. We of today seem to gaze out into an endless void, but for the Egyptians the heavens were peopled. From the east the celestial bark emerged, its passengers renewed to life.

Almost at the foot of the cliff lay the island of Elephantine (near present-day Aswan), seat of the lords of the First Nome, which was at that time the southernmost boundary of Egypt. Elephantine was an important base of the tottering Old Kingdom, and probably in Sabeni's time the only actively functioning province. Its nomarchs, as Scharff says, "conducted a lively caravan trade with the lands to the south, from which they imported precious goods of many kinds, in particular ivory and leopard skins—which were at that time used for priests' vestments" (Scharff and Moortgat, 1950, p. 70).

There is only a narrow terrace in front of the entrance to the tombs. A steep flight of steps leads up to it from the banks of the Nile, and in the center of the 404 stairway are two stone rails on which the sarcophagus rested as it was drawn up the cliffside. Thus it followed its symbolic wandering from light into darkness. Even without a valley temple, the sequence of the final royal journey of the Pharaohs was retained, with its causeway, funerary temple, tomb. Its impressiveness is in this instance strengthened by the wide cosmic view.

There were many variants of the ways in which the nomarchs cut their funerary chambers and tombs into the rock face, and numbers of these plans are given by Vandier (1954, II, pp. 293–357).

263. ROCK TOMB OF TWELFTH DYNASTY NOMARCH WAH-KA II: *The covered causeway leads from the fertile land to a pylonlike structure. Behind this is a square, colonnaded court, with stairway leading from its center to a small transverse hypostyle. Within is a longitudinal hypostyle approached by some steps. Beyond this the tomb chapel. Qaw el Kebir. Drawing after Steckeweh*

Later stage: Mentuhotep's mortuary temple and the nomarch tombs of the Middle Kingdom

The rock-tombs at Beni Hasan in Middle Egypt (Newberry, 1893), with their magnificent wall paintings, show distinct traits of the deeply penetrating ground plan (*Langraum*).

The Middle Kingdom nomarchs of Elephantine constructed their luxurious sepulchers within the sand-blown cliffs near Aswan, next to those of their Sixth Dynasty forebears and at approximately the same height. The most beautiful of

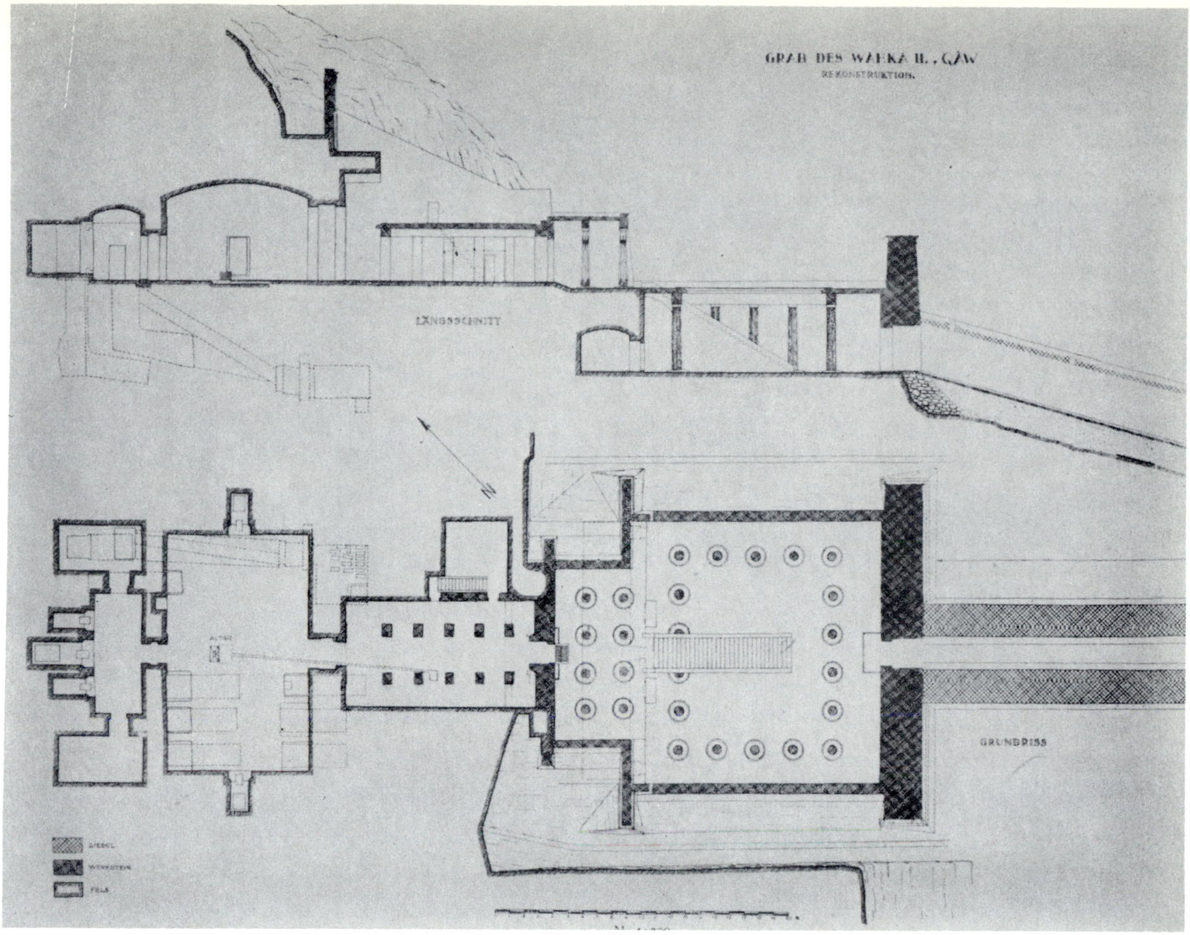

264. SECTION AND GROUND PLAN OF TOMB OF WAH-KA II *showing vaulted mortuary chapel cut into the rock. The strong emphasis on the longitudinal axis with its three levels hints at the later development—on a royal scale—of Hatshepsut's mortuary temple. After Steckeweh*

these was built by Sarenput I, with a generously wide forecourt. It is tunneled deep into the cliff face but has no stepped terraces (Müller, 1940, pp. 15–51).

Among the forerunners of Hatshepsut's Deir el Bahari temple are the immediately adjacent funerary temple of King Mentuhotep, of the Eleventh Dynasty, and the rock-tombs of the nomarchs of Qaw el Kebir, built at the peak of the Twelfth Dynasty. These, with their terraces, are nearer the conception of the mortuary temple of Queen Hatshepsut.

Mentuhotep's terraced mortuary temple

Neb-hepet-ra Mentuhotep, restorer of power to the Pharaohs and founder of the Middle Kingdom, was the first to make the city of Thebes a royal resi-

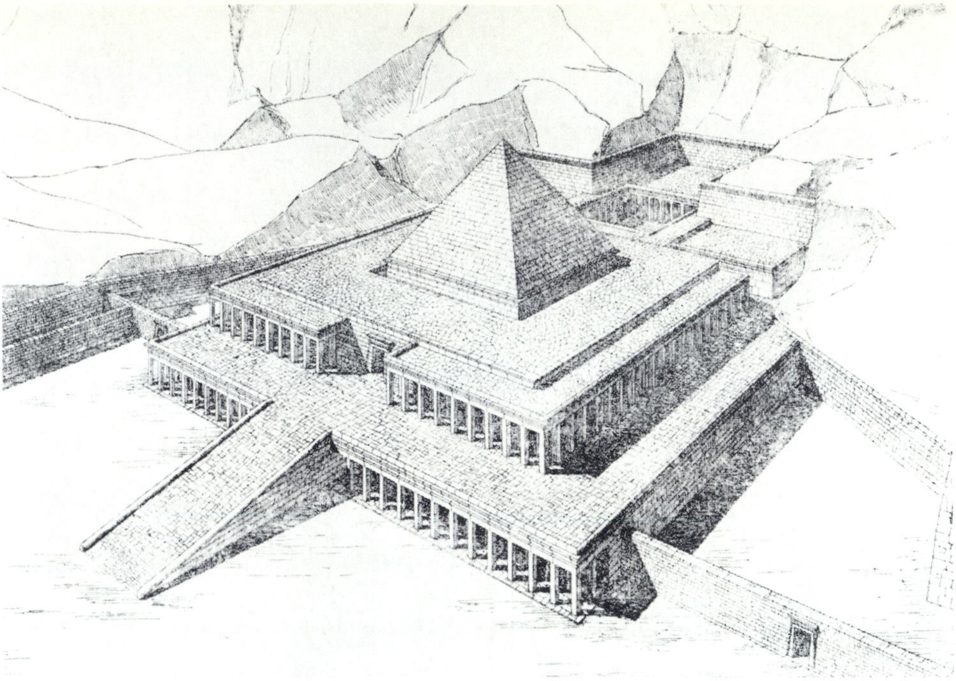

265. KING MENTUHOTEP'S MORTUARY TEMPLE, ELEVENTH DYNASTY: *The reconstruction shows unusually extensive use of porticoes on three sides; very large ramp leading to raised terrace; massive pyramid rising from center of second-level colonnaded hypostyle. Inner court (behind) leads to tombs of Mentuhotep's wife and daughters, cut into the rock face. Deir el Bahari. From Naville*

266. MENTUHOTEP'S MORTUARY TEMPLE TODAY: *View outward from inner court through the hypostyle, with the square substructure of the pyramid in the background*

dence. He built his tomb across the river from it, in the rock amphitheater of Deir el Bahari. Winlock, who has done so much to clarify the confusing history 413 of the Middle Kingdom, said: "Before Neb-hepet-rē^{c} united the Two Lands he had started to build his mortuary temple under the western cliffs at Thebes on a scale larger than that of any of his ancestors" (1947, p. 38).

The building gives the impression of many deliberate alterations: "A close inspection shows that, as finally finished, it had undergone innumerable changes in its plan" (p. 40). The ancient royal sequence—valley temple, causeway, mortuary temple—can again be recognized, though in some ways it is unclear. Despite its impressive grandeur, the structure lacks architectonic unity.

Mentuhotep's valley temple now lies beneath cultivated ground. The walled but roofless causeway, about 35 meters wide and 1200 long, led up to the temple court, which was surrounded by a high boulder wall. This court was of considerable size, and its dimensions recall the grand scale of Zoser's temple complex at Saqqara. Behind it rose the complex of the mortuary temple. Most unusual, in terms of Egyptian custom, was a portico of twenty-six columns which projected from its colonnaded hall.

An unusually broad ramp rose from the temple court to a second terrace, on left which stood the focus of the composition, the mortuary temple. Right and left of this ramp, sycamore and tamarisk trees were planted in deep pits of soil sunk into the desert sand: a sign of intimacy, of life brought into a zone of death, later to be developed by Hatshepsut.

Because it was raised upon a terrace, the portico of the temple court assumed far greater importance. It became an ambulatory surrounding three sides of the temple, which was itself enclosed within a massive wall. Within, the square hypostyle was a truly luxuriant forest of columns. It continued as a narrower, partly roofed, pillared court, behind which another, final hypostyle was excavated from within the rock wall. Along its sides niches were hewn out for six princesses. The site of Mentuhotep's actual tomb is not known with absolute certainty (ibid., p. 41).

This entire ground plan is an extreme version of the deeply penetrating rock tomb (*Langraum*), corresponding to the later nomarch tombs of Qaw, but here raised to royal magnificence.

The substructure of its low pyramid sat squarely in the midst of the great hypostyle hall. It rose ponderously—one might even say inorganically—above the flat roofs of the hall, and represented the result of many changes of plan, possibly brought about by the need to retain some ancient rite. Thus the greatest monument of the Middle Kingdom is a *Langraum* in ground plan and is pyramidal in elevation. This architectonic contradiction is probably one of the reasons it did not become a new building type.

Mentuhotep's mortuary monument gives the impression of a huge porticoed temple. Several such Egyptian temples exist: the temple at Medinet Habu near Thebes, Hatshepsut's temple at Wady Halfa, Amenhotep III's temple on the island of Elephantine, and others (Borchardt, 1938). Among the most delightful
364 is the small repository pavilion of Sesostris I, surrounded by a portico of squared pillars and adorned with delicate reliefs. Chevrier reassembled this little pavilion at Karnak, with infinite toil, from a number of remnants (Lacau and Chevrier, 1956). Mentuhotep's mortuary temple is, however, by far the largest porticoed building of Egypt. In the long run, this external exposure of colonnades does not seem to have accorded with the Egyptian mentality. Shadow-forming elements on the exterior of buildings are far more in keeping with the Greek perception.

The rock-tombs of the nomarchs of Qaw

During the Twelfth Dynasty another and more important precedent for the temple of Hatshepsut appeared in the rock-tombs of nomarchs of the Tenth Nome, at Qaw el Kebir. This was one of the most fertile of the provinces, situated in the middle of Egypt about thirty-five miles south of Assiut. According to G. Steindorff, the tombs date from the peak period of the Twelfth Dynasty (Steckeweh, 1936, p. 8); according to Scharff, they date from the middle of this dynasty (Scharff and Moortgat, 1950, p. 103), which would be somewhere around 1900 B.C.

In marked contrast to the tombs at Aswan from the Sixth and Twelfth Dynasties, those at Qaw are almost in ruins. Only from reconstructions made by H. Steckeweh can we gain an impression of their architecture.

The tombs were of three nomarchs, Wah-ka I, Ibu, and Wah-ka II. The lar-
408 gest was that of Wah-ka II. It started with a pylonlike brick structure. This corresponded to the valley temple. Then came the causeway, leading through a pylon with sloping walls into a court surrounded by a proto-Doric colonnade. In the middle of the court, a broad flight of steps led up to a second terrace on which
409 stood two rows of columns, each formed like four bundles of papyrus reeds. This narrow terrace lay across the complex like a barrier in front of a slightly raised hypostyle whose ten pillars formed a colonnade projecting into the rock, while its roof created a third terrace platform. All this was just an architectural pre-

267. MORTUARY TEMPLES OF HATSHEPSUT AND MENTUHOTEP: *Mentuhotep's temple is ideologically based on the pyramid and internally oriented; Hatshepsut's, with its three generous terraces, embraces the external landscape. The first two terraces are approached by ramps. In 1922, when H. E. Winlock made this picture, the innermost sanctuaries were incompletely excavated. Deir el Bahari*

lude, but the prelude has now become the main theme of the composition. From the third terrace one entered within the rock itself, into the chamber for offerings and burial rites. This great chamber, cut deep into the rock, was completely free of columns and was roofed by a high, segmented vault. From it one entered the most secret parts of the tomb.

The special feature of this structure and of its two immediate neighbors, the tombs of Wah-ka I and Ibu, is their clear sequence of terraces and the emphasis laid on the longitudinal axis. At the same time each separate zone was "announced by a distinct front elevation" (Steckeweh, 1936, p. 32). Here was an experiment in working with different levels on a small scale but with a purely architectural basis.

"We find ourselves," says the excavator, "in the largest and most beautiful private structure known from the period before the New Kingdom . . . the summit of provincial art in the Middle Kingdom" (p. 31). What appears here on a small scale and with a certain hesitation (shown by the repetition of horizontal barriers) is a foretaste of the radiant site planning of Hatshepsut's temple, where the tomb itself has vanished, and only a small funerary chapel cut into the rock indicates the original purpose of the structure. Later on in the Middle Kingdom, Sesostris III (1878–1842 B.C.) took the reins of office firmly into his own hands and the princely tombs of the nomarchs disappeared. From that time on, they had no significant architectural influence.

We stand at the beginning of the fifteenth century B.C. The Hyksos have been expelled and the New Kingdom founded by the Eighteenth Dynasty, which was to rule for more than two hundred years (1552–1302 B.C.). Its Pharaohs possessed sharply determined and contrasting personalities: rugged conquerors like Tuthmosis III; Hatshepsut, equal in greatness, though feminine and peace-loving; Amenhotep IV (Akhenaten), utterly different again, a religious puritan and iconoclast; finally the young Tut-ankh-amon, near the end of the dynasty, the splendor of whose funeral trappings gives a glimpse of the intricately subtle luxury of an overweary royal court.

Queen Hatshepsut ruled about two decades (1490–?1469 B.C.), but we do not know exactly how and when her reign ended.

Theoretically, the position and title of Pharaoh could only be assumed by a man. This explains why almost all the many statues of Hatshepsut in her terrace temple show her with a manlike shape. Only her face reveals her female charm.

Hatshepsut, her strongly feminine nature hemmed in by the inflexible laws of Egyptian protocol, was first married to her physically frail half brother, Tuthmosis II. He died a few years later. An infant, Tuthmosis III, son of Tuthmosis II by a concubine, then became Pharaoh. At first, Hatshepsut ruled as regent on behalf of this stepson, who later became Egypt's greatest warrior king. But soon, basing her claim upon her superior direct descent from a queen of royal blood, Hatshepsut proclaimed herself ruler of the two lands—Upper and Lower Egypt. She became Pharaoh, adopting both the title and the official dress and insignia.

Hatshepsut and Senmut

Into her life of solitude came Senmut. He gradually rose, step by step, until he became the "greatest of the great" (Winlock, 1942, p. 150). He possessed two rare talents seldom found together: he was a great artist and a great administrator. All the key positions of the kingdom were in his hands. His architectural genius is what concerns us here. It is always difficult to give vent to any personal expression when, as in Egypt, a strong and in itself splendid tradition prevails. To enable an individual voice to be heard, as it was at Deir el Bahari, great strength and courage were necessary. Only when there is a close accord between architect and client, and when the architect is able to bring to life something

268. HATSHEPSUT'S MORTUARY TEMPLE: *Ramp from second terrace. This second broad ramp leads to the third terrace with its sanctuaries*

already slumbering in the mind of the client, is it possible for a strong conceptual imagination to find a solution within the bounds of an all-powerful tradition.

This is a general truth that has particular relevance for Egypt. The close col-
Part VII laboration of King Zoser and Imhotep, a universal genius not unlike Senmut, resulted in the birth of stone architecture. Now, in the Eighteenth Dynasty, another and even closer collaboration can be observed between Hatshepsut and Senmut. What made this blossom was the close spiritual and corporal affinity between Hatshepsut and her steward.

Senmut possessed almost unlimited power. He was the Steward of Amonf which meant he was administrator of all the vast estates of the great temple of Karnak. He was "Overseer of All of the Works of the King in the Temple of

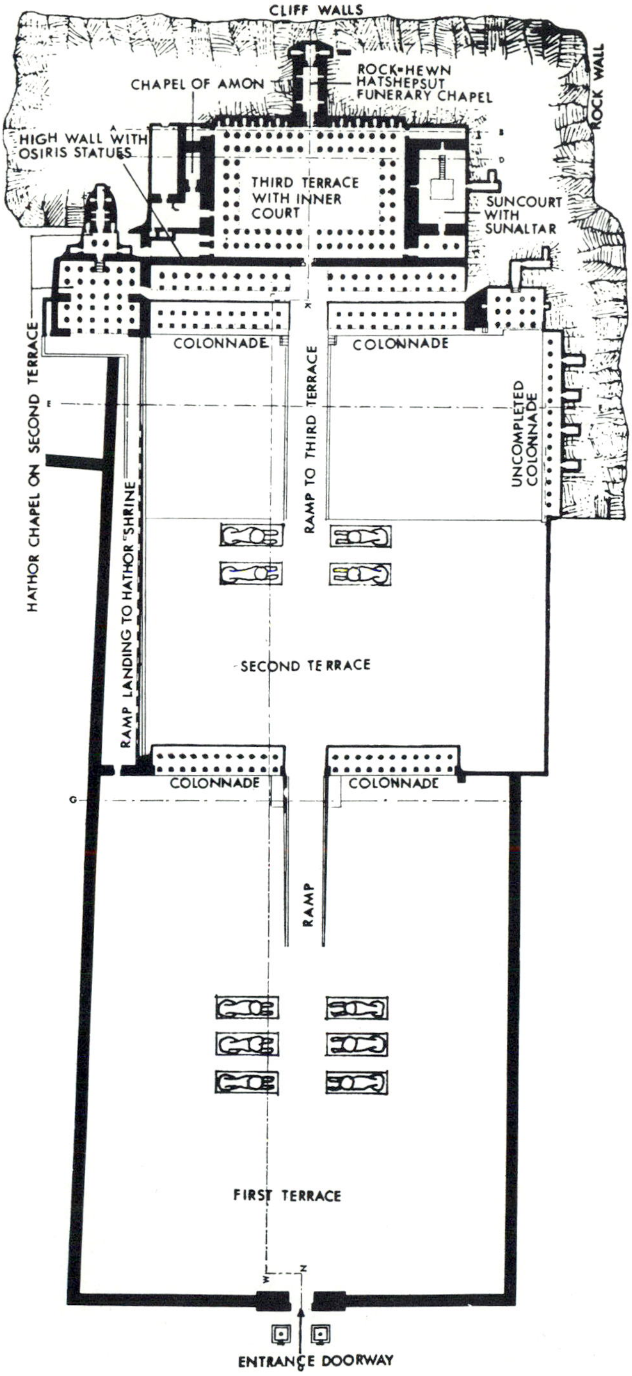

269. GROUND PLAN OF HATSHEPSUT'S TEMPLE. *After Naville*

Amon," and finally, "Overseer of Overseers of All of the Works of the King" (Winlock, 1928, p. 50). In other words, all responsibility for both design and execution was united in the hands of a genius. Senmut brought to realization the qualities of Hatshepsut's nature. This we can see at Deir el Bahari—a unique event in the history of architecture.

Senmut had official entry to the most private sphere. Hatshepsut made him high steward of her own household and also "Superintendent of the Private Apartments, of the Bathroom, and of the Royal Bedrooms as well" (p. 52). Besides this, he was chief guardian of Hatshepsut's daughter Neferu-ra, who died
420 as a child and with whom Senmut is often portrayed in block statues.

All these high offices were known to everyone. More revealing are the hidden indications of their relationship. When Senmut prepared his second tomb, tunneling toward the sacred precincts of the temple, he placed an inscription upon its marvelously designed astronomical ceiling, linking his own name with that of the queen, and even with that of the god Horus: "Long live the Horus . . . the King of Upper and Lower Egypt, 'Maatkare' [Hatshepsut], beloved of Amon, who lives, and the Chancellor, the Steward of Amon, Senmut" (p. 57). This might have appeared an even greater blasphemy to an Egyptian than the fact that Senmut, mere mortal, had his portrait painted behind every door in the temple of Deir el Bahari.

Although Senmut and Hatshepsut had to be buried in different places, their sarcophagi were identical.

270. RED GRANITE SPHINX OF HATSHEPSUT: *From the second terrace of her temple*

271. SPHINX HEAD OF HATSHEPSUT: *Even deliberate mutilation could not destroy the charm of her face*

Egyptian inscriptions are invariably reticent when it comes to the personal sphere. We have little more than indirect hints of the relations of the queen with her steward. In one of the quarry foundation deposits was an alabaster shell inscribed with the name of Hatshepsut, and with it, a little alabaster saucer on which was the name of Senmut (p. 38).

"As is usual only for highly born married couples, the names of Senmut and Hatshepsut were inscribed next to one another upon beads found in the foundation deposits of the terrace temple" (Hermann, 1959, p. 47). Even more revealing are some enigmatic symbols on the shoulders of two block statues of Senmut with the little Neferu-ra, which are now in the Berlin and Cairo Museums. Senmut, squatting, throws his cloak around the little princess. A perspicacious study by É. Drioton discloses that the two names of Queen Hatshep-

☞ below

272. BLOCK STATUE OF SENMUT *with the little princess Neferu-ra*

sut are here presented as a cryptogram (1938). On one shoulder, Senmut replaced the cartouche that normally encloses the royal names by a representation of the vulture-goddess Nekhbet, who since the days of Zoser had always been shown hovering protectively above the king. This vulture he then transformed into symbols that formed a cryptogram for the first name of the queen: Maatkare (p. 235, fig. 17). On the other shoulder stands the fantastic figure of a god, bearing symbols instead of a head. This signifies the second name of the queen: Hatshepsut. Drioton says that Senmut states with pride that he himself engraved the signs "following the ideas of my heart and with my own hands" (p. 231). In other words, secretly to carve the names of one's queen as cryptograms upon a statue is not very different from cutting the initials of one's beloved into the bark of a tree.

We do not know the circumstances under which Queen Hatshepsut ended her reign, nor the causes of the downfall and death of Senmut during her last years. She has not been too favorably handled by Egyptologists. She was certainly a "vain, ambitious, and unscrupulous woman" (Hayes, 1959, II, p. 82), and Vandier writes that "Queen Hatshepsut was too busy with the domestic difficulties she had created for herself by her own ambitions to interest herself [like Tuthmosis III] in the affairs of Asia" (Drioton and Vandier, 1938, p. 382). Hatshepsut did not trouble herself overmuch about Asia. Hers was not the character of a world conqueror. She came between two warrior kings, Tuthmosis I and Tuthmosis III, Egypt's most aggressive conquerors. To measure her by the yardstick of these two war heroes is to compare two diametrically opposite approaches to life. Hatshepsut was a profoundly feminine woman. Here lay her genius. "Violence and bloodshed had no place in her make-up. Hers was a rule dominated by an architect" (Winlock, 1928, p. 52). What she longed for and worked for was—in a word—peace upon earth.

This is apparent in the beautiful reliefs behind the colonnades of her temple terraces. These scenes stand as a silent protest against all bombastic representations of a victorious Pharaoh slaughtering his enemies—from those of Narmer to those of the Ramessides. When Hatshepsut depicted regiments marching with trumpets, drums, and banners behind the colonnade of the lowest terrace, it was to acclaim the ceremonial erection of one of her obelisks in the temple of Karnak. When, on the second terrace at Deir el Bahari, she showed the equipping of an expedition, it was one she sent to the land of Punt to bring about the peaceful exchange of Egyptian manufactures for ebony, leopard skins, incense, and sweet-smelling trees for the temple of Karnak—and perhaps also for Deir el Bahari. In the hypostyle hall of the Hathor shrine at Deir el Bahari, we find a favorite subject, repeated in other parts of the temple: "It is a festive procession of soldiers, carrying arms, boughs of trees, and sacred standards. These men are called 'the dancers of the royal boats.' They . . . enliven the navigation or the festival by dances and songs" (Naville, 1901, p. 2).

Slowly this view of the queen has gained acceptance. Hatshepsut's personality was not only her private affair. She made it visible and left it recorded for all time. As early as 1933, Junker (p. 110) pointed out that Hatshepsut's name had become unusually deeply embedded in the history of the country, and Hermann brings out her wider ideological and personal background. Her ancestral line on the female side had close relations with Crete, and Hatshepsut "seems to have inherited a special cultural tradition from her female forebears. The most noteworthy aspect of her reign—its determinedly peaceful policy—

273. HATSHEPSUT NURTURED BY HATHOR: *Relief on the south wall of the Hathor chapel with Hatshepsut in the likeness of a young boy drinking from the udder of the divine cow*

274. HATHOR AS THE DIVINE COW: *Relief on the north wall of the Hathor chapel showing Hathor, the "Golden one," with the sun disk between her horns and the sistrum (menit) around her neck, standing majestically upon her sacred boat beneath a canopy. The two figures of Hatshepsut as well as her cartouches were chiseled out by Tuthmosis III*

275. DOUBLE-HEADED HATHOR COLUMNS: *These two columns stand in the first hypostyle to the Hathor chapel*

can be seen not only as an expression of her femininity but also as similar to the conception of peace held by the Cretan-Minoan culture" (Hermann, 1959, p. 38). The unwalled cities of Crete were based on peaceful mercantile trading across the seas. "A newly awakened love of sea adventure, which one would like to associate with the queenly tradition of Crete, is hinted at in her great trading expedition to Punt" (p. 39).

Reliefs behind the peristyle in the center of the second terrace depict Hatshepsut's fanatical determination to legitimate herself as Pharaoh, since each year added to the age of the young Tuthmosis III and threatened her position. Her only weapon was her legitimacy. It was not enough that she had inherited royal blood both from her mother and from her father: She presented herself here as the direct daughter of the god Amon, who had visited her mother in her father's guise.

Undoubtedly Hatshepsut was vain. On the whole, Deir el Bahari has but a single theme: Hatshepsut. Anything else is ancillary. Just as a woman conscious of her beauty never tires of gazing at herself in a mirror, the queen placed statues of herself everywhere, in every position, standing, kneeling, with an offering in her hands, as a sphinx, or as Osiris.

Normally, such a number of self-portraits in metamorphosis would become irritating, but here they are handled with such sculptural quality that irritation never arises. Further, one recalls the words engraved in the rock, which were probably a true description of her at the time she commenced the temple, probably the fifth year of her reign: "To look upon her was more beautiful than anything; her splendor and her form were divine; she was a maiden, beautiful and blooming" (Winlock, 1942, p. 144).

The structure of the temple

The plan developed steadily: "When Hat-shepsūt and her architect, Sen-Mūt, planned to build a temple on the West of Thebes, the only imposing structure there was this temple of Neb-hepet-Rē^{c} [Mentuhotep], the first Theban king of all Egypt. Its plan was their logical model, and the space beside it an inviting site. Clearly their ambitions did not, at first, rise to the point of attempting anything as large as the temple of the founder of Thebes. . . . Before Sen-Mūt was finished he had built a temple of which the actual structure, not counting its courtyard, covered over three times the area called for in his original plan— 413
making its floor over double that of Neb-hepet-Rē^{c}'s temple—and had altered nearly every feature except the general scheme of terraces with colonnaded porches." (Winlock, 1942, p. 135). The ancient sequence was maintained: valley temple, causeway, mortuary temple, and, finally, the funerary chapel piercing into the rock face. But an entirely different architectural form emerged. Here everything is freer, more delicate, more open than in any other Egyptian architectural complex, before or since.

There were three terraces, extending from the edge of the cultivated lands 262 col
right into the cliff wall. Parts of them were cut directly out of the rock. Broad,

gently sloping ramps connected one terrace with another in regal composure. The most striking aspect of the whole complex was its upward direction. True, the lowest terrace was walled about and entered through a doorway, and the
417 uppermost, which led into the rock wall, was shielded by a wall. These were ritualistic precautions. But they were organized so that they in no way impaired the spatial freedom of the layout. This was due to the grandiose dimensions of the terraces themselves; to the relationships set up between the vertical colonnades and the horizontal expanses; and to the articulation of the walls.

The second terrace appeared the largest and most open. It must have been the last resting place of the procession before it entered the enclosed inner sanctuary. Every year the small wooden statue of Amon departed in his sacred bark from the darkness of his cell in his temple at Karnak to visit Hatshepsut's temple and to be installed in the chapel dedicated to him within the rock face behind the uppermost terrace.

Sandstone sphinxes of modest size stood to right and left of the processional way leading up from the rim of the cultivated lands. Within the temple precincts they were succeeded by very large and beautiful sphinxes of red granite.
418 One, assembled from many fragments, is now in the Metropolitan Museum, New York: "Over eleven feet in length and weighing in the neighborhood of seven and a half tons, our reassembled sphinx is a massive piece of architectural sculpture" (Hayes, 1959, II, p. 93).

If ever a place was organized to accommodate a large number of privileged persons, it was the second terrace. The view opened out, so that the eye could gaze far into the wide landscape, across the Nile to the temples on the opposite bank. The gold-sheathed pyramidion of Hatshepsut's obelisk at Karnak is said to have been visible from here.

To the right, the rock bastions immediately behind the colonnade draw the
519 eye irresistibly upward. Into this scenery, enlivened by the most daring asymmetry, a formal element was introduced: a colonnade of proto-Doric columns upon the north side. It was never completed.

One was now fully prepared for the actual purpose of the building complex: the rites for the dead. Behind the colonnaded hall to the right is a small but well-preserved shrine of the jackal-headed Anubis. To the extreme left,
261 col projecting slightly forward from the long colonnade, is the rock-hewn, vaulted shrine of Hathor. Great care was devoted to this shrine because of the special significance of the goddess Hathor as guardian of the necropolis of Thebes. Its spatial refinement exceeded that of any other part of the temple.

There was already a Hathor shrine at the north end of Mentuhotep's neighboring temple, visited by both earlier and later generations. It was excavated by Naville, who found a well-preserved sculpture of Hathor as a cow within a painted barrel vault. This vault and cow are now in the Cairo Museum. Hathor 81 is shown in her original bovine form, striding out from the papyrus swamps of the west to give direct protection to the king.

Hathor also often appears in her cow form on the delicate reliefs of her shrine in Hatshepsut's temple—and in ways that show again the queen's determined personality. Certainly she is sometimes shown as a goddess, with a long scepter in her hand, receiving offerings. But the scenes in which she appears as a cow are more arresting, as when she licks the outstretched hand of the queen, the meaning being explained in the text: "To kiss (lit. to smell) the hand, to lick the divine flesh; to endow the king with life and purity (or happiness)" (Naville, 1901, p. 3).

The grace and dignity with which the divine cow stands in her sacred boat 423 sheltered by a canopy on the wall of the deepest part of the shrine, hewn into the rock face, bears comparison with the best prehistoric animal engravings. The queen appears three times, each figure defaced by Tuthmosis III. First she stands beneath Hathor's head, "with the appearance of a grown-up man, and wearing the insignia of royal power" (p. 5). Next she crouches as a youth beneath Hathor's belly, drinking from her udder while Hathor declares: "I have suckled thy Majesty with my breasts. I have filled thee with my intelligence, with my water of life and happiness. I am thy mother, who formed thy limbs and created thy beauties" (p. 4). On the right of the panel Hatshepsut stands in her own form, presenting offerings of wine, fruit, vegetables, and meat.

In the farthermost recess of the shrine are the only undefaced representations of the queen. In one she is again shown as a young boy suckled by Hathor, and 422 this may have escaped erasure because a relief of Hatshepsut and Tuthmosis, kneeling one behind the other with offerings of milk and wine, is placed just above the adjacent opening to a small niche. Within this niche, immediately around the corner from the divine Hathor with the young Hatshepsut, Senmut could not resist placing his own figure.

The Hathor shrine of Hatshepsut's temple is organically integrated into the complex, but it could be directly approached from the valley by a gently sloping ramp, as is easily seen from the model. Upon the smallest surface, at the extreme 429 south end of the terrace, is a sequence of chambers hewn out of the rock, increasing in height, accompanied by ramifications of subtly modeled side cham-

276. BUST OF OSIRIS STATUE *with the face of Hatshepsut. From the third terrace*

277. OSIRIS STATUE ON THIRD TERRACE: *This reassembled statue with mutilated face stands before the high wall of the third terrace, protecting the sanctuaries within*

278. MODEL OF UPPER TERRACES: *The ramp leading up from the second terrace to the palisade of Osiris statues before which a long and generously wide terrace gives an unhampered view across the Nile valley. To the extreme left an independent entrance from ground level to the Hathor chapel is indicated. Within the right-hand inner court stands a sun altar*

279. PRESENT STATE OF THIRD TERRACE: *An Osiris statue, the partly reconstructed wall, and, in the foreground, the open terrace*

261 col bers and terminating in a barrel-vaulted niche. In front of this sequence stand
424 two hypostyles, one of them with two squared pillars surmounted by double-headed Hathor capitals, facing east and west.

A second ramp leads to the third and uppermost terrace: the innermost sanctuaries enclosed within a high wall. Against this wall stood a row of tall,
428 polychrome Osiris statues, all bearing the face of the queen.

A narrow granite entrance gave access to these innermost sanctuaries, but in front of the forbidding wall with its Osiris statues, place was left for a generous terrace running the whole width of the temple, giving a last all-embracing out-
429 look over a sun-bathed world—a fitting setting for a luxury hotel of the twentieth century.

The wall signified the end. Around the inner court stood an assembly of sanctuaries, concentrating the real purpose of the project at a single point.

The whole temple was dedicated to Amon-Ra, guardian of all mortuary temples of the New Kingdom dynasties. The different chapels which lay to right and left on this upper terrace display nothing out of the usual, architecturally speaking. The vaulted funeral chapel for Hatshepsut and her father, Tuthmosis I, hewn deep into the rock, is the culminating point of the composition and leads directly back into darkness.

Inseparability of sculpture and architecture

The position assigned to this mortuary temple at Deir el Bahari in the whole realm of Egyptian architecture varies. But the synthesis of sculpture and architecture here achieved had no parallel in Egypt, either earlier or later. It was far removed from the oppressive near view of the colossal architecture of later Pharaonic temples. At Deir el Bahari all was subordinated to the human scale and to the distant view. The sculpture does not dominate the architecture, nor does the architecture dominate the sculpture. They complement one another. They have become indivisible.

To unite sculpture and architecture so that each enhances the other instead of being intent upon leading its own independent existence is one of the most delicate of all problems. Very seldom is the union achieved. When it is, we have one of those rare and blessed occasions when architect and client are of one mind and wish to give expression to the same idea.

The subtlety of the cohesion between sculpture and architecture at Deir el Bahari cannot be grasped at first sight. One senses it through the disposition of

280. NORTHWEST CORNER, SECOND TERRACE: *Natural rock bastions hover above the man-made structure in an ever-menacing gesture. This architecture, like the pyramids, is conceived in cosmic terms, but at this happy moment it never transcends the human scale*

forms rather than through the forms themselves, much as one senses what lies between the lines of a well-written book. This unity cannot be understood unless one realizes the close relation of architecture and sculpture to religion. Much later, in the Gothic cathedrals—themselves the end products of a long period of development—thought and form were again blended into a synthesis.

A strong sculptural contrast was consciously sought on the third terrace. The palisade of polychrome Osiris statues formed the protective wall of the sanctuary, excluding all the uninitiated, but its presence was scarcely felt. Each colossal statue of the usually forbidding god of death bore the youthful face 428
of the queen. Although color was elsewhere used with great restraint, these figures were painted to be seen from a distance, with "the long, curved Osirian

beard, painted blue. . . . Their throats and faces are red with white and black eyes and blue eyebrows, and the various attributes which they wear or hold are red, blue, and yellow" (Hayes, 1959, II, p. 91).

In this mortuary temple, Hatshepsut was most frequently represented in the mummified form of Osiris, lord of the underworld: her arms crossed over her
428 breasts; her right hand holding the scepter *was*, a shepherd's crook with a straight stem that was believed to bring its owner wealth and prosperity; her right hand holding the sign of life, *ankh*, and a flail.

After the upsurge of the cult of Osiris, toward the end of the Old Kingdom, the god of death and his symbol—eternal renewal—became of greater significance. In this temple he was first depicted in the two gigantic statues on either
429 side of the lowest colonnade; then in the row of polychrome statues on the upper terrace; finally in niches let into the rock. Always the mummified form predominated, bearing the face of the queen.

Rows of Osiris statues were no innovation. Series of them had already ap-
366 peared in temples, as in the hypostyle of Hatshepsut's father, Tuthmosis I, at Karnak. But the disposition of the crowning row of Osiris statues at Deir el Bahari was far more exciting. Here they were placed on the outer side of the wall of the innermost sanctuary, both protecting it and—in their mass—proclaiming it far across the fertile land. The treatment of the figures is handled with unusual skill. A moment's comparison with later clumsy Osiris statues will show their grace. Moreover, they were not mechanical replicas of one another. In their faces, despite all mutilations and hieratic formality, the charm and beauty of the queen break through, with her great eyes and ripe lips. These details show the tremendous care taken over normally routine pieces of architectural sculpture.

Freestanding statues—sculpture in the round—had no place in Egypt. The wall always stood behind them like a protecting shield. The only freestanding
419 sculptures at Deir el Bahari were the sphinxes that bordered and protected the processional way.

The low reliefs at Deir el Bahari are not placed upon the outer faces of the buildings. They lie concealed behind the double colonnades of the open courts. They are executed with the greatest freshness and, even for Egypt, they breathe an air of rare felicity.

That Hatshepsut was able to hold Tuthmosis III in check and reduce him to the role of a prince consort, though his empire later extended from the Fourth Cataract of the Nile to the Euphrates, is a measure of the intensity which must have possessed her spirit. But he took a heavy revenge. Only years of bitter pent-up fury can begin to explain his frantic destruction of Hatshepsut's sanctuary in his determination to obliterate all memory of her. Her figure and her name were chiseled out of almost every relief. Her sphinxes were smashed to pieces. "The destruction gang," writes Winlock in his exciting account of the excavations, "first threw them all on their sides and then hammered them on their hips with a big maul until they snapped asunder at their weakest points. . . . [The bits] were carried off to the nearest hole and dumped into it" (1942, p. 77).

From nooks and crannies, the Metropolitan Museum expedition retrieved many fragments and pieced them carefully together. As a result, the museum's collections now provide a rare insight into the splendor of the sculptures of this temple (Hayes, 1959, II, pp. 82–106).

Buildings and nature

Everything in Hatshepsut's temple betrayed the human touch. Though its purpose as a memorial temple was fully expressed, one cannot conceive of a more majestic processional way. Its ruins even today show with what mastery its sequences of ramps and terraces expressed the eternal Egyptian concept of an upward wandering into the hereafter. The relaxation achieved here contrasts 262 col strongly, not only with the neighboring temple of Mentuhotep, but also with 410 the stepped ziggurats built in Mesopotamia half a millennium earlier. 226

Just as Osiris, the god of death, bears in his hands the symbol of life, with its hope of an eternal existence, so this mortuary temple was free from any odor of 428 the grave. It was reminiscent of a pleasure garden for eternity. Everything was light and airy, right up to the topmost sanctuary fronted by the palisade of Osiris figures. How the terraces themselves were planted we do not know, but trees grew in parts of the courts and on either side of the temple ramp, and "to supply the green so dear to the Egyptian's heart, there were two shallow papyrus pools surrounded by little circular flower beds on either hand as one approached the ramp to the upper terraces" (Winlock, 1942, p. 90).

In relation to the grandeur of its dimensions, there is here a refinement of architectural detailing that recalls Zoser's temple complex at Saqqara. In contrast to the reliefs, which never lost their delicacy of touch, Egyptian architecture was destined to be drawn into a gigantism that became increasingly apparent in the hypostyles and courts of the later temples.

Hatshepsut and the Cosmic Inner Court

Neither the delicate orchestration of elements nor the embracing openness of the temple at Deir el Bahari had any continuation in Egypt. The intention here expressed was too early for its period, just as, in the earliest beginnings of architecture, an attempt at the development of interior space was crushed by a dominant development of the external relations between objects. A similar freedom in the disposition of open colonnades and gardens only reappears in the Roman pleasure villas displayed on the frescoes of Pompeii. But again the impulse was short-lived. It rose again and finally came to full flower in the baroque period. Yet one must beware of imputing any identity of intention. To perceive a horizontal axis at Deir el Bahari and derive it from the temple of Karnak, as has been done, runs contrary to Egyptian mentality. A rational connection from point to point was far from their way of thinking. Even in Hatshepsut's temple the first court is surrounded by a high wall. Like all Egyptian architecture, Deir el Bahari is oriented vertically upward. What appear to us as horizontal planes are mere pauses on an eternally upward-moving path. This is expressed with great daring by embedding a finely articulated human
262 col structure within the immense verticality of this great rock amphitheater, which draws the eye up to its summits. No one in the baroque period would have been so intrepid as to confront his building directly with the wildness of nature. The existence of the baroque depended on the subordination of the environment to the horizontal axis: the plane was master.

518 ff A great human problem lies concealed in the architecture of Hatshepsut's temple: how to confront the unformed with the formed without allowing the formed to be reduced to insignificance.

PART XI SUPREMACY OF THE VERTICAL

THE VERTICAL AS DIRECTIVE

Our attitude to the vertical has become automatic and anchored in the unconscious. From a limitless range of directions and angles, one was chosen and became the standard to which all others must be compared and to which all must bear some relation.

Without thinking, we automatically organize the structure of a building, a sculpture, a relief, or a painting with reference to its relation to the vertical. It is unnecessary to stress that this is no more than a first approach to the phenomenon of art—no more than a starting point. Even so, it is its organizing principle. Styles are changing but the vertical remains.

It would be a worth-while piece of research to show how the supremacy of the vertical lost some of its hold in the painting of the nineteenth century. Paul Cézanne liked to paint houses whose walls lean aslant for no obvious reason. In his landscapes he often took pleasure in depicting trees whose trunks depart from the vertical; in many of his portraits the heads are noticeably tilted out of the perpendicular, and in his seated figures the right angle between trunk and thighs is enlarged so that the figures appear to slide off their seats—something his contemporaries could never accept.

More interesting, perhaps, would be a study of the role of the vertical in our own time. Even the optical revolution around 1910, which threw out so much when it denied the general validity of the laws of perspective (and with this the static viewpoint), held fast to the organizing principle of the vertical. The latter served, however, other purposes than before: it was partly instrumental in shaping a new space conception.

This is announced in the early cubist pictures of Picasso and Braque. They perforated horizontal perspective space by abolishing the organization of the picture in depth, tipping it into the vertical and removing it from the realm of direct optical grasp. This gave rise to a transparency and intangibility which announced a new space conception. That verticality provided the scaffolding for this new structuring of space is an indication of the many meanings the concept can have.

It is unnecessary to compare in detail a still life done in 1929 with a painting
of an offering table of the Middle Kingdom. But they have one important method
438 of presentation in common. An Egyptian "still life"—with its bread, fruit, and
439 meat provided for the dead—and a still life by Braque—with wine bottle, pipe,
and guitar upon a café table—both negate perspective depth by tilting the

horizontal plane into the vertical. In some respects the Egyptian painter employs this technique more radically than the painter of 1929, who wished to achieve another purpose, to represent hovering space.

Piet Mondrian always believed that his paintings, which had no relationship to actuality, were neutral forms—*formes neutres*. But in reality, the heavy black bands that held the subtle off-balance of colored squares and rectangles cried aloud their vertical-horizontal relation. His forms were only neutral in the sense that we accept the vertical-horizontal relation as so self-evident that it *is* "neutral." Also, with Mondrian the organizing principle of the vertical served, in its own way, to build up the new space conception. He had strong theosophic interests and it may be that, unknown to him, cosmic symbolism mingled with his intentions, as it did in the strongly geometric works of the Egyptians.

In a way, the new space conception broke through under the shelter of the vertical, whose predominance as an organizing principle slowly dissolved. Kandinsky's compositions bear witness to this. In his works just after 1910, with their completely free disposition of forms, the vertical-horizontal relation is merged into a multidirectional cosmos.

Besides art, modern science has also widened our horizon. We begin to sense the relativity of the vertical-horizontal, to realize that our relation to the vertical is not self-evident or the only possible way to portray order. It exists neither in the spatial multidirectionality of the cosmos nor in primeval art. It is a special case, like Euclidean geometry, which stands in very close relationship to it.

The selection of one dominant direction is foreign to both prehistoric and primitive man. Prehistoric man did not divide the world into components, though certain elements became prominent that were never renounced throughout primeval art: multisignificance and transparency, an absence of concern for past and future, and a freedom of disposition within a setting of apparent chaos.

Before the advent of recorded history, a far-reaching change occurred in the development of vision: instead of all directions being equal, the vertical became dominant. This was nothing less than an optical revolution.

Verticality as a co-ordinating principle is not confined to the early high civilizations. It had its roots in the antecedent neolithic world. Somehow this organizing principle must be tied up with the evolutionary process of the human spirit. It occurs over the whole world, even when no direct contact is traceable between different cultures. It is possible to detect two stages among extant primitive civilizations, or as one prefers to say today, "archaic" civilizations. Certain

281. TABLE OF OFFERINGS, *stele of Mentuweser: The horizontal plane of the table is tilted into the vertical. Abydos, Twelfth Dynasty*

primitive peoples still hold to the prehistoric multidirectional lines and planes, and others accept the supremacy of the vertical. Among the first are the Australian aborigines, to some extent the Negroid peoples, and also the Eskimos. The art of the North American Indians, however, is organized upon a strongly marked vertical-horizontal basis.

The vertical is the line of movement.

Movement downward, movement upward. Directed downward: a lead plummet, the force of gravity, sunbeams. Directed upward: a connecting link with the cosmos. Forms which have come to express this are the pyramid, the ziggurat; monoliths in the form of a stele, an obelisk, a menhir.

The horizontal is the line of repose. It denotes the basis, the balance of scales in equilibrium. A horizontal position of rest was given to the Egyptian earth-god Geb, a vertical position to the air-god Shu, who separated him from the sky-goddess Nut. Vertical and horizontal belong together. One is the corollary of the other. They cannot be thought of independently. 131

282. GEORGES BRAQUE: *"The Round Table." The horizontal plane is tilted into the vertical. 1929*

THE VERTICAL AND MYTHOPOEIC THINKING

The origin of verticality is deeply anchored in mythopoeic thinking. It is the most obvious symbol pointing from earth to heaven—from earthly existence to the abode of the gods.

The forms taken by the vertical are very different. Their meaning is always a link with invisible powers, whether the godhead itself, the totem, or the ancestors "which are not annihilated by death but must be maintained and nourished. . . . Thus the spirits of the dead demand food and care . . . they demand a habitation of some material nature which can, as it were, take the place of the lost body. . . . From the primitive point of view, the gravestone was filled with strength . . . as the abode of the procreating force of the ancestral spirits" (Kaschnitz-Weinberg, 1944, pp. 12–14).

The megalithic culture, which was related to the emergence of the vertical, covered no specific period of time. It was a stage of development with widespread ramifications in time as well as in space, that always had close sacred associations with stone monuments. It was distributed throughout almost the entire world. It is not certain how far back it reached or how many meanings were bound up with the standing stones. In Palestine, not far from where the river Jordan flows into the Dead Sea, perhaps the oldest steles have been found, as well as dolmens (table-like resting places for the dead placed upon vertical blocks). In Africa—Nubia, Ethiopia, Madagascar; in Indonesia; in the Middle East and the Far East; in South America, including Easter Island—everywhere the remains of megalithic culture can be found.

At the peak of the Fourth Dynasty, Egyptian architecture undoubtedly had a megalithic character—e.g., the square monolithic columns of the pyramid 255 col temples at Giza, of which only Chephren's valley temple still transmits the original impression. Blocks used for the outer walls became more and more 311 bulky, as in the temple of the Sphinx (next to the Chephren temple), and in the mastaba, El Faroun, of Shepseskaf, last known king of the Fourth Dynasty, which lies between Saqqara and Dahshur. These gigantic blocks as well as, to some extent, the blocks and casings of the Fourth Dynasty pyramids, have megalithic traits, but refined and polished as befits a highly differentiated civilization.

In Europe the best-known centers of the megalithic culture are Stonehenge and Brittany. Both are latecomers in comparison to the Near East, falling into the first half of the second millennium B.C. In Brittany the menhirs (Breton:

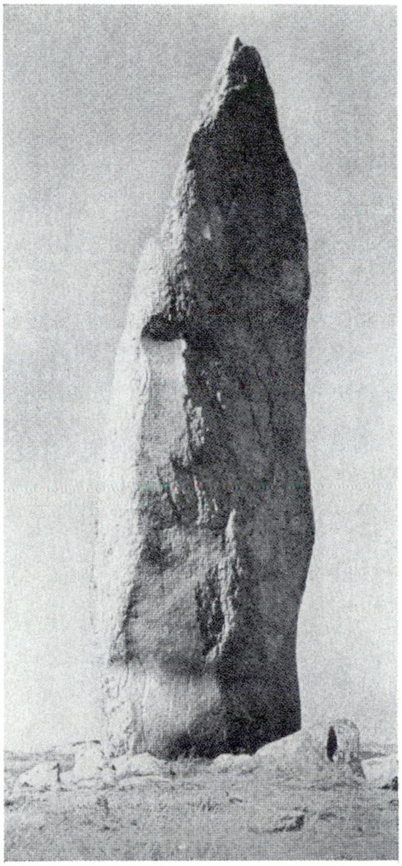

283. MANEUROCK MENHIR: *A rough stone needle tapers upward, rising to sixty-five feet. Quiberon (Brittany), latter part of second millennium* B.C.

284. OBELISK OF TUTHMOSIS I: *Obelisks stood in pairs before the pylons of the New Kingdom temples, except for Tuthmosis III's obelisk behind his festival hall*

Menhirs and obelisks are both products of a striving to express religious aspiration by means of a monolith. The Celtic menhirs were originated by barbarous tribes, the obelisks by a highly refined civilization

men = stone, *hir* = tall) are as much as sixty-five feet high. These upright 441 monoliths taper toward the top and are more or less regularly quadrangular in section. It seems probable that in France and England they were connected with animal or human sacrifices as well as with fertility cults.

The custom of sacrifice and invocation, which in Indonesia is even today bound up with the erection of menhirs, is evidence of a strongly held belief that the stone is imbued with life.

Even now, Breton legends attribute to certain menhirs powers of growth, of wandering down to the stream, of giving forth sounds and mutterings. James Joyce, who felt the magic attraction of these monuments, made *Finnegans Wake* —that modern legend of humanity—open with a dialogue between two menhirs whom he named Mutt and Jute.

Coincidences seem to occur in modern art, popular creation, and slumbering prehistoric remembrances. One of the comic strips in American papers has long had two characters called Mutt and Jeff, one tall and one short, who are continually in difficulties. This was certainly known to Joyce, whose dialogue between these two giant stones, Mutt and Jute, is carried on in a kind of dream language, expressing ambiguous half-formed words and speech. It is more utterance than talking. Words have not yet become detached from the stone block, from the silence of nature. The dialogue begins (1939, p. 16):

"Jute.—Yutah!
Mutt.—Mukk's pleasurad.
Jute.—Are you jeff?
Mutt.—Somehards.
Jute.—But you are not jeffmute?
Mutt.—Noho. Only an utterer.
Jute.—Whoa? Whoat is the mutter with you?
Mutt.—I became a stun a stummer.
Jute.—What a hauhauhauhaudibble thing, to be cause! How, Mutt?"

Each utterance has associations and inner meanings, such as it might have possessed in the primeval ages and certainly had during the first high civilizations. Egypt, especially, liked to give many-sided significance to its signs—an inheritance from prehistory.

A single prehistoric example may be taken from the Magdalenian period to exhibit the bond between man and the invisible powers: a totem or a fetish on a right wooden pole—the bird on a stick from the cavern at Lascaux (Dordogne).

It was painted in the most secret place in the cavern, probably the shrine of the cult, and was placed in a highly dramatic context. This is very rare. (The question of the relation between the man in a bird mask and the wounded bison has been discussed earlier.) Is the bird on the stick a totem or a clan symbol? Perhaps both. In any case it shows that the concept of a magical protector goes very far back in human consciousness. I:507 ff

During the course of millenniums, this concept engendered the emblems of the forty-two Egyptian provinces, or nomes. On the obverse side of the slate votive palette of Narmer, standards of Egyptian nomes are borne before the victorious king upon long poles: two falcons (there were several falcon nomes), Upaout, the jackal, and one blown-up bladder which is thought to represent a placenta. As in the ships depicted upon Nagadah pottery, these standards sometimes hang downward like ribbons. Probably in the course of political development, the original fetish or totem of a clan was taken over by an entire province. However below

285. USES OF THE VERTICAL: *a) bird on a wooden pole, from the cavern of Lascaux, Magdalenian period; b) standard-bearers from the Narmer palette, with emblems of the provinces; c) phoenix (Benou) on the monolith (benben) which first emerged from chaos (fig. 220); d) two tall poles before a First Dynasty shrine (fig. 239)*

this may be, these animals, plants, and (to us) lifeless objects, persisted as the standards of the nomes from the protohistoric period until the end of Egypt's existence as an independent state.

On the rock walls of the Wady Hammamat—the shortest route from Upper Egypt (Coptos) to the Red Sea—are late prehistoric engravings of strange spirit-boats with poles and emblems, some with arrowheads like those on Nagadah pottery (Winkler, 1937, fig. 2).

The image of a shrine of Neith, goddess of fertility and war, is preserved from the First Dynasty. Another shrine of the same period has two astonishingly tall
443 poles standing before the little building. Here, in its most primitive form, is the verticality expressed by the tremendous flag masts and obelisks which (in their
441 final monumental version) stand before the temple pylons of the New Kingdom.

With the onset of theological interpretation, vertical stones became the primeval hill which first arose from chaos and was identified with Atum, god of creation.

The obelisk was the final outcome of a process of increasing geometric abstraction. Its *Urbild*, in the form of a rough monolith, was found by Moret en-
344, 443 graved upon the shoulder of a kneeling Second Dynasty statue (1935–38, p. 624). Moret was well aware that this irregular monolith, topped by a flat stone, could not be identified with the final form of the obelisk, but he nevertheless believed the obelisk to be the culmination of this Heliopolitan baetyl "in its role as image of the sun" (p. 625). Its relations with the sun—its shape still
337 towerlike but now full size, in three dimensions—appear in the sun sanctuaries of the Fifth Dynasty.

In its final New Kingdom form of a slender stone needle, the obelisk was esteemed by later conquerors of Egypt (Persians, Romans, and on to Napoleon) as a rare and precious trophy. But when obelisks were re-erected in foreign lands they were used—like the horizontal axis—in a completely different way.
380 In Egypt, they stood directly in front of the monumental pylon walls. In Europe, they were placed isolated in space, as signposts marking the centers of important urban squares (the Lateran and the Piazza San Pietro in Rome, the Place de la Concorde in Paris), or the termini of long streets. No one used the device with more forceful effect than the great planner of baroque Rome, Pope Sixtus V, 1585–90 (Giedion, 1954, pp. 97–100).

The obelisk, with its extreme reduction of materiality, is the supreme manifestation of the vertical.

The supremacy of the vertical is by no means always connected with an emphasis upon or a striving after height. It is a universal organizing principle. Ever since the acknowledgment of its superiority over all other directions, it has reigned supreme throughout all periods up to the present day.

Styles change, the vertical remains. Nor is its function as an organizing principle limited to the field of art. From the beginning, it gave rise to combinations basic to the development of the science of geometry, from which arose the perception of the axis, symmetry, and the sequence.

Many religions show an obvious longing to express their relation to the cosmos, to the world beyond, by—if the phrase be permitted—an upward glance transmuted into stone. The form this desire assumes changes and develops, from a simple fetish on a pole, or a modest stele, to the elaborate structure of a pagoda, or the filigree of a Gothic spire.

This longing to soar upward is present in the pyramids. It is first expressed in the dramatic building-up of the entire complex of which the pyramids are the climax: valley temple, causeway, mortuary temple, pyramid. Yet the dimensions of the pyramids and the balanced association of their height with all other dimensions show that their striving after height is in equilibrium with the entire complex. This follows from the Egyptian desire for symmetry and harmony, which was sedulously maintained in every field of artistic endeavor.

The axis and symmetry

The axis is an imaginary line, to which all points upon a surface, a solid, or a space bear a certain relation, usually in the sense of a mirror reflection. In addition, a single solid or a system of solids can rotate about it (the world axis, wheel axles).

Primeval art knew of no axis. Eternally in movement like the wandering I:514 ff herds, primeval art is far removed from any stable and static order.

The axis, a line not tangible but only imagined, came into being because of a need to establish relationships. But not universal relationships—only the interdependence of all parts within a system through their relation to a center line. The place of the axis in science, in organic and inorganic morphology, or in astronomical relations, is outside our field. Here we touch only upon its role in the development of art.

Supremacy of the Vertical

Symmetry is bound up with axiality; one is not conceivable without the other. right Two figures are symmetrically in relation to a central axis when point by point they are organized in relation to it, and when the lines linking corresponding points stand at right angles to it.

A form is symmetrical when its two halves, right and left of the axis, would cover one another if folded together. This is called bilateral symmetry. Each half is the mirror of the other. The mirror image hesitatingly started to become an essential law of sculpture and architecture at the dawn of history. It began with the first monumental buildings and acquired a powerful orchestral fullness upon the front elevations of the temples of the New Kingdom, with their tall 375, 380 pylons, flag masts, obelisks, and colossal seated statues of the rulers. All those parts were arranged in pairs in mutual reflection, while the high door in the center brought out and emphasized the axis.

Today, science has given wider scope to the notion of symmetry than ever before. It is applied as a classifying principle to the world of phenomena. A crystallographer has described symmetry as "the regulator of knowledge. By this we mean that man recognizes and perceives the world through the clue of symmetry" (Engelhardt, 1949, p. 210).

In mathematics, in botany, in zoology, in crystallography, in atomic structure—thus both in organic and inorganic fields—symmetry is accepted as an organizing principle. Physical chemists have distinguished fourteen different types of symmetry, mathematicians even more. The strength of scientific interest in the subject may be seen in the series of articles in *Studium Generale* (1949, pp. 203–78), wherein well-known scholars describe the role of symmetry in their respective fields of knowledge.

Mathematicians have made the strongest use of the concept of symmetry, since they have studied that wide area of "groupings" that are a kind of mathematical symmetry, as Andreas Speiser proved (1927, pp. 10–12). Understandably, ornamental motifs provided almost the only object of precise investigation that art had to offer to mathematicians. Speiser limited ornament to seven categories of band patterns supposedly comprising all the possibilities; however, periods such as the late Gothic and the rococo slipped through his fingers.

The most universal concept of symmetry was expressed by the mathematician Hermann Weyl in his Princeton lectures (1952). He did not merely chase after ornamentation; he also attempted to enter upon the domain of art in general. One can sense how hard it was to express this mathematically. Weyl was also careful not to go into the filigreelike classification so beloved of present-day investigators of symmetry. He kept to the three major categories of symmetry that were already known, but he gave them a more profound meaning.

Bilateral symmetry is the form most interesting to the mathematician. Weyl traces "the strict bilateral or heraldic symmetry" from Sumer to the Greek and Christian periods (pp. 5–24). This mirror-image symmetry was the latest form to be developed and was relatively seldom used in the early high civilizations. Yet it has become in our minds almost identical with the whole concept of symmetry.

Translatory or shifting symmetry results from a rhythmic repetition of forms, and is by far the oldest type; we shall show that it goes back to prehistory. It arises from the horizontal shifting of a given form, as in linear ornamentation, when the motif repeats again and again. For present purposes it seems better to use the term "sequence." This is the most important means of compositional order.

Rotational symmetry comes about when a motif turns through a certain angle before repeating itself: 60, 90, 180 degrees. It too appeared earlier than bilateral symmetry, though its use is more limited. It was used most effectively on the ceramics of the fourth millennium, a period of transition from prehistory to history.

From the very beginning, Weyl recognized the nature of symmetry as a balancing relationship. "*Ebenmass* is a good German equivalent for the Greek symmetry; for like this it carries also the connotation of 'middle measure'. . . . The image of the balance provides a natural link to the second sense in which the word symmetry is used in modern times: *bilateral symmetry*, the symmetry of left and right, which is . . . a strictly geometric and, in contrast to the vague notion of symmetry discussed before, an absolutely precise concept" (pp. 3–4).

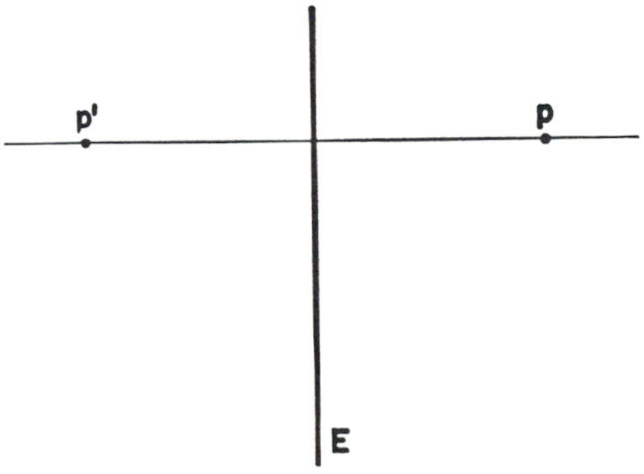

286. AXIAL OR BILATERAL SYMMETRY *arises from the use of the vertical as an organizing principle. Every object has a mirror reflection on either side of an imaginary axis. "Reflection in* E *[the axis] is that mapping of space upon itself,* $S: p \rightarrow p^1$*, that carries the arbitrary point* p *into this its mirror image* p^1 *with respect to* E" (*Weyl, 1952, pp.* 4–5)

287. PYRAMIDION OF AMENEMHAT III: *The material of this pyramidion, indestructible gray basalt, emphasizes eternity. All lines and surfaces eternally ascend to a single point. From the site of Amenemhat's pyramid at Dahshur, Middle Kingdom*

Axis and symmetry in architecture

With the coming of architecture—volumes shaped by the human hand—the vertical axis made its appearance and at once became the unrivaled organizing principle. The grandeur and purity with which it was expressed in the pyramids was never attained in later periods.

Intangible but almighty, the vertical axis mounts from the center of the square at the base to the peak. The pyramid, simultaneously "tomb of the king and temple of the great god" (Spiegel, 1953, p. 285, par. 425), is the place
89 ff in which the god, the king, and the Ka—that curious and ambivalent conception

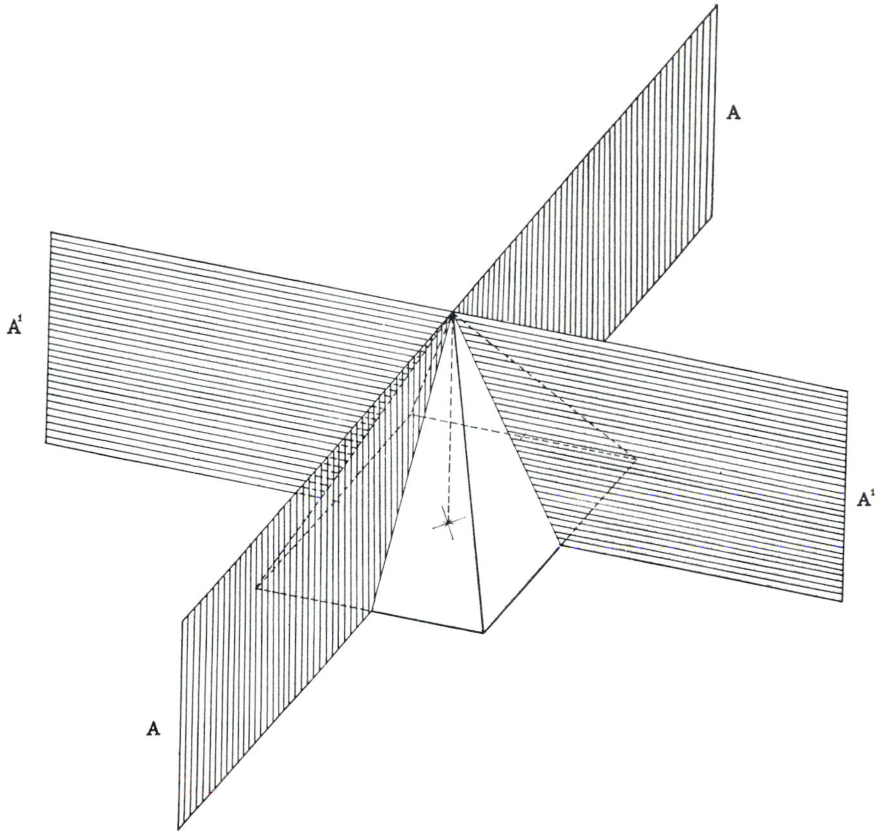

288. PYRAMID AND MEDIAN PLANES: *The axis of a pyramid can be extended to form median planes cut through its apex. One pair of such planes can be cut diagonally through the corners. Another pair* (AA–A^1A^1) *is cut at right angles to the base, on the direct east-west and north-south orientation of the pyramid*

—merge into one another. It is the beginning of the ladder to heaven up which the god-king ascends. At the pyramidion, the peak of the pyramid, all lines and all surfaces converge at a single point, rushing toward it without pause, without deviation, from their onset. Here they become one with the vertical axis, whose height gives the key to the inner relations of the pyramid structure.

Of more than eighty pyramids, only one peak with an inscription is preserved: the pyramidion of King Amenemhat III, which was found lying on the east side of his pyramid at Dahshur. It is fashioned of "indestructible basalt" (Schäfer, 1904, p. 84); each side of its base measures 1.85 meters and its height is 1.40 meters. It crowned a pyramid clad with limestone over an inner core of

left

brick. We are here at the waning of the Middle Kingdom (ca. 1800 B.C.), at the end of the age of pyramid building. The subtle treatment of the relief of the beautiful winged solar disk on this dark granite peak is reminiscent of the high artistic level of Middle Kingdom jewelry. The inscription on the eastern face reads: "Opened is the face of the King Amenemhat, he sees the 'Lord of the horizon' (the sun-god) as he traverses the heavens" (ibid.).

This indestructible monument was no more intended for the eyes of mortals than were the statues of the gods in the darkness of the cella. No one upon the ground could possibly read this small inscription. Here began contact with eternity: converse with God.

How hesitantly axial symmetry came into use at the beginning of the Third Dynasty can be seen in the powerful complex of Zoser at Saqqara. Its only
274 entrance is placed, completely asymmetrically, at the southeast end of a 550-meter boundary wall. This small entrance leads directly through a covered
250 col colonnade to the great inner court, which extends laterally from it, and then
251 col on to the step pyramid, which again is placed to the side and not upon the axis of the entire complex. This connection of strongly vertical and rectangular structures with asymmetrical harmony can be followed even in details.

In the Fourth Dynasty, the axis appeared in its full determination in the pyramid temples. In no other remaining monument does this appear with such force as in the ground plan of the valley temple of Chephren. A masterpiece of the dominating system of symmetry around a central axis is there unfolded.
325 The separated entrances for Upper and Lower Egypt are placed symmetrically about this axis and, following the leitmotiv of the double entrance, smaller and larger passages are developed symmetrically and in solemn orchestration build up the new concept of axiality.

The axis and symmetry had already appeared as the leading principle of the
Part v earliest monumental architecture: the Sumerian temple. It seems to have been far more difficult to organize an entire complex upon a rigid horizontal axis; this was apparently contrary to the inner orientation of the early civilizations. In most cases it was avoided: Chephren's valley temple, for example, led sideways into the causeway, and this dark covered passage terminated sideways and slantwise at his mortuary temple immediately in front of the pyramid.

When Ramesses II completed Amenhotep III's temple at Luxor, fronting the large new extensions with his great pylon, he did not rationally continue the
393 horizontal axis established by his forebears. His new axis followed more subtle considerations.

During the New Kingdom, alleys of sphinxes lined the sacred ways leading from one sanctuary to another (Karnak to Luxor, Karnak to the temple of Mut) before 355 as well as the processional way from Karnak to the Nile landing for the sacred barge. But the horizontal axis was not then used in the manner that has become second nature to us since the baroque period—the manner expressed in the gardens of Versailles, where the horizontality of the infinite terrestrial vistas symbolizes the monarch's hold over the country.

The horizontal axis of Hatshepsut's mortuary temple—the most felicitous axial development of Egypt—indicates the upward path of the processional way enveloped within the rock cliffs of the Libyan desert. Its orientation was not 262 col terrestrial but toward a cosmic infinity.

The median plane

The axis can also be developed into an axial plane that takes the form of an automorph (mirror image) divided into two identical halves. This form of plane is known as a median plane.

One can determine four median planes cutting through the apex of a pyramid. 449 They appear upon the square of the base as an axial cross. One pair of these planes cuts through the four corners of the pyramid; the other (AA–A^1A^1) stands at right angles to the sides of the base. This axial cross is very important in the orientation and meaning of the pyramid. It expresses the cardinal directions—north, south, east, west—upon which the pyramid was oriented. The north-south direction was exactly fixed—within minutes of a degree.

The view to the east—to the sun and the fruitful land of the Nile—meant, at the same time, life. The Sphinx also looks toward the east—to the rising of 72 the sun. The word "west" at once brought to an Egyptian mind the kingdom of night and of the dead. Westward stretched the desert and the city of the dead in the shadow of the pyramid, with the mastabas of the nobility: certainly one of the earliest examples of gridiron town planning. This appears in the lovely colored lithographs of Lepsius' monumental volumes (1849–59) perhaps even 505 more strikingly than in Reisner's photograph taken from the Chephren pyramid. The whole tremendous expanse is here encompassed: to the east of Cheops' great pyramid the ribbon of fertile land along the Nile, westward the city of the dead, and the immense desert within which all is embedded.

289. PREHISTORIC SEQUENCE OF STAGS: *The antlered stags grow out from the rock face and are not, as has been supposed, swimming through a river. Prehistory never depicted environment. Lascaux, Magdalenian period*

SEQUENCE AND THE VERTICAL

A sequence is a succession of identical or similar elements along a horizontal plane or line. The mathematicians, as we saw, consider the sequence a kind of
467 symmetry: translatory symmetry. Translatory or shifting symmetry, which can be continued endlessly, is, in the artistic sense, scarcely acceptable as symmetry. Impulses of time and rhythm enter, and it is better in this case to talk of sequences: for instance, from the artistic point of view, it is better to interpret the repeating columns of the Doge's palace in Venice—one of Weyl's examples of translatory symmetry—as a sequence.

It is not rewarding to consider sequence as a kind of symmetry in art. The essence of a translatory sequence, in contrast to bilateral symmetry, lies in its progression. It can continue without limit. It involves the factor of time. The

290. PREHISTORIC BONE ENGRAVING OF HORSES' HEADS: *The repetition in sequence served to strengthen a spell. Magdalenian period*

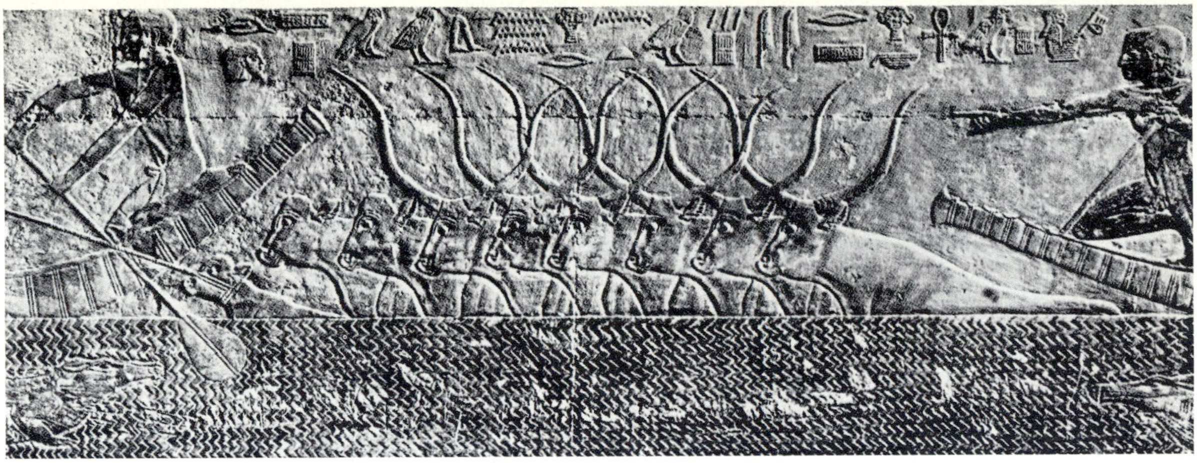

291. EGYPTIAN SEQUENCE OF CATTLE *being driven across a river. Up to the end of the first high civilizations the dynamic, movement-suggesting symmetry of sequence prevailed over static axial symmetry. Tomb of Ti, Saqqara, Fifth Dynasty*

effort of the mathematician to discover the lawful limitations of art is confined to the structure of ornamental patterning. But the sequence, as it appears in Egyptian or Sumerian reliefs, neither desired nor permitted the repetition of absolutely identical forms. As soon as we enter the wider field of art, the mathematical theory of groupings becomes too narrow. The mathematical definition of a sequence as a band or a part of a plane between two parallel lines can be used in connection with the art of the high civilizations. But it is too restricted for primeval art, where no parallel lines or plane surfaces exist. Yet the sequence was present from the beginnings of art: it is far older than symmetry.

Repetition, the essence of sequential succession, was employed in art of the Magdalenian period. One of many examples is a bone engraving showing a sequence of horses' heads. The repetition here was to give added force to the conjuration. Another example is a beautifully drawn frieze of stags, one behind the other, from the cavern of Lascaux. The frequent explanation that these stags are crossing a stream fits perfectly a Fifth Dynasty relief of cows in the tomb of Ti at Saqqara, but is rather strange for prehistory.

left
left
above

Pottery and sequence

Sequence, in the strict mathematical sense, could only develop after the vertical and horizontal had become accepted as an organizing principle.

A horizontal base line is closely related to the development of painted pottery. Detailed research into the use of the sequence and primitive symmetry should yield interesting insights. Only a few hints are offered here.

The shapes of the first handmade—later wheel-formed—pots, beakers,

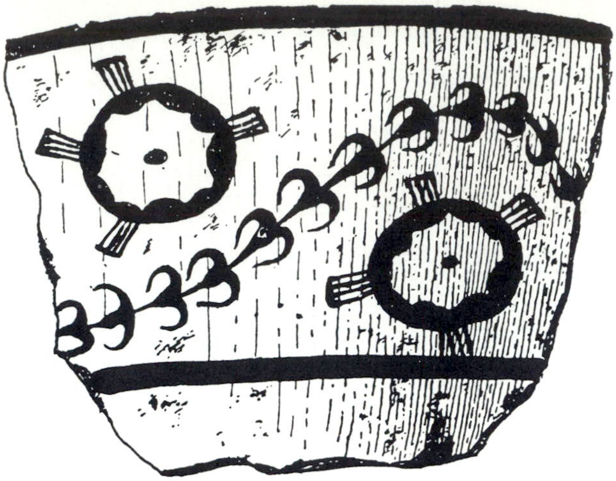

292. DIAGONAL SEQUENCE OF BULLS' HEADS: *Painted in black on greenish pottery vessel. The curving sequence still floats in space, but the horizontal limits are already well marked. Two large suns accompany the undulating chain. From Tepe Kazineh (just south of Tepe Musyan, Iran), fourth millennium. From Gautier and Lampre*

293. SLENDER BEAKER FROM SUSA: *Strongly accentuated horizontal bands separate different areas, as on the later Uruk vase (fig. 64). The center is reserved for the abstract representation of an ibex with immense horns and an hourglass body. Other smaller animals, also referring to resurrection, race round the vessel in sequential order. Susa, style I, fourth millennium*

294. IBEX ON FRAGMENT OF YELLOW POTTERY: *Black-painted figures with greatly elongated bodies drawn in a single stroke, short legs, and gigantic, backward-curving horns. Tepe Kazineh. From Gautier and Lampre*

plates, storage jars, funeral urns, etc. were naturally bilaterally symmetrical. As the potter's wheel came into use and the vessel rotated before the eyes of its maker, the fingers would almost be impelled to impress parallel bands or wavy lines upon the emerging vessel. But it was not quite so simple as that. Presiding over the decoration of these vessels stood a symbolic meaning of forms, which is for the most part lost to us.

Decoration on early pottery is either longitudinal in direction or is freely disposed on the surface. In Hassuna, one of the earliest villages of northern Mesopotamia, tall jars were found with incised (not painted) triangles placed vertically or at random.

In Part V, when speaking of the relations between architecture, pottery, and abstraction, we referred to a black beaker of around 3500 B.C. from Tepe Gawra, stratum XIII, not far from that jewel of earliest architecture, the northern temple, and concluded that abstraction was the common root of architecture and pottery. The same vessel may be instanced here with reference to its rhythmic division by repeated groups of vertical lines. 200

This early vertical organization of the surface was increasingly superseded by horizontal sequences between broad horizontal bars, as in the pottery from Iran (e.g., Sialk) or northern Mesopotamia (e.g., Nineveh). The perfection of the handmade pots found in the primitive round stone huts of the fifth or early fourth millennium (as at Arpachiyah in northern Mesopotamia) is astounding. Their abstract ornamentation ran in circular bands—checkered patterns, sequences of triangles, wavy lines, dots, etc.—around the vessels and around the inner sides of the bowls. All was now submitted to the discipline of strongly

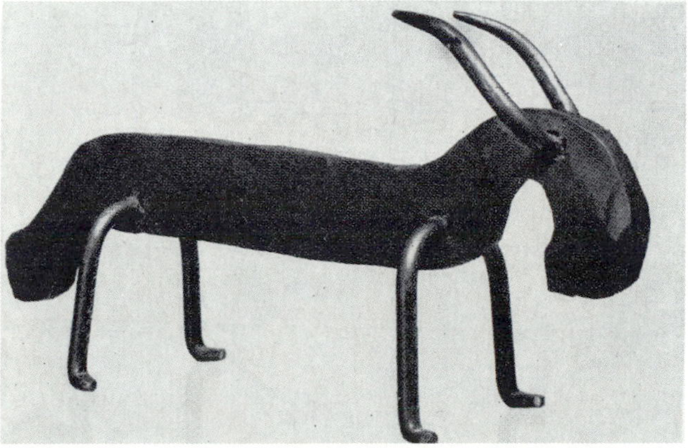

295. FLAT WROUGHT-IRON BULL: *These long-bodied, short-legged bulls, with exaggerated horns and heads bent low to protect the home against evil spirits, are still placed above the hearths in villages of the Upper Engadine valley (Switzerland)*

marked and separated horizontal base lines. In one region, which stretches from the Iranian plateau, near the Caspian Sea, to Mesopotamia, there was an influx of artistic intensity during the fourth millennium. It is evidenced by a new material, a new technique, and a new shaping of forms. Pottery bowls, beakers, and jars of great variety and excellence appeared, apparently out of nothingness.

In the pottery of the early fourth millennium, still within the prehistoric period, the desire for sequence was marvelously interwoven with a restless urge for movement. Naturalistic and abstract symbolic forms of enigmatic significance were represented simultaneously.

From the primitive scratching technique of the Hassuna vessels it is a great 454 leap to the painted shards found at such remote places as Tepe Musyan, about 150 kilometers west of Susa. In the eighth volume of J. de Morgan's *Mémoires de la délégation en Perse* (Gautier and Lampre, 1905, pp. 59–148), an excellent description of this little-known development can be found. Here is a rare instance of the sudden display of a new richness. A lively fantasy, never cramped by schematization, has enabled us to see into the stages of an unfolding repertory of abstract representations: stars, plants, gazelles, ibexes, birds, even insects, are shown in forms naturalistic to abstract. Ibexes and goats appear

296. ROTATIONAL SYMMETRY ON A SAMARRAN PLATE: *Women with flying hair and scorpions whirl in frenzied rotational symmetry, but still maintain the freedom and the hovering space of primeval times. Fourth millennium. Drawing after Braidwood, et al.*

297. HORNS ARISING FROM A BLACK CIRCLE: *No bodies. The vigorously drawn horns occupy the outer surface of this breast-shaped bowl, so that the whole area is concentrated on bringing new life and strength to the dead. Iran, fourth millennium*

with long-drawn-out bodies and gigantic horns. "The body is drawn in one long curved line . . . the horns, back-curving, extend over the whole length of the subject, which is short-legged and entirely without grace" (p. 123), as the excavators remark. 454

This abundance of forms is organized in a great variety of sequences drawn, sometimes rectangularly, sometimes diagonally, in a chain across the surface.

Supremacy of the Vertical

If we take the pottery of Hassuna and Tepe Musyan to be rough (almost "peasant") work, it would appear that places like Samarra and Susa had already acquired excellence of draftsmanship and a decisive approach to the horizontal-vertical problems of the sequence.

An audaciously slender vessel makes its first appearance. The famous Susa 454 beaker in the Louvre (Susa I style) is fraught with a striving after height. It displays an early use of precisely separated bands. A heavy base line is surmounted by the main area with its monumentally abstract version of an ibex with large horns. This animal is framed by strong double lines which use the old motif of lengthwise decoration. Above it, again between horizontal lines, are dogs (?) whose bodies are stretched out in full flight. They are said to represent hunting dogs, but this appears doubtful. Finally, above this, and again separated by horizontal lines, is a sequence of abstract birds, whose necks are pulled out vertically as much as the bodies of the "dogs" are horizontally.

The center of this beaker is certainly the ibex within its strong frame, yet the vessel demonstrates that the whole striving for movement of primeval times is still alive. See how the ibex moves to the left, the "dogs" to the right, and the birds again to the left. Like a fluid melee of different ingredients glimpsed separately for an instant before they flow into one another, past and future formations can be sensed in this slender beaker without in any way reducing its own artistic strength.

298. SEQUENCE OF IBEXES AND SCORPIONS: *The ibexes (or goats) have abstract bodies and oversized horns. The upside-down mirror juxtaposition is a heritage of prehistoric methods of representation. Impression from an Early Dynastic cylinder seal*

There is, of course, no direct relation between these Iranian ceramics and
a flat, hammered-iron bull, with head bent low for defense against evil spirits, 455
which is still placed above the hearth in villages of the Upper Engadine valley (Switzerland). Its long-stretched body and shortened legs are among the survivals that linger on in the human mind.

On prehistoric plates from Samarra (Herzfeld, 1930, pp. 11–22) figures and 456
animals were flung into a whirling frenzy: women with flying hair, scorpions with their tails swung back, all as if caught in the centrifugal motion of the potter's wheel.

Sequence? No horizontal base lines confine these eight scorpions and four women. They still carry with them the freedom of direction of primeval times and also its hovering space. But their centrifugal organization contains the seed of the sequence and of rotational symmetry.

The whole outer surface of a fourth-millennium breast-shaped bowl is fully 457
occupied by three pairs of vigorously designed horns that spring like plants from a dark disk instead of a body. Their rotational symmetry induces a forceful motion, symbolizing the life and strength they give to the dead. Between them are enigmatic abstract signs, probably frogs, symbols of newly awakened life.

Cylinder seals and sequence

The smallness of the available surface of a seal and the brittleness of the materials employed—quartz, malachite, crystal—induced a kind of artistic shorthand. The Mesopotamian development remained until the end under the spell of the cylinder seal. Its invention came about before that of script and was related to the invention of the wheel: the potter's wheel and the wagon wheel. All were based on the transformation of discontinuous steps into a continuous revolving motion. André Breton, the surrealist poet, regarded this revolutionary change from the additive movements of walking to an endless rotation as mankind's most important invention.

The cylinder seal was rolled along upon a surface of moist clay. Its impressions could be mechanically reproduced again and again at will, and etched upon the memory by repetition.

The impressions of a cylinder seal fit the definition of a sequence as a repetitive pattern between two parallel lines. Its composition first consisted of a simple repetition of single objects, as shown in our example from the Early Dy- left
nastic period. But with the advent of mythology, scenes came to be depicted,
such as the frequently reproduced fight of a hero with two attacking beasts. In 65

this scene the hero forms a vertical axis, with the two animals symmetrically disposed to right and left springing up to create a triangular composition.

Within a few centuries the seal had developed from a primitive impression denoting ownership of a jar of wine or oil to the finest achievement of Sumerian art and, later, of the art of Akkad, Babylonia, and Assyria. The manifold scenes depicted on the seals of different periods afford the best insight into the religious and ritual background of Mesopotamia. The use of the cylinder seal spread throughout the then known world: to Egypt, Asia Minor, Crete, Greece. It persisted through all the fateful changes in this area: through the Sumerian and Akkadian regimes, and the dynasties of Babylon and Assyria, almost until Alexander the Great brought this greatest Oriental empire to an end. But the importance and artistic refinement of the cylinder seal in Sumer and Babylon were never matched.

Sequences of human figures

The representation of human figures never played a major role in prehistory, yet rough sequences of human beings can be found on Magdalenian bone engravings,
32 such as that showing the ritual burial of a bison.

In Mesopotamia, sequential compositions of human figures occur in almost all
121 periods. An alabaster vase from Uruk, three feet tall, displays the monumental use of the sequence at the beginning of the third millennium. Here the sequence
119 dramatizes the festival of Inanna. As we recounted earlier, four bands of increasing size correspond to the relative importance of the subjects treated, as well as to the newly established hierarchy: plants, animals, men. The lower two bands show plants and animals, the upper two a sequential procession of bearers of offerings, culminating in the actual presentation of the offerings in the broadest band around the top of the vase. The influence of the cylinder seal, rolling out its continuously repeated sequences, can be recognized.

The two inward-tilting panels of the Standard of Ur (ca. 2500 B.C.) are each separated into three parallel bands. On one of these a long line of cloaked
right soldiers is presented in rigid sequence. The technique used is a colorful inlay of pieces of shell set in bitumen.

It is a long step from the intensity of Mesopotamian seal impressions to the oversize reliefs that line courts, passages, and throne rooms of the palaces of the last kings of Assyria. The figures have become vacuous—like overenlarged photographs that have lost all their original intensity.

299. SEQUENCE OF SOLDIERS, STANDARD OF UR: *Part of one of the tilted panels, showing a sequence of kilted and cloaked soldiers represented in shell pressed into bitumen; ca. 2500* B.C.

The principle of sequential order never vanished from this area, for it was taken over by the Persians, who ended the historic existence of Mesopotamia. In their great palaces at Persepolis, Darius I and Xerxes built two monumental stairways leading from the audience hall of Darius and the hundred-pillared throne room of Xerxes to the general palace quarters upon a higher level. The wall behind them is spread with reliefs of tribute bearers seemingly ascending the stairways. They come from all parts of the empire and include, as two millenniums earlier, a line of guardsmen in strict sequential order. We are now only a below

300. SEQUENCE OF SOLDIERS, PERSEPOLIS: *Part of the reliefs lining the monumental stairways of the palaces of Darius I and Xerxes. Fifth century* B.C.

301. EGYPTIAN SEQUENCE: *Wooden models of bearers of offerings. Three tall and slender women, two bearing provisions and live ducks, follow an overseer. From a tomb in Deir el Bersheh, Middle Kingdom*

few decades from the riders on the Parthenon frieze. Frankfort stresses the plasticity in the Mesopotamian figures which, with the greater refinement of garments and other details, betrays the hands of the Greek craftsmen brought in by Darius from his Ionian campaigns (as recounted in a large inscription replete with overweening self-acclamation). But there can be no doubt that the stiff verticals of the petrified guests, marching along the wide walls of the staircase between strongly defined parallel bands of rosettes, still follow the same rules of composition as the cylinder seals more than two millenniums earlier. But the early artistic impetus of the latter, long clouded over, has now become stereotyped. No importation of artists from all the parts of the then known world could breathe life into this stiff pomposity.

We are at the end of an epoch. The relaxed attitudes of the riders to the Panathenaean festival a generation later demonstrate how great a distance had already been traveled from the rigidity of the oriental despots.

Sequence in Egypt

In the early period, Mesopotamia and Iran present a far wider range of information on the development of the sequence than does Egypt. In Predynastic times and even during the First and Second Dynasties, Egypt's artistic energy was concentrated upon perfection of form and craftsmanship. Its undecorated vessels of hard stone have no counterparts in Sumer. Even at this early period they express that essential demand of the Egyptian mind for a never-ending existence.

The sequence appears in Egypt in full expansion at the opening of the pyramid age. Upon the walls of Sneferu's valley temple at Dahshur is a frieze of young women with outstretched arms—all identical—each bearing a platter of gifts and the *ankh*. They represent the different provinces of Egypt and can only be distinguished from one another by the provincial emblems above their heads. These slender maidens are the first known Egyptian representation of bearers of offerings: a motif that was further developed during the Middle Kingdom and that never entirely disappeared.

During the Fifth Dynasty a magnificent display of scenes was created in the mastabas of the nobles. Sometimes a single incident covers an entire wall—Ti 466 hunting in the marshes—sometimes a scene unfolds along several parallel bands separated by narrow strips. These principles were retained in the reliefs and paintings of the Middle Kingdom and the New Kingdom.

Mastery in rendering female grace is achieved in the finely carved wooden models of offering bearers from a Middle Kingdom tomb (Deir el Bersheh). Three slender, long-legged maidens march behind an overseer. Two of them left have the right arm pressed close against the side, with a live duck struggling in the hand, and carry a box of provisions on the head.

Architecture and sequence

Mesopotamia

After many experimental stages, upright walls, meeting each other at right 178 ff angles, became the standard elements of a house.

The brick, the first standardized building material, had to go through a similar period of groping before it acquired the standard form that remained unchanged for five thousand years. The birthplace of the brick was Iran, at the end of the prehistoric period, but its real homeland was Mesopotamia, and the evolution of its standard form can best be traced there.

This country, which invented the means of changing discontinuous movements into a mechanical rotation, formed its crisply rectangular bricks in wooden molds: rectangular boxes into which clay (or clay mixed with straw) was pressed, then knocked out and left to dry in the sun.

Supremacy of the Vertical

The precise parallelepiped form of the brick was not exclusively the product of purely functional reasoning. It arose also from the demands of abstraction, rationalized under the spell of the vertical. Vertical walls composed of rectangular bricks formed large plane surfaces. How should these be organized, especially in the case of temples, which demanded a monumental distinction?

192 ff The walls of the early Mesopotamian temples, both inside and outside, were treated as a sequence of recessed panels. Their parallel vertical ridges gave the wall surface a pattern of light and shadow and that plasticity so beloved of the people of Mesopotamia both in the south and in the north. The refinement already achieved in the Al 'Ubaid period around 3500 B.C. is indicated in the
196 northern temple of Tepe Gawra XIII and the archaic Uruk temples. This we have already dealt with, since there one could directly trace the gradual refinement of the buttress—architecture's first means of reinforcement—to an articulation of recessed panels. In the levels below stratum XIII at Tepe Gawra, the walls of houses and sanctuaries are still reinforced by clumsy buttresses. A similar development could be traced at Eridu in the south, where simple buttresses
191 strengthened the walls of the oldest known sanctuary.

How elaborate the modeling of the temple wall had become by around
203 3000 B.C. can best be seen in the large temples A–D at Uruk. Though only fragments of their ground plans are preserved, these show the great depth to which the paneled niches were hollowed out. The play of light along the sequence of recessions must have given the temple a most impressive plasticity.

This bold modeling was not developed further. One has to leap to the time of Hadrian to find similar tendencies. Neither the white temple at Uruk nor any
202 other Sumerian sanctuary gave its walls such strongly plastic expression.

Egypt

At the dawn of history, the Nile valley adopted the Mesopotamian sequence of recessed niches together with many other innovations. When the Horus kings
118 conquered Lower Egypt, the recessed panels of the palace façades had already become a symbol. Similarly, the mastabas and cenotaphs of the kings of the
271 First Dynasty used recessed paneling for their superstructures and enclosure walls. Zoser made a striking use of the system when he surrounded his mortuary
248 col complex at Saqqara with the first high wall of limestone.

254 col Only with the appearance of the true pyramid in the Fourth Dynasty was there a breakaway to the immaculate plane surface, which never afterward van-
341 ff ished from Egyptian architecture. It epitomized the deepest inner strivings.

The penetration of the vertical into Egyptian art was as fanatical as the effects of perspective representation in the Renaissance. The reliefs and sculptures of the Old Kingdom were completely under the spell of the new discovery. Everything focused upon it.

Two examples illustrate this penetration: a relief from the tomb of Ti, dating from the Fifth Dynasty, and one of the sculptured groups of King Mycerinus with two goddesses, from the Fourth Dynasty.

Relief: Ti hunting among the papyrus reeds

Ti, the highest official of several kings, a great landowner, and priest of Ne-user-ra's sun temple at Abu Gurob some miles south of the Giza pyramids, 335 is depicted more than life-size, standing erect in his Nile boat, strictly vertical 466 as was the rule for the standing human figure both earlier and later. He stands alone like a god upon his small boat, his staff in his hand, watching his servants corner a hippopotamus with spears. Their poles and their movements are depicted in rigid parallels. The power of the master is reflected by their small scale. The three boats glide on a strictly horizontal water surface indicated, as always in Egyptian representations, by a precise sequence of vertical zigzags. The back- 453 ground is formed by a wall of soaring, closely packed vertical lines, somewhat like corrugated cardboard, but when one looks more closely, their triangular profiles become clear. They are the papyrus reeds of the Nile swamps. As in a similar relief from the tomb of Mereruka, freedom is allowed only to the deni- 467 zens of the transparent river, and to the birds along the upper edge of the relief, though their nests on the papyrus blossoms are arranged in almost parallel rows. Only a hunting chameleon and some birds in flight are permitted freedom of direction. In the New Kingdom, this primeval liberty was still granted to the birds flying across the ceilings of many tombs.

The regal gesture of the great man, strengthened by the background of vertical stems, indicates that in the structure of the state everything now had its ordered hierarchical position.

302. TI HUNTING IN THE PAPYRUS MARSHES: *Relief on the north wall of the chapel of Ti's tomb. All is governed by the vertical. Saqqara, Fifth Dynasty. From Steindorff*

303. SAILING THROUGH THE MARSHES: *Detail from the tomb of Mereruka. Here also the papyrus stems are represented by closely packed vertical lines. Saqqara, Sixth Dynasty*

Sculpture: Mycerinus with two goddesses

The vertical also forms a constituent element of three-dimensional sculpture. A
vertical axis passes through the human body, to which everything appears
magically bound. This is the line of intersection of two vertical planes crossing
each other at a right angle. All parts of the body are projected upon, or parallel
167 ff to, these intersecting planes. For three millenniums the method of composition
through vertical planes was maintained. One of the secrets of Egyptian art was
that this extreme artistic discipline never became locked into schematic rigidity.
Sculptures and reliefs continued to emanate a grace that carries with it a breath
simultaneously of life and of inaccessibility. One of the groups of King Mycerinus
right accompanied by two goddesses, found in the valley temple belonging to his
pyramid, indicates the growing use of the vertical as an organizing principle for
sculpture in the round.

290 Instead of the lonely darkness of King Zoser enthroned in his serdab, or the
326 solemnity of Chephren in his valley temple, we have a group of three persons, a
human group that appears to approach the onlooker—the face of the Pharaoh
strongly modeled as though addressing the spectator rather than eternity. In
this triad the king is accompanied by Hathor and a somewhat smaller figure
personifying the goddess of one of the nomes. Here we are concerned exclusively
with the compositional order of this sculpture; we have already dealt with the
111 ff Hathor nudes of the Fourth Dynasty as the earliest representations of the beauty
of the female body.

Upon the base of another of these groups (Museum of Fine Arts, Boston) is
an inscription in which the goddess Hathor says: "I have given to you all good
offerings of the South forever" (Smith, 1960, p. 43). This shows that the
goddess of the province in this triad serves the same purpose as representations
462 of worldly goods, or of servant girls bearing laden baskets on their heads.
Three other triads found with this also represented provinces of Upper Egypt,
and it is not unlikely that there were originally statues representing all the
Nomes of Upper and Lower Egypt. Through these the king would have been
able to draw upon the whole country for nourishment after death" (p. 46).

In these triads the symbol takes on an anthropomorphic form. It changes into
a human relationship. The gods become humans and the humans become gods.
80 ff Hathor, originating in Upper Egypt (Denderah), was at first the divine cow,
the primeval mother, closely related, as always, to the king. After she became
the goddess of love, she retained only the last remnants of her primeval shape.

304. TRIAD OF MYCERINUS: *King Mycerinus, the goddess Hathor, and the goddess of a nome. A vertical axial plane passed through the human body frontally and laterally constitutes the basis of the composition*

In these triads she still wears as headdress a pair of horns with the solar disk between them. Her open left hand rests gently against the open right hand of the king. Her right hand, in the customary manner, is firmly clenched. The king wears his insignia: the white crown of Upper Egypt, the royal beard, and the royal apron. Apart from this he is naked. The whole group has a quality of human purpose, as though they are on their way to an agreed destination.

The vertical axis provides the germinating inner strength of each of these figures and a framework for the whole composition. The three vertical axes of the triad are made even stronger by the vertical-horizontal planes that accompany them. The group, carved in gray-green slate, is freed from the block but retains the vertical plane as a dominating background. This is strengthened by the horizontal base upon which—as always—the feet stand flat. Thus a striking L-shape, jutting from the wall and the floor, intensifies the vertical-horizontal organization.

These are just the first primitive evidences that leap immediately to the eye. The way the supremacy of the vertical works in the inner evolution of art is more secret and more complex; for behind it stands a play of relationships that, without being pompous, one can call universal. Many scholars have brought these relations to light.

The starting point is always the plane surface. The vertical engendered the plane: then the vertical plane became a picture plane. Never before and never since has the vertical plane acted with such strength as a constituent element of the composition.

482 ff To this is linked the invention of the squared grid, which was traced out upon unfinished reliefs and sculptures and from which were developed far-reaching relationships between human forms, proportions, and the Egyptian system of measurement.

It was deeply rooted in the Egyptian mentality that geometric and arithmetic considerations could not arise from a limited setting. In a seldom quoted passage from the *Republic*, Plato puts forward a concept of geometry that can be termed completely Egyptian in the sense of the relations between geometry and the form of the pyramids. He must have learned this as a Greek initiate into the Heliopolitan priesthood.

It is true that Plato first speaks of the practical use of geometry to mark out a site, but then he proceeds to its true purpose: "The real object of the entire study is pure knowledge . . . the knowledge of that which always is and not of a something which at some time comes into being and passes away . . . geometry is the knowledge of the eternally existent . . . it would tend to draw the soul to truth" (VII 527 B; tr. Shorey, 1946).

Egyptian discoveries, as far as we can gather from their writings and monuments, were based on relationships often as surprising as far-reaching. This is apparent in the Egyptian system of numbers. If an Egyptian wanted to express a fraction, he did not use absolute values as we do. Instead of the fraction 6/7, for instance, he would give a relation to the total unity: 1 — 1/7. The Egyptians "made use only of fractions with the numerator 1, with the sole exception of 2/3, for which they had a special symbol. When they divide a line into 7, the result is *one* seventh which is to be regarded rather as a *quality* than a *quantity*. The remainder is not 6/7, but a complementary fraction (i.e., 1 — 1/7). In this way an intimate relationship arose between the original whole and the part, between the part and its complementary fraction" (Kielland, 1955, p. 10).

The Egyptian acted similarly when he had to determine the slope of an angle, which was of great importance, for example, in the case of the pyramids. He worked it out through relationships, not directly. In the interpretation of one of the most important mathematical sources of the Middle Kingdom, the *Rhind Papyrus*, Borchardt draws attention to the method of determining angles. The starting point is the right-angled triangle. Its height remains constant (28 fingers). Its base is variable. The angle of inclination is determined by the specific length of this base (1893, pp. 15–16).

The Egyptians, with their strong visual sense, took to geometry more readily than to arithmetic. With them everything was related to perception, quite otherwise than with the calculation-minded Mesopotamian peoples. The Babylonians reckoned the angle by the number of its degrees, and the division of the circle was related to their sexagesimal system of numbering that divided the hour into 60 minutes and 3600 seconds (Neugebauer, 1945, p. 12).

In the Egyptian method of establishing the size of an angle, one senses the geometer on the building site setting up his triangle everywhere, for example to control the slope of the pyramid, while the Babylonian division of the angle into degrees is far more closely related to the stargazing astronomer.

The right-angled triangle

The vertical cannot be conceived of in isolation. It is indicated by auxiliaries to which it is inseparably connected: the horizontal and the intervening angle of ninety degrees. From the reciprocal interdependence of these three components the right-angled triangle arises, composed of a vertical and a horizontal line with their terminal points connected. This encloses a new element: *a plane*. As the vertical became supreme over all directions, the right-angled triangle rose to prime importance. It exercised an almost magical attraction as discoveries were made of its hidden properties and laws. It is not too much to say that here lay the starting point of geometrical thinking.

The imagination of this period saw the right-angled triangle not only as a geometric phenomenon with special properties upon which man could meditate, but as completely bound to a mythopoeic spatial relationship.

This was expressed for the first time, in staggering dimension, by the pyramids, and nowhere more impressively than in the great pyramid of Cheops. 257 col No other pyramid has so intrigued scholars over the last one hundred and fifty years. Its decisive right-angled triangle lies hidden from the eyes of the layman. It only appears when a plane perpendicular to the square plane of the base is cut through the apex of the pyramid. 478 Its catheti are formed by the vertical height of the pyramid (h) and the horizontal base that connects the end point of h with one of the square sides of the ground plan. The practical value of this triangle will be immediately evident: it determined the angle of slope that governed the form and appearance of the pyramid. But it also signified much more.

The Pythagorean theorem: relations between lines and planes

In the realm of geometric ratios, the jump from relationships between lines—i.e., the proportions of their lengths—to relationships between planes and lines is particularly informative.

The theorem that bears the name of Pythagoras aims at establishing, in a

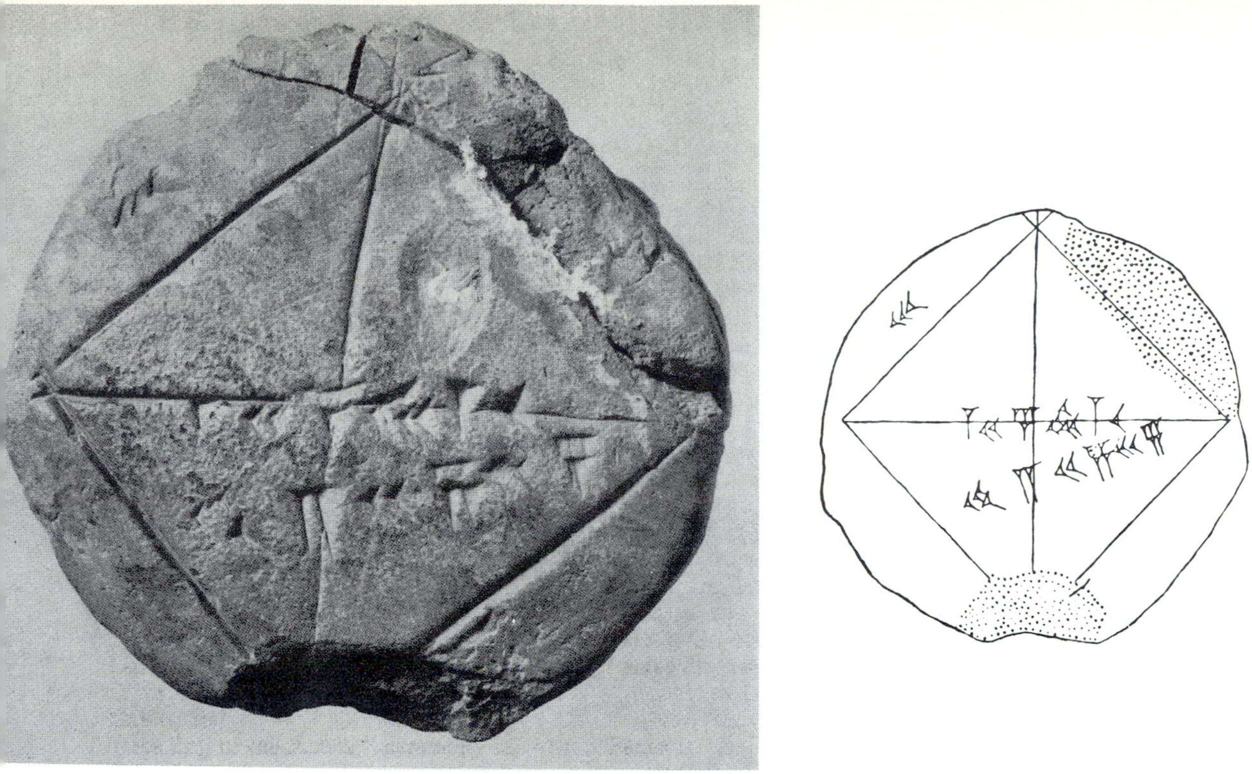

305. CLAY TABLET WITH CUNEIFORM SCRIPT: *The Pythagorean theorem in Babylonia; ca. 1600* B.C. *"We know today that all the factual mathematical knowledge which is ascribed to the early Greek philosophers was known many centuries before" (Otto Neugebauer). With drawing*

specific case, relationships between lines and planes beyond those immediately visible to the eye. Let us for a moment forget the statement of this theorem: that in a right-angled triangle the sum of the squares on the shorter sides (catheti) equals the square on the hypotenuse. Let us instead approach it from a methodological point of view. What interests us is the method of thinking expressed here, a method which is never held up by details but always follows the scent further, making unexpected leaps to discover relationships: in this case, the relations between the sides of the right-angled triangle and the squares built up on them.

The Pythagorean theorem fits into the Egyptian climate of thought. Here is the relation between horizontal, vertical, and right angle. Here is their relation
to the square, which had such an extraordinary fascination for the imagination 348
of that time. The circle and the curve, apart from a few specific exceptions, are banished from Egyptian art. We do not know much about the magical meaning the Egyptians attributed to the square. Its relation to the number four, regarded as the holy number, is obvious. In this sense it becomes the powerful basis for

the pyramid. From the triangle which is formed by placing a vertical plane, parallel to one of the sides of the square, through the apex of the pyramid, new relations were developed. The Pythagorean theorem is closely linked to the form and proportions of the pyramid.

It is significant that the right-angled triangle formed the starting point both of the Pythagorean theorem and of the golden section. But neither is mentioned in the *Rhind Papyrus.* Borchardt asserts cautiously that one should not assume any knowledge of the Pythagorean theorem among the Egyptians.

Otto Neugebauer, the leading investigator of exact knowledge in the high civilizations of antiquity, goes further. No known source, according to him, speaks of the relation between the squares on the catheti and that on the hypotenuse in Pythagorean form. Nevertheless, it appears quite possible that Egyptian geometry was aware of the content of the Pythagorean theorem (1934, p. 122). Later, Neugebauer put the case more strongly: "It seems to me evident, however, that the traditional stories of discoveries made by Thales or Pythagoras must be discarded as totally unhistorical. . . . We know today that all the factual mathematical knowledge which is ascribed to the early Greek philosophers was known many centuries before, though without the accompanying evidence . . . which the mathematicians of the fourth century would have called a proof" (1951, p. 142). In its stead there existed in Babylon an interest in problems of approximation. A small tablet with cuneiform writing, now in
473 the Yale Babylonian collection, shows a square with its two diagonals. From the accompanying figures, it follows that the length of the diagonals ($\sqrt{2}$) was computed from the length of the sides. The tablet dates from about 1600 B.C. Whether the Pythagorean theorem, the knowledge of which it confirms, was known earlier, hidden in the interrelating measurements of the pyramids, and whether it had crossed the borders of Mesopotamia in exact form, is left to the individual imagination. Bearing in mind how influences in the artistic realm went back and forth between Mesopotamia and Egypt, not only during the early dynasties but even in Predynastic times, the isolation of this knowledge appears at least unlikely.

The golden section and the pyramid

Among the qualities hidden within the right-angled triangle are the proportions of the golden section, which from their unique characteristics are also called *divina proportione.* The term goes back to the Franciscan friar Luca Pacioli, who in 1509 published in Venice a book with the title *Divina Proportione.* It may even be that the expression was first used by his friend Leonardo da Vinci, with whom Pacioli was in close contact in Milan in 1496 and 1497 when he was writing his book and Leonardo was painting his *Last Supper.*

The golden section consists of the division of a straight line into two unequal parts, in such a way that the smaller part is in the same ratio to the larger part below as the larger part is to the whole. The smaller part is called the minor, the larger the major, and the golden section therefore consists of the following proportion:

$$\text{Minor} : \text{Major} = \text{Major} : (\text{Minor} + \text{Major})$$
$$AD : DB = DB : AD + DB$$

Thus the golden section presented a special means of mediating between contrasts, "because in the golden section two extremes are related by an intermediate proportion" (Pfeifer, 1885, p. 190). In this apparently simple statement lies hidden a many-sided play of relations, as well as many unique properties which were noted by the seventeenth-century astronomer Johannes Kepler, who first used the terms "major" and "minor."

The use of ϕ to represent the golden section was first introduced around 1910 by an Englishman, William Schooling. "The symbol ϕ given to this proportion

306. THE GOLDEN SECTION

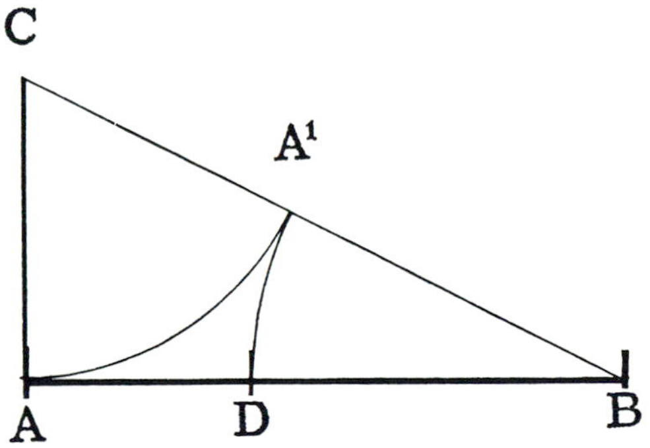

was chosen partly . . . because it is the first letter of the name of Pheidias, in whose sculpture this proportion is seen to prevail when the distances between salient points are measured" (Cook, 1914, p. 420).

The question immediately arises: Is it due to a conscious or an unconscious use of the golden section that this proportion recurs so frequently in architecture? The great role it plays in the pyramids rules out any accidental use of the laws of proportion. It is certain that its logical deductions were first set down by Euclid in the third century B.C. on Egyptian soil in the form of propositions, proofs, and conclusions, and that its practical utilization can be established throughout the Egyptian development.

One can repeatedly observe that Egyptian thinking was far removed from logical demonstration. It is fruitless to search for it. Neugebauer stresses that the Pythagoreans, whose dependence on Egyptian knowledge is well known, held the golden section in high esteem, but that no Egyptologist has ever found it mentioned in any hieroglyphic text (1934, p. 122, footnote). Elaborate investigations have been made, those by Else Christie Kielland for example, which have shown with surprising penetration that the organization of an Egyptian relief, sculpture, or piece of furniture is based on a universal, though often complicated, application of the golden section (1955).

The division of a line by the golden section is achieved quite simply. The starting points are the vertical, the horizontal, and a right-angled triangle whose
475 longer cathetus (*AB*) measures twice the length of the small one (*AC*). Swinging the small cathetus onto the hypotenuse, we find point A^1. A second curve from the point A^1 to the long cathetus *AB* gives point *D* which divides *AB* in the proportion of the golden section. The simple method of the division is reminiscent of that by which the Egyptians determined the inclination of an
471 angle: keeping the height constant and varying the base line.

The absence of any written records about the meaning of the pyramids has given rise during this and the last century to fantastic theories of their central location on the globe; to the reading into them of mysterious prophecies; and to assumptions that they were not tombs but rather a crystallization of the scientific knowledge of the time. These theories were often based on inexact or even false measurements. The attractively illustrated volumes by the Astronomer-Royal for Scotland (Smyth, 1867) remain among the best known. They have been sufficiently judged.

Fantastic astronomical messages have also been read into the dimensions of the great pyramid: an assertion that the distance of the sun from the earth is one thousand million times the height of the pyramid, or that, from other of its dimensions, the radius of the earth and even the climatic changes of the ice age can be deciphered (Moreux, 1923).

Borchardt in 1922 ignored everything not already pinpointed by documentary evidence, and Noel F. Wheeler in 1935 was even more rationalistic. Certainly distinctions between "journalistic rubbish and scientific statements" (p. 5) are necessary, but it is doubtful whether one can reject as "hair-raising formulae . . . all founded on the same sand as the rest" (p. 293) everything that cannot be measured with a yardstick, since doing so contradicts the nature of Egyptian thought. When, much earlier, a great Egyptologist like E. A. W. Budge stated that the pyramids were built "as a *tomb* and as nothing but a tomb" (ibid., p. 303), it was a trite projection of a materialistic point of view into a world in which everything turned on relationships, on multiple meanings, on the interpenetration of the spheres of the here and the hereafter.

We cannot decipher the symbolic meanings inherent in the dimensions of the pyramid. But sometimes their presence shines through. Lauer, despite his thoroughly critical approach, does not categorically reject everything for which no documentary records exist. In his chapter "Théories: Les Prétendus Secrets des pyramides" he carefully selects those for which direct relationships can be found (1948, pp. 110–60).

The pyramid and its planes

It is in the nature of the golden section that it automatically introduces a continuity of proportions and an infinite series of harmonic reflections. M. Ghyka (1927) has investigated the properties of the golden section more carefully than anyone else of the present day. This endless continuity of related proportions may be the reason why the lines and planes of the great pyramid are always disclosing new aspects of the golden section.

First came a relationship of the planes known since antiquity. Tradition, though no direct proof, asserts that this knowledge goes back to Herodotus, who learned it from the priests of Heliopolis.

The starting point is the triangle that results from slicing the pyramid in two on a line parallel to one of its sides. This triangle forms the surface of a half- 478
section of the pyramid. The so-called equation of Herodotus states that the square of the height (h^2) equals the area of one of the sloping side triangles:

$$h^2 = bx$$

Here b equals half the base and x the center line of the sloping side triangle. This assertion thus contains a relation between the absolute height of the pyramid, its base, and its sloping sides. Moreover, by means of a simple deduction it becomes clear that in the median triangle the catheti (height of the pyramid, h, and b, half of its base) stand in the ϕ relationship (Lauer, 1948, p. 191). This was discovered, or rather rediscovered, around the middle of the nineteenth century. The line x of this triangle, running from the middle of the base to the

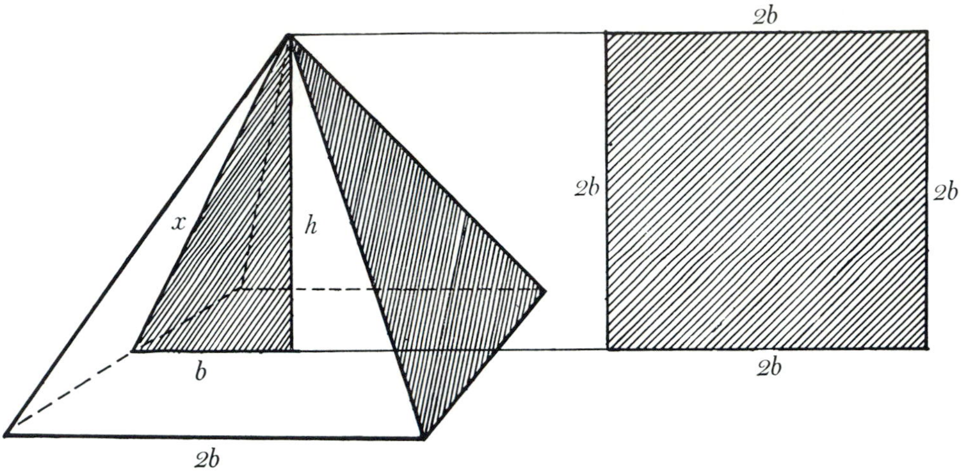

307. THE EQUATION OF HERODOTUS ($h^2 = bx$): *This expresses the relationship between the height of the great pyramid and the surface of one of its constituent triangles. The square of the height equals the area of one of these triangles*

apex of the pyramid, at the same time establishes the important angle of elevation.

The golden section also governs the relations of the actual surface planes of the pyramid to one another. The surface of the square base is in the same ratio to the sum of the four sloping triangles as these are to the total surface area. Lauer reports (p. 158) that this relationship was discovered from simple observation by K. Kleppisch, a Warsaw engineer.

We can touch only lightly upon the connections of π and the golden section. There have been copious discussions as to how much the Egyptians knew of the value of π, the relation between the circumference and the diameter of a circle. It stands to reason that, with their method of thinking, they would express it only as a ratio, in the form of a fraction. It can be asserted that "the relation of the perimeter of the base of the great pyramid to twice the height equals π" and further that "the relation of the area of the base to the area of the median section equals π" (ibid., p. 192). In confirming this, Lauer adds the remark of a mathematician, Paul Montel, who had drawn his attention to a little-noticed connection between π and ϕ:

$$0.618 = \frac{1}{\phi} = \left(\frac{\pi}{4}\right)^2 = \left(\frac{3.1416}{4}\right)^2 = 0.617$$

thus, one might say, closing the chain of relationships (ibid.).

SCULPTURE AND THE VERTICAL PLANE

The Egyptian sculptor did not create his work from the rough stone. He started from a block hewn into the shape of a prism. A squared grid was marked on its 480 sides. On the front of the prism he would draw the figure *en face*, on the sides in profile, all according to the canon. Only then would he start his sculptural work. From the beginning, the relief or statue was enclosed in the rectangular block, in complete contrast to the method of a Lysippus or a Michelangelo.

What rules did the chisel obey?

The Dane, Julius Lange, saw the constituent law of Egyptian sculpture to be the unconditional maintenance of a vertical plane, slicing centrally through the body. This "law of frontality," as he called it, was universal, and no deviations were permitted. Lange expressed his law for three-dimensional sculpture as follows: "Whatever position the figure assumes the rule applies that the central plane which can be supposed to lie lengthways through the human body, through the backbone, the crown, the nose, the breastbone and the sexual organs, and which cuts it in two symmetrical halves, must retain its position in one plane, and cannot be turned or bent one way or the other" (quoted by Kielland, 1955, p. 23).

Basically, the law of frontality merely states that Egyptian sculpture is governed by the vertical plane. But in what planes are the limbs arranged? How are the arms and legs treated?

This is answered by Schäfer's investigations. He accepts Lange's law of frontality. In one place he even calls it a "brilliant discovery" (1929, p. 53), but he feels it is incomplete and elaborates his concept of a "straight view" which contrasts with Greek art of the fifth century B.C. "Though they employed quite different methods, it is certain that these [Egyptian] draftsmen were convinced that they had always represented nature as faithfully as possible. Although of course their physical eye, like any normal eye, registered the foreshortenings, they nevertheless neglect these apparent impressions and unconsciously record what their mental eye tells them, what they know about the nature of the body, or, not to lay too great a stress on the intellectual element, what lives in their imagination as reality. Therefore I characterize their method of drawing as 'the presentation of the straight view!' " (p. 34)

The term "straight view" serves to underline the contrast with a foreshortened or (as the Egyptians would perhaps have put it) a distorted portrayal of an object, such as was presented in Greek art and, nearly two thousand

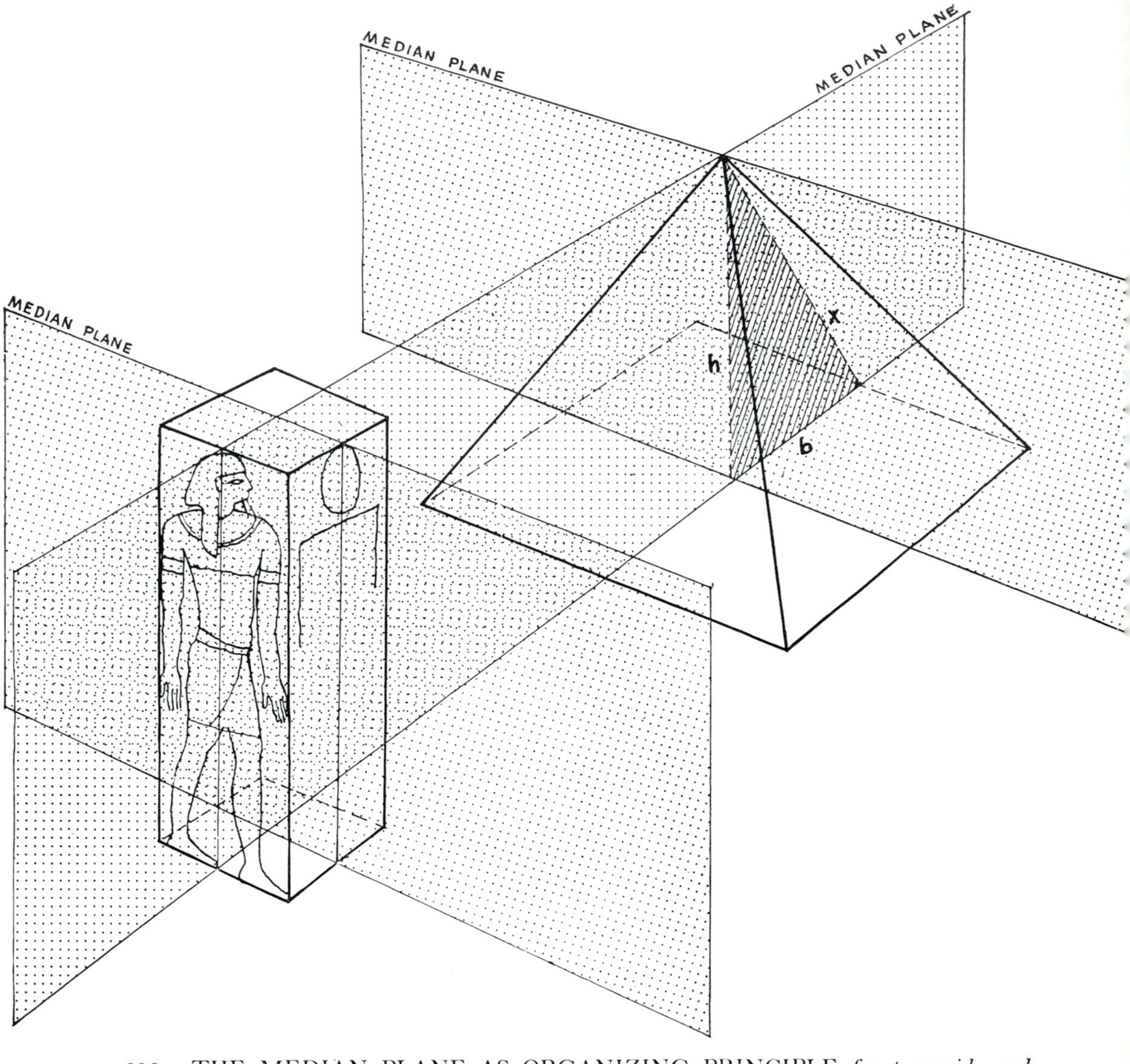

308. THE MEDIAN PLANE AS ORGANIZING PRINCIPLE *for pyramids and Egyptian sculpture*

years later, was developed still further in perspective representation. The expression "straight view" means that the parts of an object are depicted in their natural size and proportions. In this representation of "what their mental eye tells them" Egyptian art continues the primeval tradition, though absolute freedom of the creative imagination is now strictly limited to "straight view" presentations upon predetermined vertical parallel planes.

"Consequently," says Schäfer, "a 'pre-Greek' statue, that is, one based on a 'straight view' conception, is on the whole composed out of four views standing at right angles to each other: a straight front and back view and two straight side views" (p. 36). All the parts—head, torso, arms, and legs—remain within a framework of vertical planes. From this he develops his amplification of Lange's law of frontality. Human beings and animals "have two decisive dimensions to their perception. One lies in the widest contour of the front view of the head and torso, the other in the widest contour of the lateral view. . . . The resulting main directions, standing at rest at right angles to each other, fascinate the imagination of the pre-Greek artist to such an extent that the composition of his statues, even when portraying movement, is determined by two planes crossing each other at right angles. His "straight view" conception of the exterior surface of the parts of the body and limbs is related to and laid in these planes, or in invisible parallel planes, in a process similar to that by which he handles the planes in a relief" (ibid.).

In other words, the imaginary vertical axis of a standing figure becomes the line along which the two planes intersect at right angles. Thus, in addition to a single frontal plane, Schäfer recognizes that the figure is also governed by a plane standing square to the first: a kind of spatial axial cross. The line of intersection of these planes in the original rectangular block becomes the axis of the figure, and "invisible" parallel planes are added along which the limbs are arranged.

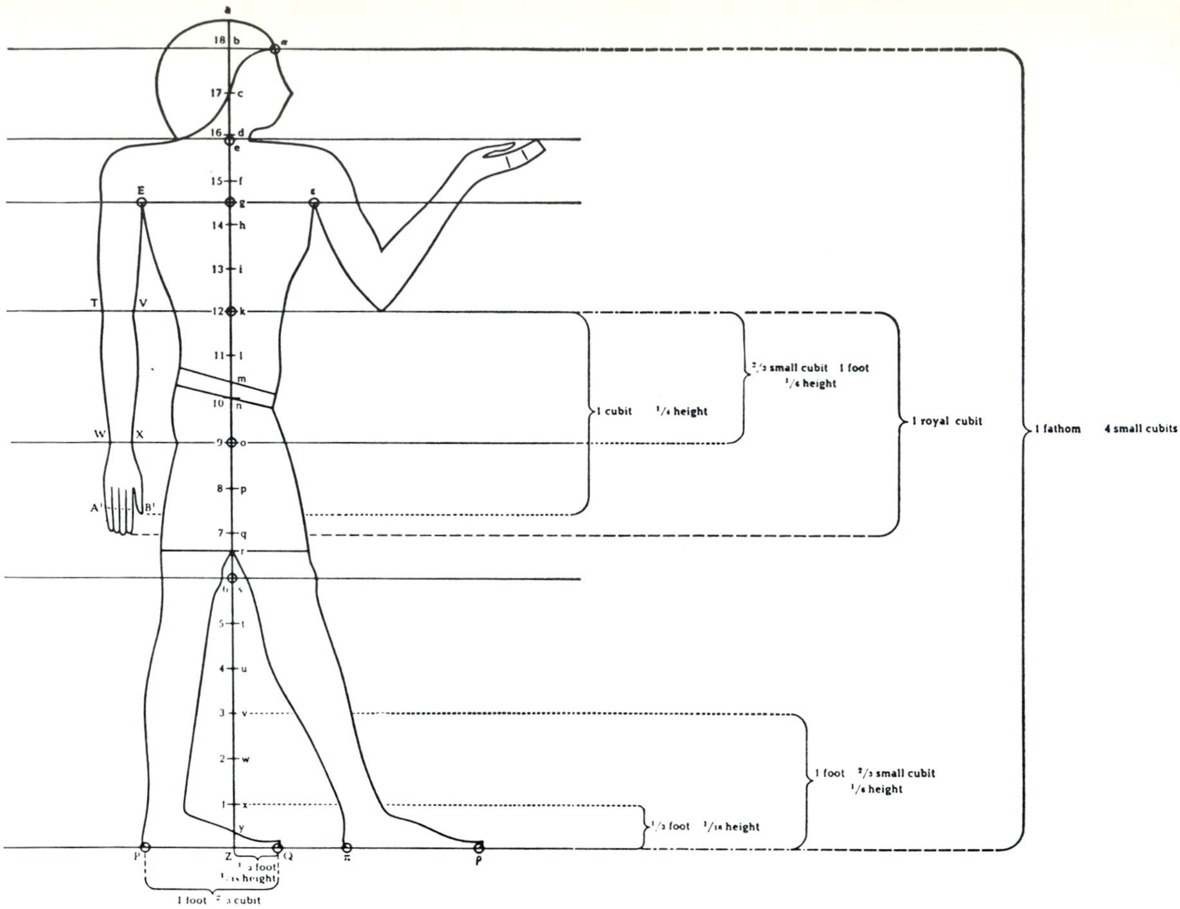

309. EGYPTIAN CANON OF HUMAN PROPORTIONS: *In the Old Kingdom the vertical axis passed through the navel. The dimensions and relations of different parts of the body are indicated by horizontal lines. From Iversen, after Lepsius*

THE MEANING OF THE SQUARED GRID

What is the meaning of the squared grid which the Egyptians invented for the execution of their reliefs and sculptures in the round?

More than a century ago, Lepsius, on an expedition to Egypt in 1842–46, recognized that the rows of figures ranged one above the other in an unfinished tomb in Saqqara were overlaid by a grid. Since then more than a hundred similar examples have been found.

above

Lepsius did not stop at this discovery. He noticed that the center line of the individual figure was emphasized as its vertical axis and was cut through by six horizontal lines. The foot was marked by two red dots. From these observations he developed his canon, i.e., a fixed system of proportions by which the unchanging relations of different parts of the human body were firmly established. As early as 1849 he announced: "Now for the first time we were able to distinguish sharply and clearly the different epochs of Egyptian art, each with its own personal character, up to then often unrecognized, so that their very existence was denied. . . . I cite as one of the most important particulars, that in unfinished monuments I have found numerous examples of three different canons of proportion for the human body" (p. 20). These were from the Old and Middle Kingdoms and, with a complete change in the principles of subdivision, also from the New Kingdom. Thus Lepsius made the "fundamental observation"—as Erik Iversen calls it—that the relationship between the height, length of the arms, length of the foot, etc., simultaneously expressed units of the Egyptian measuring system (1955, p. 11).

Lepsius' expedition, which, on the recommendation of Alexander von Humboldt, had been sponsored by the King of Prussia, resulted in an inventory of the then known Egyptian monuments which was published in twelve gigantic

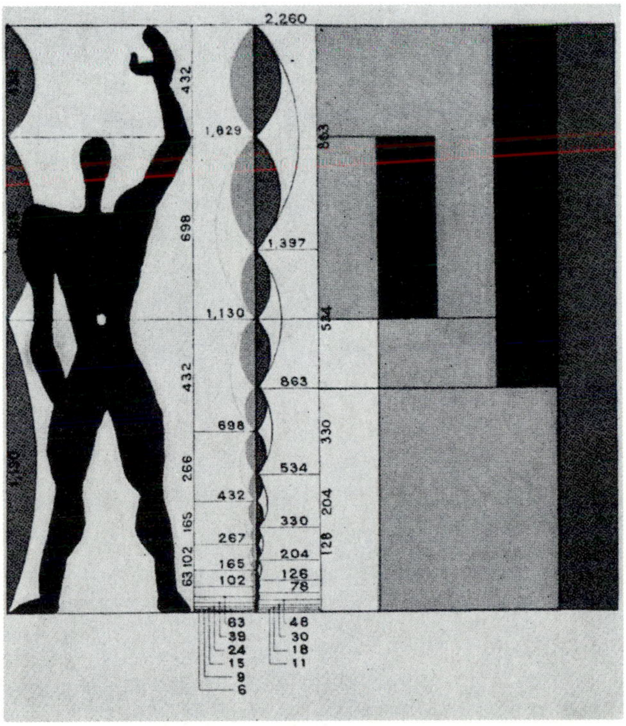

310. THE MODULOR, LE CORBUSIER: *In 1947 Le Corbusier's Modulor system reintroduced a canonlike relationship between the different parts of the human body "universally applicable to architecture and mechanics." From Le Corbusier*

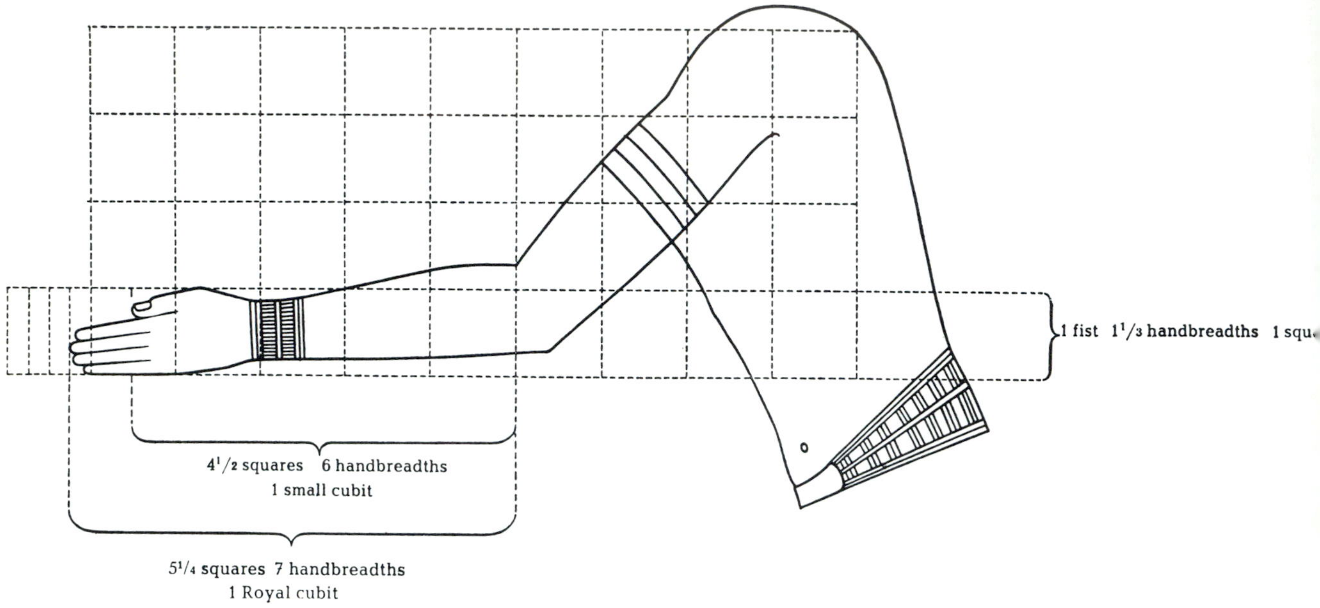

311. THE FIST AS THE BASIC EGYPTIAN MODULE: *The sides of the squared grid were identical with the fist* (1⅓ *handbreadths*). *The "royal cubit" measured seven handbreadths* (5¼ *squares*) *from elbow joint to finger tips, the "small cubit" six handbreadths* (4½ *squares*) *from elbow joint to the tip of the thumb. From Iversen, after Lepsius*

volumes of plates, including some superb colored lithographs and drawings of details (Lepsius, 1849–59), and in rich treasures for the Berlin Museum. Commentaries based on his notes and diaries were published only after his death (ed. Naville, 1897–1913). Even more important were the thoughts which Lepsius formulated on the nature of Egyptian art, thoughts which are still valid, or rather, whose meaning has been rediscovered today. He was one of the first to investigate the relationships which occur in all representations of the human body from the Old Kingdom until the end of the Egyptian era. He possessed something of the universal outlook of eighteenth-century philosophers and historians that continued into the first part of the nineteenth century: Jacob Burckhardt, almost a contemporary of Lepsius, is another example.

But the materialistic approach of the following generation brushed aside Lepsius' findings. Leading Egyptologists, such as Maspero and G. Perrot, dismissed them with the facile explanation that the squared grid was merely the easiest way to transfer a drawing onto the stone.

It is only today that the deeper meanings of Lepsius' observations are being honored and developed; only now do we realize that in Egypt the proportions of the human body, the measuring system, and the divisions of the squared grid were closely related. This conception serves Iversen as the starting point for a more defined approach. He contradicts the assertion of Perrot and Maspero that the squared grid is only a *mise aux carreaux:* a tool with no other purpose than to facilitate the reproduction of the representation (1955, p. 54).

This remark about the setting into squares (*mise aux carreaux*) is not without interest. It shows once again how even distinguished scholars unconsciously transfer certain customs of their own day to the Egyptian mentality. The nineteenth-century painter's custom of facilitating the transfer of a sketch onto canvas by means of a squared grid has little connection with the Egyptian grid, which was bound up with the inner organization of the picture. The painter's grid is based on completely different premises, traceable to the Renaissance and the invention of perspective as established by the generation of Florentine artists around 1400. Undoubtedly the nineteenth-century painter's use of the grid represents an adulteration of Leone Battista Alberti's invention of the squared grid as an "optical veil": the draftsman observed an object through a vertical transparent tissue covered with a squared netting and transferred it onto a similarly squared piece of paper. Albrecht Dürer indicated this method most vividly in his book *Underweysung der Messung mit dem Zirckel und Richtscheyt* (1525), where, among other examples, he shows how a woman's figure lying 486 in extreme foreshortening is transferred onto the drawing paper, using a squared grid scratched upon glass. This representation of an object as it appears, and not as it is, contains within it the notion of particularity and modern individualism. Both are alien to the Egyptian canon of relationships.

What were the relations between the Egyptian squared grid, the proportions of the human body, and linear measure?

The starting point was the standing human figure. The units of measure upon which all proportions were based were the hand and the arm: that part of the body which produces and creates things.

The squared grid based on the human handbreadth

The basic measure of the hand was the closed fist. This appears again and again in Egyptian statues, often holding a symbol of authority or an amulet, but sometimes without either. The fist became the basic module for all proportioning. This explains Iversen's brilliant equating of the side-lengths of the squares of the grid with the fist. The fist is measured over the knuckles across the breadth of the hand, including the thumb: "In all the grids the fist is equal to the side-length of the square" (1955, p. 33). Once the relation between the side-length of the grid and the fist had been determined, other proportions of the body could be expressed by it.

We are indebted to Iversen for the insight we now have into the theoretical background of the squared grid as well as into the relation between the side-length of the square and the fist, which was still unknown to Lepsius (1884, p. 100).

The dimensioning of the human figure

The outstretched hand and arm was another favored gesture throughout Egyptian art. From this was derived the decisive linear measurement: the cubit.

The "small cubit" was measured from the elbow to the tip of the thumb. It
484 consisted of six handbreadths. Each handbreadth was again divided into four fingers. The scale was still further elaborated by the organic subdivision of the fingers into, according to Lepsius, units almost as small as millimeters. The small cubit was the normal linear measure of the "old canon." In the old canon
right human height was measured from the sole of the foot to the point where the wig or head covering joins the forehead.

Both the small cubit and the handbreadth were related to the squares of the grid: the cubit measured 4½ squares, the handbreadth ¾. The human body in the old canon measured 18 squares; i.e., 18 fists, or 4 cubits, or 6 feet (a foot comprises 3 squares), or 24 handbreadths. This indicates the interlacing and interplay of proportions, form, and linear measure.

The divisions of the small cubit are known to us directly through its marking

312. THE SQUARE GRID OF THE RENAISSANCE: *Artist drawing a reclining woman in perspective: woodcut by Dürer. The square grid which Alberti invented in the early fifteenth century assisted in the perspective reproduction of objects as they appear, rather than as they are*

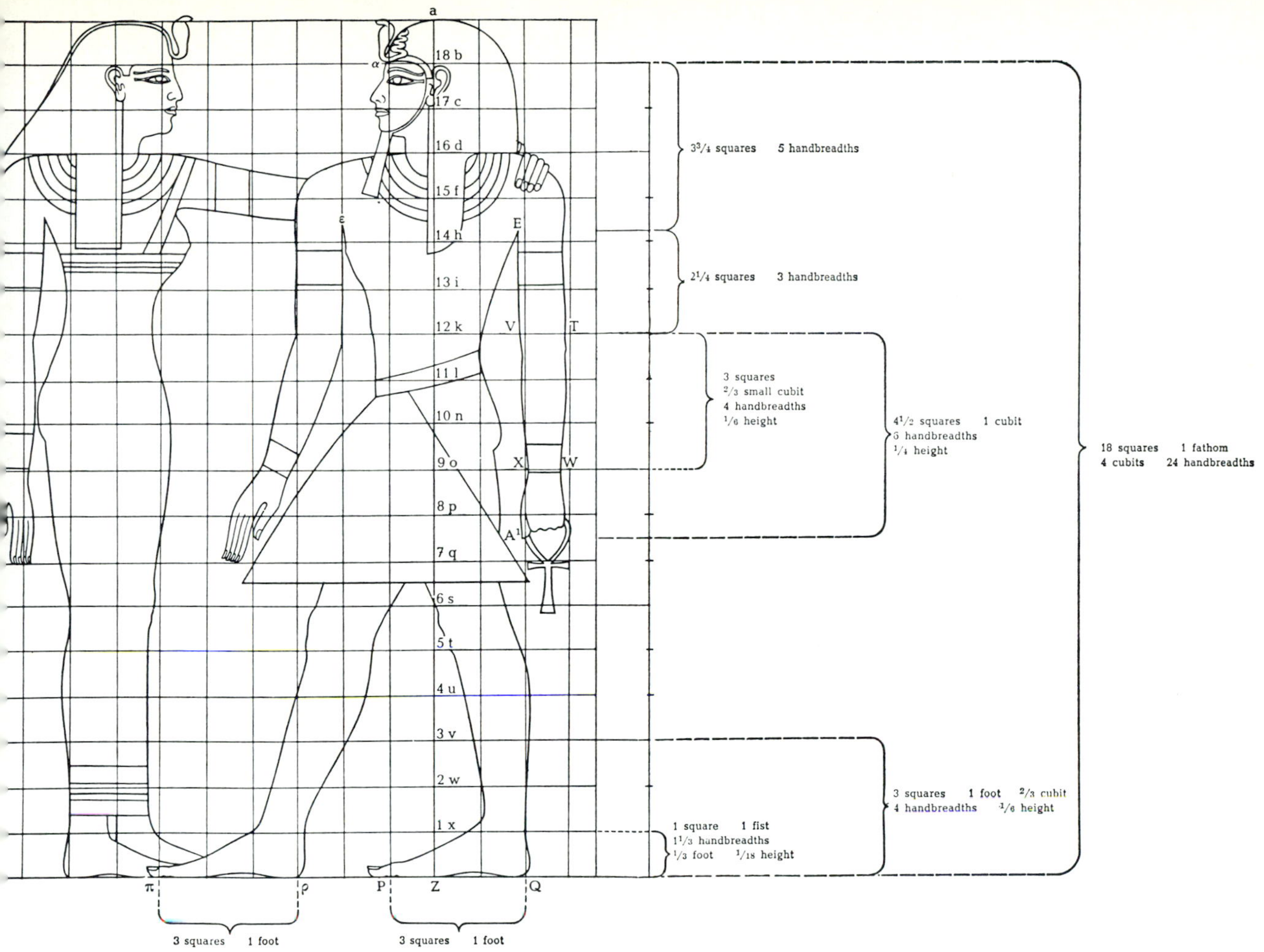

313. THE HUMAN BODY AND THE SQUARE GRID IN EGYPT: *The square grid served to establish the absolute proportions of the human body. For instance, according to the "old canon," the human body measured eighteen squares (4 small cubits) from the soles of the feet to the forehead. From Iversen, after Lepsius*

on extant measuring rods (one of them in the British Museum), and through the description of Herodotus (II, 149; tr. 1949, Powell, p. 181), who identified it in general with the Greek cubit which was divided similarly (Lepsius, 1884, p. 5).

Alongside the small cubit there was also the large "royal cubit," which exceeded the former by ⅙, or a handbreadth, and was measured from the elbow to the tip of the middle finger, comprising 7 handbreadths. "The Egyptian designation of this cubit as royal already tells us that it is a particular cubit, distinguished from the ordinary one and consequently additional. This addition, however, was very old, older than the oldest stone monuments, for it was employed upon them. The marking on measuring rods apart, it is found exclusively in connection with building works. . . . I have explained the name of the 'royal cubit' in this way, and I maintain that all massive erections, namely the pyramids and temples, were executed in the name of the king" (ibid., p. 18). It may perhaps be remembered that the Egyptians measured the inclination of a slope by employing a standard dimension for the vertical and varying the horizontal measure. The vertical was always 28 fingers high, which corresponds exactly to the royal cubit. The royal cubit suppressed the small cubit completely during the Saite period in the seventh and sixth centuries B.C. Human height was then measured from the sole to the eyelid, comprising 21 squares, or 4 royal cubits.

As Lepsius pointed out, the cubit spread throughout the Mediterranean basin and the Middle East. The Greek measuring system was taken over from Egypt: "To be sure, the Greeks did not take the Egyptian cubit as the main standard of their linear system from the Egyptians, but established as such the *foot,* on their own initiative. Among the Egyptians this measure appeared not as a foot but as two-thirds of a cubit, or simply two-thirds, and remained in the background, seldom coming into use" (ibid., p. 33).

It seems that in Greece a certain relationship also existed between the artistic canon and the linear measure, as may be concluded from the "metrological relief" in the Ashmolean Museum (Michaelis, 1883, p. 336). Above a man with outstretched arms is a footprint in curious isolation. The distance between the tips of his middle fingers appears to be closely related to the proportions of the Egyptian canon of the Late Period, since it equals the height from sole to eyelid, which comprised four royal cubits (Iversen, 1955, p. 59).

below

The relations and proportions of the canon all derive from natural observation, as do the linear measurements. In contrast to the meter, the cubit is a human measure, originating in the relation between hand, arm, and human height.

314. GREEK METROLOGICAL RELIEF: *Upper part of the body of a youth with outstretched arms, indicating the standard length of a fathom. A foot, the measure really used by the Greeks, is shown above the right arm; ca. 450* B.C.

PROPORTIONS IN ARCHITECTURE

Architecture is composed both of immediately visible forms and of an interrelationship between its elements, creating an integrated whole from a number of isolated parts. Here lies the function of proportions.

A sensitive eye can often instinctively sense when a oneness has been achieved among all parts of a building: its ground plan, shaping of spaces, and plastic elements. But such an optical survey is somewhat primitive and superficial. The interplay of proportions is less visible than the immediate forms and outlines.

The loss of a capacity to integrate parts into a comprehensible whole is not merely a shortcoming of our period but a perilous deficiency. Without it we are unable to attain a civilization in equipoise. Translated into architecture, this deficiency appears in the absence of one of its basic necessities: the conscious use of proportions. Misled or undisciplined individualists may believe in a haphazard rule of thumb, but real architecture cannot come into being unless all its parts are integrated, just as a building cannot be made to stand erect without someone's knowledge of construction.

Whatever earlier period is considered (classical, medieval, Renaissance), it will be found that all projects in all their parts—horizontal, vertical, spatial—were submitted to the invisible interplay of proportions.

No architecture is more imbued with proportions than that of Egypt, which stood at the beginning. One of the reasons is that proportions were then inseparably bound up with symbolic meanings.

The Egyptian demand for an embracing oneness in its conceptual image of the world could not be halted when it came to architecture. It came to the fore in the scrupulously careful cosmic orientation of the great pyramids. The ceremony of "Stretching the cord" (knotted at intervals of 3, 4, and 5 to form a right-angled triangle) was performed by the Pharaoh himself at the erection of all important sanctuaries. The value laid upon safeguarding the corners of a building is shown by the square holes found by Winlock at the mortuary temple of Mentuhotep at Deir el Bahari: "At each of the four corners of the foundation trench a hole some three feet square was dug. On the appointed day—with the king present in person, in all probability—the priests approached one corner of the temple and placed in the hole the head, a leg, and a rib of a freshly slaughtered ox. Beside it they laid some conical loaves of bread . . . saucers filled with barley, figs, grapes . . . round cakes, and half a dozen miniature wine jars. All this was doubtless accompanied by prayers that the king, who would one day be buried in the temple, should never feel the pangs of hunger or of thirst" (1942, p. 51).

An Egyptian sanctuary was always conceived as a unity, and so no details exist that are without significance. It made no difference that the temples were growing organisms. Each part that was added was integrated into the whole by the use of the same system of proportions. Just as the proportions of the human figure were submitted to a grid based on the dimensions of the human hand, all proportions in architecture were related to the same basic system. This is not contradicted by the fact that proportions could be applied in many different ways.

Even before 1900, Choisy had recognized the use in Egyptian architecture of the equilateral and the golden section triangles (1899, I, pp. 51–57).

In the 1920's E. Mössel (Mössel, 1926) "discovered the use by the Egyptian architects of the summation series of Fibonacci or Lamé 1, 2, 3, 5, 8, 13, 21" (Badawy, 1961, p. 1), which comes so close to the golden section proportions. The series which bears the name of Leonardo Fibonacci, a thirteenth-century Italian professor, reappears again and again in the proportions of Egyptian architecture, and one can without difficulty assume that it was already known and used by the Egyptians: "It must be remembered that what we know about the mathematics and the science of the Egyptians is what they chose to let us know" (p. 9). Science was kept secret and hidden like the statue of a divinity.

In the 1950's the research of Badawy and R. A. Schwaller de Lubicz gave a detailed insight into the proportional organization of Egyptian buildings. Badawy did this in an unpublished work on ancient Egyptian design, Schwaller de Lubicz in three volumes devoted to the careful study of a single building complex, the temple of Luxor, entitled *Le Temple de l'homme* (1957).

In a paper to the Twenty-fifth International Congress of Orientalists at Moscow, Badawy gave a summary of some of his ideas on "the relation of the parts to the whole and the interrelation between the different elements" (Unpublished Mss.). Egyptian complexes, such as the large New Kingdom temples which grew by accretion—new parts being added in front of the earlier structures—continued to follow exactly the same system of proportions, even if separated by several hundred years. Badawy describes as "harmonic design" the system based on certain recurrent dimensions occurring in ground plan and section which can be expressed by a constructional diagram using isosceles triangles and squares. "Both systems, the arithmetic of Fibonacci and the graphic system of the golden section, were combined to achieve harmonic design in architecture according to fixed rules capable of being transmitted to teaching without the help of writing."

In our period many architects, still imbued with a nineteenth-century romantic individualism, believe that their personal artistic instincts do not need the control of any system of proportions. Some, but comparatively few, work, like Mies van der Rohe, with a basic additive module recurring throughout a structure. Le Corbusier, like Picasso or Miró, has an inner relation with artistic experiences which has long vanished from the work of the *routinier* painter or architect. He has derived from the subconscious his system of the Modulor, combining the 483
arithmetic and geometric systems of Fibonacci and the golden section adapted to the dimensions of the human figure and, from there, applied to architectural proportions. He has consistently employed this system in his architecture.

The cubit as a basis of architectural proportions

As we mentioned earlier, the Egyptians invented grids, based on the dimensions 485 ff
of the human hand, to establish the correct proportions of the human body in painting, relief, and sculpture. Proportions in architecture were based on the 484
length of the human forearm: the cubit. Thus Egyptian architecture is a projection of the proportions of the human body and limbs transposed into a larger —but still human—scale. This is especially true of the great temples. Man and man's artifacts were closely interlocked.

Badawy carefully limited himself to the methodological use of proportions leading to a "harmonic system of architectural design" (1961), just as Iversen followed through the use of a squared grid to determine the proportions of the human body (1955, p. 33).

Schwaller de Lubicz stressed the symbolic implications inherent in the proportional organization of the whole of a great temple. The graphic analysis in his second volume is of superb precision. One may not be willing to go so far as to compare the meaning of a Christian cathedral with the profoundly different religious outlook of the Egyptians. One may also feel extremely cautious about accepting the idea that different parts of the Luxor temple reflect different stages of human growth: that the proportions of the innermost sanctuary represent those of a *nouveau-né* or that one can find the proportions of an adult skeleton in the entire complex, including its latest additions (1957: II, pl. XV; III, pp. 57–62).

Supremacy of the Vertical

Schwaller de Lubicz's volumes are not normally found in the bibliography of any serious Egyptologist, yet his fundamental point of the relations between symbolic meaning and the use of proportions cannot in the long run be excluded from earnest consideration. His influence upon Robichon and Varille, who were particularly concerned with the cosmic implications of the Egyptian temple, led to a further refinement of Egyptian excavations and was a contribution to the neglected studies of the symbolism which permeates all Egyptian architecture, down to the setting of every stone.

PART XII THE FIRST ARCHITECTURAL SPACE CONCEPTION

THE INTANGIBILITY OF SPACE

It is possible to give physical limits to space, but by its nature, space is limitless and intangible. Space dissolves in darkness and evaporates in infinity. To become visible, space must acquire form and boundaries either from nature or by the hand of man.

The intangible phenomenon of space has always fascinated man—even disturbed him. Like abstraction and the symbol, the origin of the concept of space lies embedded in Greek thought. Archytas, one of the Pythagoreans, wrote on the nature of space, though his work is lost except for a few fragments. Plato's *Timaeus,* which contains his deepest mythopoeic thinking, deals with the construction of the universe and develops a cosmology. Plato transports us to a point "before the beginning of years," when time was not and "the earth was without form and void" (tr. Bury, 1952, introduction). Involuntarily one senses the influence of Egyptian thought, well known to Plato from his long stay in Heliopolis. Gradually we follow the process by which the cosmos was developed out of chaos.

I:514 ff

Plato conducts us with the aid of his two concepts, the eternal and the temporal, here called the model and the copy: "One of them being assumed as a Model Form, intelligible and ever uniformly existent, and the second as the model's Copy, subject to becoming and visible." But here, he says, "the argument seems to compel us" to add to these two images a third: "a Form that is baffling and obscure. What essential property, then, are we to conceive it to possess? This in particular, that it should be the receptacle, and as it were the nurse, of all Becoming" (49A–B). Later he adds: "While it is always receiving all things, nowhere and in no wise does it assume any shape similar to any of the things that enter into it. For it is laid down by nature as a moulding stuff for everything, being moved and marked by the entering figures, and because of them it appears different at different times" (50 C).

Plato never actually employs the word "space," but we concur in the view, held by many scholars of ancient philosophy, that the substance of which he is speaking was in fact no other than space, "the Receptacle of this generated world," which if we describe as "invisible and unshaped, all-receptive and in some most perplexing and most baffling way partaking of the intelligible, we shall describe her truly" (51A–B).

One can sense here Plato's hesitancy before the intangibility of this "essential property" which is the "receptacle . . . of all Becoming." In this "invisible and unshaped" medium he places all things that emerge and that change. This is the first time man attempted to define the intangible phenomenon of space. The approach is a metaphysical one, but it also encompasses the psychic content of space.

In the realm of architecture, space is experienced by means of observation, in which the senses of sight and touch are interlocked. In the first instance this is a simple statement of fact. But through the relations of the most diverse elements and the degree of their emphasis—straight or curving lines, planes, structures, massivity, proportions, forms of all kinds—a matter of simple physical observation can be transposed to another sphere. These diverse elements are seen suddenly as a single entity, as a oneness imbued with spiritual qualities. This transformation of a physical fact into an emotional experience derives from a higher level of our faculty of abstraction.

ARCHITECTURAL SPACE CONCEPTION

It is light that induces the sensation of space. Space is annihilated by darkness. Light and space are inseparable.

If light is eliminated, the emotional content of space disappears, becomes impossible to apprehend. In the dark there is no difference between the emotional evaluation of a chasm and of a highly modeled interior.

The essence of space lies in the interaction of the elements that confine it. The diverse ways in which these parts have been formed and related to one another is the substance of the history of architecture.

Though space is intangible, between man and space there is a psychic relationship. This changes continuously, sometimes in nuances, sometimes fundamentally. The relation between man and man-made space appears in his space conception. Like his attitude toward the state and his attitude toward the world, the latter is bound up with the nature of his period. But it is possible for a certain space conception to persist over long ages and to indicate the links that bind prolonged periods together, as is the case with the Egyptian and Sumerian civilizations.

A space conception is instinctive and finds its expression in the way man places three-dimensional objects in relation to one another. For the most part, he is unconscious of the space conception to which he responds. This is why the space conception of a period can give insight into man's attitude toward the cosmos, toward nature, and toward eternity.

Recently the exact sciences also appear to have found the need to investigate changes in space conception "and its corresponding theories" in connection with the history of scientific thought and physics. In the preface to *Concepts of Space* Max Jammer writes: "*It is my firm conviction* that the study of the history of scientific thought is most essential to a full understanding of the various aspects and achievements of modern culture. Such understanding is not to be reached by dealing with the problems of priority in the history of discoveries, the details of the chronology of inventions, or even the juxtaposition of all the histories of the particular sciences. It is the history of scientific thought in its broadest perspective against the cultural background of the period which has decisive importance for the modern mind.

"The concept of space, in spite of its fundamental role in physics and philosophy, has never been treated from such a historical point of view" (1954, pp. v f.).

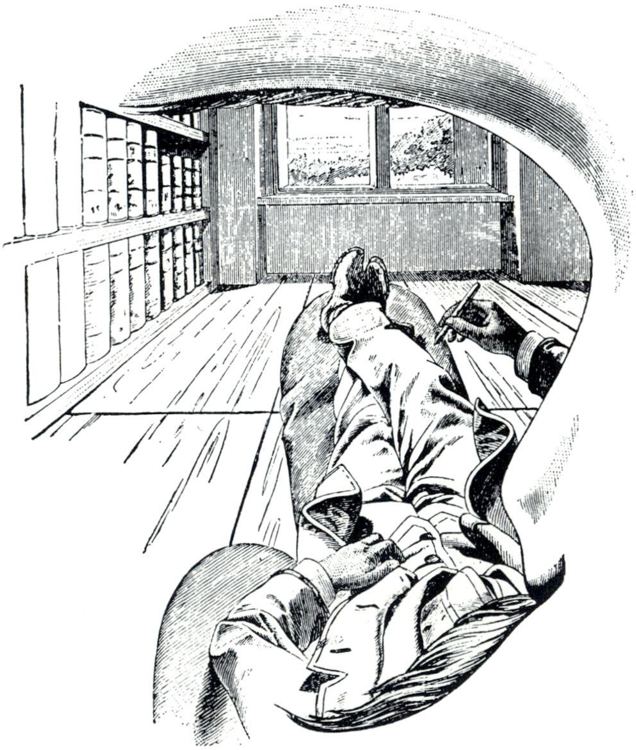

315. ONE-EYED FIELD OF VISION OF RECUMBENT MAN: *Lying outstretched upon a couch, his view framed by the arch of his eyebrows, his nose, and his mustache. Foreshortened perspective is based upon a a single-vision static viewpoint. Drawing by Mach*

Static and dynamic space

Ernst Mach, the Viennese physicist and mathematician, had, as early as 1885, gone deeply into the space sensitivity of the eye and the relation of visual apperceptions to each other and to psychical elements. In a famous sketch he depicted the static field of vision of a person lying at ease. In foreshortened perspective he drew a man lying upon a sofa, his field of vision framed by the arch of his eyebrows, his nose, and his mustache. Eyebrows, nose, and mustache, accordingly, appear gigantic. As in the early Renaissance, the spatial depth is indicated by the progressive foreshortening of the limbs, and even the drawing hand is already dwarfed. left

Dynamic space

It immediately became apparent that the static viewpoint of someone lying upon a sofa was insufficient. It began to be recognized that the natural field of vision was dynamic—in other words, that the perception of space could not be bound to

316. PAUL KLEE: *"Die Scene mit der Laufenden." Elimination of the single viewpoint and introduction of a dynamic perception of space through the roving eye of a moving observer. Drawing, 1925*

a single viewpoint. Movement played a decisive role in the perception of space. Many theories were developed in this context. One of them conceived perception of space (seeing in depth) as the perception of a time difference (Arnold, 1949, p. 26). Another measured reaction time: the time that elapses between the onset of a stimulus and the corresponding bodily action (Pauli, 1941–42, pp. 177–92).

It would be most interesting to have a means of gauging dynamically moving space as it appears when walking through it. This would involve the continuous, difficult-to-grasp changes of space and of the object within it that come into the field of vision of a walking man. These have been symbolically expressed by contemporary artists.

497 In Paul Klee's *Scene mit der Laufenden* (Scene with Running Woman; 1925), he did not lay the main emphasis upon the successive phases of her bodily movements passing through time. This had been done by the Futurists, Giacomo Balla for example, or Marcel Duchamp in his *Nude Descending a Staircase* (1912). Klee went a step further. He incorporated changes in the form of the surrounding space while it was being crossed. The space and the running figure depict this psychic-physical reality as an overlapping sequence of phases. This is a dynamic experience of space: a dynamic perception of space in depth. It moves beyond the realm of mathematical analysis of movement. An increasing spatial experience is expressed in the same way as the transparent organic growth of a fruit in another of Klee's pictures.

From the time of Paolo Uccello—that early Renaissance master of foreshortened perspective—to Mach's eyebrows and mustache, distance in space was conceived of as seen from a static viewpoint.

In the contemporary conception of space, interest is concentrated upon the roving viewpoint of the moving observer: space which is absorbed by the mind in continuous dynamic movement.

Similar observations have been made by the neurologists. According to the neurologist V. von Weizsäcker, perception has no absolute and permanent frame of reference (1943, p. 16). "We have had to learn meanwhile, that we cannot perceive or even think of Nature without bringing in something which is simply our own individual and highly personal truth. Today the individual approach and personification have become governing conditions of what was formerly considered objective Nature, wholly independent of man. We do not only exist in time and space, but time and space also exist within us, and there is therefore an inevitable interconnection between inner and outer agitation" (p. 27).

This assertion that space and time also exist within us, that we are not merely immersed in them, and that there exists an interrelation "between inner and outer agitation" is the best explanation of Klee's *Scene mit der Laufenden.* The 497 picture is not simply concerned with the sequential development of single or composite movements, such as the stages of walking, as the Futurists brought them into consciousness through transparent and kinetic analyses. It is concerned with the simultaneous presentation of the dynamic space that comes into being through the changing relations of space to the person moving through it.

This introduction of the changes noticed simultaneously by the observer and the observed has also an important role to play in architectural space conception.

Research into architectural space

Consideration of space as a material for artistic representation arose in the Renaissance, the moment rationally scientific perspective drawing made it possible to bring space onto a two-dimensional picture plane. Although this consideration had the task of submitting the reception of perspective to a subtly intuitive refinement, it always dealt in perspective in depth. In a university lecture Hans Jantzen followed this development through four hundred years (1938) throughout which interest centered upon the representation of space in painting. But in 1890 a strong impetus arose to bring architectural space into consideration. Leading art historians began to find the analysis of formal shapes insufficient and too coarse. They recognized Plato's space, as a receptacle of all becoming, to be an essential ingredient of architectural expression.

The first definite investigations into space as a constituent element of visual art occurred in the last decade of the nineteenth century. They were made by an Austrian, Alois Riegl (1858–1905), a Swiss, Heinrich Wölfflin (1864–1946), and a German, August Schmarsow (1853–1936). Each of these three great scholars in his own fashion contributed to advances in this field.

Riegl made far-reaching contributions, despite the fact that he died very young. His was the most universal conception. Few conceptions have been so fruitful for research in art history as his conception of the *Kunstwollen.* This was the battering-ram used against the leading materialistic aesthetic of Gottfried Semper, which had held the stage for sixty years. Riegl was, as he stated in his *Spätrömische Kunst-Industrie,* first published in 1901 in a little-known professional journal, "so far as I can see the first . . . who has perceived art as the outcome of a definite and conscious *Kunstwollen* [artistic volition] which asserts itself in conflict with the requirements of custom, material goods, and technical skills" (1927, p. 9). The excitement resulting from the work of these three men was limited to the German-speaking world. Art historians and archaeologists from other countries, on both sides of the Atlantic, considered, and in part still consider, preoccupation with so intangible a subject as space to fall outside the confines of earnest scholarship. In Italy it is only in recent years that space has become recognized as a constituent element of architecture.

In 1888 Wölfflin, in *Renaissance und Barock*, had set the tone by announcing the meaning of space as something absolute, a note which had never been heard before. In this early work, whose language places it among those rare publications on art history which do not age with time, a space conception is nowhere directly mentioned, but it pervades the entire work. Again and again the inseparable connection of "space forms" with the "life of a period" is pointed out and the effect of intangible form upon the psychic interpretation of spatial form demonstrated. One may also suggest that the lean strength of Wölfflin's language had great influence on Riegl and Schmarsow. Wölfflin was a direct disciple of Jacob Burckhardt. He stood nearest to the latter in his inner conception of the high Renaissance, though from the beginning Wölfflin linked this with the baroque. He was perhaps by nature the last Renaissance man. He sought throughout his life for quietness and composed dignity, and his main interest centered in the extension of the Renaissance into the nineteenth century. This was the period in which were rooted the five pairs of ideas set forward in so masterly a manner in his *Kunstgeschichtliche Grundbegriffe* (1915).

Though Riegl was primarily concerned with the minor art of Roman provinces, his historic vision ranged over a far wider field even from the start, and broadened into universality. He traced *Raumbildung*—formation of space—from the pyramids to early Christian art. For the first time an art historian dared to observe Egyptian architecture with other eyes than those of the archaeologist. For this he used the polarized notions of vision and touch: optic and haptic. These refer back to a general functioning of the senses and were not derived from a specific style. The touch of an object gives it its plastic form. Vision brings in the optical concept of its appearance. This vision/touch (optic/haptic) categorization deals with a generalized human apperception of the external world and is capable of universal application.

In fact—though much later—the same notion was employed in modern mathematics. Gilbert de B. Robinson defined it as follows: "Our concept of *physical space* is the result of a desire to order our experiences of the external world.

. . . Our experience of the external world comes to us through our senses, and of these our sense of *vision* and our sense of *touch* seem to be the most significant" (1946, p. 5).

Riegl's notion of space is equally fruitful, though his exploration of it is rather hampered by tradition. He assumes the observer of space to be motionless, and thus to have a static space conception like that defined and presented by Mach in 1886. The ideal observer is thus nailed to a fixed viewpoint, both for interior and for exterior space.

The third of these trail blazers, Schmarsow, considered the limitation to a single viewpoint too one-sided and not sensitive enough to human perception. To perceive an object fully, the observer must have a continually changing viewpoint. Already in 1893, in his opening lecture at Leipzig, "The Nature of Research into Architectural Space," Schmarsow had glimpsed the innermost nature of the formation of architectural space. In his main work on the fundamental concepts of art (1905), he states definitely: "Both the basis and the unalterable determinant in the definition of architecture as art must thus be its *formation of space* (Raumbildung). Architecture is a space-former from start to finish: its nature is created by this notion" (p. 184; italics mine).

In this work Schmarsow analyzes some of Riegl's beliefs in a not unfruitful polemic, saying in his foreword: "Because of its critical discussions, I attach myself, in the first instance, to the highly important and learned work of Alois Riegl, *Spätrömische Kunst-Industrie* (Vienna, 1901), since this, following the stated intention of its author (p. 139), is mainly devoted to a discussion of the principal problems" (p. iv).

Schmarsow is incited to develop a productive analysis, and he widens the field by bringing in a dynamic instead of a static observation of space. A building must be circled—"wandered around"—and its interior space must be "wandered through": a requirement also constantly emphasized in Wölfflin's lectures. As he expressed it orally, architecture demands to be gone through. Schmarsow was the first to bring definitely to the fore the dynamic conception of shaped spaces. We shall see that this concept leads us to a positive evaluation of the first architectural space conception which was not accessible to Riegl, and which occurred long before scientists had recognized the dynamic process of vision and linked it with the component of time.

If Riegl had laid the foundation for the comprehension of a work of art in *Kunstwollen*, and for a work of architecture in touch and vision, Schmarsow took the initiative in broadening it. It is completely wrong to see the teaching of

Wölfflin, Riegl, and Schmarsow as purely formalistic, physiological observations, as has occasionally happened. Riegl's notion of *Kunstwollen* and Wölfflin's *Lebensgefühl* (feeling for life; vitality) should make this clear enough. They all sought, in their own way, to encompass the total structure of a period.

A space conception is but the disclosure of architectural intent. The architecture of the first high civilizations, which is everywhere saturated with symbolism and mystical meaning, can only be comprehended when related to its space conception.

SPACE CONCEPTION IN PREHISTORY AND THE ARCHAIC CIVILIZATIONS

We have sought gradually to bring out those elements whose combination built up the first space conception: abstraction, the supremacy of the vertical, the plane surface, volumes in space. These things, susceptible to vision and touch, were also fraught with symbolic meanings that are far from simple. As so often
Part II in the archaic high civilizations, they are pluralistic, they have manifold meanings. On the one hand their symbolic background was bound up with a grandiose
396 ff cosmic outlook: with the movements of the stars, with the eternal cycle of the day, with constant wandering and movement. On the other hand they were tied
320 ff to an exceedingly rigid social hierarchy, which was again drawn into the cosmic aspect.

The entire archaic outlook, like that of prehistory, assumed the oneness and
33 ff inseparability of the world. One world, in which the animal was part of the community, rising even to divinity, and not yet regarded as an inferior creature.

Despite this, there is a profound difference between the space conception of
1:Part VI prehistory and that of the high civilizations. We questioned earlier what differentiated the space conception of prehistory from that of today.

Primeval art was a rock art. Caverns and cliffs have curving surfaces that change continually in form and direction. This multiplicity of form, this infinite
1:529 ff freedom of directions, these endlessly changing surfaces were part of the being of primeval art, which was closer to nature than any other but yet knew how to allow for human individuality.

The freedom of surfaces corresponded with the freedom of direction. Vertical and horizontal had not yet achieved predominance. The eyes of primeval man, like those of contemporary primitives (the Eskimo, for example), held all directions in equal esteem. Representations that are to our eyes vertical—animals that seem to be falling or standing on their heads—were not so intended. They cannot be interpreted on the principles of vertical co-ordination. To primitive eyes, such animals are simply standing near one another. **1:522** **1:417**

The freedom of approach to all directions and surfaces, like the frequent transparent, interpenetrated animals, has long enough misled people into seeing cavern art as chaotic and lacking all composition. There is no need to discuss this here. Of recent years, French scholars have been making statistical investigations of the laws of composition, the division and combination of animal types and animal groups, and have discovered an astounding accordance in their placement at particular points in the caverns. This does not result from following rational laws of composition in our sense. **1:517** **1:518**

The consequences of the rigid hierarchical organization of archaic society can be recognized also in the supremacy of the vertical, selected from among the multiplicity of directions. It was the vertical which symbolized the human posture in contrast to that of the animal: man was beginning to believe himself to be ruler of the earth. **Part XI**

Just as one direction was chosen from all others to become an organizing principle, so also the endless variety of rock surfaces became one—one smooth unbroken plane. This abstraction is also applicable to Sumer, but it was only in Egypt that the rigorously even surface became exclusive: the immaculate absolutism of the planes of the pyramids, with their total rejection of any detailing. The plane surface never disappeared from Egyptian architecture or art, either in the temples of the New Kingdom or in the sunken reliefs, whose delicate articulation, woven directly into the surface, was so close to the Egyptian temperament. **153 ff**

The pure surfaces become volumes: pyramids, pylons, obelisks. From the standpoint of authoritative architecture as it developed after the Roman vaulted structures, these volumes do not fall within the realm of architecture. The highest aim of Western architecture has been the formation of hollowed-out space: interior space. This was Riegl's view. He had always in mind a domed space, which best expressed in monumental form the hollowing-out of space. But interior space of this kind was unknown to the architecture of the first high civilizations. Their attitude toward the vaulting problem can be briefly stated.

At the origin of architecture—in Egypt as well as in Mesopotamia—there was a period when the house of god, the temple, was conceived as an interior space **190 ff** similar to the newly developed dwelling house. Still, for Riegl, later Egyptian art was a spaceless art: "The architectural ideal of ancient Egypt is most purely expressed in that typical mortuary monument, the pyramid. Before whichever of its four sides the observer places himself, his eyes are accorded just the unified plane of an equilateral triangle, whose sharply cutoff sides in no way suggest their union with a three-dimensional body behind." Under the spell of the fixed viewpoint, Riegl could only see the single intangible surfaces and came to the conclusion that "the pyramid is more a picture than a structure" (1927, p. 36).

This is where Schmarsow enters. From the start, he had been concerned with the changing viewpoint and, consequently, a dynamic apperception of space: "The less we are inclined to behave as one-eyed creatures, satisfied with a single viewpoint, the more we shall become accustomed to changing our viewpoints so as to encompass the material individuality of things from all possible angles. . . . In Riegl's analysis the main thing, bodily substance and verticality . . . eluded him" (1905, pp. 16–17).

Riegl had recognized the great importance of the plane surfaces as the constituent element of the pyramid. His further conclusion that the significance of these planes lay in their intangibility can no longer be accepted.

It is part of our nature that every human product, no matter what it is, must be bound to its own time and place. It may, however, contain seeds capable of later development. These exist in astonishing number in the work of Riegl. What has changed is our approach to surfaces, volumes, and space.

Pyramids, planes, and volumes

The pyramids stand on the rim of the desert. Below them stretches the fertile
right valley, behind them a limitless waste of sand. Life and death, an exuberant fertility and an eternally sterile land, come together without compromise.

In one respect the pyramids are unique. No later period has ever attempted to make use of so subtle a simplicity to express its irrepressible urge to link human fate with eternity. It is this absolute simplicity and perfect precision that transforms the logic of numbers into enigma and mystery.

The enormous, highly polished triangular planes repel any disturbance of the dead. The pyramids were undisturbable symbols, seats of the god-kings. Their huge, immaculate surfaces formed a mirror for the ceaselessly changing atmosphere. They displayed what the eye only partially perceives. They reflected all that passes between earth and sky—all the infinite, delicate changes of the mov-

317. VOLUMES IN SPACE: *The cosmic unity between pyramid, sky, and the limitless desert. From Lepsius*

ing hours. They gather the light even today, though their surfaces are now rough and granular. The play of ever-changing light imbues them with eternal motion. Their color and form passes through every phase: almost complete dematerialization in the midday glare, enormous weightiness in the evening shadows, a black triangular plane soaring vertically upward in the starlit night.

257 col
256 col

An unbiased eye that had never beheld a pyramid—Riegl's observer, say—would not automatically complete its volume. The plane surfaces acquire an existence of their own. In reality, only one or at most two of the triangles can be perceived at one time. Through the changing light they somehow become detached from the solid body they form.

The Ka was, in a somewhat similar manner, thought to be independent of man. It was part of him and yet simultaneously apart. It could enter and leave his body. The upward-soaring triangles of the pyramid seem to possess this same independent entity.

We have begun to understand this phenomenon. The sculptor Brancusi, explaining the ability to be simultaneously part of a body and yet separate from it, has said: "I think a true form ought to suggest infinity. The surfaces ought to look as though they went on forever, as though they proceeded out from the mass into some perfect and complete existence" (*Time*, Nov. 14, 1955, p. 88).

At the peak of the pyramid age, pyramids were seldom in isolation. The three right great structures at Giza are organized in a somewhat diagonal association. Their sloping surfaces operate in changing relationships and seem to release themselves from the volumes to which they are tied. The drama of this interplay only becomes apparent when one stands before the early pyramid of Medum, or Zo- 251 col ser's step pyramid, long enough for their influence to be appreciated. These pyramids stand isolated in grandiose relationship to the cosmos. But the archi- 507 tectonic power of a pyramid achieves its climax when there is an interplay of volumes.

What happens is much the same as what we earlier described, in reference to Rockefeller Center, New York, 1931–37, as the "grand play of volumes and surfaces" (Giedion, 1954, p. 755), which is something quite different from the single viewpoint of the Renaissance. In Rockefeller Center the dense concentration of the slablike skyscrapers makes it easier to see how their radiating planes appear to detach themselves from the central core. But what happens is in principle the same.

Like the individual planes, the effect of the volumes is not limited to their actual physical limits. They also exert a certain radiation. Even though it cannot be directly measured, it exists like the area of an electromagnetic field. Our eyes record it and it is apparent in our psychic reaction. This occurrence is again recognized today, since the interplay of gigantic high-rise apartment houses has become a daily experience.

The notion of architecture has been extended. The conception of architecture as synonymous with the creation of interior space has seemed too narrow and has been overthrown. The same radiation that gives a hollowed-out interior space its psychic form (its *Gestalt*) emanates also from volumes. The difference is that these do not radiate inward toward an interior space, but stream out into the cosmos.

Its close bond to the eternal presence of the cosmic is the finest bequest of Egyptian architecture. It is the most complete expression of the interconnection of cosmic and human: of eternal presence and temporal change.

The question whether the pyramids are architecture or sculpture answers it-

318. THE THREE PYRAMIDS OF GIZA: *"L'architecture étant le jeu savant, correct et magnifique, des volumes sous la lumière"* (*Le Corbusier*)

self. Indeed, the very question is rooted in the conception of architecture as synonymous with interior space. What architecture means today, Le Corbusier expressed clearly in 1923: "Architecture being the masterly, correct, and magnificent play of masses brought together in light, the task of the architect is to vitalize the surfaces that clothe these masses" and to use the surfaces to accentuate and amplify forms (tr. 1927, p. 37).

The first architectonic space conception is an architecture of volumes in space.

Interior space and lighting

Many elements of the ground plans of the great temples of the New Kingdom
320 ff already existed in germinal form in the pyramid temples of the Fourth Dynasty. The first of the offering and mortuary temples, immediately alongside the pyramid, served much the same purposes as the later versions. Rites were performed and sacrifices offered in the first for the dead king, in the others to honor Amon.

258 col The glory of the New Kingdom, the hypostyle halls of the great temples, had
250 col a forerunner in Zoser's long entrance hall, though this was not then developed further. Riegl recognized the unique feature of these covered halls. He saw that they were not interior spaces in the later accepted sense at all. No attempt was
right made to form a space. They were filled with a forest of columns. Their dimensions and their limits could not be accurately appreciated: "The visual effect of the distant walls, ceiling, and floor would have created an impression of space which would certainly have caused the Egyptians the utmost discomfort. Thus the halls were thickly filled with a forest of close-standing supporting columns, so that all planes which could have operated as space-forming elements were dissected and split up. As a result one's impression of the space, despite its con-
389 siderable size, was greatly diminished, and the eye was held by impressions of the individual columns" (1927, p. 37).

Spatially, the relief-covered walls are nonexistent. The rows of columns press so closely against them as to split up their surfaces. It is scarcely possible for the eye of the camera to find a position from which to photograph the reliefs. This is why Riegl speaks of Egypt's "space phobia" (ibid.).

Hypostyles did not form an enclosed space for a congregation of believers, like that of a Christian basilica. They were only entered by the highest in the land and were not resting places even when used for the celebration of important
396 ff rites. They were places of passage for the wandering of the god from shrine to shrine, and were dimly lit.

The attitude of the Egyptians toward interior space can be inferred from their handling of columns and lighting.

Columns

The great hypostyle halls with their forests of papyrus-columns, blue-painted ceilings, and dim lighting were not conceived as enclosed interior spaces. This is everywhere apparent from their tectonic treatment. The papyrus-columns, which
247 col, 259 col terminate in buds or flowers, do not represent a supporting scaffolding, as col-

319. AVERSION TO INTERIOR SPACE—GREAT HYPOSTYLE, KARNAK: *Columns of the side aisles of the great hypostyle, whose 134 colossal papyrus columns fill the void of the hall so that no interior space can develop. This was strengthened by offsetting the column centers in alternate rows*

320. WINDOWS FILLED WITH STONE GRILLES: *In the throne room of King Merenptah the light filtered through small slits, as in the great hypostyle at Karnak. Memphis, Nineteenth Dynasty*

umns do in Greece. Schäfer once remarked that "the Egyptian columns appear as freely growing plants, without indicating that their heads act as supports. . . . The Egyptians, like the Babylonians, considered the temple ceiling as a heavenly vault. In Egypt, even Zoser's artists painted the hall ceilings with stars" (1929, p. 31).

It is also significant that the architrave was never developed further in Egypt. Its form never changed with that of the columns (Jéquier, 1924, p. 168). Columns and beams stand in an architectonic relation as supports and loads. But an aesthetic stress was never laid upon such a relation, as in Greece, where the columns openly support the temple, whose pitched roof and ornamentation strengthen its significance as the house of God.

right

In the imagination of the Egyptians the flat-roofed hypostyle appeared open to the sky even when covered over.

Lighting

The way light is directed and modulated is of the utmost consequence for a space conception, for it is light and space-limiting forms that give flesh and bones to an architectural complex.

From Zoser's mortuary complex to the great Ptolemaic temple at Edfu, from the beginning to the end, the Egyptians felt the need of a dimly lit, half-dark space. In the first authentically constructed interior space, Zoser's entrance hall, the windows of the side walls consisted of small slits, so that only a small amount

279

321. PAPYRUS-BUNDLE COLUMNS, LUXOR: *The Egyptian column lays no emphasis upon the relations of load and support, but appears to stand freely in space. West side of court of temple of Luxor*

of light should penetrate. In Chephren's three-aisled valley temple, the only
326 temple from the Fourth Dynasty whose lighting can be securely established, the
sun's rays also enter through narrow horizontal slits near the ceiling. Similarly,
370 in Tuthmosis III's festival hall at Karnak the aisle was lit only from high-placed
openings, even though these were somewhat larger.

The principle of the half-dark space was also retained in the great hypostyles.
259 col In the hypostyle of Karnak, the aisle was lit from high, inset stone grilles with
narrow vertical slits which let in the light as through a filter. There were also
small holes in the ceiling blocks. The throne room of Merenptah, of the Nine-
510 teenth Dynasty, in Memphis, had the same dim illumination as in earlier times.

Vaulting in the archaic civilizations

Domes and barrel vaults might easily go unmentioned here, since they played no part in the monumental architecture of the first high civilizations. Nor did they play any in Greece. The intersecting opposition of verticals and horizontals was common to all these civilizations that laid little value on interior space.

At the same time, vaults and domes were employed from the very beginning of architecture, and the oldest pointed arch, found in Eridu, goes back to the fourth millennium.

A hut of reeds or a house of clay becomes more complicated when built with
rectangular, vertical walls. Reed mats or a mixture of mats and clay take on the
374 form of a curved vault far more readily than that of a flat roof at right angles to
the walls. That this was not alone due to the greater ease of construction is
shown by various hieroglyphs from the First Dynasty that depict a sanctuary in
the shape of an animal with horns and tail. "The covering in the shape of an animal's back, becomes an irregular vault" (Badawy, 1954, p. 63).

The great buildings of Memphis must have presented a tremendous difference
from these primitive huts, yet they too were roofed with wood, having walls of
288 brick and matting. The stone façades of Zoser's complex at Saqqara give some
right notion of their appearance, ending as they do in a shallow curve stressed by a
molding. These Zoser buildings terminate the earliest development. By the time
of the Fourth Dynasty they had become obsolete and given place to a more direct
expression of verticals and horizontals.

Even today, reed buildings of considerable size are erected in Mesopotamia,
120 like those on the Sumerian relief of the sacred stables of the goddess Inanna. A
similar building appears upon a fragment of ebonite as a primitive Egyptian

322. CURVED PARAPET OF SHRINE: *Fragments of the curved parapet surmounting one of the shrines in the Heb-Sed court of Zoser's mortuary complex, Saqqara*

shrine of the First Dynasty. Almost all basic forms of vaulting—dome, barrel vault, and arch—are found here. This diminutive temple was the abode of a god or of a sacred animal. In Mesopotamia, even in the second half of the third millennium, a temple was rebuilt with barrel vaulting and ventilation inlets (Tell Asmar). 204

In Egypt also there are evidences of early vaulting. At the opening of our present century, J. Garstang found tombs in Upper Egypt with curved arches and barrel vaults, incorporating both the corbel vault and the segmented arch (1904, pl. 14). It is typical of the stagnant vault construction of Egypt that the Nineteenth Dynasty vaults of the Ramesseum, about twelve hundred years later, were still constructed just as primitively from a double arch. 515

Recently, in Saqqara North, Emery found that both vaulting methods—the corbeled and the segmental—existed in very modest dimensions in the late First

Dynasty. The subsidiary burial of a sacrificed servant (Tomb 3500) was roofed
273 "with a leaning-barrel vault of brick resting on a ledge. . . . With the roofing of the grave a high, vaulted superstructure was raised above it" (1958, III, p. 102).

Even more interesting is the large barrel vault that Emery found connected with the tomb of Horus Aha (Tomb 3357) in the so-called model estate: "One of the most extraordinary features is the long barrel vault running down the full length of the avenue between the two buildings. . . . Here, for the first time, we have evidence of the actual appearance of monumental buildings of the First Dynasty that is not based on . . . conjectural reconstruction (1954, II, p. 171).

The typical Egyptian vault, like the Sumerian, was the corbel vault in which the courses of bricks or stones project inward as they are laid on top of one an-
305 other. These are found on a grand scale in the tomb chamber of the Medum pyra-
308 mid, and rise to an impressive height in the bent pyramid at Dahshur, which
318 contains a series of rectangular vaults. In the Grand Gallery of the Cheops pyramid, where the walls narrow to the summit, the corbel vault attains its most monumental form. Jéquier remarked correctly: "This is not a vault but a roof greatly extended in height" (1924, p. 311).

The avoidance of curved and circular forms in such monumental structures was almost inevitable in the period of the supremacy of the vertical. It is decisive that these vaulted tombs were eternally inaccessible and in perpetual darkness.

Circular domes surmounting the tomb chambers can be found in quantity in the Middle Kingdom. A single example, the tomb of Seneb at Giza, is known from the Fourth Dynasty.

Vaults remained unimportant in the New Kingdom. They were never visible from outside. They were chthonic images: caverns in the heart of the earth. The cow Hathor, the mother-goddess and protector of the dead, steps out from her
81 barrel vault on a relief in the chapel of Amenhotep III.

Hatshepsut also built a Hathor chapel into the rock. The vault that closed it was still a corbel vault, though the edges of the individual projecting blocks are
261 col smoothed off to form an arch: "By diminishing those parts which project, equilibrium is assured while scarcely anything is taken from strength" (Choisy, 1904, p. 68). The same principle was later employed in the temple of Sety I at Abydos to construct vaults over seven chapels for various gods and the deified king. These adjacent barrel-vaulted chapels were also in darkness. The small square openings in the vault—in the opinion of Amice Calverley—were only for ventilation.

323. MUD-BRICK BARREL VAULTS OF WAREHOUSES: *The Ramesseum, mortuary temple of Ramesses II. Thebes, Nineteenth Dynasty, thirteenth century* B.C.

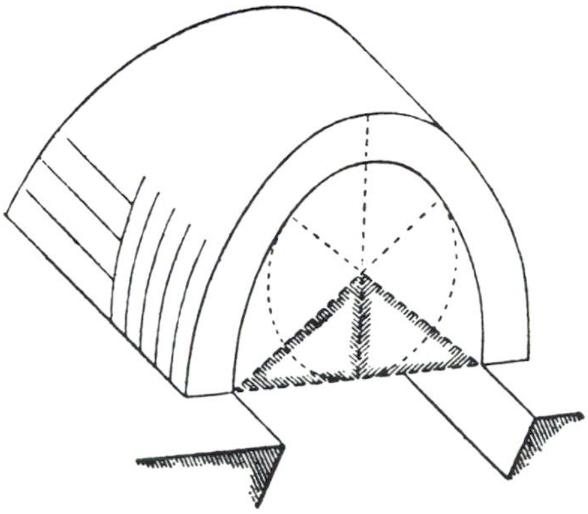

324. CONSTRUCTION OF RAMESSEUM BARREL VAULTS: *Neither the material used nor the methods of construction had changed throughout fifteen hundred years. Drawing by Choisy*

325. BARREL VAULTS AS SUBSTRUCTURE IN BABYLON: *Barrel vaults served as an invisible foundation for the Hanging Gardens of Semiramis. Sixth century* B.C.

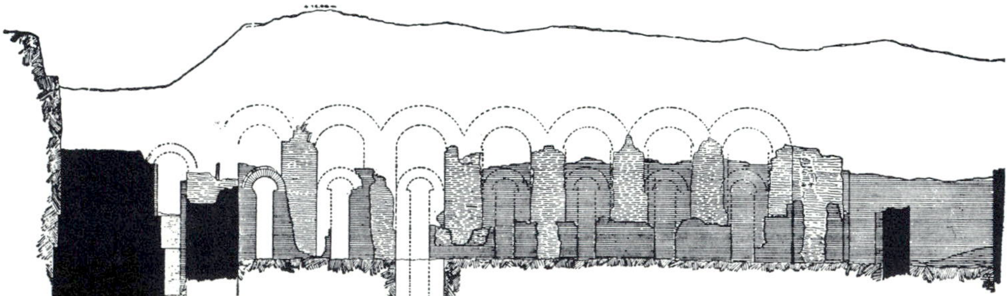

326. HANGING GARDENS OF BABYLON: *Reconstruction. From Koldewey*

In daily life the vault served as the most convenient form of shelter. The storage chambers of the Ramesseum in Thebes are among the best preserved. Their vaulting consists of sloping superimposed brick courses, each course strengthened by those lying above it. Choisy has shown this very clearly. This construction is still primitive and reminds one in principle of the double vaults and "leaning-barrel vaults" of the First Dynasty, found by Emery. **left**

Lack of interest in the external appearance of vaults was common to all the archaic cultures. The two tiers of seven barrel vaults that supported the legendary Hanging Gardens of Babylon had a timid span of ten to eleven feet. Koldewey, the excavator of Babylon, commented that the vaulting construction "shows clear signs of tentative and inexperienced work" (1913; tr. Johns, 1914, p. 94). This was in the sixth century B.C., at the end of the whole development. **left**

This means that vaulting never rose to symbolic heights, either in Egypt or Mesopotamia. It was never externally stressed or even made visible. It remained underground, unlit. Space and light belong together. Without light space disappears. For the dome to arrive at its renowned position in architecture, light had to be brought into the interior and stress laid upon the external appearance of its monumental form. For this a completely different space conception was necessary.

The cosmic orientation of the inner court

Inner courts, unroofed enclosures within a building, can have various meanings. In a monastery of the Middle Ages, the cloister was for meditation and contemplation. The courtyard of a Gothic castle was the only open space in which a man could feel safe from attack. The courtyards of Renaissance palaces retained the tradition of building around an open space, but gave it a festive character.

The enormous apartment-house projects of the nineteenth century, wishing to make maximum use of the site, created a number of interior courts degraded to the unworthy purpose of serving as light-wells. This was the lowest ebb of a long development.

The inner court was created in Egypt, but its significance was quite different from that of later times. From the beginning to the end, the Egyptian inner court was oriented toward the cosmos.

The standard form of the pyramid, the discovery of the beauty of the human body—particularly the female body—and the formation of the inner court all took place during the rise of the Fourth Dynasty.

The First Architectural Space Conception

The large courts of Zoser's complex are not inner courts in an exact sense.
274 They are plazas surrounded by different buildings. The inner court itself first
328, 330 appears in the three mortuary temples of Cheops, Chephren, and Mycerinus.
These were immediately adjacent to the pyramids. Reconstructions made by Lauer and Ricke from the scanty remnants of these three temples throw light upon their organization and meaning.

The mortuary and veneration temple, approached only by the long causeway, signified the place of transition before the dead king took on his existence as a god: "The door to the veneration temple opened the way to the world of stars in which the soul of the king appeared in the form of a heavenly deity" (Schott, 1950, p. 199). This was symbolically expressed in architectural terms when the twilit causeway, after passing through some intervening chambers, opened into the sun-filled inner court—the only place in the whole complex which was fully open to the sky and into which light could pour unhindered. It was framed by square columns between which—in Chephren's temple—were seated statues of the king. These courts were forerunners of the great courts of the Theban temples where, more than a millennium later, they achieved their monumental form.

The temples of the New Kingdom had two orientations. Their horizontal orientation pointed out that existence is an eternal wandering, both in life and death. Each part of the temple was a place of passage, except for the innermost
before 355 sanctuary in which dwelt the god himself, and even there the sacred ship lay
alongside the cella, ready to carry the small wooden statue from one temple to another.

Their vertical orientation was as directly related to the cosmos in the covered hypostyle halls as in the open courts. The architecture of the rectangular court
393 f of Amenhotep III's temple at Luxor shows this well. Before the sanctuary stands
a roofed hypostyle with four thickly arrayed rows of papyrus-columns. The fourth wall is absent, so that the hypostyle opens directly upon the wide inner court surrounded by identical columns of rose granite, creating a unity of unusual power.

The ceilings of both the hypostyle and the columned porticoes have the same symbolic treatment. The columns are like plants growing up to the blue sky, with no desire for expression as bearing members. This remains the case wherever temples were built, up till the end of the Ptolemaic period and into Roman times.

Earlier than this, at the beginning of the New Kingdom, Senmut achieved a daring individual solution, heightening to the utmost this upward striving of the

327. THE COSMIC INNER COURT: *Northwest corner of second terrace of Hatshepsut's mortuary temple; the peristyle surmounted by towering rock cliffs*

Egyptian sanctuary. Upon the second, main terrace of Hatshepsut's mortuary
417, 431 temple at Deir el Bahari he erected two wings of columns: the west wing, divided
by the wide ramp that leads up to the third terrace, and the uncompleted north
519 wing whose single row of columns forms part of the soaring cliff face. Between
them an asymmetric transformation of the earlier inner court lies open to an uninterrupted view over the valley of the Nile and the great arena of cliffs.

The third and uppermost terrace was protected by a high wall. The visitor was
led slowly upward to the entrance into an enclosed court surrounded by columns,
429 with shrines for Amon, Tuthmosis I, and Hatshepsut cut deep into the rock face.
335 This court with its sun altar is nearer to the sun sanctuary of Ne-user-ra than to
328 the inner courts of the Fourth Dynasty. The upward thrust has been pushed to
its limit by a great architect who had the courage to bind unhesitatingly together
the formed and the unformed by coming dangerously near to the lofty organ-pipe
towers of the rock bastions.

From the close relation of abstract architectural forms and undisturbed nature comes a unity from apparently contradictory forces, as everywhere in Egyptian religion. "No Greek temple," commented Ricke, "which sought to express its active organic monumentality by contrasting its tense form with an inorganic rock wall, would be able to achieve monumentality in such a setting, no matter how large and noble its form. The form of the Egyptian temple of Hatshepsut seems to have crystallized out of the rock arena" (1944, p. 17).

The architectural wisdom of the entire complex is not limited to its visible form. Like a true poem, its strength does not lie only in an accumulation of sonorous words, but rather in the inexplicable manner in which they become part of an inner meaning. In the drive for a higher aspiration, the genius of this architect was kindled to an amalgamation of form and site. This rare achievement is not limited to certain periods. It is always one of the highest aims of architecture.

With this we reach the end of the periods that have directly concerned us here, but the problem of constancy and change does not end, and it seems inorganic to end abruptly as though these periods stood in isolation. A few fragmentary remarks therefore follow, regarding later developments.

It is the nature of an architectural space conception to encompass a wide time span which is itself made up of a number of very different periods. An architectural space conception has a far more general nature than painting or sculpture. The architecture of Egypt and Greece shares the same space conception, but the sculpture of Egypt and Greece is fundamentally different. On the other hand, an architectural space conception embraces far greater differences within its span than the other arts do. Various strongly contrasting periods have the same basic approach to architectonic space. In this context, both the pyramids of Giza and the Acropolis at Athens express a similar relation to inner and outer space. Neither the Greeks nor the Egyptians ever developed interior space with the same intensity they expended on relating their architecture to the cosmos.

Since the beginning of architecture there have been only two basic space conceptions, as Riegl and Schmarsow recognized. A third, which embraces characteristics of both and yet, in certain ways, proceeds further than either, is now in the making.

The first stage embraced both the archaic high civilizations and also the Greek development. Sculptural objects—volumes—were placed in limitless space.

The second stage of architectural development opened in the midst of the Roman period. Interior space, and with it the whole vaulting problem, became the highest aim of architecture. In the space conception of this second stage, the notion of architectural space was almost identical with the notion of hollowed-out interior space. From late antiquity on, hollowed-out space—circumscribed interior space—was the finest achievement of the art of building.

The greatest skills have been devoted to modeling interior space, and in methods of vaulting, imagination has had its greatest freedom of expression. Thus the various means of vaulting interior space indicate the evolution of this stage of architecture.

The Roman Pantheon, with its partial forerunners, marks the beginning. The second space conception encompasses the period between the building of the great Roman vaults, such as the thermae, and the end of the eighteenth century.

A third stage of architectural development was foreshadowed at the beginning of the nineteenth century. This century acted as a transition period. Apparently all stylistic forms were indiscriminately employed, together with means of shaping interior space borrowed from every period (as Paul Frankl recognized). But in the more anonymous structures of this century there lie indications and hints that could only acquire artistic content and life with the opening of the third space conception at the beginning of our century.

The third space conception contains elements of both the first and second stages. It has discovered again the emanating properties of volumes in space, without relinquishing the modeling of interior space. The integration of these two basic elements gives rise to new ones that betoken a third stage of development.

The first architectural space conception

The first architectural space conception can be briefly summarized:

The primeval space conception, with its freedom of all directions, and the
1:514 ff absolute absence of compromise with which it placed objects in space with no regard to their limits or to their relation with their neighbors, persisted throughout prehistoric times.

Shortly before the emergence of the historic period, a fundamental revolution occurred in the realm of vision. Instead of an unlimited number of directions, relations were restricted to one: to the vertical, with its necessary complement
Part XI the horizontal. The beginning of architecture coincides with the rise to supremacy of the vertical, the right angle, the axis, and symmetry. The disappearance of the freedom of all directions involved the disappearance of the freedom of all surfaces. The smooth, shadowless plane surface emerged, and with it a totally new beauty.

The first architectural space conception was concerned with the emanating power of volumes, their relations with one another, and their interaction. This binds the Egyptian and Greek developments together. Both proceed outward from the volume, although the Greek temple, with its shadow-creating porticoes and its elaborately plastic entablatures and pediments, is as different from the Egyptian temple as a flat Egyptian sunken relief is from a Greek statue fully modeled in the round.

The Egyptians also had temples with surrounding porticoes. Borchardt has examined these exhaustively, since they represent certain first steps toward the Greek temple. These Egyptian temples were either repositories for the solar boat or side chapels, and were rare.

The Greek temple stands like a crystal in space. Even so, the little regard paid to its interior space links it with its Egyptian forebears. Riegl once observed that both lacked those simplest means of communication between interior and exterior: windows (1927, p. 39).

The inner courts of Egyptain temples, with their upward orientation, were directly related to the cosmos. Simultaneously the temples were directed earthward. They were the umbilical cord that linked historic to primeval times. For the Egyptian, the darkness of night was not anxiety-ridden, as it is for us. The Egyptian was trustful of the darkness as the area traversed each night by his sun-god upon his eternal journeying. Darkness was where contact with supernatural forces could be established. In primeval times, the most sacred symbols had been hidden in the most inaccessible parts of caverns. It was not different in the Egyptian temple. The most holy place, with the little procession-statue of the deity, was a dark cella at the farthest end of the temple. Only the Pharaoh, the son of god, and the high priest had access to it.

The Ka statues of the dead kings stood in darkness, like that of King Zoser, waiting in his serdab on the north side of his pyramid. Those visiting him could 290 ff at most catch a gleam from his crystal eyes. The dark night of the pyramid passages, the enclosed temple sanctuary, and the twilit hypostyles express the same attitude. They explain the Egyptians' position toward interior space. Both Sumer and Egypt could construct interior space when the need arose, even vaulted space, but they had no interest in it.

Interior lighting, which became such a decisive form-giving medium in conjunction with the vaulting problems of the second space conception, was almost completely ignored by the Egyptians. Thus it is understandable that Riegl stresses the "space phobia" of the Egyptians, and that W. Worringer describes their architecture as "pre-spatial."

The second architectural space conception

There were vaults from the time architecture began, but their powers of heightening religious and secular experience were not known until Imperial Rome. These powers appeared in conjunction with the symbolic relating of interior space to the cosmos, much as the powers of volumes in space (ziggurats and pyramids) were manifested in the first high civilizations. Under the turning cupola of Nero's "golden house," which depicted the movement of the stars and is known only from coins (Boëthius, 1960), the emperor was identified with the creator of the universe. A similar scene appeared in the throne room of Domitian.

The dome of Hadrian's Pantheon at the beginning of the second century signalized the complete breakthrough of the second space conception. From that time on, the concept of architectural space was almost indistinguishable from the concept of hollowed-out interior space. Since Roman times, changing periods developed vaulting to express their different emotional needs. The simple barrel vaults and domes of Hadrian's villa in Tivoli led to the development of complicated interpenetrating spaces.

Byzantium continued the development. The golden dome of the Hagia Sophia with its band of light was conceived of as having been let down from heaven, the symbolic canopy of the cosmos.

In the perforated Ravenna churches of Justinian, great interest was taken in so modeling internal lighting as to strengthen the shaping of architectural space.

In the Gothic cathedrals this was carried further, with great sublety. The modeling of light was part of their meaning.

There is an immense difference between an Egyptian temple and a Greek temple, yet both fall within the first space conception: volumes standing in space, indifference toward interior space. In the second space conception, differences appeared in construction and in the significance of the modeling of interior space. The symbolic content of the domes of the Pantheon, the Hagia Sophia, the buildings of the Renaissance, and the late-baroque domes of Borromini, Guarini, and Balthasar Neumann is vastly different, yet all of these are encompassed within the great curve of the second space conception.

Both these stages are manifested by their space conceptions. But in developments that span such great periods of time, such different places and peoples, and such different systems of society, this can only take the form of a flowing, over-all envelopment, allowing for very different expressions of content. A many-sided evolution flows on from the pyramids to the Parthenon, though glaring contrasts spring to the eye: in scale, form, plan, and structure. The continuity of a definite space conception is uninterrupted. This is the bedrock upon which, unknown to their creators, the two great architectural epochs are founded.

Riegl's assumption that the supreme goal of architecture, since the Pantheon, has been design of interior space has not been questioned. At the same time, one cannot overlook the diversified modeling of exterior volumes by means of light and shade. This began during the first space conception, in the modeling of the Greek temples, and had its most dramatic development in the flying buttresses, perforated spires, and concave portals of the Gothic cathedrals. These were also volumes, but they acted like arrows directing the eye to the interior. Closer research into the relations of interior and exterior space in the second space conception, and into the rare cases when the whole building was treated as a sculpture, might show us some connecting links between the second and third conceptions.

The third architectural space conception

During the Renaissance, Western man was highly interested in exploring optical perspective in terms of the appearances and foreshortening of objects.

In our period, preoccupation with the appearance of objects has given way to another problem. Researches into the nature of space have replaced concentration upon physical appearance. It is probably not too much to say that every artist—certainly every sculptor—is concerned with the exploration of space and with ways of seizing hold of this intangible medium. Alberto Giacometti's striding figures create space all about them, having reduced their own forms to the utmost. The *surfaces dévelopables* of Antoine Pevsner simultaneously absorb and emanate light. Jacques Lipchitz made an early attack upon the solid volume, and dissolved his figures into fluidly curving lines of force that define simultaneously internal and external space. The dematerialization of the solid volume can now be observed in the work of almost all contemporary sculptors.

It was Alexander Archipenko who, in 1909 to 1915, indicated what was to prove the decisive direction for later sculptors. He brought out the plastic possibilities of dematerializing solid volumes. In his bronze figures solid and void, inside and outside, flow continuously into one another. He describes this as the modulation of space and the concave. His continuous intangible transitions from firmly molded convex volumes to concave interiors symbolize this modulation.

As a result of Archipenko's interaction of natural forms and abstraction, some of his statues appear to have only one breast. Though this is common in Egyptian reliefs, the reasons are quite different. The experience of two millenniums of molding interior space lie behind Archipenko's statues. His plastic interplay of interior and exterior space anticipated, to a certain degree, the architectural tendencies of the 1960's.

Volumes in space

Buildings, like sculptures, radiate their own spatial atmosphere, and we have again become sensitive to the emanating power of volumes in space. Today the architect has to deal with problems of relating the volumes of high and low structures. As at its first beginnings, architecture is again approaching sculpture and sculpture is approaching architecture. They are almost ready to be integrated.

Interior space

The modeling of interior space continues, but there is a profound change in the approach to its vaulting. During the second space conception, the ceiling was conceived as resting firmly upon its supporting walls. The focus of a vaulted ceiling was at its highest point, in the center. In the third space conception, the vaulted ceilings of some of its most advanced buildings seem to hover above the walls, as in Le Corbusier's pilgrimage chapel at Ronchamp (1955), where a concave ceiling rises up to the walls, the separation stressed by a narrow band of glass. In other words, the former place of maximum height is now the lowest. The curve, rising up to the walls, indicates that it does not stop there but expands farther into space, like a bird with outspread wings. Eggshell-thin concrete vaulting helps realize these new demands.

This is only one of the possibilities. Many others exist—we are only at the beginning. It is possible that our period may develop various kinds of vaulting. How the third space conception will proceed cannot be foreseen, but its general directions are apparent. The task of the historian is not merely to elucidate the past, but also to recognize the signs that lead into the future.

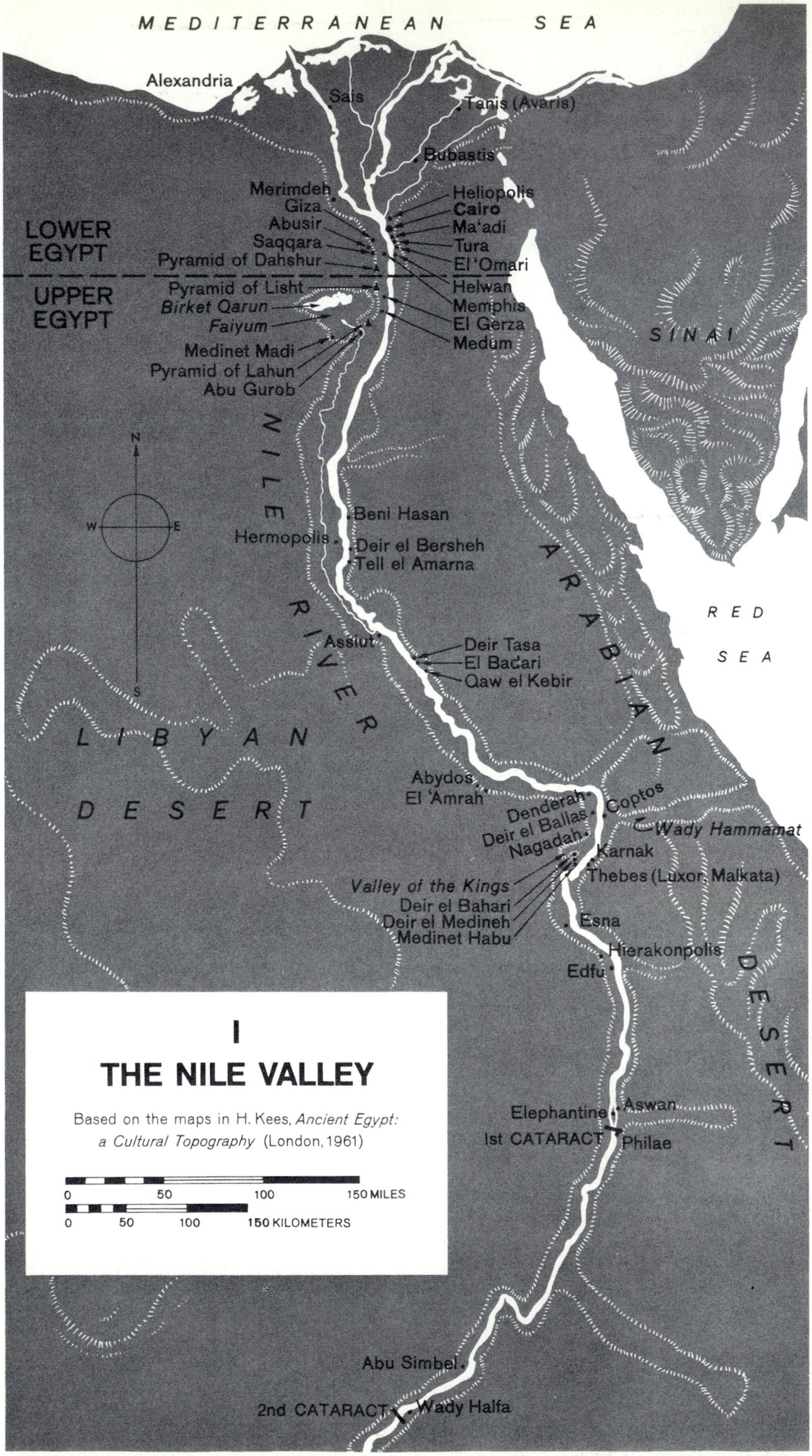

I
THE NILE VALLEY

Based on the maps in H. Kees, *Ancient Egypt: a Cultural Topography* (London, 1961)

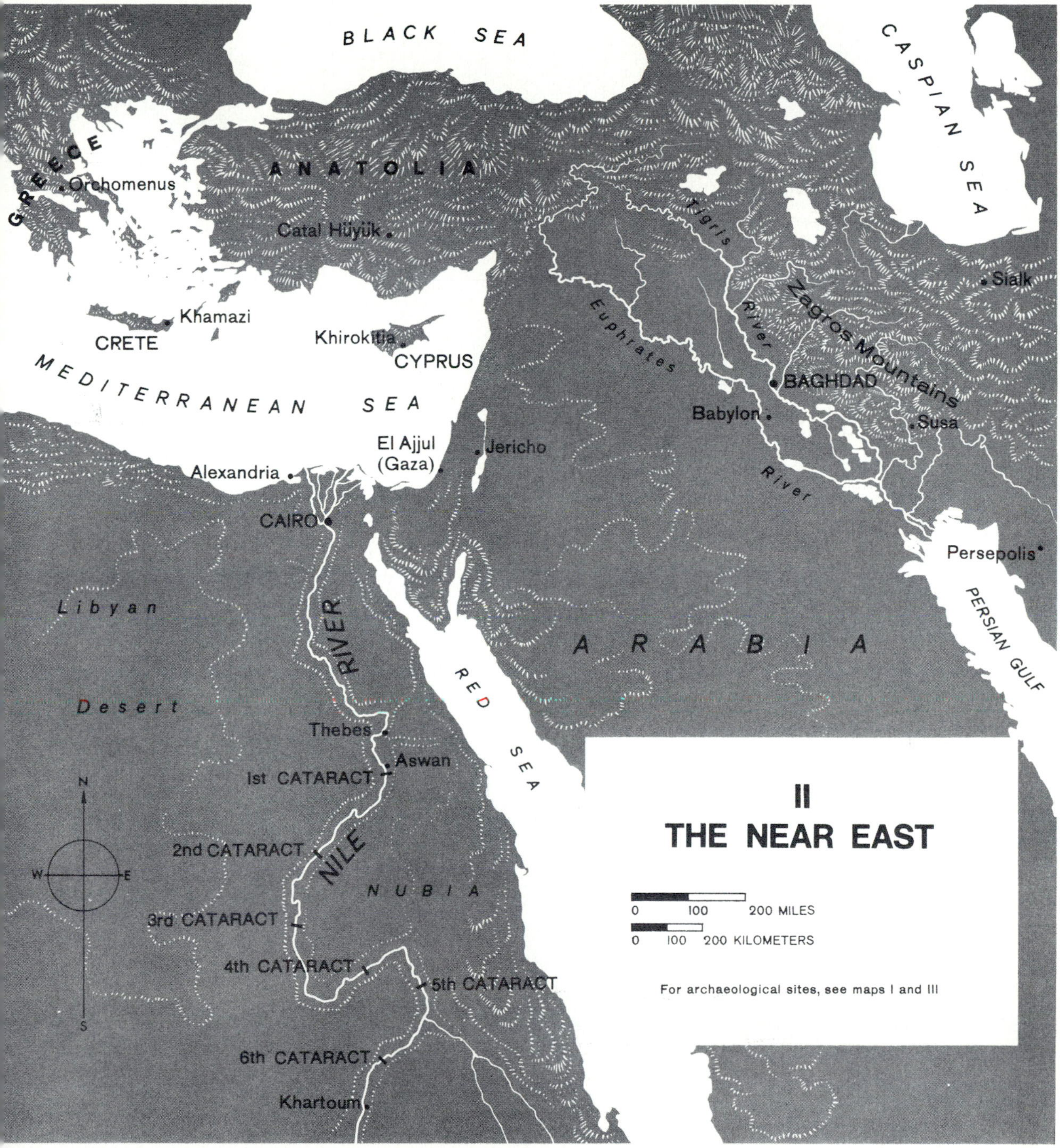
BLACK SEA
CASPIAN SEA
GREECE
Orchomenus
ANATOLIA
Catal Hüyük
Khamazi
CRETE
Khirokitia
CYPRUS
MEDITERRANEAN SEA
Tigris River
Euphrates River
Zagros Mountains
Sialk
BAGHDAD
Babylon
Susa
El Ajjul (Gaza)
Jericho
Alexandria
CAIRO
Persepolis
PERSIAN GULF
Libyan Desert
NILE RIVER
ARABIA
RED SEA
Thebes
Aswan
1st CATARACT
2nd CATARACT
NUBIA
3rd CATARACT
4th CATARACT
5th CATARACT
6th CATARACT
Khartoum
N
S
W
E
II
THE NEAR EAST
0 100 200 MILES
0 100 200 KILOMETERS
For archaeological sites, see maps I and III

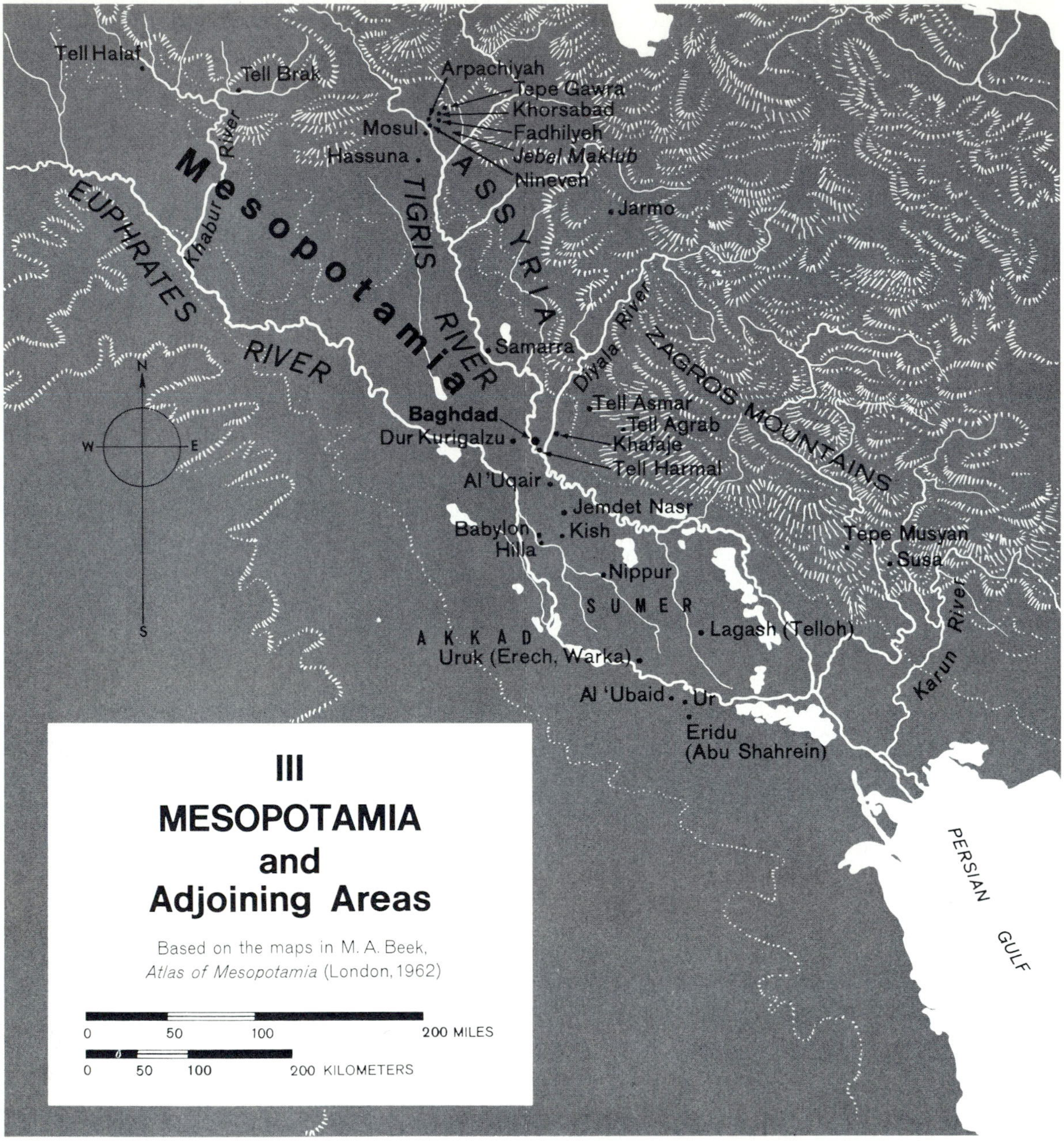

III
MESOPOTAMIA and Adjoining Areas

Based on the maps in M. A. Beek, *Atlas of Mesopotamia* (London, 1962)

LIST OF ILLUSTRATIONS

LIST OF WORKS CITED

INDEXES

LIST OF ILLUSTRATIONS

Abbreviated descriptions are given, with names of museums or other collections and sources of photographs (P) and drawings. Unattributed drawings were prepared under the author's supervision. The plates are from photographs by the author, as are the text illustrations credited "S. G." In the margins of the text, indicates an illustration on the page referred to.

PLATES

ILLUSTRATIONS IN THE TEXT

LIST OF WORKS CITED

Albright, W. F. 1946: *From the Stone Age to Christianity*. Baltimore. 2nd edn.

——— 1954: "A Survey of the Archeological Chronology of Palestine from Neolithic to Middle Bronze." In: *Relative Chronologies in Old World Archeology*, ed. R. Ehrich. Chicago.

Aldred, C. 1950: *Middle Kingdom Art in Ancient Egypt*. London.

Amer, M. See under Menghin, O.

Amiet, P. 1951: "La Ziggurat d'après les cylindres de l'époque dynastique archaïque," *Revue d'assyriologie et d'archéologie orientale* (Paris), XLV.

——— 1953: "Ziggurats et 'culte en hauteur' des origines à l'époque d'Akkad," *Revue d'assyriologie et d'archéologie orientale* (Paris), XLVII.

——— 1959: "Brève Communication," *Revue d'assyriologie et d'archéologie orientale* (Paris), LIII.

Andrae, W. 1939: "Vorderasien," *Handbuch der Archäologie* (Handbuch der Altertumswissenschaft, Abt. 6), text vol. I. Munich.

Arkell, A. J. 1955: "An Archaic Representation of Hathōr," *Journal of Egyptian Archaeology* (London), XLI.

Arnold, W. 1949: *Das Raumerlebnis in Naturwissenschaft und Erkenntnistheorie*. Nuremberg.

Badawy, A. H. 1937: *Der Gott Chnum*. Glückstadt, Hamburg, New York.

——— 1954: *A History of Egyptian Architecture*, I. Giza.

——— 1961: "The Harmonic System of Architectural Design in Ancient Egypt," *Deutsche Akademie der Wissenschaften zu Berlin: Mitteilungen des Instituts für Orientforschung*, VIII.

——— "Ancient Egyptian Design: a study in harmonic proportions" (Unpublished Mss.).

Baqir, T. 1944: "Excavations at 'Aqar Qūf, 1942–1943," *Iraq* (London): *Supplement*.

Barb, A. A. 1953: "Diva Matrix," *Journal of the Warburg and Courtauld Institutes* (London), XVI.

Barguet, P. 1953: (a) "L'Origine et la signification du contrepoids de Collier-Menat," (b) "La Structure du temple Ipet-Sout d'Amon à Karnak du Moyen Empire à Aménophis II," *Bulletin de l'Institut français d'archéologie orientale du Caire* (Cairo), LII.

Baumgärtel, E. 1955: *The Cultures of Prehistoric Egypt*, I. Revised edn., London.

Beckerath, J. von. 1961: "Bemerkungen zur chronologischen Tabelle über die pharaonische Zeit," *5000 Jahre ägyptische Kunst*. [Ausstellung in Villa Hügel, Essen.] Essen.

——— 1962: "The Date of the End of the Old Kingdom," *Journal of Near Eastern Studies* (Chicago), XXI.

Bégouën, H. and Breuil, H. 1934: "De quelques figures hybrides (mi-humaines, mi-animales) de la caverne des Trois Frères (Ariège)," *Revue anthropologique* (Paris), XLIV.

Bissing, F. W. von. 1949: "Baumeister und Bauten aus dem Beginn des Neuen Reichs," *Università degli studi di Pisa: Studi in memoria di Ippolito Rosellini*, I.

Bleeker, C. J. 1956: *Die Geburt eines Gottes*. Tr. from the Dutch by M. J. Freie. Leiden.

Boëthius, A. 1960: *The Golden House of*

Nero. (Jerome Lectures, Fifth Series.) Ann Arbor, Mich.

Boll, F. 1903: *Sphaera.* Leipzig.

Bonnet, H. 1952: *Reallexikon der ägyptischen Religionsgeschichte.* Berlin.

Borchardt, L. 1893: "Wie wurden die Böschungen der Pyramiden bestimmt?" *Zeitschrift für ägyptische Sprache und Alterthumskunde* (Leipzig), XXXI.

——— 1905: *Das Re-Heiligtum des Königs Ne-woser-re,* ed. F. W. von Bissing. I: *Der Bau.* Berlin.

——— 1907: "Das Grabdenkmal des Königs Ne-User-Rēc," *Wissenschaftliche Veröffentlichung der Deutschen Orient-Gesellschaft* (Leipzig), VII.

——— 1922: *Gegen die Zahlenmystik an der grossen Pyramide bei Gise.* Berlin.

——— 1928: *Die Entstehung der Pyramide.* (Beiträge zur ägyptischen Bauforschung und Altertumskunde, I, 2.) Berlin.

——— 1932: *Einiges zur dritten Bauperiode der grossen Pyramide bei Gise.* (Beiträge zur ägyptischen Bauforschung und Altertumskunde, I, 3.) Berlin.

——— 1938: *Ägyptische Tempel mit Umgang.* (Beiträge zur ägyptischen Bauforschung und Altertumskunde, II.) Cairo.

Bothmer, B.; Müller, H. W.; and De Meulenaere, H. 1960: *Egyptian Sculpture of the Late Period, 700 B.C.–A.D. 100.* [Catalogue of an exhibition at The Brooklyn Museum.] New York.

Braidwood, L. S. See under Braidwood, R. J.

Braidwood, R. J. 1957: *Prehistoric Men.* (Chicago Natural History Museum, Popular Series.) 3rd edn., Chicago.

———; Braidwood, L. S.; Tulane, E.; and Perkins, A. L. 1944: "New Chalcolithic Material of Samarran Type and its Implications," *Journal of Near Eastern Studies* (Chicago), III.

——— and Howe, B. 1960: "Prehistoric Investigations in Iraqi Kurdistan," *Studies in Ancient Oriental Civilization,* 31. Chicago.

Breuil, H. 1952: *Quatre cents siècles d'art pariétal; les cavernes ornées de l'âge du renne.* Montignac. Tr. by M. E. Boyle: *Four Hundred Centuries of Cave Art.* Montignac, 1952.

See also under Bégouën, H.

Brugsch, H. 1883: *Thesaurus Inscriptionum Aegyptiacarum,* I. Leipzig.

Brunner, H. 1936: "Die Anlagen der ägyptischen Felsgräber bis zum Mittleren Reich," *Ägyptologische Forschungen* (Glückstadt, Hamburg, New York), III.

Bull, L. S. 1923: "An Ancient Egyptian Astronomical Ceiling-Decoration," *Bulletin of the Metropolitan Museum of Art* (New York), XVIII.

Bulle, H. 1907: "Orchomenos," *Abhandlungen der philosophisch-philologischen Klasse der Königlich Bayerischen Akademie der Wissenschaften* (Munich), XXIV, 2.

Burckhardt, Jacob. 1868: *Force and Freedom: Reflections on History.* Tr. anon. New York, 1943.

Capart, J. and Werbrouck, M. 1930: *Memphis à l'ombre des Pyramides.* Brussels.

Caton-Thompson, G., and Gardner, E. W. 1934: *The Desert Fayum.* London. 2 vols. (text and plates).

Champdor, A. 1957: *Babylone.* Neuchâtel. Tr. and adapted by E. Coult: *Babylon.* London and New York, 1958.

Chevrier, H. 1936: "Plan d'ensemble de Karnak," *Annales du Service des Antiquités de l'Égypte* (Cairo), XXXVI.

——— See also under Lacau, P.

Choisy, A. 1899: *Histoire de l'architecture,* I. Paris.

——— 1904: *L'Art de bâtir chez les Égyptiens.* Paris.

Contenau, G. 1927, 1931: *Manuel d'archéologie orientale,* I and II. Paris.

——— 1947: *La Magie chez les Assyriens et les Babyloniens.* Paris.

COOK, T. A. 1914: *The Curves of Life.* New York.

COONEY, J. 1945: "Identification of Three Old Kingdom Sculptures," *Journal of Egyptian Archaeology* (London), XXXI.

COTT, P. B. 1935–36: "An Egyptian Sculpture of the Fourth Dynasty," *Worcester Art Museum Annual* (Worcester, Mass.), I.

CUMMINGS, E. E. 1963: *73 Poems.* New York.

DARESSY, G. See under GAILLARD, C.

DEBONO, F.: "Les Fouilles du Service des monuments de l'Égypte, saison 1950" (Unpublished Mss.).

DELOUGAZ, P. 1940: *The Temple Oval at Khafājah.* (Oriental Institute Publications, LIII.) Chicago.

——— and LLOYD, S. 1942: *Pre-Sargonid Temples in the Diyala Region.* (Oriental Institute Publications, LVIII.) Chicago.

Description de l'Égypte. 1809–22. Paris. 5 vols.

DE MEULENAERE, H. See under BOTHMER, B.; MÜLLER, H. W.

DHORME, E. 1949: *Les Religions de Babylonie et d'Assyrie.* 2nd edn., Paris.

DIKAIOS, P. 1953: *Khirokitia.* London, New York, Toronto.

DIMICK, J. 1958: "The Embalming House of the Apis Bulls," *Archaeology* (New York), XI.

DRIOTON, É. 1938: "Deux Cryptogrammes de Senenmont," *Annales du Service des antiquités de l'Égypte* (Cairo), XXXVIII.

——— 1941: Review of B. Grdseloff, "Das ägyptische Reinigungszelt," in *Annales du Service des antiquités de l'Égypte* (Cairo), XL, fasc. 2.

——— and VANDIER, J. 1938: *Les Peuples de l'Orient méditerranéen.* II: *L'Égypte.* Paris.

DUNHAM, D. 1950: *El Kurru, the Royal Cemeteries of Kush,* I. Cambridge, Mass.

——— 1956: "Building an Egyptian Pyramid," *Archaeology* (Cincinnati), IX.

DÜRER, A. 1525: *Underweysung der Messung mit dem Zirckel und Richtscheyt.* Nuremberg.

EDWARDS, I. E. S. 1961: *The Pyramids of Egypt.* Revised edn., London. (Also Pelican paperback, Harmondsworth and Baltimore, 1961. The London edn. is cited herein.)

ELIADE, M. 1949: *Traité d'histoire des religions.* Paris. Tr. R. Sheed: *Patterns in Comparative Religion.* New York, 1958.

EMERY, W. B. 1949, 1954, 1958: *Excavations at Sakkara: Great Tombs of the First Dynasty.* I, Cairo. II and III, London.

——— 1956: "An Egyptian Queen's Tomb of 5,000 Years Ago," *Illustrated London News,* June 2, 1956.

——— 1961: *Archaic Egypt.* Harmondsworth and Baltimore.

ENGELHARDT, W. J. VON. 1949: "Symmetrie," *Studium Generale* (Heidelberg and Berlin), II.

ERMAN, A. 1887: *Ägypten und ägyptisches Leben im Altertum.* Tübingen. Tr. H. M. Tirard: *Life in Ancient Egypt.* London and New York, 1894.

FAKHRY, A. 1959: *The Monuments of Sneferu at Dahshur,* I: *The Bent Pyramid.* Cairo.

FALKENSTEIN, A. 1941: *Topographie von Uruk.* (Ausgrabungen der Deutschen Forschungsgemeinschaft in Uruk-Warka, III.) Leipzig.

——— and SODEN, W. VON. 1953: *Sumerische und akkadische Hymnen und Gebete.* Zurich and Stuttgart.

FAULKNER, R. O. 1955: Review of L. Greven, "Der Ka in Theologie und Königskult der Ägypter des Alten Reiches," in *Journal of Egyptian Archaeology* (London), XLI.

FECHHEIMER, H. 1927: "Eine ägyptische Tierstatue aus der Ersten Dynastie," *Kunst und Künstler* (Berlin), XXV.

FIRTH, C. M. 1925: "Excavations of the Department of Antiquities at the Step Pyramid, Saqqara (1924–1925)," *Annales du Service des antiquités de l'Égypte* (Cairo), XXV.

——— and QUIBELL, J. E. 1935: *Excavations at Saqqara: The Step Pyramid.* With plans by J.-P. Lauer. Cairo. 2 vols. (text and plates).

FRANKFORT, H. 1933a: *The Cenotaph of Seti I at Abydos*, I. With chapters by A. de Buck and Battiscombe Gunn. (Thirty-ninth Memoir of the Egypt Exploration Society.) London and Antrim, N. H.

——— 1933b: "Tell Asmar, Khafaje and Khorsabad," *Oriental Institute Communications* (Chicago), XVI.

——— 1934: "Iraq Excavations of the Oriental Institute 1932/33," *Oriental Institute Communications* (Chicago), XVII.

——— 1939a: *Cylinder Seals.* London.

——— 1939b: *Sculpture of the Third Millennium* B.C. *from Tell Asmar and Khafājah.* (Oriental Institute Publications, XLIV.) Chicago.

——— 1948: *Kingship and the Gods.* Chicago.

——— 1954: *The Art and Architecture of the Ancient Orient.* (Pelican History of Art.) Harmondsworth and Baltimore.

FROBENIUS, LEO. 1933: *Kulturgeschichte Afrikas.* Zurich.

GAILLARD, C., and DARESSY, G. 1905: *Catalogue général des antiquités égyptiennes du Musée du Caire*, XXV: *La Faune momifiée de l'antique Égypte.* Cairo.

GARDINER, A. 1961: *Egypt of the Pharaohs.* Oxford.

GARDNER, E. W. See under CATON-THOMPSON, G.

GARNOT, J. S. F. 1948: *La Vie religieuse dans l'ancienne Égypte.* Paris.

GARSTANG, J. 1904: *Tombs of the Third Egyptian Dynasty.* Westminster.

GAUTHIER, H. 1931: "Les Fêtes du dieu Min," *Publications de l'Institut français d'archéologie orientale* (Cairo): *Recherches d'archéologie, de philologie et d'histoire*, II.

GAUTIER, J.-E., and LAMPRE, G. 1905: "Fouilles de Moussian," *Mémoires de la délégation en Perse*, VIII. Ed. J. de Morgan. Paris.

GHIRSHMAN, R. 1957: "The 'Tower of Babel' Now Completely Excavated," *Illustrated London News*, July 13, 1957.

GHYKA, M. 1927: *Esthétique des proportions dans la nature et dans les arts*, II. Paris.

GIEDION, S. 1954: *Space, Time and Architecture.* (The Charles Eliot Norton Lectures for 1938–1939.) 3rd edn., Cambridge, Mass.

——— 1962: *The Eternal Present*, I: *The Beginnings of Art.* (The A. W. Mellon Lectures in the Fine Arts, 1957.) New York (Bollingen Series XXXV:6) and London.

GOLOMSHTOK, E. 1938: "The Old Stone Age in European Russia," *Transactions of the American Philosophical Society* (Philadelphia), XXIX.

GONEIM, M. Z. 1956: *The Buried Pyramid.* London, New York, Toronto. (Published also as *The Lost Pyramid.* New York, 1956.)

GRAZIOSI, P. 1942: *L'Arte rupestre della Libia.* Naples. 2 vols. (text and plates).

GRDSELOFF, B. 1941: "Das ägyptische Reinigungszelt," *Études égyptiennes* (Cairo), IV, fasc. 1.

GREEN, F. W. See under QUIBELL, J. E.

GREVEN, L. 1952: "Der Ka in Theologie und Königskult der Ägypter des Alten Reiches," *Ägyptologische Forschungen* (Glückstadt, Hamburg, New York), XVII.

GUNN, B. 1926: "Inscriptions from the

Step Pyramid Site," *Annales du Service des antiquités de l'Égypte* (Cairo), XXVI.

HAINES, R. C. 1956: "Where a Goddess of Love and War was Worshipped 4000 Years Ago: The Temple of Inanna," *Illustrated London News*, August 18, 1956.

HALL, H. R. and WOOLLEY, C. L. 1927: *Ur Excavations*, I: *Al-'Ubaid*. (Joint Expedition of the British Museum and of the Museum of the University of Pennsylvania to Mesopotamia.) London.

HASSAN, S. 1953: *The Great Sphinx and Its Secrets.* (Excavations at Giza, VIII, 1936–37.) Cairo.

HAYES, W. C. 1953, 1959: *The Scepter of Egypt*, I and II. New York and Cambridge, Mass., resp.

——— 1962: "Egypt to End of Twentieth Dynasty," in *Chronology*. Cambridge. (The Cambridge Ancient History, revised vol. I, Ch. VI, pp. 3–23.)

HEINRICH, E. 1936: *Kleinfunde aus den archaischen Tempelschichten in Uruk.* (Ausgrabungen der Deutschen Forschungsgemeinschaft in Uruk-Warka, I.) Berlin.

HELCK, W. 1962: *Die Beziehungen Ägyptens zu Vorderasien im 3. und 2. Jahrtausend v. Chr.* (Ägyptologische Abhandlungen, V.) Wiesbaden.

HERMANN, A. 1959: *Altägyptische Liebesdichtung*. Wiesbaden.

HERODOTUS. Tr. J. E. Powell. (Oxford Library of Translations.) Oxford, 1949 (vol. I).

HERZFELD, E. 1930: *Die Ausgrabungen von Samarra*, V: *Die vorgeschichtlichen Töpfereien von Samarra.* Berlin.

HIRMER, M. See under LANGE, K.

HÖLSCHER, U. 1912: *Das Grabdenkmal des Königs Chephren.* (Veröffentlichungen der Ernst von Sieglin-Expedition, I.) Leipzig.

——— 1943: "Der Erste Pylon von Karnak," *Mitteilungen des Deutschen Instituts für Ägyptische Altertumskunde in Kairo* (Berlin), XII.

HOPFNER, T. 1913: "Der Tierkult der alten Ägypter nach den griechisch-römischen Berichten und den wichtigeren Denkmälern," *Denkschriften der Kaiserlichen Akademie der Wissenschaften in Wien, philosophisch-historische Klasse* (Vienna), LVII, 2.

HOWE, B. See under BRAIDWOOD, R. J.

HURRY, J. B. 1928: *Imhotep.* 2nd and revised edn., Oxford.

IVERSEN, E. 1955: *Canon and Proportions in Egyptian Art.* London.

JACOBSOHN, H. 1939: "Die dogmatische Stellung des Königs in der Theologie der alten Ägypter," *Ägyptologische Forschungen* (Glückstadt, Hamburg, New York), VIII.

JAMMER, M. 1954: *Concepts of Space.* Cambridge, Mass.

JANTZEN, H. 1938: "Über den kunstgeschichtlichen Raumbegriff," *Sitzungsberichte der Bayerischen Akademie der Wissenschaften, philosophisch-historische Abteilung* (Munich), 5.

JEANNERET, C. E. See LE CORBUSIER.

JÉQUIER, G. 1922: *L'Architecture et la décoration dans l'ancienne Égypte*, II: *Les Temples Ramessides et Saïtes de la XIXe à la XXXe dynastie.* With photographs by V. de Mestral-Combremont. Paris.

——— 1924: *Manuel d'archéologie égyptienne.* Paris.

——— 1946: *Considérations sur les religions égyptiennes.* Neuchâtel.

JOYCE, J. 1939: *Finnegans Wake.* New York.

JUNKER, H. 1933: "Die Ägypter," (*Geschichte der führenden Völker*), III: *Die Völker des antiken Orients.* Freiburg.

——— 1959: "Die gesellschaftliche Stellung der ägyptischen Künstler im Alten Reich," *Sitzungsberichte der Österreichischen Akademie der Wissenschaften, philosophisch-historische Klasse* (Vienna), CCXXXIII, 1.

——— 1940: "Vorbericht über die siebente Grabung . . . auf der vorgeschichtlichen Siedlung Merimde-Benisalâme vom 25. Januar bis 4. April 1939," *Akademie der Wissenschaften in Wien, philosophisch-historische Klasse* (Vienna and Leipzig): *Anzeiger*, LXXVII.

KAISER, W. 1956: "Zu den Sonnenheiligtümern der 5. Dynastie," *Mitteilungen des Deutschen Archäologischen Instituts, Abteilung Kairo* (Wiesbaden), XIV.

KANTOR, H. J. 1944: "The Final Phase of Predynastic Culture," *Journal of Near Eastern Studies* (Chicago), III.

——— 1952: "Further Evidence for Early Mesopotamian Relations with Egypt," *Journal of Near Eastern Studies* (Chicago), XI.

KASCHNITZ-WEINBERG, G. VON. 1944: *Die mittelmeerischen Grundlagen der antiken Kunst.* Frankfurt a. M.

KEES, H. 1941: "Der Götterglaube im alten Ägypten," *Mitteilungen der Vorderasiatisch-Ägyptischen Gesellschaft* (Leipzig), XLV.

———1956: *Totenglauben und Jenseitsvorstellungen der alten Ägypter.* 2nd edn., Berlin.

KENYON, K. M. 1957: *Digging Up Jericho.* London.

KIELLAND, E. C. 1955: *Geometry in Egyptian Art.* London.

KING, L. W. 1912: *Babylonian Boundary-Stones and Memorial-Tablets in the British Museum.* With an atlas of plates. London.

KOLDEWEY, R. 1913: *Das wieder erstehende Babylon.* Leipzig. Tr. Agnes S. Johns: *The Excavations at Babylon.* London, 1914.

KRAMER, S. N. 1956: *From the Tablets of Sumer.* Indian Hills, Colorado. (Published also as *History Begins at Sumer*, Anchor paperback, New York, 1959. The Colorado edn. is cited herein.)

——— 1959: "Sumerian Literature and the Bible," *Studia Biblica et Orientalia* (Rome), III.

LACAU, P. 1926: "Sur un des blocs de la reine provenant du IIIe pylône de Karnak," *Annales du Service des antiquités de l'Égypte* (Cairo), XXVI.

——— and CHEVRIER, H. 1956: *Une Chapelle de Sésostris Ier à Karnak.* Cairo.

LAMPRE, G. See under GAUTIER, J.-E.

LANGE, K. and HIRMER, M. 1955: *Ägypten.* Munich.

LANZONE, R. V. 1883: *Dizionario di mitologia egizia*, III. Turin.

LAUER, J. P. 1936: *Fouilles à Saqqarah: La Pyramide à degrés*, I, II. Cairo.

——— 1948: *Le Problème des pyramides d'Égypte.* Paris.

LE CORBUSIER (pseud. of C. E. Jeanneret). 1923: *Vers une Architecture.* 2nd edn., Paris. Tr. F. Etchells: *Towards a New Architecture.* New York, 1927.

——— 1953: *Œuvre complète, 1946–52.* Zurich.

LEEUW, G. VAN DER. 1933: *Phänomenologie der Religion.* Tübingen. Tr. J. E. Turner: *Religion in Essence and Manifestation; a Study in Phenomenology.* London, 1938.

LEGRAIN, G. 1916: "Le Logement et transport des barques sacrées et des statues des dieux dans quelques temples égyptiens," *Bulletin de l'Institut français d'archéologie orientale du Caire* (Cairo), XIII.

——— 1929: *Les Temples de Karnak.* Brussels.

LENZEN, H. 1939: "Ein Marmorkopf der Dschemdet Nasr–Zeit aus Uruk," *Zeitschrift für Assyriologie und vorderasiatische Archäologie* (Berlin), XLV (N.S. XI).

——— 1942: *Die Entwicklung der Zikurrat von ihren Anfängen bis zur Zeit der III. Dynastie von Ur.* (Ausgrabungen der Deutschen Forschungsgemeinschaft in Uruk-Warka, IV.) Leipzig.

——— 1949: "Die Tempel der Schicht Archaisch IV in Uruk," *Zeitschrift für*

Assyriologie und vorderasiatische Archäologie (Berlin), XLIX (N.S. XV).

LEPSIUS, K. R. 1849: *Denkmäler aus Ägypten und Äthiopien* [Vorläufige Nachricht über die Expedition, ihre Ergebnisse und deren Publikation]. Berlin.

——— 1849–59: Ibid. (plates). Berlin. 12 vols.

——— 1897–1913: Ibid. (text). Ed. E. Naville. Leipzig. 5 vols in 3.

——— 1884: *Die Längenmasse der Alten*. Berlin.

LLOYD, S. 1933: "Model of a Tell El-'Amarnah House," *Journal of Egyptian Archaeology* (London), XIX.

——— 1947: "The Oldest City: A Pre-Sumerian Temple Discovered at Prehistoric Eridu," *Illustrated London News*, May 31, 1947.

——— and SAFAR, F. 1943: "Tell Uqair," *Journal of Near Eastern Studies* (Chicago), II.

——— 1945: "Tell Hassuna," *Journal of Near Eastern Studies* (Chicago), IV.

——— See also under DELOUGAZ, P.

LUCAS, A. 1948: *Ancient Egyptian Materials and Industries*. 3rd and revised edn., London.

MACH, E. 1886: *Beiträge zur Analyse der Empfindungen*. Jena. Tr. C. M. Williams: *The Analysis of Sensations and the Relation of the Physical to the Psychical*. Chicago and London, 1914.

MACKAY, E. 1929: "A Sumerian Palace and the 'A' Cemetery at Kish, Mesopotamia," *Field Museum of Natural History* (Chicago): *Anthropology Memoirs*, I.

——— See also under PETRIE, W. M. F.

MALLOWAN, M. E. L. and ROSE, J. C. 1935: "Excavations at Tell Arpachiyah 1933," *Iraq* (London), II, 1.

MARIETTE, A. 1855: "Renseignements sur les soixante-quatre Apis trouvés dans les souterrains du Sérapéum," *Bulletin archéologique de l'Athénaeum français* (Paris).

——— 1856: *Choix de monuments et de dessins*. Paris.

——— 1857: *Le Sérapéum de Memphis découvert et décrit*, III. Paris.

MASPERO, G. 1913: *Egyptian Art*. Tr. E. Lee. London.

MASSOULARD, É. 1949: "Préhistoire et protohistoire d'Égypte," *Travaux et mémoires de l'Institut d'ethnologie* (Paris), LIII.

MELLAART, J. 1963: "Excavations at Çatal Hüyük, 1962, Second Preliminary Report," *Anatolian Studies: Journal of the British Institute of Archaeology at Ankara* (London), XIII.

MENGHIN, O. 1939: "Die ältere Steinzeit (Eiszeit)," *Handbuch der Archäologie* (Handbuch der Altertumswissenschaft, Abt. 6), text vol. I. Munich.

——— and AMER, M. 1932: *The Excavations of the Egyptian University in the Neolithic Site at Maadi. First Preliminary Report*. (Egyptian University Faculty of Arts Publications, 19.) Cairo.

MERCER, S. A. B. 1952: *The Pyramid Texts in Translation and Commentary*, I, III. New York, London, Toronto.

MEYER, E. 1925: *Die ältere Chronologie Babyloniens, Assyriens, und Ägyptens*. Stuttgart and Berlin.

——— 1957: *Earliest Intellectual Man's Idea of the Cosmos*. London.

MICHAELIS, A. 1883: "The Metrological Relief at Oxford," *Journal of Hellenic Studies* (London), IV.

MONTET, P. 1952: *Les Énigmes de Tanis*. Paris.

MOORTGAT, A. 1945: "Die Entstehung der sumerischen Hochkultur," *Der alte Orient* (Leipzig), XLIII.

——— See also under SCHARFF, A.

MORET, A. 1935–38: "L'Influence du décor solaire sur la pyramide," *L'Institut français d'archéologie orientale du Caire* (Cairo): *Mémoires*, LXVI, fasc. 2 (*Mélanges Maspero*).

MOREUX, T. 1923: *La Science mystérieuse des pharaons*. Paris.

MORGAN, J. DE. See under GAUTIER, J.-E., and LAMPRE, G.

MÖSSEL, E. 1926: *Die Proportion in Antike und Mittelalter*. Munich.

MÜLLER, H. W. 1940: "Die Felsengräber der Fürsten von Elephantine aus der Zeit des Mittleren Reiches," *Ägyptologische Forschungen* (Glückstadt, Hamburg, New York), IX.

——— See also under BOTHMER, B.

MURRAY, M. A. 1934: "Ritual Masking," *L'Institut français d'archéologie orientale du Caire* (Cairo): *Mémoires*, LXVI, fasc. 1 (*Mélanges Maspero*).

——— 1952: *The God of the Witches*. New edn., London.

NAVILLE, E. 1901: *The Temple of Deir El Bahari*. (Nineteenth Memoir of the Egypt Exploration Fund.) London. Part IV.

——— 1910: *The XIth Dynasty at Deir el-Bahari*. London. Part II.

NELSON, H. H. 1940: *Medinet Habu*, IV: *Festival Scenes of Ramses III*. (Oriental Institute Publications LI.) Chicago.

NEUGEBAUER, O. 1934: *Vorlesungen über Geschichte der antiken mathematischen Wissenschaften*, I: *Vorgriechische Mathematik*. (Die Grundlehren der mathematischen Wissenschaften, LXIII.) Berlin.

——— 1945: "The History of Ancient Astronomy: Problems and Methods," *Journal of Near Eastern Studies* (Chicago), IV.

———1951: *The Exact Sciences in Antiquity*. Copenhagen, Princeton, London.

NEUMANN, E. 1955: *The Great Mother; an analysis of the archetype*. Tr. from the German by R. Manheim. New York (Bollingen Series XLVII) and London.

NEWBERRY, P. E. 1893: *Beni Hasan*. (First Memoir of the Archaeological Survey of Egypt.) London. Part I.

——— 1924: "Egypt as a Field for Anthropological Research," *British Association for the Advancement of Science* (London): *Report of the Ninety-first Meeting, Liverpool, 1924*.

NILSSON, M. P. 1943: "The Rise of Astrology in the Hellenistic Age," *Lunds Astronomiska Observatorium* (Lund, Sweden): *Meddelande*, Ser. II, 111 (Historical Notes and Papers, 18).

OTTO, E. 1938: "Beiträge zur Geschichte der Stierkulte in Ägypten," *Untersuchungen zur Geschichte und Altertumskunde Ägyptens* (Leipzig), XIII.

PALLIS, S. A. 1956: *The Antiquity of Iraq*. Copenhagen.

PARKER, R. A. 1950: "Calendars of Ancient Egypt," *Studies in Ancient Oriental Civilization, 26*. Chicago.

PARROT, A. 1948: *Tello: vingt campagnes de fouilles (1877–1933)*. Paris.

——— 1953: *La Tour de Babel*. Revised edn., Neuchâtel. Tr. from the 1953 edn. by E. Hudson: *The Tower of Babel*. (Studies in Biblical Archaeology, II.) New York, 1955.

PAULI, R. 1941–42: "Die stereoskopische Reaktionszeit," *Zeitschrift für Psychologie* (Leipzig), CLI.

PERKINS, A. L. See under BRAIDWOOD, R. J.; BRAIDWOOD, L. S.; TULANE, E.

PETRIE, LADY (H. U.). 1927: *Egyptian Hieroglyphs of the First and Second Dynasties*. London.

PETRIE, W. M. F. 1892: *Medum*. London.

——— 1896: *Koptos*. London.

——— 1901: *The Royal Tombs of the Earliest Dynasties, 1901*. (Twenty-first Memoir of the Egypt Exploration Fund.) London. Part II.

——— 1903: *Abydos*. London. Part II.

——— with WAINWRIGHT, G. A., and MACKAY, E. 1912: *The Labyrinth, Gerzeh, and Mazghuneh*. (British School of Archaeology and Egyptian Research Account Publications, 21.) London.

PEYRONY, D. 1934: "La Ferrassie," *Préhistoire* (Paris), III.

PFEIFER, F. X. 1885: *Der goldene Schnitt und dessen Erscheinungsformen in Mathematik, Natur, und Kunst.* Augsburg.

PIANKOFF, A. 1957: *Mythological Papyri.* Tr. and with an introduction by A. Piankoff; ed., with a chapter on the symbolism, by N. Rambova. (Bollingen Series XL:3.) New York.

PLATO. *The Republic.* Tr. Paul Shorey. (Loeb Classical Library.) Cambridge, Mass., and London, 1946 printing. (vol. II.)

——— *Timaeus, Cleitophon, Critias, Menexenus, Epistles.* Tr. R. G. Bury. (Loeb Classical Library.) Cambridge, Mass., and London, 1952 printing. (vol. VII.)

POGO, A. 1930: "The Astronomical Ceiling-Decoration in the Tomb of Senmut," *Isis* (Bruges), XIV.

PRITCHARD, J. B., ed. 1950: *Ancient Near Eastern Texts Relating to the Old Testament.* Princeton.

QUIBELL, J. E. and GREEN, F. W. 1902: *Hierakonpolis.* (Egyptian Research Account, Fifth Memoir.) London. Part II.

——— See also under FIRTH, C. M.

RADCLIFFE-BROWN, A. R. 1952: *Structure and Function in Primitive Society.* London.

RAVN, O. E. 1939: *Herodots Beskrivelse af Babylon.* Copenhagen. Tr. M. Tovborg-Jensen: *Herodotus' Description of Babylon.* Copenhagen, 1942.

REISNER, G. A. 1931: *Mycerinus: the temples of the third pyramid at Giza.* Cambridge, Mass.

——— 1936: *The Development of the Egyptian Tomb Down to the Accession of Cheops.* Cambridge, Mass.

RICKE, H. 1944: *Bemerkungen zur ägyptischen Baukunst des Alten Reichs,* part I. (Beiträge zur ägyptischen Bauforschung und Altertumskunde, IV.) Cairo.

——— 1950: Ibid., part II. (Beiträge zur ägyptischen Bauforschung und Altertumskunde, V.) Cairo.

——— 1954: *Das Kamutef-Heiligtum Hatschepsuts und Thutmoses' III. in Karnak.* (Beiträge zur ägyptischen Bauforschung und Altertumskunde, III, 2.) Cairo.

RIEGL, A. 1927: *Spätrömische Kunst-Industrie.* Vienna.

ROBINSON, G. DE B. 1946: *The Foundations of Geometry.* (Mathematical Expositions, 1.) 2nd edn., Toronto.

RÖDER, G. 1928: "Eine neue Darstellung des gestirnten Himmels in Ägypten aus der Zeit um 1500 v. Chr.," *Das Weltall* (Berlin), XXVIII.

ROSCHER, W. H., ed. *Ausführliches Lexikon der griechischen und römischen Mythologie.* Leipzig, 1884–1937. 6 vols. in 9. Vol. 4, 1909–15.

ROSE, J. C. See under Mallowan, M. E. L.

RÖSSLER, H. 1952: "Kraftwesen der Pyramiden," *Technische Rundschau* (Bern), Oct. 17 and 24, 1952.

RUST, A. 1958: *Die jungpaläolithischen Zeltanlagen von Ahrensburg.* Neumünster.

SAAD, Z. Y. 1951: "Royal Excavations at Helwan (1945–1947)," *Supplément aux annales du Service des antiquités de l'Égypte* (Cairo), XIV.

SAFAR, F. See under LLOYD, S.

SCHÄFER, H. 1904: "Miscellen: Die Spitze der Pyramide König Amenemhets III," *Zeitschrift für ägyptische Sprache und Altertumskunde* (Leipzig), XLI.

——— 1919: *Von ägyptischer Kunst, besonders der Zeichenkunst,* I. Leipzig.

——— 1929: "Die Leistung der ägyptischen Kunst," *Der alte Orient* (Leipzig), XXVIII, 1/2.

SCHARFF, A. 1939: "Der alte Orient: Ägypten," *Handbuch der Archäologie*

(Handbuch der Altertumswissenschaft, Abt. 6), text vol. I. Munich.

——— 1941: "Die Frühkulturen Ägyptens und Mesopotamiens," *Der alte Orient* (Leipzig), XLI.

——— 1947: "Die Ausbreitung des Osiriskultes in der Frühzeit und während des Alten Reiches," *Sitzungsberichte der Bayerischen Akademie der Wissenschaften, philosophisch-historische Klasse* (Munich), 4.

——— and MOORTGAT, A. 1950: *Ägypten und Vorderasien im Altertum.* Munich.

SCHEFOLD, K. 1959: *Griechische Kunst als religiöses Phänomen.* Hamburg.

SCHIAPARELLI, E. 1884: "Il significato simbolico delle piramidi egiziane," *Atti della Reale Accademia dei Lincei CCLXXXI* (Rome): *Memorie della classe di scienze morali, storiche e filologische,* XII, 3rd series. (Also published as a separate reprint, Rome, Turin, Florence, 1884.)

SCHMARSOW, A. 1905: *Grundbegriffe der Kunstwissenschaft.* Leipzig and Berlin.

SCHMÖKEL, H. 1957: "Geschichte des alten Vorderasien," in: *Handbuch der Orientalistik,* ed. B. Spuler. II: *Keilschriftforschung und alte Geschichte Vorderasiens.* Leiden. Part III.

SCHOTT, S. 1950: *Bemerkungen zum ägyptischen Pyramidenkult.* (Beiträge zur ägyptischen Bauforschung und Altertumskunde, V.) Cairo.

SCHWABE, J. 1951: *Archetyp und Tierkreis.* Basel.

SCHWALLER DE LUBICZ, R. A. 1957: *Le Temple de l'homme apet du sud à Louqsor.* Paris. 3 vols.

SCHWEITZER, U. 1948: "Löwe und Sphinx im alten Ägypten," *Ägyptologische Forschungen* (Glückstadt und Hamburg), XV.

——— 1956: "Das Wesen des Ka, im Diesseits und Jenseits der alten Ägypter," *Ägyptologische Forschungen* (Glückstadt, Hamburg, New York), XIX.

SETHE, K. 1916: "Von Zahlen und Zahlworten bei den alten Ägyptern," *Schriften der Wissenschaftlichen Gesellschaft* (Strassburg), XXV.

——— 1928: "Altägyptische Vorstellungen vom Lauf der Sonne," *Sitzungsberichte der Preussischen Akademie der Wissenschaften, philosophisch-historische Klasse* (Berlin), XXII.

——— 1929: "Amun und die acht Urgötter von Hermopolis," *Abhandlungen der Preussischen Akademie der Wissenschaften, philosophisch-historische Klasse* (Berlin), 4.

——— 1930: "Urgeschichte und älteste Religion der Ägypter," *Abhandlungen für die Kunde des Morgenlandes* (Leipzig), XVIII, 4.

SIMPSON, W. K. 1957: "A Running of the Apis in the Reign of 'Aha and Passages in Manetho and Aelian," *Orientalia* (Rome), N.S. XXVI.

SMITH, W. S. 1949: *A History of Egyptian Sculpture and Painting in the Old Kingdom.* 2nd edn., London.

——— 1958: *The Art and Architecture of Ancient Egypt.* (Pelican History of Art.) Harmondsworth and Baltimore.

——— 1960: *Ancient Egypt as Represented in the Museum of Fine Arts, Boston.* 4th and revised edn., Boston.

SMYTH, C. P. 1867: *Life and Work at the Great Pyramid.* Edinburgh. 3 vols.

SODEN, W. VON. See under FALKENSTEIN, A.

SPEISER, A. 1927: *Die Theorie der Gruppen von endlicher Ordnung.* (Die Grundlehren der mathematischen Wissenschaften, V.) 2nd edn., Berlin.

SPEISER, E. A. 1935: *Excavations at Tepe Gawra,* I. (Joint Expedition of the Baghdad School, the University Museum, and Dropsie College to Mesopotamia.) Philadelphia.

SPELEERS, L. 1923: *Les Figurines funéraires égyptiennes.* Brussels.

——— 1935–38: "La Signification des pyramides," *L'Institut français d'archéologie orientale du Caire* (Cairo): *Mémoires,* LXVI, fasc. 2 (*Mélanges Maspero*).

SPIEGEL, J. 1953: *Das Werden der altägyptischen Hochkultur.* Heidelberg.

STECKEWEH, H. 1936: *Die Fürstengräber von Qâw.* With contributions by Georg Steindorff. (Veröffentlichungen der Ernst von Sieglin-Expedition, VI.) Leipzig.

STEINDORFF, G. 1913: *Das Grab des Ti.* (Veröffentlichungen der Ernst von Sieglin-Expedition, II.) Leipzig.

STOCK, H. 1959: "Das Sonnenheiligtum von Abusir," *Neue deutsche Ausgrabungen im Mittelmeergebiet und im vorderen Orient.* Berlin.

STONE, L. A. 1927: *The Story of Phallicism,* I. Chicago.

TERRACE, E. L. B. 1961: "A Fragmentary Triad of King Mycerinus," *Bulletin of the Museum of Fine Arts* (Boston), LIX.

THAUSING, G. 1948: "Zum Sinn der Pyramiden," *Österreichische Akademie der Wissenschaften, philosophisch-historische Klasse* (Vienna): *Anzeiger,* LXXXV.

THOMPSON, M. S. See under WACE, A. J. B.

TOBLER, A. J. 1950: *Excavations at Tepe Gawra,* II. (Joint Expedition of the Baghdad School and the University Museum to Mesopotamia.) Philadelphia.

TULANE, E. See under BRAIDWOOD, R. J.; BRAIDWOOD, L. S.

VAN BUREN, E. D. 1935: "A Problem of Early Sumerian Art," *Archiv für Orientforschung* (Berlin), X.

——— 1949: "Discoveries at Eridu," *Orientalia* (Rome), N.S. XVIII.

VANDIER, J. 1952, 1954–55: *Manuel d'archéologie égyptienne,* I and II. Paris.

——— See also under DRIOTON, E.

VARILLE, A. 1954: "Quelques Charactéristiques du temple pharaonique," *Le Musée vivant* (Paris), 1, 2.

WACE, A. J. B., and THOMPSON, M. S. 1912: *Prehistoric Thessaly.* Cambridge, England.

WAINWRIGHT, G. A. See under PETRIE, W. M. F.

WEISSBACH, F. H. See under WETZEL, F.

WEIZSÄCKER, V. VON. 1943: *Wahrheit und Wahrnehmung.* Leipzig.

WERBROUCK, M. See under CAPART, J.

WETZEL, F., and WEISSBACH, F. H. 1938: "Das Hauptheiligtum des Marduk in Babylon, Esagila und Etemenanki," *Wissenschaftliche Veröffentlichung der Deutschen Orient-Gesellschaft* (Leipzig), LIX.

WEYL, H. 1952: *Symmetry.* Princeton.

WHEELER, N. F. 1935: "Pyramids and their Purpose," *Antiquity* (Gloucester, England), IX.

WIEDEMANN, A. 1912: "Der Tierkult der alten Ägypter," *Der alte Orient* (Leipzig), XIV, 1.

WINKLER, H. A. 1937: *Völker und Völkerbewegungen im vorgeschichtlichen Oberägypten im Lichte neuer Felsbilderfunde.* Stuttgart.

——— 1938: *Rock-Drawings of Southern Upper Egypt,* I. London.

WINLOCK, H. E. 1928: "The Egyptian Expedition, 1925–1927," *Bulletin of the Metropolitan Museum of Art* (New York), XXIII, 2, sec. II.

——— 1942: *Excavations at Deir el Bahri 1911–1931.* New York.

——— 1947: *The Rise and Fall of the Middle Kingdom in Thebes.* New York.

WINTER, E. 1957: "Zur Deutung der Sonnenheiligtümer der 5. Dynastie," *Wiener Zeitschrift für die Kunde des Morgenlandes* (Vienna), LIV.

WISEMAN, D. J. 1959: *Cylinder Seals of Western Asia*. London.

WOLF, W. 1931: *Das schöne Fest von Opet*. (Veröffentlichungen der Ernst von Sieglin-Expedition, V.) Leipzig.

WÖLFFLIN, H. 1888: *Renaissance und Barock*. Munich.

——— 1915: *Kunstgeschichtliche Grundbegriffe*. Munich. Tr. by M. D. Hottinger from the 7th German edn.: *Principles of Art History*. New York and London, 1932. (Also Dover paperback.)

WOOLLEY, C. L. 1927: "The Excavations at Ur 1926–7," *The Antiquaries Journal* (London), VII.

——— 1931: "Excavations at Ur, 1930–1," *The Antiquaries Journal* (London), XI.

——— 1934: *Ur Excavations*, II: *The Royal Cemetery*, plates. (Joint Expedition of the British Museum and of the Museum of the University of Pennsylvania to Mesopotamia.) Oxford.

——— See also under HALL, H. R.

WORRINGER, W. 1908: *Abstraktion und Einfühlung*. Munich. Tr. M. Bullock: *Abstraction and Empathy*. London, 1953.

GENERAL INDEX

A page reference preceded by an * asterisk indicates an illustration. Important concepts are printed in SMALL CAPITALS. See also the Index of Concepts (for Vols. I and II), following this index.

A

General Index

General Index

General Index

N

O

P

Q

R

T

INDEX OF CONCEPTS

The chief discussions of concepts both in the present volume and in Vol. I, *The Beginnings of Art*, are here indexed to facilitate comparative study of the two.